THE BRITISH EMPIRE
BEFORE THE AMERICAN REVOLUTION
VOLUME VII

THE GREAT WAR FOR THE EMPIRE

THE VICTORIOUS YEARS

1758–1760

THE BRITISH EMPIRE
BEFORE THE AMERICAN REVOLUTION
VOLUME VII

THE GREAT WAR FOR THE EMPIRE

THE VICTORIOUS YEARS, 1758–1760

BY

LAWRENCE HENRY GIPSON

B.A. (OXON.), PH.D., D. LITT., F. R. HIST. S.

RESEARCH PROFESSOR OF HISTORY

LEHIGH UNIVERSITY

MCMXLIX
ALFRED A. KNOPF
NEW YORK

THIS IS A BORZOI BOOK,
PUBLISHED BY ALFRED A. KNOPF, INC.

THIS BOOK IS DEDICATED *to the memory of one whose firm loyalty to the truth of history transcended all lesser loyalties, the late* A. G. DOUGHTY, *Deputy Minister and Keeper of the Public Records of Canada.*

Preface

NEITHER the title of this volume of the series, *The Great War for the Empire: The Victorious Years, 1758–1760*, nor that of its predecessor, *The Great War for the Empire: The Years of Defeat, 1754–1757*, has the exactness that is the ideal of every student of history. For example, victories were recorded for British arms during the earlier years of the war that, in spite of the more resounding defeats, paved the way for the triumphant conclusion of Anglo-French hostilities in North America that came in 1760; while defeats in the later years, both in the broad field of strategy, short of an actual trial by combat, and on the field of battle itself, were experienced by the forces of the Crown, and some of these defeats were of such a nature as to call into question at the time whether or not victory against their formidable opponents was obtainable in the bitter contest going on in the New World. Nevertheless, upon the basis of the available evidence and thinking in terms chiefly of the American scene, it is clear that the first four years of the fighting left the French in control of much territory that had not been previously held, with a dominating influence over most of the more warlike Indian tribes of eastern North America and with a reputation of invincibility in arms; just as it left the British despondent and writhing under the series of blows rained upon them by the enemy during these same years. It is equally clear that the last three years of the American war witnessed the steady deterioration of this earlier French prowess: the loss in each of these years of one or more vitally strategic positions; the gradual withdrawal of Indian support, which had been so important a factor in pressing back British frontier settlements; and, finally, in the last year of the war, not only the dire shortage of matériel for continuing the struggle but the desertion from the ranks of the hard-pressed troops of practically all the Canadians. In contrast to this, during these latter years there gradually took place a mighty concentration of British military forces in North America under generals who could and did utilize them to advantage; both British regulars and American provincials, moreover, became at last adept in wilderness fighting; and, withal, such ample resources of every variety were made available to the armies for the successful prosecution of the war that, in spite of doubts that arose at times in the minds of men, its outcome could hardly be questioned. Yet the dramatic contest that ended at the gates of Montreal in September 1760 is but half told if one limits one's vision to the unfolding of events in America.

One may, indeed, assert with confidence that had it not been for the relentless and effective exertion of British naval predominance on the high seas, for the unchallenged superiority of English heavy industry and British colonial agriculture, now turned to warlike purposes, over French heavy industry and Canadian agriculture, and for the equal superiority of the pound sterling over the livre and, with it, British credit over French credit in the world's money markets, there would have been no military collapse in New France such as took place in 1760. Nor would there have been — something that is of utmost importance to bear in mind — any such emphasis placed, as was placed by the court at Versailles, on the war in Germany. There the great French land forces could be utilized — as these forces could not possibly be in North America under existing handicaps — with at least the expectation that, as a result of the successful termination of the Continental war, in which France had comparatively little direct interest, any losses that might be sustained overseas would be recovered in a mutual return of territory at the peace treaty and, beyond this expectation, with the hope that the end of the war would leave the nation in an even stronger position not only in Europe but as a world power than that enjoyed before the outbreak of hostilities. But an analysis of the above factors, so decisive in determining the outcome of the war in America — when operating in combination with large numbers of troops with dearly bought battle experience and under the leadership of those in whom they could have confidence — must be reserved for future consideration.

The war in North America was won, not by aggregations of hardy frontiersmen fighting in Indian fashion — important as were the services of many of the provincials after receiving the exacting training of rangers, and of others who aided in making roads, in building boats, in transporting supplies, and in other ways — but by those who, all in all, adhered rather closely, as will be noted in this volume, to traditional European techniques of carrying on war. In this connection the role of the British heavy-artillery train for the battering of forts impervious to musketry fire was of decisive importance both in the psychological effects of its presence and in its actual use. The garrisons of Fort Duquesne, Fort Niagara, Ticonderoga, and Crown Point and those of the great fortresses of Louisbourg and Quebec, as well as the French army concentrated at Montreal, were in no instance starved into surrender by siege operations; but either through fear of the play of this artillery upon them, against which they had no defence — as at Forts Duquesne, Ticonderoga, and Crown Point and at Montreal — or through the systematic demolition of the fortifications — as at Niagara, Louisbourg, and Quebec — these places were won.

Further, in open warfare on the field of battle, even the French with their long experience in wilderness operations adhered with remarkable fidelity to the canons of traditional military science and tactics, while at the same time utilizing the Indians and Canadians for raiding enemy settlements and for scouting purposes. The battles of Ticonderoga in 1758, of Montmorency and of the Plains of Abraham of 1759, and of Sillery of 1760 showed the same great attention given to the classical requirements for troop formations — with the same stress placed upon the distribution of heavy- and light-armed units to form the center, flanks, and reserves, and for the placement and utilization of field artillery — as in the battles that were at the same time being fought in Europe. When Abercromby at Ticonderoga failed to bring up his guns and establish batteries to support his English grenadiers and Scottish Highlanders in their desperate attack upon the French entrenchments, he not only committed an unpardonable military blunder but turned his back upon over two centuries of tactical teaching and practice and thereby displayed his incompetence as a commanding officer. This does not imply that the manner of carrying on war in Europe was not modified in some respects in America as the result of wilderness requirements — as evidenced, for example, by the emphasis placed upon the use of rangers for reconnaissance purposes — but rather that it was found that men trained in the European manner of fighting and provided with European weapons of war were best suited to command armies that faced one another even here in the New World during the years of deadly

conflict. Again, it is a testimony to the value placed by such commanders upon rigid training and equally rigid military discipline that
when it came to the ordering of charges or assaults against the entrenched enemy, involving an advance into the open with fire reserved until at point-blank distance from the foe, in every instance
it was the European regular who was thus employed, rather than the
less rigidly trained and disciplined colonial. The war may, indeed,
be truthfully called a European conflict in a New World setting;
only when one grasps that fact is it possible to evaluate the full significance of the processes involved in bringing it to a termination.

The present volume is concerned with military operations in
North America after William Pitt first took over the direction of
affairs. While this is logical, there is included in it material covering
the year 1757 that should have found a place in the preceding volume if the chronological limits announced for these volumes had
been rigidly adhered to. Such adherence, however, was found to be
impracticable by reason of restrictions placed, under war-time conditions, on the size of books when Volume VI was produced. In fact,
before the publisher could embark upon the printing of the manuscript of that volume it was necessary to eliminate two of the chapters and compress others. It may be mentioned in passing that one
of the chapters dropped subsequently appeared in the *American
Historical Review* under the title: "British Diplomacy in the Light
of Anglo-Spanish New World Issues, 1750–1757," and the other in
the *Canadian Historical Review* under the title: "A French Project
for Victory Short of a Declaration of War, 1755."

As indicated in the Preface of Volume VI, the war in North America that terminated in 1760 was characterized by the movements and
clashes of no large armies. Some of the most important successes
credited to both the British and the French in its course were secured by the use of comparatively small bodies of troops. Yet there
can be no question that there was at stake one of the greatest prizes
ever contended for by rivals in arms — a prize, in fact, that makes
the conquests of an Alexander the Great, a Cæsar, or a Napoleon
sink almost into insignificance; for it was nothing less than the continent of North America. In treating of military developments that
led to the winning of this continent by the British, care has been
given to deal with the more important logistical, strategical, and
tactical problems in a manner such as is demanded by a generation
of readers who have been made acutely aware of the fact that the

waging of war is a science as well as an art and who expect far more from the present-day historian than narration, even with brilliant description of the setting of events.

For materials used in writing the present volume, it is not only a great pleasure but a duty to indicate my very great obligations to the Public Record Office, the British Museum, the Library of Congress, the Public Archives of Canada, the Huntington Library, the Clements Library, the Manuscript and Map Division of the New York Public Library, the Historical Society of Pennsylvania, the Ridgeway Library, the Pennsylvania Historical Commission, the Pennsylvania State Archives, Massachusetts State Archives, the Massachusetts Historical Society, the New York Historical Society, the Archives of the State of New York, the Maryland Historical Society, the Newberry Library, the Princeton University Library, and the Lehigh University Library. Moreover, it would have been impossible for me to have worked through the masses of materials freely placed at my disposal had it not been for the kindly aid of both directors and assistants at many of these places, who eased my labors in searching for fugitive documents and in countless other ways. To mention all of those who helped to smooth my path, however, is impracticable in this preface: the catalogue of names is too large, and to mention but a few would be to make an invidious distinction — something that my sense of gratitude to the rest will not permit. Not least in importance among the institutions that made this volume possible are Lehigh University and the Lehigh Institute of Research. Without the freedom from teaching and administrative work, and without the generous financial support, granted by them, it would simply have been impossible to have proceeded with this large undertaking which is designed to make its appeal not so much to the readers of popular literature as to those who are seeking to understand and to evaluate facts in their historical setting.

It should be here emphasized, as was stressed in the preceding volume, that the quantity of material bearing upon the subject matter of this volume is so vast that simply to list it comprehensively would require a book in itself. As the footnotes will indicate, only those original materials were used, as a rule, that carry the greatest weight of authority; as for original materials of secondary importance, these were utilized on occasion largely for narrative or descriptive purposes. The warm reception given to the first volume of *The Great War for the Empire* by thoughtful readers has encouraged me to feel that the present volume will be equally welcomed.

Before closing the Preface one duty remains. It is to make a very belated acknowledgment to Professor C. H. McIlwain of Harvard University for a misconstruction in Volume IV of this series (page 230, footnote 8) of a statement made by him in his scholarly Introduction to Wraxall's *An Abridgement of the Indian Affairs* (p. xxi) with reference to the decisive influences promoting Anglo-French rivalry in North America in 1754. This rivalry was based primarily, not so much on competition for the fur trade, which I thought Dr. McIlwain indicated was the case, as for territory, it would seem — a view that has been consistently emphasized in the volumes of this series and with which he heartily concurs.

L. H. G.

"Rotha"
Panther Road
Rydal, Pennsylvania
November 1, 1948

Contents

CHAPTER I

PITT, THE GREAT COMMONER, COMES TO POWER

THE COLONIAL LINE OF DEFENCE

CHAPTER III

THE LOSS OF FORT WILLIAM HENRY

CHAPTER IV

THE CHECKMATING OF LOUDOUN

CHAPTER V

THE EUROPEAN SCENE. PITT'S REVERSAL OF POLICY

Chapter VI

A WINTER'S INTERLUDE IN NORTH AMERICA

Chapter VIII

ABERCROMBY MEETS HIS MASTER. FRONTENAC

CONTENTS xxvii

CHAPTER IX

FORBES BUILDS A ROAD TO VICTORY

CHAPTER X

THE CONTINENTAL COLONIES AND THE WAR, 1759

Chapter XI

CONSOLIDATION OF BRITISH POWER SOUTH OF THE ST. LAWRENCE, 1759

Chapter XII

WOLFE ASCENDS THE ST. LAWRENCE

CHAPTER XIII

THE PIERCING OF THE HEART OF NEW FRANCE

CHAPTER XIV

THE CULMINATION OF THE WAR IN NORTH AMERICA

Maps and Plans

CHRONOLOGY

1757

April	6	The fall of the Pitt-Devonshire ministry.
June	29	The Pitt-Newcastle ministry takes office.
July	18	Frederick defeated by Daun at Kolin.
	25	Cumberland's defeat at Hastenbeck.
Aug.	5	Loudoun gives up the Louisbourg Expedition.
	9	The surrender of Fort William Henry.
Sept.	8	Cumberland signs the capitulation of Kloster-Seven.
	22	British capture of the Island of Aix.
Nov.	5	Frederick's victory at Rossbach.
	12	The French destruction of German Flats.
Dec.	5	Frederick's victory at Leuthen.

1758

Feb.	28	British naval victory off Cartagena, Spain.
April	3	Hawk's naval victory in Basque Roads.
	11	The Anglo-Prussian subsidy treaty.
June	8	Wolfe lands at Gabarus Bay.
	23	Prince Ferdinand's victory at Crefeld.
July	4	Abercromby launches his campaign.
	8	British defeat at Ticonderoga.
	26	The French surrender Louisbourg.
Aug.	7	The British capture of Cherbourg.
	27	Bradstreet's capture of Fort Frontenac.
	27	The indecisive Battle of Zorndorf.
Sept.	11	British defeat at Saint-Cas, France.
	14	Colonel Grant defeated near Fort Duquesne.
Oct.	12	The French repulse at Loyalhanna.
	13	Frederick's defeat at Hochkirch.
	24	The Easton, Pennsylvania, Indian Treaty.
Nov.	24	The French destruction of Fort Duquesne.

1759

June	14	Admiral Durell arrives off Ile d'Orléans.
	25	Wolfe and Saunders join Durell before Quebec.
July	24	The French defeat at La Belle-Famille.
	25	The French surrender of Fort Niagara.
	26	The French destruction of Fort Ticonderoga.
	31	The French destruction of Fort St. Frédéric at Crown Point.
	31	Wolfe's attack at the Montmorency.
Sept.	13	Wolfe's landing at the Foulon.
		The French defeat on the Heights of Abraham.
	17	The surrender of Quebec.

1760

April	28	The British defeat of Sillery Woods.
May	15	The arrival of the British relief at Quebec.
Aug.	25	Amherst captures Fort Lévis.
		Haviland captures Fort Isle-aux-Noix.
Sept.	7	Vaudreuil surrenders Canada to Amherst.

THE BRITISH EMPIRE
BEFORE THE AMERICAN REVOLUTION
VOLUME VII

THE GREAT WAR FOR THE EMPIRE

THE VICTORIOUS YEARS

1758–1760

CHAPTER I

Pitt, the Great Commoner, Comes to Power

EW MEN of historical importance present so many paradoxes as does William Pitt in the course of his public career.[1] A hater of corruption in government, he was raised to power by the influence of corruption, occupying with an easy conscience a seat in Parliament as the representative of more than one rotten borough; the bitter denouncer of Walpole's policy of granting pensions, he saw nothing morally reprehensible in accepting for three lives a pension of £3,000 from the King for himself and his descendants; a man of the people — "the Great Commoner," as he was called — he was in no way common: unapproachable except on his own conditions, at times insufferably arrogant, he was unwilling to work in office with other men as equals; he had to dominate his colleagues in government or would go into opposition to them. Called by Frederick Harrison "the greatest orator who has ever trod the floors of Parliament," yet there has survived no authentic specimen of his oratorical powers that would entitle him to a place among any of the really great orators of the past. In fact, his greatest oratorical outbursts,

---

[1] Among the lives of Pitt the following are the most important for the period under discussion: F. S. Thackeray: *History of the Right Honourable William Pitt, Earl of Chatham* (2 vols., 1827); Albert von Ruville: *William Pitt, Graf von Chatham* (3 vols., 1905; translated into English by H. J. Chaytor and M. Morrison, 3 vols., 1907); Basil Williams: *William Pitt, Earl of Chatham* (2 vols., 1913); Brian Tunstall: *William Pitt, Earl of Chatham* (1938); Frederick Harrison: *Chatham* (1905); Lord Rosebery: *Chatham, Early Life and Connections* (1910); and Kate Hotblack: *Chatham's Colonial Policy: A Study in the Fiscal and Economic Implications of the Colonial Policy of the Elder Pitt* (1917).

like the one in connection with which Horace Walpole declared: "Pitt surpassed himself, and then I need not tell you that he surpassed Cicero and Demosthenes," came from the heart rather than from the head; and while it thrilled his fellow commoners for its subtle wit, its sarcasm, its vivacity, and its eloquence, it neither enlightened nor determined foreign policy and was quietly interred by the author himself when he finally ascended to high office and assumed the grave responsibilities of leadership. For, characteristically, with burning conviction he at one period denounced state policies that at a later period he defended with equal conviction. As a foremost supporter of the exalted place of Parliament under the constitution of the realm, he nevertheless in later years, in the midst of the American crisis, was led to belittle its powers, and especially its most essential power, the right to the exercise of which power in the name of the nation had called it into existence in the thirteenth century. One is therefore not surprised that the man acclaimed as the chief architect of the modern British Empire, whose influence in war laid its broad foundations, should in the peace that followed have helped mightily to shake it to its very foundations. For in his sweeping denials of the power of Parliament to levy taxes on all British subjects, beneficiaries of the national defence, he unwittingly placed a deadly weapon in the hands of the aspiring colonials that was to be used not only to strike at the concept of the unity of sovereignty within the Empire but to sever the ties that hitherto had strongly bound the thirteen continental colonies to the mother country.

Yet Pitt's fame is secure. While it is true that he ascended to high office as the result of a corrupt system, his conduct both in public life and in retirement was so unblemished as to be almost unprecedented in an office-holder of his period. While it is equally true that in debate he treated his opponents at times with gross unfairness, hurling at them outrageous charges that could not be sustained simply because they were untrue in the terms in which he framed them, he was singularly free from harbouring malice against others and at all times exhibited a burning, pure, even if on occasions misguided patriotism that stirred the faith of all Englishmen, friend and foe alike. In fact, his most distinguished contribution to England was not in the halls of Parliament but in the privacy of his closet; not in glittering and impassioned declamation, in connection with which his tall, gaunt figure, his terrifying "beak," his piercing eyes, and his well-modulated voice held crowded galleries in hypnotic trance, but in the painstaking detail with which he planned in semi-seclusion his defence of the British Empire and his onslaught against that of France; in the meticulous care that he lavished on each major strategic move in the process of the war; in the faith that he inspired in the men of the army and navy that what he asked them to do would be accomplished with the means that his forethought had placed at their disposal; and, finally, in the fact that he lifted the nation from the depths of despondency in defeat to a high point of exaltation as the result of the series of tremendous victories won over the enemy in the four corners of the globe. If his reputation as a statesman has suffered with the passing of years, his reputation as the leader of an embattled nation at a period of one of its gravest crises is still at a pinnacle. Child of a prosaic century that in spite of itself produced giants, he takes his place beside the greatest of them.

William Pitt was born in the Borough of Westminster in 1708 and was educated at Eton and at Trinity College, Oxford. Although af-flicted with gout from his youth, he chose the army as a career and secured a cornet's commission in the dragoons. Physically incapaci-tated from undergoing the rigors of actual military operations, he became, nevertheless, deeply interested in theoretical military sci-ence and absorbed the contents of the available treatises [2] — some-thing that was later to have great significance. But this quiet ac-tivity was cut short when in 1734 he found himself in a position to enter Parliament as a member from Old Sarum in Wiltshire. For burgage tenures in this rotten borough had been purchased by his nabob grandfather, the eccentric "Diamond" Pitt, doubtless to give added respectability to one who had made a large fortune in India as a free trader and speculator in diamonds and who thereupon had retired to a fine country estate in England to become one of the landed gentry. When the grandson took his seat in Parliament early in 1735 he was twenty-seven years of age and possessed all the con-fidence of youth. Attaching himself to the group of so-called Boy Patriots headed by Lord Pulteney, he went into opposition to the Wal-pole administration and rallied to the support of Frederick, Prince of Wales, who was more bitterly hostile to his own father, George II, than George had been as Prince of Wales to his father during the latter's reign. From the time of his maiden speech, delivered in 1736,

---

[2] Shelburne's "Autobiography," in the Life of William, Earl of Shelburne (p. 57), by Lord Fitzmaurice.

to the fall of Walpole in 1742, he was, as an orator, feared by his opponents and acclaimed by his supporters and the public at large. His position in international affairs was that of a supernationalist on such issues as the Hanoverian subsidy treaty and the Convention of 1739, signed with Spain but never ratified by Parliament.[3] In domestic affairs it was that of a purist seeking to rid the country of the abominations of the administration. He magnified rumours into actual fact, charging that the Minister had plundered and betrayed the country and had then plunged it into a dangerous war in order to prevent an inquiry into his conduct — like a thief who burned the house he had robbed so that in the ensuing confusion he might escape. Today, to the student conversant with the period — after taking fully into account everything that was untoward in the government of Great Britain — the utterances of the fiery orator leave an impression of such utter irresponsibility in flinging the most damning charges against his political enemies that there is no surprise that George II and his advisers were most reluctant to see the author of them admitted to any post that would require a cool head and sagacious and constructive statesmanship.

With the change of administration, Pitt was ignored when it came to the filling of offices by the Wilmington-Carteret ministry and went into opposition. Not until February 1746, with the Pelhams now entrenched in office and looking for popular support, was he admitted to even a minor post, that of joint Vice-Treasurer and Receiver General and Paymaster General of all of His Majesty's revenues in the Kingdom of Ireland; however, in May of the same year he was elevated to the much more important post of Paymaster General of His Majesty's land forces and retained it until the time of his dismissal late in 1755.[4] There is no evidence that he ever took any interest in the routine administration of his office — he was not a financier. But he won the respect of all groups for his refusal to profit financially by his position as did both his predecessor and his successors during their incumbency. Further, it provided him with a substantial income that permitted him to support himself as a member of Parliament and also to deepen his knowledge of international affairs and army administration under war-time conditions during the War of

[3] For Pitt's attack on the Spanish Convention of 1739, delivered on March 8 of that year, and his attack on the Hanoverian subsidy on December 10, 1742, see *Parliamentary History*, X, 1280–3; XII, 1033–6.

[4] See Volume I of this series, pp. 111 and 119–20.

the Austrian Succession. For a period of nine years he was part of the Pelham machine. Ever considering his present appointment but a stepping-stone to greater responsibilities in government that would come through consistent support of the ministers, he used his eloquence to further measures that he had previously denounced. Now he helped to drive through Parliament subsidy measures for the support of a Hanoverian army in Flanders, now he defended treaties with both Bavaria and Spain and, in relation to the treaty with the latter country, admitted that he had previously been wrong in insisting that it must contain a clause prohibiting Spain's right of search of British vessels. No longer a supporter of the Prince of Wales, he was strongly opposed by Frederick's supporters in the general election of 1747, and it required the personal presence of Newcastle at the Seaford election, with the lavish entertainment of the voters and with the Duke's personal presence at the returning office, to secure this seat — all of which, it was later charged in the House of Commons, was in violation of repeated resolutions of the House of Commons and an obstruction to the freedom of election. Yet when a petition was presented that the election be invalidated on these grounds, it was treated by Pitt as beneath consideration and as the occasion for a jest.

Such glaring inconsistencies present William Pitt in an unfavourable light. He was in truth an opportunist,[5] and employed, or permitted to be employed in his behalf, the tools of an opportunist. It may also be affirmed that in opposition to government — whether it was as a rather cocky young man before he came into the government in 1746, or as a mature leader after his resignation in 1761, or as an aging valitudinarian after he finally gave up all thought of continuing in office in 1768 — he does not appear to advantage, irrespective of the unrestrained acclaim of his admirers. In considering his place in history, however, his irresponsibility in opposition, as was previously suggested, was offset by his high sense of responsibility when in power; the questionable means that were used to secure his elevation is also offset by the fact that these were characteristic of the age and that he took good care as a rule not to be personally involved in the sordid traffic in votes by which he benefited and that seemed to be necessary if he were to attain his objectives as a political figure. Nevertheless, in 1741 he threw his support to George Lyttelton in the Oakhampton election after promising to

---

[5] Shelburne's "Autobiography," *loc. cit.*, p. 60.

support the candidate of the Prince of Wales, and in 1747 was present at the notorious election at Seaford.

In 1754, upon the death of Henry Pelham, it seemed that at last a policy-framing post was within Pitt's grasp, but his hopes were blasted, in spite of his steady support of the government — as the result not only of the King's opposition to the man who had permitted himself to refer to George's principality in Germany as a "despicable electorate," [6] but also doubtless of Newcastle's unwillingness to see one in the office of Secretary of State for the Southern Department who might get quite out of control and thereby strike at the foundations of the "system" that he was supporting and even at his own leadership in public affairs. Baffled for the moment and embittered, Pitt at the same time was kept in Parliament through the interest of the Duke, who now in the general elections placed at his disposal a seat for Aldborough, in Yorkshire, a Pelham family borough. In spite of this, the public was soon regaled with the spectacle of one holding a not unimportant office in the government determined to thwart its policies. But effective resistance to it was not easy. Seeking a temporary alliance with George Fox, another disappointed aspirant for high office, and veering again as in his youth in the direction of Leicester House, where with the death of Frederick in 1751 young Prince George and his mother, the Dowager Princess, were holding forth in opposition to Newcastle, did not yield results in the way of gathering important support. In fact, he lost a part of his previous following when he now broke politically with some of his closest family connections, established by his marriage into the Grenville family, which took place at this period, and when George Lyttelton and George Grenville accepted public office. Nevertheless, he could at least raise his voice in Parliament against Newcastle, who, incidentally, had made it possible for him to do so. The subsidy treaties contracted by the ministry at this time gave him the opportunity, which he seized. Previously he had blown cold and then hot on the question of subsidies to foreign powers and now he blew cold again — in his blast against the treaties signed at this juncture with Russia and Hesse-Cassel — in a debate that took place in November 1755. As recorded by Horace Walpole, his speech — thinking in terms of present-day standards — was not only waspish but turgid, even bombastic, loaded with distortions of the plain facts and unjustifiable innuendoes directed against the ministry. Little did

---

[6] For Pitt's address of December 10, 1742, see *Parliamentary History*, XII, 1033–6.

he realize, at the time, that he himself was destined to wax even hotter for subsidy treaties when made the responsible minister two years later than he had ever waxed cold against them; that he was to make them cardinal features of his foreign policy while waging victoriously the Great War for the Empire. Little also did he realize — in charging that, if the treaties were passed providing total subsidies of less than £155,000, "his Majesty would not be able to sleep in St. James for the cries of a bankrupt people" — that he himself would before many years be urging with all his eloquence the annual payment to the house of Prussia alone of a subsidy of £800,000, which he would then declare a great and prosperous nation could well afford to pay; nor that when he scorned the protection of Hanover as in no wise in the national interests, he himself would eventually come to demand, in the name of national interest, that Prince Ferdinand's army, protecting Hanover and other states in alliance with Great Britain, must be supported to the limit so that France could batter herself to exhaustion in western Germany and thereby be unable to provide a proper defence of her vast empire.

After the treaties had been approved by an overwhelming majority in the Chamber, Newcastle and the King were free to deal with the recalcitrant orator, who was promptly dismissed from his post. Now reduced in circumstances, depending upon a legacy from his grandfather of an annual value of £200 and one from the former Duchess of Marlborough of £400, he was led to accept from his brother-in-law, Lord Temple, a gift of £1,000 a year "until better times," in order to maintain for his family their accustomed standard of living while he busied himself with the task of undermining the ministry. This he succeeded in accomplishing during the year following his dismissal, thanks largely to the adverse fortunes of war, a consideration of which has been given in the preceding volume of this series. As a chief means to the end in view he aimed at arousing deep suspicion of the government as then constituted even when on occasion he supported its proposals.[7] The unthinking public was finally led to believe that the ministry was not only hopelessly incompetent, but unpatriotic if not disloyal; that the leaders after

---

[7] Perhaps the most impartial biographer of Pitt, in referring to his attacks at this period, justly declared: "We are staggered by the large number of untenable assertions which he made, by the unjustifiable charges which he heaped upon the ministry. . . . Of the impartial examination of facts there is no trace. . . . Pitt desired nothing but power for himself . . ." (Albert von Ruville: *William Pitt, Earl of Chatham*, trans. by H. J. Chaytor, I, 378).

being permanently barred from public office richly deserved to be brought to trial. Everything was wrong with the government, nothing right. Yet Pitt was very careful not to attack his monarch when, for example, the Hanoverian estimates were brought in. In his own words, a fundamental distinction must be made: ". . . nothing but good flowed from the King; nothing but ruin from his servants." [8] When in May 1756 a request of the Commons was made for one million pounds for war expenses, he put the blame for hostilities solely upon the shoulders of the ministry in saying, what simply was untrue:

> "that we had provoked before we could defend, and neglected after provocation; that we were left inferior to France in every quarter; that the [previous] vote of credit had been misapplied to secure the Electorate; and that we had bought a treaty with Prussia by sacrificing our rights." [9]

Yet it was true that in 1755 Braddock had failed, Boscawen had failed, Hawke had failed, each in his appointed task. Although French merchant ships by the scores had been captured and thousands of French sailors, the British Isles, defended by only a few regiments, were nevertheless highly vulnerable to invasion by a nation with two hundred thousand soldiers in arms, who under favourable weather conditions might, in spite of superior British sea power, find a landing and by quick action possess themselves of the British capital and metropolis of the Empire. Therefore, as a defensive measure, Hanoverian and Hessian troops were brought over in the spring of 1756 when secret information disclosed French plans of invasion. This wise measure designed to quiet the very reasonable fears of the people was also denounced by Pitt, who declared: "Those who supported such measures would bear the marks on their foreheads" [10] — putting them among the accursed of mankind. In May of the new year came the defeat of Byng, in June the loss of Minorca, in August the surrender of Oswego.

No ministry could easily survive such a series of checks and blows to national pride. Although eight thousand men had been added to the army, although work in the shipyards was being pushed to add to British naval strength, the people at last turned violently against the ministry. Newcastle was mobbed at Greenwich, and at West-

---

[8] Horace Walpole: *Memoirs of the Reign of George II*, II, 188.
[9] *Ibid.*, II, 194.
[10] *Ibid.*, II, 188.

minster the rabble took up the refrains of a song that chanted the Duke to the block and Byng to the yardarm. The ministry began to disintegrate. Attorney General Murray, a tower of strength in the House, insisted on translation to the peerage, as the Earl of Mansfield, and on the vacant office of Chief Justice of the King's Bench, and in October he entered the House of Lords; in the same month Secretary of State Fox handed in his resignation. Thus the two most capable and skilful defenders of the government policies were no longer to be counted on in the great national forum. Newcastle was faced by a hopeless task.

In the light of developments that have been considered, William Pitt was not unaware that all eyes were upon him in the fall of 1756. He had the London mob, but he also had the London livery companies and merchant princes, together with Leicester House, men of the army and the navy, and many of the clergy.[11] Even the King realized the importance of restoring faith in the government so badly shaken by events and cast an inquiring gaze in his direction. Could this man so contemptuous of the efforts of others be now entrusted with the guidance of the war? Could one who had spoken repeatedly in bitter opposition to the support of the electoral possessions and of subsidies in general be now counted on to raise his voice in behalf of them? It was inconceivable to George that Pitt would do "my business." If not, what then? No one had the answer. On October 19 he was privately sounded out by Lord High Chancellor Hardwicke as to his willingness to come into the government [12] and, if so, upon what terms.

In reply he stated that he would take office, but would not serve under Newcastle, nor would he bind himself not to impeach the ministers should they resign from their posts. This meant that he wanted a perfectly free hand in taking over the war — free from dictation by St. James's and, incidentally, equally free from dictation by Leicester House.[13] As for Newcastle, Pitt seems to have reasoned

---

11 See *Memoirs of a Celebrated Literary and Political Character* [Richard Glover], *from the Resignation of Sir Robert Walpole in 1742 to the Establishment of Lord Chatham's Second Administration in 1757; Containing Strictures on Some of the Most Distinguished Men of that Time*, pp. 71–2.

12 George Harris: *Life of Lord Chancellor Hardwicke; with Selections from His Correspondence, Diaries, Speeches and Judgments*, III, 76–7.

13 See the *Grenville Papers, being the Correspondence of Richard Grenville, Earl Temple, K.G., and the Right Hon. George Grenville, Their Friends and Contemporaries*, I, 177.

that were the Duke left in office, he himself would not, on the one hand, have the necessary freedom of access to the King nor, on the other, be able to persuade the heir presumptive, Prince George, and his adviser, Lord Bute, that he had not secretly connived with the Duke in making certain unpopular appointments to the Prince's household.[14] Pitt now began reversing himself. On October 21 he sought a meeting with Lady Yarmouth, the King's mistress, whom heretofore he had scorned.[15] At this conference he indicated his willingness to assume office, but also his firm determination to exclude Newcastle. Yet at the same time he left a very strong hint that this step would not mean that Hanover had lost "*all* its friends." This doubtless helped to clear the mind of George on one vital point — he did not need to be persuaded of Pitt's essential integrity of character. Again Hardwicke waited upon Pitt to seek to move him from his determination to eliminate the Duke, but without success. Now at last reconciled to the loss of Newcastle's services, the King commissioned Fox to see if Pitt would form a joint ministry with him. But the latter rebuffed him with abruptness, indicating that he would not act with Fox.[16] Although Fox was now urged by the Earl of Granville to try to form an administration, he did not feel himself sufficiently strong to do so and declined the task.

At this point the young Duke of Devonshire stepped into the picture at the request of George and took up the thread of negotiating with Pitt, which lasted many days. Pitt himself had felt under necessity in planning a ministry to offer the Treasury to some one of the leading nobility "whom the Whigs would look up to," and preferred the Duke. He was therefore ready to talk to him. According to Horace Walpole, Pitt, who was still rather isolated, "wanted friends for places, more than places for his friends," consisting as the latter did largely of those attached to the Grenville family, together with a few stray followers such as Legge, who had been dismissed as Chancellor of the Exchequer at the same time that Pitt had been dismissed the preceding year. His lack of capable supporters is indicated most clearly in his about-face respecting Sir Thomas Robinson, who had surrendered the Secretaryship of State for the Southern Department to Fox in 1755. At the time of Robinson's appointment in

---

[14] Albert von Ruville, *op. cit.*, II, 56.

[15] Horace Walpole, *op. cit.*, II, 259–60.

[16] *Ibid.*, II, 262. See Fox's letter to Bedford of October 30, 1756, *Correspondence of John, 4th Duke of Bedford*, II, 205.

1754, Pitt had in contempt declared: "He [the King] may as well send his jack-boot to govern us." [17] But now he proposed to Devonshire to bring him back to occupy the very same post. For himself he sought to become Secretary of State for the Northern Department, with the dismissal of the Earl of Holderness from this post. But when this was reported to the latter, he declared with spirit that he would resign "as the other great persons were to do" — unless this were inflicted as a punishment, in which case he would refuse to do so until his "crime" had been proved. This greatly comforted the King, who still abhorred the thought of seeing Pitt "and of telling the only secrets that he had to a man whom he never would let into his closet." [18]

As a result Pitt had finally to agree to keep Holderness in his highly confidential post, embracing as it did relations with the states within Germany as well as with Austria and Russia. Devonshire, while accepting the post of First Lord Commissioner of the Treasury, had, nevertheless, to agree to restore Legge, whom he disliked and distrusted, as Chancellor of the Exchequer. Pitt himself now accepted the southern Secretaryship of State, placed one of his brothers-in-law, Earl Temple, at the head of the Admiralty, and another, George Grenville, as paymaster of the navy, and still another, James Grenville, on the Treasury Board. [19] Yet so few of his followers were in Parliament, and those that were there were faced with such great difficulties in being re-elected, that he had either to leave or to place in high office a number of friends of both Newcastle and Fox. Such men were Granville, Halifax, Barrington, Gower, Charles Yorke, and Bedford. Still Newcastle, Hardwicke, Anson, and George Lyttelton were retired and Fox, in spite of his intrigues, was excluded.

Like many another man, the Duke of Newcastle, after twenty-four years in office, was a poorer if wiser man, with the value of his personal estate cut from £30,000 to £13,000, [20] as the result of the steady drain on his resources in maintaining a majority in Parliament favourable to his policies and a suitable table for foreign dignitaries and others with a claim to his hospitality. Yet he left office not without the good wishes of many and the admiration of some, par-

[17] Horace Walpole, op. cit., II, 263–6.

[18] Ibid., II, 266–7.

[19] For two letters from Temple to Pitt having to do with filling leading posts in the government, see Correspondence of William Pitt, Earl of Chatham (ed. W. S. Taylor and J. H. Pringle), I, 186–95.

[20] Horace Walpole, op. cit., II, 272.

ticularly the representatives in London of foreign powers. For example, the Bavarian Ambassador Haslang, writing home the day after the Duke's resignation, predicted that the new ministry would not last long and that the nation would be obliged to appeal again to him. He then went on to say:

> "This minister who has sacrificed more than half of his wealth in a service of thirty years has demanded no other recompense than the title of Duke for his nephew and heir [Lord Lincoln]. . . . His correctness and his disinterestedness will continue to be his praise." [21]

On December 4 Pitt received the seals of office, and the Devonshire-Pitt ministry came into existence, swept into power by the demands of the people, and with the blessings of the young court at Leicester House. Men sought at this juncture a national saviour, and Pitt alone among leading men of affairs could not be blamed for some setback in either the present or the preceding war and he alone had ventured to set forth his own plans as infallible in rejecting those of the government. Now, freed from the presence of the hitherto ubiquitous Newcastle, he at last was to have an opportunity to prove what he could do. But his situation was by no means ideal: the King treated him with coldness, if not suspicion; his hold on Parliament was very tenuous; his hold on the Cabinet Council equally so. How now would he fulfil all those promises and expectations, many of which seemed to conflict with realistic, statesmanlike policy? [22] The Austrian Ambassador, Count Colleredo, writing to Kaunitz on November 26, put his finger on the embarrassments facing his administration in pointing out that

> "if attempt should be made to change methods of administration and to strike out new paths, opposition will certainly be offered by the members of the former ministry . . . and their adherents in Parliament." [23]

In fact, the lack of unity in the ministry-to-be was evident at the opening of Parliament on December 2 before the new appointments were announced. In reply to the address from the throne Devon-

---

[21] Haslang to the Bavarian ministry, November 12, 1756, quoted by von Ruville, op. cit., II, 64.

[22] George Lyttelton to his brother, November 25, 1756, Memoirs and Correspondence of George, Lord Lyttelton, from 1734 to 1773 (ed. by Sir Robert Phillimore), II, 536.

[23] Quoted by von Ruville, op. cit., II, 68.

shire in the House of Lords supported the expression of thanks, moved by Earl Gower, about to become Lord Privy Seal, for the bringing in of foreign troops as a defence in the emergency — something that Pitt had bitterly opposed; in the House of Commons the reply by Charles Townshend, about to become Treasurer of the Chamber in the King's Household, significantly omitted this, although the speech plainly called for some reference to it.[24] Pitt in his own speech walked a tightrope. He could no longer blast his old opponents; instead he stressed the importance not only of an effective militia, now that the King had announced that the Hanoverians would be sent back to the Electorate, but of building up the navy, in view of the growing maritime strength of the French; indeed, he spoke with unwonted moderation.

With the announcement of the new ministry there was a scurry for seats. Pitt, in surrendering his seat for Aldborough, the gift of Newcastle, had sat for Buckingham, the two seats of which were controlled by the Grenville family. He was obliged to vacate it, however, in favour of James Grenville, appointed as one of the Lords Commissioners of the Treasury and in need of the position. He succeeded at this juncture in securing one of the Oakhampton seats, previously held by his brother Thomas, and later by George Lyttelton, now transferred to the House of Lords. This he occupied until he was returned from Bath in July of the following year.

At last in power after so much striving, Pitt was able — in spite of the miserable state of his health — to set about the task of energizing the British war effort. This was far from simple. As Secretary of State for the Southern Department he had no direct connection with the German war or direct responsibility for it; this lay within the jurisdiction of the Secretary of State for the Northern Department. It is true that he could bring pressure upon the King and Holderness by a threat of resignation, in opposing a specific step or policy. It is equally true, however, that should he appear to act as a check upon such a step or policy previously approved by the King's inner circle, he might, were it considered a matter of sufficient importance, be forced out of office. While clearly not a prime minister, at the same time he was expected to speak for the Cabinet Council as a whole in the House of Commons — at the same time that Dev-

---

[24] *The Parliamentary History of England from the Earliest Period to the Year 1803* (compiled by T. C. Hansard), XV, 771–9; *Grenville Papers*, I, 182; *Lyttelton's Memoirs*, II, 542–3; *Glover's Memoirs*, pp. 75–6; *Horace Walpole's Memoirs*, III, 166.

onshire was expected to exert himself to see that a majority of the members of the two houses of Parliament were favourably disposed to the government. Pitt's position, in fact, was one of uneasy balance. Yet within a not too restricted area his powers were very real: he could issue orders to the Admiralty with respect to naval operations; he could likewise issue them to the Secretary at War, in so far as these related to land operations against France and in the New World. He accordingly approved measures to continue the upbuilding of the navy and the army. In this connection he took a step of major importance in approving the recruiting of Highlanders, whose superb fighting qualities now made them an asset of extraordinary importance to the State, just as these same qualities had previously made them, as once disaffected subjects, a constant peril.[25] As a result, early in the year 1757 two battalions of a thousand men each were easily raised by Simon Fraser, son of Lord Lovat, who was executed for treason in the Scottish rebellion of 1746.[26] Subsequently other Highland battalions came into existence and were signalized for their bravery and loyalty.[27]

Pitt before he came to power had very much at heart the retrieving of the critical situation in North America, vividly impressed upon all Englishmen by the defeat of Braddock and the fall of Oswego. He now laid his plans to turn the tables on the French by the capture of that most strategic place, the great fortress of Louisbourg on Cape Breton Island. In preparation for this he wrote in December to Lord Loudoun, commander-in-chief of the regular forces in North America, and to Governor Lawrence of Nova Scotia, informing them that a squadron and armed forces would be sent to Halifax early in the spring.[28] Early in February of the new year he also addressed a circular letter to the governors of the other northern colonies asking their hearty co-operation in order to act offensively against the enemy

---

[25] It is of interest that the Duke of Cumberland, who fought the Highlanders at Culloden in 1746, was favourably disposed ten years later toward the idea of employing them in the King's service and transmitted to Pitt a paper embodying this project which had been submitted to him (Francis Thackeray: *History of the Right Honourable William Pitt, Earl of Chatham*, I, 268).

[26] *Bedford Correspondence*, II, 242. Previous to this period, it may be noted, we have the impressive record of the loyal Highland "Black Watch," or the 42nd regiment.

[27] James Browne (*A History of the Highlands*, IV, 133–384) gives an excellent account of the Highland regiments down to 1812.

[28] *Correspondence of William Pitt when Secretary of State with Colonial Governors and Military and Naval Commissioners in America* (ed. Gertrude S. Kimball), I, 1–2, 14.

in Canada [29] and another to all the governors in North America calling upon them to assist Rear Admiral Holburne, who would be in charge of the squadron.[30] This would be responsible for convoying ships to America carrying eight thousand regulars, who would be used not only to overwhelm Louisbourg but to energize the campaign against Crown Point and Ticonderoga in the Lake Champlain region. Together with these plans for offensive action Pitt likewise took steps for the defence of South Carolina, threatened, according to reports reaching him, by a movement of the French eastward from Louisiana. This was done by ordering Montgomery's Highlanders to South Carolina to assist in its protection.[31] Further, to secure British interests in the East Indies he dispatched a small squadron to that area under command of Commodore Stevens, and to do the same for the West Indies, another squadron under Admiral Cotes.[32] Finally, for the safety of the mother country — especially in view of the fact that he was determined to send many of the best British regiments to America and had insisted before agreeing to take the seals of office that the Hanoverian and Hessian soldiers in England should be returned home — he had his supporters introduce a militia bill in the House of Commons. This measure, like the previous one of the spring of 1756, was at length passed by the House of Commons after much amendment and then held up in the House of Lords; but, unlike the former bill, it succeeded finally in getting the approval of that body after still further drastic amendment.[33]

The explanation of Pitt's willingness to leave the British Isles without much protection on land in order to promote his program in America was that he had now become convinced that France was not in a position nor in the mood to attempt their invasion.[34] He also

---

[29] Letter of February 4, 1757, *Documents Relating to the Colonial History of the State of New York* (ed. E. B. O'Callaghan), VII, 216.

[30] Letter of February 19, *Pitt Correspondence*, I, 9–10.

[31] See his letters to Montgomery and Governor Lyttelton dated March 31, 1757, ibid., I., 27–9.

[32] John Entick: *The General History of the Late War*, etc. (London, 1765), I, 152.

[33] *Parliamentary History*, XV, 782. The bill was not enacted into law until after the retirement of Pitt from the government in April (John Entick, op. cit., I, 131–42).

[34] Andrew Mitchell, British Minister to the court of Frederick of Prussia, in writing to Holderness from Dresden on December 9, 1756, relayed the substance of a conversation that he had with Knyphausen, who before the break between France and Prussia had for years, as Frederick's representative in Paris, had the most confidential relations with such French leaders as the Duc de Belle-Isle. Knyphausen made clear why Belle-

had confidence in the ability of the royal navy to make such an attempt disastrous to the enemy. With these developments there went hand in hand the education of Pitt in the problems of continental Europe, where war on a large scale was now a fact.

After Frederick II had invaded Saxony, under circumstances described in the preceding volume of this series,[35] he proceeded to blockade the army of that principality at Pirna in order to reduce it by famine rather than destroy it by an assault upon its almost inaccessible entrenchments along the Elbe. At the same time he ordered Field Marshal von Schwerin, who had been encamped in the County of Glatz, taken from Maria Theresa in the preceding war, to invade Bohemia from that quarter and Field Marshal Keith with a second army to invade the Kingdom from Saxony, each moving in such manner as would cover the Austrian Generals Brown, entrenched at Kolin, and de Piccolomini, at Königgrätz.[36] Then leaving Pirna under close investment, he joined the army under Keith and on December 1, 1756 encountered the Austrians at Lowositz in an indecisive engagement. Soon after this event — with the hope of Austrian aid dissipated — the Saxon army at Pirna surrendered as prisoners of war and, with this, the King Elector Augustus III left for Poland, and the Electorate was treated as a conquered province: its soldiers were forcibly embodied in the Prussian army, its archives and treasury were looted, and enormous exactions were laid upon the people. This indignity visited by one of the states within the Holy Roman German Empire upon a member state could not be overlooked by the Imperial Aulic Council and the Diet. Frederick was ordered to appear before these bodies at Ratisbon, and when he failed to do so was condemned for contumacy, and the Imperial fiscal was ordered to notify him that he was put under the ban of the Empire and had forfeited all the dignities and possessions which he held under it, and that his subjects were now absolved from their allegiance to him. To carry out the sentence the Circles of the Empire were called upon to furnish their proper contingents of men and money.[37]

Isle's plan of throwing fifty thousand men across the Channel could not at this juncture of affairs be carried out and why the marshal was strongly opposed to making the attempt with a small force (*Pitt Correspondence*, ed. Taylor and Pringle, I, 206–9).

[35] *The Great War for the Empire: The Years of Defeat, 1754–1757*, pp. 420–5.

[36] *Politische Correspondenz Friedrich's des Grossen* (ed. Albert Naudé), XIV, 85–7.

[37] Advices from Ratisbon, September 23, reprinted in the *Pennsylvania Gazette*,

But this was not all that resulted from Frederick's aggressions. Louis XV now notified Maria Theresa that he would come to her aid with two armies numbering over a hundred thousand men, and Czarina Elizabeth, true to her engagement to assist the Empress Queen in case she were attacked by Prussia, put sixty thousand men in motion under General Apraxin. Sweden also threw in her lot with the other three powers and the Empire to humble Frederick. While the Russians moved against East Prussia, the French armies passed over the Rhine, one of them, under Marshal d'Estrées, pressing into Westphalia in northern Germany, and the other, under the Prince de Soubise, to the south so as to bring direct support to the Austrians. The only forces that the King of Prussia could now rely upon outside of his own was a body of Hanoverians and Hessians numbering between thirty and forty thousand men. Clearly, in view of this vast combination, not only was Prussia in mortal danger, but so were Hanover and Hesse.

When the news had first reached England of Frederick's invasion of Saxony in August 1756, there was dismay and indignation.[38] The King thought first of an open denunciation of the act, but was prevailed upon to put aside any such plan.[39] The ministry realistically adjusted itself to the changed situation of a *fait accompli*[40] and to the idea that instead of peace on the Continent for years to come — as had been fervently hoped might be the case as the result of the Convention of Westminster, signed on January 16 in London — there was to be war, with not only the King's German possessions probably involved, but also Great Britain. George for a time was hopeful that the former might be spared, and sought from Maria Theresa, for whom previously he had made so many sacrifices, a guarantee of Hanoverian neutrality. This, however, was opposed by France, the armies of which demanded a free passage through the Electorate, as Frederick previously had demanded of Saxony — something that the King as Elector was unwilling to consider.[41]

December 16, 1756; "The History of the Present War," *The Annual Register for the Year 1758*, pp. 14–15; John Entick, op. cit., II, 225.

[38] The *London General Evening Post* of September 11, 1756, in referring to the conduct of Frederick, declared that "some People in exalted stations are not a little chagrined at this Turn of Affairs in the [Holy Roman German] Empire." Nevertheless, it pointed out why an alliance with Prussia was more advantageous than with Austria.

[39] See Volume VI, page 424, of this series.

[40] See the letter of Michell, Prussia's chargé d'affaires in London, to Frederick, dated September 14, 1756, *Politische Correspondenz*, XIII, 470–1.

[41] Richard Waddington: *La Guerre de sept ans*, I, 160. For the conditions attached

Meanwhile the Newcastle ministry as early as September — realizing that only an effective military force would be likely to protect Hanover from violence, if not from devastation, and that for good or ill England must in the expanding war side with Prussia — had begun negotiations with Frederick for the creation of an army for the defence of northwestern Germany, to be composed of some thirty thousand troops drawn from Hanover, Hesse, and Brunswick, reinforced by eleven thousand Prussians, all under the command of Ludwig Ernst, Duke of Brunswick.[42] But the ministry became involved in the crisis that led to its resignation, and with the coming of Pitt to office the only step that was immediately taken involving the Continent was the decision to send home the foreign troops. In face of what seemed to be the new Minister's neglect of the interests of Hanover and Prussia, menaced as these states were with the overwhelming forces of Austria, France, and Russia, Frederick by the end of the year came to feel that in Pitt he had no friend, but an enemy,[43] and was resolved that if he could not depend upon British aid, he would take the drastic step of dismantling his powerful fortress of Wesel in Westphalia, which guarded his possessions there as well as the approach to Hanover from the west, and would concentrate his attention on the defence of Brandenburg-Prussia.[44] Should this happen, the fate of Hanover would be sealed.[45]

Late in November the King of Prussia had forwarded to London through Mitchell a *"Project de Campagne pour l'Armée des Alliés."* This had stressed the extreme threat of a powerful French army to be sent, according to reports, against Hanover and had made clear at the same time that by utilizing the Hanoverians and Hessians returning to the Continent from England, by adding to these forces troops to be obtained from Brunswick and Gotha as well as from Prussia, a force of some fifty-four thousand men could be assembled

---

to the proposed convention of neutrality for Hanover prepared by the Danish Minister Rantzau and the Minister of Maria Theresa, see Walpole, op. cit., III, 12–13.

[42] Albert von Ruville, op. cit., II, 87.

[43] Richard Waddington, op. cit., I, 173.

[44] Albert von Ruville, op. cit., II, 88.

[45] Andrew Mitchell, British Minister to Prussia, writing to Holderness on December 9, stated that Knyphausen, who knew the plans of the French so well as the result of his long residence in Paris, declared that the French had assured him that once they reached Hanover, they would treat this principality as well as Westphalia "in the same manner as Louis XIV did the Palatinate" (*Pitt Correspondence,* ed. Taylor and Pringle, I, 209).

to oppose the enemy's advance from this quarter.[46] But for weeks there was inaction. Then toward the end of December, when relations with the King of Prussia were reaching a crisis, as was indicated, the new ministry gave its assent to the project, without, however, taking any steps at the time to put it into motion. In fact, even Pitt now had come to see the value of a European war of diversion; [47] yet this meant subsidies. Early in the new year his ministry also took another step in repudiation of his earlier expressed views against both subsidies and the use of foreign troops to aid in the defence of the British Isles, when on January 16, 1757 it was decided to offer Denmark an annual subsidy of one hundred thousand pounds for the use of eight thousand Danish troops in Great Britain or Ireland.[48] These troops, it was felt, would now be needed in view of the announcement of the plans for the withdrawal of the Hanoverians and Hessians insisted upon by Pitt.

When William Pitt on February 17, 1757 faced his first Parliament after coming to office, he showed that his education in the field of foreign affairs was proceeding. No longer did he talk, as he had done while in opposition the preceding year, about letting the French overrun Hanover and then indemnify, if need be, the King for the loss of his patrimony. Now, in presenting the King's message to the Commons, he appealed for "extraordinary supplies" to prevent that catastrophe, especially in view of the formidable preparations of France and her allies, which

> "threaten with the most alarming consequences Europe in general; and as these most unjust, vindictive designs are particularly and immediately bent against his majesty's electoral dominions, and those of his good ally the King of Prussia, his majesty confides in . . . his faithful Commons, that they will cheerfully assist him in forming and maintaining an army of observation for the . . . defence and preservation thereof, and enable his majesty to fulfill his engagements with the king of Prussia, for the security of the empire, against the eruption of foreign armies, and for the support of the common cause." [49]

---

[46] *Politische Correspondenz*, XIV, 63–6.

[47] Basil Williams: *The Life of William Pitt, Earl of Chatham*, I, 304, and also his *The Whig Supremacy, 1714–1760*, pp. 335–6.

[48] Pitt was not able to be at the meeting because of illness. But there is every reason to assume that the decision could not have been made without his consent. For a discussion of this see C. W. Eldon's *England's Subsidy Policy toward the Continent during the Seven Years' War*, pp. 87–8.

[49] *Parliamentary History*, XV, 782–3. Horace Walpole wrote regarding this episode

He could not have been right both in 1756 and in 1757; and one must affirm that he was right in now accomplishing what has been characterized by one of his biographers as "perhaps the most conspicuous *volte-face* in the whole of his many-sided career." [50] It seems that at last he was fully aware that Hanover must be defended and Prussia supported if his own program for aggressive action against the French on sea and in the New World was to bear fruitage. In the debate that followed the message he eulogized Frederick and swallowed without too wry a face Fox's veiled taunt in reminding him that Pitt himself had at one time asserted "that the German measures of last year would be a mill-stone about the neck of the minister" (Newcastle) and in expressing the hope that "*this German measure* would be an ornament about the [new] Minister's neck!" [51] Strangely enough, Fox's derisive hope respecting Pitt's altered policy regarding Germany was fulfilled. For in the eyes of the latter it came to be neither a halter nor a millstone but, indeed, an ornament about his neck. As to his demand for a subsidy of £200,000 for the maintenance of Hanoverian troops to protect the Electorate, this was voted unanimously by Parliament.

It will be noted that at the time of the dismissal of Pitt from his post as paymaster in November 1755, although he had declaimed against Continental subsidies, Parliament had supported these in principle, and the new Parliament was as firmly committed to the idea of the necessity of them in implementing an effective foreign policy. Pitt certainly could not oppose this body in 1757 if he wished to retain his office, nor could he now, while remaining a member of the Cabinet Council, oppose the king. His position, as has been indicated, was far from firm. In fact, he refused the title of minister given to him by Fox, in rather weakly insisting in open debate on the Hanoverian subsidy that "he had neither ministerial power nor influence" and that the most he could do was to say: "This I will do — that I will never do." [52] His insecurity, in spite of

---

(*Memoirs of the Reign of George II*, II, 313): "One cannot say which was the most ridiculous, the richest Prince in Europe begging alms for his own country [Hanover], or the great foe of that country becoming its mendicant almoner. The next day he [Pitt] opened the message, the purpose of which was to ask 200,000l.; and he endeavoured to torture some consistence out of his conduct, sometimes refining, and when that would not do, glossing it over with what he would have put off for confident honesty."

[50] Frederic Harrison: *Chatham*, p. 87.
[51] Walpole, *op. cit.*, II, 314.
[52] Walpole, *op. cit.*, II, 314.

his dramatic reversal of views, became increasingly evident: his support, hesitant as it was, of Byng — condemned to death, but temporarily reprieved — lessened his popularity among the masses of the people, who had become convinced of the admiral's cowardice in battle — a capital offense; [53] his close connections with the court of young Prince George offended both the King and the Duke of Cumberland; [54] again, his manner of declaiming in the royal presence palled on his royal master, "a man of plain sense," who "neither used ornament in discourse nor admired it"; [55] finally, his consistent coldness toward the Duke of Cumberland, high in the esteem of the monarch, further undermined his position. For George felt that his crown in England had been saved in 1746 by his son's victory at Culloden and now looked confidently to him to save the Electorate in Germany in 1757.[56] But Cumberland had little faith in the ministry as then constituted to support him adequately as the newly designated commander of the Army of Observation, in spite of the granting of limited supplies to that end by Parliament; and, according to Horace Walpole, he only agreed to undertake the difficult and dangerous mission at the price of the dismissal of Pitt. As for the King, "could his Majesty hesitate," queries this accomplished writer, "between an unwelcome servant and a favourite dominion?" [57]

George did not long hesitate; in fact, he not unwillingly agreed to sacrifice Pitt. On April 5, therefore, after Temple had already been turned out of office, by royal command Pitt was called upon to surrender to His Majesty the seals of office. The makeshift ministry thus came to an end.[58] Three days after this event the Duke set out for Harwich to embark upon an enterprise that was destined to deprive him not only of the favour of his father but of his reputation as a military commander and also to consign him to obscurity for most of the remaining years of his life.

It would be futile to traverse minutely the maze of negotiations that ended on June 29 in the establishment of the Pitt-Newcastle

---

[53] Von Ruville (op. cit., II, 104–6) is exceedingly severe on Pitt for not throwing the full weight of his influence upon the side of Byng and justice: see also Volume VI of this series, pages 414–16.

[54] The Earl of Bute, writing to Pitt on March 2, 1757, addressed him as "My dearest Friend" (Pitt Correspondence, ed. Taylor and Pringle, I, 223–4).

[55] Walpole, op. cit., II, 378.

[56] Ibid., II, 376.

[57] Ibid., II, 377.

[58] Lord Waldegrave: Memoirs from 1754 to 1758, p. 106.

ministry.[59] The King sought to establish a Newcastle-Fox administration, but it was impossible to reconcile the quite irreconcilable
elements that were proposed from time to time for the various offices.
Meanwhile Pitt rose to a new height of popularity. He and his
friends, who had demanded a parliamentary inquiry into the conduct of the Newcastle ministry over the loss of Minorca but also had
permitted the matter to slumber for months while in office, "now
agreed to push the scrutiny into the military part with great ve-
hemence." [60] The public was delighted. At last the guilty people who
had been entrenched in high places should be brought to justice.[61]
The inquiry began with a blare in the House of Commons on April
19, but inevitably soon descended into "pantomime, from which
nothing was intended, expected, or produced." [62] In fact, at worst,
Newcastle, Anson, and others were, one must affirm, only guilty, if
guilty at all, of poor judgment with respect to defensive measures
taken in 1756, with so many factors, ponderable and imponderable,
influencing the decisions arrived at that even today it is difficult to
say to what extent the old ministry was to blame for the series of
untoward events — among these the surrender of Minorca — emphasized in the preceding volume of this series. But this was not evident
at the time of the institution of the inquiry, and people with a
burst of enthusiasm took to their hearts the defender of the national
honour who had just been forced out of office. The London Common
Council led the way in presenting to Pitt the freedom of the city
in a gold box, to be followed by a score of other cities. Seldom has
a private citizen in England been the recipient of such marks of respect and affection as was the man once again acclaimed as "the
Great Commoner." But the popular hero took good care during the

[59] For an intimate account of the efforts to form a new ministry by one sympathetic
toward Fox, see Horace Walpole, op. cit., III, 1–31.

[60] Ibid., III, 3–4.

[61] "Britannicus," in writing to the New-York Gazette from England at the period
of the beginning of the investigation, declared: "If we take a Review of our public
Transactions for the last twelve Months, we shall be forced to confess it to be a Year
of the most Dishonour to the Crown, of the most Detriment to the Subject, and of
the most Disgrace to the Nation, that ever blemished the Annals of Great-Britain. . . .
But whether the Treachery, Negligence, or Incapacity of those in Power hath been
the Cause of our Losses, and Dishonour, it doth not alter the Effect . . ." (reprinted
in the Pennsylvania Gazette of June 16, 1757).

[62] Walpole, op. cit., III, 7–11. For the resolutions relating to the loss of Minorca
approved by the Commons on May 3, including the last, which indicated that no
greater assistance, consistent with the safety of His Majesty's dominions, could have
been sent to the Mediterranean than was sent, see Parliamentary History, XV, 822–7.

debates on the inquiry not to pin the blame for Minorca on any particular man. It was clear that if he were again called upon to serve the state he would be obliged to work with some of those responsible for the decisions of the preceding year. But still he had to face the opposition of Cumberland's friends as well as Newcastle's in the royal closet.

After the plan for a Newcastle-Fox ministry had fallen to the ground, the King called upon the latter to provide an administration. But his weakness was equally evident. Newcastle's friends would not serve with him, and Lord Mansfield, on June 11, in returning to the King the exchequer seals to be turned over to Fox,[63] strongly advised the King against the step. Acting upon this sound advice, His Majesty inadvertently cleared the way for the return of Pitt.

As early as the middle of May, Pitt and Hardwicke had met "*by chance*," as Walpole describes it, to see if a Newcastle-Pitt coalition could not be formed.[64] Pitt's terms were very high — such as to exclude the Duke from interfering in either foreign or domestic affairs. But the latter, who had for years enjoyed great power, was not prepared to negotiate for a master, and the negotiations were broken off. Again, after seven weeks of futile effort to establish a ministry of some sort,[65] Newcastle and Pitt, in the presence of Hardwicke, engaged in an interview, but could come to no agreement.

Then on June 4 young Prince George brought the two men together in his own drawing-room at Leicester House in the presence of Bute. Pitt was more reasonable on this occasion, but there were still points of difference that could not be bridged. Not until Fox had accepted defeat on the 11th, with the King especially critical of Newcastle, was a further attempt made by the young court; then Lord Chesterfield was commissioned to make a last effort to heal these differences so that an orderly government might be established. Out of these final negotiations came the famous Pitt-Newcastle coalition ministry, which took office on the 29th. Again Pitt was obliged to reverse himself. In forming the Devonshire-Pitt ministry he had announced that he would not serve with Newcastle and was adamant on that point; he also had bitterly opposed Anson. Now he not only agreed to share with the Duke the power of chief minister

---

[63] Walpole, *op. cit.*, III, 29–30; George Harris, *op. cit.*, III, 131–2; *Bedford Correspondence*, III, 245–6.

[64] Walpole, *op. cit.*, III, 14.

[65] *Correspondence of Chatham* (Taylor and Pringle), I, 227–36.

upon the basis of a division of responsibilities, but, according to Walpole, took the initiative in restoring Anson to his old post as First Lord of the Admiralty.[66] In each instance his reversal was wise. The men co-operated with him and proved in the end a source of strength. For in Newcastle he found a great stabilizing force that permitted him to act with confidence in those naval as well as in military matters that lay within his jurisdiction and to carry measures through Parliament that, without the assistance of an astute and experienced political manager, he might not have been able to carry — such as the raids along the coast of France, which were not very popular either in the House or outside of it.

In forming the joint ministry each of the leaders was obliged to yield on certain points: neither wanted Fox as Paymaster General, but each had to give way to satisfy the King and Cumberland. Pitt had to accept the restoration of Holderness, Newcastle's close friend, to the Northern Department, but insisted on the inclusion of Temple in the ministry, despite the Duke's reluctance and the King's positive dislike of the Earl; [67] and the latter was now made Lord Privy Seal, an appointment that did not involve frequent appearance in the royal closet. Sir Robert Henley took Hardwicke's old place of Lord High Chancellor and in doing so gave up his seat for Bath, which Pitt coveted and now secured and thereupon held until transferred to the House of Lords as the Earl of Chatham in 1766.[68] By this shift he was at last freed of dependence upon rotten boroughs and their managers and could feel a new independence in more ways than one as he now went into action to perform one of the most signal services to the British Empire that can be credited to any Englishman.

---

[66] Walpole, op. cit., III, 32. Von Ruville, following John Almon (Anecdotes of the Life of William Pitt, Earl of Chatham), leaves the impression that Hardwicke, Newcastle's friend, suggested Anson for the Admiralty and was supported by the Duke and Bute, whereupon Pitt gave way (op. cit., II, 129).

[67] Lord Waldegrave, op. cit., pp. 113, 128.

[68] Parliamentary History, XV, 308, 1086; George Harris, op. cit., III, 144.

The Colonial Line of Defence

WITH THE CLOSE of the year 1757 in America there were few rosy tints in the horizon to encourage the English-speaking colonials. Everywhere they were on the defensive, and this was particularly true along the western frontiers.

Georgia and South Carolina had at their doors powerful and war-like Indian tribes, the Creeks and the Cherokee. They were also subjected to hostile influences from such French outposts as Fort Toulouse on the Alabama and the newly constructed Fort Massac on the lower Ohio just below the mouth of the Tennessee, in each of which there were garrisons of regular troops. Further, the Shawnee, now bitter enemies of the English, endeavoured to drive these two great confederations into the arms of the French by going into their villages and seeking to stir up their young men to launch attacks against the settlements.

How hopelessly weak the colony of Georgia was may be indicated by a letter written by Lieutenant Governor Ellis to the Board of Trade on October 5, 1756, in which he pointed out the defenceless condition of the inhabitants of that province: "The Frontier, instead of being covered by Forts, is entirely destitute of any, at least, that are not in ruins." [1] He then went on to indicate that there were not only no forts as a defence, but no artillery, no ships of war, and not one person under arms within the colony, except a company of but forty men of the South Carolina Independents. While there might be, he calculated, as many as eight hundred of the settlers capable of bearing arms, yet they were scattered throughout a wide extent

---

[1] P.R.O. Board of Trade, Georgia, 26, B. 24.

of country and therefore could not be rallied even in an emergency. As a result, the colony was wide open to attack, and only the Lower Creeks, held in a precarious alliance, stood between it and hostile thrusts from Louisiana.

It is true that toward the end of November of that year, in answer to the continuous appeals of Ellis for aid, His Majesty in Council ordered five hundred muskets with bayonets and the necessary ammunition to be sent to Georgia and to be placed in the hands of the inhabitants.[2] But even this assistance did not provide the province with a fighting force, although it did to some extent give to the inhabitants living in many isolated groups some means of protection. Yet in the spring of 1757 the forts still remained in ruins.[3] The cause of this utter incapacity of the people to care for themselves is set forth by the Governor in bald terms:

> "To this weakness and insecurity may in great measure be imputed the little progress this colony has made, notwithstanding the great & frequent helps it has had from England; for in a Country that is exposed to every kind of outrage & injustice within & from without to every sort of depredation & attack how can we expect that people will trust themselves & their property? incessantly uneasy, incessantly in alarm no person that has anything to lose or is exempt from the terms of a jail will come among us." [4]

The province of South Carolina was much more prosperous and much better able to defend itself than was Georgia. Its militia was numbered in 1756 at 8,400 and those enrolled in the companies were provided with good arms. Yet it was largely paralysed from taking aggressive action. The Negroes, many of them real jungle blacks, outnumbered the whites seven to one.[5] As a result of an intense fear of a slave insurrection, only a fraction of this potential strength was available for service on the frontier and none for operations in North America beyond the bounds of the province.[6] A purely defen-

---

[2] P.R.O., B.T., Georgia, 26, B. 38.

[3] Ellis, writing to the Board of Trade on March 11, 1757, declared: "It were greatly to be wished that those little forts which were intended to secure our frontier, such as Augusta upon this River [the Savannah] & Argyle upon the Ogechec, as well as the fortifications on the Islands toward the Spaniards were put in a defencible condition. — At present they are quite in ruins & are rather marks of our weakness than power" (P.R.O., B.T., Georgia, 27:12).

[4] Ibid.

[5] British Museum, Additional Manuscripts, 33029, folio 357.

[6] Loudoun to Lyttelton, April 24, 1757, C.O. 5: 48. The unnamed author of a "Plan for the Protection of Carolina & Georgia," under date of October 16, 1756, ex-

sive program was therefore all that was envisioned by the South Carolina Assembly.[7]

Consistent with this view, that body appropriated money for the reconstruction of Fort Prince George on the Keowee in the area of the Lower Cherokee towns and also for a fort long contemplated in the Over Hills Cherokee country.[8] However, before Lyttelton, who succeeded Glen and arrived in Charleston on June 1, could proceed with the building of the latter, a small body of Virginians under Major Andrew Lewis appeared at Chote — lying on the banks of the upper Tennessee in the Over Hills, and a few miles from this important and strategically located "place of refuge" for the Indians — and built in July 1756 a small log fort. After accomplishing this feat in aid of the common cause, Lewis and his men returned to Virginia rather disillusioned about securing Cherokee aid in protecting their own frontier, and leaving the fort without a garrison.[9]

plained that the Negroes "were offered their freedom on the occasion of the last invasion from St. Augustine, which caused numbers to desert, & the whole force & attention of the Province to prevent an insurrection" (ibid.). Governor Lyttelton seems to have written this.

[7] It is true that the author of the "Plan for the Protection of Carolina & Georgia," who it would seem by internal evidence was Governor Lyttelton, as indicated in the preceding footnote, outlined a project whereby all the colonies to the southward of Pennsylvania should join in an aggressive movement against Louisiana. This was to be done by raising a force of eleven thousand white men and four thousand Indians. These, spearheaded by a thousand regulars and a train of artillery to be sent from England, would move first against Fort Condé at Mobile, the soldiers going by water and the Indians by land. After this, New Orleans would be attacked. With the success of the enterprise, the entire expense of which would be borne by Great Britain, he thereupon proposed drastic treatment of the French inhabitants: "I recommend sending the Garrison & all other Inhabitants to Old France, & giving their Houses, Furniture, Implements for Agriculture, Improved lands, & everything else belonging to them, except their Cloaths to the irregulars that is, the Provincial troops engaged in the expedition, & three years' full pay, subsistence & Cloathing to both Officers & private men, upon Condition that they will reside there, to which must be added the expence of sending them their wives, children, & slaves. By these means a powerful Colony will be planted at once" (ibid.).

[8] Before the arrival of Lyttelton, Glen had taken steps toward the building of this fort. His various negotiations with the Assembly over this and the financing of it are fully set forth in the "Journal" of the upper house of Assembly for the year 1756 (see under date January 20, February 20, March 26, and May 15, 1756). The "Journal" is available to students in the Microfilm Division of the Library of Congress.

[9] For a very fine account of these transactions see J. R. Alden: John Stuart and the Southern Colonial Frontier, Chapter iv. The Virginia fort, according to Colonel Bouquet, writing to Lord Loudoun from Charleston on August 25, 1757, was "a meer bubble, constructed to humour the Indians. It is a square of 30 paces, wth two little Bastions and small Gorges of 4 feet & Garrison'd by a single old Cherokee who lives there." He went on to explain its uselessness: "Its proximity to Fort Loudoun wou'd

Late in September Captain Raymond Demeré, with the military engineer De Brahm, moved with a force of South Carolina Independents and provincials into the Over Hills and, after some little controversy, determined upon the site for their own fort. Like the Virginia post, it was constructed on the banks of the Tennessee, but some seven miles below the former and still closer to Chote. It was also very much more of a fort. Fort Loudoun, as it was named, represented the extreme western extension up to this time of the authority of South Carolina, for it was at least five hundred miles from Charleston. But this purely defensive policy did not end the worries of the provincial government. Among the Over Hills Cherokee there was a rather strong pro-French group, with its center at Tellico (Telliquo), west of the Tellico Mountains (the present Unoka Mountains), but east of the fort. According to Lyttelton, writing to Lord Loudoun on February 19, 1757, this group, having been "debauch'd" by the French, had made their submission to the latter. In the same letter he also told of a report that a party of French and their Indians, as a result of this submission, were coming into the Over Hills country with presents for the Upper Cherokee and that they would endeavour to build a fort at old Hiwasse (Highwasse), which lay well to the east of Tellico.[10]

To guard against such dangers, the Governor summoned to Charleston the redoubtable Upper Cherokee leader Attakullakulla, or Little Carpenter as he was called by the whites.[11] He, with over sixty followers, appeared after proper delay and for a period of over two weeks engaged in a series of conferences with Lyttelton and his advisers, which lasted from January 3 to February 17. In these the Governor made clear the great advantages that all the Indians in alliance with the English enjoyed over those in alliance with the French, who were utterly unable to supply their needs. Even the Upper Creeks living about the French Fort Toulouse had to rely

---

equally render it useless at Such a Distance, even if it was a good place" (*Bouquet Papers*, Pennsylvania Historical Commission, 1941, Series 21631, p. 66. The series number relates to that carried by the original papers, which are among the Additional Manuscripts in the British Museum, reproductions of which are in the Library of Congress. These were utilized by the historical branch of the Works Progress Administration in preparing them for publication).

[10] Loudoun Papers, No. 2865, Huntington Library.

[11] For the previous activities of Little Carpenter see Volume IV of this series, pages 70–81.

on the English for goods, he declared. In reply Little Carpenter stated that he had no notion of making peace with those he had always been killing, and then added:

> "I love to spill the blood of enemies, therefore . . . my advice to my young Fellows shall be, fall on, fall on; we have kill'd a great many of the French & their Indians & have made their blood run down Tanassee River. I will go home & do the same with the French as you said in your talk the Great King's Ships had done with theirs. . . ." [12]

But the Cherokee were clearly of two minds rather than one. While deputies of the Over Hills Tellico faction were in Canada to consummate a firm treaty of friendship with the Governor General, some two hundred from the Lower Towns went to Virginia in the spring of 1757 to engage in raiding operations in the direction of Fort Duquesne. As will be noted in the course of this volume, Cherokee sentiment was destined to fluctuate until in 1759 anti-English feeling swept even through the Lower Towns and the Over Hills Indians converged on Fort Loudoun and its defenders.

South Carolina, however, was destined to be defended, not by its own militia, but principally by troops on the royal establishment. As a nucleus there were the three Independent Companies of regulars generally stationed on the borders of the province.[13] Then on June 15 a battalion of the Royal American Regiment under Colonel Bouquet put in its appearance at Charleston, accompanied by the two hundred Virginians; and later in the year came Montgomery's Highlander regiment of a thousand men. As against this support of almost two thousand regulars maintained out of the royal exchequer, this flourishing colony, in spite of the fact that it had agreed to raise a regiment from among its militiamen, the latter, as indicated, num-

---

12 In a letter from Lyttelton to Loudoun, April 5, 1757, Loudoun Papers, No. 3290.
13 In the early spring of 1757 the three Independent Companies permanently stationed in South Carolina totalled two hundred and eighty-one men. They were distributed as follows: one hundred were at the new Fort Loudoun; twenty-nine were at Fort Prince George on the Keowee; fifty-two were at Fort Frederica on St. Simon Island off the southeastern coast of Georgia; thirteen were holding Fort Augusta, also in Georgia; twelve were at Fort Moore on the upper Savannah; six were posted at Fort Johnston at the entrance of the harbour of Charleston; and six were at Fort Frederick; finally, sixty-three were held as a reserve and for the immediate protection of the metropolis (report by Francis Halkett, dated February 23, 1757, Loudoun Papers, No. 5649).

bering over eight thousand, but quite inactive, and in spite of the
fact that it had under arms by June of that year two companies of
provincials of sixty men each, was not to make good its promise.[14]
The truth is that the men of the province were too prosperous to
want to bother with military service even to ensure the safety of
their families and possessions. They had enjoyed the King's protection for years through the presence of the Independents along their
borders, and now, in the midst of a great war, they expected that this
royal solicitude for their welfare would be continued to meet their
needs. Colonel Bouquet testified: *"They're Extremely pleased to
have Soldiers* [15] to protect their Plantations but will feel no inconveniences from them, making no difference between a Soldier & a
Negro." [16]

This spirit of dependency upon the Crown to provide for their
welfare was manifested in other ways. When Bouquet arrived with
his regulars in South Carolina, he was surprised to find one of the
fairest American cities "quite defenceless," with the forts in ruins and
a great part of the heavy guns used in the batteries — sent earlier by
the Ordnance Department — even without carriages, "some buried
in the Sand, and the people living in all the security of a profound
peace!" [17] Yet there was no peace, but a great war. When approached
to enlist in the provincial regiment, South Carolinians, however,
would plead, according to Governor Lyttelton writing in the fall of
1757, either illness or pressing business on their lands. His statement
in this connection is illuminating:

[14] Lyttelton to Loudoun, June 13, 1757, Loudoun Papers, No. 3672. On June 22
Lyttelton appeared before the Assembly to notify the two houses of the arrival of the
troops sent for the protection of the province. He declared: "Gentlemen, our most Gra-
cious Sovereign had on his part . . . done all that in your warmest Wishes you could
have hoped for. Our Fellow Subjects have also done theirs; it remains for you to do
yours . . ." (upper house of Assembly "Journal," pp. 51–3). On June 30 a bill for
granting £140,000 current money came from the Commons House of Assembly to the
upper house to provide five companies of one hundred men each as well as two additional companies of two hundred men each. The former were to be employed in the
general service of North America, if so needed; the latter for the defence simply of
South Carolina. On July 4 it was agreed that all the companies should be of one hundred men each; and on July 6 the bill was signed by the Governor (ibid., pp. 57–9).
But the men could not be found to enlist.
[15] Underlined in the original.
[16] Bouquet to Loudoun, August 25, 1757, Bouquet Papers (Pa. Hist. Com.), Series
21632, p. 64. Bouquet then went on to remark that "every body appears well disposed
to the common Defence of the Country (as far as it does not interfere with private
Interest or Conveniences)" (ibid., p. 67).
[17] Ibid., p. 66.

"I esteem it a great Happiness to this province that a considerable a number of Regulars is now here, & rather as I believe it beyond a doubt that our own people however they might prove in irregular Service wou'd be altogether unfit for the defense of this Town [Charleston] if the Enemy should form an Enterprise against it, or in Garrison duty in any other Place that shou'd be besieg'd. . . ."[18]

Even as late as the middle of October the colony had not succeeded in enlisting as many as seventy men in its provincial regiment, to be composed of seven hundred men. The members of the militia simply would not voluntarily serve, and the Assembly was unwilling to agree to Bouquet's proposal that out of this numerous group a sufficient number should be drawn by lot for duty in the regiment for a period of from two to three years.[19]

What was equally scandalous was the determination of too many of the people to profit by the presence of those who had come to save them from what seemed to be great impending dangers, by making exorbitant charges for everything required by the regulars for their sustenance and protection against the weather. Only reluctantly and after great delay was it agreed, in the face of widespread sickness and death among the soldiers living exposed to the elements, to build barracks.[20] What is more, when North Carolina raised two companies to aid the sister province in the defence of its frontiers and the men were ready to embark for Charleston, the orders had to be revoked. For not only were there no conveniences, no quarters, no supplies available for them to the southward, but what was worse, the South Carolina Assembly made it virtually impossible for them, according to Governor Dobbs, to bring in their own supplies for nourishment of these troops:

"Had we sent our companies to Charles Town we would have been in great distress to have paid them. . . . Everything we would send at above 60 per cent Loss; they had laid a Tax equal to a Prohibition on our Naval Stores, and refused to take it off even so far as to pay the Troops we sent. The Beeves I sent all took Distemper, and Mr. Stead Agent Victualer said they [the South Carolinians]

---

[18] Lyttelton to Loudoun, October 20, 1757, Loudoun Papers, No. 4675.
[19] Bouquet to Loudoun, October 16, 1757, Bouquet Papers (Pa. Hist. Com., 1941), Series 21631, p. 109.
[20] Bouquet to Loudoun, June 23, 1757, Bouquet Papers (Pa. Hist. Com., 1941), Series 21631, p. 15.

would not pay for burying them, and if they had lived we should have lost above 60 per cent upon the first Cost."[21]

North Carolina therefore also settled down, with the two colonies to the southward, to a purely defensive posture in 1757, with the two companies of provincials placed on garrison duty at Fort Johnston at Cape Fear and at the two little forts at Ocracoke and at Topsail Inlet on the coast.[22] Fort Dobbs, to protect the western settlements situated on a branch of the Yadkin, was also kept in good condition and was garrisoned by forty-six effective men and officers.[23] In truth, the colony was poor, its currency highly depreciated, and its militia, theoretically numbering almost thirteen thousand[24] according to the rolls, was but half-armed. It was much farther removed than its neighbours, however, from the dangers that the war involved.

As for Virginia, which served as a protection to North Carolina, its leaders in public life had after Braddock's defeat turned again to the youthful George Washington. He, as a result of his two campaigns toward the Ohio, was now accounted the most outstanding military leader in the Old Dominion, if not in the entire South. What doubtless appealed to his fellow Virginians was not only his unimpeachable character, his high social standing, his commanding and soldierly bearing, but his spirit of resolution and enterprise, which even two defeats had not dampened. Writing to his mother soon after the disaster at the Monongahela, he breathed the spirit that was destined eventually to make his memory forever cherished among Americans:

"If it is in my power to avoid going to the Ohio again, I shall, but if the Command is press'd upon me by the genl. voice of the Country, and offer'd upon such terms as can't be objected against, it would reflect eternal dishonour upon me to refuse it. . . ."[25]

---

[21] Dobbs to Loudoun, September 20, 1757, Loudoun Papers, No. 4502.

[22] Ibid. Artillery and ordnance stores were at this period granted by His Majesty for Fort Johnston (Colonial Records of North Carolina, ed. W. L. Saunders, V, 831).

[23] The fort was described in a report to the Assembly in December 1756, as an "Oblong Square fifty three feet by forty. . . . In height Twenty four and a half feet. . . . The Thickness of the Walls which are made of Oak Logs regularly Deminished from sixteen Inches to Six, it contains three floors and there may be discharged from each floor at one and the same time about one hundred Musketts" (ibid., V, 849).

[24] Ibid., V, 603.

[25] Writings of George Washington (ed. J. C. Fitzpatrick), I, 159.

Soon after this he was made colonel of the Virginia regiment and with great enterprise set to work to recruit it.[26] With the nucleus of the regiment already established at Fort Cumberland and after setting up temporary headquarters there in September, he proceeded to distribute his men along the frontier in such a way as to offer the best possible protection to the outlying but deserted settlements from the flying detachments of the French and their Indians. By the beginning of January of the new year he was able to write to Governor Dinwiddie from his now permanent headquarters at Winchester that his troops, some one thousand in number, were being trained in the method of Indian fighting, "and hope in a little time to make them expert." He then went on to say:

"I have already built the Forts on Patterson's Creek, (which have engaged the chief of the Inhabitants to return to the Plant'ns) and have now ordered Captain Waggener with 60 Men to build and Garrisin two others, (on places I have pointed out high up) on the South branch [of the Potomac], which will be a means of securing near a 100 Miles of our Frontiers, exclusive of the Command at Fort Dinwiddie, on Jackson's River."[27]

Washington saw no prospect, however, with the small force at his disposal, of acting other than simply on the defensive, especially in view of the fact that this was the settled policy of Maryland and, as he himself pointed out, was likewise "the full determination of the Pennsylvanians; so there can be no hope of assistance from that quarter."[28] It was at this critical juncture of affairs that he was under the strong impulsion again to resign his commission — now as the result of his quarrel over rank with Captain John Dagworthy.[29] The latter had had a King's commission and was at the time commanding some thirty Maryland men garrisoned at Fort Cumberland — where also were contingents of the Virginia regiment — and would not recognize Washington's Virginia commission. An appeal was made to General William Shirley,[30] and to determine the matter as speedily as possible, with Dinwiddie's permission, Washington, look-

---

26 After the selection of the officers, each captain was instructed to raise thirty men, each lieutenant eighteen, and each ensign twelve, to be embodied in sixteen companies (ibid., I, 163–7).

27 Ibid., I, 286.

28 Ibid., I, 286.

29 Ibid., I, 289–90.

30 See Dinwiddie's letter to Shirley, January 24, 1756, Dinwiddie Papers, I, 328–31.

ing every inch the colonel in his resplendent uniform secured for the occasion, appeared in Boston, where the general was temporarily stopping, and fully gained his point. Again in April 1756, feeling that his best efforts to care for the safety of the frontier were not being properly supported by the Virginia Assembly, he was once again fully determined to resign his post and place the problem thereby squarely in the lap of that body; but he was dissuaded from doing so in view of the news arriving by express of the presence of bodies of French and Indians within the outlying settlements and of the "general consternation" of the distressed inhabitants fleeing for safety.[31]

Hurrying back to Winchester, he found everything in confusion and proceeded to send out strong patrols from Fort Cumberland and from Winchester. This, however, did not prevent the settlers west of the Blue Ridge living on the South Branch of the Potomac from streaming eastward. Even in the neighbourhood of his own head-quarters people were being destroyed. In fact, so little faith did many of the frightened inhabitants have in the ability of the Virginia armed forces to protect them that the colonel informed the Governor that

> "numbers in the neighbourhood hold Councils and cabals to very dishonourable purposes, and unworthy the thoughts of a British subject. Despairing of assistance and protection . . . they talk of capitulating and coming upon terms with the French and Indians. . . ."[32]

He also pointed out to his friend John Robinson, Speaker of the House of Burgesses and treasurer of the province, that a large and strong fort must be built at Winchester. For it was "now the farthest boundary of this county, — no inhabitants beyond it; and if measures are not taken to maintain it, we must retire below the Blue Ridge in a very short time."[33]

In May there came a lull in the frightening incursions as reports were received that the enemy had returned to Fort Duquesne, and in that month preparations were made to build a chain of forts to protect the frontiers. But it was not until the latter part of June that the work was effectively begun — after Fort Voss, a strong post on the upper waters of the Roanoke, was burnt and captured and the

---

[31] Washington to Robert Hunter Morris, April 9, and to Dinwiddie, April 16, 1756, *Writings of Washington*, I, 309–12.

[32] Washington to Dinwiddie, April 24, 1756, *ibid.*, I, 330.

[33] *Ibid.*, I, 339.

inmates massacred — with Captain Hogg detailed by Washington to begin the most southern portion of the chain and to move northward, building these security havens at designated places, while other parties from Winchester and Fort Cumberland started from the northern limits and worked southward. But it was heartbreaking work carried on in the midst of renewed savage incursions. To aid in it, the Assembly drafted men from the militia to assist the regiment in fort-construction and in the defence of the areas most infested by the enemy. But the enlistments were for very brief periods, and when the time of the enlistment had expired the draftees would return home, leaving the refugees from the frontiers, and also the forts, without any proper protection. Many did not wait for the end of their term of service. When ordered to march to an area of danger, they would simply disappear. According to Washington, "it was common for twenty or more to desert of a night.[34]

In an effort to inspirit his troops he addressed them about the middle of August with great fervour, urging them to show "Willing Obedience to the best of Kings, and by a strict Attachment to his royal Commands, demonstrate the Love and Loyalty we bear to his sacred Person. . . ." [35] But even this deep devotion expressed by him for his King and the cause that he himself had so much at heart failed to alter the attitude of defeatism that seemed to have gripped the souls of the people of the frontier counties. Indeed, most of them seemed to be thinking almost exclusively of their own safety and were therefore indisposed to come to the aid of their neighbours. Writing to Lord Fairfax from Winchester the latter part of August, the colonel gave a graphic picture of conditions:

"When Hampshire [County, now in West Virginia and embracing the settlements on the South Branch of the Potomac] was invaded, and called upon Frederick [County] for assistance, the people of the latter refused their aid, answering, 'Let them defend themselves as we shall do if they come to us.' Now the enemy have forced through that country, and begin to infest this, those a little removed from danger are equally infatuated; and will be, I fear, until all in turn fall a sacrifice to an insulting and merciless enemy." [36]

34 Washington to Dinwiddie, August 4, 1756, ibid., I, 421.
35 Letter from Winchester, August 17, 1756, Pennsylvania Gazette, September 16, 1756. The "Address," as printed in both the Ford and the Fitzpatrick editions of Washington's Writings, was taken from the Proceedings of the Massachusetts Historical Society, XIV, 264, where the letter is modernized.
36 Ibid., I, 448.

In the face of these difficulties, which would have overwhelmed a weaker man, a man of less versatility and less ability to command, the colonel of the Virginia regiment persisted, even in the face of criticism from some of those in authority, such as Dinwiddie, who had no adequate conception of the enormous perplexities as well as the hazards involved in the task. As a result, by November of the year 1756 Washington was able to indicate that, in addition to a strong fort at Winchester, called Fort Loudoun,[37] there were sixteen defensible places, including not only forts but stockades and block-houses available for the security of the inhabitants.[38] These were designed to be located sufficiently near to one another so that patrols from one could get in touch with other patrols and assistance could be sent to any of them under attack. This meant that they were so located that when the chain was completed they would be about eighteen miles apart, with especially large concentrations of troops at Cox's (Cockes's) Fort on Patterson's Creek, well to the west of Winchester and beyond the South Branch; at Dickerson's (Dickson) Fort on Jackson's River, a tributary of the James; at the rebuilt Fort Voss on the upper waters of the Roanoke; at Fort Maidstone on the upper Potomac, near the mouth of the Cacapon, which flows into it; at Fort Dinwiddie, also on Jackson's River, as was Dickerson's; and at Fort Loudoun, the headquarters at Winchester — in the order of the need for concentration.[39] In spite of all this, Washington was compelled to indicate to Dinwiddie in November that the misery of the frontier settlers was such that "the whole back country is in a general motion toward the southern colonies; and I expect that Scarce a family will inhabit Frederick, Hampshire, or Augusta [counties], in a little time." [40]

---

[37] The student should bear in mind that there were three forts with this name: one was on the Tennessee, built by South Carolina; another in Pennsylvania, built by that province on Conococheague Creek, which flows southward into the Potomac; and the third at Winchester, in Virginia.

[38] For Washington's statement concerning the forts already constructed and those desirable to build, according to the plan drawn up, see his "A Plan of the Number of Forts, and strength necessary to each, extending entirely accross our Frontiers, from South to North" ibid., I, 490). L. K. Koontz in Appendix I of his Virginia Frontier lists the forts built along the western settled borders of the province during the war. Subsequent research has necessarily provided some correction of the efforts here made to identify the posts, a number of them having been temporary structures.

[39] Writings of Washington, I, 490. For a plan of Fort Loudoun see The George Washington Atlas (published by the Bicentennial Commission, 1932), Plate XIII.

[40] Writings of Washington, II, 4.

In truth, the heroic efforts of the Virginia regiment, labouring through winter and summer, seemed to be unavailing as the new year dawned. Writing to Captain James Cunningham, an aide-de-camp of the Earl of Loudoun, on January 28, 1757, Washington declared:

> "The French grow more and more Formidable by their alliances, while Our Friendly Indians are deserting Our Interest. Our [that is, the Virginia] Treasury is exhausting, and Our Country Depopulating, some of the Inhabitants fly entirely of [off], while others Assemble in small Forts destitute (almost) of the necessary's of Life to see what Measures will be concerted [by the government in London] to relieve their Distresses." [41]

Later, in the spring, in a letter to his kinsman Richard Washington of London, he wrote in a spirit, it is apparent, of some despondency:

> "I have been posted . . . for twenty Months past upon our cold and Barren Frontiers, to perform I think I may say impossibilitys, that is, to protect from the Cruel Incursions of a Crafty Savage Enemy a line of Inhabitants of more than 350 Miles in extent with a force inadequate to the taske. . . ." [42]

Indeed, the conception behind this purely defensive attitude was repudiated by the future Father of his Country, in favor of an aggressive move upon the enemy's powerful stronghold, Fort Duquesne, lying menacingly at the forks of the Ohio. He was persuaded, he affirmed, that three thousand men under good regulation to be furnished by the three middle colonies of Virginia, Maryland, and Pennsylvania might not only advance westward to fortify and secure the passes of the Appalachians, but even take possession of the Ohio, cut the communication between the French fortress and the Great Lakes, and thereupon make themselves masters of a place that had become "the Terror of these Colonies." [43]

Washington had to admit, however, in a long statement prepared for enlightening Loudoun on the discouraging southern frontier situation, that the Virginia Assembly then, as previously, was absolutely opposed to any such move on the part of the provincials,[44] in-

---

41 Ibid., II, 5.

42 Letter of April 15, 1757, ibid., II, 22.

43 Letter to Captain Cunningham previously cited, ibid., II, 5.

44 Washington, in enumerating the difficulties that faced him, pointed out that the Assembly, in "restraining the forces from marching out of the colony, or acting offensively," had framed a bill by which it was impossible for the officers to exercise

volving as this did great risks in sending its poorly trained forces against professional soldiers. For in case of serious defeat the great and prosperous province would be left without protection, as easy spoil for the enemy. He also had to admit to Dinwiddie, at this same period, the mutinous condition of many of his troops, some of whom were flogged severely by the decision of a recent general court-martial, while others even came under sentence of death.[45]

That the Virginia regiment had cause for deep dissatisfaction is clear in view of the fact that the men had received no new allotment of clothing from the government of Virginia since March 1754. They were still anticipating a supply at the beginning of 1757. Those who deserted, covered with nothing but rags, according to the young colonel, fixed in the mind of the public "Such horrid impressions of hardships they had encountered, that no arguments could remove these prejudices, or facilitate the recruiting service." [46] To fill up the ranks, vagrants had been impressed by Act of Assembly when volunteers failed. But "these abandoned miscreants," as Washington called them, embraced every opportunity to effect their escape. Then the Assembly in the face of the continued ravishing of the frontier by the enemy had decided to bring the number of the Virginia regiment up to fifteen hundred men, as has been previously indicated, by drafting from the militia. This did not prove effective, however, since the rich by paying ten pounds were exempted, with "many of the poorer sort absconding." [47] Labouring under these manifold handicaps, the depleted regiment had nevertheless performed, as has been shown, a useful service. During the year 1756 it had engaged in over twenty skirmishes with the enemy, suffering casualties of almost a hundred killed and wounded, and by its activity had so protected the inhabitants of the province that not one half as many people were lost as were in the neighbouring colonies.[48]

The year 1757 was, in fact, one of deep gloom and harassment for Washington and his regiment. In the spring of that year his officers signed a "Remonstrance" to Governor Dinwiddie pointing

discipline over the soldiers should they be taken out of the area where they were supposed to act on the defensive (Washington to Loudoun, January 1757, Loudoun Papers. No. 2659. The original Washington letter should be used rather than the defective copy printed in the *Writings of George Washington* in the Fitzpatrick edition).

[45] Washington to Robert Dinwiddie, January [12], 1757, *ibid.*, II, 1.

[46] Washington to Loudoun, January 1757, *op. cit.*

[47] *Ibid.*

[48] Again according to Washington (*ibid.*).

out that, unlike those colonials under arms for a stated period, they had been in continuous service for three years and yet were deprived of "the Benefits common to British Subjects." They went on to declare that

> "We are defending part of the Domain of Great Britain . . . that we want nothing but Commissions from His Majesty to make us as regular a Corps as any upon the Continent . . . we labour under every disadvantage, without enjoying a single Benefit which the Regulars do." [49]

But the regiment was destined to remain on the provincial establishment. During the early months of the year there was comparative quiet along the lengthy Virginia frontier, with only desultory attacks by small parties of French Indians. Then in the month of April, as the result of repeated urging on the part of the Virginia authorities, some four hundred southern Indians appeared at Fort Loudoun: Cherokee, Catawba, Tuscarora, and those from smaller tribes. Dinwiddie ordered them to divide into scalping parties and move in the direction of Fort Duquesne, not only to secure scalps and prisoners, but to obtain intelligence respecting the movements of the enemy and their strength at the French fort. [50] These reinforcements were welcome, as the Virginia regiment at this juncture was reduced to but four hundred men, who were attempting to guard the three hundred and fifty miles of frontier. [51] In fact, on account of the fewness of its defenders, the Governor ordered Washington to desert most of the long line of forts and to concentrate his forces at but seven of them. [52]

The order for concentration was sensible, and doubtless it was felt that with so large a body of Indians now in service the outer settlements would be saved from many of the savage forays of the preceding year. Yet most of the Indians who arrived in Virginia made hardly more than a single expedition before they determined to re-

---

[49] Enclosed in Washington's letter of April 16, Writings of Washington, II, 25-7.

[50] Dinwiddie to Loudoun, May 2, 1757, Dinwiddie Papers, II, 616-17. Writing to Pitt on May 14, the Governor avowed that scalping parties were "a barbarous Method of conducting Warr, introduc'd by the French, wch we were oblig'd to follow in our own Defence" (ibid., II, 620).

[51] Ibid., II, 618.

[52] At Fort Loudoun at Winchester, Fort Maidstone at the mouth of the Great Cacapon River, which flows into the upper Potomac, Fort Edwards on Capon River, Fort Pearsall and Fort Buttermilk, both on the South Branch of the Potomac, Fort Dickinson on the upper James, and Fort Voss on the upper Roanoke (ibid., II, 622).

turn home. The reason the Catawba gave was perfectly correct: that the French Indians were raiding their own country to the south and they therefore had to leave to protect their wives and children.[53] As for the Cherokee, about one hundred and eighty in number, they were very difficult to keep under control and were guilty of "many Disorders" as they passed through the country and even accused the Virginians of "perfidy and deceit" when their exorbitant demands were not readily met by Washington and his officers.[54] One of the difficulties of the situation was that "the different colonies [were] struggling with each other for their assistance." For not only had Virginia bargained with them, but also Maryland and Pennsylvania, with the result that, realizing their importance, they acted, according to Washington, "very insolently." [55] It was perhaps with not a little sense of relief that the colonel saw many of them follow the Catawba and Tuscarora back to their own towns. Nevertheless, the more dependable remained and began bringing in some scalps and prisoners. By means of the latter information was gained as to the strength of Fort Duquesne, where it appeared by the testimony of the French prisoners that there were some six hundred European troops together with a smaller body of Indians.[56] The number of Indians was soon increased.

As a result the commandant of the fort, Marchand de Lignery (Lignerie, Liniery), a veteran of the Great Lakes region who had displaced Dumas at the forks of the Ohio, now sent out a party of some two hundred French and Indians in the hope that it might surprise and capture Fort Cumberland.[57] Reports of the movement were carried to Maryland, Pennsylvania, and Virginia by friendly Indians, who insisted that a strong army with artillery was moving over Braddock's road to the attack. There was general consternation for a time. It seemed that the fort was doomed, weakly garrisoned as it was by a small body of troops. But the Frenchman in charge of the expedition, a M. de Montizambert de Niverville, fell ill, his

[53] Dinwiddie to Loudoun, May 18, 1757, ibid., II, 629. As soon as the presence of the Catawba was discovered among the raiding parties the English sent out, the commander of Fort Duquesne directed a number of his own Indians to go into the Catawba country (Vaudreuil to de Moras, July 12, 1757, Documents Relating to the Colonial History of the State of New York, X, 581).

[54] Washington to John Robinson, May 30, 1757, Writings of Washington, II, 43; Dinwiddie to Pitt, June 18, 1757, Dinwiddie Papers, II, 641.

[55] Washington to Dinwiddie, June 10, 1757, op. cit., II, 48.

[56] Washington to Colonel Stanwix, June 12, 1757, ibid., II, 60.

[57] Vaudreuil to de Moras, July 12, 1757, N. Y. Col. Doc., X, 581.

force split up into raiding parties, and only some twenty of his followers reached the vicinity of the fort.[58] From this time on, however, until late in the winter of 1757 the bloody raids continued,[59] with parties of English and Cherokee counter-raiding in the area of the forks of the Ohio, but with minor success. In the midst of the alarm Dinwiddie ordered the militia of the neighbouring counties to march to Winchester.[60] But most of them arriving were without arms, ammunition, or provisions, and although offered wages by Washington to forward the work of completing the fortifications at Fort Loudoun, they were, according to him, "deaf to this or every other proposition . . . to the interest of the Service."[61] But in the face of such "flagrant breach of the law and a total contempt of Orders" on the part of the militia, the colonel could only write to the Governor to demand that this deplorable insubordination be made the subject of inquiry.

At this point it should be made clear that at the meeting of the governors with Lord Loudoun in Philadelphia early in the year it was agreed that all the forces operating in the area affected by the presence of the French at Fort Duquesne should be under the control of an officer of the regular army who was to be stationed with a battalion on the frontiers of Pennsylvania, as perhaps the most critical point. The officer in charge was Colonel John Stanwix, of the 60th regiment, a highly competent professional soldier. Up to the period of the alarm over the safety of Fort Cumberland, Washington had been kept in ignorance of this arrangement by Dinwiddie, who had seen fit to issue all orders to him. Now, however, he informed Washington that as Stanwix was commander-in-chief, his orders must be obeyed without regard to any others received.[62] This must have brought a sense of relief to Washington, who had long been irritated by the Governor's petty interference in military matters upon which he was not fully informed. Especially was he reassured in his precarious situation since Stanwix was prepared to march to his assistance on any emergency.

On July 15, to give his superior a true understanding of the condi-

---

[58] Ibid.
[59] On July 7 the commandant of Fort Duquesne wrote with jubilation to Vaudreuil that the different parties he had sent out had recently brought in some two hundred prisoners or scalps (Vaudreuil to de Paulmy, September 7, 1757, ibid., X, 670).
[60] Dinwiddie Papers, II, 643.
[61] Washington to Dinwiddie, June 27, 1757, Writings of Washington, II, 79.
[62] Dinwiddie to Washington, June 24, 1757, Dinwiddie Papers, II, 654.

tion of the troops under his command, he proceeded to write with great frankness to this estimable soldier. In his long letter, among other things, he stated:

> "Militia, you will find, Sir, will never answer your expectation; no dependence is to be placed on them; They are obstinate and perverse . . . ordered to certain posts for . . . the protection of the Inhabitants, [they] will, on a sudden, resolve to leave *them*, and the united vigilance of their officers can not prevent them."

But this was not his only trouble. The regiment was sadly depleted, and to bring it up to twelve hundred the Assembly had agreed to draft men out of various counties. Washington in his letter then turned to this tender subject:

> "No man I conceive was ever worse plagued than I have been with Draughts . . . sent from the several counties in this Government, to complete its Regiment: out of 400 that were received at Fredericksburgh, and at this place, 114 have deserted. . . . I have a Gallows near 40 feet high erected (which has terrified the *rest* exceedingly), and I am determined if I can be justified in the proceeding, to hang two or three on it, as an Example to others." [63]

This he proceeded to do in the case of two deserters, one of whom had deserted twice and the other Washington described as "one of the greatest villians on the continent." [64]

In spite of the fact that Washington continued to be plagued by desertions after the men had received clothes, arms, and bounty money,[65] he did succeed in retaining enough of the draftees so that by the middle of September he had in the regiment some seven hundred — yet five hundred short of the number promised by the government.[66] But he was unable to prevent a continuance of the "horrid devastations" of the enemy that began in June and mounted in intensity.[67] Writing in October to Stanwix, who was also having his troubles in Pennsylvania, he declared:

---

[63] Washington to Stanwix, July 15, 1757, *Writings of Washington*, II, 97.

[64] Washington to Dinwiddie, August 3, 1757, *ibid.*, II, 118.

[65] Washington to Dinwiddie, September 17, 1757, *ibid.*, II, 126. In this letter he refers to the desertion of thirteen out of twenty-nine drafts from Lunenberg County.

[66] *Ibid.*, II, 127.

[67] Lord Fairfax wrote to Loudoun on October 2 relative to the "unhappy situation in the back parts of this Colony." He stated that a fortnight ago a party of Indians came within twelve miles of Winchester and his own plantation and scalped or carried away thirty-four men, women, and children. Although Washington sent out some of his soldiers and the county some of the militia, they saw no Indians and returned after burying the dead (Loudoun Papers, No. 4570).

"To think of defending a frontier, as ours is . . . with only seven hundred men, is vain and idle. . . . I am, and have for a long time been, fully convinced, that, if we continue to pursue a defensive plan, the country must be inevitably lost." [68]

To Dinwiddie he wrote in despair late in that month that

"if there is no Expedition to the westward . . . nor a force more considerable than Virginia can support, posted on our frontiers . . . there will not, next campaign I dare affirm, be one soul living on this side the Blue Ridge the ensuing autumn . . . an incredible number of Inhabitants has fled in consequence of the two last incursions of the enemy. . . . I do not know on whom this miserable and undone people are to rely for redress." [69]

But the Virginia Assembly was still convinced that no force that could possibly be raised within this province and those adjoining would be prepared to undertake the task, without risk of another great disaster like that of 1755 of marching against the French at the forks of the Ohio. What is more, the people of that fair province, like those of South Carolina, were so much concerned with their private affairs that, out of between one and two hundred thousand white people, the able-bodied of whom made up a numerous county militia, [70] Washington was forced to rely upon a mere handful of devoted men, as well as others who were not so devoted but feared the gibbet prominently displayed as a warning at headquarters, to care for the safety of those who remained at home.

If Virginia, perhaps the most populous if not the most prosperous British colony in North America, was indisposed to risk the effort of trying to dislodge the French from Fort Duquesne, still less were Maryland and Pennsylvania. Of the latter two, Maryland with a population in the fall of 1756 estimated at 180,000 white people, [71] had under arms in the late spring of the new year but 250 men. [72] This was true in spite of the ravishing of the western settlements of the province by the French and Indians and the consequent deser-

---

[68] *Writings of Washington*, II, 145.

[69] *Ibid.*, II, 151.

[70] The population was estimated in 1755 at 230,000 people in the official report to the Board of Trade, wherein the number enrolled in the militia was placed at 27,000 men (*Dinwiddie Papers*, I, 387).

[71] Proceedings and Acts of the Assembly of Maryland, September 23, 1756, *Archives of Maryland*, LII, 608.

[72] *Ibid.*, IX, 1.

tion of the flourishing area of the lower Conococheague, far to the east of Fort Cumberland, during the fall of 1756, when the Maryland contingent at that fort had also been withdrawn and Fort Frederick, near the Potomac on the site of the present town of Hancock, was designated by the Assembly to serve thereafter as the most westerly defence of the province. In the spring of 1757, however, as a result of a conference of the Governors of Pennsylvania, Maryland, Virginia, and North Carolina with Lord Loudoun in Philadelphia, it was agreed that Virginia should send four hundred men to the assistance of South Carolina and that, as a consequence of this relief, Maryland should assume the full responsibility of garrisoning Fort Cumberland, containing as it did a large deposit of the King's military supplies.[73] This seemed to be a very reasonable proposal, in view of the fact that the fort was in Maryland. Yet when Captain Dagworthy, under orders of Governor Sharpe, returned to the fort with one hundred and fifty men late in April to serve as the garrison, this aroused the most violent protests within the Assembly. For that body took the position that the fort was of much greater protection to Virginia than to the part of Maryland that was still settled, and forthwith determined to withdraw all financial support from even their own soldiers so long as they remained on guard at this place.[74] Indeed, throughout the rest of the war the province remained rather ignominiously on the side lines, as it were, with the Assembly choosing to elevate its rather trivial grievances against the Proprietor far above the tremendous challenge that the presence of the French and Indian pressure on the western borders presented to all American colonials. The mere fact that the more thickly populated parts of the province were fairly well protected by the long line of defences erected to the southward by Virginia and to the northward by Pennsylvania and therefore enjoyed a sense of security and immunity from danger does little to mitigate the conduct of those in control of the Assembly, who apparently reflected the attitude of the leading planters and merchants. The latter simply did not want the war to interfere with their private activities and the making of war-time profits.

In Pennsylvania, with a long undefended frontier like that of Virginia exposed to the merciless visitations of the French and Indians,

---

[73] Governor Sharpe to Lord Baltimore, Philadelphia, March 23, 1757, *ibid.,* VI, 533.

[74] Sharpe to Colonel Stanwix, May 8, 1757, *ibid.,* VI, 550–1.

the defeat of Braddock's army came as a great shock. To all except
the most confirmed of the pacifistic groups, the need for providing
adequate protection for the frontier settlements was now brought
home sharply. On July 20, soon after news arrived of the disaster,
the Governor, Robert Hunter Morris, sent to the Assembly a notification that, as an encouragement for those who would engage in a
common enterprise with the neighbouring colonies for the purpose
of removing the French from the Ohio, the Proprietors were prepared to offer some six or seven hundred thousand acres of good
land, advantageously situated from the point of view of transportation and markets; [75] this, at the current rate at which lands similarly
located were selling, would amount to the neighbourhood of some
ninety thousand pounds Pennsylvania currency, according to the
Governor.[76] Ignoring this really generous offer, the Assembly in its
turn, to provide for defence, was led to bring in a bill to appropriate
the sum of fifty thousand pounds to be raised by a tax on *all* estates,
real and personal — including the Proprietarial lands. This led to a
deadlock, such as had previously occurred between the Governor
and the Assembly. For the Governor was forbidden by his instructions from the Penn family to approve the taxation of their lands
by the Assembly.[77] The Proprietors, however, were willing to make
voluntary contributions out of their resources for the common ends
and welfare.

But the Indians did not await the settlement of the new-old dispute. In November 1755 came the massacre of the Moravians and
their Christian Indians at Gnadenhütten, — in the region of the upper Lehigh.[78] Elsewhere along the frontiers there were isolated kill-
ings and the burning of homes. In the face of this confusion, this

---

[75] Every colonel was to receive one thousand acres, every lieutenant colonel and
major seven hundred and fifty, every captain five hundred, every lieutenant and ensign
four hundred, and every common soldier two hundred, in addition to his pay and other
perquisites provided for in the service (*Pennsylvania Colonial Records*, VI, 504, 539).

[76] *Ibid.*, VI, 540. The offer was extended, according to Thomas Penn, writing to
the Board of Trade on November 17, 1755, to embrace three thousand men who for
thirty years would enjoy exemption for paying quit-rents (C.O. 5:1274).

[77] As John Marshall later pointed out, the power to tax is the power to destroy.
The Pennsylvania Proprietors took the position that their status as grantors of all land
in Pennsylvania removed them necessarily from the power of the legislature to tax
them. In the words of Morris to the Assembly: "You cannot, therefore, without inter-
verting the order of things, have a Power over those from whom you and every one
else in the Province derive all the power they have" (*ibid.*, VI, 541).

[78] *Pennsylvania Archives* (first series), II, 521-2.

inertia, on the part of the government, the settlers, "driven to distraction, came down and demanded Protection of the Legislature in the most peremptory Manner." [79] Indeed, the citizens of the newly established town of Reading in a memorial sent to the Governor reflected the general attitude of the frightened frontier population. In it they declared:

> "If we are not immediately supported, we must not be sacrificed and are therefore determined to go down to Philadelphia with All that will follow us, and Quarter ourselves on its inhabitants and await our Fate with them." [80]

Then and only then was the Assembly brought to action. Retreating temporarily from the high grounds that it had taken and in order to reach an accommodation with the Governor, it agreed that the province should grant £55,000 "for the King's use, on terms that could be consented to," with the Proprietors prepared on their part to make a contribution of £5,000 for the same purpose.[81] In order to square this act of appropriations with their testimony, the Quaker majority saw to it that the bill made no mention of plans for warlike activity on the part of the government of the province. The money was appropriated for purchasing provisions for the King's forces, for erecting and maintaining "posts," for the paying of expresses, for the clearing of woods, for the support of the Indians, and for "other heavy charges for the King's use." Thereupon a comprehensive program was undertaken and carried to completion with the building of a chain of forts and blockhouses that ultimately extended from the upper Delaware to the Potomac, with here and there strong places such as Fort Augusta at Shamokin, where the east and west branches of the Susquehanna unite, and at other critical points.[82]

This work was carried out by a volunteer force of a thousand men formed into companies. But they were under no effective discipline. The Assembly — dominated by members of the Society of Friends, who were supported by other pacifistic groups as well as other groups

---

[79] Governor Morris to the Board of Trade, February 1756, C.O. 5:1274, Bundle V, 166. For the "Remonstrance" likewise of the Mayor and the Council of Philadelphia of November 25, 1755, see the *Pennsylvania Archives* (eighth series), V, 151–3.

[80] Quoted by J. Bennett Noland in his *General Benjamin Franklin*, p. 12.

[81] C.O. 5:1274, Bundle V, 166; *Pennsylvania Archives* (eighth series), V, 4158–9; *Statutes at Large of Pennsylvania*, V, 201–12.

[82] *Pennsylvania Archives* (first series), II, 557 et seq. See also Index under "Forts."

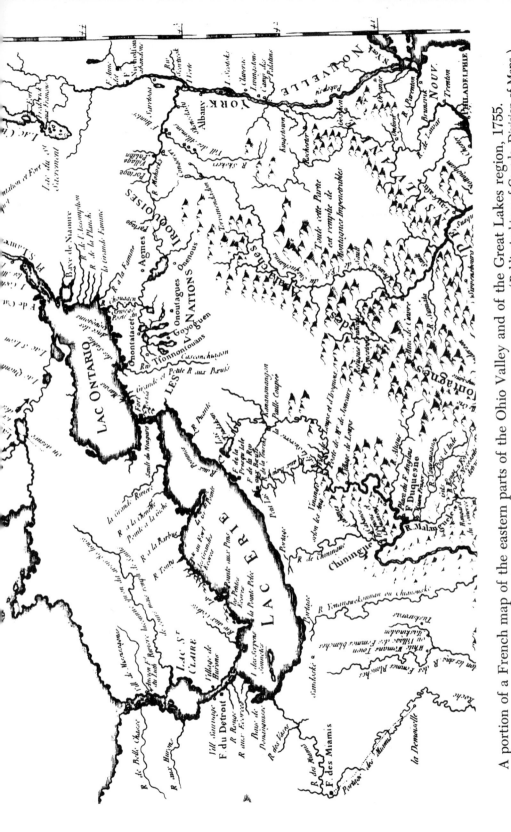

A portion of a French map of the eastern parts of the Ohio Valley and of the Great Lakes region, 1755.
(Public Archives of Canada, Division of Maps.)

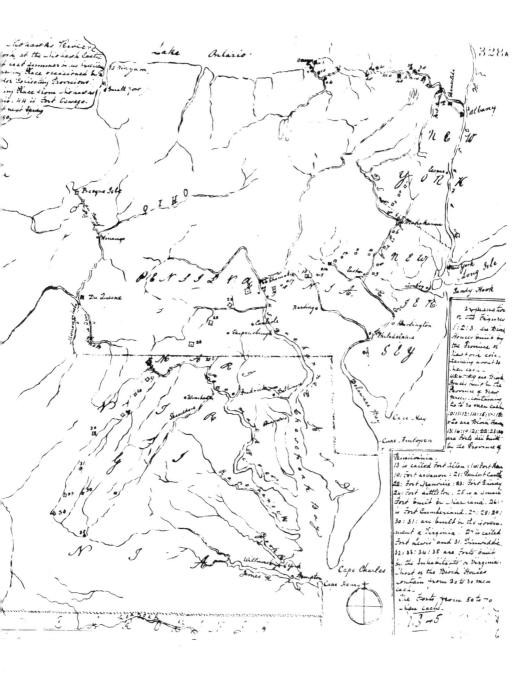

William Alexander's manuscript sketch of the western forts and posts, 1756.
(Public Archives of Canada, Division of Maps.)

that were reluctant to serve in arms even in this emergency [83] — was unwilling to pass any law that provided any element of coercion. As a result it was difficult, if not impossible, to hold popularly elected military officers as well as the men to their duty when this became disagreeable and arduous.[84] To the Assembly such "matters of compulsion" as an effective military law were unlawful; to the Governor the absence of such a law made it impossible to guarantee the protection of the province.[85]

Thus the utmost that the Assembly of Pennsylvania could be brought to undertake as a responsibility was the guarding of the more thickly settled part of the province. An offensive movement on the part of those colonies most seriously affected by the presence of the French and Indians at Fort Duquesne — such a movement as the Pennsylvania Proprietors sought and were prepared to support liberally — was not attempted and would not be considered. Even these purely defensive measures were so very defective that the

---

[83] Isaac Norris, the Speaker of the Assembly, writing to Robert Charles on October 5, 1755 (Norris Letter Book, p. 83, the Hist. Soc. of Pa.), declared: "Our Elections are now over and the Governer [sic] is like to meet ye same Sentiments and nearly ye Same Faces for one year longer." In the elections of the preceding year, out of a total of thirty-six members only eight were not under the control of the Society of Friends (Pennsylvania Magazine of History and Biography, XXIII, 516–20). For the list of representatives elected in October 1755, see the Pennsylvania Archives (eighth series), V, 4087–8, 4093.

[84] C.O. 5:1274, Bundle V, 166. The "Act for the Better Ordering and Regulating such as are Willing and Desirous to be united for Military Purposes within this Province" (Statutes at Large, V, 197–201), passed on November 22, 1755 by the Pennsylvania Assembly after much debate and also after many violent petitions had been received, observed in its preamble that it was undesirable for great bodies of men to gather voluntarily on any occasion of alarm without any authority or discipline, and then declared: that it would now be lawful for those freemen who saw fit to form themselves into companies to choose by a majority of votes their company officers; these in turn by vote should choose their regimental officers; the latter, in conjunction with the Governor, should thereupon draw up articles of war and, when these were freely subscribed to by the volunteers, should enforce them — provided that such articles were comfortable to the military laws of Great Britain, in so far as a volunteer force could be compared with standing troops; further, that no youth under twenty-one and no indentured servant should be enlisted without consent of parents or masters; and, finally, that no volunteer should be compelled to go more than three days' march from the settled parts of the province or be kept more than three weeks at garrison duty without his expressed permission. The act was repealed by King in Council July 7, 1756 (C.O. 5:1274, Bundle V, 186).

[85] The student should consult the article by Theodore Thayer: "The Quaker Party of Pennsylvania" (Pa. Mag. of Hist. and Biog., LXXI, 19–43), in which the writer insists that the reluctance of the Pennsylvania Assembly to pass urgent defence bills was not because of the pacifism of the Quakers.

Governor was now convinced of the necessity for parliamentary intervention in the affairs of the province. He requested this and was supported by a petition to the King signed by numbers of leading inhabitants. This petition was referred to the Board of Trade for consideration. After due hearings, at which the London agent and also legal counsel for the Assembly were present, this body on March 3, 1756 drew up a representation to the Lords of the Committee of the Privy Council. This emphasized how very improper and inadequate were certain of the acts of the Assembly relating to the defence of the province and recommended the repeal of this legislation.[86] The Board also repudiated vigorously the contention of the Assembly that under the charter "in case of any Emergency, the Proprietor was obliged . . . to defend them" (that is, the people of the province.[87] It declared that

> "the Legislature of every Country is in Duty bound, by the Original Constitution, Frame and Compact of Government, to support and defend that Government, and those who are subject to it; . . . that the Measures alledged by the Assembly to be intended to this end are improper . . . and that there is no Reason to hope that proper or effectual Measures will be taken, while the Majority of the Assembly consists of Persons whose avowed Principles are against Military Services, however Necessary for the Security and Defence of Government, who have declared by publick Acts, that it is a Violation of a Fundamental of the Constitution, and a direct Breach of Privilege, to compel Persons to bear Arms, or to find or Provide for such as will do Military Service in their Stead, and who, tho' not a sixth Part of the Inhabitants of the Province, are yet, contrary to the Principles, the Policy, and the Practice of the Mother Country, admitted to hold Offices of Trust and Profit, and sit in the Assembly, without their Allegiance being secured to the Government by Sanction of an Oath; and therefore we see no Remedy to the Evils so justly complained of by the Petitioners, unless by the Interposition of an Act of the *British* Legislature, agreeable to the Opinion of His Majesty's Attorney and Solicitor General [in the year 1744] . . . when the defenceless State of this Province was under your Lordships Consideration. . . ."[88]

---

[86] "An Act for punishing Mutiny and Desertion" and "An Act for the better ordering and regulating such as are willing and desirous to be united for Military Purposes."

[87] The report of the Board of Trade, the recommendations of the Lords of the Committee, and the final action of the Privy Council in repealing the laws in question are presented in Franklin's *Pennsylvania Gazette* for October 21, 1756.

[88] *Ibid.*

Clearly the government of the mother country was getting ready to take drastic action for the protection of the lives and property of the inhabitants of Pennsylvania, and also to bring them into more active participation in the war. It now was proposed to compel by act of Parliament everyone occupying public office or a seat in the Assembly to take an oath — a measure that would have had the effect of eliminating permanently from public life in the province every conforming member of the Society of Friends. The imminence of this move was brought home to influential members of the Society in England. They finally agreed that they would bring pressure to bear upon their brethren in the Pennsylvania Assembly to resign their seats voluntarily if the British ministry on its part would agree not to raise such an impediment to American Quakers in public service in normal times.[89] The ministry accepted this pledge. As a result of this understanding, in the annual election of 1756 fourteen Church of England men were chosen to the Assembly together with seven Presbyterians, four "Call'd Quakers, but not Owned by the Society," one Baptist, one Lutheran, and a Moravian — making twenty-eight who had no scruples respecting war measures, as against eight Quakers who were pacifists, out of a total of thirty-six members.[90]

Meanwhile, in the face of the brewing storm against them, the Assembly in the spring of 1756 had bent sufficiently before it to take steps to strengthen the law regulating the conduct of the soldiers in the pay of the province. For on April 15 the Quaker majority departed sufficiently from their doctrine of noncoercion to pass an act, in place of the useless law of the preceding year that had been repealed by His Majesty in Council, that extended to Pennsylvania the same procedures and punishments laid down in the British statute relating to mutiny and desertion passed by Parliament in the twenty-

---

[89] This agreement had been reached before the Board of Trade made its representation, according to a letter written by Thomas Penn to Provost William Smith of the College of Philadelphia on February 15, 1756 (Smith Mss., Hist. Soc. of Pa.).

[90] "Members of the House of Assembly in Philadelphia as they stood October 14th, 1756," Hist. Soc. of Pa. Transcriptions. Those elected in October are listed in the *Pennsylvania Archives* (eighth series), VI, 4383. According to the *Pennsylvania Gazette* (October 7, 1756): "We hear there are sixteen of the People called Quakers, and that the Remainder are of the Church of England, and other Denominations. Of those elected, two Quakers from Bucks County and two from Chester County at the beginning of the session of the legislature after the October elections resigned their seats 'at the request of our Friends' and their places were taken by those with no scruples respecting War-like Measures" (*Pennsylvania Archives*, eighth series, VI, 4385–6).

eighth year of George II.[91] What is more, steps had also already been taken — as a result of private initiative and the decision reached by the non-pacifistic commissioners appointed to disburse the funds that had been granted by the Assembly — to enlist the services of friendly Indians as well as others to make war on those hostile red-skins who had been ravaging the outlying settlements of the provinces. By popular subscription seven hundred pieces of eight were raised as a reward for those who would bring to Philadelphia the heads of Shingas and Captain Jacobs, leaders of the hostile Dela-wares.[92] Further, the commissioners in charge of the military funds [93] determined now to support the Governor in an open declaration of war against the enemy Indians and to allot money for the payment of prisoners and even of scalps secured from among the natives. As a result, on April 9 they set up a schedule of rewards for these.[94] But little enough was achieved by the above measure, at least for some months. The French and their Indians continued their savage raids: on July 30 Fort Granville on the Juniata River was destroyed.[95] Al-

---

[91] 7 Ruffhead, 576. For the Pennsylvania law see *Statutes at Large*, V, 219–21. The law was to expire on October 30 of the same year. Upon the expiration of this act, on November 6, another act, to expire the following March 25 and in almost identical terms, was passed, but it in addition, significantly, included a clause that permitted the punishment of crimes committed by soldiers while under the earlier act to be carried out during the life of the later law (*ibid.*, V, 266–8).

[92] See the advertisement in the *Pennsylvania Gazette* of January 1, 1756.

[93] They were Isaac Norris, the Speaker, James Hamilton, former Governor of the province, John Mifflin, Benjamin Franklin, Joseph Fox, John Hughes, and Evan Morgan.

[94] For every male Indian prisoner, one hundred and fifty Spanish milled dollars; for every female Indian prisoner, one hundred and thirty; for every scalp of a male Indian over ten years of age, one hundred and thirty; and for every scalp of a female Indian, fifty (*Pennsylvania Archives*, first series, II, 619, *Pa. Col. Rec.*, VII, 78–9). Two of the commissioners, John Mifflin and Joseph Fox, Quakers in good standing up to this time, were now disciplined by the Society. On April 30, 1756 at a monthly meeting of Friends, when they refused to admit the error of their ways, they were finally disowned. The minute drawn up is of interest to the student. The first part of it reads as follows: "The Overseers [of the monthly meeting] inform'd the Meeting they had dealt with John Mifflin & Joseph Fox for being concern'd in promot⁸ & advising to the late Declaration of War against the Indians, offering Rewards for scalping them, & other Military Preparations in open Violation of that Testimony of Peace ever profess'd by us since we were a People & that there does not appear any Grounds of Hope of our convincing them of their Error, as they urge it to be the Result of their Judgement after mature Consideration, and express a Desire that Friends should give themselves no fur-ther Trouble with them" (Shippen Mss., in the possession of Roland S. Morris of Philadelphia).

[95] The enemy burned this post and carried a number of people who had sought its protection into captivity. The attack was made while the garrison was protecting some

most all of those inhabitants of Cumberland County who still remained in their homes fled eastward at this juncture, and those in the western part of York County also took flight and followed their example when reports arrived about sporadic attacks in that area.

Only one act of heroism on the part of the Pennsylvania volunteers lifted the gloom in the summer of 1756. On July 30 Colonel Armstrong with a small force of three hundred moved out of Fort Shirley — located on Aughwick Creek, which flows northward and then empties into the Juniata some miles west of where Fort Granville had stood on the banks of that river — and, passing silently over the famous Frank's Town Traders' Path, arrived in the neighbourhood of the important Indian town of Kittanning on the Allegheny River.[96] Here it was that the notorious Delaware chief Captain Jacobs held forth, and here likewise many prisoners captured by the Indians were held for ransom. Early in the morning of August 8 Armstrong delivered a surprise attack on the village, burnt most of the houses containing large stores of ammunition, released a number of prisoners, and succeeded, in spite of heavy losses sustained, in destroying some thirty or forty warriors.[97] The effect of this might have been important upon the attitude of the hostile western Indians had not the news spread like wildfire that Oswego on Lake Ontario with its forts and its regiments of colonials had fallen into the hands of the French on August 14. Everywhere in the back country the English, in spite of Armstrong's feat, were now held in contempt by the Indians. Even before the fall of the great trading center the French had boasted, according to reports received in Albany, that its conquest "would secure to them the quiet Possession of Pennsylvania, and give them a free Entrance into the Province of New-York." [98] There was danger of this. Even the Germans on the Pennsylvania frontier were now brought into an attitude of hostility to their government by Saur's pacifistic newspaper, the *Pennsylvanische Berichte*.[99] Conrad Weiser in a letter to the Governor at this period

of the inhabitants who were seeking to harvest their crops (*Pennsylvania Gazette*, August 19, 1756).

[96] Kittanning was located about twenty-five miles above Fort Duquesne.

[97] For a detailed account of this episode see Armstrong's letter written to Governor Denny on September 14, 1756, the *Pennsylvania Archives* (first series), II, 767-73; also the *Pennsylvania Gazette*, September 23, 1756. On the question of the death of the Indian Captain Jacobs see the *Western Pennsylvania Magazine of History*, XVII, 121-3.

[98] See Albany advices of August 19, *Pennsylvania Gazette*, August 26, 1756.

[99] Saur, in the editions of August 16 and 29 of his paper, had charged, contrary to

emphasized the disaffection existing among many of these settlers, who did not hesitate to declare

> "that it would be yᵉ most prudent measure they could take, in case the French and Indians shou'd continue to have so great success, to propose an accommodation on condition of being rendered secure in their Possessions." [100]

In view of the dangerous situation of the province and the difficulties that Robert Hunter Morris had faced in seeking to secure co-operation from the Assembly, the Pennsylvania Proprietors had thought best to relieve him of his onerous duties and to appoint in his place a military man who might have better success in establishing a proper defence for the province. As a result, Lieutenant Colonel William Denny of the regular army was named,[101] and on August 20 he took the oath of office before the Governor's Council.[102] This, with the disappearance of most of the Quakers from the Assembly, already noted, seemed to be a good augury for the future. It was also high time for a change in attitude on the part of the Assembly; for the enemy continued their blows on outlying settlements. As Fort Shirley, with the destruction of Fort Granville, was in a position of dangerous isolation, it was evacuated in July. In Cumberland County — after many of the inhabitants were induced to return to their farms on Conococheague Creek beyond the Kittatinny Mountains and near the later site of Fort Loudoun [103] — the Indians made a surprise attack and succeeded in killing a number of settlers and soldiers and in taking others prisoner. This was early in November. At the same time shocking reports came from Berks County, east of the Susquehanna, where the enemy massacred and burned even in the area about Fort Lebanon.[104] One chief difficulty was that the provincial troops, according to Governor Denny, were lacking

---

fact, that the Indians had turned against the English because their lands had been taken away without compensation.

[100] Pa. Col. Rec., VII, 245.

[101] On May 7, 1756 Denny received a commission from the Proprietors to act as Lieutenant Governor, and on May 17 this was approved by an order in council (C.O. 5:1274, Bundle V, 169).

[102] Pa. Col. Rec., VII, 220–1.

[103] Fort Loudoun was built very close to McDowell's Mill, a well-known landmark of this period, which had been provided with a palisade for protection of the settlement.

[104] Pennsylvania Gazette, November 11, 1756.

"any kind of Discipline, each Man was humoured by his Officer, scarce two in a Company were of one Opinion and the Men could not be got to march against the Indians, and if the Savages by any accident came upon them they did not stand to their Arms but fled and increased the Panick amongst the Inhabitants which thereby became general." [105]

It was at this critical juncture that a regiment of regulars was consigned by Lord Loudoun to the Pennsylvania defences. Also in an effort to win back the Delawares, most of whom had joined the Shawnee in making war on the English, a conference was arranged at Easton to include those of the tribe who had not as yet gone on the warpath.[106] Denny attended this with an escort of regulars in their striking uniforms and with their military band and some of the provincial soldiers. Teedyuscung, so-called King of the Delawares, came down from the Indian town of Tioga (now Athens, Pennsylvania) and acted as spokesman for the small group of Indians. He admitted that some of the young men had struck the English and discoursed rather fully on old grievances such as the Walking Purchase. The Governor sought to bring the Indians to an accommodation, especially to cease hostilities and release all English prisoners, and offered compensation for whatever the Indians thought had in the past been wrong and unjust. But nothing could be done, because there were few Indians present, if any, who could set up any valid claims. Recognizing this fact, Teedyuscung could only declare that the following year he would seek to bring to the government the sense of those Indians who felt that they had a grievance. The conference was complicated, it may be added, by the presence of a body of Quakers, headed by Israel Pemberton, who not only sought to see that justice was done to the natives but encouraged them, so Conrad Weiser, the interpreter for the English, insisted, to lodge complaints.[107] In fact, the real grievance of the Delawares did not come into the open at the conference. This grievance was that at the command of their superiors, the Six Nations, they had left the area of the Walking Purchase — the valleys of the Delaware and the

[105] Denny to Loudoun, November 12, 1757, Loudoun Papers, No. 4793.

[106] Most of the Delawares present came from New Jersey. For the Easton Indian Conference of 1756 see P. A. W. Wallace's Conrad Weiser, pp. 459–65. The official text of the conference is in the Pa. Col. Rec., VII, 313–38.

[107] Ibid., p. 461. See also Theodore Thayer: Israel Pemberton, King of the Quakers, pp. 183–4.

Lehigh — and had settled on the upper Susquehanna, where they had been told that they would be undisturbed; in spite of this promise, they had had to face recently the intrusion upon their hunting grounds of a large body of Connecticut settlers. The latter, members of the so-called Susquehanna Company, had purchased lands in the northern part of Pennsylvania from the Iroquois chiefs during the Albany Conference in 1754, and in defiance of the claims of the Pennsylvania Proprietors were busy with plans for a settlement, including the survey of these lands.[108] Why this did not become a subject of discussion at the conference is quite clear. Four Mohawks, representatives of the Six Nations, were present and were on the outlook for any attempt on the part of the Delawares to question the overlordship of the latter.[109] Thus the problem of making peace with the Delawares was complicated both by the active intrusion of the Quakers into the conference and the confusion arising from this, and by the fact that the people against whom these Indians had a very real grievance — the Connecticut people — were under treaty protection from the Iroquoian Confederation.

The relief that now came to the province and lasted for months was brought about, not so much by the presence of a battalion of regulars, the Royal Americans, or by any change of heart on the Indians, but chiefly because of the withdrawal of the energetic French leader Dumas and most of his forces from Fort Duquesne before the setting in of the winter season. For supplies were low and only a skeleton force could be retained at the fort. There was little subsistence for the Indians, who now were encouraged to scatter to their villages, as in previous winters, to pass the period of snow and ice.

Thus the government of Pennsylvania, with the coming of the year 1757, felt that all that it could possibly do was to maintain a line of defence that in the upper areas of the province was confined to the region east of the Susquehanna and that pivoted upon Fort Augusta at the forks of the Susquehanna, where at all times a rather strong body of troops was concentrated. It may be added that to the north and east of the Pennsylvania defence line, and connected

---

[108] See Weiser's "Memorandum" of November 26, 1756, printed by Wallace (op. cit., pp. 462–4).

[109] When Weiser was informed of the real grievance by a small group of Delawares, including their own interpreter, Deedemy, and asked why they did not discuss this at the conference, the latter replied that they "were afraid of the Minquo that were there, least [sic] they might misrepresent the story when they come home" (ibid.).

with it, was a series of some six small blockhouses erected by New Jersey to the east of the Delaware, each garrisoned by twenty or thirty men, to guard against the movement of Indians down that river and along the famous Minsi Path. Those in turn were connected with and supported by three blockhouses built by the New York authorities along the upper waters of that stream.

During the spring of 1757 things remained quiet along the Pennsylvania frontier, but by the summer the border, as in Virginia, was again aflame. Colonel Conrad Weiser of the Pennsylvania volunteers, stationed on the frontiers, reported in July that almost every day people were killed and scalped even in the vicinity of the flourishing settlement of Tulpehocken, where he had his own home, and that the inhabitants were moving *en masse* to the shelter of the new town of Reading.[110] That the Delawares were deeply involved in these outrages was clear, in spite of the promise of Teedyuscung at Easton the preceding fall that he would hold his young men in check until a permanent peace could be established. There was indeed great urgency to bring this about, and already the chief had been invited by Governor Denny to come again to the former treaty town with as many of his followers as he could gather together who had not gone on the warpath, so that all matters of dispute between this tribe and their brothers the Shawnee and the English could finally be settled.

It was not until July 21, however, that the Indians appeared, to the number of three hundred, and among them members of the Six Nations, who, as previously indicated, felt they had a deep interest in any agreement that might be reached between the Delawares and the government of Pennsylvania. Once again Israel Pemberton and members of the Friendly Association were on hand in full force and insisted on the right to participate in the deliberation. According to both Conrad Weiser and George Croghan, both great friends of the Indians, they introduced an element of serious discord into the proceedings by encouraging the Indians to go back into the past and bring forth ancient claims regarding lands that had for a long time since been settled.[111] In the words of Weiser: "At this Treaty

---

[110] Weiser to Denny, July 12, 1757, *ibid.*, p. 474.

[111] For the position of the Friendly Association the student should consult the "Address of the Trustees and Treasurer of the Friendly Association" presented to Governor Denny on July 13, 1757 (*Pa. Col. Rec.*, VII, 638–46), and also Charles Thomson's *An Enquiry into the Causes of the Alienation of the Delawares and Shawnese Indians* (Philadelphia, 1757).

the Indians learned our Weakness, by being Informed of our Divisions." [112] Croghan, who was the official provincial interpreter, went
further in denouncing the interference of the Quakers, who even
after the treaty, he declared:

> "Still continue to sett up Teedyuscung against yᵉ Governor. . . .
> Shure those people Must be Mad, for in My opinion they are Seting
> up yᵉ Indians to Claime yᵉ Whole Province, and Indeed if we Should
> be unsuccessfull in this Warr, they may Say all yᵉ English Coloneys
> belongs to them; how Long yᵉ Government att home will Suffer yᵉ
> Quakers to Actt yᵉ part they have hither to Don, I Cant Say, Butt if
> Long permited, I fear thire Conduct in the End will Nott be found
> for yᵉ Good of his Majesty's Subjects in America." [113]

Bedevilled by the mistaken zeal of the association and by Teedyuscung's arrogance as the result of its encouragement, the conference went from bad to worse. At one time it was feared that open
violence would take place in the town. In the course of one of the
chief's harangues, however, great confusion suddenly broke out
among the Indians. According to Weiser, one of the other Delawares, seeing the dangerous drift of Teedyuscung's arguments, began denouncing his chief in the following terms:

> "We thought we came to make Peace with our Brethren the English,
> but you continue to quarrel about yᵉ Land affair which is Dirt, A
> Dispute we did not hear of till now." [114]

What is more, the representatives of the Six Nations began showing
great anger toward him in questioning the land settlements. As a result, he quickly ceased his bluster and suddenly told the surprised
Governor that the Indians were now ready to make peace and
would no longer press ancient matters. Copies of the old land deeds
were now presented and their accuracy verified by the clerk for the
Indians, who was Charles Thompson; the chief declared he was
satisfied; and the presents were given, with everything ending har-
moniously on August 4, at Easton.[115]

---

[112] Weiser to Denny, October 27, 1757, *Pennsylvania Archives* (first series), III,
314. In this letter Weiser points out the weaknesses of the "Address" of the Friendly
Association and its dangerous tendency.

[113] Croghan to ——, December 18, 1757, *ibid.*, III, 319; see also Wallace, *op. cit.*,
p. 488.

[114] *Ibid.*, p. 483.

[115] For the proclamation of peace with the Delawares and Shawnee by Denny see
the *Pennsylvania Gazette* of August 11, 1757.

But in spite of all fine words there was no peace with the Delawares and Shawnee who had moved within the orbit of French influence. The news of the fall of Fort William Henry at this time set the Indians on fire as had the fall of Oswego the preceding year. When Weiser returned from the conference to his frontier post, he was overwhelmed with the bad news coming in of continual Indian attacks on isolated settlements — of scalping, killing, taking prisoners, and burning habitations.[116] Yet it must not be thought that all the Pennsylvania forces were idle, in spite of the charge of the Assembly that the inhabitants had received no protection from them.[117] As Colonel John Armstrong made clear in a public letter written in Cumberland County on September 12, at least the troops under his command there, in conjunction with Stanwix's regulars stationed at Carlisle, had been busy scouring the woods, sending out parties and also spies as far as the Allegheny Mountains and even beyond, as well as in protecting people during the harvest. He insisted that where troops were stationed in that area no inhabitants had fallen into the enemy's hands.[118] As a matter of fact, most of the serious raids during the summer and fall of 1757 were directed by the enemy against the area to the east of the Susquehanna that was under the protection of the provincials commanded by Colonel Weiser. The Indians, under the leadership of a few daring Frenchmen, would at this period move through the deserted Juniata Valley, from Fort Niagara or one of the forts on the upper Ohio or on Lake Erie, then cross the Susquehanna — perhaps so as to strike the Shamokin Trail and from there move through the Swatara Gap or at any one of a number of other points either above or below Fort Augusta — to carry out their destructive missions, and then return to their base of operation.[119] These raids could not be prevented by the small forces stationed at the posts stretching from the Susquehanna to the Delaware, much to the despair of Weiser.[120]

116 See the *Gazette* for August 11 and 18, September 1, October 13 and 27, and November 3 for accounts of these terrifying visitations. For example, from Lancaster County came the account at the end of August: "That there is nothing but Murdering and Captivating amongst them by the Indians." The same was equally true of Berks County.
117 Address of the Assembly to the Governor, September 28, 1757, *Pa. Col. Rec.*, VII, 744.
118 This is printed in the *Pennsylvania Gazette*, October 13, 1757.
119 Denny to Loudoun, November 10, 1757, Loudoun Papers, No. 4794.
120 Weiser in a letter to Richard Peters from Heidelberg, in Berks County, on October 4, declared: ". . . I have been very Buisy with writing to the Comanding offi-

The obvious answer to this was the organization of an expedition that would have as its objective the destruction of the French forts, from which flowed all these tribulations that overwhelmed communities in even the more settled part of the province. Yet one may search the records of the Pennsylvania Assembly without finding the slightest suggestion in favour of such an aggressive move on the part of those who controlled its proceedings.

We now have a picture in some detail of the defensive posture of British North America to the south of the Mohawk River at the close of the year 1757. It has seemed important thus to stress this, since it relates to one of the most profound misconceptions embedded in American history and tradition: that Americans felt at this critical period that with their own resources they were fully prepared and were even destined to retrieve the great misfortunes that the war during the past four years had brought to them. It is clear that this was not the case. Yet if they felt their incapacity to do so, who would reclaim for them those great areas that they had previously been busy settling before the war interfered and that now lay desolate and deserted, far west of the line of forts that stretched with intervening patrol areas for hundreds of miles — from the region to the west of Esopus (now Kingston), New York, along the borders of New Jersey, through central Pennsylvania and on to the Potomac, and then down the Valley of Virginia into North Carolina? How would it ever be possible for them, in addition to reclaiming this region, to be free again to move beyond the great western barriers of the Appalachians to plant their homes?

It was to William Pitt, who through his superb leadership, his mobilization of the manpower, the military and the financial resources of the mother country, and, finally, through his capacity to instil a spirit of co-operation, at least temporarily, and also of confidence, in the minds of the all too individualistic Americans, that the chief credit for supplying the answers to these questions must be given. Strange as it may seem, this perhaps greatest of all of their benefactors, the one above all others who guaranteed to them a great future on this continent, where they could dwell in security; this statesman who was willing to sacrifice almost every other consid-

---

cers of the several forts under my Care. It is now Come so farr that murder is Comited allmost every day; there never was such a Consternation among the people. . . . I have neither men nor a sufficient n'br of officers to defend the Country" (*Pennsylvania Archives*, first series, III, 283).

eration for the promotion of their future welfare — an attitude quite
devoid of all sinister or cynical ulterior motives — this champion
who supported them even in rebellion and believed in them in season and out, now as leader of His Majesty's government and then as
leader of the opposition, was never properly recognized by Americans of his own generation or by their descendants. While monu-
ments by the hundreds have been erected to lesser men here in the
broad expanses of the United States, where is that monument, outside of the place named in his honour at the forks of the Ohio by
those of the regular army and a few small towns and counties, which
worthily expresses a sense of gratitude or, if not gratitude, at least a
sense of some appreciation for his great services to the American
people? When, indeed, will this people at length free itself of that
hoary distortion of the plain facts of history that would make the
war that is now being described, not one entered into by the mother
country primarily for the purpose of protecting the vital interests of
the American colonials, but rather just another episode in the history
of an aggressive, rapacious, grasping, calculating British imperial-
ism, as Thomas Paine saw it, and as Bancroft proclaimed it to be?

But, as we shall note in the course of this volume, even Pitt, the
organizer of victory in the Great War for the Empire, had to face
checks and disappointments in carrying out his project of overwhelming the French in the New World — a project that he pursued with a fixity of purpose little short of an obsession.

CHAPTER III

The Loss of Fort William Henry

A S HAS BEEN INDICATED in the first chapter of this volume, there was confusion and indecision in England during the first half of the year 1757, with the question of the permanency of the ministry and then its reorganization hanging in the balance until the joint ministry of Pitt and Newcastle was firmly established early in the summer. This situation at home was bound to have its effect on the American summer campaign. It was not until May 1 that Lord Loudoun, as will be noted subsequently, received Pitt's final orders. In fact, the year was destined to end in great gloom for the British. On the other hand, for the French in North America it was counted as the fourth year of victories — in spite of the loss of Fort Beausé-jour in 1755 and the failure of Dieskau, later in that year, to dis-lodge the British forces from Fort William Henry, with the conse-quent capture of that hapless general in the Battle of Lake George. In 1754 the English post at the forks of the Monongahela had been seized and Fort Duquesne erected as a barrier against the move-ment of the British colonials west of the Appalachians; also in that year Fort Necessity had been captured and with it the forces under Washington and MacKay; in 1755 Braddock's army, made up largely of regular British troops, received a disastrous defeat in which the general himself was mortally wounded; in 1756 the great British trading emporium on Lake Ontario with its supporting forts had fallen and its large garrison taken captive; and in 1757 Fort William Henry, a dagger pointed toward the very heart of the French Empire, was destined likewise to fall. Indeed, there seemed to be every indication for those guiding the destinies of New France that the war was being won, so far as the contest in North America was concerned. Even accepting the vast inequality of potential man-power and economic assets that remained in favour of the British colonials, the French in Canada saw other factors overbalancing these in significance and could appeal to history respecting the ability of a small yet martial people to hold in awe and even on oc-casion to conquer a vast empire, as Alexander overran Persia.

The confidence of French leaders in North America was based upon the fact that the English on the continent were non-military in outlook. Moreover, the latter, although in the midst of war, were motivated by a purely defensive attitude, such as impelled them to withdraw from the western settlements to the more thickly inhab-ited areas in Virginia, Maryland, and Pennsylvania and there to set up posts and barriers. This confidence was likewise increased by the fact that whereas in New France there was unity of control and every resource could be mobilized and directed to its maximum military effect, in the British colonies there was no such unity and no such ability to command and concentrate resources. Each colony was thinking primarily of its own particular interests and safety and each retained much of the old peace-time jealousy of its neighbours. With this there went hand in hand a wide dispersion of authority: some of it was in the hands of the commander-in-chief of the British forces in North America; some of it in the hands of the provincial governors; but most of it was retained by the respective colonial assemblies. All this represented a tremendous wastage of energy, whatever its great merits might be in times of peace. Again, there was every indication that the American phase of the war would be won in wilderness fighting. Here these French leaders saw them-selves in a position of decisive advantage: French regulars had much more the spirit of adventure than had the British regulars; Canadi-ans were unsurpassed in their ability to operate in a wooded coun-try; and, finally, by the beginning of 1757 almost every important Indian nation living within reach of the area of hostilities was in full alliance with the French King, or was considering such an alliance, or was committed to a policy of neutrality — and the Indians, while of little use against fortified places, were by long experience adept at bush fighting, raiding, and scouting. This drift of Indian tribes away from the English and into the French camp must at this point be considered briefly.

In 1754 came the defection of the Ohio Valley Delawares, the Shawnee, the Mingo, and the Miami or Twightwee in favour of the French. The French could already count upon the support of the Abenaki and Micmac in old Acadia; of the Caughnawaga or Praying Iroquois settled in Canada; of the Hurons and other groups in the region of Fort Detroit; of the ferocious Chippewa or Saulteurs, the Missisauga, kinsmen of the latter, the Ottawa, the Nipissing, the Algonkins, the Menominee or Folles Avoines, and the Potawatomi in the upper Great Lakes region; of the Illinois and other Indian groups on the upper Mississippi; and of the very numerous Choctaw in the lower Mississippi basin. Only the Chickasaw on the upper waters of the Yazoo River and the Catawba, living close to the settled parts of the Carolinas — neither of these tribes large or powerful — could be counted on to side actively with the English. The Upper and Lower Creeks, the Alabama, the Cherokee in the South, and the Six Iroquoian Nations in the North, each sought a position of strict neutrality in the war, in spite of the fact that the two last named were supposed to be in alliance with the English. There were, in fact, signs to indicate that both the Cherokee and the Six Nations — each of Iroquoian stock — were in the latter half of the year 1756 preparing to follow other Indian groups and shift to a French connection.

Reference has already been made in the preceding chapter to the sending of Cherokee deputies from Tellico in the Over Hills to Canada for securing an alliance. These Indians had been encouraged to act through a letter addressed to them from Governor General Vaudreuil and secretly transmitted by a Canadian who had been adopted into the nation.[1] As a result of this, in the fall of 1756 deputies left for Montreal, but were diverted to Detroit, where their distant kinsmen and fellow Iroquoians, the Hurons, were living. Arriving there, after some delay, early in the new year, they appeared before the French commandant, Lieutenant de Muy, and his allies the Hurons and Ottawa, and asked for French protection. If their wants could be supplied, they declared that they would strike the English. They affirmed that these were the sentiments of nine of the Cherokee villages and that thirty other villages were only waiting for their return to decide. De Muy, instructed by the Governor General how to reply to them, while encouraging them to resist the

---

[1] Vaudreuil to Machault, April 19, 1757, Documents Relating to the Colonial History of the State of New York, X, 539.

English was unable to guarantee to them the satisfaction of their needs so long as they remained in their present location. To Vaudreuil, in thus giving the commandant his instructions, it was a matter of the greatest urgency that this powerful nation should be given "an asylum" under firm French protection; to that effect he also later addressed his superior Machault, French Minister of the Marine,[2] declaring that this asylum, he felt, might be provided by the establishment of a post at the falls of the Ohio, where Louisville is now located. De Muy therefore strongly urged the Indians to migrate. The Cherokee, after presenting a belt to the Hurons and also another to the Ottawa, asking that the latter should let their tomahawk fall very heavily on the English and not turn it against them, departed for home well pleased with their reception at the hands of the French, but without otherwise committing themselves.

At about the same time that the Cherokee deputies were moving northward for their conference at Detroit, representatives of all the Six Nations except the Mohawks were journeying to Montreal to treat with the Governor General and Montcalm. There were some one hundred and eighty of them in all. On December 13 in the presence of a group of Canadian Indians — the Caughnawaga, the Ottawa, the Potawatomi, the Nipissings, and the Algonkins[3] — they asked for peace and friendship and also for forgiveness for their past offences. To show their dislike for their traditional allies they trampled underfoot medals some of them had accepted from the English, and the Oneida even presented to their brethren the Cayuga a belt from which an English scalp was suspended.[4] They also asked to be permitted to make war on the Chickasaw and Cherokee. Vaudreuil, while well disposed to their striking at the former, who never ceased their hostility to the French, cautioned them to hold their hand when it came to the latter, with whom, as has been noted, he was then negotiating. When they informed him that the Palatine Germans living on the Mohawk River were alienated from the English and sought an alliance with the Six Nations against them, he encouraged this[5] and also called upon them to show the sincerity of

2 *Ibid.*

3 "Account of the Embassy of the Five Nations," annexed to Montcalm's letter of April 24, 1757, *ibid.*, X, 555–63.

4 *Ibid.* For additional details of the conference the student should also consult the *Journal du Marquis de Montcalm*, ed. Abbé Casgrain, pp. 122–45.

5 That there was some truth in the message of the Iroquois that the Palatines settled on the Mohawk were far from happy in their relations with the English is indicated by

their professions not only by destroying the English posts in their midst but by bringing the Mohawks into the accord. Nor did all the responses come from Vaudreuil or from Montcalm, who seems particularly to have caught their imagination. The Nipissings, the Ottawa, and the Potawatomi, each in turn, warned the Six Nations that if they played false, their mats would be bloody. Deeply impressed with the prowess of a people who had in one year cleared the English from the trans-Appalachian region and captured Fort Necessity with its defenders, who had the next year almost destroyed a splendid British army sent to retrieve the earlier defeat on the upper waters of the Ohio, who had only that very year overwhelmed the English at their prized Oswego, and who could truly boast of the devoted friendship of so many of the other great tribes of Indians, the deputies of the Iroquoian Confederation turned back to their homes. To Montcalm this embassy was the most important development "that had occurred in a long time. . . ." [6]

Well might the French in Canada feel at the beginning of 1757 that their future indeed was bright, in view of the great revolution in the relations of the Indians along the English western borders, all in their own favour. Also, of even greater significance to them was the fact that the authorities at home had been busy for years siphoning some of the very finest of the regular troops into New France. In 1750 the number there stood at eight hundred; by the beginning of 1757 it had reached six times that figure; and when the reinforcements for the latter year that had been requested by Vaudreuil and granted had arrived, it would be over eight times as many — in precise figures 6,600, exclusive of officers. [7] These superb soldiers — used as a nucleus and supported by the colonials, the Canadian militia, and a cloud of Indian allies — would constitute a formidable force for either defensive or offensive operations. Even before receiving the promised reinforcements the Governor General

---

information given to Sir William Johnson early in the spring of 1757 by a friendly Onondaga called Corn-Milk. After Johnson pledged to keep his identity concealed, the Indian informed him that the Germans of Burnitfield had sent a letter the preceding fall to the French Governor by an Oneida Indian, complaining of the ill treatment they had received at the hands of the English troops passing and repassing that way, and that "as they looked upon themselves to be in Danger as well as the Six Nations, they were determined to live and die by them, & therefore begged the protection of the French" (Johnson Papers, ed. James Sullivan, II, 679–80).

[6] N. Y. Col. Doc., X, 563. The official minutes of the conference are to be found in ibid., X, 499–518.

[7] "Ministerial Minute on the French Force in Canada, 1757," ibid., X, 523–6.

determined to strike at Fort William Henry, defiantly erected on the edge of Lake Sacrament, renamed Lake George by the English and menacing the French control of the waters of this lake and their forts at Ticonderoga and Crown Point.

From this fort, in fact, on January 17 of the new year a band of about eighty rangers under the famed Captain Robert Rogers had moved, for reconnaissance purposes, silently through the woods and snow to the west of the lake and had suddenly appeared on the shore line midway between the two French forts. Thereupon it had attacked a party of Frenchmen and, after securing prisoners, which had been its chief objective, had made good its retreat, in spite of the efforts of the commandant at Ticonderoga to destroy it, involving as this did a bloody engagement in a deep ravine.[8] It was obvious that the English had in hand some plan for striking at the two French forts and were seeking information as to their strength.[9] To thwart them and to destroy, if possible, the large concentration of military stores and equipment at Fort William Henry, Vaudreuil commissioned his brother, François-Pierre Rigaud, Governor of Trois Rivières, to head an expedition against it. With two hundred and fifty regulars, three hundred colonials, six hundred and fifty Canadian militia, and three hundred Indians — in all, some fifteen hundred men — he moved late in February, still in the midst of winter, over the frozen waters of Lake Champlain and Lake George, and on March 18 was in the neighbourhood of the fort. Equipped with snow-shoes and sledges, the troops also brought with them some three hundred scaling ladders for carrying the fort by storm, since they lacked artillery for making a breach in its walls.[10]

But the defenders of Fort William Henry were on the alert and were under the command of an excellent soldier, the military engineer Lieutenant Colonel William Eyre of the 44th regiment, called by Vaudreuil "an officer of consummate experience in the art of War." [11] The designer and builder of this fort, Eyre was prepared

---

[8] "Journal of Capt. [Robert] Rogers, Scout, January 15th, 1757," Loudoun Papers, No. 2704, Huntington Library.

[9] Rogers before killing his prisoners, whom he could not carry back in his perilous retreat, ascertained that there were at Ticonderoga three hundred and fifty regulars, two hundred Canadians, and forty-five Indians, and some six hundred regulars at Crown Point (ibid.).

[10] "Declaration of Guillaume Chasse and John Victor, prisoners, of March 23, 1757," Loudoun Papers, No. 3146.

[11] N. Y. Col. Doc., X, 542. His eminence as military engineer was widely acclaimed

to defend it to the limit of his resources with his garrison of five
hundred regulars, plus a body of rangers. Very early on the morning
of the 19th the distant noise of axes was heard, and far out on the
lake a light flickered; the alarm was thereupon given and the troops
rushed to man the guns and also took up their positions on the ramparts with their small arms. Still in the midst of darkness, the French
now approached the fort and proceeded to set fire to the largest of
the lake sloops and to hundreds of bateaux drawn up on the lake
shore. Eyre's artillery, however, began playing upon them, forcing
a temporary retirement. But they soon returned and enveloped the
fort and from rocks and trees rained a steady and heavy musketry
fire upon the defenders throughout the day. When darkness again
intervened, they at length succeeded in destroying by fire the long
line of bateaux. Again retiring out of range of the artillery fire with
the coming of the dawn, they now, on the 20th, sent a small party
under the Chevalier Mercier with a red flag to summon Eyre to surrender the fort. In this summons Rigaud asserted that the fort had
been built on lands belonging to His Most Christian Majesty, much
to the regret of the French, who were averse to carrying on war in
these parts — perhaps referring to the old Albany-Montreal neutrality of earlier wars. They were therefore prepared, he indicated, to
be lenient with the garrison and would agree to permit it to march
out with the honours of war, should it surrender peaceably, and
would even guarantee to protect it from the Indians; otherwise this
protection could not be promised when the fort was carried by assault.[12]

Eyre replied that his force was prepared to resist to the last extremity. In fact, so resolute were the defenders and so merciless
was the fire of the heavy guns and musketry that all attempts to
scale the fort were foiled. The French, however, burned the sawmill, the rangers' quarters in the picketed enclosure not far from
the fort, set fire to the storehouses and to the hospital on the other
side of it; and for a time it seemed that the soldiers' barracks would
also be consumed by the violent heat; fortunately, there was no

---

among the English (Captain John Knox's *Historical Journal of the Campaigns in North
America for the Years 1757, 1758, 1759, and 1760*, I, 388, 395; II, 133, 405).

[12] Rigaud de Vaudreuil to the commandant of Fort George, Loudoun Papers, No.
3109. According to the testimony under oath of two French prisoners, Guillaume Chasse
and John Victor, in case the fort had to be taken by assault the French were to grant
no quarter; the heavy guns of the fort were to be turned against the defenders, the survivors put to the sword, and the fort blown up (*ibid.*, No. 3146).

wind to carry the flames. After finally succeeding in burning a large vessel still on the stocks, the assailants withdrew on the 23rd.[13] Hunger and continued exposure to the most severe winter weather seen in years compelled their withdrawal after six weeks spent without cover and only when their supply of provisions for fifteen days had at length reached exhaustion.[14] While the fort had not been captured, as had been hoped, yet the expedition was held to be a real success. Writing to Machault, Vaudreuil declared with enthusiasm: "Fort George is actually isolated; its exterior establishments no longer exist, and General Lawden's [Loudoun's] beautiful and immense preparations have been calcined by the flames at a trifling expense. . . ."[15] Its destruction at the hands of the French had to wait, however, until the month of August.

In turning now to the situation of the British colonials, it is clear from what has been said in the preceding chapter that most of them sought to ignore the fact that they were confronted with one of the most dangerous situations in all their history. Governor Jonathan Belcher, writing to Lord Loudoun at the beginning of the new year, offered a partial explanation when he affirmed: "Your Lordship is sensible that the People in these Colonies are quite unused to War and Martial Discipline. . . ."[16]

George Gardner of Newport, Rhode Island, sheriff of Newport County and a captain of one of the militia companies, communicating also with the commander-in-chief at this same period, pointed to the desolation of the American frontiers, with over fifteen hundred of their inhabitants carried into captivity by bands of the enemy as evidence of their weakness. Seeking to explain the failure of the Americans during these earlier years of the war, he raised the question:

> "Is it not, My Lord, that all seek their own, every Man his private Gain, persuing a distinct and seperate Interest from that of his Majesty and the public? Some indeed glory in their Extraordinary

---

[13] Eyre to Gage, March 24, and Eyre to Webb, April 6, 1757, ibid., No. 3151 and No. 3299.

[14] Montcalm to d'Argenson, April 24, 1757, N. Y. Col. Doc., X, 547–50. On their return over the glaring snow and ice one third of the detachment became quite blind temporarily, Canadians and Indians as well as regulars, and had to be led by their comrades; at the end of forty-eight hours, however, with the use of simple remedies their sight returned (ibid.).

[15] Ibid., X, 543.

[16] Loudoun Papers, No. 2630.

Vigilence in draining the Continent of Thousands of its Inhabitants (Deserters included) to carry on certain Schemes [that is, privateering] for private Gain."

He calculated that at least ten thousand able-bodied men had been taken away from the defence of the continent to serve in privateers and other vessels, lured by inducements of possible large gains, and further asserted that deserters from the army "get off to sea [after receiving the enlistment money] almost as fast as they can be recruited." He then asked:

"How can we expect, My Lord, to make any Head against his Majesty's Enemies while a Contrary party are intervening, bribing and corrupting his Soldiers to Answer their own private Ends; all the Laws hitherto made, My Lord, have not been sufficient to prevent the Enemy's receiving large supplies of provisions from the Continent?" [17]

Indeed, the royal navy as well as the army was plagued by the desertion of those who were lured to sail on the privateers. In New York the ships of war and transports intended to be used by Loudoun for his campaign against Louisbourg were tied up at the docks late in the spring because of the wholesale desertion of sailors, enticed by owners of privateers who had already brought to that port prizes valued at over two hundred thousand pounds. These deserters, concealed in the city pending their sailing away in the privateers, were only recovered when the general determined to surround the city with three battalions while Sir Charles Hardy made a house-to-house search.[18]

It would not be far from the truth to affirm that in this supreme crisis in North America, which directly affected the life of every man, woman, and child, colonials by and large expected the mother country to bear the chief burden of protecting them and their interests, while leaving them undisturbed in their pursuits. Even in those colonies which were the most active in providing men and provisions the practice of padding accounts that were rendered to Loudoun for payment out of the royal treasury was so prevalent that he was impelled to write to Pitt that "it is the constant Study of every Province here, to throw every Expence on the Crown, and

---

[17] *Ibid.*, No. 2618. No colony was more committed to privateering than was Rhode Island. For this see H. C. Chapin: *Rhode Island Privateers in King George's War.*

[18] Loudoun to Pitt, May 30, 1757, *Correspondence of William Pitt,* I, 69.

bear no part of the Expence of this War themselves."[19] This disposition to lean heavily on the mother country may be illustrated by
the most powerful of all the colonies, Massachusetts Bay. After the
news of the disastrous defeat of Braddock's army in 1755 and in
view of the great difficulty that this populous province faced in providing for the defence of its frontiers, the General Assembly represented to His Majesty the absolute necessity of sending over regiments of regulars from the mother country to assume the main task
of garrisoning the numerous outlying posts of the province.[20] This
step was only taken, the legislators pointed out, because not only
did they have to deal with the Canadians and the Indians, "but the
Treasure and Regulars from Old France are employed against them
and the Province has already Exerted itself so beyond its ability
that in their own strength they can proceed but little farther." At
the same time they made clear that although Massachusetts Bay
had supplied for the "general Good many more Men than all the
other Colonies together" — some eight thousand, in fact —

> "our People are not calculated to be confined in Garrisons or kept in
> any particular Service; they soon grow troublesome & uneasy by
> reflecting upon their Folly in bringing themselves into a State of
> Subjection when they might have continued free and independent."

They therefore petitioned that "those Fortresses which may be
erected for the Defence of his Majesty's Territories" should be garrisoned by "his Majesty's Regulars rather than by American Troops,
tho' in the pay of the Crown."[21] Such was the attitude in 1755 of the
colony with the greatest reservoir of manpower of any within the
British Empire, and, as indicated in the preceding chapter, most
colonials at the beginning of 1757 seemed to reflect a similar purely
defensive attitude and a disposition to look to the mother country
for a solution of the problem of the protection of their vital interests from an aggressive enemy.

---

[19] Loudoun to Pitt, May 3, 1757, ibid., I, 57.

[20] The following were the chief posts that had been erected for the protection of
the province by the fall of 1755: Fort Halifax on the Kennebec, the fort at Brunswick,
Fort Frederick at Pemmaquid, the post at the mouth of the River St. George, the post
at Saco, Fort Dummer on the western extremes of New Hampshire, but when built,
within Massachusetts Bay, together with Fort Massachusetts and the posts at Pontoo-
such, at Charlemont, at Colerain, and at Fall Town (House of Representatives, October
30, 1755, Williams Mss., Vol. I, No. 188, Mass. Hist. Soc.).

[21] "A Representation of the Case of his Majesty's Province of Massachusetts Bay,"
under date of September 26, 1755, B. M. Add. Mss., 33029, folios 206–9.

It is clear, however, that British regiments confined to garrison duty — to a mere defensive policy — would never win the war in North America. As will be noted in the chapter to follow, the commander-in-chief of all the armed forces on the continent, Lord Loudoun, soon after the disaster at Oswego in 1756, had made up his mind that the only way to deal with the enemy effectively was to strike boldly at him by means of an amphibious operation in the North Atlantic — an operation that he had determined to lead in person. This meant that while he and his second in command, Major General Abercromby, would be engaged in it, Brigadier General Webb must, under the rules of military precedence, be left in general charge of frontier defence. And this was a misfortune.

Webb, it is true, had served in the Coldstream Guards, had fought with Ligonier's force at Dettingen, had acquitted himself honourably at Fontenoy, and had proved himself to be highly proficient at military paper work, but withal he seemed to have utterly lacked the fire, the spirit, and also the coolness and sound judgment for an independent command. He had been thrown into a panic on his expedition up the Mohawk the preceding year when moving to the relief of Oswego, and by the beginning of 1757 he had become a confirmed hypochondriac.[22] In the events to follow, his timidity, his indecision, and his errors in the tactical and strategical arrangements of the troops under his immediate orders are almost unbelievable in one with so much military experience and with so high a command.[23] While he was thoroughly justified in not risking an all-out attempt against Ticonderoga and Crown Point[24] — espe-

[22] Loudoun, writing to Cumberland on January 4, 1757 (Loudoun Papers, No. 2637), referred to Webb in the following terms: "I mentioned Mr. Webb being ill; he was about a fortnight ago, Attacked with a very slight fit of palsy, which did not last a Minute, and to another would have been of very little Consequence, but all his People have died of that disease, and he is still low and down, and I cannot get his Spirits up; I am very much afraid, that he will be an infinite loss to the Service, for the Country is so immensely wide, we must have people we can depend on, in different places. . . ."

[23] The student should consult Pargellis (Lord Loudoun in North America, pp. 243–51) for a very careful and competent analysis of Webb's blunders.

[24] Loudoun in writing to Pitt under date of March 10 made clear that "for the Security of this Country" he was placing Webb in command "for the defence of Fort William Henry, and Fort Edward, and the Security of the Magazines at Albany" (Correspondence of William Pitt (ed. Kimball), I, 18). In his "Queries" to Loudoun, Webb states: "We are, I presume to Act on the Defensive. We take our Camp at Fort Edward which is the best Situation and Securest manner of Posting Ourselves? Can any demonstrations be made toward Wood Creek?" In reply Loudoun stated that Webb was "to Act Offensively or Defensively, as the situation, or Intelligence of the Enemy will

cially in view of the small number of regular troops available who would be expected to bear the brunt of the assaults,[25] and also of the authentic information that came to him of the gathering at Ticonderoga of several regiments of French regulars — he should at least have set to work with utmost diligence to seek to make himself undisputed master of Lake George. He should also have collected and posted at Fort William Henry a sufficient body of troops so as to permit him to keep the enemy in a state of apprehension by means of a series of strong feints directed by water against the French fort and in general should have thoroughly consolidated his positions not only at the lake but at Fort Edward by drawing in most of the troops posted in the Mohawk Valley when it became apparent by the beginning of May that the French were making no preparations for a descent of that river.[26] But he did none of these things. What is more, stationed as he himself was at Fort Edward, he kept Fort William Henry so weak that, instead of serving as a constant British threat to the enemy, it rather became a natural pawn and lure to them.

Webb was seriously handicapped, of course, in one respect — a handicap for which to some extent he himself was responsible as the result of his destruction of the forts on the upper Mohawk and his precipitate flight thereupon in 1756. He could not command any important Indian support. Five of the Six Nations quite refused it, and as for the Seneca, the farthest removed from British influence, many of their young men had previously gone southward with the French and the Northern Indians and had "struck" the English.

Permit" (Loudoun Papers, No. 3474). But this offensive action did not manifestly include a campaign against the French forts. Only, in fact, when Loudoun had received a false report in June that all French troops in Canada were being concentrated at Quebec did he indicate to Webb the possibility of a move against Ticonderoga and Crown Point (Loudoun to Pitt, June 17, 1757, Pitt Correspondence, I, 76).

[25] As will be made clear in the course of this volume, the British commanders-in-chief in North America were very reluctant to assign to the provincials tasks that would almost inevitably result in heavy losses. This was not the result of any great solicitude for the preservation of the lives of American colonials, but rather a firm conviction that heavy casualties sustained by the forces of a colony would discourage others from it from volunteering.

[26] Lieutenant Thomas Butler, stationed with a small force of provincials at Oneida on the upper Mohawk, wrote to Sir William Johnson on April 26 — after the Indians had earlier spread many false alarms and rumors: "They [the scouts] say there is no such thing as an Army Coming this way as yet . . . but we may depend & be assured, that a vast great Army of French & Indians are now out to attack Fort William Henry" (Johnson Papers, IX, 692).

Sir William Johnson during the spring of 1757 had done his best to bring them into active participation and to offset the influence of the Montreal conference of the preceding fall, but he had largely failed. While the Indians themselves, in conferring with him, stressed their "dangerous Situation," he was convinced that this was not the true explanation: it could be found in the following facts:

> "Our Ill Success hitherto hath intimidated them. Our Methods of Carrying on the War is not according to their Methods, And the present Prospect of Our Affairs doth not seem to please them. Hence they are not prejudiced in our Favour, but seem to think We are going wrong, and therefore will not go with Us. In short, without some striking Success on our Side, I believe they will not join us." [27]

Yet it is equally true that not many of the Six Nations — outside the group that the Abbé Piquet (Picquet) could command at La Présentation on the upper St. Lawrence and the Praying Iroquois settled in Canada — supported the French in their Lake Champlain campaign in the summer of that year, to a consideration of which we must now turn.

To Governor General Vaudreuil the winter attack on Fort William Henry changed the situation of New France and rendered it "as advantageous as it was critical," in view of Loudoun's determination, according to information brought to him, which he had accepted at its face value, to throw a large army in the spring of the year against Ticonderoga.[28] His Indian informants and scouts who hovered about the English forts late in the spring of 1757 indicated that the enemy was slowly repairing the damage done by Rigaud, but there was "neither bateau nor wagon at Fort George, nor at Fort Lydius" (Fort Edward). The garrison of the latter fort, he was told, consisted of but three hundred men, many of them ill, while that of the former had been supplemented by but three companies of regulars and some militia.[29] By June 1, he had become assured that Loudoun had given up all plans for an offensive in the area of Lakes George and Champlain and was committed to an operation against Louisbourg with the aid of a fleet of fifteen ships. This situation, he declared in a letter to the Minister of the Marine written on June 1, offered him a most favourable opportunity to lay siege to Fort William Henry

---

[27] Johnson to Edmund Atkins, June 21, 1757, *ibid.*, IX, 785.
[28] Vaudreuil to the Keeper of the Seals, April 22, 1757, *N. Y. Col. Doc.*, X, 543.
[29] Vaudreuil to the Minister of the Marine de Moras, June 1, 1757, *ibid.*, X, 566–7.

and he indicated that he was summoning the Indians of the upper Great Lakes region and was expecting at least twelve hundred of them. His only great cause of anxiety was the lack of provisions for his troops, a supply of which he was awaiting from France now that the river was free of ice.[30] But he was impelled to give up hope of securing this aid in time and therefore turned to the limited resources of the colony. The Canadians, he was able later to report, were so impressed by the preparations being made to strike at the English that in patriotic fervour they voluntarily gave up the little reserves of pork and flour they had put aside for their own livelihood and were subsisting on Indian corn, milk, and vegetables.[31] By this means the Governor General was able to make available for the Marquis de Montcalm ample provisions for a limited period in full anticipation that with the success of the expedition the great stores of food supplies provided for the English garrisons at Fort William Henry and Fort Edward would fall into the hands of the French.

By July, while the provision ships from France had failed to arrive, other ships brought reinforcements of troops.[32] In the course of the summer some thirty-five hundred made their appearance to strengthen the military position of New France.[33] Everywhere there was an atmosphere of buoyancy in the colony. Men looked forward to the speedy termination of the war here in North America, which had gone so favourably for them. Montcalm in July wrote to the Minister of the Marine and Colonies, de Moras, that while he sought an early recall in order to return to France and to his family, should there be at the peace an interval between the news that it had been made and the departure for France of the troops, he would like to be permitted to go into the interior in the area of the Great Lakes and the Ohio in order to make a survey, "with military and political views" as his objectives.[34]

Never had there been at Quebec or at Montreal, in view of this happy anticipation of an early and advantageous peace, such scenes of social animation as occurred during the winter and spring of 1757. The Governor General, Intendant Bigot, Montcalm, the Chevalier

---

[30] *Ibid.*

[31] Vaudreuil to de Moras, July 12, 1757, *ibid.*, X, 585.

[32] Montcalm to the Minister of War de Paulmy, July 11, 1757, *ibid.*, X, 573.

[33] Intelligence sent by Colonel Peter Schuyler, a prisoner at Quebec, under date of October 4, 1757 by Joseph Morse, Chatham Mss., Volume XCV (Canadian Archives Transcripts).

[34] Montcalm to de Moras, July 11, 1757, *N. Y. Col. Doc.*, X, 578.

de Lévis, and others vied with one another in the brilliance of their
entertainments as great receptions, dinners, balls, and suppers followed one another in an endless succession. Montcalm until Lent
had open house three times a week and always at least sixteen people at his table, at which gatherings colonials mixed with Frenchmen, and the ladies, with sparkling wit and beautifully robed,
spread their charms.[35] For a military man he was delighted with the
performances of his own regular troops and had also come to have
a deep admiration for the Canadians. In one of his animated letters
he exclaimed: "What a Colony! What a people, when called on!
They all possess talent and courage at bottom. . . ."[36]

He also had come to appreciate the part that the Indians could
play in the approaching campaign. Writing to the Minister of War
on July 11, he observed:

> "Last month a thousand Indians arrived from the upper country;
> many of them came from 4 to 500 leagues. . . . Our Indians are
> equally capable of determining in a quarter of an hour the gain or
> loss of an affair."

He then went on to remark:

> "I have been obliged here to gratify the Indian Nations, who will
> not leave [for the campaign] without me. . . . On the day before
> yesterday I was [away from Montreal] to chant the war and made
> a feast for the Indians of the Lake of the Two Mountains; Yesterday,
> for those of the Sault St. Louis; to-day held a Council with the
> Upper Indians. I [shall] hold a general Council to reunite them
> all, by presenting them with a large Belt of Wampum in the name
> of the Great King, for whom they entertain the most profound re-
> spect and veneration." [37]

With the Indians, both domiciled and savage, now properly ex-
cited, and with other military preparations completed, Montcalm
and his staff left Montreal and arrived on July 18 at Fort Ticonderoga, where there was assembled by the end of the month an
army of over eight thousand eager, confident fighters, including
some two thousand Indians, supported by a train of artillery.[38] Soon

[35] A clear picture of the social life at Montreal and Quebec is given in the *Lettres
de Montcalm à Madame de Saint-Véran, sa mère, et à Madame de Montcalm, sa femme,
1756, 1757*.

[36] Montcalm to de Moras, July 11, 1757, *N. Y. Col. Doc.*, X, 577.

[37] *Ibid.*, X, 574–5.

[38] "Journal of the Expedition against Fort William Henry," and Bougainville to
de Paulmy, August 19, 1757, *ibid.*, X, 599, 606. Among the domiciled Indians the

there was action. Marin led two hundred of his far-western Indians boldly through the forest into the very vicinity of Fort Edward and, according to Montcalm, "carried off a patrol of ten men, and swept away an ordinary guard of 50 like a wafer; went up to the enemy's camp under Fort Lydius [Edward] [where] he was exposed to a severe fire [by massed British troops] and retired like a warrior. The enemy, whose conduct has been as timid as ours has been bold, did not follow." [39] The party did not bother to take prisoners, but returned with a collection of forty English scalps. Not to be out-done, Langlade, in support of a French colonial detachment under Lieutenant Corbière, led his ferocious Ottawa and Saulters as well as Christian Abenaki along the western borders of Lake George. After waiting in ambush on both shores of the lake at Sabbath Day Point, at early dawn on the 27th the party discovered a flotilla of twenty-two barges containing three hundred and fifty New Jersey and New York provincials moving up Lake George in the direction of the French encampment. The troops, under command of Colonel Parker of the New Jersey regiment and of five captains, had left Fort William Henry to attack the French outposts at Ticonderoga and to burn a mill at the falls. Suddenly raising their blood-cur-dling war whoop and as suddenly pouring a withering fire upon the occupants of the barges, the Indians in their swift-moving canoes immediately closed in for the kill. The provincials, apparently para-lysed by fright and surprise, offered almost no resistance as the boats were overturned by the savages. Most of those who were not drowned were taken captive. Parker and perhaps one hundred men made their escape.[40] After this victory there occurred a repetition of the horrid festivity that took place when the Ottawa and Saulters captured Pickawillany; for these Indians now proceeded to engage

---

French Christian Iroquois and some Oneidas from the Six Nations constituted the single largest group; the next largest was the Abenaki; there came in addition Hurons (also Iroquoian), Nipissings, Algonkins, Amalicites led by the famous Abbé Piquet of Présentation, and a few Micmacs from old Acadia, to a total of over eight hundred. Among the Upper Country Indians the largest group was made up of Ottawa, led by the famous Langlade, who in 1752 had overwhelmed La Demoiselle at Pickawillany with his Indians. The Saulters (Chippewa) were also well represented, as were the Folles Avoines (Menominee) and the Potawatomi. There were also Foxes, brought by Marin from Green Bay on Lake Michigan, together with the Sauk (Sac), Iowas, Loups, Puant (Puan), and a sprinkling of other wild Indians, numbering in all close to one thousand (ibid., X, 607–8).

[39] Montcalm to Vaudreuil, July 27, 1757, ibid., X, 591.

[40] Ibid. Webb to Loudoun, August 1, 1757, Loudoun Papers, No. 4020; for other accounts see also N. Y. Col. Doc., X, 599, 647.

in a cannibalistic feast after having killed and boiled one of the English prisoners, in spite of the fervent protests of Father Roubaud, Jesuit missionary to the St. Francis Indians, who was quartered among the Ottawa at the time.[41] Indeed, Montcalm's aide-de-camp Bougainville, while admitting the fact, could only say that it could not be prevented; for had force been used to check these Indians, they, he affirmed, would have immediately gone home in a rage [42] — and the French had other business for them.

On July 29 the forward movement against the English fort began. Between that date and August 1 the artillery train, the munitions, the provisions, two hundred and fifty bateaux, and two hundred canoes were portaged over the Carrying Place by the soldiers in the absence of horses and oxen. Already on the 29th Chevalier de Lévis started with a force of two thousand Frenchmen and five hundred Indians to skirt the western shore of Lake George by land; then two days later the rest of the Indians departed in their canoes; and on the first day of the new month Montcalm and the main part of the army took to the water. Now was the time, if ever, for the English to have met the threat by the operation of a heavily armed lake force. This, through a reasonably alert patrol of the comparatively narrow lake, could have sighted the French flotilla and then have blasted it with cannon-fire while keeping well out of range of the French musketry. But such a patrol did not exist. The available vessels were only two old sloops and five whaleboats. As a result, the French, with no interference,[43] reached the southern shore of the lake at the point of rendezvous, four leagues to the west of the fort. At dawn on August 3 the army moved forward by land and water preceded by a cloud of Indians and by ten o'clock Fort William Henry and the outlying entrenched camp were surrounded by some five thousand troops and two thousand Indians, and their fate was sealed.[44]

---

[41] See Roubaud's letter of October 21, 1757, quoted by Parkman: *Montcalm and Wolfe*, I, 482–3.

[42] *Journal de l'expédition contre le Fort George du 12 juillet au 16 août*, 1757.

[43] After Webb left Fort William Henry on his inspection trip, boats were sent out each night to observe any movement of the enemy. Only on August 2, when the enemy was but four miles from the southern shore, was its advance detected. But the scout boats were attacked and only five of the occupants escaped to land early on the morning of the 3rd (Loudoun Papers, No. 6660).

[44] Perhaps the best account of the campaign has been left by Bougainville. See his long letter to de Paulmy of August 19, 1757, N. Y. Col. Doc., X, 605–16.

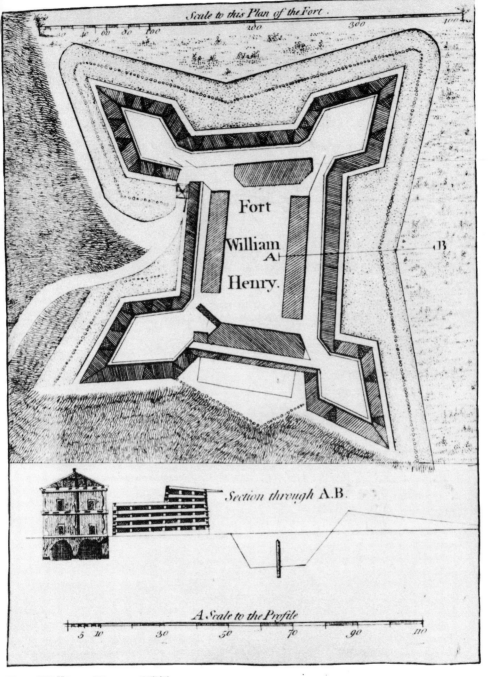

Fort William Henry, 1757.

(From Ann Rocque's *A Set of Plans and Forts in America*, 1765.)

A. The Dock | C. Fort William Henry | E. The Enemys 1.ᵗ Battery | F. Their 2.ᵈ Battery of 10 Guns | G. Their Approaches
B. The Garrison Gardens | D. The Different Morass | of 9 Guns & 2 Mortars | and 3 Mortars | H. Two Intended Batterys

A PLAN of
Fort William Henry
and the
English Camps
& Retrenchments
with the
French different Camps
and Attack there upon

C

B

N

D B

D B

B
C

A

PART OF LAKE GEORGE

A Scale of this Plan of 100 Yards.

100 300 500 700

G

H
F

G

E

K

I. The Place where they | the main Body of ye Army | M. M.ʳ de la Corne with | English Troops Encamped | Retrenchment was made
landed their Artillery | L. M.ʳ de Levis Camp with | 1500 Canadians & Indians | before they was ordered by Gⁱ | O. the bridge over ye Morass
K. M.ʳ Moncalms Camp with | 3000 Regulars & Canadians | N. The Ground where the | Wedd to the Place where the | P The English Retrenchment

The siege of Fort William Henry, 1757.

(From Ann Rocque's *A Set of Plans and Forts in America*, 1765.)

Meanwhile General Webb, left temporarily by Loudoun in supreme command of the British land forces in this area and to the southward, had arrived at Fort Edward on June 24. Although clothed with great responsibility after taking over his command in April,[45] he apparently before leaving Albany, his headquarters, on June 23, had known nothing of the French preparations at Ticonderoga and elsewhere for an invasion; nor was he aware that the control of Lake George, with all that it implied, had passed from the English to the French, with work proceeding in a leisurely fashion on but two new war galleys, still on the stocks when the blow fell. On his way up the country, however, he was informed by a French prisoner brought in by the Indians of great activity at Ticonderoga, with the concentration there of lake boats and artillery.[46] But he does not seem to have become unduly apprehensive. Early in July two French deserters from this fort also confirmed the report of the prisoner, and on July 10 still another prisoner indicated that there were now five battalions of troops encamped about it and that General Montcalm was expected there at any moment "with the main body of the army." [47] Even this ominous report did not stir Webb into action. Only on the 25th — a month after his arrival at Fort Edward — did he see fit, accompanied by Lieutenant Colonel Young of the Royal Americans, Colonel Montrésor of the Royal Engineers, and Captain Ord of the Royal Artillery, to go to inspect Fort William Henry, where Lieutenant Colonel Monro of Otway's regiment, the 35th, was in command. After surveying the situation he then decided to follow Loudoun's recommendation to abandon the old encampment to the southwest of the fort and to concentrate the troops there on a rocky eminence, known as Titcomb's Mount, to the southeast of it, just across the road leading to Fort Edward and therefore commanding this approach. He accordingly issued orders to Monro covering this point.

On the 28th he also sent a party of rangers in three whaleboats under command of Captain Israel Putnam, of later Revolutionary War fame, to reconnoitre the lower part of the lake. Putnam returned that same day with the report that at the first of the nar-

45 For his instructions under date of April 26 and his "Queries" and Loudoun's answers of the same date, see Loudoun Papers, No. 3474 and No. 3478.

46 Webb to Loudoun, April 1, 1757, ibid., No. 4020.

47 Ibid.

rows, only sixteen miles away, they detected a concentration of the enemy on either shore.[48] The following day, with his mission completed, Webb hastily left for Fort Edward and thereupon, now thoroughly alarmed, "in view of the motions of a large French army this way," [49] proceeded to send out appeals for help to the Governors of New York, Massachusetts Bay, Connecticut, and Rhode Island. He also ordered Lieutenant Colonel Young to reinforce Monro at Fort William Henry so as "to complete the Number of Troops there to 2000." [50] The commander of the fort, the day before Webb left him, pleaded in vain for a proper reinforcement to be sent without delay; in this connection he pointed out that he had but eleven hundred men with him fit for duty and that the fort was the critical point in any movement of the enemy in the Lake Champlain area against the British positions:

> "Because if they are repuls'd, in their Attempt, upon Fort William Henry, the affair will be over; But if they take it, I wont Say the taking of Fort Edward will be the Consequence, but I think it will be a great step toward it. As they will then have a road to bring their Cannon." [51]

All that Webb could be prevailed upon to do was to agree to provide two hundred regulars of the Royal Americans and eight hundred Massachusetts Bay provincials. Yet even this small reinforcement did not appear until the evening before the investment of the fort and was therefore not available to help strengthen the breastworks at the new encampment.

With respect to the strength of the place, it may be emphasized that Fort William Henry was laid out with some care by Colonel Eyre, as was indicated in the preceding volume of this series. In the form of an irregular square with four bastions, it was some one hundred and thirty yards at its greatest length. On the northeast point it was washed by the waters of the lake and on the southeast front protected by an untraversable marsh over which a bridge had been constructed to connect with the road to Fort Edward; the other two sides were surrounded by moats surmounted by palisades; beyond

---

[48] Ibid., No. 6660.

[49] Webb to de Lancey, July 30, 1757, and Webb to Pownall, July 31, 1757, ibid., No. 4003 and No. 4010.

[50] Ibid., No. 4020.

[51] "Queries to General Webb by Lieutenant Colonel Monro, and Webb's Answers, July 28, 1757," ibid., No. 3994.

these moats stretched an open space for perhaps eight hundred to a thousand yards, called the gardens, protected by placing the trunks of half-burnt trees one on top of another. The elevated entrenched camp that dominated the fort was separated from it by a great marsh; the camp's east side was also bordered by a marsh, and the entrenchments of it, like those of the gardens, consisted of trunks of trees.[52] It therefore seemed to possess in the hands of a determined and capable garrison, furnished with adequate artillery and other matériel, considerable power of resistance against a superior force. When the French began their siege of the fort on August 3, Colonel Monro had under his command — to face a powerful force of seven thousand five hundred enemy — six hundred and forty men of the regular regiments, one hundred New York Independents, and about twelve hundred provincials — the latter made up of contingents from Massachusetts Bay, New Jersey, and New Hampshire — together with one hundred and forty rangers and sixty carpenters and sailors.[53]

It may be noted that before the French made their advance, and while the designs of the English in the Lake Champlain area were still masked and uncertain, five battalions of French regulars were placed at Ticonderoga and but one at Crown Point, with other troops stationed at such points as at Fort St. Jean leading up to Montreal. This was a sound tactical arrangement. On the other hand, Webb's distribution of troops was as faulty as that of Montcalm was correct. With some seven thousand troops available in the New York area — made up of regulars and provincials [54] — not many more than eleven hundred of them were on July 30, according to the returns, stationed at Fort William Henry, while at Fort Edward — a much stronger and in other respects a less vulnerable place — at the same date there were almost thirty-five hundred.[55] Even after he had sent a thousand of the garrison to Monro's support, he still must have retained at Fort Edward and close at hand a great numerical superiority over the Fort William Henry garrison, with other large contingents of troops stationed at Saratoga, Stillwater, Half Moon, and Albany. Moreover, thousands of New Eng-

---

[52] Richard Waddington: *La guerre de sept ans*, I, 261.
[53] Loudoun Papers, No. 4367.
[54] Stanley Pargellis, *op. cit.*, p. 244.
[55] *Ibid.*, p. 245. Webb on August 5 claimed that only sixteen hundred men fit for duty were stationed at Fort Edward (Loudoun Papers, No. 4081). If this were so, he must have sent some of his troops southward.

land and New York militia were available in an emergency and were being kept in a state of alertness for that purpose. It was therefore inexcusable on his part that, after the information given through deserters and prisoners of the gathering of much of New France's armed might at Ticonderoga, he did not send out his call for assistance without a moment's delay. Had he done so, there would have been plenty of time to have concentrated a very respectable force of some five or six thousand of his most seasoned soldiers at Fort William Henry, while still holding other troops to guard Fort Edward and the connecting posts between that fort and Albany. His procrastination and the faulty distribution of troops, therefore, were factors in his failure to carry out his promise to Loudoun made in his letter of August 1 that he would,

> "upon any Intelligence of the near approach of the Body of the Enemy, move up with the Remainder of the Army and endeavour to dispute their Landing, or make a Stand with the whole on some advantageous Ground, after having thrown a sufficient Garrison into each of the Forts." [56]

Instead of doing so, he now, in reply to Monro's call for help, pleaded lack of proper information! [57] Yet this timid man on the same day that he did so had his aide-de-camp warn Captain Christie at Albany that the "enemy is landed with a large army to attack Fort William Henry." [58] In the end he was impelled to leave its defenders to their fate, while continuing vainly to promise support and victory. [59]

After Montcalm had drawn his line securely about the fort, he sent an officer with a white flag to Monro demanding in courteous language, but with a veiled threat of dire consequences in case of refusal, that the garrison should peaceably surrender. [60] In this message he referred to his numerous army and to his superior artillery — as fate would have it, much of the latter apparently of English make and laboriously brought from the Monongahela and from Os-

---

[56] Ibid., No. 4020.

[57] Webb to Monro, August 3, 1757, ibid., No. 4032.

[58] Ibid., No. 4033.

[59] For example, Webb's aide-de-camp, Bartram, wrote on August 6 to Monro: "We have now got together . . . three Armies of five thousand Men in different parts of the woods. We shall set out in the night with the whole join'd together and make no doubt of cutting the enemy entirely off. I am, Dear Sir, till I have the pleasure of seeing you to partake of the victory. P.S. We shall bring a field train" (ibid., No. 4106).

[60] For this see ibid., No. 6660.

wego.[61] Monro's reply was a firm refusal to yield the fort, which he expressed his determination to defend to the last.[62] In the first three days of the siege there was almost uninterrupted cannonading from each side, while the French were at the same time busy erecting a battery of heavy cannon and mortars, which went into action on the 6th. On the 7th Montcalm sent another flag of truce with a message stating that he had intercepted a letter that Webb had sent and was sending it over to Monro to show that for his own part "he chose to carry on the war like a Gentleman." [63]

This letter, the last to be received by Monro from Webb before the surrender, indicated that the latter did not think it prudent to attempt to assist him until reinforced by the militia of the colonies, in view of the strength of the enemy. He therefore suggested that, should he not be able to give timely assistance, Monro could surrender. "You might," he stated, "be able to make the best terms . . . Left in your power." [64] While Montcalm may have thought that the contents of the letter would have settled the affair, the unknown writer of "Transactions at Fort William Henry," describing the siege, declared:

> "Before the appearance of this Letter, we were constantly animated with the Thoughts of the General's speedy arrival, and a large body of Troops to our assistance; Yet, when undeceived, not a single man seem'd daunted, nor was there the least mention made of Capitulating until it was impossible to defend the Fort twenty-four hours longer. . . ." [65]

The grim and unequal fight thereupon continued. One factor ultimately served to determine the issue: the disintegration of the artillery of the fort.[66] Before the capitulation all the heavy ordnance — the thirty-two-pounders and the eighteen-pounders — had either burst or split, as well as some of the guns of lesser calibre. This lessened the power of resistance. Many of the provincials also were submitted to the ordeal of enemy fire for the first time in their lives

---

[61] Ibid., No. 4020.

[62] His actual statement, in contrast with the embellished accounts of it, is in ibid., No. 4038.

[63] "Transactions at Fort William Henry, August 3–9, 1757," ibid., No. 6660.

[64] Ibid., No. 4041.

[65] Ibid., No. 6660.

[66] See ibid., No. 6660, and also Lieutenant Colonel Williamson to Monro, August 4, 1757, and "Return of Ordnance Fit for Service at the Time of the Capitulation," ibid., No. 4061 and No. 4395.

apparently and, according to Monro, did not do their duty "with regularity or resolution," in contrast to the coolness of the regulars.[67] On the morning of the capitulation the Massachusetts Bay regiment of eight hundred under Colonel Frye indicated to their leader "that they were quite worn out, & wou'd stay no longer, And that they wou'd rather be knock'd in the Head by the Enemy, than stay to Perish behind the Breastworks." When this was reported to Monro by Frye, the former declared it would be proper "to make an Example of such People." Upon which Frye replied that "it was the declaration of the whole body in general." [68]

By the morning of the 9th the enemy had finished two batteries only one hundred yards from the fort and were preparing to carry it and the entrenched camp by a grand assault.[69] For five days and nights their defenders had had no moment of sleep or rest; their hope of succour from Fort Edward had now vanished, as had their hope of effective resistance, and the Massachusetts Bay line determined to go on no longer. Monro, informed by a body of his officers of this and of the critical situation in general at the camp, therefore decided to call a council of war. As a result of its unanimous decision he was brought to agree to capitulate on the best terms procurable.[70] A white flag now appeared over the fort; the firing ceased on both sides; and in the unearthly stillness that took the place of the roar of battle Lieutenant Colonel Young proceeded from the fort to the camp of Montcalm. By one o'clock the terms of surrender had been agreed upon.

These were as distinctly honourable to the English as they were advantageous to the French, providing as they did that the former were to march from the fort and entrenchment with their arms and personal effects and with all other honours of war and were then —

---

[67] Monro in his "Memorandum" of November 7, 1757 states: "The Provincials [the New Jersey and New Hampshire troops] in the Fort, behav'd Scandalously; when they were to fire over the Parapet, they lay down upon their faces and fir'd straight up in the air." As for the Massachusetts Bay troops, according to him, until the morning of the capitulation they did their duty better than the other provincials (ibid., No. 5309).

[68] "Remarks upon some Particulars of the Siege," by Colonel Monro (ibid., No. 4479). "I'm sorry to say it, tho' with great truth," declared the sturdy colonel, "that in general, the Provincials did not behave well." It may be suggested that he was perhaps expecting too much from poorly trained and poorly disciplined soldiers.

[69] See the "Journal of the Expedition against Fort William Henry," and Bougainville's long letter to de Paulmy, August 19, 1757, N. Y. Col. Doc., X, 598–618.

[70] Council of War in the camp near Fort William Henry, August 9, 1757, Loudoun Papers, No. 4158.

as a protection from the Indians — to be escorted to Fort Edward
by a detachment of French troops and also by some of the officers
and interpreters attached to the native contingents. As for the
wounded and the sick who could not march, they were to be placed
under the protection of Montcalm. The victors for their part were
to possess the fort and all ordnance except one six-pounder, together
with all the munitions and provisions; further, it was agreed that all
prisoners, whites and Indians, taken by the English on land since
the beginning of hostilities in North America were to be safely delivered at Ticonderoga within three months; and, finally, that the
English garrison was not to serve against His Most Christian Majesty
or any of his allies for the space of eighteen months.[71]

Would that these honourable terms had been as honourably kept!

Before the capitulation was finally agreed upon and signed, the
Marquis de Montcalm indicated that he could not give his pledged
word that its terms would be respected before he met the chiefs of
the Indians in a general council. This was immediately held, and at
it he asked them to consent to the above stipulations and to promise
that they would restrain their young men. They unanimously agreed
to both requests. Thus a splendid victory for the French was cli-
maxed by a humane surrender.

"Unhappily for the renown of Montcalm and his army," writes
Waddington, the great French authority on the history of this war,
"this fine feat of arms was terminated by a horrible massacre which
followed the evacuation of the place."[72] Relying entirely upon
French sources,[73] this honest historian refers, first of all, to the massacre of the sick and wounded,[74] as well as the Negroes and Indian
allies at the fort, by the Canadian Indians, with Frenchmen looking
on, and then to the beginning of the march of the garrison, with

[71] For the "Articles of Capitulation" see N. Y. Col. Doc., X, 617–18.
[72] Waddington, op. cit., I, 263.
[73] "Receit du Père Roubaud, Missionary to the St. Francis Indians," and the
"Journals" of Captain Desandrouins, the military engineer, and of Captain Malaries
(Macartie) of the regiment of Béarn — all of whom were witnesses of what took place.
[74] Dr. Miles Whitworth, a surgeon in attendance at Fort William Henry, signed an
affidavit for Governor Pownall on October 17, 1757 stating that he was caring for about
thirty sick and fifty-seven wounded men at the fort at the time of the surrender; that
the French sentinels to guard them were withdrawn early on the morning of the 10th;
that he saw the French Indians drag these unhappy people out and murder and scalp
them in the presence of French troops posted not more than forty feet away; and that
there were several Canadian officers present, among them La Corne, and that "none protected the said wounded men" (Loudoun Papers, No. 4658).

Indians crowding about menacingly and not one person who had authority over them present to control them, and with only two hundred French regulars of the regiments of La Reine and Languedoc as a protecting escort. But an ordered march, as contemplated and guaranteed in the terms of surrender, he makes clear, was impossible; the Indians demanded the packs from the backs of the soldiers and, consuming the rum and brandy found in some of them, "became veritable tigers in their fury"; they threw themselves upon the women and children of the soldiers,[75] some of whom they began killing; and they stripped and made prisoners of all the rest who did not seek safety in wild, uncontrolled flight or retreat to the fort.[76] Montcalm, de Lévis, and Bourlamaque were roused from their sleep and hurried forth. The interpreters, officers of the Indians, missionaries to them, and Canadians were ordered to set to work to tear the English from the hands of their executioners. The latter, "drunk with blood and slaughter would no longer listen to any one," and many of them knocked their prisoners on the head rather than turn them over; a great number dragged them into their canoes and escaped.

Montcalm, to do him credit — after permitting, however, this monstrous scene through lack of proper safeguards of those he had solemnly promised to protect — in his despair finally bared his breast and cried out in midst of the crazed savages: "Since you are rebellious children who break the promise you have given to your Father and who will not listen to his voice, kill him first of all!" [77]

At last a semblance of order was re-established and many of the intended victims were rescued. Four hundred, however, were carried away. Some of them were massacred en route to Canada. Even in Montreal "in the presence of all the city," the Indians killed one of

---

[75] Vaudreuil, in writing to de Moras on September 7, speaks of the "great number of women" among the garrison (N. Y. Col. Doc., X, 633). According to eyewitnesses, not only were most of the soldiers stripped stark naked and some were killed, but they describe a scene hard to record: "The throats of most, if not all the Women were cut, their Bellies ripped open, and their Bowels torn out, and thrown upon the Faces of their dead or dying Bodies . . . the Children were taken by the Heels, and their Brains put out against the Trees or stones, and not one of them saved. Some of the Fugitives that reached New York on this Day, affirm this, as what they saw, in the whole or in Part, Executed before they Escaped" ("Printed by Order," New York, August 19, 1757, Pennsylvania Gazette, August 25, 1757).

[76] Colonel Frye of the Massachusetts Bay regiment, stripped of arms and outer clothing, left an account of his flight (Frye to Thomas Hubbard, August 16, 1757, Parkman: Montcalm and Wolfe, II, Appendix F).

[77] Waddington, op. cit., I, 266.

their captives, put his body in a kettle, and, most monstrous of all, "forced these unhappy compatriots to eat of it." [78] The number of those who fell victim to the Indians will probably never be known with accuracy, although — including the sick and wounded soldiers, the numerous women and children, and those dispatched on the way to Montreal — it was probably not less than two hundred and may have greatly exceeded that number.[79] French authorities tended to minimize the figures and also the whole incident.[80] Ultimately, with the departure of the Indians with their booty, the way was secure for the return, now under proper escort, of Colonel Monro and some fourteen hundred of his soldiers who had either been rescued from the Indians or had retreated into the fort for safety.[81]

Although Montcalm had been ordered by Vaudreuil to take and to destroy not only Fort William Henry but also Fort Edward, he was not prepared to undertake the latter task, which would have been infinitely more difficult than the one completed. For he would have been obliged to operate with few Indians, since most of them could not be kept after the termination of the enterprise on Lake George; again, in spite of the existence of a road from the lake to Fort Edward, it would have required three hundred horses to pull the artillery over the six leagues,[82] and these were utterly lacking since the Indians had killed all at the fort together with the cattle in the course of the siege; further, the Canadians were insistent that they be allowed now to return to harvest their crops, which were more precious than gold to the inhabitants of Canada and also

---

[78] *Ibid.*, I, 268.

[79] Large numbers of the provincials headed through the woods for their homes and not back to Fort Edward.

[80] Vaudreuil, writing to de Moras on September 7, affirmed that in the disorder but six or seven English soldiers were killed (*N. Y. Col. Doc.*, X, 634). Montcalm, writing to de Paulmy on August 15, confines himself to the statement: "I cannot conceal from you that the capitulation has unfortunately suffered some infraction on the part of the Indians. But what would be an infraction in Europe, cannot be so regarded in America" (*ibid.*, X, 598).

[81] It is an interesting fact that those in authority in the northern colonies, most directly affected, tended to minimize, as did the French, the tragedy that followed the capitulation, but not for the same reasons, one may affirm with confidence. Undoubtedly the probable psychological effects upon the plans for recruiting new forces in America, of giving emphasis to real facts concerning it, weighed heavily in the balance. In other words, they were apparently inclined to leave the matter of presenting the truth to those who would later prepare the chronicles of the war. Again, the military reputation of certain high leaders was involved. They would be disinclined to emphasize the real nature of the disaster that befell those under their direction.

[82] Doreil to de Paulmy, August 14, 1757 (*N. Y. Col. Doc.*, X, 596–7).

to those in authority; [83] and, finally, it was realized that at Fort Edward there were concentrated many times more soldiers than had been stationed at the fallen fort.[84] Therefore, after levelling the fort and destroying the entrenchments on Titcomb's Mount, the French troops made a gradual withdrawal back to Ticonderoga, Crown Point, and Montreal. Never before was the prestige of French arms in North America so high — and never would it be so high again — as it was in the fall of the year 1757.

As to Fort Edward, Webb's frantic appeals for help were promptly answered. Soon there was converging on that place a very large force, some of the New England militia even riding on horseback to its support. As a result, some seven thousand men were concentrated there not long after the capitulation of Fort William Henry.[85] Other thousands were by that time in motion in that direction. All of which only serves to illustrate the fact that Webb had shown the grossest incompetence in the utilization of the resources at his command. That he was relieved of his office and called back home is not surprising; nor is it, that in his later military service in Germany he was treated by his fellow officers with scant respect.[86] It is therefore almost inexplicable that he continued to enjoy the favour of men of high influence in the government and received, after leaving America, more than one promotion.[87] Yet one must admit he did possess at least real competence at desk-work under a superior, and this rather than field service seems to have occupied his attention.[88]

[83] Montcalm to de Paulmy, September 8, 1757, enclosing an extract of a letter from Bigot dated August 16 (ibid., X, 631).

[84] According to French estimates, there were six thousand English troops at Fort Edward (Doreil to de Paulmy, August 14, 1757, ibid., X, 596).

[85] See the communication from New York under date of August 15, 1757 in the Pennsylvania Gazette, August 25, 1757. The sender refers to a letter received stating "that they were 7000 strong last Thursday at Fort Edward; that great numbers were going up to them. . . ."

[86] Writing in French to Amherst from the British camp near Giessen on September 30, 1759, he declared: "I have been, as you know, treated like a dog and I have room for complaint against some of your friends" (Amherst Papers, Packet 32, Canadian Archives Transcripts).

[87] In June 1759 he had attained the permanent rank of major general of cavalry, and in June 1761 he became a lieutenant general (Gentleman's Magazine, XLIII, 541).

[88] Deputy Quartermaster General Sir John St. Clair, when given command of the provincial troops of Massachusetts Bay by Governor Pownall in the midst of the alarm, wrote to Loudoun on August 7, 1757 a letter that would reflect not only on Webb but on himself as well when entrusted with an independent command: "What a foolish figure a military man makes when he is left alone" (Loudoun Papers, No. 4119).

Happily, the winning of the war was not to depend upon British successes in the Lake Champlain region, but largely upon developments elsewhere. To a consideration of these events we must therefore now turn.

CHAPTER IV

The Checkmating of Loudoun

IN THE PRECEDING VOLUME the activities of the commander-in-chief of the British forces in North America, Lord Loudoun, have been described in so far as these related to the campaign of 1756; also in the two preceding chapters of the present volume repeated reference has been made to him. His reputation, which, it may be pointed out, was very high indeed when he arrived in North America, was destined to go into a total eclipse, if not by the end of the year 1757, at least before he was recalled to England in the spring of the following year — and into obscurity. It is the purpose of the present chapter to follow with some little care his role while in the process of preparing for and carrying out the campaign of 1757, so that the reader may have before him some of the more pertinent facts upon the basis of which a valid judgment of him as a military leader can be formed.[1]

Loudoun was distinctly not the type of general to take unnecessary risks, at least if he realized they were such; his earlier military experience in Europe in a subordinate position had apparently impressed upon him the idea of caution. In other words, he was willing to fight, but only under conditions that offered a fair prospect of success; meanwhile, in making his preparations for the campaign in 1757, he sought to maintain the morale of his precious regulars and

---

[1] It is only in our own day that a careful analysis of the problems that Loudoun faced has had the effect of bringing to bear upon his career in the New World a really just and not unsympathetic understanding that makes clear how shallow was much of the torrent of criticism directed against him in both England and America. For this very detailed analysis the student is referred to Stanley M. Pargellis's scholarly *Lord Loudoun in North America.*

at the same time to enlist the hearty support of the colonial authorities. In the working out of his plans it is true that he found it at
times necessary to traverse colonial interests with respect to such
tender matters as the quartering of troops, the enlisting of indentured servants, and the embargo of merchant ships; but any student
who has had the patience to cover his voluminous correspondence
will be apt to affirm that he was not unreasonable in his demands
and, in fact, could make the best possible case for them, if the war
in North America was to be brought to a speedy conclusion.

In the summer of 1756, in the face of disaster on land, Loudoun
had come to the conclusion that the only way to master the enemy
in North America was to strike boldly at the heart of New France —
the capital city, Quebec.[2] He had continued to adhere firmly to this
view at least for some months [3] and even in the early spring of the
year 1757 was still hoping to secure the approval of his plan by the
Cabinet Council.[4] As against a hazardous amphibious enterprise, a
land expedition, he indicated to his friend the Duke of Argyle,
would be still more hazardous:

> "By going to Quebec . . . success makes us master of every thing;
> . . . by fighting across the land the troops must be exposed to a
> thousand accidents. . . . They must be mentain'd at an immense
> Expense, if 'tis possible to mentain a great boddy in that Country,
> and if we have all the Success we can hope, we can get no further
> next Campaign than to Lake Champlain." [5]

But Pitt was not of that mind. While willing to admit that a land
expedition against New France presented too many problems, he
was strongly committed to the idea of assaulting first of all the fortress of Louisbourg, standing menacingly at the entrance of the Gulf
of St. Lawrence. With that threat once removed from the approach
to the great river itself, he would then direct the New World forces
of Britain against Quebec. These tasks, he was convinced — in spite
of the success of the New England troops during the preceding war
in making themselves masters of Louisbourg — were such as must
be assigned largely to regular troops, especially in view of the con-

---

[2] Loudoun to Cumberland, August 29, 1756, *Military Affairs in North America,
1748–1756, Selected Documents from the Cumberland Papers in Windsor Castle* (ed.
Stanley Pargellis), p. 233.

[3] Loudoun to Cumberland, October 2, 1756, *ibid.*, pp. 235–7.

[4] Loudoun to Pitt, March 10, 1757, *Correspondence of William Pitt* (ed. G. S.
Kimball), I, 14–22.

[5] Letter of January 9, 1757, Loudoun Papers, No. 749, Huntington Library.

centration of French regular battalions on Cape Breton Island and at Quebec and near-by Montreal. On December 22 he had written to Loudoun of the King's intention of sending a land force of eight thousand men and a strong squadron to North America to partici-pate in the next year's campaign, and on February 4 he informed the commander-in-chief that there would be placed at his disposal some seventeen thousand regular troops, including those that were already in North America. With these amply supplied with artillery and supported by a stronger fleet, Loudoun, he felt, should find himself in a position to "push with vigor an offensive war," which could only be decisive by the capture of the two French strongholds. As soon as the reinforcements had arrived in America, therefore, Lou-doun was first of all to attack Louisbourg by land and sea with a force sufficient to carry it. Should this work be accomplished by the end of May or early in June, he was then to move up the St. Law-rence against Quebec.[6] Thus, while Loudoun had asked to be per-mitted to move directly against the capital of New France, he was now ordered by Pitt to direct his forces first of all against Louis-bourg.

Yet all of those who composed the Cabinet Council of the new ministry did not see eye to eye with the Secretary of State for the Southern Department. The Duke of Cumberland, in particular, was strongly committed to a policy of supporting the plan advanced by the American commander-in-chief.[7] As a result, on March 13 Pitt's positive orders were modified by an order of the Council [8] and a new instruction was sent to Loudoun, which, while indicating that as between a move against Quebec and one against Louisbourg the latter was considered by His Majesty to be the more practicable, at the same time rested the final decision on Loudoun's own judgment in making clear that "His Lordship is nevertheless, to use His Dis-cretion with regard to which of the two above mentioned Attempts He shall judge it most advisable first to proceed." [9]

[6] Ibid., No. 2765. However, Pitt stated that "As success may depend upon circum-stances in both these enterprises that may not be known in England, His Majesty is pleased to leave some latitude" to Loudoun's discretion and judgment "to decide on the time and manner of carrying these attempts into execution."

[7] Cumberland to Loudoun, March 21, 1757, Military Affairs in North America, 1748–1756, pp. 325–7.

[8] There was present at this meeting Cumberland, Pitt, the Lord President, Bedford, Devonshire, Holderness, Earl Temple, and the Chancellor of the Exchequer.

[9] Chatham Mss., Volume XCV (Canadian Archives Transcripts); Loudoun Papers, No. 3076.

The division of opinion in the Cabinet Council on the first objective in the campaign of 1757 was also reflected, it may be emphasized in passing, among Loudoun's American advisers and confidants during the early months of 1757.[10] The most outspoken and effective arguments advanced against the proposal of the commander-in-chief to strike "at the root," Quebec, came from Thomas Hutchinson, a member of the Massachusetts Bay Council and one upon whom Loudoun was relying heavily at this period to help bring to the ensuing campaign the fullest measure of support from New England. Taking up Loudoun's argument in favour of the campaign up the St. Lawrence, he replied in rebuttal: "An attempt upon Quebeck is infinitely more hazardous than an attempt upon Louisburgh; the navigation to the former is extremely difficult & no English Pilots are well acquainted with it." He then went on to point out that were Louisbourg to remain in the hands of the French while the English squadron and transports proceeded up the St. Lawrence, a great part of the Louisbourg garrison could be used to strengthen a French fleet or an army that the French King might send over. Such a force could be used by the enemy either to follow the English expedition up the river or to coast along the undefended Atlantic seaboard, ravaging the seaports of the English colonies at will as far down as South Carolina, with the probability also that Nova Scotia would be taken over by the French once again. But with Louisbourg disposed of, the French would be deprived of the only place on the seaboard where their ships could shelter and rendezvous and the crews be refreshed. He therefore sounded a warning that if Louisbourg were by-passed, it might be the ruin of the English fleet and army in the St. Lawrence, should the expedition return from the river worn out and dispirited. Finally, in countering Loudoun's argument about the possibility of the enemy's moving by

10 This point is emphasized in a letter to James Abercromby by an unknown soldier who was an officer in the regular service under Prevost's command and who wrote from New York on May 30. After stressing this division in point of view he adds that "almost all our War Captains, particularly the Natives, are for Quebec, they say that would be striking at the roots & the branches must fall — they make light of the navigation and all other obstacles, — they are only for destroying this metropolis as an effectual means of ruining Canada & securing a great Majority of Indians & lastly that this attempt would prevent the french from attacking the frontier, a local consideration which weighs much with the good folks of this City & province." Others, he finds, however, were inclined to favour beginning with Louisbourg; to these people, "venturing up the St. Lawrence with such a garrison and harbour behind us, should we fail [would be] a hazardous experiment" (Chatham Mss., P.R.O., Vol. XCV, Canadian Archives Transcripts).

land down against the colonials if the expedition should be concentrated against Cape Breton Island, he replied that a part of the forces raised should remain for a defence until the outcome of the attempt on Louisbourg was known.[11]

That the weight of these objections to a Quebec expedition was not entirely lost upon Loudoun is indicated by his reply to Hutchinson. While he still pointed out the danger to which the northern colonies might be exposed during the operations against Louisbourg, he nevertheless added: "I enter the less into the Argument at present, as the point is . . . in Suspense till the next Packet arrives, which I hourly expect."[12]

It was on May 1 that the Pitt letter of February 4 appeared, with definite orders to attack Louisbourg. Two days after receiving it, the general replied, apparently without any disappointment that his own project had been overruled: "I am extremely happy to find, that the preparations I have made, and the plan I have prepared for, in a great Measure, Co-incides with the Orders I have now received. . . ."[13] Indeed, after receiving at Halifax on July 9 the instructions of March 13 that would permit him to use his own discretion, he did not feel disposed to turn aside from the plan for the investment of Louisbourg in accordance with Pitt's earlier orders. Moreover, it is by no means clear that he was at all anxious to risk an attack on Quebec at the time that he received the news that he had been given liberty to choose his objective. In fact, a false report was brought from Canada in June by one of the officers of Rogers's famous Rangers, who had escaped from captivity, that the French, having received accounts of British preparations to the southward, "were assembling all their forces at Quebec, to defend their Capital."[14] It is quite obvious that, had he been willing to risk such an attack and had failed, his position would have been wholly untenable. It is equally obvious, of course, that should he fail in an at-

---

[11] Hutchinson to Loudoun, March 14, 1757, Loudoun Papers, No. 3070.

[12] Loudoun to Hutchinson, April 11, 1757, ibid., No. 3335.

[13] Letter of May 3, 1757, Pitt Correspondence, I, 53. Miss Kimball in her Introduction to the Correspondence of William Pitt (p. xxx) laboured under a misconception that Loudoun himself had made the suggestion that he should "with all dispatch" invest Louisbourg and that Pitt, as a result, accepted the idea. That this misconception was prevalent in England in the spring of 1757 is made evident by the general, who, writing to Cumberland on August 16, after the attempt against that place had been given up, declared that such a report was being circulated at home (Loudoun Papers, No. 4240).

[14] Loudoun to Pitt, June 17, 1757, Pitt Correspondence, I, 75–6.

tempt to carry out Pitt's original orders respecting Louisbourg, his position would be little less embarrassing, in view of the fact that the imperious Minister had set his heart upon a successful summer campaign in America to retrieve the failures of the earlier years of the war, and also of Loudoun's expressed preference for undertaking the Quebec enterprise.

As to the comparative merits of the two plans, not only did men differ then but students of American military history do so today.[15] This much may be said: namely, that had Loudoun sought as his first objective the capture of Quebec and had his expeditionary force been repulsed and the supporting fleet seriously weakened and damaged while in the waters of the St. Lawrence, any such concentration of French naval power in the gulf as actually took place at Louisbourg in the spring of 1757 might have led to one of the greatest military disasters in the annals of British history. Doubtless the time-honoured rule that it is unwise to permit an enemy to maintain a powerful position athwart the bases of communication and supply of an advancing force is sound as a military precept, and the principle of due caution therefore demands the elimination of such a hazard before further advance is attempted. Yet it is equally clear that had Loudoun decided to go ahead with his original plan and had he been successful, not only might the New York frontier have enjoyed immunity from attack, but the campaign in North America might have been shortened by some two or three years. Was the great risk involved one that should have been taken? Loudoun was willing to take it, at least up to March 1757, while Pitt and Hutchinson fell back upon the principle of the protected advance. The latter principle, as we know, was to govern the British North American strategy at that time and in the years to follow.

While it is clear that both Pitt and Loudoun were placing their chief reliance upon the ability of the British regulars to bear the brunt of the fighting in acting as the spearhead for the advances into enemy territory, they also looked to the colonial line to supple-

---

15 Dr. Stanley Pargellis has presented in his *Lord Loudoun in North America* (Chapter IX) by far the best defence of the Loudoun strategy as against that proposed for the campaign of 1757 by Pitt and Hutchinson. He indicates that the Pitt alteration threw out of balance Loudoun's carefully conceived plans for the defence of the frontiers of New York in permitting Montcalm to concentrate for his successful attack upon Fort William Henry. It led also to a superfluity of provisions at a point where they could not be utilized and to confusion in other respects, largely as a result of the Minister's secretiveness.

ment the efforts of the former and also to take a place of real responsibility in the defence of the frontiers, along with small contingents of professionals. Pitt, for example, on February 4 called upon the governors of the northern colonies to furnish at least the same number of troops for the ensuing campaign as were provided the preceding year,[16] and those of the colonies to the south and west of New Jersey to raise as large a number of troops "as possible."[17] In each case, while asking that the enlistments should be free of limitations such as had hitherto rendered the provincial troops ineffectual for the service, he promised that all that the colonial assemblies would be expected to meet in the way of expenses involved in the raising and maintenance of these contingents would be the costs of recruiting the men and their "pay, arms, and clothing." He also indicated in a later communication that as South Carolina, according to reports, was especially threatened by the enemy, he would send to its support a regiment of Highlanders.[18]

Loudoun, before knowing that Pitt had taken office, had already stationed a battalion of regulars in Pennsylvania to help stabilize the situation there. Also, with respect to the very critical New York frontier, he had determined on his own initiative, as was noted in the preceding chapter, to post there for the period of the ensuing campaign about eighteen hundred regulars — later changed to some twenty-three hundred — to be reinforced by some six thousand provincials, which combined force was to act primarily on the defensive, as were the forces to the southward.[19] Thus he looked to aggressive action on only one front — an amphibious operation of which he would assume personal direction.

Still proceeding under his original instructions, early in the new year Loudoun had called a gathering of commissioners of the New England colonies at Boston in order to make sure of the support required from these colonies according to his plans. His position was somewhat delicate; for he was obliged to confront those who had been associated intimately with General Shirley for many years and who had shown great sympathy for the latter, facing as he did the hostility directed against him by Loudoun himself and other officers of the regular army. His first move was a monument of tactfulness.

---

[16] *Documents Relating to the Colonial History of the State of New York*, VII, 216.
[17] *Pitt Correspondence*, I, 5–6.
[18] *Ibid.*, I, 28–9.
[19] Pargellis, *op. cit.*, p. 211.

For he called to his aid in a confidential capacity the influential Thomas Hutchinson, Shirley's son-in-law, who, as indicated, was a member of the Massachusetts Bay Provincial Council and who had deeply at heart the successful conduct of the war in North America. It was he — appointed to act as one of the commissioners from his own colony,[20] the most influential colony by far — who drew up for Loudoun the framework of a proper message to be delivered to the assembled commissioners.[21] Again, Loudoun showed his tact in the character of the address that came out of Hutchinson's and his own efforts. While stressing the causes of the misfortunes that had lately befallen the British in North America in the course of the war and while calling upon the commissioners not to place hampering restrictions upon the use of the provincial troops wherever the service seemed to demand it — an important point, in view of the unwillingness of these troops to serve with the regulars during the campaign of the preceding year — he at the same time declared:

> "You may depend upon my treating your men with all that tenderness & indulgence which will consist with the necessary order & discipline & that I will employ them whenever there shall be room for it in such services as shall be most suitable to their genius & the way & manner of fighting to which they have been used & that they shall be discharged at farthest at the Experation of the term for which they are raised."

Further, he made clear to them that he would not ask for the number of troops raised for the service by the New England colonies in 1756 — some seven thousand [22] — but would be satisfied with a total

---

20 Loudoun Papers, No. 2695.

21 For Hutchinson's letter to Loudoun of January 21, 1757 enclosing his draft of the address see *ibid.*, No. 2693; for the draft itself see *ibid.*, No. 2694; for the finished document and two intermediate drafts see *ibid.*, No. 2728; a copy of this is to be found among the Williams Mss., Vol. II, No. 4, at the Massachusetts Historical Society.

22 Loudoun to Fox, February 7, 1757, Loudoun Papers, No. 2802. Pitt's decision to request the colonies to duplicate for 1757 the numbers that had been raised in 1756 was of course not known to Loudoun at the time of his own decision. When made aware of this request, he wrote to the Massachusetts Bay Council on May 2 — Lieutenant Governor Phips had passed away on April 4 — suggesting that since it was very unlikely that the additional troops could be levied and equipped by the time they would be needed, one way to comply with his orders, in spirit at least, was to have the militia properly armed and supplied with ammunition and under a standing order to march to the aid of General Webb's troops whenever the latter should call for assistance (*ibid.*, No. 3527). A letter almost identical with the above was addressed to the governors of the other northern colonies the following day (*ibid.*, No. 3548).

of only four thousand, based upon the proportions for each colony previously established.[23] In light of the disaster that befell the forces in the Lake Champlain area, this decision, while designed to appeal to the economy-minded New England assemblies, was undoubtedly unfortunate.

Nevertheless, the immediate effects of the general's address were all that he could have desired, especially in view of the hostile attitude manifested by the New England governments in the course of the 1756 operations about Lake George. While the commissioners found it impossible to agree among themselves upon the quota that each colony should furnish,[24] Loudoun had so established himself in their confidence, at least momentarily, that they each in turn called upon him to set the quotas. This he did,[25] and was gratified to find that in the end the four assemblies agreed to honour his decision.[26]

Loudoun had also determined to meet the governors of the more southern colonies at a conference in Philadelphia in February in order to "Concert a Proper Plan to be carried on there for their Mutual Security and defence." In this again he showed wisdom. For his invitation was directed to all of them, including Lyttelton of South Carolina and Reynolds of Georgia,[27] thus avoiding the mistake that Dinwiddie of Virginia had apparently led Braddock to make at the Alexandria conference of 1755. While neither of the

---

[23] Ibid., No. 2728.

[24] For example, the Rhode Island commissioners pointed out that the population of Massachusetts Bay was held to be 206,000; that of Connecticut, 130,000; while that of New Hampshire and of Rhode Island was but 36,000 each. Upon this calculation they therefore insisted that Massachusetts Bay should furnish, out of the 4,000 provincials, one half of the total; Connecticut, 1,300; New Hampshire, 333; and Rhode Island, 334 (ibid., No. 2776). On the other hand, the Massachusetts Bay commissioners made clear that since their province was keeping in its pay at least 800 men for its "immediate protection and defence" and, in addition, was employing 300 men on its two vessels of war, its due proportion of the 4,000 should not be more than 1,750 provincials out of the total (ibid., No. 2767).

[25] Massachusetts was asked to contribute 1,800 men; Connecticut, 1,400; Rhode Island, 450; and New Hampshire, 350. For a tabular statement of the quotas requested by Massachusetts Bay, Connecticut, and Rhode Island respectively, see Pargellis, op. cit., p. 215.

[26] Governor Hopkins, who, as one of the Rhode Island commissioners, finally vigorously supported Loudoun's request for 450 men from that colony — as against 334, which the colony contended was its proper quota — declared later in writing to the general that his zeal and endeavours for the service "have been charged on me as Crimes" (Loudoun Papers, No. 3482).

[27] For his circular letter to the southern governors see ibid., No. 2653.

governors of the two most southern colonies could arrange to come — although each felt honoured by the invitation, the rest of them appeared. There was a delay of almost a month, however, after their arrival before the conference got under way. For Loudoun found it impossible to reach Philadelphia as early as anticipated. Nevertheless, it began on March 15 and lasted a fortnight, with Denny of Pennsylvania, Sharpe of Maryland, Dinwiddie of Virginia, and Dobbs of North Carolina on hand, together with Colonel George Washington, who desired to confer with Loudoun on the problems confronting him in connection with his command in western Virginia. Each of these men was requested to submit his own general plan of defence of the southern areas; a free discussion of the merits of the individual proposals was then encouraged. After this Loudoun submitted his own general plan, shaped in the light of the various suggestions made in the conference, and also covering such matters as quotas of troops to be furnished by the colonies and the disposition of these along the frontiers. As this latter topic has already received detailed treatment in the second chapter of this volume, all that is desirable at this point — in striving to comprehend the strategical and tactical ideas of Loudoun in 1757 — is to make clear that he felt it important to strengthen the ability of the more southern colonies to resist the encroachments of the enemy by cantoning in this area some twelve hundred regulars, including the two hundred men of the Independent Companies of South Carolina. These troops would therefore be in a position, he felt, to aid the provincial contingents — set at 3,500 men as the total to be raised among these colonies [28] — wherever most needed. In fact, before the conference ended it was agreed that over one half of the regular force to be left in this area and some thirteen hundred provincials should be concentrated in South Carolina to protect that province from a threatened attack and that the remainder of the regulars should operate along the very troubled borders of Pennsylvania. This disposition of the troops was heartily endorsed by the assembled governors.

It may be asserted that Lord Loudoun reached the peak of his prestige in North America at the termination of the Philadelphia

[28] Loudoun requested Pennsylvania to provide 1,400 men; Maryland, 500; Virginia, 1,000; North Carolina, 400; and South Carolina, 500. The minutes of this conference are printed in the Colonial Records of North Carolina (ed. W. L. Saunders), V, 750-2).

conference. In coming into Pennsylvania he not only received a very congratulatory address from the Assembly,[29] but was the means of terminating a serious deadlock between Governor Denny and that body which involved the appropriations necessary to maintain the provincial volunteer forces.[30] Having also arrived at a harmonious agreement with the assembled governors, who were thereupon pledged to use their best exertions to secure through their respective assemblies the means for implementing their decisions, he returned to New York to continue his preparations for the year's campaign. The significance of his labours at Boston and at Philadelphia has been well described by a leading authority on this period of American colonial history:

> "This was the first time in the history of the colonies that a British commander-in-chief, endowed with suitable powers and acting on his own initiative, had undertaken to direct the military resources of eleven colonies as a unit in a general plan of operations [and had been responsible for] the posting of men along a fifteen hundred mile frontier from New Hampshire to Georgia. . . ." [31]

That there was failure of these defensive plans in the area of Lake George can hardly be justly charged to Loudoun, outside of the leniency of his demands on New England. He certainly left Webb, as has been indicated in the preceding chapter, a sufficient force, actual as well as potential, to have made a much more powerful defence than was made, with twenty-three hundred regulars and some fifty-five hundred provincials, without including the thousands of northern militia readily available in an emergency. In other words, up to his departure for Nova Scotia with his expeditionary forces, his handling of the military situation was certainly sound and was characterized by a good deal of patience in dealing with the colonial governments. This was intermixed, it is true, with firmness, especially when it came to the shelter needed and demanded for his troops during the winter season of 1756–7 and reluctantly provided by the colonial authorities, and to other measures, such as the embargo placed upon colonial vessels in the spring of 1757 — so vital in spite of its unpopularity, in order to keep supplies and information from the enemy and to provide an adequate pool of transports for

---

29 *Pennsylvania Archives* (eighth series), VI, 4535–6.
30 Denny to Thomas Penn, April 10, 1757, *ibid.* (first series), III, 117–20.
31 Pargillis, *op. cit.*, pp. 212, 227.

carrying troops to their destination, Louisbourg. His deep solicitude for the success of the campaign of 1757 led him into great and sustained exertions, so that one of his officers was led to remark that "his Lo$^{p:s}$ great anxiety makes him take all on himself from morning to night, in so much that its surprising how he holds it out." [32] In writing to the Earl of Halifax early in June he gives one something of an idea of the sweeping nature of his responsibility as commander-in-chief in North America:

> "I have been so hurried this whole winter, first with the Opposition I met with every where in putting the troops into winter quarters; then I was obliged to go to Boston, to meet with the New England Governments; from thence I was obliged to repair to Philadelphia, to settle Military matters with the Southern Governors; besides which, I have the providing for one army in South Carolina, another in the back parts of Pennsylvania; and a third in the back parts of this Province [New York], at the Forts; besides the providing and Embarking the troops" [for the Louisbourg expedition].[33]

As early as the middle of May Loudoun had the regiments that he would take with him from New York ready to embark, and on the 21st they were placed on board the transports. But meanwhile he and Sir Charles Hardy, in command of transports, had received reports of the presence of enemy ships of war off the Atlantic coast. He therefore felt impelled, on account of the great risk involved, to delay the movement of the troop ships that were without proper naval convoy until some news had arrived of the appearance of the British fleet and the transports bearing the regiments Pitt had determined to send to the New World. He was left in no doubt, however, about that minister's deep interest in the success of the campaign and of his willingness to strip England of much of the country's defences in order to make the year's campaign in America a success.[34]

In fact, the transports chartered to carry the regiments designated to go to America left the Thames for Spithead in February; on the

---

[32] To James Abercromby from ——, New York, May 30, 1757, Chatham Mss., Vol. XCV (Canadian Archives Transcripts).

[33] Letter of June 3, 1757, Loudoun Papers, No. 3785.

[34] Baron Cathcart wrote to Loudoun in February, after a long conversation with Pitt, that the minister "had so much at heart the support of the colonies that he almost seemed to think that if there was a scarcity of troops, as there seemed to be, and your Cause must either be starved or this island left bare, he rather would run the Danger this Nation would run at home than that which the Colony's would run without a very considerable reinforcement" (ibid., No. 2858).

17th of that month Vice Admiral Holburne, who was to command the ships of war as well as the transports sailing from Spithead for Ireland to embark the troops, was obliged to anchor at St. Helen's on the Isle of Wight in the face of persistent westerly winds. These winds continued without cessation for some two months,[35] and it was not until April 26 that Holburne and Commodore Holmes were able to cast anchor in the "Cove of Cork." [36] With the fleet came the transports and the officers who would command the troops to be embarked, among them Major Generals Hopson and Lord Charles Hay. Immediately the work of placing on board some fifty-two hundred men and equipment began.[37] On the 8th of May Holburne signalled the departure, and the fifty transports, convoyed by fourteen ships of the line and a frigate, started across the Atlantic. On June 6 Holburne reported — by means of a merchantman bound for England — that for the past fifteen days he had met with contrary winds and bad weather.[38] In fact, not until July 10 was he able to reach Halifax.

Meanwhile Loudoun and Hardy waited impatiently at Sandy Hook for news of the arrival of Holburne in American waters. During the interval two cruisers were sent out to scout and to report the presence of the enemy; then — almost a month after the soldiers had been embarked — when the way to Halifax seemed to be clear, it was determined to run the risk of sailing, hoping against hope that none of the large ships of the enemy would appear. Therefore on June 20 the vessels, numbering over one hundred, raised anchor and with about six thousand men aboard, together with provisions for a six months' campaign and other matériel, and all but defenceless, moved out of the Hook.[39] "If they [the French Navy] meet us,"

---

[35] Holderness to Loudoun, April 8, 1757 (ibid., No. 3316). Captain John Knox, who was waiting with his regiment at Cork, refers in his Historical Journal of the Campaigns in North-America in the Years 1757, 1758, 1759, and 1760 (London, 1769, I, 14) to "an obstinate set of contrary winds, that had retarded us in Ireland about two months after our arrival at the port of Embarkation. . . ."

[36] Ibid., I, 5; Holburne to Pitt, April 25 and May 17, Pitt Correspondence, I, 34–5, 60–1.

[37] There were embarked the second battalion of the Royals and the 17th, 27th, 28th, 43rd, 46th, and 55th regiments — the battalion of one thousand, and the others each listed at seven hundred men (Knox, op. cit., I, 7). These troops, all stationed in Ireland, received their orders to move to Cork early in February, and the seven regiments arrived there before the 26th of that month (ibid., I, 3).

[38] Pitt Correspondence, I, 73. Knox refers to a "dreadful storm" that struck them on May 13 (op. cit., I, 9).

[39] "Journal of a Voyage to Halifax on the intended Expedition under the Com-

Loudoun had already warned Pitt, "there is an end of the troops that go from hence" (New York).[40] For they could depend for convoy on only the slow-moving *Sutherland,* of but fifty guns, the *Nighten-gale* and *Kennington,* of but twenty, and two sloops. Happily, the voyage of ten days was made without incident, with no sign of an enemy ship of war, and soon after the armada had appeared at Hali-fax it was joined by units of Holburne's fleet and on July 10, as al-ready indicated, the rear admiral himself arrived on his flagship, the *Newark,* with the remainder of his vessels bringing with him the forces from the British Isles under the command of Major General Hopson and other officers. Loudoun now had under his immediate orders some sixteen regiments of regulars, including the three al-ready stationed in Nova Scotia, an artillery train, and some compa-nies of rangers under Robert Rogers — making a total of between fourteen and fifteen thousand fighters; he had also at his disposal some seventeen ships of the line, together with sixteen other vessels: frigates, sloops, bomb-ships, and a fire-ship.[41] What would or could he do with this splendid force? [42]

The answer to this question was provided by the French. Early in the year it was felt at Versailles that the British would make an attempt against Louisbourg, and it was therefore determined to pro-vide that place with naval strength so powerful that it would be safe from any threats of the enemy.[43] Then, as secret-service and other reports were received, the ministry became convinced that the British would strike at Canada "from the sea" and that Cape Breton Island would be subject first of all to attack. It therefore seemed more than ever imperative that there should be a heavy concentra-tion of naval forces at Louisbourg as early as possible in the spring.[44]

---

mand of Lord Loudoun, 1757," Chatham Mss., Bundle 78 (Canadian Archives Tran-scripts).

[40] Loudoun to Pitt, May 30, 1757, *Pitt Correspondence,* I, 71.

[41] The "Journal of a Voyage to Halifax . . . 1757" (*op. cit.*) gives an exact list of the ships and other information; see also Richard Waddington: *La Guerre de sept ans,* I, 251, and Julian S. Corbett: *England in the Seven Years' War,* I, 169.

[42] The unknown author of the "Journal of a Voyage to Halifax . . . 1757," who was, however, clearly a British officer, declared: "I never saw finer Forces than the Regiments and in particular Lord Blakeney's who shined among the Rest." He also reported "the Fleet and Army were exceedingly healthy" at the time of their arrival at Halifax.

[43] President of the Navy Board to Governor de Drucour and Intendant Commissary Prevost, March 2, 1757, *Canadian Archives Report* (1905), I, Part VI, 241–2.

[44] President of the Navy Board to de Drucour, March 31, 1757, *ibid.*

To provide for this Vice Admiral the Chevalier de Beaufremont (Beauffremont) was ordered in December to make his way at the beginning of the year with a squadron to St. Dominique, which Machault thought was in danger, with instructions that should this island not be threatened before the month of April he was then to sail for Louisbourg.[45] It was also determined to send du Revest from Toulon with another squadron to the latter place, and even a third more powerful squadron from Brest under the command of Comte Dubois de la Motte, with the expectation that these squadrons would be united under de la Motte in this Cape Breton harbour by the middle of June.[46] De Beaufremont, late in January and before the British had re-established the blockade at Brest, slipped out of that port with five ships of the line, including the *Tonnant*, an eighty-gun ship and one of the finest in the French navy, and made his way to the West Indies.[47] With everything temporarily quiet in that area, he started from Cape François on May 4 with his squadron, arrived off Cape Breton Island on the 28th, and entered Louisbourg on the 31st.

Du Revest early in April moved out of Toulon with four ships of the line but was forced by contrary winds to put back into Málaga. This gave Rear Admiral Saunders, waiting with his squadron at Gibraltar, an opportunity to meet him. The naval engagement that took place in the Mediterranean near the straits was largely limited, however, to a long-distance bombardment. In fact, Saunders with three seventy-gun ships and a fifty was hardly a match for du Revest's powerful *Hector*, a seventy-four, supported by three sixty-fours, the latter having a fire-power equal to an English seventy; further, his ships were foul, while the French ships had been newly cleaned and easily outsailed the British ships. By this means they passed safely by Gibraltar and into the Altantic, while Saunders was compelled to enter the port of Cádiz to refit.[48] Although the French squadron was reported to be within sixty leagues of the

[45] Memorandum from the King, December 20, 1756, *ibid.*, p. 232; the King to Beauffremont, December 21, 1756, *ibid.*; Machault to Beauffremont, December 21, 1756, *ibid.*

[46] President of the Navy Board to de Drucour, June 30, 1757, *ibid.*, p. 243.

[47] Besides the *Tonnant*, there was the *Défenseur* and the *Diadème*, both seventy-fours, and the *Eveille* and the *Inflexible*, both sixty-fours. See Barbier's "Journal," 1757 (*ibid.*, I, Part VII, p. 3) and the "Journal" of the *Inflexible* (*ibid.*, Vol. I, Part VIII).

[48] London Gazette, May 20, 1757; J. S. Corbett, *op. cit.*, I, 157; "Journal" of Barbier (*op. cit.*).

Grand Bank on April 30,[49] it was not until June 5 that it was in the neighborhood of Cape Breton Island and not until the 19th that three of the ships entered Louisbourg, delayed as the result of unfavourable winds and fogs.

De la Motte, meanwhile, sailed from Brest May 3 with nine ships of the line and three frigates without interference from Temple West, whose blockading squadron had been swept off the station by a gale,[50] and after a voyage without incident entered the harbour of Louisbourg on June 20, where the admiral now took command. There were thus successfully concentrated at Cape Breton Island eighteen ships of the line, together with frigates and privateers, all ready for action, undoubtedly the most powerful naval force that up to that time had been seen in the New World — taking into consideration both the number of the ships, their quality and armament. Three of them, the *Tonnant*, the *Formidable*, and the *Duc de Bourgogne*, were eighty-gun ships; they were supported by six of seventy-four guns and seven of sixty-four guns.[51]

Writing from Louisbourg on June 28, a correspondent expressed the confidence of the men there: "We have eighteen men of war in the harbor under the command of M. Dubois de la Motte. . . . This formidable army puts us at ease respecting all the attacks the English would make in that quarter." [52] In fact, far from being anxious for the safety of Cape Breton Island, they now were thinking of aggressive measures against the British on the mainland and, according to the same writer, "everybody already wants Acadia to belong to us. . . ." [53]

This buoyancy of feeling was not limited either to those at Louisbourg. When Louis XV was made aware of the success of the great strategy of concentration of naval power in the North Atlantic, he

---

[49] President of the Navy Board to de Drucour, June 30, 1757, *Canadian Archives Report* (1905), I, Part VI, 243.

[50] *Ibid.* See also Waddington, *op. cit.*, I, 251, and Corbett, *op. cit.*, I, 160.

[51] See the list of ships contained in Barbier's "Journal" (*op. cit.*). Barbier was second captain on the *Formidable*.

[52] *N. Y. Col. Doc.*, X, 572. An officer of the *Inflexible* in his "Journal" shows that de la Motte, anticipating an attempt of the enemy to land at Miré Bay, to the north of Louisbourg, had concentrated heavy detachments to block the road, which led through deep woods and ravines, while at the same time six hundred Indians were ranging about Gabarus Bay. He writes: "We were quite prepared to receive the enemy at all points. We could have wished . . . that they had executed their plan, of which we were well informed" ("Journal" of the *Inflexible, op. cit.*).

[53] *N. Y. Col. Doc.*, X, 572.

expressed the hope that de la Motte would not hesitate to move out of the harbour and boldly attack the fleet of the enemy,[54] thus reversing the characteristic French naval strategy of defensive warfare on the high seas. Further, to support the garrison and the naval forces, fourteen of the King's vessels were loaded with provisions in the various ports of France and sent without escort to Cape Breton in the hope that they would elude the British.[55] Most of these arrived. The defences of Cape Breton were therefore at this juncture of affairs at the highest point of preparation, with new fortifications constructed after 1749 about Louisbourg and arrayed with powerful batteries [56] and a fleet riding in the broad expanse of the harbour with fire-power adequate to place beneath the water any but the greatest of the British ships. Indeed, so confident was de la Motte in his ability to defend the island, even with reduced strength and with sickness among his crews, that he determined to send to Canada some of the transports, convoyed by two of his ships of the line, with the regiment of de Berry that he had brought out from France — and this was done. He thereupon settled down to await the British attack, and while waiting used his sailors to help erect additional fortifications.[57]

When Holburne and Hopson joined Loudoun and Hardy at Halifax on July 10, none of them was fully aware of the real French

[54] President of the Navy Board to de la Motte, June 30, 1757, *Canadian Archives Report* (1905), I, Part VI, 243. Under his instructions issued to him on April 9, de la Motte was "as a prime consideration to protect the place that the enemy desired to attack and menace." Yet "if the opportunity was presented, he might profit by his numerical superiority that he was supposed to have over the English in attacking and destroying their fleet; but upon this point the King left to his judgment what he felt it possible to do without compromising the forces confided to him, the preservation of which is so essential to the Navy" (Instructions of April 9, 1757, Waddington, *op. cit.*, I, 252).

[55] Six of these vessels were captured in European waters; most of the rest, however, apparently arrived (President of the Navy Board to de Drucour and Prévost, July 27, 1757, *Canadian Archives Report*, 1905, I, Part VI, 243).

[56] Among the additional fortifications erected at Louisbourg after taking it over from the British in 1749, according to the testimony of Francis Piggot, a Halifax pilot who spent six weeks in Louisbourg in 1755, was a battery on Black Rock designed to accommodate twenty-five 42-pounders and to dominate both the best landing-place — White Point in Gabarus Bay — and the entrance to the harbour and also overlooking the swamp that the New England troops in 1745 were obliged to traverse in establishing the siege. Black Rock had also been levelled, the Grand Battery strengthened, as also the walls about the city, and another battery was erected on the beach at the southeast end of the town (Minutes of a Council of War held at Halifax, July 23–31, 1757, Loudoun Papers, No. 3984).

[57] Waddington, *op. cit.*, I, 252–3.

strength at Louisbourg. Nor had a definite plan for the campaign against Cape Breton been evolved. It is true that before Holburne left England the two men who had acted as Governors of Cape Breton Island during the brief period when it had been in British possession — Vice Admiral Sir Charles Knowles and Major General Hopson — were called upon to give their views of the best way to attack Louisbourg. Each agreed that if the French were in real force on the island and determined to resist, the difficulties facing the invaders would be very great even without the presence of a French fleet, and should one be at hand in the harbour of that stronghold, they were both convinced that an attack by sea would be out of the question. In fact, they both took the position in a signed statement that

> "Shou'd but 5 or 6 [French] ships of the Line Gett there, all attempts by sea wou'd be vain, for they may keep out a hundred; nor do I think a siege by Land cou'd be carried on whilest a Squadron is in the Harbour, because after a breach is made the men who are to assault that breach, must march under the fire of all the Ships; unless there were forces enough to build batterys to Sink those Ships or drive them away, and carry on the Siege too." [58]

On July 12 the Knowles-Hopson memorandum was placed before Loudoun for consideration. Already some swift-sailing schooners had been sent out to "look into Louisbourg" and one of them, commanded by Captain Gorham (Goram) of the Nova Scotia rangers and "A good Pilot of the Place," brought back a report that there were in this Cape Breton harbour ten ships of the line and four frigates.[59] To verify this report, Loudoun now sent out the previously disabled H.M.S. *Arc-en-Ciel*, under command of Captain John Rouse, whose own ship, the *Winchelsea*, was apparently not suited to the enterprise. Rouse ever since 1744 had sailed these waters and knew them. He returned the next day, however, without securing any information since the harbour of that port was enveloped in fog. Two days later he again ventured forth, this time in H.M.S. *Success*, supported by the brig *Concord* of Philadelphia, Captain Ash, and

---

[58] The statement was framed by Knowles and endorsed by Hopson. In the Loudoun Papers (No. 3682) Knowles alone is credited with it; the Cumberland Papers in Windsor Castle call it a "Joint Proposal by Admiral Knowles & Colo^el Hopson, concerning an attack upon Louisbourg" (Pargellis: *Military Affairs in North America, 1748–1765*, pp. 310–13). For Hopson's "Private Thoughts, relative to the Attack of Louisbourg, 1757," in which he points out the great hazards an invasion may involve, see *ibid.*, pp. 302–10.

[59] "Journal of a Voyage to Halifax . . . 1757," *op. cit.*, Bundle 78.

two smaller vessels. It was hoped that they might take as a prize some craft sailing from the enemy's stronghold and, with it, prisoners in order to obtain further facts. They succeeded in securing a French fishing schooner, the crew of which declared, as had Gorham, that there had been ten ships of the line at that place, together with fourteen frigates; but that five of the line-of-battle ships and two frigates had gone to Quebec.[60] An effort to view the harbour, likewise, by Rouse, was once again unsuccessful as the result of continued fogs enveloping it. No decisive step, it was felt, could wisely be taken until more definite data had been gained.

Meanwhile the troops, many of them now suffering from sickness, had been landed and very properly put through exercises somewhat comparable to the type of training given to commando troops in the recent war. A large garden was also prepared to supply the forces engaged in the siege with fresh vegetables, so vitally necessary to keep away scurvy and other deadly ailments and for the recovery of the sick and wounded. Again, sloops and frigates under Captain Gorham attempted to gather the desired information, but returned on the 20th still baffled by the fog. On the 23rd Loudoun called a council of war, which, with adjournments, sat through the remainder of the month hearing testimony and weighing the grave issue as to the course of action to be pursued. There were present Vice Admiral Francis Holburne, Rear Admiral Sir Charles Hardy, Commodore Charles Holmes, and Captain Thorpe Fowke, representing the royal navy, and Major General James Abercromby, Major General Peregrine Hopson, and Major General Lord Charles Hay, representing His Majesty's land forces.

It should be stressed before analysing the work of the council of war that Loudoun was not bound by its decisions, but possessed full freedom to use his best judgment. In other words, in framing his instructions to the general, Pitt was very careful — especially in light of the unpopular decisions that Byng had made the preceding year based upon the advice of councils of war — to free Loudoun of any necessity to feel hampered in this fashion. It may be equally stressed, however, that no commanding officer would lightly brush aside the matured views of those who would be expected to assume the chief responsibility in carrying out his orders if these ran contrary to their own convictions on crucial matters. Loudoun's method of procedure in the course of these solemn deliberations was above criticism. He

---

[60] *Ibid.*

determined that those whom he had summoned to advise with him should be in possession of all pertinent facts, in so far as these were obtainable. He first of all, therefore, laid before the council of war all the papers that he had received from the ministry as well as Holburne's instructions and other important papers, which were carefully read and considered. Thereupon he summoned before the council all those with particular knowledge of the region.

Governor Lawrence of Nova Scotia, who for years had acted in this area in his military and civilian capacity, as major, then colonel, and then Governor, was first called upon to give his views. He was persuaded, he declared, that only a very considerable force could now reduce Louisbourg and that it would be more proper, if an attempt were made, to land at a distance to the north of the city on Miré (Miray) Bay rather than where the New England troops landed in 1745 at Gabarus Bay to the south and west of the city. His views were shared by Captain Scott, who had also seen service in this region for many years and who knew Cape Breton Island well. Yet both admitted that were the troops to land at Miré they would be obliged to traverse a long road lined on either side by a dense growth of trees and unsuited, on account of a succession of deep hollows, for transporting siege artillery over it. Nevertheless, both felt that this great hazard was less than that of attempting to land at Gabarus, and Lawrence particularly stressed the fact that the best time for disembarking a large force on Cape Breton was early in June. Captain Rouse, an experienced navigator in those waters, favoured in turn Gabarus as a landing, but admitted under questioning that, in case of bad weather intervening in the course of the operations, the ships of war must sail away and leave the troops and transports to the mercy of any French fleet riding in the harbour. Captain Bond, of H.M. sloop *Speedwell,* for seven years on the coast, and Captain Loring, who acted in the operations in 1745, were each in turn questioned without getting much light on the problem, but Captain St. Loe, of the 40th regiment of foot, likewise acquainted with the island, but not with the French preparations to receive a foe, was very confident that troops and matériel could and should be landed at Gabarus and that an attack was practicable. He was followed by Captain John Bradstreet — to become famed for his capture of Fort Frontenac in 1758 — who had spent two years at Louisbourg and who likewise knew Cape Breton well and was present at the landing of the Americans in 1745. Bradstreet also favoured Gabarus for this operation and felt that conditions were not unpromising for it. His testimony, however, touched very lightly on the problem of landing troops under unfavourable weather conditions. In all some twenty-one witnesses were heard in the course of the proceedings, among these experienced pilots who had navigated the waters for years. Some expressed confidence in the success of an operation undertaken at the time, but none was in possession of information as to the present strength of the enemy fleet, and those who favoured an attack with the present forces did so upon the assumption that the French ships of war that might be in the harbour were of much less strength than the fleet under command of Holburne.

The most disturbing testimony brought before the council of war came from Lieutenants George Phillips of H.M.S. *Centurion* and Cosby of H.M.S. *Oxford*. Each was on board a Dutch ship that had left Surinam in the late spring for Amsterdam, and while in passage in Latitude 44° 5′ west, each saw sailing westward and to the south of him a fleet flying no colours, eight of which were very large ships and "from their build — and particularly from their heads" — seemed to be French. Lieutenant James Ferguson of H.M.S. *Northumberland* also testified that on July 3 he had been sent by Lord Colville, operating off Nova Scotia, to board a Marblehead fishing schooner returning from the banks and that the master of it declared that a few days before he had been informed by the master of another Marblehead vessel that on June 22 he saw off the Green Bank

> "Twelve sail of large ships . . . which hoisted English colours, but that he [the master of the schooner] took them to be French Men of War standing for Louisbourg; and the reason he gave for their being French . . . was because he saw them pass over that Bank, which is a rout [*sic*] to Louisbourg."

A prisoner of war taken on July 14 off the Gut of Canso, one Petit Grave, also declared that before he was captured he had spoken to the master of a French shallop that had just left Louisbourg, who stated that at that time ten or twelve ships of war were in the harbour there. All of which information, inconclusive as it was, pointed strongly to the presence of a large French fleet at the very place to be attacked.

Before the council of war concluded its work Loudoun put certain leading questions to Holburne respecting the degree of support

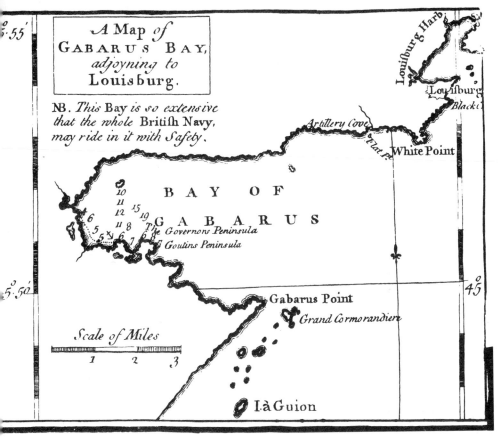

map of Gabarus Bay adjoining to Louisbourg.

that the latter was prepared to offer in case a landing on the island were attempted. The admiral agreed not only to assist in the disembarkation of the troops and the siege train but also to aid in the manning of the batteries during the siege. He also, upon further questioning, declared "that whenever the troops begin to land to form the siege of Louisbourg, that the Fleet should Anchor, and remain so in the Bay at all hazards. . . ." This could only mean that so important did he consider his duty to guard the transports and the troops that, in case of a storm, he was prepared to risk the loss of his entire fleet, which might well be driven into the shallow water by the prevailing southeasterly winds and hopelessly grounded. Finally, on July 31, Loudoun put the question of the choice under present conditions of an attack on Louisbourg or on Quebec, permitted under his last instructions. In reply, the council "was unanimously of the opinion, That the Attack should be made on Louisbourg." [61]

One incident that took place in the course of the council of war may be mentioned that for obvious reasons was not included in the minutes but that is of importance. The veteran Captain George Scott — one who had spent many years in Nova Scotia and who, with very special knowledge of conditions on Cape Breton Island, had testified before the council, as previously indicated, on July 23 — sent to Loudoun on the 28th, after much searching of heart, an unsigned letter in which he pointed out that he was convinced that "we have neither time nor numbers equal to the undertaking." His reasoning was impressive: to get out of Halifax by the utmost exertions and under most favourable conditions would take, he estimated, over a week; another week must be allowed for getting to Louisbourg, taking into account the prevailing fogs; then should

---

[61] "Minutes of a Council of War held at Halifax, July 23–31, 1757," Loudoun Papers, No. 3984. This was signed by all the members of the council of war. Lord Charles Hay put in the following reservation: "As Quebeck is deem'd Impracticable by yᵉ Majority of yᵉ Council." It may be added that Lord Hay during his stay at Halifax, both in the council of war and out of it, acted in a manner so irresponsible as to lead Loudoun and others under him to question his sanity. He apparently favoured an attack on Louisbourg without considering any of the risks involved and was very outspoken, casting insinuations against all those who wanted to see clearly all the factors in the problem of reducing that stronghold. Many of the Loudoun Papers relate to this. See, for example, copies of letters between Lord Hay and Lord Loudoun of August 6 and 7, 1757, ibid., No. 3901; Loudoun to Holderness, August 5, 1757, ibid., No. 4072; see also Hay to Pitt, September 15, 1757 and February 26, 1758, Chatham Papers, XXXIX, 108–13 (Canadian Archives Transcripts).

the weather be ever so favourable, the better part of still another week must be spent in landing the troops and their baggage; after this time eighteen or twenty days at least would be required for carrying ashore the stores and the cannon and for securing a proper encampment against surprise; thus, supposing that the weather were perfect and that the enemy permitted these operations to go on undisturbed, it would be at least the end of the first week in September, he concluded, before any essential blow could be struck. But this supposition was based on premises that must be questioned; especially that the French had either forgotten the art of war or were weakly manned, which was far from likely, he pointed out, considering the time that fate had given them to prepare everything for receiving the British. He calculated that, including Indian forces that were available as well as the services of hardy inhabitants, the French might be able to depend upon as many as 10,900 defenders; he also calculated that they must have a very powerful naval force in the harbour since they had felt free to send five or six ships of war, according to reports, to Quebec. "Fabius, my Lord," he then cautioned, "by his wise delay, saved Rome and may properly be said to have laid the Foundation for the destruction of Carthage." Let the British, he urged, follow his example. Instead of facing the "numberless difficulties" by a present attack, let Louisbourg harbour be blocked with the fleet during the fall. Then in the spring the enemy would be very low-spirited and in want of everything — a condition that always prevailed to his knowledge even when the English markets on the North American continent were open to them before the war — while the British troops already here in America, and well supplied with all necessaries, would be in high spirits and have the whole summer before them for reducing not only Louisbourg but even Canada.[62]

Scott's advice was sound and, it is of interest to note, it was fully in line with the basic strategy finally adopted by the British relative to the conquest of Cape Breton Island. Yet Loudoun, after the conclusion of the council of war, was not prepared to turn aside from an assault on it without an effort. Great stores of fascines, hurdles, and gabions — so essential for the building of breastworks on rocky

---

[62] Loudoun Papers, No. 4024. On August 23 Scott admitted to Loudoun his authorship of the anonymous letter. He then wrote freely that if the fleet would winter in America and be off Louisbourg very early in the spring, that place would be in Loudoun's hands by July 1 of the next year (ibid., No. 4295).

ground — had been brought into Halifax and placed on board ships designated for the purpose; on August 1 the artillery, stores, and other heavy baggage followed; the next day over eleven thousand effective troops were embarked by brigades at different wharfs.[63] It was determined that Holburne, whose fleet on July 23 was formed in line of battle in three squadrons, should now sail with the first favourable wind with his entire force to Cape Breton and challenge the French fleet to come forth from the harbour and fight it out. Until the outcome of this hoped-for engagement should be settled, the troops were meanwhile to remain on the ships at Halifax ready to move in the transports at a moment's notice.[64] While the admiral was busy with his preparations to depart, there arrived in Chibouctou Bay the French schooner *Surprise*, captured by Captain Edwards of the *Gosport* of Newfoundland on July 11 and having on board not only papers that were discovered, but French prisoners as well. These papers, addressed to the French ministry, indicated that twenty-two ships of the line, besides frigates, were in Louisbourg harbour, that a garrison of four thousand men were "intrenched up to their necks," and that a battery of twenty-five guns with mortars had been arranged so as to give any landing force the warmest of receptions.[65] When Edwards had examined the second captain of the captured vessel, the latter had corroborated the contents of the dispatches and gave the names of the ships that he particularly recollected. His testimony was fairly accurate.[66]

The embarkation of the troops at this juncture seems to have brought "General Concern" among the officers of the army and navy, who apparently were fully aware of the reports that were being circulated among the higher staff officers respecting the strength of the enemy. This led Loudoun to write on August 2 to Holburne, the latter on board his flagship the *Newark*, in disapproval of these murmurings; he asked the admiral on the following day, however, his opinion whether the forces at their disposal were sufficient to at-

---

[63] Knox, *op. cit.*, I, 21–2.

[64] *Ibid.*, I, 23.

[65] *Ibid.*

[66] The French officer lists two ships not given by Knox and gives two sixty-fours and one seventy-gun ship rating as a seventy-four (testimony of M. Pierre Mendibouze, August 5, 1757, Loudoun Papers, No. 4069). Apparently after he had left Louisbourg the *Bizarre* and the *Célèbre*, each sixty-fours, were sent to Quebec to convoy the de Berry regiment (*Canadian Archives Report*, 1905, I, Part VI, 244). The captain of the *Surprise* stated that eight ships had come from Toulon, which was inaccurate, unless he counted the smaller support vessels (Loudoun Papers, No. 3901).

tempt the reduction of Louisbourg with any probability of success. While Holburne denied that he had knowledge of such murmurings within the navy,[67] he did in a separate communication in reply to Loudoun's letter of the 3rd indicate that the intelligence secured by Captain Edwards had corroborated other intelligence previously received and then went on to state that "it is my Opinion there is no probability of succeeding in an attempt upon Louisbourg at this advanced Season of the Year. . . ."[68]

This confirmed Loudoun's own conviction that, taking everything into consideration, the attack should be postponed. The soundness of his judgment, in the light of all that is now known relative to the respective strength of the two forces, cannot be questioned. But he must have realized, in coming to this decision, that he would court attacks on his courage and generalship — and he was not mistaken.[69] For in writing to the Earl of Holderness on August 5 he assumed full responsibility for giving up the campaign for the year and made clear that he would leave in Nova Scotia, and particularly in the area of Fort Cumberland — the former French Fort Beauséjour — a sufficiently large force to guard against an attack and that the rest of the troops would be carried to New York to be used in supporting Webb as circumstances might direct before going into winter quarters. But he could not conclude his letter without affirming:

> "that had the fleet and the Succours not been prevented, by contrary winds, from arriving in April, as I am informed by the Secretary of State they were intended, My Master might have been in Possession of Louisbourg very early in the Season, with a very small loss of His Troops."[70]

While the above disposition of the army of invasion was being made, Hardy with his squadron sailed for Louisbourg to reconnoitre, and early in the morning on the 20th of August, with the temporary clearing of the fog, he was able to get a view of the French fleet resting in the harbour and to count seventeen ships of

[67] Holburne to Loudoun, August 4, 1757, ibid., No. 4047.

[68] Ibid., No. 4063.

[69] See, for example, "Journal of a Voyage to Halifax . . . 1757," op. cit., Bundle 78, and A Letter to a Friend on the Affairs of America, published in London in the fall of 1757, which was a very bitter attack filled with distortions of the real facts.

[70] Loudoun Papers, No. 4073; see also Loudoun to Webb, August 7, 1757, ibid., No. 4250.

the line besides frigates that "made a very fine appearance." Then the thick fog closed in again and he was obliged to stand off the land. He also observed near Louisbourg several encampments, "one very large." In reporting to Loudoun on August 24 he declared: "There appears to be every preparation necessary for your reception and such a one that in my opinion would have ended with the ruin of our Army, if a landing had been attempted." [71]

Holburne, likewise, writing the following day to the general, expressed himself still stronger in congratulating him on

> "The escape, I may say the whole Army has had, for I realy am of oppinion the whole would have been cutt off. . . . The ships would mostly have too, as we must have staid for your protection. . . . I am sure your Lordship ought to have the Thanks of our Good King and Country. . . ." [72]

As so large a French fleet, if left to operate without interference in American waters, might have created great devastation along the coast to the southward, Holburne continued at his station in Chibouctou Bay until well into September, sending out from time to time speedy cruisers to observe the enemy. About the middle of that month, in hope of drawing at least a part of their fleet out for an engagement, he set sail for Cape Breton and sent cruisers close to the harbour with the desire of enticing their ships out. But they did not move. Whereupon the entire fleet moved in the direction of Louisbourg and in so close that the admiral was able to confirm Hardy's observation. But still the French fleet remained at anchor. [73] It now became obvious that de la Motte was thinking, with the near approach of the winter season in that area, simply of getting back to France, having performed his greatest service to the King and not desiring to risk his ships. The British admiral, however, continued cruising off the enemy coast until on the 24th, when but ten leagues south of Louisbourg, a southerly hurricane of tremendous force suddenly struck his fleet and continued unabated until the next day, relentlessly driving the ships toward the shore. Reporting the incident to Pitt, he declared that had the storm continued for one day more, "every ship . . . must unavoidably have been lost." [74]

[71] Hardy to Loudoun, August 24, 1757, Chatham Mss., Bundle 95 (Canadian Archives Transcripts).
[72] Holburne to Loudoun, August 25, 1757, Loudoun Papers, No. 4311.
[73] Holburne to Pitt, September 17, 1757, *Pitt Correspondence*, I, 106–10.
[74] Holburne to Pitt, September 29, 1757, *ibid.*, I, 114–15.

As it was, one was sunk and twelve were demasted; [75] the crews of others, to save their ships, threw their cannon into the sea. Thus the great British offensive in North America for the year 1757 collapsed, with the army headed for garrison duty in the colonies at certain strategic points and the fleet now for a time a helpless, almost defenceless thing.

In taking into account the factors that led to the humiliating collapse of the British campaign of 1757 in the New World, one must bear in mind that the French in that year enjoyed a great advantage that would not always come to them: the ports of France used for the fleet and the transports were far enough to the south to avoid the paralysing effects of the powerful antitrade winds that blew for weeks on end across the southern ports of Ireland and England during the spring. They had also the great advantage of the protection given to Cape Breton Island by dense fogs that persisted almost without interruption from the latter part of June into the late fall.[76] These factors permitted Louisbourg, with the arrival of the three French squadrons and three additional battalions of foot soldiers, to enjoy a degree of security that it never before in its history possessed and, it may be added, would never again enjoy.

But beyond these advantages that nature bestowed, the fact must be recognized that Louis XV was well served in America in that year by his ministers at home and his sea and land officers across the Atlantic. They directed the power entrusted to them with great skill and determination; they prepared in good season the relief for Louisbourg and the reinforcements for Canada; and they utilized to its maximum every material resource that they possessed. For example, they saw that every inhabitant in New France capable of bearing arms and not enjoying special exemptions should render service and that the regular troops and the men of the navy were alert and vigilant and competently commanded; they secured for their land operations the support of almost every powerful Indian tribe to the east of the Mississippi River and used that support with great effect; and they freely assumed risks on both land and sea, but limited these to attainable objectives — and achieved them. Indeed, they could have declared to their royal master at the end of the

---

[75] John Entick: *History of the Late War*, II, 394.

[76] Loudoun, in writing to Holderness and Pitt on October 17, declared that during the whole period that he was in Halifax there were not "Six clear days" (Loudoun Papers, No. 4239).

summer's hostilities: We have in this fourth year of the war in North
America held the British in check on all fronts and have even forced
them back on some of these; and in the course of the operations we
have left Fort William Henry — that dagger pointed at the very
heart of New France — a shambles. Our enemies, on the one hand,
possess a foothold on the continent that, in spite of all their efforts,
is now limited to a narrow band of land stretching along the Atlantic
seaboard from Nova Scotia to Florida; while we, on the other, remain masters of the great waterways. We are still determined to see
that they remain where they are and that the fleur-de-lis continues
to wave over the valleys of the St. Lawrence, the Ohio, and the Mississippi, as well as over the Great Lakes waterway system. They
may retain the eastern rim of North America; we shall retain its vast
interior.

CHAPTER V

The European Scene. Pitt's Reversal of Policy

FRENCH MILITARY POWER reached its highest point of effectiveness in 1757 both in America in the fourth year of the Great War for the Empire and in Europe in the second year of the Seven Years' War.[1] At the close of that year it must have seemed to all detached observers that hostilities must soon come to a close in favour of the great coalition of powers, supported largely by French subsidies, that Great Britain and the British Empire, Prussia, and the little states of Hanover and Hesse-Cassel were obliged to face. France with its overseas possessions, Austria with its dependencies, the Imperial Circles of Germany, Russia, and Sweden, not only were arrayed against them in overwhelming force but everywhere were victorious. On one hand was gloom and foreboding; on the other almost unrestrained joy and confidence. As the two wars were so closely related before their partial fusing into one in 1758, it is of great importance, before turning to the course of events that is the chief concern of this series, to trace rapidly the progress of the Seven Years' War in Europe during the years 1757 and 1758.

France, to honour its treaty with the Empress Queen Maria Theresa, early in 1757 assembled two armies that were sent across the Rhine for the purpose of bringing the promised aid to Austria

---

[1] John Entick in his *General History of the Late War* (1765) wrote (II, 191), in describing the situation that confronted Pitt when he resumed power in the summer of 1757, that "he found the enemy more powerful . . . in America, more formidable on the continent of Europe, and with a more respectable navy, than at the commencement of the war."

against the King of Prussia and of seizing Hanover as a pledge that when the war came to an end, whatever gain the British might make at the expense of the French Empire would be cancelled in order to secure the return of that principality to its hereditary ruler, George II. With the northern army of some eighty thousand men, the French Marshal d'Estrées flooded through Westphalia in northern Germany and approached the Weser, where the Duke of Cumberland, who had left London early in April to take over command of the Army of Observation — composed of some forty thousand Hanoverians and Hessians and a reinforcement of some five thousand Prussians — was guarding that strategic river. In spite of his great inferiority in infantry, cavalry, and artillery, the Duke was anxious to dispute the passage of that river, but he was obliged to conform to the views of the electoral council of Hanover. This body, doubtless impressed by the fact that the King of Prussia was under the ban of the Empire, was determined "to keep clear of any operations and connections, which might expose the Electorate to a criminal process in the Imperial courts; and to act only on the defensive. . . ." [2] As a result, the allied army was impelled to retreat over the Weser. Again the Duke sought to make a stand, but he was overruled. In the words of a contemporary historian:

"Forbearance and non-resistance were . . . the maxims of the Hanoverian chancellery. Their own innocence, inoffensive conduct, and the justice and right of protection, which an Electorate can demand under the capitulations of the Golden Bull, were insisted upon, as arguments for the security of Hanover and its dependencies, against France. . . ." [3]

Therefore, without hindrance from a single man, the great French army swept over the Weser on July 10 and 11. It also gathered up

---

[2] *Ibid.*, II, 259.

[3] *Ibid.*, II, 263. It is important for the student to bear in mind that King George was determined at this period that the war that had been proceeding since 1754 on sea and in North America between Great Britain and France should not be confused with what he called "the second war" that broke out in Europe in 1756 between Prussia and Austria, involving as it did Saxony and the rest of the German states as well as France, Russia, and Sweden. When the French army advanced beyond the Rhine and moved toward the Weser, he published to the world "the just motives, which compelled him," as Elector of Hanover, "to repel force by force. . . ." He proclaimed in this pronouncement that the war between England and France "both with respect to its causes, and its end, is entirely foreign to his Majesty, as Elector of Hanover, and to his Hanoverian dominions. . . ." (For this proclamation see *ibid.*, II, 162–5.)

Emden, in East Friesland, the only seaport at that time under the dominion of the King of Prussia.

Cumberland was in a most embarrassing and extraordinary situation before the world. He could throw up in disgust his command of an army supported entirely by British subsidies. That would mean the total disintegration of that force, so desperately needed at the very moment by the King of Prussia as a protection to Brandenburg; it would also mean the abrupt end of the Duke's military career. Or he could try to save his forces until the electoral chancellery had made up its mind to fight. He chose the latter course. As a result, he again retreated northward and eastward while the French now spread out over southern Hanover and began to levy heavy contributions on the towns, which they paid to escape plundering by the French soldiers. Then and only then were his hands freed sufficiently by the chancellery to give battle to the enemy. The engagement took place at Hastenbeck on July 24 and 25. When his left flank was turned as the result of the bad conduct of Hanoverian grenadiers posted on it, again he was obliged to retreat, but in good order. Now was the critical moment, when still free to manœuvre, to have left Hanover to its fate and to have retired to the powerful fortress of Magdeburg on the Elbe. But here again the Hanoverian chancellery interfered, now deeply apprehensive for the fate of the principality. The archives of the Electorate had been hurriedly transferred from Hanover to Stade, lying near the mouth of the Elbe, far to the north of Magdeburg; these, it was insisted, must be protected at all hazards. Again unable to follow his own conceptions of a proper defensive campaign, the Duke now slowly retreated northward so as to offer the desired protection to Stade and, each time that he halted, took up a strong position, which he held until the flanks of his very inferior army were about to be turned by the enemy, and then retired — always with an eye to the safety of Stade. At the mouth of the Elbe were four British warships. He calculated that they at least might bring to him the desired support in taking up his post at Stade; but again his weakness did not permit him to extend his lines so as to include a strategically located fort below this city on the Elbe, which the French seized, and by so doing deprived him of any possibility of aid from the small British squadron. Now, at last cornered, with no possibility of further retreat or of effective resistance, and urged by the Hanoverian ministry to capitulate on terms that would save the army and the precious archives and leave the Electorate in a position of "strict neutrality," he was led to submit. Through the intervention of the King of Denmark, the capitulation of Kloster-Seven was signed on September 8, 1757.[4]

This famous capitulation, incidentally, brought to a close Cumberland's military career and gave to the French the desired occupation of both Hanover and Hesse, as well as Brunswick. It also deprived Frederick of Prussia of all assistance from these quarters. For it provided that all hostilities between the French and the Army of Observation should cease; that the auxiliary troops of Hesse, Brunswick, Saxe-Gotha, and Lippe should be sent home, but not as prisoners of war; that Cumberland and his Hanoverians and Prussians should retire to the east of the Elbe, outside of a few thousand men permitted to be posted at Stade; and, finally, that the French should remain in possession of all the posts and regions where they were then in control, until peace should be made.

Free, according to the terms of the capitulation, to march in the direction of Berlin, the French, under the command of the Duc de Richelieu, who at this juncture superseded d'Estrées, moved into the Electorate of Brandenburg and busied themselves making exactions upon the towns and cities that lay in the wake of their advancing columns. But this, at the time, was only one of the worries that faced the King of Prussia. Early in April he had started his operations with the determination to overrun Bohemia and bring the war to a rapid close. Three of his armies moved upon Prague, and near that place his forces met the Austrians under the command of Prince Charles of Lorraine. The bloody battle at last went in Frederick's favour; whereupon he proceeded immediately to lay siege to Prague. Field Marshal Daun, however, some twenty miles away, moved forward slowly with another Austrian army of some sixty thousand to Kolin, not far to the east of the invested city. In spite of the fact that Daun's position was remarkably strong and that he possessed a heavy superiority over the Prussians in artillery, the King of Prussia, with only some thirty-four thousand men available for the attack, decided on June 18 to risk battle with him. This time Frederick's good fortune, or, rather, sound judgment, deserted him as he hurled the flower of his highly disciplined troops again and again against the parked batteries and natural defences of the Austrians, only to be driven back each time with frightful slaughter. Defeated in his efforts, faced with enormous losses, there was but one thing

---

[4] This is given by Entick (ibid., II, 276–80).

to do, and that was to give up the siege and retreat from Bohemia. Then, while he was busy reorganizing his forces, came the news of Cumberland's defeat on the 26th at Hastenbeck and that of the march of one hundred thousand Russians into East Prussia. Hardly had the King of Prussia at length arrived at Leipzig in Saxony with his army when other bad news came in: his forces in East Prussia had suffered defeat late in August. If that were not enough of adversity, shortly afterward he was informed of the capitulation of Kloster-Seven and then soon came tidings that the Austrians were streaming into Silesia from the south. Marching to the aid of Field Marshal Bevern's weak force in that duchy, he was likewise advised that Berlin had been raided and plundered by an Austrian force and also that western Brandenburg was being overrun by the French. The end of Prussian resistance seemed to be at hand.[5]

The news of this series of calamitous events not only reached Frederick; it also reached London. In an endeavour to draw the French forces back home and out of Germany and to strike at the same time a heavy blow to the steady growth of French naval power, Pitt conceived the idea of sending a powerful expeditionary force against the important naval base of Rochefort on the Charente, which flows into the Bay of Biscay, where at least ten or a dozen ships of the line were harboured and where a great arsenal and numerous magazines were located. This, if overrun and destroyed, would be a major blow to France's sea power and to the enemy's overseas possessions; it would also adversely affect Brest, Port L'Orient, and Rochelle to the north and Bordeaux and Bayonne to the south. It was understood that this base was weakly fortified and weakly defended by troops. After taking into consideration various factors involved, the Cabinet Council was led to give its assent to this enterprise as the best method of relieving the pressure upon the King of Prussia while at the same time remaining free from direct British interference in the war in Germany.[6]

Eighty-four hundred foot soldiers and marines were set aside for this amphibious operation, together with thirty warships, including sixteen line-of-battle ships, and fifty-five transports for the troops and siege equipment. These were to assemble at the Isle of Wight in July. Owing to the mismanagement of the contractors, it was not

---

[5] Entick gives the reader a reasonably accurate account of these Prussian reverses.

[6] Horace Walpole (*Memoirs of the Reign of George II*, III, 44–5) suggests that the Cabinet Council was cowed by Pitt into endorsing the move.

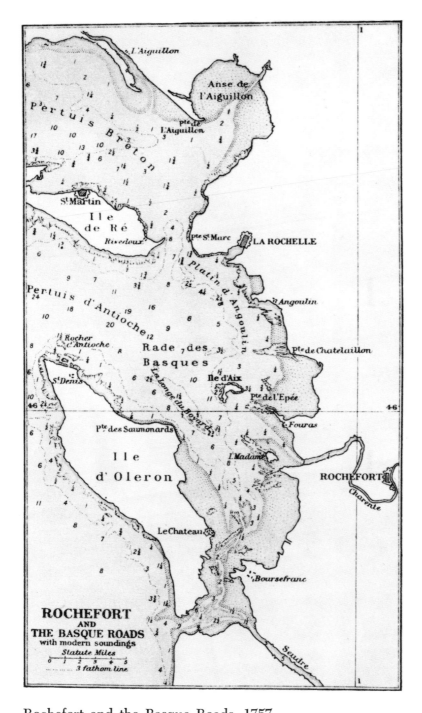

Rochefort and the Basque Roads, 1757.
(From J. S. Corbett's *England in the Seven Years'
War*, with the permission of Longmans, Green & Co.)

until early in September that the transports arrived at Cowes,[7] and it was not until the 8th of that month that the fleet at last, joined by the transports, was able to leave Portsmouth. Then contrary winds had to be faced, so that the fleet did not appear off the island of Ré until the 22nd of that month, and it was not until the day following that the fort of the little island of Aix was submitted to bombardment. Captain Richard Howe, now transferred from the *Dunkirk* to the powerful *Magnanime*, a captured French ship, drove his vessel close to the shore and, in spite of heavy shelling from the battery on land, silenced it with his salvos, and soon afterward the fort struck its colours. But the capture of the island, covering both Rochefort and Rochelle, was destined to bring the expedition to an end. Neither Generals Sir John Mordaunt and H. S. Conway, who commanded the land forces, nor Admirals Hawke, Knowles, and Brodrick, in charge of the navy, felt that conditions were favourable, with the season already too far advanced for safe naval operations, to accomplish more than had been done. Therefore, in spite of a tentative agreement, based upon the recommendation of Colonel James Wolfe that Fort Fouras on the mainland and guarding the mouth of the Charente be attacked, and even after the men had actually been placed in boats for the attempt, this stroke was called off as far too hazardous for those involved, because of the heavy surf and the shallowness of the water, which would prevent any sort of artillery support from the navy.[8] Thus ended the expedition that had cost the British people a million pounds.[9]

The student surveying the events of the year 1757 must be cautioned against falling in line with many of the rather irresponsible contemporary denunciations levelled against both Pitt and the commanding officers for setting on foot such an enterprise as that against Rochefort and for concluding it without any notable success.[10] War

---

[7] *Correspondence of Chatham* (ed. Taylor and Pringle), I, 242.

[8] Wolfe was very critical indeed of the hesitation displayed by both the naval and the military leaders on this expedition and even expressed shame at being on the expedition and declared "there never was people collected together so unfit for the business they were sent upon — dilatory, irresolute, and . . . very unsoldier-like or unsailor-like" (Wolfe to his mother, October 17, 1757, and Wolfe to Major Rickson, November 5, 1757, Beckles Willson: *The Life and Letters of James Wolfe*, pp. 335, 339).

[9] The reader should consult Corbett's excellent account of the expedition in his *England in the Seven Years' War*, I, 206–22.

[10] There was a conviction, for example, held by many in England that the reason the leaders gave up the attempt to reach their objective was that there existed some secret

holds many risks, uncertainties — and imponderables. It demands
of leaders great resourcefulness and a willingness to test new conceptions that may hold promise of results without committing the
cause they are supporting to unnecessarily great hazards. The enterprise that failed may be compared to a large modern commando
raid. Had it succeeded without too great loss of life and naval
strength, it would have more than justified this expenditure and
also that of the national wealth. The probabilities of success were
based upon the observations of a competent military engineer, one
Captain Clerke (Clerk, Clark), who visited Rochefort in 1754.[11]
There proved to be, however, certain factors that doomed the enterprise to failure. One of these was the timidity and hesitation of both
the elderly Mordaunt and Hawke. Had Wolfe and Howe been in
control, one may affirm that had there been failure it would at least
have shed some glory on the English army and navy — and there
might have been success. The enterprise, nevertheless, served one
useful purpose: it thoroughly alarmed the French people and
brought home to the French ministry the fact that the western ports
must not be stripped of defences in favour of prosecuting the war
in Germany, and it led to the movement of very considerable forces
from central France in the direction of the coast.[12] The extent to
which this and subsequent raids diverted attention from the east
to the west and held battalions in western France that might otherwise have been used in Germany served an important strategic pur-

relationship between their faltering and the capitulation of Kloster-Seven, and, in fact,
this constituted a gesture to the French in the direction of a general pacification. This
was so expressed by Thomas Potter in writing to Pitt on October 11 and also by Alder-
man Beckford in addressing the Minister on October 22 (*Correspondence of Chatham*,
I, 277–81). The Earl of Chesterfield, writing to his son on October 10, declared: "Suspicions, you may be sure, are various and endless; but the most prevailing one is, that
the tail of the Hanover neutrality, like that of a comet, extends itself to Rochefort"
(*Letters of Philip Dormer Stanhope, 4th Earl of Chesterfield*, ed. Donamy Dobrée, V,
2248). The truth is that the water about Fouras was so shallow that in approaching it
some of Hawke's ships got aground; yet the fort was beyond the reach of ship fire, and
the surf was such that the navy could not promise that any of the soldiers who might
be landed could be taken off again (Beckles Willson, *op. cit.*, pp. 332 et seq.).

[11] Captain Clerke's letter to Sir John Ligonier under date of July 13, 1757 is given
by Entick (*op. cit.*, II, 286–9). Lord Fitzmaurice, who later became the Earl of Shelburne and who participated in the expedition, referred in later years to "the goodness
of General Clerke's intelligence" in his "Autobiography" (see Lord Fitzmaurice's *Life
of William, Earl of Shelburne*, I, 72).

[12] For a list of the contingents of French troops shifted to the west of France from
September 29 to October 4, 1757, see Corbett, *op. cit.*, I, 228.

pose. For the same number of men sent to the aid of Frederick as was assigned to the raid on Rochefort — assuming that at this juncture Pitt and the nation had been disposed to participate actively in the war in Germany — would have counted for little in view of the fact that Prussia had arrayed against it forces that totalled almost one half a million soldiers.

Thus as October 1757 drew to a close, there seemed to be little doubt that the two wars in which France was involved were being won by this nation and its numerous allies. In North America strategic Fort William Henry had fallen; Loudoun had been thoroughly checkmated and compelled to give up his enterprise against Louisbourg; and great stretches of the regions previously settled by the colonial British along their western frontiers had been deserted. In Europe, Minorca was still in enemy hands; the western ports of France — the scene of feverish activity in bringing support to French overseas possessions — were all still open; the Electorate of Hanover, the Margravate of Hesse, the Duchy of Brunswick, all had given up the struggle and were now occupied by French troops; the western portion of the Electorate of Brandenburg was likewise overrun; one hundred thousand Russians were in East Prussia; the Swedes had invaded Pomerania; the Austrians were pushing the Prussians out of Silesia; Frederick had suffered a great loss of prestige in the disastrous defeat he had experienced at Kolin in Bohemia at the hands of Marshal Daun and in his retreat from the walls of Prague; finally, the army of the Empire, strengthened by the forces of the Prince of Soubise and numbering over forty thousand men, was advancing into Saxony from the west in command of the Duke of Saxe-Hilburghausen, to enforce, as general *Feldzeugmeister* of the Empire, the decrees of the Diet against Frederick.

Then early in November, as winter was about to close in on all of northern Europe, the King of Prussia, who had previously scattered his forces so as to defend as many places as possible, suddenly, by means of forced marches, concentrated at Leipzig all available troops with the determination to come to grips with the combined Imperial-French army. On November 5 a battle took place near Rossbach and, in spite of a numerical superiority of two to one enjoyed by the enemy, Frederick, by the skilful use of his cavalry supported by his infantry, struck with such terrifying force the allied wing seeking to envelop his left flank that this led ultimately to the utter collapse of the opposing forces. Late in the afternoon they fled from the field of battle in great disorder, and out of Saxony. But there was no rest for the Prussians, in view of the desperate situation in Silesia. With little delay the King started his already wearied army into motion and led it one hundred and seventy miles to the east in twelve days. Arriving in northwestern Silesia, he joined the defeated forces of Prince Bevern. Thus reinforced, he now moved against Breslau, which had capitulated to the Austrians, and in doing so came face to face again with the Austrian Count Daun. The latter was in possession of greatly superior forces as at Kolin and was now so confident of the outcome of a battle with the Prussians that he rashly left his strongly fortified camp and appeared at Leuthen, to the west of Breslau, on December 5. Once again Frederick showed his superb military genius by crushing the left flank of his foe, which, as at Rossbach, just a month before to the day, had attempted to encircle his flank; once again his cavalry carried the honours of the day as Daun after the most desperate resistance fled from the field of battle, leaving one third of his army behind as dead, wounded, or prisoners.

The Battle of Leuthen not only brought to an end the year's campaign but with that of Rossbach changed profoundly the general military situation in Germany. The way was open for the capture of Breslau and other Silesian towns, with the Austrians retreating to Königgrätz in Bohemia. The great Russian army, after repulsing Lehwaldt in East Prussia, but unable to live off the country, now retreated from the Kingdom. Their retreat was followed by that of the Swedes from Prussian Pomerania; the French army under the Duc de Richelieu, operating in western Brandenburg, having become increasingly demoralized, likewise evacuated its conquests and retired westward; and, finally, the Imperials withdrew into southwest Germany in order to recover from the disaster that overtook them at Rossbach. Such was the general military situation at the end of 1757 — so changed from that of three months earlier. Such are the fortunes of war!

It should be made clear that when Frederick of Prussia was apprised of the Convention of Kloster-Seven, he wrote a personal letter to George II in which he declared:

> "You are the cause of all the misfortunes that are ready to fall upon me. I never would have broken my alliance with France, but for

your fair promises. I repent not of my treaty with your Majesty; but do not shamefully abandon me to the mercy of my enemies, after having brought upon me all the powers of Europe." [13]

To this blistering communication, which told only half the story, the British monarch replied on September 20 assuring the royal sender that it was certainly not for lack of interest in Prussia's unhappy situation that the capitulation had taken place and that he himself as Elector was overwhelmed with chagrin because of his inability to bring assistance to His Prussian Majesty; but as King of England he could assure him that that country might be depended upon to do everything humanly possible to sustain him.[14] George, in reality, seemed to think for a time that all hostilities, both in America and in Europe, might be terminated by extending what appeared to be the rather liberal terms of the Convention of Kloster-Seven so as to bring about a general armistice. But he was soon undeceived. The French considered themselves in too favourable a position in general to hear of a precipitate peace.

As for the Hanoverians, they, like their Elector, were not slow in being disillusioned respecting the neutrality convention, with the French now in control of all strategic places within the Electorate and its dependencies except Stade, and daily increasing their demands. Indeed, they came to realize that the "neutrality" that they hoped would give them peace and security gave them neither and was, in fact, intolerable. They therefore called upon Great Britain, which they held to be "the cause of their misfortune," to rescue them from their unhappy state.[15] George, in turn, as a German Imperial Elector, likewise appealed to the Diet for aid and protection from the "unprovoked attack" by the French on his Electorate.[16] He also determined that, since the enemy had not honoured the terms of the Convention, he as Elector would declare it broken and would at the same time summon once again into the field the Army of Observation — no longer under his son, but now under the command

---

[13] This is not given in the *Politische Correspondenz Friedrich's des Grossen*, but is printed in Entick, *op. cit.*, II, 416.

[14] *Politische Correspondenz Friedrich's des Grossen*, X, 424; see also the circular letter of September 16 that Holderness sent to the representatives of the foreign powers residing in London respecting the Convention (Entick, *op. cit.*, II, 416–17).

[15] *Ibid.*, II, 431.

[16] This document, as well as the preceding one, is to be found in Entick (*ibid.*, II, 417–26).

of Prince Ferdinand of Brunswick. This was done.[17] Although the new commander showed commendable energy and dislodged the French from some places, he was unable to prevent Richelieu from settling down in winter quarters within the Electorate and from carrying out severe measures against the inhabitants. When the new year dawned, the enemy was still in control there.

The policy that the British ministry would pursue in the future relative to events on the Continent was ultimately determined as the result of the education of Pitt in the broad field of strategy, such as was called for in the waging of a world war. In this process no man in a position of similar responsibility was ever called upon more frequently to eat his own passionate words or to reverse his own determined position than was this Minister as the result of the unfolding of events in Europe. With the overrunning of the Electorate of Hanover by the French, he no longer referred to it as "contemptible," no longer was disposed, as earlier, to leave it to its fate with the idea of making some indemnification to the King for its losses.

As the bad news continued to arrive, Hardwicke and Newcastle thought that British regiments should be sent to strengthen Cumberland's Army of Observation, but Pitt was opposed.[18] Newcastle also wanted to grant immediate large subsidies to the King as Elector, but Pitt desired to postpone consideration of this until the new year; [19] he was won over to the Duke's point of view as to subsidies, however, early in August as the situation in Hanover continued to deteriorate [20] and agreed to a grant of £100,000 to the Electorate and a smaller grant to Hesse-Cassel to keep them fighting; he also accepted the view that the King of Prussia must have a very large grant. But nothing was done to aid Frederick at the time. After the

---

[17] For George's declaration as Elector of Hanover in denouncing the Convention see *ibid.*, II, 435–9. The King's position at this period was very inconsistent. After Cumberland's reverse at Hastenbeck in July, he determined to seek peace for Hanover and took steps to secure the support of Austria; when the Duke in September finally concluded the Convention of Kloster-Seven — acting on the full powers granted to him by his father and in line with what he felt were the King's desires — George insisted that his son had signed contrary to his orders and placed the latter in disgrace. For a comprehensive discussion of this see C. W. Eldon's *England's Subsidy Policy toward the Continent during the Seven Years' War*, pp. 96–101. The King's declaration that the Convention of Kloster-Seven no longer was operative is given by Entick (*op. cit.*, II, 435–9).

[18] Newcastle to Hardwicke, July 26, 1757, B.M., Add. Mss., 32872, folio 340.

[19] Hardwicke to Newcastle, August 4, 1757, *ibid.*, folios 441–2.

[20] Newcastle to Hardwicke, August 6, 1757, *ibid.*, folios 465–7.

news of the Kloster-Seven capitulation reached England the Minister demanded that George repudiate it. This was done, as has been noted. With the assembling of Parliament on December 1, in his speech from the throne the King appealed to that body not only to support him in his efforts to preserve his hereditary possessions but to grant to Prussia adequate financial assistance.[21] This was agreed to without serious debate. In fact, the news of the victory at Rossbach had made Frederick an almost universal hero in England and people at large called loudly on the government to aid him in his struggle against a veritable cloud of enemies; they also now saw the need of rescuing Hanover from the grasp of the French.

The King of Prussia not only demanded British subsidies but also a British fleet in the Baltic and British soldiers to support Prince Ferdinand. Although Newcastle was prepared in January of the new year to send some twelve thousand troops, Pitt was opposed, as he had consistently been, in principle, to sending British soldiers to fight on the Continent. He had, in fact, declared to the Commons on December 14 that he "would not send a drop of our blood to the Elbe, to be lost in that ocean of gore." [22] While George as well as Newcastle sought to persuade him to change his mind, he refused to do so at the time. Nevertheless, by the end of March he had receded sufficiently from his position to agree to send a small force to the seaport of Emden in East Friesland. The chief direct aid to the King of Prussia throughout the war, however, was destined to be in the form of subsidies, and on April 11 a treaty was signed making provision for them. By this treaty both Frederick and George — the latter in his capacity as Imperial Elector as well as King — covenanted:

> "That neither of the contracting powers shall conclude any peace, make any truce, or enter into any treaty of neutrality, of what kind soever, without the participation of the other." [23]

---

[21] The Parliamentary History of England (T. C. Hansard), XV, 830.

[22] Horace Walpole, op. cit., III, 88.

[23] Entick, op. cit., III, 74-5. The treaty, consummated in London, was signed by Henley, Granville, Newcastle, Holderness, Hardwicke, and Pitt for King George, and by Knyphausen, former Prussian Ambassador to France, and Michell, secretary to the Prussian London legation, for the King of Prussia. The debate over the Prussian treaty in the House of Commons is given in Parliamentary History (XV, 783–803). Unfortunately, it was placed in the year 1757 by Hansard in connection with the discussions relative to the Westminster Convention rather than in its appropriate place in the year 1758.

Thereupon it was agreed that His Britannic Majesty should pay to the agent of the King of Prussia the sum of four million German crowns, or £670,000, during the period of a year. This sum Frederick was to employ in keeping up his forces, "which shall act as may be most for the common cause." [24] In addition to the substantial direct aid granted to Prussia, the Cabinet Council by a separate "Declaration" agreed to assume the entire support of Ferdinand's army of fifty thousand troops, as well as five thousand additional soldiers that George as Elector promised to furnish. [25]

Between January 23 and April 20, 1758, in fact, a series of grants was made to the Electorate and to the Margravate of Hesse-Cassel amounting in all to £1,191,894. [26] This was in addition to huge appropriations for supporting the war that Britain was waging with France. Pitt, who, when in opposition, saw with violent alarm the prospect of national bankruptcy in the granting of rather trivial sums in 1756 to support Britain's allies on the Continent, now felt that the Kingdom could easily afford in 1758 to appropriate during the spring session of Parliament over ten million pounds. [27] Heavy duties on all malts and an extraordinary tax of four shillings on the pound upon all lands, personal estates, offices, and pensions were provided; the sinking fund was raided; a great loan of four and one half millions was floated, based upon the granting of annuities, and another half million was secured by a lottery, and eight hundred thousand by the issue of exchequer bills paying interest; a special tax on dwelling houses and a window tax were also levied. With these and other devices a total of over eleven million pounds was raised to support the government in its various commitments. [28] It is this tremendous national effort to protect the Empire, combined

---

[24] Frederick, in communicating with Prince Ferdinand, stated on April 12 — after the treaty had been agreed upon but before he had received news of its signing — that he had a new treaty with the King of England and then declared: "I had desired to add to it the sending of English troops to Germany but this is a note that I cannot sound, because Pitt is afflicted with fantasies in his head" (Politische Correspondenz Friedrich's des Grossen, XVI, 375). Writing again to the Prince two days later, the King expressed his agreeable surprise to learn that eight or nine hundred English troops had arrived at Emden to garrison and defend that port as well as other parts of East Friesland (ibid., XVI, 383).

[25] Frederick to Prince Ferdinand, April 18, 1758, ibid., XVI, 390. For the "Declaration" see Newcastle Papers, B.M., Add. Mss., 32879, under date April 8, 1758.

[26] Annual Register, 1758 (ed. R. and J. Dodsley, 1761), I, 127–30.

[27] The total grant up to and including June 10 was £10,486,457 (ibid., I, 138).

[28] Ibid., I, 132–7.

with an equal effort on the part of Britons under arms, that is described by American traditionalists as Great Britain's cynical, selfish, grasping policy in the direction of world conquest.

With this unprecedented support guaranteed for the armies of Frederick and Ferdinand for the campaign on the Continent in 1758, it was not long before the latter took the field. Reinforced by a body of Prussian horse, the Prince moved over the Oder and against the French in Hanover. The latter now were under command of the Comte de Clermont, who had displaced the Duc de Richelieu. Everywhere they gave way; only on the Weser at Hoya and at Minden was there any effective resistance, which, however, was overcome. In extreme need of all supplies, the enemy had lost their earlier morale and eagerness to fight and in the month of March began their retreat toward the Rhine in three widely separated columns, evacuating all of their late conquests. Reaching the broad river, they passed over and into the Austrian Netherlands and France — with the exception of a small force under Clermont, who was determined to retain the fortress of Wesel, but later was obliged to desert even that. Likewise to the north in East Friesland, when Commodore Holmes appeared before Emden with a small squadron, that place was evacuated and a regiment of British troops proceeded to garrison it. Thus ended ingloriously the French invasion of Germany.

Now came Prince Ferdinand's chance to move westward with his army. He had determined to carry the war into the enemy's country before its demoralized forces could be reorganized. On June 1 he therefore crossed the Rhine with a contingent and by the 7th his whole army was over that hurdle, with the French continuing to retire. Then at Crefeld they decided to make a stand, and the battle was joined on the 23rd. While their left wing was crushed and forced to flee, the rest of their army, nevertheless, was able to retire in good order and was soon greatly reinforced by fresh troops. As a result, it seemed wise for the Prince to retire, while he still had the opportunity, back across the Rhine, especially in view of the fact that the Prince of Soubise, whose forces had also been greatly augmented, was still posted in southern Germany and was showing signs of activity in the direction of Hesse-Cassel. This he did early in August, and later was joined by a British army of over seven thousand men composed of five superb regiments of horse — considered to be the best-equipped cavalry in Europe — and four of foot.[29] These troops for the most part had been hurriedly sent to Emden in July and placed under the command of the Duke of Marlborough and Sir George Sackville for the express purpose of reinforcing the Prince.

The realities of the Continental situation, in other words, compelled Pitt to put aside sentiment in favour of logic and to give way even on this most crucial issue. Here at last — and in spite of all the Great Commoner's declamation and protestation to the contrary — there took place the fusing in large measure of the overseas Great War for the Empire with the European Seven Years' War, which Newcastle had steadily contended was inevitable.[30] During the next four years, therefore, the people of Great Britain were called upon by their government to provide fully for the various large military enterprises on land and sea outside of Europe, as well as for an army there, and to underwrite the cost of keeping the forces of Hanover and Hesse-Cassel in the field and much of the cost involved in Prussia's military activities.[31] In fact, they did even more than this. To form a diversion in western Europe such as would relieve the pressure of the French upon Germany as well as strike at communications with the French Empire, the Cabinet Council, on Pitt's initiative, had determined again to raid the French coast,[32] where, as the result of last year's alarm at Rochefort, considerable forces were stationed at various points for the protection of the vital seaports.[33] Late in May two squadrons were in readiness to sail on this mission, and on June 1, the very day that Ferdinand had begun his movement to cross the Rhine, they moved out of Portsmouth. The ob-

---

[29] William Beckford to Pitt, July 10, 1758, Chatham Correspondence, I, 329; Entick, op. cit., III, 175.

[30] D'Abreu to Wall, March 3, 1757, Chatham Correspondence, I, 296–7.

[31] By the spring of 1758 Britain was supporting two hundred and eighty-four thousand men of land and sea forces — not counting the support given to the King of Prussia — and was maintaining over three hundred ships of war (Entick, op. cit., III, 96).

[32] This determination was in fact embodied in the "Declaration" that formed a part of the subsidy treaty with Prussia (Newcastle Papers, B.M., Add. Mss., 32879, under date of April 8, 1758). Indeed, Frederick had by February come to see the value of a really powerful diversion on the French coast (Memoirs of Sir A. Mitchell, I, 401). The objective, Saint-Malo, was strongly recommended to Pitt by Ligonier, Marlborough, and Sackville in a paper that detailed the advantages of a strong attack in this area. The secret instructions to Marlborough, signed May 20, 1758, quotes at length from this paper ("Expedition to the Coast of France, 1758," Shelburne Papers, 37:11, Clements Library).

[33] Corbett, op. cit., I, 254–5.

jective was the port of Saint-Malo, on the English Channel. According to the plan adopted, Anson with a very powerful fleet of twenty-two ships of the line, supported by eight frigates, was to take post to the westward of the actual operations so as to be in position to cover these from interference on the part of a French fleet that might move out of Brest.[34] The other squadron, placed under command of Richard Howe,[35] who, commanding the *Magnanime*, had won the only laurels in the expedition against Rochefort, consisted of smaller ships of the line, with frigates, sloops, bomb-ketches, fire-ships, as well as a hundred transports with troops and, finally, auxiliary vessels, making up a great armada of over one hundred and fifty sails.

This operation, one of the largest ever launched against the shores of France until the twentieth century, involved a total of at least thirty-four thousand men, including those who manned the ships.[36] It was hoped that the land forces at the moment under command of the Duke of Marlborough and Sir George Sackville, both with a reputation for daring and bravery, and with Ligonier joint authors of the plan, would be able to seize this seaport with the support of Howe's fleet and thereupon hold it with proper naval support. Located, as it is, on a granite island and at the time connected with the mainland only by a long and narrow causeway, it seemed to be a logical objective, especially since it was far enough to the north to influence the movement of troops that might otherwise be let loose against Ferdinand in his operations west of the Rhine. Everything went well at the beginning of the operation. The troops were landed on June 2 and 3 at Cancale, on a bay to the east of Saint-Malo, without serious opposition. After forming an entrenched camp they began their slow march westward;[37] and on the 7th the light horse raided the little port of Saint-Servan, adjacent to Saint-Malo, and with lighted torches set fire to and destroyed sixty-six ships, most of them merchantmen, resting in the harbour, and then at near-by Solidore accounted for "upward of a hundred" more, besides enormous quantities of naval stores, which also went up in flames.[38] But, unfortu-

---

[34] For Anson's instructions see Shelburne Papers, 37:12.

[35] For Howe's secret instructions, *ibid.*, 37:14.

[36] Corbett, *op. cit.*, I, 272.

[37] Writing to Pitt on June 11, Marlborough was forced to admit that the country, filled with thick hedges and ravines, was "entirely different from what I had heard it represented" (Shelburne Papers, 37:38).

[38] *Ibid.*

nately, there was no proper road to permit the movement of the siege artillery directly across the land to Saint-Malo, powerfully fortified, with walls too high for scaling. Again, rumors began to arrive of the gathering of large French forces, amounting to some ten thousand men, according to Marlborough.[39] In the face of this complex situation, both he and Sackville, no longer in a frame of mind for taking great risks,[40] agreed that it was desirable to let well enough alone and to re-embark the troops. Therefore on the 12th, just ten days after the first landing, this was done. After making threatening moves against Havre, at the mouth of the Seine, against Caen, Harfleur, and finally Cherbourg, with supplies growing short and the soldiers sickly, they then returned to Spithead early in July to restock and recruit.

Although the expedition fell short of Pitt's hopes, its psychological effects on the population of western France and on the government at Versailles were undoubtedly profound. Convinced that this was the case, the ministers determined to send out Anson and Howe once more without delay. As for Marlborough and Sackville, these two men had had their fill of such military operations and, immediately upon their return to England, brought pressure to bear upon the ministry to be sent to Germany to command there the British forces allotted to that theatre of war.[41] As has already been noted, this was done. Pitt, as a result of this shift, was now forced to employ for the next diversionary attack on western France Lieutenant General Thomas Bligh, who at first had been designated to the command in Germany and who had just arrived from Ireland. An elderly man, quite unsuited for the task, his choice, however, was almost inevitable, not only because of his rank but in view of the fact that he had been summoned to England to take over a command that was given to another and it was felt that the morale of the army would be adversely affected were he again brushed aside. He was instructed [42] to land his troops at or near Cherbourg, on the coast of Normandy, and, if possible, to destroy this port together with the ships riding in the basin as well as all magazines and arsenals. The forces at his

---

[39] *Ibid.*

[40] Shelburne, in his "Autobiography," writes that on this expedition "Lord George Sackville's cowardice was notorious to the whole army" (Fitzmaurice, *op. cit.*, I, 75).

[41] Sackville, according to Dodington (*Diary*, p. 410), declared "he could no longer go Buccaneering."

[42] For Bligh's instructions see Entick, *op. cit.*, III, 177–80; for his commission see Shelburne Papers, 37:89.

command were reduced by three regiments from those commanded
by Marlborough. This was not illogical since he was not to attempt
to hold — only to destroy and thereupon to depart.

Under Vauban, in the days of Louis XIV, Cherbourg had been
fortified in the most modern fashion and provided with a wall carried to a great height, but these defences had been demolished soon
afterward and the protection of the town now rested in five forts
located on the bay. Against it the expeditionary force sailed from
the Isle of Wight on August 1; not until the 6th, however, were the
ships able to approach it, because of adverse winds. Thereupon a
landing was made some two leagues to the west of the port, in spite
of the presence of some three thousand of the enemy horse and foot.
The following day, with the horses and artillery safely ashore, the
march on Cherbourg began, and as the troops approached the town,
the weak garrison fled, leaving it quite undefended.[43] Entering it,
Bligh soon made himself master of the surrounding forts and then
proceeded methodically with the work of destruction. All batteries,
forts, magazines, and stores were wrecked; twenty-seven ships went
up in flames; and the engineers even proceeded to blast the solid
masonry of the basin and jetties.[44] The task consumed a week. While
this was going on Bligh's soldiers became thoroughly demoralized,
apparently as the result of the discovery of large wine magazines,[45]
and there followed a breakdown of discipline, with consequent excesses at the expense of the inhabitants — something that Marlborough had sternly guarded against.

Meanwhile, the military governor of Normandy, Maréchal de
Luxembourg, stationed to the south and west at Granville, hurried
toward Cherbourg when the news came of the attack and began to
organize the forces that he had gathered at his camp twenty miles
away for a counterattack. But before he was ready to move up for
action, the entire British force re-embarked on August 16, leaving
behind them a scene of misery and desolation. In the words of one
of the inhabitants: "The memory of this descent will cause a shudder
to the end of time to all those to whom history shall tell what we saw
and suffered." [46]

Returning to England, the force again left on the 18th of the

---

[43] Bligh to Pitt, August 7 and 8, 1758, *ibid.*, 37:116, 118.
[44] Bligh to Pitt, August 15, 1758, *ibid.*, 37:123.
[45] Entick, *op. cit.*, III, 185.
[46] Quoted by Corbett, *op. cit.*, I, 296.

month and headed once more for Saint-Malo, leaving behind a nation rejoicing in this recent success.[47] But, on account of contrary
winds that forced the fleet back, it was not until September 3 that
Howe appeared at Saint-Lunaire Bay just to the west of his immediate objective. Seven thousand troops were landed here, with the
idea apparently of carrying them on flat boats protected by bomb-
ketches to the port of Saint-Servan, so close to the fortifications of
Saint-Malo that it could be bombarded from that point.[48] But this
was found to be impracticable. Meanwhile the weather became unfavourable and the fleet was exposed to such great danger that the
commodore was compelled to shift both the warships and the transports three leagues to the westward to the Bay of Saint-Cas. Bligh's
troops now moved somewhat inland to secure supplies without meeting with much interference.[49] But soon news began to come in of
the gathering of a very considerable French force to oppose them.
As a result, with little artillery and in a position of hourly growing
danger, it was decided to retreat to the ships.

Overconfident as he apparently was, however, the old general,
instead of making a forced march to get in contact with the fleet,
rested his troops on the night of the 10th. This gave an opportunity
for the Duc d'Aiguillon, military governor of Brittany, to hurry up
from Brest with nine battalions of foot and some squadrons of horse,
together with militia picked up on the march. These, while avoiding
an action, hung on the British flank until Bligh, finally reaching
Saint-Cas on the 11th, attempted to re-embark his force. Thirsting
for revenge for the insults they had suffered, the French at last came
to the attack. From the steep hill surrounding the little bay they
started to pour a murderous artillery fire upon the British troops
gathered on the beach. While some of the lighter ships moved in
close and played their guns on the enemy with considerable effect,
it was only by the heroic action of the crews of the fleet that most
of Bligh's men were finally placed on board flat-bottomed boats and
carried to the ships. To encourage the sailors exposed to heavy fire,
Howe set an example of bravery, standing upright in one of the
rescuing craft that moved to the beach. In spite of all, at least six

---

[47] On September 16 a grand procession, with drums beating and fifes playing, proceeded to the Tower of London, carrying on gun-carriages the highly ornamented brass
cannon and mortars captured at Cherbourg (Entick, op. cit., III, 190–200).

[48] Ibid., III, 193–5; Howe to Pitt, September 7, 1758, Shelburne Papers, 37:141.

[49] Bligh did not plan to embark his troops immediately, "but to stay in the country
according to circumstances" (Bligh to Pitt, September 8, 1758, ibid., 37:142).

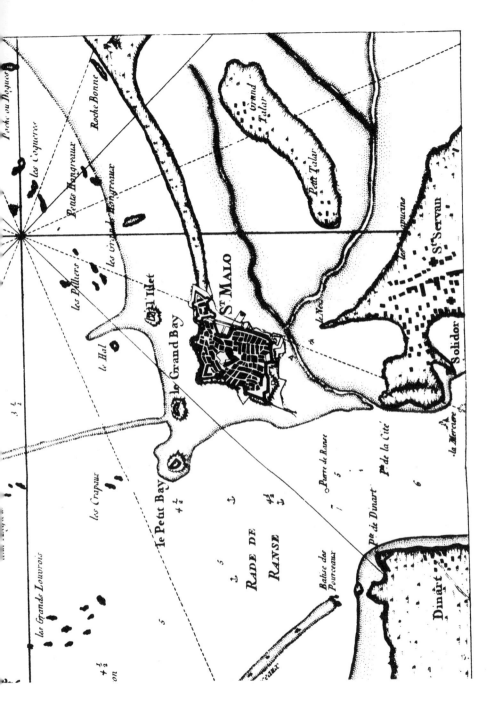

St. Malo and its approaches.
(From *Le Petit Atlas Maritime Recueil de Cartes et Plans des Quartre Parties du Monde*, 1764, Clements Library.)

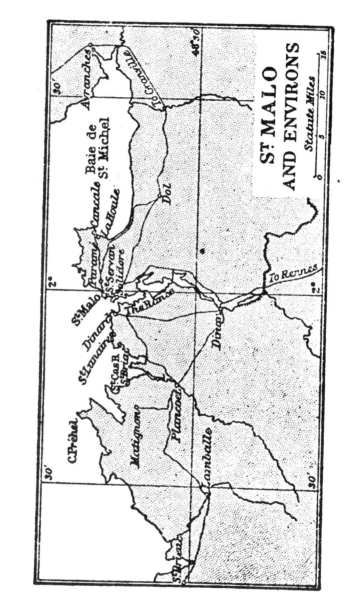

St. Malo and St. Cas Bay, 1758.

(From J. S. Corbett's *England in the Seven Years' War*, with the permission of Longmans, Green & Co.)

hundred of the rear guard, which fought with supreme courage, were taken prisoner, and the dead on the beach and in the water numbered hundreds, if not thousands as the French claimed.[50]

Unfortunately, the news of the unhappy ending of the raid, "despirited the people of England," [51] who could not clearly appreciate the strategical value of keeping the western coasts of France in a perpetual state of alarm and by this means immobilizing large numbers of the regular troops of the enemy that might otherwise feel free to move into the eastern theatre of war.[52] Pitt was therefore impelled to bow before the storm of disapproval of such raids; he was also influenced in his decision by the fact that nowhere could he find, at least in the Old World, a military man with the proper qualifications who could wisely be put in command. Clive in India and Wolfe still in America had these in abundance, but they had no counterparts in the armed forces at home or in Germany. In fact, by the time the expedition had returned to the home ports Pitt was thinking in terms of concentrating on another against Martinique, as well as the even more vigorous prosecution of the campaign in North America and therefore needed all the resources at his command for these objectives.[53] Before turning to developments in the

---

[50] See the account of the affair as published at Paris on September 22 in Entick (op. cit., III, 215–19). These give the total British losses as some four thousand men. The Annual Register, 1758 (p. 69), gives the figures as four hundred prisoners and six hundred killed and wounded. Bligh, in his dispatch written on board the Essex on September 13, declared: "We have lost between six and seven Hundred Men, killed, drowned, and taken Prisoners" (London Gazette, September 18, 1758). The last figure is by all other evidence much too small. A strict censorship over the affair was established by the government, and the military dispatches were lost, as Corbett (op. cit., I, 301) makes clear, so that it is difficult to arrive at exactness. Howe in his dispatch to Pitt written on board the Essex on September 12 presents the activities of the navy (Shelburne Papers, 37:145). For a long and vivid account of the fight by the rear guard, see that by William Tryon, written September 12, 1758 (Clinton Papers, Volume I, Clements Library).

[51] Walpole (op. cit., III, 136) reflected the popular temper in referring to the expedition in the following terms: "The folly of this exploit, the inhumanity of exposing gallant men to carnage for no end imaginable but to satisfy the obstinate ostentation of a Minister . . ." and again: "Such was the conclusion of Mr. Pitt's invasions of France, the idleness or fruitlessness of which took off from the judgment of his other attempts and successes. . . ." Shelburne, in his "Autobiography," takes issue with this point of view. All that was needed for the success of the expedition, he affirmed, was a good commander (Fitzmaurice, op. cit., I, 76–8).

[52] Corbett (op. cit., I, 303) calculated that as many as seventy or even eighty battalions of French regulars were held in western France at this period for the protection of the coasts.

[53] Chatham Correspondence, I, 355.

New World, however, it is important to consider briefly the progress of events in Germany, and particularly the activities of Frederick of Prussia, who in 1758 was compelled to face a coalition of enemies as powerful as that which confronted him in Germany the preceding year. For it was clear that the outcome in Germany of the two wars now so largely fused into one would profoundly influence the future of the British Empire.

Early in April the King of Prussia — assured, as the result of the retrograde movement of the French army, now under attack by Prince Ferdinand, that he need not worry about developments to the west and also assured of the financial support of Great Britain — began his military activities for the year. Quickly moving upon the one fortress in Silesia still in the hands of the Austrians, Schweidnitz, he invested it and within two weeks secured its surrender. Thus the master once again of all Silesia — an earlier conquest from the Empress Queen — as well as of Saxony — his most recent conquest, from the Elector and King of Poland — he felt that he was at last in position again to carry the war into the enemy's country and to move upon the great fortress of Olmütz. This was therefore besieged. But again he had to deal with Daun, who, instead of giving battle, proceeded to cut off his convoys bringing up provisions and destroy all the forage in the area, upon which his cavalry was dependent. So serious, in fact, became his position by the beginning of July that he was forced to raise the siege. Instead of retreating, however, he advanced rapidly into Bohemia, where he laid his hands, as anticipated, upon various enemy supply depots, took possession of Königgrätz, laid it under contribution, and then moved swiftly back into Silesia.

It was indeed high time that he returned to his possessions, for two powerful Russian armies were entering the New Mark of Brandenburg and must be dealt with. But it was not until the latter part of August that he was able to appear with his army on the lower Oder northeast of Cüstrin, which the Russians were besieging. Then on the 25th he confronted the enemy — drawn up in the form of an enormous square and buttressed by tiers of batteries — near Zorndorf, where one of the most bloody battles of the Seven Years' War took place. Again it was the Prussian cavalry that saved Frederick from defeat after his infantry had retreated before the furious Russian assaults. From nine in the morning until seven in the evening the carnage continued. But the following day the enemy slowly began their retreat toward the Polish frontier, leaving behind in the hands of the Prussians their great artillery train, their military chest, and many prisoners.

Although Frederick was freed of this menace from the east, other members of the great coalition were active. Again the Imperials were in Saxony, entrenched at Pirna; again Daun moved his Austrians also into Saxony as well as into Silesia, and once again the King of Prussia was called upon to save the situation to the south, which was far too serious to be faced by the forces under command of his brother, Prince Henry, who was covering Dresden. After marching southward and after resting and re-forming his troops, and with but thirty-seven thousand men available for the service in hand, he met Daun at Hochkirch, near Bautzin, on October 13 and again through overconfidence almost suffered an irretrievable defeat at the hands of that skilful general. In fact, had not his cavalry kept open a way for his all but surrounded infantry and artillery to escape, he must have surrendered. As it was, he left behind over seven thousand of his men killed, wounded, or prisoners, and among the dead were two of his best generals, the Scot Keith and Prince Francis of Brunswick. But there was no time for mourning the bitter loss. Silesia had to be relieved, and the King marched into that duchy — leaving behind his victorious but slow-moving opponent — freed it from the grasp of the Austrians, and then turned back swiftly into Saxony to save Dresden from Daun and Leipzig from the Imperials. Again both Austrians and Imperials retreated southward toward Bohemia rather than fight out the issue, and as the winter of 1758 closed in, Frederick, as the result of another year of almost unparalleled exertions, could again breathe freely with respect to the safety of his old and new possessions — both those that were hereditary and those that he had conquered.[54]

But we must now consider the progress of events in the New World and also seek to determine, among other things, to what extent the struggle in Europe was affecting that in North America.

---

[54] For detailed accounts of the developments in Europe, Entick, as a contemporary authority, is still valuable; among later historians Waddington's monumental work should be consulted, as well as Schaefer's *Geschichte des Siebenjährigen Krieges* and Curt Jany's *Geschichte der Königlich-Preussischen Armee*, Vol. II, the last a work by a military expert.

CHAPTER VI

A Winter's Interlude in North America

IN THE PRECEDING CHAPTER emphasis was placed on the degree to which the government of His Most Christian Majesty was occupied in the course of the second and third years of the Seven Years' War in Europe in bringing support to its allies and in fending off the savage British raids against the coasts of France. It was also occupied with the problem of carrying military and other kinds of relief to the King's overseas possessions and, together with this, in keeping open the long lines of communication with them, which as time passed became increasingly difficult in view of a British sea supremacy that, instead of receding, was constantly, although slowly, increasing. But this fact of tremendous significance was not, and perhaps could not be, apparent to North American colonials at the close of 1757 — a year that had brought to them such bitter disappointment and discouragement.

Potentially the British colonies undoubtedly had the strength, with little or no direct aid from the mother country, to drive the French out of the advanced positions they had taken at the expense of the frontier settlers and traders. But their strength could not be mobilized, for reasons that have already been made clear. Further, after three years of fighting they lacked the necessary confidence in their own ability and all but universally resigned themselves to the idea that this task, so all-important to their own welfare, must be the responsibility of regular soldiers. Indeed, during the winter of 1757–8 most of their long northern and western frontiers, as will be noted, were guarded by British troops, over ten thousand of whom were now concentrated on the continent in preparation for the campaign of 1758.[1] It is, in fact, probably accurate to state that there were several times as many British soldiers protecting the continental colonies during the winter of 1757–8 as there were provincials actually under arms during the same period.

The provinces of Georgia and South Carolina, it may be pointed out, were able to relax in security by reason of the presence of Montgomery's regiment of Highlanders, five battalions of the 60th under Colonel Bouquet, and the three Independent Companies attached to this area — all maintained out of the British exchequer.[2] Although the Assembly of South Carolina had agreed in the spring of 1757 to provide a regiment of troops for its own protection, Bouquet, the officer in command in this area, was obliged to state in November that the province had not as yet raised a hundred men,[3] and in February of the next year he declared:

> "The Carolina regiment will never be raised, as they have not got yet upwards of 200 men, most of them of the worste Kind: their Cloathing has been ordered from England, and they are so naked that they cannot be employed on any duty, and Scarce be exercised unless the Sun shines very bright." [4]

Not only was the Assembly negligent in this respect, not only did the substantial planter class continue to refuse to perform military service even to ensure its own protection, when it could be provided by the King, but their treatment of the soldiers who had come to perform that essential service was such as to arouse deep indignation. While the provincial government was prevailed upon in October to build barracks for one thousand of the men, most of whom were living in a most exposed condition, it refused until late in the year, and only as the result of serious protests, to furnish them with those necessaries which always were expected and customarily provided, such as barrack utensils, bedding, and firewood.[5]

---

[1] Loudoun in his report to Holderness and Pitt, under date of October 17, 1757, gives the figure as 12,700, but these included some regulars captured by the French both at Fort William Henry and on the high seas (Loudoun Papers, No. 4239, Huntington Library).

[2] Loudoun to Pitt, October 17, 1757, ibid., No. 4239.

[3] Bouquet to Governor Ellis, November 12, 1757, Bouquet Papers (Pa. Hist. Com., 1941), Series 21632, p. 121.

[4] Bouquet to Colonel Forbes, February 1, 1758, ibid., Series 21632, p. 140.

[5] See the Representation of the Field Officers to Colonel Bouquet, December 2, 1757, ibid., Series 21643, pp. 16–18.

Lord Loudoun, then in New York, was impelled, in face of this shabby treatment of his men by the South Carolinians, to make clear to Governor Lyttelton that the troops were sent

> "to the rich, flourishing Province of South Carolina . . . on their own Sollicitation, for their own Defence, when they, as well as all the World, thought themselves in Danger, and . . . those troops are Maintained entirely at the Expence of the Mother Country." [6]

What is more, the provincial treasurer, acting under orders, made the unprecedented demand that provisions brought in to supply these troops, who were busy during the winter weather building fortifications for the province, should be subject to the high duties levied on such imports. This led Bouquet to frame a strong remonstrance to the Assembly early in the new year. [7]

North Carolina, largely protected as this province was by the troops and defences maintained within the neighbouring provinces, did not seem to be in need of keeping under arms any large number of men. Therefore but three companies of fifty men each of those previously raised were held in order to do garrison duty in the two forts on the coast and two on the frontiers.

In Virginia the situation remained critical as winter came on, as it had been since the start of the Indian raids against the province in June, with scalping parties still surprising unguarded groups of settlers. [8] Yet Washington, who had gone through four years of campaigning in devoted service to the cause, could not be blamed. He had, in fact, been tireless in his activities as colonel of the Virginia regiment. But with a long frontier to defend he was given to command but four hundred and twenty-four men fit for duty, [9] out of a militia that totalled twenty-five thousand, as indicated in an earlier chapter of this volume — a shameful thing for the Old Dominion! These precious few troops, moreover, had to be widely distributed to provide the minimum protection. [10] The only favourable aspects of

---

[6] Loudoun to Lyttelton, December 6, 1758, Loudoun Papers, No. 4954.

[7] Bouquet's Petition to the Assembly, January 19, 1758, Bouquet Papers (Pa. Hist. Com., 1941), Series 21632, pp. 137–8. It may be pointed out that the remonstrance, at the request of the Assembly, was changed to a petition.

[8] Dinwiddie to Loudoun, December 1, 1757, Loudoun Papers, No. 4930.

[9] Washington's "Return" of the troops on the frontier, December 1, 1757, ibid., No. 6765.

[10] The troops were distributed among the following forts and palisaded places: Fort Edwards, Fort Baldwin, Fort Dickinson, Fort Young, Fort Dinwiddie, Fort Cloyd, Fort Voss (now named Fort Lyttelton), Town Fort, Fort Harness, Fort Holland, Power's

the situation were that after the early part of December the enemy was less active along the western frontier and that Washington's superior, Colonel John Stanwix, with most of a battalion of the 60th regiment of regulars posted at Carlisle in Pennsylvania and with other troops at York, Lancaster, and Reading and at Annapolis in Maryland, was well prepared to send men to his assistance in case of serious need.

As for Maryland, the Assembly remained adamant, in that it would not support in any way the troops of the province that had been sent to garrison Fort Cumberland, although the place was within the colonial boundaries. It also denied the right of Loudoun, as the commander-in-chief in North America, to determine the disposition of the troops raised by the province, in spite of the fact that the other colonies had generally agreed to this, and the New England colonies, New Jersey, and Virginia had readily sent, and North Carolina was prepared to send, troops under orders outside of the limits of these colonies for the general defence.[11] In view of this remarkable display of irresponsibility on the part of the Assembly and the weakness of the defensive position of both Maryland and Virginia, Loudoun resolved at the close of the season's campaign to place within the colony of Maryland five companies of his regulars. He also gave orders to Colonel Stanwix to supply Captain Dagworthy's company, if necessary, with provisions to maintain it at Fort Cumberland and, should these troops withdraw from it as the result of the pressure of the Assembly, to garrison it either with a contingent of the Virginia regiment or, if this was impossible, to place there three hundred regulars. In doing so he stressed its strategic value, serving as it did as "a barrier against the enemy inroads and also an entry into the country the French have usurped from the King." [12] Dagworthy happily held on to his position in spite of the attitude of the Assembly, and early in December was able to thwart an attempt by a body of French and Indians to seize the fort [13] — a stronghold that in spite of its importance had been, ac-

Mill, Fort Patterson, Fort Mendenhall, Fort Evans, Fort Capon, Fort Pearsall, Fort Pleasant, and Fort Kirkendall (ibid.).

[11] Governor Sharpe to Loudoun, October 21, 1757, ibid., No. 4670; also the same to the same, December 22, 1757, Maryland Archives, IX, 113–15; and the address of the upper house to Sharpe of December 16, 1757 protesting the attitude of the lower house (Loudoun Papers, No. 5019).

[12] Loudoun to Stanwix, November 3, 1757, Loudoun Papers, No. 4743.

[13] Dagworthy to Stanwix, December 11, 1758, ibid., No. 4997.

cording to Stanwix, "disclaimed" not only by Virginia and Pennsylvania but, as has been noted, by Maryland as well.[14]

It should be added that when the regulars arrived at Annapolis, the Assembly refused to make arrangements for quartering them and adjourned in that month, leaving them without any provisions made for their shelter, such as other colonies had done when contingents of the King's troops went into winter quarters within their borders.[15] In other words, the planters of Maryland, as well as those of South Carolina and Virginia, were too busy with their personal affairs in the boom war years to care to be discommoded in any manner by the urgencies of the war that, in their own most vital interests, had to be fought to a conclusion. That they all wanted a favourable outcome of it cannot be questioned; but they wanted someone else to assume the chief risks, while they watched their slaves and indentured whites plant and harvest their fertile fields in tranquillity, well removed from the scenes of terror along their own frontiers. For example, on December 15 the lower house of the Maryland Assembly, in addressing Governor Sharpe, referred to the expectation that it had had the previous spring "That his Majesty's Forces would act offensively to the Westward" and in that hope had increased the number of its troops to five hundred so that those who might not be needed for the immediate defence of the frontier inhabitants could join in such an expedition.[16]

Pennsylvania, in spite of its traditional pacifism, was by the winter of 1757 making a far greater contribution in manpower to the protection of its frontiers than any of the colonies to the southward.

[14] Stanwix to Loudoun, November 13, 1757, *ibid.*, No. 4825. For the position of the Maryland Assembly respecting Fort Cumberland see its address to Governor Sharpe of December 15, 1757 (*ibid.*, No. 5017). In it the point was emphasized that the fort was "between Eighty and Ninety Miles from the Settlements of the Westwardmost Inhabitants of this Province. . . ."

[15] The Annapolis Corporation to Sharpe, December 22, 1757, *ibid.*, No. 5060; the address of the upper house to Sharpe, December 16, 1757, *ibid.*, No. 5019.

[16] *Ibid.*, No. 5017. But even this small measure of co-operation with the regulars who might proceed against Fort Duquesne was not possible on the part of the province, according to the upper house. This, because of the settled determination of the lower house, was to clog the supply bill for maintaining the provincial troops with "such absurd Restrictions" upon the control of the latter as to leave little doubt that "it was framed with a View to evade the granting of any money." In rejecting the bill of the lower house the upper house declared: "the only Provision . . . which has the least Tendency toward a Union, or can conduce to an uniform Plan of Mutual Assistance, and Defence, is that, by which the Forces raised in the respective Governments are subjected to one Direction in their military Operations" (Address to Sharpe, December 16, 1757, *ibid.*, No. 5019). But this view the lower house would not accept.

During this period the province maintained on foot twenty-five companies, totalling over twelve hundred men, who were stationed at sixteen posts stretching from the upper Delaware to the south-western limits of the province, with some eight companies stationed at Fort Augusta, a place of great strategic importance, and with one or two companies, or even less, at other posts.[17] In addition to this, Colonel Stanwix, with a battalion of the 60th regiment, stationed at Carlisle, had general charge of the defence of the region to the west of the Susquehanna and was loyally supported by gallant Lieutenant Colonel Armstrong, who commanded the provincials in that area. That critical region was, in fact, so effectively patrolled that the raiding enemy was only able to pick off groups of settlers who, failing to comply with Stanwix's orders, neglected to apply for guards of soldiers when engaged in their harvest. Writing to Loudoun on November 10, Governor Denny declared:

"The whole Country join in acknowledging the protection that Colonel Stanwix has given them by sending out frequent ranging Parties, and that Gentleman is pleased in his Letters to me very much to approve Lieutenant Colonel Armstrong's Conduct and commends the behaviour of the Provincial Officers and Soldiers for being indefatigable in doing their duty on their scouting Parties." [18]

In other words, only in that region to the east of the Susquehanna outside the area covered by Stanwix and Armstrong were the French raids effective and continuous, as the Indians fell upon the increasingly contracted outlying settlements.

But the idea of putting an end to those savage forays, by the destruction of Fort Duquesne through the combined efforts of the

[17] The forces were distributed at the following posts from south to northeast: at Fort Loudoun, Fort Littleton, Fort Morris at Shippensburg, and at Carlisle, all to the west of the Susquehanna; at Fort Augusta at the forks of it; at Fort Hunter, above Harris's Ferry on the east bank of the river; at Fort Swatara to the east twenty-four miles in Bethel Township; at Fort Henry, fourteen miles to the northeast of Swatara; at Fort William, near the forks of the Schuylkill, twenty-two miles northeast of Fort Henry; at Fort Allen on the Lehigh at the mouth of Mahoning Creek, forty-two miles northeast of Fort William and connected with it by the small Fort Everit at Allamangle (Allemingle) and a blockhouse; finally, at Wind Gap, and Depuis (De Pews), and at two other blockhouses to shelter the more settled parts of Northampton County on the upper Delaware and lower Lehigh. The attempt to defend the Juniata River valley had been given up, with the destruction of Fort Granville and the desertion of Fort Shirley on Augswick Creek (Pennsylvania Archives, first series, III, 339–41; see also for the location of the forts Nicholas Scull's "Map of the Improved Part of Pennsylvania," undated but prepared about the year 1759).

[18] Loudoun Papers, No. 4794.

people of the colonies chiefly affected, was no more seriously considered by the government of Pennsylvania than by the governments
to the southward — in spite of the fact that such an authority on
boundaries as Lewis Evans, surveyor and map-maker, had made
clear that this fort was well within the bounds of the province and
had so placed it in 1755 in his famous *Map of the Middle British
Colonies*.[19] As previously emphasized, it was felt at the time by
colonials by and large — and very rightly, it may be added — that
such a move must rest primarily upon an army of highly trained
troops, accompanied by military engineers and a siege train. And
with the coming of winter there appeared signs that the commander-
in-chief of the British forces in North America was contemplating
just such a move. For it is clear that gradually there was concentrated within the province — at Philadelphia, in the secure eastern
part of it, and at Reading, Lancaster, and York, in areas affected by
raids — other contingents of regulars than those at Carlisle. Most of
these troops, while in quarters awaiting the next campaign, were
so deployed as to serve therefore as an additional protection against
the winter forays of the enemy.[20]

The populous and prosperous though small colony of New Jersey,
freed from possible dangers of slave uprisings, had been requested
by Loudoun for the campaign of 1757 to vote one thousand men.
But the Assembly would not go beyond five hundred. In agreeing
to raise even this small number it was found that the people were
so much occupied with their domestic concerns and were so prosperous, as the result of the high war prices secured for the products
of their farms, that, in spite of the greatest inducements offered to
secure this modest contingent out of a population not far from
seventy-five thousand, it was necessary to recruit in Pennsylvania.[21]

---

[19] For this map see Gipson: *Lewis Evans*, Part IV.

[20] For Loudoun's notification to Denny, dated October 2, 1757, of the coming of
these contingents, see Loudoun Papers, No. 4567. That Loudoun was contemplating an
aggressive move in using Pennsylvania as a base of operations is also indicated by the
report that St. Clair made to him in the fall of 1757 on the condition of the roads in
that province, particularly those that led to the frontiers (Report dated September 21,
1757, *ibid.*, No. 4510).

[21] The New Jersey Assembly authorized, in the words of Colonel Stanwix, stationed
at the time in Philadelphia, "the vast reward of twelve pounds levie Money, great pay
or full Cloathing for eight months service only in the Jersey Provincials." These unprecedented inducements had the effect of putting a stop to all other recruiting in Pennsylvania until the required New Jersey contingent had been raised (Stanwix to Loudoun,
April 20, 1757, *ibid.*, No. 3407).

These forces when raised were placed at the disposal of General Webb, who was commissioned by Loudoun, as has already been made clear, to defend the approaches to Albany.

New Jersey was, of course, fairly well protected by its neighbours, although raiding parties passing over the Minsi Path did, it is true, occasionally penetrate the system of blockhouses erected for its greater security on its northern and western borders. With the conclusion of the campaign in the fall of the year, the provincial force in the general service was sent home by Loudoun, who indicated to the government of this colony, as well as to that of the other northern colonies, that his greatest need was for a small but active body of rangers for winter service, to be employed in the region of Lake Champlain and the valley of the Mohawk. New Jersey's allotment for this special levy was only one hundred men, and these were promptly raised. But having done this, the province, because it had discharged the returning regiment, found that it was without troops to garrison the blockhouses, since volunteers for this service could not be induced to re-enlist or present themselves. Consequently President John Reading of the Provincial Council [22] was impelled to appeal to Loudoun to send some of his regular troops to perform this duty.[23] The general, however, very properly pointed out that the regulars were brought to America for offensive action and consequently could not assume the responsibility of protecting each colony from small raiding parties, which, he made clear in this connection, must rest upon the inhabitants of the individual colony.[24]

The province of New York, it goes without saying, was from the beginning, and continued to be almost to the end of the war, one of the most critical of the areas in North America. By reason of its central location and the insistent problems of defence of its frontiers, its metropolis became Loudoun's headquarters, and within the limits of the colony at all times a considerable body of regular troops was therefore maintained. One might have thought that this would have been highly gratifying to the people of the province, but this was not so. Not only did they bitterly resent the placing of an

---

[22] Governer Belcher died in the fall of 1757; the Lieutenant Governor, under a commission that still seemed to be good, was Governor Pownall of Massachusetts Bay. Reading therefore acted temporarily with limited powers as the chief executive.

[23] Reading to Loudoun, December 12, 1757, *ibid.*, No. 5004.

[24] Loudoun to Reading, December 15, 1757, *ibid.*, No. 5018.

embargo by order of the general on their shipping, as well as the shipping of the other colonies, as a preliminary step to the invasion of Cape Breton, but they also vigorously protested Loudoun's efforts, with the public houses full, to secure temporary quarters in private homes for his soldiers who had arrived after a winter's sea voyage and were destined soon to embark with him. The writer of a pamphlet that appeared in London in 1758 entitled *The Conduct of a Noble Commander in America Impartially Reviewed* [25] emphasizes the hatred that these measures aroused against the general among the inhabitants. The writer, obviously close to him and perhaps a member of his staff, says with reference to the quartering issue: "The people, tho' they had been sensible enough of their dangers, & tho' they look'd on these troops as destined for their lasting Security, would have treated them with a rigour desgraceful, even if shewn toward the Prisoners of an Enemy." In face of the refusal of the magistrates and their insistence on the rights and privileges of the people as Englishmen, Loudoun ordered in this emergency "a fair & equal" distribution of the men in public and private houses.[26] In turn, the Albany merchants, who in earlier wars had continued to trade with the French Indians and to take an attitude of "neutrality" toward the hostilities going on, were now quite cut off from a very lucrative business. It was under these circumstances perhaps too much to expect them, prone to lawless ways, to be either happy or favourably disposed toward the commander-in-chief, who made their city one of the chief concentration points for the armed forces.

With the fall of Fort William Henry, Loudoun, who had given up his plan to attack Louisbourg, returned on September 1 to the colony, accompanied by a large part of his army. His immediate objective was to take charge of the defence of the more settled part of it. For the Lieutenant Governor of the province, de Lancey, had found to his sorrow and mortification that the militia of the colony could not

---

[25] This was published in London in 1758; for this see the *London Magazine*, June 1758; and also the Abercromby Papers, No. 403, the Huntington Library, where it is reproduced.

[26] The writer, in defending the general in taking this measure, states: "He always spoke with great Respect of their natural & political rights, but he would not sacrifice to them the Lives of the Soldiers." Happily, the people, while inconvenienced, found the soldiers under such strict orders that their conduct was unexceptionable, according to him (*ibid.*). It may be added that the editor of the *London Magazine* voiced the view that Loudoun was to be complimented for acting with "consummate prudence."

be depended upon for this work. In fact, when the alarm over the French success at Lake George had been sent out by General Webb, he had ordered the militia of Queens, Westchester, the Highlands, New York City, and Albany County to Fort Edward. Some of the men actually arrived there, it is true, but others moved forward slowly, until most unexpectedly the whole body "except those of the County of Albany . . . deserted in a most mutinous manner." [27] Montcalm happily did not, as already noted, make any further advance and, after destroying the fort at Lake George, retraced his steps to Canada.

Blocked in 1756 from making any progress against the French, again blocked in his plans during the summer of 1757 for an amphibious campaign, Loudoun was determined, if humanly possible, to do something during the remainder of the year. Immediately on arriving in New York he called upon Deputy Quartermaster General Sir John St. Clair to give his opinion of the feasibility of an expedition during the late fall and early winter against Ticonderoga and Crown Point. This experienced officer, who had carried a heavy responsibility during Braddock's campaign, presented a report on September 2. In it he pointed out that, under the most favourable conditions, it would not be possible to lay siege to Ticonderoga before the middle of November; [28] this meant that the investment of that place and Crown Point must be carried out under winter conditions; he therefore gave as his judgment that, in view of the advanced season, no more could be done than "to secure our Frontiers in the best manner we can from further Insults" by distributing the regiments in the region above Albany and that of the Mohawk Val-

---

[27] De Lancey to the Assembly of New York, September 2, 1757, New York Colonial Mss., 85: 11b, N.Y. State Archives. The Lieutenant Governor stated with reference to the wholesale desertion: "This step whether arising from Cowardice or disgust or whatever other Motive deserves a very severe animadversion, more especially as it was taken at a time when the enemy were still at Fort William Henry only fourteen miles distant Fort Edward" (ibid.).

[28] St. Clair's plan, similar to the one that he had prepared for Shirley in 1756, called for the marching by land of a corps of five thousand men to Ticonderoga and the transporting of the artillery and provisions by water. He calculated that it would require the remainder of the month of September to concentrate the troops and the provisions at Lake George; the month of October, he thought, would be consumed in constructing the necessary bateaux and flat-bottom boats and in bringing up the artillery to the lake front; then five days must be allowed for the water carriage on the lake to the falls, and thereafter ten days to transport the whole from the landing at the falls to Ticonderoga (Loudoun Papers, No. 4391).

ley.[29] The day after this report was written, Webb also wrote from Albany pointing out that there was not a single British vessel of any kind left on Lake George; he expressed the view, however, that troops, at least, without artillery, could be marched to the west side of it, to Ticonderoga, along the path used by the enemy in making their late campaign against Fort William Henry. At the same time he observed that the French still had at, or near, their fort, according to the report of two escaped English prisoners, six battalions of troops, most of whom, however, were expected soon to go into their winter cantonments.[30]

It appears that Loudoun now for a time put aside the thought of a winter campaign along the northern borders of New York.[31] In October, however, he embraced the idea once again.[32] As the plan matured, it seemed best to him to include but three thousand regulars and a thousand rangers, with provisions and equipment for only an attack on Ticonderoga. The provisions and equipment, as well as artillery, would be transported on carts and sledges over the frozen lake and was to include some twenty-four-pounders, some eighteen-pounders, and also mortars. It was later decided that five hundred Indians were also to be recruited for the adventure. The soldiers were to travel either on snowshoes or behind those equipped with them.[33] Loudoun expected to lead the raid in person and, in doing so, to live as the common soldiers would be obliged to do, without the shelter of a tent. Many other matters dealing with the over-all strategic scene in North America compelled him, however, to turn the enterprise over to young but energetic Lord Howe, who had arrived in America with Holburne in July and was now colonel of the 55th regiment.[34]

---

[29] Ibid.

[30] Ibid., No. 4391.

[31] His letter to Governor Denny of September 7 is concerned solely with providing winter quarters for the troops (ibid., No. 4419); in writing to Holburne on the 18th he indicated that since it was beyond his power to attack the enemy yet this season, the troops not stationed in Nova Scotia and in South Carolina would be used for protecting the northern and middle colonies. "All I have to do is to secure the country from a second attack this year and repair the losses and have everything prepared to take Fortune by the Forelock whenever they Leave a Hole for me to Creep in at" (ibid., No. 4494).

[32] Loudoun to Cumberland, October 17, 1757, Pargellis: Military Affairs in North America, 1748–1765, pp. 400–2.

[33] Abercromby to Loudoun, December 30, 1757, Loudoun Papers, No. 5151; see also for other details ibid., No. 2112 and No. 2914.

[34] In the instructions given to Howe in December the number of troops to be employed was not specified, but was to be agreed upon by him and Abercromby. In case

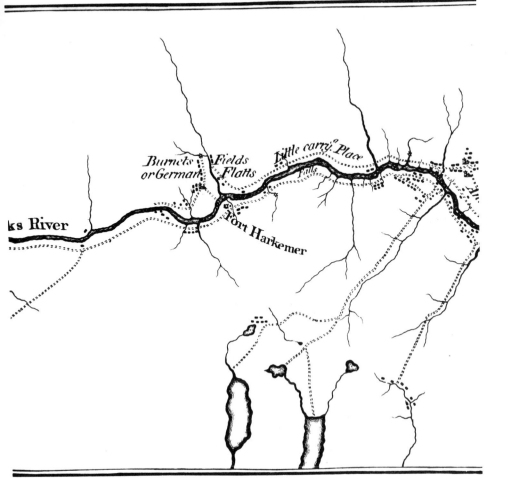

Fort Herkimer and German Flats.
(From Thomas Mante's *History of the Late War in North America, 1772.*)

But the expedition planned for the month of February did not materialize. The snowshoes to be made at Fort Edward by the ranger Robert Rogers and his men were not ready when almost everything else was prepared,[35] and an unprecedented snowfall of great depth led to its abandonment.[36]

Only up the Mohawk, in fact, was there any sign of action, and this came as the result of the initiative of the enemy. Early in November Ensign Picoté de Bellestre and the Sieur de Lorimer at the head of three hundred marine troops, together with Canadians and Indians, moved eastward from Lake Ontario into the country of the Oneida. Passing by five abandoned English posts on the upper Mohawk, they finally arrived in the neighbourhood of Fort Herkimer, situated on the south bank of that river, where Captain Townshend was posted with some two hundred men of the 22nd regiment.[37] On the 11th, avoiding the fort, the party crossed the stream to the north side and remained encamped in the woods overnight and then very early the next morning burst in upon the flourishing Palatine settlement of German Flats, protected by some five small blockhouses. At first there was some resistance as the French and the Indians with their war whoops rushed forward; but the Mayor of the village, Johan Jost Petrie (Petery), soon opened the doors of one of the forts and asked for quarter. The rest of the

---

of success against Crown Point and Ticonderoga, he was to destroy the two forts after taking away all the cannon that could be moved (ibid., No. 5171).

[35] Rogers was expected to construct for the expedition seven hundred snowshoes, and also seven hundred metal "ice-creepers," to fasten on the shoes of soldiers, as well as three hundred hand sleighs (Abercromby to Loudoun, February 14, 1758, ibid., No. 5595).

[36] This is treated in some detail in B. G. Lœscher's The History of Rogers' Rangers, I, 233-5.

[37] Loudoun to Pitt, February 14, 1758, Correspondence of William Pitt (ed. G. S. Kimball), I, 183.

The French have left us a clear description of Fort Herkimer, which they called Fort Kouri. It was a large three-story stone house with portholes at each story and likewise in the basement for the purpose of cross-firing. It was also provided with some small pieces of artillery and was roofed with planks and shingles. Some thirty feet distant from it was a ditch six feet deep and seven in width. The crown of the ditch inside its circumference was surmounted with palisades "in an oblique form; within the palisades was a parapet of earth raised to such a height that the soldiers behind it could fire over the palisades; a feature of the parapet that strengthened the defences was that it was so constructed as to form four bastions, as it were, that flanked each other." Within the enclosure, in addition to the large building, was a smaller one used as a barrack and guard house ("Topography of the Country between Oswego and Albany," 1757, Documents Relating to the Colonial History of the State of New York, X, 676).

defences were likewise delivered without the loss of a soul. Thus the village was now at the mercy of the enemy.[38]

The attack came as an almost unbelievable surprise to these Palatines, who, abiding in a false sense of security, were under the conviction that they had succeeded in establishing a firm agreement of neutrality with the French and their Indian allies — reference to which has already been made in an earlier chapter. When warned by Townshend the preceding day that intelligence had been received of the approach of the enemy, they "obstinately" refused to obey his orders to seek shelter within Fort Herkimer; for they were persuaded that the capture of the fort alone was the objective of the French and that they themselves would receive no injury.[39] But now came the bitter disillusionment while they as prisoners witnessed for a period of forty-eight hours the systematic destruction of the settlement, as houses, barns, granaries, and sheds went up in smoke and thousands of livestock were either killed or driven off.[40] Only on the 13th, with the work of devastation progressing and while many of the French and Indians were very drunk,[41] did Townshend feel that he was in a position to send a party across the river to seek to interfere with the saturnalia of destruction. But nothing was accomplished to pay for the loss of lives. Moreover, the fort, were it depleted of defenders, was itself liable to fall a prey to the fury of the enemy. The commander, in fact, when danger threatened, had sent out a call for aid from the troops stationed on the lower Mohawk. This relief, made up of Highlanders stationed at Schenectady and some militia, moved forward under the command of Lord Howe. Although Howe showed the most commendable energy in gathering and marching his troops,[42] upon his arrival

---

[38] For Bellestre's account see *ibid.*, X, 672–4.

[39] See Captain Thomas Williams's statement dated December 9, 1757, Loudoun Papers, No. 4973. The reluctance of the Palatines to enter the fort may be attributed to the fact that they did not want to provide grounds for an accusation by the French and Indians that they had taken sides in the war and were not neutral.

[40] Bellestre estimated that he destroyed more grain at the Flats "than the Island of Montreal produced in years of abundance"; that the same was true of hogs; that three thousand horned cattle, the same number of sheep, fifteen hundred horses, and other property valued at over 1,500,00 livres was likewise destroyed or carried off (*op. cit.*, X, 673–4).

[41] Howe's report to Loudoun (Loudoun Papers, No. 4835).

[42] See Howe's two letters to Loudoun written from Fort Johnson and Fort Hendrick, both on November 14, 1757 (Loudoun Papers, No. 4829 and No. 4830); also see Loudoun to Pownall, November 17, 1757 (*ibid.*, No. 4853), telling of Howe's return to Albany; Loudoun to Pitt, February 14, 1758, *Pitt Correspondence*, I, 184–5.

at the fort, there now lay across the river — in place of a once prosperous community of several hundred settlers, accounted "generally
rich," living in a land "as fertile . . . as any perhaps in the
world" [43] — only blackened ruins and desolation and the silence of
death. For the enemy, with at least a hundred and fifty prisoners —
men, women, and children — and loaded with booty, including some
fifty scalps, had already departed.[44] One disturbing factor in this
bloody raid that came to light was the information that many of
the Oneida of the Six Nations were deeply implicated as active
participants.[45]

Thus the German-speaking population in upper New York was
made to realize, as did that in western Pennsylvania to their sorrow,
that even the most inoffensive and humane behaviour toward the
Indians allied with the French could not save them from attack.
As a result, when in December information was brought by friendly
Indians to the extensive settlement on the Schoharie that a body
of French and Indians was planning to attack it some time in January, the inhabitants immediately sent a delegation to General
Abercromby at Albany begging him to send some of his troops to
protect them and informing him at the same time that their families
were already deserting the region. To support that "flourishing and
valuable Settlement," the general ordered detachments from Howe's
and Murray's regiments to march to its assistance. To aid in their
coming the settlers offered to supply sleighs, and upon their arrival
gladly opened their stone houses for the accommodation of the
men and as gladly "agreed to erect everything for their own
defence under the direction of Captain Abercromby" [Abercrom-
bie].[46]

Before turning to a brief view of the situation in New England
at the end of 1757, it may be well to refer at this point to one problem that faced the commanding officers in charge of the New York
area. This was the conduct of the American rangers. Men from
western New Hampshire and western Massachusetts had had much
experience in woodcraft; they were hardy and brave. It was therefore determined by General Shirley in 1755 to organize some of

---

[43] N.Y. Col. Doc., VII, 341.

[44] Ibid., X, 697, 705. Some of the settlers succeeded in reaching the safety of the
fort; others, in attempting to do so, were, unhappily, drowned (ibid., X, 678).

[45] Loudoun to Pitt, February 14, 1758, Pitt Correspondence, I, 184–5.

[46] General Abercromby to Loudoun, December 29, 1757, Loudoun Papers, No.
5144.

them into three companies to engage in scouting.[47] Under such leaders as the redoubtable Robert Rogers and his brother Richard, and also John Stark and Israel Putnam, both of later Revolutionary War fame,[48] they did excellent work in carrying out reconnaissance, bringing in prisoners, and intercepting small parties of the enemy. When Loudoun took over command, he continued them in the service and added an additional company. They were, it may be pointed out, on a very different footing from the provincial forces, for they were really auxiliaries of the regular army, and as members of it took the oath of fidelity and were supposed to be subject to the "Rules and Articles of War." [49] Their pay was high; they received, in addition, substantial bounties for every Indian scalp, were clothed and armed after 1756 in a manner most suited to the work they performed,[50] and were maintained in all respects at the expense of the Crown. So valuable did they seem to be that Loudoun determined in October 1757 to have more of them for winter scouting and, in agreeing to send home the provincial forces raised by the northern colonies, asked each of these colonies at the same time to furnish a contingent of experienced rangers amounting in all to eleven hundred.[51] But the weakness of such a service shortly became evident. Too many of the men of the older companies were wild and undisciplined; like the Indians, they scouted only when they felt like doing so, and also like the latter they appeared to be excessively fond of rum, and when drunk were dangerous and riotous. Sent out in November of that year from Fort Edward with Captain Stark to secure French prisoners in the neighbourhood of Ticonderoga, they showed a very bad spirit, resenting, apparently, the fact that Captain Abercrombie of the 42nd regiment was in chief command. Only Robert Rogers apparently had the slightest

---

[47] For the history of the rangers during the early years of the war see B. G. Lœscher: *The History of Rogers' Rangers*, Vol. I, *The Beginning, January 1755 to April 6, 1758*; Robert Rogers's "Journal" in *Reminiscences of the French War; Containing Rogers's Expeditions* (1831); *Journal of Major Robert Rogers* (Dublin, 1769).

[48] Putnam after serving under Rogers accepted a commission in the Connecticut forces.

[49] Robert Rogers to Loudoun, October 25, 1757, Loudoun Papers, No. 4701. Rogers in this long communication outlines the methods employed by the rangers in their scouting activities. It is of great value to those interested in the techniques of backwoods warfare.

[50] Lœscher, *op. cit.*, Appendix B.

[51] New Hampshire was to furnish 50; Massachusetts Bay, 350; Rhode Island, 100; Connecticut, 300; New York, 200; and New Jersey, 100 (Loudoun Papers, No. 4414).

control over them, and he, on account of illness, did not participate in the expedition. Instead of moving by stealth, as was so essential, they fired their guns frequently at game, and in the vicinity of the French fort permitted themselves to be discovered; then, according to Captain Abercrombie's account,

> "Captain Stark . . . set up the Indian hollow, upon which the whole party jumped up & yelled as if Hell had broke loose & all fell to firing at a few men running away. I did everything in my power to make them hold their tongues & behave as they ought to do." [52]

After returning to their camp on the island near Fort Edward, some of them showed the most serious insubordination even to their own officers, and staged a wild carousal, which led to a serious riot after three of the men were whipped for refusal to obey the commands of their own captains.[53] It seemed that this useful arm of the service was about to disintegrate, for the men were not held, as were the regulars, to a rigid discipline. General Abercromby, in fact, was, impelled to warn Rogers that should his men desert, as they seemed disposed to do, they would do so at the peril of hanging — just as was the case with the regulars. Soon after this, in order "to retrieve the Character of the Rangers," who themselves had now come to realize the gravity of their misconduct, their great partisan leader, now restored to health, secured permission from Colonel Haviland to take them out again to scout.[54] However, in view of their seeming

---

[52] Lœscher, op. cit., pp. 193–7. Captain James Abercrombie to Loudoun, November 29, 1757, Loudoun Papers, No. 4915; General Abercromby to Loudoun, December 30, 1757, ibid., No. 5159.

[53] Lieutenant Colonel William Haviland to Abercrombie, December 16, 1757, ibid., No. 6859. For the conclusions of the court of inquiry, December 8–11, 1757, see ibid., No. 4969; see also Lœscher, op. cit., pp. 197–209.

[54] Rogers in his "Journal" (op. cit., pp. 44–5) does not mention this misconduct. He made two expeditions in the neighbourhood of Fort Ticonderoga. On the first, between December 17 and 27, accompanied by one hundred and fifty rangers, he managed to capture two Frenchmen from the fort and secured information regarding the strength of the enemy there and at Crown Point, and then, after slaughtering a number of cattle, left (ibid., p. 47). According to the French account, the artillery of the fort "drove him away pretty quick," and it mentions that before he retreated he attached to the head of one of the slain oxen a letter addressed to the commandant of the fort, "the contents whereof were an ill-timed and very low piece of braggadocia" (Doreil to Belle-Isle, April 30, 1758, N. Y. Col. Doc., X, 703). Again on March 10, after his plan to surprise Ticonderoga with a party of four hundred rangers was laid aside, he was ordered by Haviland to go to the neighbourhood of the fort to secure prisoners. This he did, using skates and snowshoes. His party of one hundred and eighty on the 13th met a group of the enemy, which it defeated, but, unhappily, this was but the advanced

unreliability and lack of discipline, Lieutenant Colonel Thomas Gage offered to raise a corps of five hundred light-armed foot at his own expense that would have the mobility of the rangers and would, in fact, be made of American woodsmen, but would have the full status of regular troops and as such would be subject to all regulations applying to them.[55] Loudoun agreed to this proposal and issued orders for arming them. Thus early in 1758 on the frontier of New York there now came into existence for the first time in the history of the British army a branch of the service well adapted by experience and equipment to perform all the functions of scouts and rangers.[56] This corps took its place with the other units of the regular army in guarding the frontiers of the province and was also available to participate in the next summer campaign. It may be added, however, that companies of American rangers attached to units of regulars continued to be employed throughout the period of the war, with Rogers now elevated to the rank of "Major of the Rangers in his Majesty's Service."[57] The part these men played in the final outcome of the struggle was one of no little significance.

Of the American continental colonies, outside of Virginia, those of New England alone provided, without aid from the regular troops, for the defence of their frontiers. One must hasten to add, however, that the presence of a considerable body of regulars at Fort Edward was an important element in the protection of the western reaches of both Connecticut and Massachusetts Bay; further, a large number of these troops in Nova Scotia likewise helped to secure Maine. Of these colonies, Connecticut by the close of the year 1757 had made the best showing in the contribution of men in accordance with its population and in the steadiness of the behaviour of the soldiers. Although Loudoun called this little republican colony "a strange Government," he at the same time indicated in writing to Pitt on October 17 that it had a good man at its head

guard of some six hundred Canadians and Indians, who finally inflicted a very severe defeat upon the rangers. Rogers gave his losses as one hundred and twenty-five ("Journal," op. cit., pp. 57–8). The French accounts report that at least one hundred and forty-four scalps were taken, as well as a few prisoners (N. Y. Col. Doc., X, 698; Archives des Colonies, Canada, 1758, B. 107; 42).

[55] Gage to Loudoun, December 22 and 23, 1757, Loudoun Papers, No. 5066 and No. 5074.

[56] Pargellis: Lord Loudoun in North America, p. 305.

[57] Rogers's "Journal," op. cit., p. 65. In fact, Loudoun in January 1758 authorized Rogers to raise five additional companies of rangers.

in the person of Governor Fitch.[58] In 1756, when a requisition of some twelve hundred and fifty troops had been requested of the colony to permit a move against Crown Point, it actually furnished twenty-five hundred — when the hope of securing contingents from the middle colonies outside of New York was not realized.[59] Many of the New York contingents of that year were likewise recruited within its borders; it also provided the number agreed upon in Boston at the beginning of 1757. Then when New Hampshire in the spring of that year was indisposed to care for the protection of the settlement called No. 4 on the upper Connecticut, although within the bounds of that province, five hundred troops raised by the little colony and under the command of Lieutenant Colonel Nathan Whiting were thereupon ordered by Loudoun to march up the river to perform the service.[60] This duty was carried out in the most excellent spirit; and a similar spirit characterized the contingent of nine hundred men sent under command of Major General Phineas Lyman to upper New York, where they were placed under orders of General Webb. With the attack on Fort William Henry, upon the call of that general, there was a willing response; one fourth of the entire militia of the colony and one half of a regiment of provincials were hurriedly assembled and sent forward, many of them on horseback, only to be ordered back home. Finally, with the dismissal of the provincial forces by Loudoun at the end of the year's campaign, the colony, on request and after some discussion, made provision for three companies of rangers, numbering two hundred and eighty men, to continue in the service for the winter.[61] This response elicited from the general warm commendation.[62]

If the commander-in-chief had praise for Connecticut, he had little for Rhode Island. Its contingent in 1756 fell greatly short of the number requested to be raised.[63] Although the colony finally agreed to the requisition of four hundred and fifty men for the campaign of 1757,[64] as the result of the strong urging of Governor

---

[58] Loudoun Papers, No. 4239.

[59] Fitch to Holderness, July 20, 1757, C.O. 5:19, pp. 177–80.

[60] Fitch Papers, I, 348; Loudoun to Hutchinson, April 11, 1757, Loudoun Papers, No. 3335.

[61] Fitch Papers, I, 349; see also Loudoun Papers, No. 4633.

[62] Loudoun to Fitch, November 5, 1757, ibid., No. 4765.

[63] Loudoun to the Governor and Company of Rhode Island, January 29, 1757, Rhode Island Colonial Records, VI, 15–17.

[64] Ibid., VI, 20, 22–7, 33–7.

Hopkins, it showed its displeasure that he should have been so generous as to agree to furnish that large a number by removing him from his office "by a very great majority of votes" in the elections that came in the spring of the year.[65] Moreover, the men voted were slow in mustering and when they arrived at Albany were without arms — although three hundred of the King's arms used the preceding campaign were scattered about the colony — and the number of troops was also deficient.[66] Upon the completion of the summer campaign Loudoun called upon the colony to supply one hundred rangers in place of the provincial line that returned home, but the Assembly obstinately refused to give more than seventy, which brought from the general a sharp rebuke.[67] What disturbed him more, however, than this failure to co-operate in the common cause — especially in view of the fact that "the King at the expence of the Mother Country has sent so great a Force for your Protection [and that of the other colonies], both of Land Forces and Fleets" [68] — was that information had reached him earlier in the year of "many vessels from the ports of your province having traded with, and supplied the enemy in their own ports. . . ." [69] In fact, thousands of men were employed on the colony ships and, it may be added, their captains apparently paid little attention to royal orders, such as those involving embargoes, and both in peace and in war were largely a law unto themselves. Moreover, one problem that faced those in the colony who were disposed to co-operate loyally in the great common enterprise of the war in North America was that the people were plagued almost to death as the result of the reckless

---

[65] Hopkins to Loudoun, April 26, 1757, Loudoun Papers, No. 3482.

[66] *R. I. Col. Rec.*, VI, 70, 72. In August 1757 there were but three hundred and seventeen men credited to the Rhode Island regiment in New York, including those on furlough (G. S. Kimball: *Correspondence of the Colonial Governors of Rhode Island*, II, 257).

[67] Loudoun to Governor Greene, October 9, 1757, Loudoun Papers, No. 4615.

[68] *Ibid.*

[69] *R. I. Col. Rec.*, VI, 70. Writing to Pitt on October 17 regarding the conduct of the people of the colony, Loudoun declared, with a good deal of feeling, that "they are a Lawless sett of Smugglers, who continually Supply the Enemy with what Provisions they want and bring back their Goods in Barter for them; and their abandoned practices in many matters, make them able to give very little Aid if they were willing, to the Public Cause" (Loudoun Papers, No. 4329). In 1750 the contraband activities of the Rhode Island traders were denounced by the agents of the British West India colonies, who declared that the inhabitants of this colony traded with the French islands, "forgetting all the ties of Duty to his Majesty, the Interest of the Mother Country and the reverence due to its Laws" in reviving a trade that they had but too successfully carried on before the war (C.O. 323: O. 59–60).

depreciation of the provincial currency poured forth by the Assembly over a period of years without proper security.[70] Nevertheless, many people were apparently doing very well indeed who engaged in rapid transactions and also lawless trade. Loudoun at least, in writing to Governor Greene in October 1757, declared that he had informed himself of the ability of the colony to do its part and was aware "of the losses sustained in the War and of the profits made." [71]

Massachusetts Bay, in contrast to Rhode Island, was, all in all, active in support of the war. The necessity of its favourable outcome, in terms of the welfare of the people of the province, was realized and generally kept in mind. The most populous of the New England colonies, it furnished at all times a much larger number of provincials for the service than any of its neighbours, and these, in the main, acquitted themselves well. For the operations of 1757 eighteen hundred men were raised and sent out of the province to serve under General Webb. A large part of them under Colonel Fry helped to defend the camp near Fort William Henry, and only after the hope of speedy relief had passed did they lose spirit and determine to surrender or at least to give up the struggle. But on the fatal march toward Fort Edward, already described, many of them lost their lives or suffered cruel indignities at the hands of the Indians, as did their commander, who finally appeared at Fort Edward clad only in his shirt.

Since its early history the colony had looked with dread upon the French in Canada, and the stories of the terrible visitations of their Indian allies during Queen Anne's War were kept alive at every fireside. While all New England with the outbreak of the war wished ardently to see the reduction of Canada achieved — in the words of Thomas Hutchinson, "an object, above all others" — no colony had greater reason to feel this urgency. Moreover, as this writer points out, "the benefits expected from this acquisition were nothing more than a freedom from that distress which they were liable to, every time a war broke out between England and

---

[70] See the address of Charles Bowler of Portsmouth to the "Gentlemen of the colony of Rhode Island," April 28, 1757, Loudoun Papers, No. 3494. This refers to the distress of the widows and children, "scarce saved from starvation," and the ruin of many merchants and the fact that the farmers were seeking to get rid of their money as fast as they could since it continued to fall in value. For a brief history of this inflation see Volume III of this series, pages 70–4.

[71] Loudoun Papers, No. 4615.

France." [72] Not only were the frontier settlements liable to be ravished, but the great fishery enterprise off the island of Canso, near Cape Breton Island, employing thousands of people, would come to a halt, with consequent acute economic distress and stagnation facing the great seafaring population of the ports of the province. This conquest, it was realized, could only come by the most active participation of the mother country in the enterprise. The myth of a rapacious British Empire stretching out its tentacles from London to grasp everything in sight, including Canada, had not as yet been created and woven into the American national tradition. Indeed, the chief criticism of the people of Massachusetts Bay against the government of Great Britain in the preceding war was not that it had had designs on Canada primarily for the benefit of the people of the British Isles, as was later to be asserted and generally accepted to be true, but that it could not be brought to consider seriously such an acquisition, even with all Governor Shirley's eloquence and persuasiveness and even with Louisbourg in the grip of the New England forces. No, the men of England at the period under survey still considered the region of the St. Lawrence a forbidding area of waste lands and unendurable winters, a financial liability to any nation, not an asset. Therefore, if it were conquered and held, such an acquisition must be based on considerations more substantial than the hope of enriching the people at home. These considerations were ultimately to be advanced by such leading colonials as Benjamin Franklin at the time of the making of the peace treaty and in terms of the security of British colonials living in North America.

In view of what has been said, it is surprising that Massachusetts Bay did not follow the excellent example of its steady neighbour to the south and west, Connecticut, and extend a welcome to the troops that, returning from Nova Scotia after Loudoun had given up that enterprise, were, according to his plan, to be quartered within the colony so as to be ready at the earliest possible moment for the next year's enterprise against Canada. As had been the case in South Carolina, Maryland, Pennsylvania, and New York, there were now murmurings in Massachusetts Bay against this proposal for quartering as an encroachment on the liberties of the province. Thomas Pownall, who had recently taken over the government, sent

---

[72] See Hutchinson's *History of Massachusetts Bay from the Year 1750, until June, 1774* (London, 1838), p. 69.

a message to the Assembly that brushed aside the question whether the troops should or should not have lodgment within the colony, and raised instead another: whether the people would prefer to have the troops quartered by an act of the provincial government or simply by orders of the commander-in-chief of the British forces in North America, adding significantly: "that ye Army must & will make their own Quarters good." [73] Although the legislature, according to the Governor, had come prepared to reject "unanimously" a request for winter quarters, it now faced the dilemma realistically and voted in favour of a law that would provide by the civil authority quarters for one of the regiments, rather than have it come under terms of military law. Under this statute the magistrates agreed to turn Castle William over for the use of Loudoun's troops.

But the issue was not settled. It was necessary to recruit for the purpose of filling up the British regiments depleted by death and illness; and this work could not be carried on at the castle across the bay and far removed from the town. Not only did the local magistrates refuse recruiting quarters to parties sent to the province, but they were supported by the Assembly. On November 4 that body passed an act that, among other provisions, forbade under penalty of one hundred pounds any officer civil or military to billet a soldier or seaman upon an inhabitant of the province without his consent, other than in a public licensed house.[74] Pownall, however, was impelled to refuse acceptance of this clause in the act, since it would be from Loudoun's point of view a clear defiance of the authority of the King's commanding officer in time of war and public emergency. For the general took the position that he had the right to require quarters, not only by reason of the powers granted to him as the King's military representative, but on the explicit terms of the Mutiny Act of Parliament relating to the quartering of troops in the mother country in time of war. Writing to Pownall from New York on December 2, he declared that by the statute passed by the Assembly:

"they attempt to take away the King's undoubted Prerogative . . . they attempt to take away an Act of the British Parliament; they attempt to make it impossible for the King either to keep troops in North America, or if he kept them in his Forts to make it impossible

---

[73] Pownall to Loudoun, August 27, 1757, Loudoun Papers, No. 4319.
[74] This was embodied in the "Act for Regulating the Militia," as section 25.

for him to march them thro' his own Dominions either for the **Defence** of these Dominions or for the Protection of the Lives and **Property** of his subjects."

He then went on to show the dilemma that faced him should he acquiesce in the position of Massachusetts Bay and apply it impartially to all colonies. He declared:

> "it will really mean that the whole Troops in Connecticut, Long Island, New York, Livingston Manor, Cloverack, Esopus, Albany, Half Moon, Nestaguna, Schenectady, the Jerseys, Pensilvania, Maryland, South Carolina and Georgia must [in default of winter barracks] be turned into the streets to perish, except self preservation dictates to them as men, to save their Lives, by forcing themselves under cover." [75]

But Loudoun did not stop there. He felt that the whole future of successful military operations in North America was at stake and had determined, even before writing the above, that should the Assembly of Massachusetts Bay continue to show this spirit of recalcitrance, to march a regiment already quartered in Connecticut, another from Long Island, and a third from New York, and if need be two more from Pennsylvania, into the province and find accommodations for them there for the winter. [76]

When the Assembly met again late in November, the members therefore faced this ultimatum. Then it was that they passed a remarkable resolution. In it they took the position that they had not believed at the time that they took their former action that the British statute providing for quartering had been designed to extend to the colonies; they made clear, however, that they had not endorsed principles that would call into question the power of Parliament to pass a quartering act that would include America, and that

> "To prevent any ill consequences which may arise from an opinion of our holding such principles, we now utterly disavow them, as we should readily have done at any time past, if there had been occasion for it. . . ."

To remove all possibility of any future misunderstanding, they likewise went on record in the following words, which, it is of interest

---

[75] Loudoun to Pownall, December 2, 1757, Loudoun Papers, No. 4955.
[76] Loudoun to Pownall, November 15, 1757, *ibid.*, No. 4838.

to mention in passing, were to be utterly repudiated by them before a decade had passed:

> "The authority of all acts of parliament which concern the colonies, and extend to them, is ever acknowledged in all the courts of law, and made the rule of all judicial proceedings in the province. There is not a member of the General Court, as we know of no inhabitant within the bounds of the government, that ever questioned this authority." [77]

They thereupon proceeded to declare their willingness to pass an act of their own "agreeable to the Act of Parliament for quartering Troops that have occasion to march or quarter in the Province." [78] This was done.[79] But the point finally gained by Loudoun was not pressed home. Neither were the regiments from the south marched into the province to be wintered there as threatened, nor were Frasier's Highlanders, who had been originally destined by the general to go to the Bay colony; indeed, the latter were billeted in western Connecticut, where they were given ample accommodations without fuss or controversy in the towns of Fairfield, Milford, Norwalk, Stamford, and Stratford until they moved out for action in the spring of 1758.[80]

In turning to New Hampshire, we find a poor colony, distressed, as was Rhode Island but not to the same degree, as the result of a depreciated currency, and also with a population largely engaged in backwoods activities as well as agricultural pursuits. The lands of the province extended into the area of the upper Connecticut, where the French were active, while the region that is now embodied within the state of Vermont, still closer to the enemy, was likewise claimed, although that claim was contested by New York. When in the year 1741 its southern boundary was at last made definite, it was found that many communities previously settled by Massa-

---

[77] This resolution of January 6, 1758 is printed in full by Hutchinson, *op. cit.*, pp. 65–6; among the official documents containing it, see C.O. 5:49, pp. 198–202.

[78] Pownall to Loudoun, December 16, 1757, Loudoun Papers, No. 5022; and the Massachusetts Bay Assembly to Pownall, December 16, 1757, *ibid.*, No. 5021.

[79] For the act of December 1, 1757 see *ibid.*, No. 4931.

[80] The reader is referred to Dr. Pargellis's *Lord Loudoun*, Chapter VII, for a scholarly analysis of the issue over quartering. Since this issue, as it concerned the American colonies before the outbreak of the Revolutionary War, will be given extended treatment in a subsequent volume of this series, it seems best not to give at this point any further comment on its constitutional aspects.

chusetts Bay people were awarded to it. This proved to be an embarrassment in the war that was now being waged, especially in view of the fact that the settlement, then known as No. 4, but now as Charleston, was located just below Black River, which, flowing from the west into the Connecticut, formed an easy and favourite approach for raiding parties of French and Indians.

During the summer of 1755 the farms of the scattered inhabitants of No. 4 were attacked, and although a small patrol of twenty-one New Hampshire troops was sent for its protection, the men were enlisted for only a brief period and, after this, insisted on returning home, leaving the settlement quite defenceless.[81] When Loudoun came to Boston early in 1757 to secure aid from New England for his summer campaign, the people of No. 4 signed a petition to him asking to be placed under the protection of the forces of Massachusetts Bay but were persuaded by Colonel Theodore Atkinson, representing New Hampshire at the meeting, not to deliver it.[82] Their condition was so precarious, however, that Thomas Hutchinson, who had long befriended them and had even gone to England in their behalf after they had been separated from the province of their nativity, wrote to Loudoun during the month of March to secure for them at least a guard of some thirty or forty men to protect them.[83] The general thereupon ordered two hundred of the New Hampshire forces to this critical area. But the troops had not as yet moved up when, well over a month later, the Indians launched an attack against the settlement.[84] In fact, so difficult was it for the province to induce men to enlist to protect their own borders that Loudoun had decided before this attack to send five hundred Connecticut soldiers under Lieutenant Colonel Whiting up the river to defend the inhabitants of No. 4 as an emergency measure — reference to which has already been made.[85]

One explanation of the weakness of the province in frontier defence was that most of the members of three of the companies of rangers serving with the British regulars under command of the Rogers brothers and Captain Shepherd (Sheepard) had been raised among the frontiersmen of New Hampshire, "by which the inhab-

[81] Petition of the Inhabitants, September 8, 1755, Williams Mss., Vol. I, No. 175, Mass. Hist. Soc.
[82] Hutchinson to Loudoun, March 4, 1757, Loudoun Papers, No. 3070.
[83] Ibid.
[84] Loudoun to Governor Wentworth, April 25, 1757, ibid., No. 3462.
[85] Loudoun to Hutchinson, April 11, 1757, ibid., No. 3335.

itants near the frontier are very thin," as the New Hampshire Assembly pleaded in its resolutions.[86] The colony also contributed some three hundred and fifty men as its quota for the provincial forces raised by New England. These had been sent to Fort William Henry and about a third of them, with the fall of that fort, were either killed or carried into captivity; the remainder returning home were under a pledge not to carry arms.[87]

Nevertheless, New Hampshire was not putting forth its full strength, as is clearly indicated by its military response the following year. Further, the conduct of the troops sent to relieve Whiting at No. 4 early in September was scandalous. Some five hundred had been ordered up to that place in August by Governor Wentworth. On September 1 somewhat over two hundred of them had finally arrived; the rest dallied along the route to that extreme frontier post and then, according to reports reaching Whiting, began "running away in companies."[88] But the scandal did not stop here. The New Hampshire mounted troops that had reached the place "went off in a body" on September 2, riding away with such speed that they could not be caught and brought back. The foot soldiers that had arrived were so "very impatient of being detained" that the commander of the Connecticut forces, who had planned to leave with his troops, decided — in view of the fact that the people of the settlement and those of settlements farther down the river were "in great fear" — that he must remain.[89] Desertions continued. Early in October there were but fifty-five New Hampshire privates still at No. 4;[90] finally, late in November, the remainder of these troops deserted this important post, leaving the faithful Whiting and his Connecticut men to stand guard over it.[91]

By this survey it is clear that before the beginning of 1758 some colonies had played a very creditable role in the war, others had made an indifferent response, while still others had shown an indis-

---

[86] Resolution of May 18, 1757, *ibid.*, No. 3635.

[87] *Provincial Papers*, VI, 609.

[88] Whiting to General Webb, September 1, 1757, Loudoun Papers, No. 4375.

[89] Whiting to Webb, September 2, 1757, *ibid.*, No. 4383; Whiting to Colonel Israel Williams, September 3, 1757, Williams Mss., II, 43, Mass. Hist. Soc.

[90] "Return of troops by Major Thomas Tash, October 3, 1757," Loudoun Papers, No. 4573. According to this return, there were no New Hampshire troops at Fort Bellows; sixteen were at No. 2; twenty-nine at Fort Dummer; and none at Hinsdale — all New Hampshire outposts.

[91] Wentworth to Loudoun, December 1, 1757, Loudoun Papers, No. 4927.

position to make any effective contribution to the common cause outside the voting, from time to time, of funds for warlike purposes.[92] Yet even most of the backward and indifferent colonies were to be stirred into a display of energy and enthusiasm as the result of Pitt's dynamic appeals to them and the inducements he held out to individual Americans disposed to do their duty at this critical period.

---

[92] As colonial public finance covering this period will be rather fully treated in a subsequent volume, it does not seem proper to emphasize it at this point in the series.

CHAPTER VII

The French Tide in North America Begins to Ebb

THE YEAR 1758 was to witness a notable recession of the French tide in North America that had inundated so much of the land which, before the outbreak of the Great War for the Empire, had been the object of exclusive British colonization and trade relations. This recession came as the result of counter-movements of decisive force organized by Pitt and directed — where these were successful — by those who, with one exception, were new to the American scene. It would not be safe, however, for the historian to assert that these men were able to succeed under conditions that brought only failure to their predecessors; for conditions gradually altered. This will not be difficult to understand if one keeps clearly in mind the over-all view of a world war being waged on many fronts and shores. Indeed, at some of these points French power began showing signs of serious weakness. This was true of Canada.

The year 1757 had been one of continued military successes for the French in North America. Everywhere they had been on the aggressive except on Cape Breton Island, where a strongly defensive posture served their purposes much better. Their raiding parties had depopulated much of western Virginia, western Maryland, western Pennsylvania, and western New York; they had conquered and destroyed Fort William Henry and had become the undisputed masters of Lake Ontario and Lake George as well as Lake Champlain; and they had been so well prepared to receive Lord Loudoun's great expeditionary force directed against Louisbourg that he gave up the attempt without striking a blow. Further, they had been successful in maintaining contact with France. During the summer of 1757 forty-three ships had eluded the British fleet and arrived at Quebec by way of the strait of Belle Isle, bringing thirty-five hundred troops from France, with war stores and goods.[1]

Nevertheless, by the fall of the year Canada was suffering from an acute shortage of food. According to Colonel Schuyler of the New Jersey regiment, who was captured at Oswego in 1756 and was being held prisoner at Quebec, the inhabitants by the fall of 1757 were being limited to four ounces of bread and a little salt pork as a day's ration, although the soldiers received nine ounces, and meat twice a week, in order to maintain their strength. He predicted that by the middle of February 1758 all reserve provisions would be consumed and that the next summer would bring the most acute distress to the people, were the mouth of the river well guarded by British ships to prevent relief from arriving.[2] Indeed, as early as June of 1757, Intendant Bigot, alarmed at the growing food shortage, seized all the grain stored at Quebec and on the farms in that area, lodged it in the public magazine, and commissioned four bakers to make it up into bread. This was distributed by public authority upon the basis of individual daily allowances, as indicated.[3] So serious was the food shortage, in fact, that prisoners were sent out of Canada who would otherwise have been held, and found their way to England under flags of truce.[4] The explanation of this dearth of food in Canada lies in the fact that not only were the harvests of 1756 and 1757 there very bad indeed,[5] but, what is more, all the supply ships that sailed from France with provisions, to the number of sixteen, were, according to the testimony of the released British prisoners, captured while on the high seas.[6] It was even

---

[1] Intelligence from Colonel Peter Schuyler, a prisoner at Quebec, sent by Joseph Morse, who left Canada on October 4, 1757, Chatham Mss., Vol. XCV (Canadian Archives Transcripts).

[2] Ibid.

[3] "Journal" of Lieutenant Richard Pell, ibid., Vol. XCV.

[4] Ibid.

[5] "State of Canada in October, 1757, with some Thoughts on the Manner of Reducing it by C. Mⁿ," Amherst Private Papers, Packet 57 (Canadian Archives Transcripts) "C. Mⁿ" was apparently among the released prisoners.

[6] The writer quoted above stated that of these ships only the *Liberté*, arrived, with three thousand barrels of flour. But according to Montcalm, this statement was not true. The *Liberté*, he declared, had been selected to bring five hundred quarters of flour, but

stated that so little of the soil of the province was cultivated and so much was required of its inhabitants in the King's service that since the beginning of hostilities there was not produced in any single year enough food to maintain an army of six thousand men for a four months' campaign and still leave enough for the subsistence of the people.[7] As a consequence, no military operations of an extended nature could in any year be launched until the supply ships arrived from France, usually in either June or July, which meant that the campaigns must necessarily start fairly late in the summer season.

This problem of logistics also very much complicated another — the means of securing the continued support of the Indian tribes that had given such material aid to New France in the war. For they were actually more feared by the British frontier settlements than were the French troops. Yet these savages, coming in great numbers, as they did in the campaign against Fort William Henry, made an enormous demand on the provision supply, "taking everything at pleasure and Destroying three times the Quantity of Provisions they would eat." [8] With the growing shortage of food, the Indians could no longer be liberally supplied, with the result that they began leaving the service, "at the instigations of the English," and there seemed to be no possibility of retaining them without supplies from abroad.[9]

During the winter of 1757–8 this severe rationing continued, with the supply of flour gradually disappearing. Montcalm, writing to de Moras on February 19, 1758, declared: "The article of provisions makes me tremble. . . ." [10] Early in April, in the face of this ominous food crisis, the daily quantity of flour given to individuals

---

instead brought clothing for the soldiers (*Journal du Marquis de Montcalm*, ed. Abbé Casgrain, p. 304). The president of the Navy Board, writing to Bigot on February 28, 1757 (*Canadian Archives Report* [1905], I, Part VI, 235), had stated that the means taken to provision Canada for the year would, if they succeeded, leave the colony well provided. On July 27 he wrote to Drucour and Prévost at Louisbourg (*ibid.*, VI, 243), that there sailed for that port from France fourteen of the King's vessels laden with provisions, six of which, he stated, were captured in European waters, but he felt that the eight others must have arrived with twelve thousand quintals of flour. Yet to be sure that there would be food enough he informed Admiral de la Motte that he had sent eight additional provision vessels from Rochefort (*ibid.*, VI, 244–5). With all this effort, however, it would appear that not one of these ships carrying flour reached Quebec.

    [7] "State of Canada in October, 1757 . . . by C. Mⁿ," *op. cit.*

    [8] *Ibid.*

    [9] *Canadian Archives Report* (1905), I, Part VI, 260.

    [10] *Documents Relating to the Colonial History of the State of New York*, X, 686.

was cut in half — to two ounces. That was too little for an active person. M. Daine, reporting from Quebec on May 19, warned the Maréchal de Belle-Isle that "we are on the eve of the most cruel famine" and that large numbers of the horses of the province had already been purchased to be consumed. He affirmed that the "mechanics, artizans and day-laborers exhausted by hunger, absolutely cannot work any longer; they are so feeble that 'tis with difficulty they can sustain themselves." Before finishing his pessimistic letter, however, he received the news that five ships loaded with flour, which had sailed from Bordeaux, had arrived at the town, together with a small English prize freighted with the same commodity. The joy of the people of the city at the appearance of this relief, he was able to declare before closing his letter, was impossible to express.[11]

But it must be pointed out that, to survive, the Canadians had been obliged to consume the seed crop of wheat that was designed to be planted to ensure a harvest for the fall of 1758. Aware of this situation in France, four hundred tons of seed wheat and the same amount of rice for the subsistence of the people were placed on board three vessels at Dunkirk early in the spring and sent to Canada.[12] They were followed by other supply ships. By this means and with the heartening announcement made by the King of Spain that his subjects had the right to fish off the banks of Newfoundland and likewise full permission to carry on trade with Canada as well as with other French possessions in the New World,[13] it was felt by the authorities in old France that New France would rise above its economic difficulties and would be able for another year to triumph over its enemies, perhaps so decisively as to bring on an advantageous peace that would give to the French everything that they demanded in the way of territorial claims in the New World. Indeed, at this period they began to take steps to supply more cultivators of the soil in Canada by sending Alsatian families there who were to be given land near Quebec and provided with seeds and tools.[14]

---

[11] *Ibid.*, X, 704–6.

[12] Minister of the Marine to Vaudreuil and Bigot, March 23, 1758, *Canadian Archives Report* (1905), I, Part VI, 258.

[13] The Minister to Vaudreuil and Bigot, March 27, 1758, *ibid.*, VI, 259. Writing to Bigot on April 23, the president of the Navy Board stated that the letter would be carried to him by the "Sr. de Plazentia, commanding the Spanish vessel *La Ville de Bilbao*, chartered to carry a cargo of provisions from Bordeau to Quebec" (*ibid.*).

[14] The president of the Navy Board to Vaudreuil and Bigot, April 24, 1758, *ibid.*

It is of interest to note that such leaders as Montcalm in America were so confident of the ability of the French to maintain their advantages in North America, at least for a period of time — even in the face of the scarcity of food — that they demanded as the minimum price of peace not only the possession "of what England calls Acadia as far as the Isthmus and [of] Beauséjour" but the permanent elimination of the English from Lake Ontario, where Oswego once stood, from Lake Erie, and from all the regions west of the Appalachians, with Ohio confirmed to France and with the Five Nations and also the Indians dwelling on the Susquehanna, which flows through the heart of Pennsylvania, made quite independent of British control.[15] This obviously was not the position of a man who stared at inevitable defeat or the loss of Canada as an immediate contingency. Moreover, the Chevalier de Lévis, one of the most capable and gallant officers sent to New France during this period, took the position that the French had much greater means than the English to make sure the protection of the critical frontier of Lake George and Lake Champlain. He felt that Montreal could be easily defended, but that Albany, a town poorly fortified, was liable to fall whenever sufficient French forces were available to proceed against it; once it was captured, the regions round about would, he was persuaded, furnish adequate supplies for the maintenance of the army. He also indicated that Fort Duquesne, the most vulnerable of the French strongholds, could be protected in the future as in the past by continuously sending out raiding parties against the settlements of Pennsylvania and Virginia that would create such devastation and terror that the inhabitants, "the least warlike of all the English colonies," would demand peace. He also suggested the means for reconquering Acadia, by employing an expeditionary fleet moving up the Baie Françoise (Bay of Fundy), which would be supported by detachments of light-armed troops and regulars from Canada: "Port Royal (Annapolis Royal) once taken, we shall be masters of all of Acadia and only Halifax will remain to the English, which they cannot support." Nor was this all. He felt that the whole province of New York — and not simply Albany — could be detached from the British Empire and brought into an offensive and defensive

---

[15] Montcalm to de Paulmy, February 23, 1758, N. Y. Col. Doc., X, 691. Montcalm, it is true, felt that peace was desirable for New France in that "in the long run" — on account of the numbers of the English and the difficulty of transporting provisions and reinforcements — the province must be reduced.

alliance with France if a fleet with a considerable body of troops should appear before poorly defended New York City. He declared that the inhabitants of the province, largely of Dutch ancestry, were dissatisfied and tired of war and that they would accept the French King's protection if permitted to throw off their allegiance to Great Britain and establish a republic. This would separate New England thereafter from the southern colonies, and French forces could sustain the new republic.[16]

The French strategy for the year 1758, as it related to the use of the forces in Canada, was outlined by the Marquis de Vaudreuil in January of that year in a *mémoire* to Montcalm.[17] The latter, with the major part of the troops, was to make a powerful diversion along the frontiers of Lake George, while de Lévis with a detachment of three thousand men was so to impress the Six Nations that they would take up the hatchet against the English, and with these allies he was to destroy the remaining settlements on the Mohawk.[18] It was felt that by means of these two concerted diversions the enemy would not be able to act offensively in New York either to the north or to the west. Further, in March a plan was drafted by the military engineer the Chevalier de Mercier for the capture of Fort Lydius (Edward), which was to be carried out by Montcalm with his aid.[19] By this means it was hoped not only that the British campaign for the year would be upset but that a great advantage over the enemy would be secured.

One factor that might have had very adverse effects upon the French efforts in North America, in addition to that of the economic weakness of Canada, must, however, be mentioned at this point. It was the growing alienation between Governor General de Vaudreuil and the Marquis de Montcalm. The friction between these two high-spirited and ambitious men became very evident after the capture of Oswego in 1756, when each claimed the chief honour of it.[20] By

---

[16] Lévis to Mirepoix, September 7, 1757, *Lettres de Chevalier de Lévis, 1756–1760,* pp. 141–2, 145–6, 149–52.

[17] *Lettres et pièces militaires, 1756–1760* (ed. Abbé Casgrain), pp. 25–8.

[18] *Lettres de Lévis, 1756–1760,* p. 186.

[19] *Lettres et pièces militaires, 1756–1760,* pp. 32–43.

[20] This point has been well developed by Richard Waddington's *La Guerre de sept ans,* I, 240–1. Vaudreuil gave the chief credit of the operations to his brother, the Sieur de Rigaud, whose firm resolution he contrasted with Montcalm's lack of the same. Writing to de Moras on September 1, 1756, the Governor General stated: "If I had been less vigilant and had not sustained with firmness the orders that I had given, Chouaguen (Oswego) would still be in the keeping of the English. . . . I cannot praise

the fall of that year Montcalm was writing to the Minister of War, d'Argenson, of the "inexcusable duplicity" that Vaudreuil displayed in sending orders and dispatches so that blame would fall on Montcalm and de Lévis should affairs miscarry.[21] The following year — before the successful expedition against Fort William Henry — Montcalm, in communicating with the Minister of the Marine, de Moras, indicated that the Governor General was a man "with no character of his own, surrounded by men who seek to destroy all confidence that he might have in the general of the land forces. . . ." [22] Deeply convinced that Vaudreuil was bent on making him the scapegoat of any untoward military reverse that might take place, he also, in communicating his views of the orders given to him in January 1758 by Vaudreuil, replied on January 23 in a *mémoire* that bristled with suspicions of his superior and that pointed out to him how contradictory in nature were the instructions under which he was to operate, since one part of them could not be reconciled with other portions, and that as a whole they involved his own military reputation.[23] Thus when New France needed the greatest possible sense of unity, there existed a bitter rivalry, a personal animosity, between its highest executive and its most gifted general that boded no good for the future.

In vain did the president of the Navy Board write to one and to the other in an effort to heal the breach. He called upon Vaudreuil, in a letter dated February 14, 1758, to recognize that Montcalm had no less zeal for the service and no less talent than had de Lévis,[24] and on March 3 he appealed to Montcalm to consider that the present was "not the moment to appraise the qualities and talents of those who direct affairs. . . ." [25]

Yet despite the lack of accord in New France between its two powerful leaders, Frenchmen by and large must have felt as did Governor Thomas Pownall of Massachusetts Bay, who, in addressing Pitt at the beginning of 1758 regarding the failure of British measures in the New World, declared pessimistically:

---

too highly the great zeal that my brother, the Canadians, and the Indians showed on this occasion; without them my precautions and my orders would have resulted in a poor *démarche*" (*ibid.*).

[21] Montcalm to the Comte d'Argenson, November 1, 1756, *N. Y. Col. Doc.*, X, 491.

[22] Montcalm to de Moras, July 11, 1757, *ibid.*, X, 576.

[23] *Lettres et pièces militaires, 1756–1760*, pp. 29–32.

[24] *Canadian Archives Report* (1905), I, Part VI, 256.

[25] *Ibid.*, VI, 258.

". . . It will be seen that the loss of the Waters and Country of Ohio, The Loss of Oswego and the Naval Power of the Lakes, have entirely excluded the English from the Command in the Continent and all Power over the Indians and have confirmed the Dominion of America to the French." [26]

But let us now turn to the British plans for the prosecution of the war. Pitt at the end of the year's operations in 1757 could only, so far as the American scene was concerned, regard the aspect of things with unfeigned disgust. He had fully expected results; he had news only of the defeat of the British at Lake George, with the capture of Fort William Henry, and of the fiasco of the campaign against Cape Breton Island. Blame must fall somewhere and it fell upon the hapless head of the commander-in-chief, Lord Loudoun. In fact, it was reported that the Great Commoner came to feel that the principal reason that the latter did not make an assault upon Louisbourg was the dislike that the general had of the ministry as then constituted. [27] On December 15 at the meeting of Parliament, when the estimates for the following year came up, an effort on the part of Lord George Sackville to support Loudoun brought Pitt to his feet, and in a long speech — as reported by William Cotterell, secretary for Nova Scotia, in a letter addressed to the commander-in-chief — he

---

[26] *Correspondence of William Pitt* (ed. G. S. Kimball), I, 162.

[27] William Cotterell to Loudoun, December 8, 1757, Loudoun Papers, No. 4970. Captain Cotterell, secretary of the Nova Scotia Council, went to England after Loudoun had given up the attempt on Louisbourg, not only to recover his health but to explain the situation that made an assault upon that stronghold too hazardous under the circumstances. A man of ability and tact, he got in touch with the various leaders in the administration and sought to convince them that Loudoun's conduct was sound and for the best interest of the cause in hand (see his letter to Loudoun of September 8, 1757, *ibid.*, No. 4424, giving the substance of his interviews with Pitt, Newcastle, Holderness, Granville, Anson, Barrington, and Fox, most of whom he found inclined to be very critical of the general, although Fox approved strongly of his conduct). Loudoun's London agent, John Calcraft, summarizes the complaints against the general in a letter to him dated December 29, 1757 (*ibid.*, No. 5140). Loudoun was, in general, accused of failure not only to correspond frequently with the ministers but to send any plan for the next year's operations, and also of inactivity at the close of the Louisbourg campaign. The real causes for the demand for his recall, however, in so far as Calcraft could gather them from Fox and others, was that Pitt had been led to commit himself in his speech in Parliament and that Sir Charles Hardy, Governor of New York and naval commander, who was then in England, had spoken critically of "American matters," particularly regarding Loudoun's alleged preference for relying upon military rather than civil power to secure his ends; his failure to explore sufficiently the country and to carry out winter campaigns; his lack of consideration for the provincial troops; his slighting of colonial governors; and, finally, his responsibility for leaving General Webb too weak (*ibid.*).

"Abused both Land & Sea Officers Exceedingly, Yo^r Lordship by name he Taxed with Inactivity, tho' Your Force was greatly Superior to the enemys. . . . Said he had no hopes for this year nor cou'd have none from the next whilst the American Affairs Continued in the hands they were . . . that he cou'd Prove you had done wrong. . . ." [28]

Loudoun was doomed. In a very crisp letter dated December 30 Pitt recalled him to England and in so doing informed him that he was to turn over his command to Major General Abercromby.[29] The same day he wrote to the latter notifying him of his appointment to the supreme command of all the King's forces in North America.[30] Letters were also sent to all the governors of the continental colonies. In these the Minister called upon them to aid in all ways the considerable squadron that he would send to the New World in the spring. In other letters directed to the northern colonies he called upon them to raise within New England, New York, and New Jersey a total of at least twenty thousand men "to join a Body of The King's Forces for Invading Canada, by the Way of Crown Point, and carrying War into the Heart of the Enemy's Possessions. . . ." [31] In still other letters to all the southern colonies but Georgia he called upon them to furnish in all:

"a body of several Thousand Men to join the King's Forces in those parts for offensive Operations against the Enemy; and . . . toward

---

[28] Letter of December 16, 1757, ibid., No. 5025. Horace Walpole in his *Memoirs* declared of this speech by Pitt that he loaded Loudoun "with all the asperity peculiar to his style . . . not only nothing was done — nothing was attempted" (op. cit., III, 89).

A private letter written in London on December 20 and printed in part in the *Pennsylvania Gazette* of March 16, 1758 shows that Pitt lashed out in all directions in his speech, which was much approved by the public. It is of sufficient interest to include here some part of it. The author stated that "All this Kingdom and City are in Raptures at a Speech lately made by Mr. P— against the Officers of the Navy and Land Forces . . . wherein he sets forth their non-attendance in their different stations, their great Neglect of Duty . . . their false Musters, to the great Loss of his Majesty's Honour and the Service of the Nation that paid them; their Want of Application to Geography, the different Arts of War and Military Discipline; their Insolence to their inferior Officers, and Tyranny over the common Men; that the Nation was taxed beyond Measure to support them in their Extravagance, Idleness, and Luxury, whilst large Arrears are due to the most useful Sett of Men, and Bulwark of the English Nation, the common Sailors. . . . In short, it was the finest Oration that ever was made in an English Senate. . . ."

[29] *Pitt Correspondence*, I, 133-4.

[30] *Ibid.*, I, 134-5.

[31] *Ibid.*, I, 135-43.

removing & repelling the Dangers, that threaten the Frontiers of any
of the Southern Colonies on the Continent of America. . . ." [32]

In making these requests of the British colonials in order "to avert
. . . the Dangers impending in North America," he promised not
only to provide all those brought into the service with arms, ammunition, tents, and provisions at the expense of the King, but to
make strong recommendations to Parliament that all other expenses
that would fall on the individual colony in the way of levying,
clothing, and paying the enlisted men, should be properly compen-
sated "according as the active vigour and strenuous efforts of the respective Provinces shall justly appear to merit." [33]

Pitt was determined, it is clear, to make an unprecedented effort
for the year 1758 and by this to redeem the reputation of the army
and navy. Not only was he prepared to urge the granting of great
subsidies to Prussia, Hanover, and Hesse-Cassel for the war in
Europe, as has already been noted, but he asked Parliament to
provide supplies for sixty thousand British seamen and marines and
for over fifty thousand effective land forces — which meant the
appropriation of millions of pounds. [34]

In writing to Abercromby at the same time that he sent him
notification of his appointment, Pitt made clear that His Majesty had
nothing more at heart than "to repair the Losses & Disappointments
of the last inactive and unhappy Campaign" in North America. To
that end he informed him that most of the regiments of regulars
in the New World had been allotted to the siege of Louisbourg and
that more would be sent to join in that task, which he stated was
scheduled to begin as early as next April, should the season permit,
under an officer to be appointed under the King's particular commission. With respect to the specific responsibilities resting on the new
commander-in-chief, Abercromby was notified that without delay
he was to concert all necessary measures for the early invasion of
Canada by way of Crown Point, should this prove practicable, so
that an attempt against either Montreal or Quebec could be made in
the course of the campaign. Among these preliminary measures,
one of the most important was the construction on Lake George of
a sufficient number of boats, vessels, and other craft to restore to
Great Britain the control of that body of water and thereby facili-

[32] *Ibid.*
[33] *Ibid.*
[34] *Annual Register,* 1758, p. 127.

tate the movement, first of all, against Ticonderoga. Abercromby was also called upon to appoint Brigadier General Forbes to take charge of military operations in the southern provinces and to do all things that were necessary to promote the success of these three distinct enterprises.[35]

But while Abercromby held the title of commander-in-chief of all British forces in North America, it is clear that his chief function was not to plan the strategy of the campaign for the following year, or to give orders to the commanders of either the Louisbourg or the Fort Duquesne expedition, or even to determine the allocation of the available forces for the three enterprises to be set on foot, but simply to obey orders that the ministry would send to him from time to time, and in particular to concentrate his chief energies upon the Lake George and Lake Champlain campaign after the requirements of the other commanders had been fulfilled, according to these same orders. In fact, on the same day that the general received his two commissions for the execution of his office,[36] there came in the same packet Pitt's instructions for the disposition of the British regiments in America and also of the forces to be raised there in the respective colonies. According to these instructions, thirteen of the regiments on the royal establishment, together with recruits for them — amounting in all to over 14,000 men, not including 600 American rangers, but including the two regiments to be sent — and the great artillery train provided the preceding year for the enterprise, were allotted to the Louisbourg expedition; nine regiments with recruits and the Independents of New York, totalling about 9,500 regulars, together with the 20,000 provincials to be raised, were designated to be employed for "an Irruption into Canada"; finally, two regiments, including Montgomery's Highlanders, a battalion of the Royal Americans, and the South Carolina Independents, to which were to be added 5,000 southern provincials when recruited, were to make the drive on Fort Duquesne.[37]

Since Pitt thus contemplated the employment of over twenty-five thousand provincials, it was important in his eyes that they be rendered as effective as possible. This the Minister sought to guarantee by the new regulations, already mentioned, whereby these troops

[35] *Pitt Correspondence*, I, 143–51. See also Pitt's "Instructions" to Abercromby dated December 30, 1757, Abercromby Papers, No. 7, Huntington Library.

[36] These were dated December 28 and 29, 1757, respectively.

[37] "Disposition of the Forces in North America," by Pitt, Abercromby Papers, No. 851.

would be armed, provisioned, and sheltered in the same manner as
the regulars, all at the expense of the mother country, and also by
another regulation whereby their officers would now enjoy a new
status when serving with those on the royal establishment. Under a
warrant for settling their rank, which was dated December 30, 1757,
it was provided that for the future all general officers and colonels
serving under provincial commissions should on all detachments,
courts-martial, or other duty take rank next after all colonels with
royal commissions; and that all officers under the rank of colonel
should have rank next after those of similar rank enjoying either
the King's commission or that of the commander-in-chief of the
British forces in North America.[38] How significant this new arrangement was in the eyes of the provincial officers need only be illustrated by citing the cases of Major General John Winslow of Massachusetts Bay and his officers acting in the northern area in 1756, who
refused to serve under Loudoun when their commissions were not
honoured, and of Colonel George Washington in the southern area
in 1755, who likewise refused to accept commands from Captain
Dagworthy at Fort Cumberland.[39] The problem, however, when
thinking in terms of the most efficient military service, was not, it
must be pointed out, a simple one to resolve, and the new regulation, so favourable to provincial officers, carried implications that
were not in all respects in harmony with this conception. As a rule,
a man in the regular service spent many years in various subordinate
ranks while learning the art of warfare by campaigning and in the
ordeal of battle before attaining the rank of colonel, not to speak
of that of a field officer. On the other hand, it was necessary, under
the circumstances, when raising colonial forces, to place them under
men who, as a rule, previous to the granting of their commissions,
had been engaged in private pursuits and who therefore had had

---

[38] "Warrant for Settling the Rank of Provincial Officers," *ibid.*, No. 8.

[39] At the beginning of the war in the New World the King had issued a warrant,
dated November 12, 1754, providing that all troops serving under royal commission
"shall take Rank before all Troops, which may serve by Commission from any of the
Governors," and that "General and Field Officers of the Provincial Troops should have
no Rank with the General and Field Officers, who serve by Commission from Us." On
May 12, 1756 another warrant was issued that made some concessions to provincial officers in that it declared that all such general and field officers should take rank only as
"Eldest Captains" on all detachments, courts-martial, and other duties when serving
with those on the royal establishment (*ibid.*). Under the order of December 30, 1757
it was made clear that the earlier date of the commission of a provincial officer would
not permit him to outrank a regular officer who had the same rank.

little or no experience with actual combat service. Yet these men would now under the new regulation, if of superior rank, have the command of veteran officers and their contingents when acting together. This did not make for harmony or for an effective service. However, in the case of such seasoned and capable soldiers as, for example, Colonel Washington of the Virginia regiment, Colonels Armstrong and Burd of the Pennsylvania line, and Major General Phineas Lyman and Colonel Whiting of the Connecticut troops, men now well experienced in frontier fighting and of high capabilities, the recognition of their rank was most fitting. Nevertheless, it may be pointed out that in the actual application of the regulation, when provincials were joined with regulars in large numbers in a common enterprise, they were almost without exception under the superior command of a regular field officer,[40] who made it a rule to employ his more seasoned, battle-hardened regulars to spearhead assaults on difficult positions, especially those involving willingness to advance in the open under heavy enemy fire. In fact, for the most part the provincials, outside of the rangers, were destined to be used during the remainder of the war, when acting with regulars, not so much as front-line combat troops but as reserves in battle and for the construction of roads, the building of forts, boats, and vessels, and for the work of transport. In such employments they made a particularly important contribution to the winning of the war in North America.[41]

In turning now to a consideration of the year's operation in North America, it would be well to take up in sequence the attack on Louisbourg, then the movement against Ticonderoga, the destruction of Frontenac, and, finally, the expedition against Fort Duquesne. As a result of three of these four operations, and in spite of the disastrous outcome of one of them, French power in North America was dealt a shattering blow from which it never was able to recover.

---

[40] Two exceptions involving Major General Lyman and Colonel Sir William Johnson will be noted in the progress of this narrative.

[41] Dr. Pargellis deals with this point in his *Lord Loudoun in North America* (pp. 354–5). He also calls into question the wisdom of Pitt, with so large a force of regular troops in America, in relying at all on colonial levies. The cost of these contingents, when it came to the reimbursement of expenses of the colonies by Parliament, was very great in view of the "exorbitant pay and the high bounty of eight pounds sterling a man which many assemblies offered"; moreover, they were not only inexperienced as a group in warfare but so slow in assembling for the year's campaign as very seriously to impede the progress of military operations (*ibid.*).

In maturing his plan for the conquest of Isle Royale or Cape Breton Island, Pitt, by the fall of 1757, had come to realize the vital importance of having in North America not only an army but also a fleet ready to move against any assigned objective at the earliest possible moment with the coming of the thaw and weather suitable for large operations. He therefore reversed the instructions given to Rear Admiral Holburne that had been drawn up in February of that year and also those of July 7 and 18,[42] all three of which contemplated the return of the fleet to England with the close of the campaign. Now he ordered at least eight of the ships of the line in the best condition to remain during the winter at Halifax under the command of Sir Charles Hardy [43] — much to the displeasure, it may be mentioned in passing, of the sea officers, who had an intense dislike of the place and who naturally preferred to rest in their homes in England.

Three days after this letter was written, Holburne's fleet in the New World was battered in a very heavy storm while cruising in the neighbourhood of Cape Breton Island, with the result that a number of the ships were so damaged as to impel him to send them directly home under escort of Hardy in the *Windsor*.[44] He himself, with eight ships of the line, returned to Halifax and by the middle of the next month had them in seaworthy condition and soon after this received Pitt's September orders. As Hardy, however, had gone to England, he named Lord Colville, senior captain, to command the eight best ships of the line that were to winter in Nova Scotia,[45] and, after being assured that the French fleet at Louisbourg had at length sailed for France, returned in November to England in the least serviceable of the line-of-battle ships resting in Halifax harbour, the *Newark*.[46] He was not to reappear again in the New

---

[42] The clauses in these instructions that relate to the particular point under discussion are given by Pitt in his letter to Holburne of September 21, 1757 (*Pitt Correspondence*, I, 110–11).

[43] *Ibid.*

[44] See his letters to Pitt dated September 29 and 30, 1757, *ibid.*, I, 114–16. Hardy in his "State of the Squadron," dated September 28, 1758, indicated that of twenty ships in the fleet of from fifty-four to eighty guns only nine escaped without serious injury and one, the *Tilbury*, a sixty-gun ship, was wrecked on the coast of Cape Breton Island (Loudoun Papers, No. 4540).

[45] Holburne to Pitt, November 4, 1757, *Pitt Correspondence*, I, 125.

[46] De la Motte left Louisbourg with most of the ships on October 30; three others departed the next day ("Journal" of Barbier of the *Formidable* and "Journal" of the *Inflexible* (*Canadian Archives Report* [1905], Part VII, 12, and Part VIII, 8). Holburne, writing to Loudoun on November 10, indicated that he would in a day or two

World, and it was just as well, since before leaving it he had become thoroughly convinced that the assault on Louisbourg was impracticable by armed forces.[47] Nor was he favourable to the idea of leaving so many capital ships in the New World as he was commanded by Pitt to leave.[48]

The Minister had already decided to place Vice Admiral Boscawen in charge of the fleet that would operate in North American waters in the coming campaign; but not until early in the new year did he reach a decision as to who would command the expeditionary force against Louisbourg. He had determined, however, to send over James Wolfe — who had acquitted himself with great credit on the expedition against Rochefort — with the rank of brigadier general and to confer the same rank on Edward Whitmore [49] and also on

---

return to England with only the Newark, now being assured that the French fleet had left (Loudoun Papers, No. 4801).

[47] Holburne's letter of November 8 from Halifax to John Forbes of the 17th regiment, who was on Loudoun's staff, is so very revealing of his low opinion of Pitt's strategy that it may be given in part. He declared, evidently in low spirits, that "we want a cup of comfort, but I don't desire to see your faces this way again; act in your own spheres upon the land, & we chance them by sea; block up the river St. Lawrence & the Mississippi which our ships at Jamaica might do; don't come & leave the Continent Exposed to be ravag'd by the enemy" (Loudoun Papers, No. 4785).

[48] Holburne thought that Loudoun was the source of Pitt's order. In his letter to Forbes he declared: "I fancy his Lordship has had some hand in so many ships being left here [Halifax], but he may be assured they might [have] been just as soon from England cleaned & refitted & man'd, for I have not got a man since we arrived, but many lost both by death & desertion; & how are they [the ships] to do their duty in the spring?" (ibid.). Governor Lawrence of Nova Scotia, doubtless fully aware of Holburne's views, on November 12 wrote to the Earl of Halifax saying that the order for the ships to winter at Halifax, he perceived, was looked upon as "neither agreeable or useful." He thereupon set to work to refute the arguments advanced against this, particularly those having to do with the refitting of the ships before taking to sea in the early spring. To prove that this could be done more advantageously for the service at Halifax than in England he illustrated his point by making clear that, on the one hand, with all his efforts Holburne did not arrive in Halifax from England until July 9, while, on the other hand, Captain Marshall, who was at Halifax during the preceding winter, got his ship the Nottingham rigged and fitted for sea by the end of March (Chatham Mss., Vol. XCVIII, Canadian Archives Transcripts). Sir Charles Hardy, who was second in command of the fleet in American waters, likewise shared the views of Holburne regarding the inadvisability of keeping ships of war in the New World. On December 14, at the request of Halifax, he framed his "Proposals" for the next year's campaign against Louisbourg, which were presented to Pitt. These embodied the idea that the fleet for that operation should sail from Europe "as early as possible" and should be on the coast of Cape Breton before the French fleet could reach the island (ibid., Vol. XCV).

[49] As to Whitmore, Wolfe, writing to Lord George Sackville on February 7, 1758, soon after the promotions were made, says: "Barre, who knows Whitmore better than anybody, assures me that he has no health nor constitution for such business as we are

Charles Lawrence, Governor of Nova Scotia and a person possessed of great knowledge of Cape Breton Island. His choice of a commanding officer now fell upon Colonel Jeffery Amherst.

Amherst, forty-one years of age, had already spent twenty-three of these in the service; he had fought in Flanders, was at Dettingen and at Fontenoy, and then in Scotland on the staff of Ligonier in the War of the Austrian Succession.[50] With the outbreak of the Seven Years' War in Europe he was ordered to take over the commissariat for the Hessian troops; after this he served as quartermaster under the Duke of Cumberland in the Army of Observation and was present at the signing of the Convention of Kloster-Seven. A capable, steady soldier, he had done little, however, to distinguish himself and had never held an independent command. He had nevertheless impressed his qualities both upon the powerful Sackville family, a Kentish family as were the Amhersts, and on General Ligonier, who had been made a viscount in 1757 and, what is more, by Pitt's desire elevated to the rank of commander-in-chief of the British forces at home.[51] It may therefore be assumed that either Pitt or the King had had his attention directed by these admirers to this highly efficient soldier, who though of low rank, it is true, yet knew how to get along with other people, could obey orders with exactness, and was experienced in staff work, and whose loyalty to the Minister could not be called in question.[52] Holderness was there-

going upon; he never was a soldier, but otherwise, a very worthy gentleman" (Beckles Willson: Life and Letters of James Wolfe, p. 358).

[50] See John C. Long, Lord Jeffery Amherst, Chapter II, and the Journal of Jeffery Amherst (ed. J. Clarence Webster), "Introduction," pp. 1–6.

[51] Writing to Amherst on January 4, 1757, Sir George Sackville expressed the fear that Amherst "will be sorry to be sent for to England . . . but such is the want of officers among us that the King has very unwillingly consented to your being employed abroad in a Command of much expectation, and in which nobody is thought [as] likely to succeed as you are." He also referred in this letter to the "general approbation" of his conduct of affairs in Germany on the part of both the Hessians and the Hanoverians (Amherst Private Papers, Packet 2, Letter 3, Canadian Archives Transcripts). Ligonier, a naturalized Frenchman who fought under Marlborough against the French, writing to Amherst at about the same time, says: "You are Going to Jouir un Grand Role and if Proper Measures Signifie any thing In all appearance it will be a Glorious one to you, and of Great Advantage to this country; the Voice of the nation calls you to it, and it must be So" (ibid., Packet 2, Letter 2).

[52] Lieutenant Colonel James Murray, who was not an easy person to get along with, shows his high esteem of Amherst in writing to him on January 27, 1758. In this letter he expressed his "joy" in having part in an enterprise conducted by Amherst (ibid., Packet 2, folio 4).

fore ordered to recall him to England.[53] Upon his arrival there the latter part of February — delayed by the winter season in the Elbe — he was soon afterward commissioned "Major General of Our Forces in North America, and Commander-in-Chief of a Body of Our Land Forces, to be employed in the Siege of Louisbourg, and on other Services . . . "[54] and thereupon was given certain instructions as to the manner of carrying out the service that he had been called upon to perform.[55] As an amphibious operation, the attack upon Louisbourg, as well as subsequent movements of the combined land and naval forces, demanded the closest co-ordination of the two branches of the service, and this was especially stressed not only in these orders but in those earlier given to Boscawen.[56]

Pitt was determined that this year there should be no delay in beginning operations against Cape Breton Island. Indeed, the latter part of January Sir Charles Hardy sailed for Halifax in order to take charge of the preliminary work of sealing up the harbour of Louisbourg before the French fleet could get in. He arrived in Nova Scotia on March 19 in a ship of the line, the *Royal William*, accompanied by two frigates.[57] American newspapers not only noted Hardy's arrival and that he, with the use of the fleet that had wintered there, would begin cruising off the coast of Cape Breton,[58] but also published to all the world that Admiral Boscawen would sail early in March from Ireland with twelve ships of the line, fourteen frigates, and transports holding eight thousand troops, for the immediate investment of the French island stronghold.[59] News writers in London, moreover, boldly proclaimed in January that

---

[53] The Holderness letter reached him at Stade on January 14, 1758, but it was not until February 20 that the ship, icebound in the Elbe, was able to sail (*Journal*, pp. 29, 32). He reached London six days later.

[54] His commission was dated March 2, 1758.

[55] His instructions, dated March 3, are among the Chatham Manuscripts in the Public Record Office, Bundle 96 (Canadian Archives Transcripts).

[56] For Boscawen's instructions of January 27, 1758, which are very similar to those given to Amherst, see *ibid.*, Bundle 78, No. 8.

[57] Hardy to Pitt, March 22, 1758, *Pitt Correspondence*, I, 212; the *Pennsylvania Gazette*, April 6 and 13, 1758.

[58] It may be pointed out that Lord Colville, in charge of the ships that wintered at Halifax, had them all ready for service by the time that Hardy arrived; in fact, as early as March 17 the *Sutherland* was sent out to cruise off Louisbourg harbour (Colville to Pitt, March 20, 1758, *Pitt Correspondence*, I, 211).

[59] *Pennsylvania Gazette*, April 6, 1758. The number of troops, however, was actually only some twenty-five hundred.

twelve regiments of foot [60] were to be embarked as early as February 20 and that the fleet sailing for North America in the spring was expected "to be greatest, best mann'd, and otherwise the best equipp'd of any Fleet that sail'd from England since the last Dutch War.[61]

Boscawen, in fact, sailed for the New World on February 19 [62] with ten ships of the line and a number of frigates, but no transports, which had gone ahead under convoy carrying two regiments and military stores. With the admiral were also Wolfe and Whitmore. The latter carried instructions from Pitt to the effect that as soon as eight thousand of the soldiers designated for the Cape Breton expedition had arrived at Halifax from the mainland, he should immediately — without awaiting the arrival of Amherst — put them on board ship, together with the artillery train and supplies designed for the Cape Breton Island operations. These troops, it was stated, should be under the direct command of Brigadier General Lawrence and should be disembarked at a place considered most favourable by the latter and Boscawen. Once the landing had been effected they should proceed to Gabarus Bay — were they to go ashore elsewhere — to secure that vital approach to Louisbourg; whereupon the artillery and stores were to be landed there for the beginning of the siege.[63]

It was not until May 9 that Boscawen and Wolfe entered Halifax harbour, after eleven weeks in passage. In the words of Wolfe: "The continual opposition of contrary winds, calms, or currents baffled all our skill and wore out all our patience." [64] He might have added that, always a bad sailor, he was terribly seasick most of the time. Already there had assembled at the place most of the regiments; and Whitmore, who had gone directly to New York for the purpose of bringing up the artillery and troops from that place and from Boston, was hourly expected.[65]

---

[60] This was mere propaganda to mislead the enemy.

[61] *Pennsylvania Gazette*, April 27, 1758.

[62] *Annual Register*, 1758, p. 83.

[63] A copy of these instructions, under date of January 27, 1758, are among the Abercromby Papers, No. 20. According to these orders, Whitmore was to remain in Halifax in charge of that place. Wolfe, the third brigadier general, curiously enough, was not mentioned in them. He, of course, was much younger than either of the other men of the same rank.

[64] Wolfe to Sackville, May 12, 1758, Beckles Willson, *op. cit.*, p. 363.

[65] H.M.S. *Devonshire* brought the transports from England to New York to embark the regiments waiting there (Abercromby to Pownall, April 16, 1758, Abercromby

Meanwhile, since early in April Hardy had been patrolling the entrance of Louisbourg, in spite of fogs and storms; in fact, he had been obliged to face "the severest weather imaginable," and for the safety of his ships was compelled at times to veer away from the coast out into deep water. This gave an opportunity for a small enemy squadron of five ships of the line and three frigates to slip into the harbour.[66] However, French vessels carrying military stores and provisions were for the most part, it appears, picked up by the British fleet.[67]

By May 24 everything was in preparation for the departure of the fleet and transports for Louisbourg, with strict orders already issued to the troops [68] and with a plan of strategy adopted that was clearly based upon Brigadier General Lawrence's proposals as outlined the previous year at Loudoun's council of war.[69] This involved the initial landing of forces at Miré Bay, some distance to the north of Louisbourg; thereupon the troops, supported by those who would deliver attacks immediately to the south of Miré, would advance through the woods over a road leading southward to Gabarus, where another small force for the sake of diversion would seek to land. This main operation, it was agreed, should be in charge of Wolfe, while Monckton was to support him by attacking Lorembec (L'Orembeck) — somewhat south of Miré — with Lawrence remaining off the Gabarus Bay area in general command, as provided for

Papers, No. 167). Lawrence, meanwhile, had embarked the troops that gathered at Boston and was ready to sail for Halifax by April 17 (Lawrence to Abercromby, April 17, 1758, ibid., No. 172). On May 18 Boscawen wrote from Halifax to Abercromby that all the troops but four companies from Anstruther's and Monckton's regiments and Bragg's regiment from the Bay of Fundy had arrived (ibid., No. 264). It may be noted that the troops were all landed at Halifax and put through the same sort of commando exercises — simulated "bush fighting after the Indian manner, making fascines, raising redoubts, attacking, defending them etc" — as were the troops at Halifax the preceding year, for which much scorn was poured upon Loudoun's head by his critics ("Ensign James Miller's Memoir," Amherst Private Papers, Packet 54, pp. 18–19).

[66] Letter written from Quebec to Montreal, May 19, "Intelligence," Chatham Mss., Bundle 96 (Canadian Archives Transcripts).

[67] Wolfe to Sackville, May 12, 1758, and Wolfe to General Wolfe, his father, May 20, 1758, Beckles Willson, op. cit., pp. 364–5.

[68] For Lawrence's orders to the troops see the Abercromby Papers, No. 303; see also Lawrence to Pitt, May 23, 1758, Pitt Correspondence, I, 256–7.

[69] J. S. Corbett (England in the Seven Years' War, I, 318–19) gives Wolfe credit for this plan. But Lawrence, who knew the region, as Wolfe did not, had strongly insisted, when he appeared before the council of war held in 1757 between July 23 and 31, that the landing should be made at Miré, not at Gabarus Bay (Loudoun Papers, No. 3984).

by the instructions Pitt had given to Whitmore.[70] Four days later, with the wind, which had been very adverse for a week, now favourable, the ships moved out from Halifax and were proceeding on their way when the new commander-in-chief arrived after a tedious voyage of over nine weeks.

Amherst had been able to leave England on Rodney's H.M.S. *Dublin* on March 16. But the trip across was delayed by many incidents, among which was the capture by Rodney of a great French East India ship off the coast of Spain, and by the difficult navigation through the fogs to the New World — all to the deep distress of the general.[71] But now the fog had lifted and the *Dublin* joined the armada of one hundred and fifty-seven ships and transports headed for Louisbourg.[72]

The fate of that great stronghold, it may be said, was largely sealed on the coast of France and in the Mediterranean during the preceding winter and the spring. When de la Motte returned from Cape Breton with his fleet and anchored at Brest, his ships were veritable death-traps. Two thousand of his sailors had perished during the passage, more than half of the rest, some twenty-four hundred, were in the grip of ship fever, and the remainder were overcome with fatigue.[73] The landing of the sick had the effect of turning that seaport into a vast charnel house. It was reported that ten thousand of those congregated there perished of the plague before it ran its course, and all operations looking to the next season's campaign were thereby suspended. De la Motte, moreover,[74] who on each of his two voyages to the New World had blasted the hopes of the English, was now made to feel the weight of royal censure. He was criticized, it was asserted, for not recapturing all of old Acadia — since he arrived at Cape Breton Island long in advance of the movement to Halifax of the British fleet and the transports

---

[70] Wolfe to Sackville, May 24, 1758, Willson, *op. cit.*, p. 366.

[71] Amherst's "Journal," *op. cit.*, pp. 33–46.

[72] On the day that Amherst joined the fleet and transports he wrote to Abercromby informing him that he was sending Colonel Monckton back to Halifax to guard Nova Scotia. This letter shows how independent a command he had in that he assured the commander-in-chief that he would "take every opportunity" to acquaint him with the progress of events off Cape Breton, and "I shall be glad at all times to assure you that I am, Sir, Yours . . ." (Amherst to Abercromby, May 28, 1758, Abercromby Papers, No. 290).

[73] "Journal" of the *Inflexible* (*Canadian Archives Report* [1905], I, Part VIII, 9).

[74] "Recueil des Nouvelles de france," 1758, "Intelligence," Chatham Mss., Bundle 96 (Canadian Archives Transcripts).

carrying the regiments intended for the conquest of Louisbourg [75] — and also for not destroying Holburne's fleet when the opportunity presented itself; and he was, as a result, placed in disgrace. [76] Such was the unhappy termination of the French expedition to the New World in 1757.

The French Minister, nevertheless, determined to send out a third powerful fleet in the fourth year of the war as early in 1758 as was possible. This fleet, it was also planned, would convoy ships with two additional battalions, as well as ample supplies, so as to assure the protection of Cape Breton Island. [77] But now the British squadrons operating off the coast of France and guarding the entrance to the Mediterranean were far more successful than in previous years in making abortive the arrangements of the enemy.

In May 1757 Henry Osborne (Osborn), Admiral of the Blue, had been sent into the Mediterranean as commander-in-chief of the naval forces there, superseding in that position Rear Admiral Charles Saunders, already stationed there, who had been unable to prevent du Revest earlier in the year from moving his fleet out of the Mediterranean and to the New World. In December Osborne received intelligence that the French Admiral de la Clue was planning to leave Toulon for Louisbourg with a squadron and a reinforcement of foot soldiers. He therefore moved into the straits athwart the path of the enemy, with the result that de la Clue sought refuge for his ships in the neutral Spanish port of Cartagena. Early in February, while the British fleet was cruising slightly west of the straits, news reached it that the French admiral had been strengthened by the arrival of two more ships of the line from Toulon, which now gave him eight line-of-battle ships; but even so he did not stir from Cartagena to challenge the British squadron. In fact, he was waiting for the arrival of Admiral Duquesne with three more ships of the line, including the mighty *Foudroyant,* from the same port. With this power at his disposal he would at last be in position to sweep aside all opposition.

When Osborne received intelligence of this move on the part of

---

[75] "Intelligence from Brest," November 7, 1757, Chatham Mss., Bundle 87 (Canadian Archives Transcripts).

[76] "Intelligence from France," *ibid.,* Bundle 96.

[77] President of the Navy Board to Vaudreuil and Bigot, February 10, 1758; the same to Bigot, of the same date; the same to Drucour and Prévost, January 14, February 14, March 11, 1758, *ibid., Canadian Archives Report* (1905), I, Part VI, 255-6, 263-4.

Duquesne [78] by means of his cruisers and from the British consul at Cartagena, he and Saunders determined to prevent a union of the French squadrons by taking the entire force of fourteen ships, large and small, into the Mediterranean. Before their arrival on the 28th Duquesne appeared in the neighbourhood of Cartagena and signalled de la Clue to come out. The latter did not respond, nor could Duquesne enter, on account of the strong westerly that was blowing, until the English fleet arrived — swept forward by the same wind — and separated him from de la Clue. [79] Although the breeze was also favourable for the latter to come out and challenge the British, the French admiral was apparently under orders to avoid a combat at home in order to save his strength for the New World — at least he remained securely in the Cartagena harbour while the British turned furiously upon Duquesne's squadron. [80] The latter immediately separated and fled. Osborne, after detailing ships for the pursuit, settled down near Cartagena with the remainder of the fleet to watch de la Clue.

There were old scores to settle. Saunders had been roughly handled the preceding year by du Revest before the latter broke out of the Mediterranean to move across the Atlantic; and then in 1756 there had been the crowning humiliation of Byng's battle off Minorca. Captain Storr in the *Revenge*, supported by two other ships,

---

[78] A British secret agent at Toulon on February 3 sent out information that the *Foudroyant* was ready to sail and would leave in a day or two for Cartagena to join de la Clue, who would then have eleven ships of the line and three frigates. The informer, however, was mistaken when he said that de la Clue, after passing through the straits, would head for St. Domingue and that Duquesne would sail for Louisbourg ("Advices from France," Chatham Mss., Bundle 87, Canadian Archives Transcripts).

[79] Corbett (*op. cit.*, I, 258) indicates that there was simply at issue between de la Clue and Duquesne a question of precedence, which determined the failure of the latter to enter Cartagena. According to a dispatch from Marseille of March 4 printed in the *Amsterdam Gazette*, "M. du Quesne beat about for three Days before Carthagena, without being able to get into the Harbour" (*Pennsylvania Gazette*, May 25, 1758).

[80] I have not been able to find de la Clue's instructions. The instructions of French admirals bound for the New World, however, seem to have without exception been framed with the idea of avoiding all sea fights in European waters if this could be done without dishonour to the navy. Yet the public was not aware of this, as the following indicates: "M. de la Clue's Conduct is now the common Topic of Conversation in France, and they say, in some Measure, is similar to that of the late Admiral Byng; for de la Clue had the Wind direct from off the Shore to carry him out, for which he is inexcusable, as he saw du Quesne's Signals for joining him; instead of which, de la Clue returned Signals for him to bring his small Squadron into the Harbour, which was a Thing impossible, considering the Wind, and the [later] Situation of the English Fleet; for which they say he will be called to Account" (London Advices, *ibid.*, June 1, 1758).

started after the *Orphée;* by seven o'clock in the evening the French ship, after a bloody running fight, surrendered. Captain Rowley in the *Montague* and Captain Montagu in the *Monarch* drove the *Oriflamme* onto the Spanish shore and there left the ship to avoid breach of neutrality. Captain Gardiner of the *Monmouth,* a sixty-four, made after the *Foudroyant,* "the pride of the whole French navy," an eighty-gun ship that in 1756 had been de la Galissoniere's flagship, when Gardiner had acted as captain of Byng's flagship, the *Ramillies.* This was the rendezvous he now sought above all other things in life in order to wipe out what was felt to be a great personal disgrace as well as one for the British navy.[81] His ship, the fastest in the fleet, gained gradually on its powerful opponent. Before the engagement began, Gardiner summoned his sailors and declared, while they cheered him: "This ship must be taken; she looks to be above our match; but Englishmen are not to mind that, nor will I quit her while this ship can swim, or I have a soul left alive." [82]

At five o'clock he was near enough to open fire and was wounded in the first exchange; at seven o'clock he had closed within pistol-shot to a death-grapple; two hours later he fell mortally wounded, but lived long enough to exact a promise from his next in command never to give up the ship; whereupon the lieutenant, it is related, nailed the flag to the staff and stood by it with a brace of pistols, declaring that "he would put any man to death who attempted to come near the colours to strike them." [83] Soon afterward, in the fury of the battle, the mizzenmast of the *Monmouth* was shot away; then that of the *Foudroyant* followed, and after that its mainmast toppled. With the appearance of two other British ships of the line, Duquesne now hauled down his flag and became a British prisoner of war, and the great French battleship consequently exchanged hands to become "the terror of the French and the pride of England." [84]

---

[81] A letter written from Gibraltar on March 28, 1758 by an unknown officer on board the privateer *Volunteer* refers to the return to this port of both the *Monmouth,* bringing with it the *Foudroyant,* and the *Revenge,* bringing with it the *Orphée.* The writer says that Captain Gardiner before he departed on his mission confessed to certain friends "with great anguish of soul . . . that my Lord A[nson] had reflected on him and told him that he was one of the men who had brought disgrace upon the nation" (John Entick: *The General History of the Late War,* III, 58–9).

[82] *Ibid.*

[83] *Ibid.*

[84] *Ibid.* The *Monmouth* was manifestly no match for the *Foudroyant* under normal

As the result of this engagement de la Clue clung to his refuge at Cartagena for a month — not daring to risk the attempt to break through the straits and thereby get to Louisbourg — and then returned to Toulon and dismantled his fleet. But the French ministry was not daunted by this check, and early in March the president of the Navy Board wrote to Drucour and Prévost at Louisbourg that orders had been given for a division of the King's vessels commanded by Beaussier de l'Isle to leave Brest for that stronghold "at the earliest possible time," with the added warning that on "the issue of this campaign that of the War principally depends." [85] Hawke, who left Spithead with seven ships of the line on March 12 for the Bay of Biscay, felt that the principal concentration of enemy ships for the New World would be at Rochefort and proceeded to Basque Roads to cover that place and La Rochelle. On April 3 he saw a large fleet within the roads — some forty transports and store ships containing troops and provisions, which were escorted by seven ships of the line and seven frigates — and he headed toward them. To save this flotilla the French drove the vessels ashore and then, in order to float them again, were obliged to throw overboard not only guns but the provisions and other matériel collected for the aid of Louisbourg. [86]

While this was being accomplished, however, to the north at Brest Chef d'Escadre des Gouttes slipped out in the Prudent, his flagship, [87] and he was soon followed by Captain Beaussier with four

line-of-battle conditions and under these would undoubtedly have been quickly sunk by the latter in any exchange of broadsides. The British ship's sixty-four guns were made up of twenty-four-pounders and twelve-pounders and it had a crew of but four hundred and seventy men; on the other hand, the French ship's eighty guns were made up of forty-two-pounders and twenty-two-pounders and it had a crew of a thousand men. Captain Gardiner's tactics had the effect of wiping out much of this advantage: he approached the enemy from the rear and then moved in along beside it within pistol-shot, thus wiping out the effectiveness of the heavy French battery, the guns of which were elevated for distance firing. Still the advantage was greatly in favour of the Foudroyant.

[85] Letter of March 11, 1758, Canadian Archives Report (1905), I, Part VI, 265.

[86] Entick, op. cit., III, 60-2.

[87] An attempt was made early in March to send relief to Louisbourg. One of the ships put back to port; the other actually reached sight of Cape Breton, but was likewise obliged to return to France since it was confronted by a great ice floe that surrounded the island, which it could not break through. Des Gouttes succeeded in reaching the port toward the end of April, but only with his own ship. One hundred and fifty of his crew had perished on the voyage and three hundred had to be hospitalized (Des Gouttes to the Minister, May 6, 1756, quoted by Richard Waddington in his La Guerre de sept ans, II, 335).

ships of the line, with batteries removed, as well as a frigate, in which were a battalion of troops and supplies; and still later Captain de Chaffault sailed from the same port with two of the line and four others of the same class turned into transports and carrying still another battalion and additional stores, and he succeeded in landing his troops at Port Dauphin before sailing for Quebec.[88] The ministry, it is clear, after de la Clue's failure to break out of the Mediterranean, had determined to get at least thirteen warships into Louisbourg; [89] but in view of Hawke's activities in the Bay of Biscay, it was later decided that nine was the most that could be spared.[90] Even nine did not arrive at Louisbourg, however — a number far too few to interfere seriously with the designs of the British. In fact, there were but six warships that could reach its spacious harbour and were therefore available to participate in the defence of that strategic stronghold in its supreme hour of need, and only five of them were ships of the line, and four had come *en flûte*. Thus Osborne, Saunders, and Hawke in the Old World had destroyed the Anglo-French balance in the New, and by this means had immeasurably lightened the task that confronted Amherst and Boscawen as they moved toward Cape Breton Island on May 28. The French Minister had prophetically warned des Gouttes:

> "Upon the outcome of this campaign [for the preservation of Cape Breton Island] depends principally that of the war. Our enemies will neglect nothing to make the conquest, but you should be more than in condition to render their efforts vain and repulse them with glory for France." [91]

As has been indicated, Lawrence, Wolfe, and Boscawen had before Amherst's arrival determined upon a threefold attack on the

---

[88] Corbett, *op. cit.*, I, 316.

[89] President of the Navy Board to Drucour and Prévost, April 10, 1758, *Canadian Archives Report* (1905), I, Part VI, 266. On March 29, 1758 one employed in France in the British secret service drew up a list of ships that either had departed for Isle Royale (Cape Breton Island) or were about to depart for that island from either Brest or Rochefort. This list includes eleven fully armed vessels and twelve that were partly armed (en flûte) ("*Vaisseaux et frigates du Roy qui sont à la mer, ou sont y aller,*" Chatham Mss., Bundle 87, Canadian Archives Transcripts).

[90] President of the Navy Board to Drucour and Prévost, April 10, 1758, *op. cit.*, VI, 266.

[91] Quoted by Waddington, *op. cit.*, II, 336.

island, with the principal force landing under Wolfe at Miré Bay some distance to the north of Louisbourg.[92] The general apparently had studied the pros and cons of this plan, and may have secured the views of such men as Captain Rouse of the *Sutherland*, who for many years had sailed the waters about Cape Breton and had more than once traversed the difficult road from Miré and who was strongly committed to a unified approach to the conquest of that island by way of Gabarus Bay, where the New England provincials had landed in 1745 with his help when commanding the galley *Shirley*.[93] At least it is clear that on June 1 Amherst decided to send Major James Robertson of the 60th regiment with a frigate "to make discoveries." [94] Robertson looked not only into Louisbourg harbour but also into Gabarus Bay, where he noted "five or six small encampments of a Dozen Tents." [95] The next day the general himself entered the bay, together with about a third of the transports, and then, accompanied by Robertson, Wolfe, and Lawrence, reconnoitred its shore line in a boat.[96] The day following, with the arrival of Brigadier General Whitmore from Halifax [97] and the movement into the bay of most of the remaining transports, he announced his decision: there would be a landing "at one place instead of three."

Amherst's plan was simple. Wolfe was to land on the left of the bay at a place called Fresh Water Cove or Flat Point, west of where the New England troops had landed; he was to be supported by twelve companies of grenadiers, Fraser's Highlanders, Scott's Nova Scotia light-infantry corps of marksmen, and a body of rangers, the

---

[92] That Wolfe was apparently not fully committed to this plan of operation is indicated by his letter of May 24, 1758 to Lord George Sackville. He refers to it as "Our present notions . . ." and then goes on to state that "perhaps General Amherst may arrive in the meanwhile time enough to improve the present plan" (Willson, *op cit.*, pp. 336–7).

[93] For Rouse's views respecting Gabarus Bay as the most appropriate place of landing, see "Minutes of a Council of War held at Halifax, July 23–31, 1757," Loudoun Papers, No. 3984. Most of those who testified before Loudoun's council of war also favoured Gabarus, among them Bradstreet.

[94] "Extract of a Journal of the Proceedings of the Fleet and Army sent against Louisbourg," *Military Affairs on North America, 1748–1765* (ed. Stanley Pargellis), pp. 416–18.

[95] *Ibid.* and Amherst's *Journal*, p. 47.

[96] *Ibid.*, and a "Journal of the Proceedings . . . against Louisbourg," *op. cit.*, p. 417; Amherst to Pitt, June 11, 1758, *Pitt Correspondence*, I, 271.

[97] Monckton was sent back to Halifax by Amherst to protect Nova Scotia when he summoned Whitmore (Amherst to Abercromby, May 28, 1758, Abercromby Papers, No. 290).

last mostly from Massachusetts Bay. Lawrence, at the same time, was to approach the shore to the right of Wolfe between Flat Point and White Point with six battalions of regulars; Whitmore to the right of Lawrence was to move with a division around White Point, which is on the extreme right of the bay and to the south of the harbour of Louisbourg; finally, a number of sloops carrying Bragg's regiment, which had wintered in the Bay of Fundy, were to pass in front of Louisbourg, to secure, if possible, a footing to the north of it at Lorembec.[98] But now the weather became foul, with a great surf rolling and fog obscuring the landscape. In fact, conditions were so very unfavourable that Boscawen was advised by some of his captains, when he called one after another on board the *Namur* for consultations, that a landing could not be wisely undertaken.[99] Not until the morning of the 8th was there any diminution of the heavy swell.

Already Amherst had altered his plan. In place of a threefold attack in and about the bay, he determined on but one attack, to be led by Wolfe against the Anse de la Cormorandière (Bay of the Coromants, called by the English Kennington Cove). Lawrence's forces were to be drawn up in boats in the center behind the frigates so that, if it seemed wise, they could move either directly forward or off to the left to support Wolfe, while Whitmore's detachments, in boats off to the right, were to keep well out of gun range and either move according to the earlier plan or support Wolfe and Lawrence as ordered at the time.[100]

As might have been anticipated, the French had left no stone unturned to make the approaches to Louisbourg impregnable. De la Motte, during his sojourn in the harbour with his fleet the preceding year, had employed his sailors as well as the garrison to throw up a chain of earthworks at every landing cove east and west of the

---

[98] The orders of June 3 are given in Captain John Knox's *Historical Journal of the Campaigns in North America for the Years 1757, 1758, 1759, and 1760* (1769), I, 164–6; see also Amherst's *Journal*, pp. 47–50; and Willson, *op. cit.*, p. 372.

[99] They stressed the impracticability of the attempt in so rough a sea with the shore so well fortified. When Captain Ferguson, of H.M.S. *Prince of Orange*, "an old, brave, and experienced officer" in whom the admiral had great confidence, was summoned, he, after hearing all the arguments against the attempt, now advised Boscawen, for his "own honour and the glory of his country, to exert that power, with which he was invested." The admiral, happily, acted upon this advice and thereupon put aside the idea of demanding a general council of war to consider the desirability of giving up the attempt (Entick, *op. cit.*, III, 224).

[100] Orders of June 4, 1758, Knox's *Historical Journal*, I, 166–7.

fortress.[101] Gabarus Bay, where the New England troops had landed in 1745, received his particular attention, and at the Anse de la Cormorandière, at Flat Point or Fresh Water Cove, and at White Point there were concentrated some "heavy cannon and swivels of an extraordinary calibre," securely mounted. In addition, trees had been cut and then piled up for a distance of twenty or thirty yards in front of the entrenchments, with the branches toward the sea and interwoven to form an abatis. Behind all these defences were now posted between two and three thousand regulars, irregulars, and Indians under the command of Colonel St. Julien.[102]

To launch an attack against the bay under these circumstances with the tide still running strong seemed suicidal and yet by two o'clock of the morning of the 8th the men were in their boats and by four o'clock pushed off, led in person by Wolfe, Lawrence, and Whitmore — each division making for an apparent assigned objective, but with Wolfe alone, on the extreme left, called upon to force a landing. They were supported by the fire of six frigates, which moved as close as possible to the shore and distributed their fire all along the bay. The French could therefore not determine where the real attack would be made. As the brigadier approached Flat Point or Fresh Water Cove as though it were his objective, he got such a rain of fire at half-musket distance that his boats veered to the left of it and made for the Anse de la Cormorandière, while Lawrence now in turn made a feint as though to attack at Flat Point. But the Red Division under Wolfe soon ran into trouble as they drew near La Cormorandière: the heavy surf overturned boats, and the protruding rocks shattered others; at the same time a destructive fire from the French artillery fifteen feet above the water's edge, supported by musketry, raked them. Faced with this terrifying ordeal, even the impetuous brigadier could only see disaster for his men by proceeding farther into the cove. He therefore, it is stated, signalled for a withdrawal with his hat — it seemed that the attempt had failed.[103]

---

[101] A map made by de la Motte showing the defences that he constructed is on display in the museum erected on the site of the great fortress, which has now become a Canadian national historical site.

[102] Entick, op. cit., III, 228–9; Knox, op. cit., I, 169.

[103] Thomas Mante: History of the Late War in North America, pp. 135–6; Entick, op. cit., III, 229; see also a "Journal of the Proceedings of the Fleet," from May 28 to June 15, Abercromby Papers, No. 291, Huntington Library, and Waddington, op. cit., II, 345.

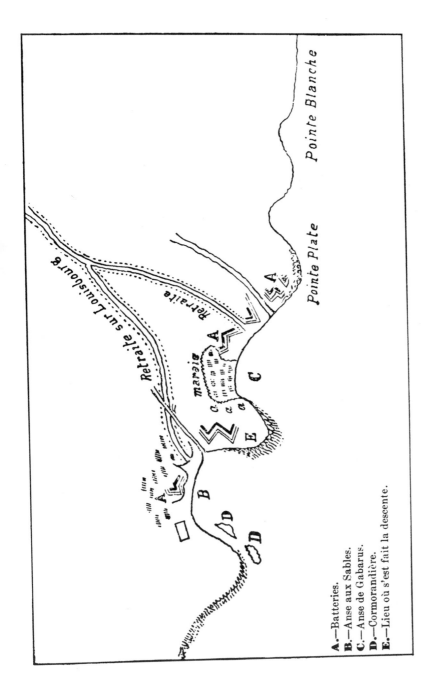

A.—Batteries.
B.—Anse aux Sables.
C.—Anse de Gabarus.
D.—Cormorandière.
E.—Lieu où s'est fait la descente.

"Descent des Anglois à Louisbourg, 1758."

(From the *Journal du Marquis de Montcalm.*)

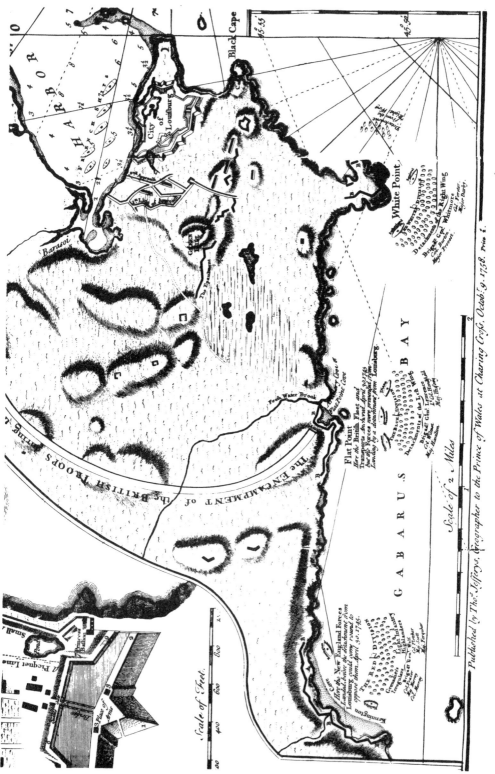

The landing on Cape Breton Island at Gabarus Bay and the siege of Louisbourg 1758

If any man ever, in popular belief, was born under a lucky star, it was Wolfe. In connection with the two greatest achievements of his meteoric career as a general — the forced landing at Gabarus Bay and his approach to the northern bank of the St. Lawrence beneath the Heights of Abraham — his success seems to have come as the result of misunderstanding, if not direct disobedience to his orders for a withdrawal by his subordinates. In the present instance, it appears that he signalled to his troops to desist in what seemed a mad attempt and to retire. But a boatload of Scott's light-infantry saw an unguarded precipitous "neck of rocks" protruding to the east of the cove and west of Flat Point, so inaccessible from the bay that the French had not felt it necessary to fortify it. Therefore, running the boats upon the rocks, they leaped ashore. The brigadier, taking in the significance of this at a glance, now signalled to the others to follow suit. His own boat made for the neck, and when he approached it he leaped into the surf and over submerged rocks to dry land.

In the face of so much activity on the part of the British boats in the area of the cove itself, this movement, somewhat hidden from the view of the defenders, was not at first perceived and gave time for the assembling of a respectable body of troops before Colonel St. Julien became aware of it; then, according to Drucour, he sought to hurl his grenadiers against Wolfe's force, but as they advanced they received such a terrible fire as to lay low almost all the French officers and as a result they retired.[104] In the confusion of the recoil the brigadier led his troops against the nearest battery playing upon them and carried it.[105]

There was now consternation at La Cormorandière as the British continued to swarm ashore, with Lawrence swinging his Blue Division away from the direction of Flat Point and following Wolfe, while he in turn was followed by Whitmore's White Division, shift-

104 Waddington, op. cit., II, 345.

105 Writing to his uncle, Major Walter Wolfe, concerning this historic landing, the brigadier declared: "It may be said that we made a rash and ill-advised attempt, and by the greatest of good fortune imaginable we succeeded" (R. Wright: Life of Major-General James Wolfe, p. 448). This position, it may be pointed out, is hardly consistent with his views held in 1757 regarding the desirability of an attempt at a forced landing against Fort Fouras, guarding the approaches to Rochefort. There he was prepared to sacrifice as many as a thousand men if need be in that hazardous enterprise (Wolfe to Major Rickson, November 5, 1757, Willson, op. cit., p. 339). In the present instance he succeeded in attaining his objective with the loss of only a small fraction of this number.

ing from the extreme right to the extreme left.[106] In fact, the fear of being cut off was so strong among the defenders of the cove where the landing was made that no order was given even to spike the cannon there before the French troops began a precipitous retreat in the direction of Louisbourg, some four miles to the east.[107] This flight from the Anse de la Cormorandière affected all the other troops posted about Gabarus Bay, with the result that they in turn began to retreat to the security of the town, only stopping to burn the barracks in the suburb of Barachois.[108] Thus with the loss of about a hundred men — either killed by enemy fire, drowned, or wounded — what had seemed impossible to achieve but an hour previous was now accomplished.[109] The Amherst strategy, fortunately, was vindicated.

While Lawrence and Whitmore were busy with the task of landing, Wolfe, accompanied by Amherst, who had reached shore, went in pursuit of the French troops as they clambered over rocks and waded through bogs; indeed, the chase, in the words of the general, was "over the Roughest and worst ground I ever saw."[110] Only when the enemy had reached the protection of the town, and the great guns in its fortifications had opened fire, did the British troops retire beyond their range. There the permanent camp was fixed by Amherst and there the soldiers were refreshed with French bread and wine that had fallen into their possession with the flight of the enemy from Gabarus Bay.[111] Whereupon, with night coming on, the weary men — after so many bitter disappointments, so many humili-

---

[106] Amherst to Pitt, June 11, 1758, Pitt Correspondence, I, 274.

[107] A French officer's "Journal," 1758, Chatham Mss., Bundle 96 (Canadian Archives Transcripts). To Montcalm, who heard of the landing on June 26 and also had received a sketch of the landing-place apparently from Franquet, who sent him the news, it was a mystery why the troops responsible for defending this part of the bay did not, after the first discharges of their artillery and musketry, rush with fixed bayonets upon the landing English and overwhelm them, and why the troops just east of the landing-place did not do likewise (Journal du Marquis de Montcalm, p. 380).

[108] So wrote La Houillère to the Minister on June 10, 1758 (Waddington, op. cit., II, 345.

[109] Amherst gives the figures in his letter to Pitt of June 11, 1758 (op. cit.). Out of the regulars a hundred and seven were casualties; out of the American rangers six were listed. One rather gruesome aspect of the assault at La Cormorandière is related by a naval officer who participated in it. He declared that after the enemy had fled, "we found the Bodies of one hundred & odd French Regulars & two Indians, which our Rangers Scalped" ("Journal of the Proceedings of the Fleet," Abercromby Papers, No. 291).

[110] Amherst's Journal, pp. 50–1.

[111] "Journal of the Proceedings of the Fleet," Abercromby Papers, No. 291.

ations and even disasters visited on British arms in North America during the past four years — could lie down to rest in a spirit of high exaltation and with the feeling of a memorable accomplishment that had proved to all the world that Briton's land troops were still men of courage and enterprise. This spirit, this feeling, was recorded by a contemporary, who, in chronicling the feat of daring of June 8, wrote: "Such was the incredible service and extraordinary achievement of *a day* that must be ever glorious in the annals of this nation. . . ." [112] But to the French military engineer at Louisbourg, Franquet, the 8th was nothing less than a *"jour fatal à Etat."* [113]

Although the entrenchments west of Louisbourg were now laid out some three miles in extent for the main encampment, the weather continued bad. Not until the 11th could any of the artillery or stores be landed. The 12th was a "most terrible day"; Wolfe, nevertheless, marched with some twelve hundred regulars and rangers around the harbour, passing by the settlements that the French had already burned, to Lighthouse Point — northeast of the city and across the basin from it — which he occupied. The enemy meanwhile had also drawn all their forces within the main fortifications, with the exception of those employed on an island battery at the entrance of the harbour — thus giving up their *Batterie Royale*, which had been so constructed to the north of Louisbourg and at the edge of the basin as to be able to play upon any hostile ships that, after silencing the island battery, ventured into the harbour. The brigadier in making this circuitous move was simply carrying out the general's previously announced plan, which was to secure a position at the lighthouse from which the British could destroy the ships in the harbour and put out of action the battery at its entrance.

To secure his position from an attack on his rear while engaged in this operation, Wolfe now sent detachments along the road to Miré Bay to take post as far north as Lorembec. [114] By the 19th his troops had succeeded in erecting a battery well sheltered by rocks; by this date he also had a second placed behind an eminence called Green Hill. While the guns and mortars now began to play upon the enemy, but little damage was done to the French fleet, which by moving

---

[112] Entick, *op. cit.*, III, 235. Mante (*op. cit.*, p. 136) writes: "No opposition, it seems, could check the animating spirit raised by the ardent desire of regaining credit, and of expunging the foul blot with which the miscarriages of successive years had stained the British colours."

[113] Montcalm's *Journal*, p. 378.

[114] Wolfe to Amherst, June 12, 1758, Willson, *op. cit.*, p. 374.

closer to the walls of the city was pretty well out of range. The island battery could be reached, however, and by the 25th its guns had been silenced.[115] With the extension of entrenchments and the erection of new batteries on the land side, together with the constant patrol, when weather conditions made it possible, of Hardy's ships before the entrance of the harbour, an iron ring was thus being forged about the city.

Louisbourg, located upon a rugged promontory to the south of the spacious harbour, was an impressive seaport over two miles in circumference. Not only was it substantially built with many of the houses, as well as other structures, of stone, but its streets were broad and uniform and at right angles with one another. There could be seen the Château St. Louis, where the Governor of Cape Breton Island and his council carried on the public affairs of the colony; there the barracks and the great parade for the soldiers; there the large hospital, some two hundred and eighty feet long, maintained by the Frères de la Charité; there the convent of the Sisters of the Congregation, who taught the children and carried on works of mercy among the inhabitants; and there, facing the open square, the church with its spire reminding men of things eternal. To the docks of the city resorted each year in time of peace, on an average, some hundred and fifty ships — far more than ever appeared at either Quebec on the St. Lawrence or New Orleans on

---

[115] Beckles Willson in his *Life and Letters of James Wolfe* indicates in a footnote (p. 373) that the French battery at the entrance of the harbour was on Goat Island and that "Island Battery" had already been dismantled. This seems to be incorrect. In a contemporary and rare map of the siege of Louisbourg in 1758 possessed by the Public Archives of Canada, Goat Island is not fortified, but to the north and west of it there is portrayed clearly the heavily fortified "*Batterie et Isle de l'Entrée.*" Amherst in his *Journal* writes on June 24 (p. 57) that "We must destroy the Island Battery, as all that can be done to the Shipping is not great"; and on the 25th he records (*ibid.*) that "in the evening the Island Battery was silenced." Entick also refers to "Island battery" firing on the Lighthouse Point and the silencing of it (*op. cit.*, III, 237–8). English mapmakers were doubtless responsible for this misconception, since they confused the names of the three islands near the harbour. The one squarely at the entrance is Battery Isle, then to the south of it is Isle aux Chèvres or Goat Island, and then to the south of this is Isle Verte or Green Island, according to the contemporary French map referred to above. In the map inserted by Willson in his volume (p. 371) Goat Island is confused with Green Island; in an undated but apparently contemporary English map by J. Henton, in the Public Archives of Canada, the most southern of the three small islands is called "Goat or Green Island"; while Mante in his *History of the Late War in North America* presents a map on which the island at the entrance is called "Goat Island and Battery."

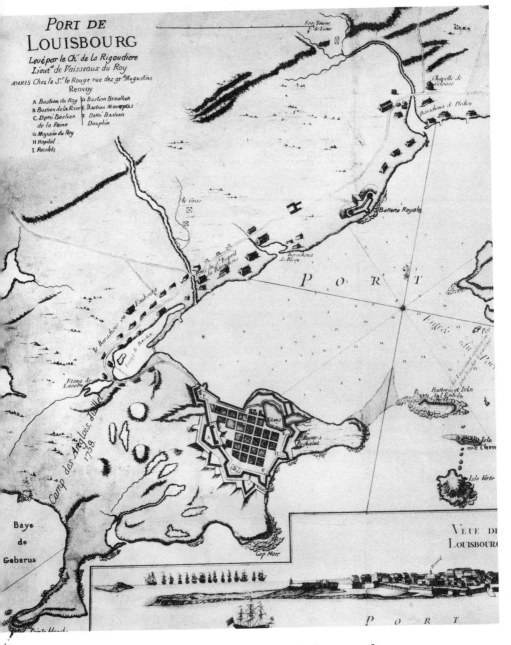

"Port de Louisbourg," 1758. By the Chevalier de la Rigaudiere.
(Public Archives of Canada, Division of Maps.)

the Mississippi; these brought not only the products of the north-
lands — cod, salmon, furs, oil, and planks — for sale and for trans-
shipment, but also those of the West Indies to be exported — rum,
molasses, sugar, tobacco, cotton, and coffee — as well as those of
the northern British colonies — wheat, flour, barrelled beef and pork,
horses, and many other commodities. Moreover, during the busy
fishing season hundreds of shallops with their crews congregated at
the wharves; for about the harbour stretching inland was a vast
number of stages for drying the cod caught in near-by waters.

One can perhaps recapture in imagination some of the movement
at Louisbourg of the thousands of people going about their daily
tasks during the summer season — fishermen, sailors, merchants,
soldiers, the men and women of the robe, and Micmac Indians —
where today, unhappily, other than the sound of the distant
breakers and the cries of sea-gulls, there is only silence — and
ruins.[116] From this latter fate the French ministry had sought to save
the city by means of powerful fortifications constructed by the military engineers Verville and Verrier at a great expense to the Crown.
On the land side the defences consisted of a glacis or steep incline
ending in a banquette or elevation from which the defenders could
fire under protection; a covered way was underneath it, behind this
stretched a moat, and towering above the moat was another parapet
with a banquette, all a part of the main ramparts. In the center of
this embattled wall stood the King's Bastion, or the Citadel, to the
left of it the Queen's Bastion and Gate and to the right of it that of
the Dauphin and the West Gate. Facing the water approach were
three other bastions. All these bastions commanding both the land
and water approaches were so constructed as to be able to deliver
a deadly cross-fire upon an attacking force. Moreover, the land approaches were either so rocky or so marshy as to make it exceedingly
difficult at most places for a besieging force to dig entrenchments
and parallels and thus to advance under protection. It is true that
these fortifications suffered from natural forces the lot of all others
of this period and were in need of constant repair.[117] Yet the French
historian Waddington was correct in stating that, in spite of all their

---

116 Alone among these impressive ruins a historical museum is now to be found.

117 Waddington (op. cit., II, 339–40) emphasizes the efforts made to keep the
fortifications in a state of repair and to strengthen them at a cost of 480,000 livrès spent
between 1754 and 1758.

defects, they were "the finest in North America making Louisbourg the advanced citadel of New France." [118] There was therefore every reason to believe that the capture of the place, well provided with provisions, could be delayed for a very long period, especially should the garrison show a much greater spirit of resistance than had been manifested in 1745 when the New England provincials brought about its surrender. [119] This would then give an opportunity, if things were favourable along the coasts of France, for the Comte de Conflans to come from Brest to the aid of the place with — according to plans that had been formulated — a great fleet of twenty-four ships of the line. [120] With this powerful force he might be able not only to scatter the invading armada but even to inflict upon it a most disastrous defeat. But Conflans was not to come, for the fleet could not be spared from the home waters in view of the well-known and ominous preparations in England for a great naval and military expedition that rumour said was to be directed against the coasts of France. [121]

Nevertheless, the forces concentrated within the American Dunkirk were sufficient of themselves to make a very good defence. There were two battalions of the Bourgogne regiment, two of the Artois, two of the Cambise (just arrived from France), two of the Volontaires Étrangers, twenty-four companies of the Canadian line, and two companies of artillery — totalling over three thousand men, and supported by twenty-six hundred sailors and marines, as well as by the male inhabitants of the city. These forces were under the

---

[118] *Ibid.*, II, 363.

[119] Montcalm, when he heard that the British in 1758 had landed on Gabarus Bay, referred in his *Journal* to the proceedings that took place in 1745 when the New England troops landed. He stated that when this took place the King's storehouses were in the neighbourhood of the bay, and as a consequence nearly all the effects in them were transported into Louisbourg and placed in the storehouses of private individuals. The city itself was surrendered as soon as it was, he charged, so that those who were storing these goods could profit by their possession. He also charged that Bigot, the King's commissaire, by failing to make any report on goods not actually in the King's storehouses at the time of the capitulation, also shared in these profits and was moreover guilty of persuading the inhabitants to petition the commandant to give up the place, which the latter did under pretext of not being able to control the people who had risen against him (Montcalm's *Journal*, p. 380).

[120] Extract of a letter written from Quebec, May 24, 1758, "Intelligence," Chatham Mss., Bundle 96 (Canadian Archives Transcripts).

[121] De Lévis, writing to d'Argenson on July 2, 1758 from Canada, declared: "Louisbourg is besieged and will be taken if M. de Conflans does not come to its aid with his squadron" (*Lettres de Lévis, 1756–1760*, p. 192).

supreme command of the Governor of Cape Breton Island, the Chevalier de Drucour.[122]

Unfortunately, within the stronghold there were divided opinions, especially as these related to the use of the fleet. On the very day of Wolfe's landing, Rear Admiral des Gouttes, in consideration of this grave development, sent to Drucour a communication embodying the views of his captains. It was to the effect that the King's ships should leave the harbour that very night, while the wind was fair and the opportunity still was open to escape; since otherwise the enemy, now on shore, would soon move around to Lighthouse Point, thus putting the vessels in danger of destruction.[123] The Governor, after holding a council of war with his land officers, replied that the Minister of the Marine had always told him that the fleet sent to Louisbourg was purposely for its defence; that its departure would be a show of weakness to the enemy; and that, "being doomed to the same fate, it is proper to run the same risks." [124] The staff of the garrison took the position, in other words, that the most important thing was to prolong the resistance; this would be impossible, it was felt, were the defenders deprived of the use of the ships and the fighters on board them.[125] The day before the silencing of the island battery on the 25th by Wolfe's guns from Light-House Point, the officers of the fleet, again through des Gouttes, appealed to Drucour for a council of war. They indicated that they had now performed the only service of which they were capable and begged that, unless they could still be really useful, they might depart with

---

122 On April 10 de Blénac was ordered to proceed to Louisbourg in the *Formidable* to command the squadron to be concentrated there. That same day a separate order was given to him to take over the general command of all troops at this place (*Canadian Archives Report* [1905], I, Part VI, 266). On May 10 he left Brest, but when he arrived off Isle Royale he found it blockaded by the enemy and returned in his ship "very happy to be able to bring to a good port the vessel which was confided to me" (quoted by Waddington, *op. cit.*, II, 336).

123 Des Gouttes to Drucour, June 8, 1758, *Canadian Archives Report* (1905), I, Part VI, 500.

124 Drucour to des Gouttes, June 8, 1758, *ibid.* The president of the Navy Board, who had received letters written from Louisbourg just after Wolfe's landing, among them a letter from des Gouttes, wrote to the latter on June 30 that his proposal and that of his captains to leave the port of Louisbourg after the descent of the English by way of the Anse de la Cormorandière was "premature and dangerous for the preservation of the place." To Drucour he also wrote on the same day that there should be no question of sending the warships away, "unless they are in danger there or they can no longer hope to save the place" (*ibid.*, VI, 267).

125 This view was expressed in the diary of the siege now in the Moreau St. Méry Collection, *ibid.*, VI, 498.

their ships.[126] The Governor and his military staff, in the words of one of the naval officers, in making reply "pretended the town was safe if we remained and went so far as to say if we sailed out they would charge the squadron with the loss [of it, should it subsequently fall]." [127] In face of this positive position assumed on the part of the land forces, the navy reluctantly submitted to the decision of the council of war that all must share a common fate.[128]

On the 29th four vessels were sunk at the entrance of the harbour to block it up; provisions and powder on board the men of war were transferred to the town, and most of the crews joined the land forces on the ramparts after the remaining five ships and a frigate had been towed as close to the fortification of the town as possible.[129] But still there was no harmony between the services. In fact, the officers of the navy charged that the defence was not being carried out with the public interest in mind. Their views on this are doubtless faithfully reflected in the "Journal" of one of them:

> "It was in effect to hold out as long as possible to raise the reputation and glory of individuals to which they sacrificed the welfare & honour of the State . . . but what displeased us most was to have it said throughout the town we had not done our duty in not destroying their [the enemy's] batteries; nor would they receive our wounded men into the hospital . . . [and we were therefore] obliged to put our sick and wounded men under tents that were exposed to the enemy's fire. . . ." [130]

In contrast to the lack of unity within the camp of the French, there was the most perfect spirit of co-operation between the British land and sea forces. Amherst's *Journal* contains many references to the hearty way that Boscawen honoured every requisition of sailors, guns, and equipment made upon him. Hundreds of veteran naval artillerymen and many of the great thirty-two-pounders were

---

[126] Representation of the ship captains of June 24, *ibid.*, VI, 500.

[127] French officer's "Journal" under date of June 22, 1758, Chatham Mss., Bundle 96 (Canadian Archives Transcripts).

[128] It is of interest to note that in the spring of 1760 the Marquis des Gouttes, according to information reaching London, was punished for his behaviour at Louisbourg by being degraded from the order of nobility; not only was his patent for his rank burned at the hands of a hangman, but he himself was sentenced to be imprisoned for twenty-one years (London advices, April 4, *Pennsylvania Gazette*, June 12, 1760).

[129] Representations of des Gouttes, June 29, 1758, *Canadian Archives Report* (1905), I, Part VI, 500; a French officer's "Journal," June 29, 1758, *op. cit.*

[130] *Ibid.*

needed for the land batteries, and these were readily transferred from the ships and thus made available to the general and Brigadier Wolfe. Thus slowly but steadily the British entrenchments were pushed forward so as to bring the heavy guns at last within battering range; wherever possible the pioneers used pick and shovel, and when this could not be done fascines, gabions, and rocks were employed to advantage. This advance of the batteries was viewed, very naturally, with dismay by the besieged. The French naval officers now proposed a grand sally against the entrenchments on the British left in an effort to destroy the most menacing of the batteries, threatening the Dauphin Bastion, by a surprise move at night. In this connection they recommended that all the launches and shallops in the harbour be employed to carry the largest possible number of soldiers across the harbour so as to strike the enemy on the flank. The land officers, however, fearing that their men, once they had landed, would then be cut off, rejected the plan as too hazardous.[131] But the entrenchments came ever closer each day to the outer French defences. On the night of July 3 on the right of the British lines the military engineer Mackellar threw up a new work but six hundred paces from the French covered way; [132] the town now began to suffer from red-hot shot, shells, and bombs; on the 6th the crowded hospital was struck by a bomb. Clearly these advanced works had to be destroyed or the city would perish.

While one or more sorties on a small scale had been made before the 9th for the purpose of destroying the British batteries, on the night of that day the most important one was made with the purpose of destroying the advanced works that now threatened the Queen's Bastion. The French, concentrating at heavily fortified Cap Noir (Black Cape or Black Rock), just to the south of the city, moved suddenly in the darkness, to the number of about a thousand, upon the British entrenchments and actually penetrated them, surprising the grenadiers and other soldiers posted there and taking some prisoners, but then quickly retreated when other British detachments appeared on the scene.[133] Nothing of importance, therefore, was accomplished. The city was indeed doomed, and from that time on,

[131] Ibid.

[132] Amherst's Journal, p. 61.

[133] According to Amherst, most of the French troops that made the sortie were drunk (ibid., pp. 63-4); according to a French naval officer, the French soldiers fired on one another, "by which we lost more men than the Enemy" (a French officer's "Journal" for July 9, op. cit.).

the heavy British guns, having full range of it and the harbour, kept up a constant fire.

On the 15th the speedy frigate *Aréthuse* escaped from the harbour and sailed for France carrying ominous tidings of the approaching fall of Louisbourg.[134] It was none too soon. For now one heavy blow after another fell upon the heads of the hapless French defenders. On the 19th des Gouttes in the name of his captains asked permission of Drucour to burn the remaining vessels, all of which had been damaged, rather than to expose them to capture,[135] but the Governor was not then willing to assume the responsibility of fixing the exact time when this should be done — that, he felt, was for des Gouttes himself to decide.[136]

The following day Wolfe opened up one of his heavy batteries against the Dauphin Bastion with great effect and succeeded in dismounting some of the French guns.[137] On the 21st at noontime a shell from his battery fell upon the French *Célèbre*, a sixty-four-gun ship, which led to the explosion of the powder magazine; in an instant the vessel was all aflame. The *Entreprenant*, a seventy-four, and the *Capricieux*, another sixty-four, were stationed so close that they also caught fire, and all burned to the water's edge. The *Prudent*, however, a seventy-four and des Goutte's flagship, was to the windward and received no damage, and the *Bienfaisant*, a sixty-four, was also saved when the cables of the burning ships were instantly cut.[138] But this great misfortune only added to the intense bitterness that existed between the land and sea officers. One of the former wrote in his "Journal":

> "The joy that the captains manifested over the loss of their ships is a sure guarantee of the pains they gave to set them on fire. They, however, desired to persuade us that they did the impossible to save their vessels, but that it was not possible. As a result they put under arrest a Captain of the Bourgogne battalion because he said that with a company of grenadiers he would undertake to save the King's ships." [139]

---

[134] *Ibid.*, under date of July 15; *Amherst's Journal*, p. 67.

[135] Des Gouttes to Drucour, July 19, 1758, *Canadian Archives Report* (1905), I, Part VI, 501.

[136] Drucour to des Gouttes, July 19, 1758, *ibid.*

[137] *Amherst's Journal*, pp. 68–9.

[138] A French officer's "Journal" for July 21, 1758, *op. cit.*

[139] Quoted by Waddington, *op. cit.*, II, 353.

The day following this disaster the great King's Bastion — the citadel — went up in flames, with the exception of the Governor's apartments, as the result of shell-fire, and from that time on, the heavy British artillery "enfiladed the whole town." One building after another was razed, helpless inhabitants as well as defenders were killed in large numbers; but still Drucour continued to resist; [140] even Madame Drucour, to enspirit the desperate defenders, went to the ramparts each day and actually took part in the firing of the cannon. The barracks at the Queen's Bastion were consumed by fire the night of the 23rd, burning "with great violence" [141] and on that of the 25th, "under cover of great fog," Boscawen sent two of his captains, Laforey of the sloop *Hunter* and Balfour of the *Aetna*, with six hundred men in boats into the harbour to seize the two remaining French ships riding at anchor there close to the walls. With loss of a few men this was done; the *Bienfaisant* was towed to the bottom of the basin and placed under the protection of one of Wolfe's batteries; but the *Prudent*, aground at low tide, could not be floated and was burnt.

With the French fleet in the harbour a thing of the past and the harbour now cleared for the entrance of Boscawen's ships, six of the latter making ready to move in and complete the destruction of the town; with the great King's Bastion on the land side a shambles, the Dauphin's Bastion no longer effective, and the Queen's Bastion now at length exposed to the fire of a great battery at last completed in front of it and ready to go into action; with only four cannon left on the ramparts that could be used; with no shelter any longer available for the wounded and for the women and children as a thousand bombs fell upon the city in a space of twelve hours — in face of this accumulation of disasters, Drucour realized that the end had come. For hope of aid from France had now disappeared. At the council of war to which he summoned his military engineer, Franquet, his leader of the regulars, Colonel La Houillère (La Houllière, Lahoulière), [142] and des Gouttes of the navy early the morning of the 26th,

---

140 A French officer's "Journal," *op. cit.*, under date of July 22; Amherst's *Journal* p. 69.

141 *Ibid.*, p. 70.

142 La Houillère had been commandant of Sales in the old province of Roussillon in southern France. He had recently arrived at Cape Breton Island on the *Bizarre* to take charge of the regulars. This was apparently not agreeable news to Montcalm. After receiving a report of his arrival at Louisbourg, the latter records in his *Journal* (p. 381):

it was finally agreed to ask for terms. A white flag was raised at the
Dauphin Bastion, and Houillère's adjutant, with all guns now silenced, left the West Gate for Amherst's headquarters to ask for
terms. Boscawen, who had come ashore, assisted in drawing them
up and they were then signed by him as well as by the general. Included in them was a demand that the garrison and the sailors and
marines on the King's ships surrender as prisoners of war.

Drucour and his advisers upon receiving the terms of capitulation
determined to reject them and thereupon sent Lieutenant Colonel
d'Anthony (d'Anthonay) with a counter-demand to the effect that
the garrison and the men of the navy be accorded the same status
as was given to the British garrison that capitulated at Port Mahon
on Minorca in 1756 and subsequently was transferred to Gibraltar.[143] He stated in this connection that if his request was refused,
the garrison was prepared to meet the general assault that the British promised. Amherst and Boscawen, however, were unwilling to
modify their terms,[144] and in turn Drucour replied that he was prepared to abide by his decision. Then Jacques Prévost, Commissaire
Ordonnateur of the island, entered the picture. In a memorial that
he had drawn up, he pointed out that the lives of four thousand inhabitants were at stake should the city, by their refusing the British
terms, be given over "to carnage and the rage of an unbridled soldiery, eager for plunder, and impelled to deeds of horror by pretended resentment at what has formerly happened in Canada." [145]
Drucour thereupon retreated from his dangerous resolve and sent
a second messenger to recall the first, and soon after d'Anthony appeared again at the British headquarters, now fully authorized to
conclude the terms. As finally signed, these provided that all armed
defenders not only of Cape Breton Island but of Isle St. Jean (to be
known later as Prince Edward Island) were to become prisoners of
war and as such were to be transferred to England on British vessels; that the two islands, with all military effects upon them, were
likewise to be surrendered; that the French sick and wounded were
to be accorded the same treatment as those of the British; and, fi-

---

"I do not know if they [the soldiers] will take a good look at him and if their discontent in this regard will not do injury to the service."

[143] Drucour to Amherst, July 26, 1758, C.O. 5: 53, folio 253.

[144] For their reply see Mante, op. cit., pp. 138–9.

[145] For this memorial see Parkman: Montcalm and Wolfe, II, 72–3. Reference of
course was made by Prévost to the massacre of British soldiers after the surrender of Fort
William Henry.

nally, that the peaceful inhabitants of the island were to be transported to France in such a manner as Boscawen should deem proper.[146]

The fall of Louisbourg, the great French bastion of the New World, was a momentous event in its bearing upon the outcome of the Anglo-French struggle for the continent of North America. Its defence by the garrison had been valiant,[147] but had failed. Never again was it destined to rise as it did after its surrender in 1745 to menace British sea power in the North Atlantic and to act as an effective barrier to the operations of an enemy in the gulf and the St. Lawrence River. Its final fate, indeed, was sealed by Pitt. Early in the spring of 1760 — after the operations against Quebec had been completed, in connection with which it had proved useful — Commodore Byron was ordered to Cape Breton Island with a body of engineers and sappers, the latter drawn from the mines of England. In the course of the next six months he ran almost fifty galleries underneath the great fortifications and then in a series of blasts these were levelled. Thus this once flourishing city, void of inhabitants and wrecked beyond repair, took its place among other great ruins of the past that serve to mark for future generations the close of one epoch of history and the beginning of another.

---

[146] For the terms see P.R.O., War Office, Series I, 5: 15. By special request Amherst and Boscawen agreed that the personal effects of the military and civil officers and others, including the inhabitants, were to be respected (Amherst Papers, Packet I, folio 26, Canadian Archives Transcripts). As to the number of inhabitants who were to be carried away as prisoners of war, Drucour did what he could to minimize the extent of the armed support given by them. Writing to Amherst the day following the capitulation, he insisted that these constituted but "a weak company of Volontaires which during the invasion and siege were working on the batteries" (C.O. 5: 53, folio 273).

[147] On November 18, 1758 Drucour drew up a memorandum covering the siege. In this he emphasized the fact that besieged strongholds are nearly always captured unless relieved and that the soldiers of the garrison had shown great valour in the defence of Louisbourg and therefore richly deserved the favour of the King (Canadian Archives Report [1905], I, Part VI, 498).

CHAPTER VIII

Abercromby Meets His Master. Frontenac

W/HEN PITT CAME to the determination to put aside the Earl of Loudoun as commander-in-chief of the British forces in North America in favour of Major General James Abercromby, he doubtless erred in judgment as he likewise did in substituting his own plans of military operations in the New World for those that Loudoun had matured.[1] It is certain that Loudoun possessed the confidence of the leading officers who served under him more fully than did Abercromby, and for good and substantial reasons.[2] A brave but canny Scot, he adhered to the sound Fabian military principle of using his resources but not squandering them; in other words, of delaying action even in the face of criticism from superiors until the favourable time for it arrived and then of concentrating his forces where they would count for the most in the realization of the ultimate objective of all military operations — the destruction of the power of the enemy. Having a great personal stake in the campaign of 1758 — the saving of his military reputa-

---

[1] These points are well developed by Dr. Pargellis in his *Lord Loudoun in North America* in the final chapter, "Loudoun and Pitt."

[2] For the views of such soldiers as Forbes, Stanwix, St. Clair, James Robertson, and James Abercrombie see *ibid.*, pp. 362–4. The following extract of a private letter "from a gentleman at New-York to a Merchant in London" undoubtedly shows the attitude of many toward Lord Loudoun: "If unblemished uprightness, unwearied diligence, uncommon spirit and capacity, joined to every amiable virtue, could give a man glory, and save him from disgrace, the *Squirrel* man of war could not have brought here on the 4th of this month, orders to recall Lord Loudoun from his command" (*Pennsylvania Gazette*, July 6, 1758).

tion, which had suffered as the result of his inability to act effectively against the enemy during the two preceding campaigns – he could be depended upon to move in for a decision. That his capacity as a soldier was of a high order is clear from his plans for the operations of 1758.

These plans were comprehensive and conceived in the light of experience with New World conditions. First he had determined to winter six of his regiments in Nova Scotia with the express purpose of using them as a spearhead against Louisbourg; these, under command of Major General Hopson, long acquainted with this region as the result of his services in Nova Scotia, would be supported by other troops from England that might possibly arrive in time to be available and by the provincial forces of New England to the number of some eight thousand. The latter were to be employed largely in the pioneer work of building roads and bridges on Cape Breton Island, once the landing had been made by his regulars. His idea was to be in position to invade the island before the French fleet could arrive and before assistance could be brought down the St. Lawrence – closed for all navigation until late in the spring – while its defence and that of Louisbourg had to depend upon no more than the garrison of two thousand that wintered there. Again, he had decided to invade Canada and strike at Montreal in person by way of Ticonderoga and Crown Point and for that purpose to throw against the two latter places twelve of his battalions of regulars, supported by American rangers, who would carry on scouting activities, leaving the work of assault to professional soldiers. His plan for this campaign envisioned the movement of those troops – already under arms and quartered conveniently for the purpose – against Ticonderoga early in May before the French could possibly reinforce that place. This could be done in view of the fact that the Hudson River was open for navigation a fortnight before the Richelieu. With no more than a thousand defenders at the most to face, the regulars could be counted upon to secure possession of the fort, which would then open the way for the seizure likewise of Crown Point. The way would then be open, he felt, to move upon Montreal. Further, he had agreed to permit Major Bradstreet to lead an expedition against Fort Frontenac, to be made up of the New York and New Jersey provincials as well as hardy bateau-men whom Bradstreet had earlier commanded in operations along the Mohawk. Finally, he had sent two regiments into winter quarters so situated that they could be put into motion against Fort Duquesne without delay as soon as weather conditions were favourable. These and the provincials from Pennsylvania, Virginia, and Maryland were to be commanded by Colonel Stanwix, who had now come to know well the country to the east of the fort and the problems involved in its assault. Loudoun had also arranged for Indian support for the Ohio Valley campaign, through arriving at an understanding with Colonel William Byrd, who had built the Virginia fort in the Cherokee country. The latter was to bring up a large body of Cherokee warriors — at least six hundred. With these and the other forces at his command Stanwix was to march so that he might be in the neighbourhood of the fort not later than the middle of June — again before the French could easily bring in reinforcements from the upper country to strengthen the small garrison that had wintered there. This would still leave time after the reduction of the fort to move against the French defences on the upper Allegheny and on Lake Erie.[3]

Pitt's plan altered fundamentally the above careful disposition of the troops. The two regiments that were preparing to march against Fort Duquesne were suddenly shifted to the Louisbourg campaign, and other troops "at 1000 miles distance" were ordered to take their places, with all the attendant delays. As a result, most of the six hundred Indians gathered for the Ohio expedition became weary of inactivity and dispersed. Again, the new plan eliminated the expedition against Fort Frontenac and provided for most of the regular regiments stationed in America to be concentrated at Halifax for the Louisbourg expedition, with only six battalions and ten companies of regulars, instead of twelve battalions, actually available for the Lake Champlain expedition. The northern provincials, outside of six hundred rangers, were ordered to go, not to Cape Breton Island, but to reinforce Abercromby's army to the number of seventeen thousand. According to Major James Robertson, who not only participated in the Louisbourg expedition but had a clear and accurate picture of the over-all operations in 1758, these provincials, "mostly press'd Men," had they been carried to Cape Breton Island

---

[3] Loudoun to Pitt, February 14, 1758, *Correspondence of William Pitt* (ed. G. S. Kimball), I, 192–4; Loudoun's plan is also to be found in Volume V of his notebooks under date January 27, 1758; these notebooks are in the Huntington Library together with the other Loudoun Papers. See also Major James Robertson to the Earl of Morton, December 19, 1758, in *Military Affairs in North America, 1748–1765* (ed. Stanley Pargellis), pp. 429–32.

would have greatly shortened the operations before Louisbourg, since the great need was for labourers for the making of roads and entrenchments; they were much better workers than the regulars, whereas, sent overland — most of them a distance of three hundred miles to the concentration south of Lake George — "half of them never joined General Abercromby," and every man who did, "but a good Soldier, was an insupportable Burthen." This slow concentration also involved great delays where speed of movement was so vital.[4]

The new commander-in-chief was a Scot, as was Loudoun, and had had a long military career. He had served as Lieutenant Colonel of the Royal Scots, was on the staff of General St. Clair throughout the campaign in Flanders in connection with the War of the Austrian Succession, took part in the expedition against Port L'Orient in Brittany, was at Hulst in the Low Countries when it was besieged, and was in the sortie that attempted to break out of that city. In January 1756 he was raised to the rank of major general in America and in June of that year arrived in New York as a member of the staff of Lord Loudoun. While he had never enjoyed an independent command up to the time of his appointment by Pitt in December 1757, his preparation for his new and great responsibility was certainly superior to that of Amherst. A kindly, tactful man, he was far removed from the tough, hard-bitten military type; he was not in the most robust health, however — although only fifty-two years of age, he had begun to feel the weight of these prematurely. Nor was he a born fighter: he lacked the spirit, the quick wit to size up situations instantaneously and to act decisively to take advantage of any opening presented by the enemy, and he also wanted the aggressiveness that characterizes without exception any great military leader. Nevertheless, with such an excellent field commander as George Augustus Lord Howe to supply what he himself lacked in the way of qualities, his campaign might have been a highly successful one had he been permitted to operate upon the basis of the Loudoun arrangements for the assault on Ticonderoga. Had he been so permitted, the war also might have been shortened by the space of a year — at least in the opinion of some of his contemporaries whose views cannot easily be dismissed.[5] But he was under orders issued by the Minister in the name of the King and

---

4 Ibid., p. 431.
5 For this view see ibid., p. 432.

was scrupulous in fulfilling them, except in the making of minor, and withal desirable, adjustments.

When, on March 4, H.M.S. *Squirrel* arrived in New York harbour bearing Pitt's dispatches of December 30 and the news of the recall of Loudoun and the appointment of Abercromby to take his place, the latter was in Albany. He proceeded to New York, however, as rapidly as possible over roads filled with a deep snow. Soon after reaching the city he sent out circular letters to all the governors of the continental colonies to supplement those addressed to them by Pitt. He called upon the northern colonies, in line with the Minister's instructions, not only to provide him with twenty thousand men for his own campaign but to institute an embargo on all ships until the Louisbourg expedition got under way.[6] As to the provincial troops to be furnished for the year 1758, he stressed the point that, whereas in former years the men who would make the best soldiers had been, as a rule, exempted from service and "only indifferent ones" had been sent, now he wanted "Men fairly drafted out of your best Militia."[7]

The response of most of the colonial assemblies was encouraging. Whereas the Governor of Massachusetts Bay had been having great difficulty in persuading the Assembly to raise scarcely more than two thousand men, to meet the quota set by Loudoun of a total of seven thousand to be furnished by the six most northerly colonies for the operations of the year 1758, now, upon the basis of the unexampled encouragement held out by Pitt that all the larger items of expense involved in levying, clothing, arming, and maintaining the provincials would be met by the mother country, the House of Representatives unhesitatingly voted "unanimously" that the province alone would provide seven thousand soldiers.[8] New Hampshire, which had already furnished a good many rangers, however, agreed, in spite of Governor Wentworth's efforts to bring the number up to a thousand,[9] to raise a regiment of but eight hundred to

---

[6] Pitt in his letter of January 11, 1758 called upon Abercromby to institute the embargo, *Pitt Correspondence*, I, 159–60.

[7] Circular letters of March 14 and 15, 1758 to the governors of the northern colonies, Abercromby Papers, No. 44, Huntington Library.

[8] See *Acts and Resolves*, IV, 135; Pownall to Pitt, March 14, 1758, *Pitt Correspondence*, I, 203. Pownall figured that if the five other colonies would do as well, this would provide Abercromby with a total of some twenty-seven thousand provincials (*ibid.*).

[9] *New Hampshire Provincial Papers*, VI, 662, 665; Wentworth to Pitt, March 26 and April 23, 1758, *Pitt Correspondence*, I, 215–17, 224.

serve not to exceed nine months; the Rhode Island Assembly voted
to recruit a thousand; [10] and that of Connecticut, always to be depended upon, resolved to supply five thousand.[11] As for New York
and New Jersey, the Assembly of the former set some twenty-six
hundred as the proper quota of the province and acted to raise that
number; [12] that of the latter would consent to raise but one thousand, a number "far short of their Abilities," in the judgment of
Abercromby.[13] Nevertheless, the total number of provincials voted
by the northern colonies for the ensuing campaign, while falling
short of the twenty thousand requested by Pitt, was at least ten
thousand more than Loudoun had asked them to procure — totalling,
as it did, some seventeen thousand six hundred men.

But Abercromby, while carrying out his orders, had little faith in
the fighting ability of the raw levies from the colonies when it came
to aggressive warfare. In a letter to Brigadier General Lawrence
written on April 30, he declared that he "must submit to better
judges how far the distribution [of troops] sent from home is equal
to the services expected," and indicated that he himself should
really have two thousand more regulars, for which he would exchange three thousand provincials. Otherwise, he did not see how
it would be possible to move beyond the southern shore of Lake
George after he had provided proper garrisons for the various places
in his area — Albany, Schenectady, the upper Mohawk, and the
critical places on the upper Hudson, Fort Edward, and the site of
Fort William Henry. He added prophetically: "I mentioned this,
that due allowance & deductions may be made to obviate Censures
& Reproaches that may be thrown out when things are not explained
& understood." [14] Before closing his letter he laid bare his apprehension that in any move against Ticonderoga he would be obliged to

---

[10] *The Colonial Records of Rhode Island*, VI, 129; Abercromby to Pitt, April 28,
1758, *Pitt Correspondence*, I, 226. Governor Hopkins claimed that there were only six
thousand men in the colony capable of bearing arms and that of this number a thousand
were already being employed on "Private Vessels of War" (*ibid.*).

[11] *Connecticut Colonial Records*, XI, 93; Fitch to Pitt, April 10, 1758, *Pitt Correspondence*, I, 222.

[12] *Journal of the Council of New York* for March 23, 1758. Governor Pownall of
Massachusetts Bay was very critical of the action of New York. Writing to Pitt on
March 23, he declared: "New York have always insisted that the proportion settled at
Albany [in 1754], in which they stood compared with Massachusetts as four to seven,
ought to be observed" (*Pitt Correspondence*, I, 213).

[13] Abercromby to Pitt, April 28, 1757, *ibid.*, I, 225.

[14] Abercromby Papers, No. 216, Huntington Library.

face "the whole regular force in Canada" unless Lawrence would make a strong feint against Quebec by sending some frigates up the St. Lawrence to burn the settlements on its lower reaches and thereby so alarm the government of New France that many of their troops would be recalled from the Lake Champlain area to defend the capital.[15] He nevertheless set to work with a good deal of energy to forward the preparations for his northern drive.

For the success of this enterprise strong Indian support was needed. On May 13 he therefore summoned Sir William Johnson to Albany with the view of concerting measures with him to this end.[16] But Johnson would guarantee at the time little assistance from the Six Nations, torn as they were between "a French & English Faction"; he had therefore to limit himself in his reply to expressing the hope that after the Indians had completed their approaching congress at Onondaga, he might be in a position to bring into the field as many as four or five hundred of the Six Nations.[17] In truth, the Indian Superintendent of the Northern District had lost so much influence with his own charges that he was even requested by a belt not only to refrain from coming to this important gathering, to which he had previously been invited, but also not to take the field in the ensuing campaign and, instead, to stay at home. In order to ascertain the true sentiments of the different nations within the Confederation Sir William, moreover, was obliged the latter part of May to send to their castles one who was more closely attached to them, Captain Jellas Fonda, bearing a brief "speech" from him indicating that he fully expected to take the field even without any Indian support.[18] But Fonda met with great obstructions in attempting to carry out his mission and at a meeting with the Mohawks and

---

[15] *Ibid.* It is of interest that this letter was not sent to Whitmore, the senior brigadier. Abercromby makes clear in a passage of it his reasons: "Here I rest it, relying that you will suggest every thing that occurs to you in Aid of us, & you will take something more upon you with your Colleague . . . who is a worthy good man, advanced in Years, without the least experience or knowledge of the State of this part of the world — On these considerations I'm persuaded he'll be very ready to take your Advice" (*ibid.*).

[16] *Johnson Papers*, IX, 900. He had already written on April 4 asking Johnson to collect as large a body of warriors as possible for this service (*ibid.*, IX, 891). Johnson on April 13 had replied that he would use his best endeavours to that end, but emphasized the necessity of providing suitable arms "should they incline to Join us in great numbers," otherwise they might turn against the British (*ibid.*, IX, 895).

[17] Johnson to Abercromby, May 17, 1758, *ibid.*, IX, 901–6.

[18] *Ibid.*, IX, 901–11.

Oneida was told that he must not proceed farther up the country as there were large numbers of French Iroquois at Onondaga.[19]

Johnson, nevertheless, persisted in his efforts to win some aid at least. Weeks passed. As late as June 22, while he still promised this aid to Abercromby, he was impelled to admit in writing to the general that the Iroquois who were to accompany him to Fort Edward had not yet arrived at Fort Johnson.[20] Meanwhile Abercromby was growing more and more impatient with the failure of Johnson to appear with his painted warriors and finally was impelled to write in surprise and in rebuke at the strange delay, adding his deep concern "at being deprived of your Aid & Assistance with the Indians at Your Back, which we stand much in need of." [21] It was not until July 5 that the baronet, accompanied by about two hundred natives, appeared in the neighbourhood of Fort Edward, some ten miles distant.[22] Finally, on July 8, the day of the decisive battle, with his numbers now increased to three hundred and ninety-five warriors, he joined Abercromby at the sawmill near Ticonderoga [23] — too late, however, for the most essential services that they could have rendered.

But other things were demanded for the success of the campaign against Canada. The provincials that had been voted by the six northern colonies, for instance, had to be raised and sent to the point of concentration. This involved time. In some colonies the troops raised were reluctant to march without arms.[24] These had been promised by Pitt in order to equip the colonials,[25] and the vessels carrying them were off Spithead on February 19 in company

---

19 Fonda's report of June 12, 1758, *ibid.*, IX, 923–5.

20 *Ibid.*, II, 851–2.

21 Abercromby to Johnson, June 24, 1758, *ibid.*, II, 853; see also John Appy to Robert Wood, July 2, 1758, *ibid.*, II, 866–70.

22 Johnson to Abercromby, July 5, 1758, *ibid.*, II, 871. The truth is that the Indians were much more interested in getting drunk than in fighting, and their squaws brought up from Albany an abundance of rum (*ibid.*).

23 The Mohawks contributed 172 warriors; the Oneida, 68; the Tuscarora, 22; the Onondaga, 30; the Cayuga, 24; the powerful Seneca, but 12; the Schoharys, 18; and the Mohikanders, 47 (*ibid.*, IX, 944–5).

24 Writing to Pitt on May 22, Abercromby declared: "I am under the greatest Difficulties imaginable for want of Arms; . . . the Provinces, knowing my Distress make a handle of it, to retard their Troops from joining me, alledging that Men without Arms can be of no Service" (*Pitt Correspondence*, I, 250).

25 In his letter of December 30 to Abercromby he stated that ten thousand arms would be provided for the soldiers of the northern provinces (*ibid.*, I, 147).

with the *Vanguard* as an escort.[26] It was not until June 14, however, that Lieutenant Governor de Lancey could write to the general from New York that they had at length arrived, together with the tents for the same purpose.[27] This was not the only difficulty. The men of Massachusetts Bay — perhaps having in mind the horrors as well as hardships that had ensued at Fort William Henry after its surrender the preceding year and, in contrast, the exhilaration of the Louisbourg campaign of 1745 and, it may be added, also the prospect of acquiring in Nova Scotia good estates that had belonged to the Acadians before their recent expulsion — were strongly committed to the idea of being sent "Eastward." In fact, both the House of Representatives and the Council brought pressure to bear upon Governor Pownall to use his influence with Abercromby to that end. When the general made clear that he was under positive orders to use them on his own expedition and in defence of the upper country, they were not at all happy.[28] This may help to explain the misconduct and lack of spirit of many of them, to which reference will be made. Abercromby did, however, fall in line with the Governor's strong recommendation that, to encourage enlistments throughout the province, the numerous deserters from the preceding campaign should be pardoned if they would agree to re-enlist for the new campaign;[29] at the same time he very politely refused the earnest request of Pownall that he be permitted to engage actively in this year's operations in a military capacity.[30]

There were, unhappily, great delays in the raising of the provincial contingents. As late as June 19 Massachusetts Bay had not se-

---

[26] Boscawen to Abercromby, May 18, 1758, Abercromby Papers, No. 264.

[27] *Ibid.*, No. 355.

[28] See Abercromby to Pownall, March 25, 1758, *ibid.*, No. 72.

[29] *Ibid.*

[30] Could any words be more tactful than the following regarding Pownall's ambitions to play a military role: "But, my Dear Governor, how can I take upon me to advise you on this Subject, when at the same Time that I shou'd be willing to gratify My own Inclinations, I might perhaps expose myself for encouraging your quitting a Place, where your Presence may be more essentially necessary; permit me therefore to abide by what I have already said on this Subject" (*ibid.*). Abercromby undoubtedly not only questioned the Governor's qualifications for an active command of troops but also shared Loudoun's feelings that Pownall was so opinionated that should his views be crossed, there would develop serious friction. That the Governor was deeply hurt at the decision that he should remain in Boston is indicated by his reply to Abercromby on April 3 (*ibid.*, No. 106): "As to my leaving my Province, I have an Instruction for that very Purpose whenever my Services may be of use else where, I was in hopes they might be on this Occasion of peculiar use. . . ."

cured the number it had agreed to provide,[31] and other colonies, such as Connecticut, experienced similar difficulties.[32] Moreover, the movement of these troops into upper New York was extraordinarily slow. When Abercromby wrote to Pitt from Lake George on June 29, he was compelled to point out that not one half of the provincials he expected to take with him for his assault on Fort Ticonderoga had arrived, and added: "There are but 500 of the Connecticut Troops at this Place, and not a single Man of the New Hampshire-men, or Rhode-Islanders, You will see by the Return the Deficiencies of the Massachusetts-Bay. . . ." [33]

These returns indicated that a total of fewer than six thousand provincials, out of an authorized twenty thousand, had, after the passing of many precious weeks, as yet appeared. Indeed, hardly more than one half of the contemplated seven thousand Massachusetts Bay troops were then on hand to be assigned their duties, and less than fifteen hundred of the five thousand Connecticut troops, including the one thousand sent up the Mohawk to Schenectady.[34] There was, of course, no time now left to turn these men, for the most part raw recruits, into disciplined soldiers. If the campaign was to be launched this year, it had to be without further delay. Including the regulars, numbering about sixty-three hundred, the rangers, and the fifty-nine hundred provincials, Abercromby succeeded in concentrating at Lake George by the first of July some twelve thousand troops — in place of an anticipated twenty-seven thousand, as Pitt had planned — together with an artillery train and eight hundred bateaux and ninety whaleboats — a transport

---

[31] Pownall to Abercromby, June 29, 1758, ibid., No. 366.

[32] "Govr. Fitches brief Acc^o. of Proceedings Respecting ye War," 1758, Fitch Papers, I, 350. As late as June 8 New Hampshire had raised only seven hundred men out of but eight hundred promised (Provincial Papers, VI, 680–1). As late as June 15 Colonel Henry Babcock of the Rhode Island regiment was writing to Governor Hopkins: "I can't but hope that the General Assembly will fall upon some method of expeditiously raising the remainder of the Troops" (Rhode Island Colonial Records, VI, 151). It appears that the colony fell some three hundred short of the one thousand the Assembly agreed to provide.

[33] Abercromby to Pitt, June 29, 1758, Pitt Correspondence, I, 285.

[34] "Return of Provincial Troops at Lake George," June 29, 1758 (Abercromby Papers, No. 400). There were 2,853 from Massachusetts Bay; 475 from Connecticut; 1,715 from New York; and 922 from New Jersey. A part of the provincials were set aside to guard the lower Mohawk: 700 from Massachusetts Bay, 1,000 from Connecticut, 700 from Rhode Island, and 600 from New York. These were placed under command of General Stanwix, who turned over his Pennsylvania command to General Forbes. Stanwix also had under him three New York Independent Companies and two of rangers (ibid., No. 359).

supply quite sufficient to carry the available troops, military stores, provisions, and artillery.[35]

By the evening of July 4 the artillery, stores, and provisions were embarked, and then, with the arrival of other contingents of provincials — to bring their number up to about ten thousand — as well as additional bateaux and whaleboats, the army, numbering about sixteen thousand souls, took to the water the following day and proceeded up the lake some twenty-five miles to Sabbath Day Point in four long columns headed by Colonel Bradstreet's bateau-men, Rogers's rangers, and Gage's light infantry, all in whaleboats.[36] These were followed by a thousand bateaux. The sight must have been impressive to the observer. "They covered the Lake from side to side, which is a Mile and a Half over at the upper End; and . . . extended from Front to Rear full seven Miles," wrote one who watched them leave the lower end of Lake George.[37] After a halt they proceeded by night to the designated landing-place — a cove just below where the French advanced guard from Ticonderoga was stationed — arriving there early on the 6th.[38]

Had Abercromby been free to march with his regulars as early in the spring as Lord Loudoun had planned to do, the outcome of the campaign might have been — in fact, most probably would have been — very different. For Loudoun, realizing, as the result of reports, that the British could move from Fort Edward to Lake George a fortnight earlier than the French could possibly move from the St. Lawrence to the head of that lake because of the difference in the climate, as has already been indicated, had in mind appearing before Ticonderoga toward the end of May with twelve regiments of regulars. These had been concentrated for this purpose, as previously stated, in the area of the Hudson and Mohawk rivers and were ready to move "on an Hour's Notice." [39] To convey them across the lake to the neighbourhood of the fort with the necessary supplies, artillery, and other matériel would have required much less in the way of transportation facilities than was necessary for the type of force that Abercromby was compelled to take with him upon the basis of Pitt's orders. It meant that the more limited number of boats of

[35] Abercromby to Pitt, May 29, 1758, Pitt Correspondence, I, 285.

[36] Abercromby's General Orders of July 3, 1757, Abercromby Papers, No. 407.

[37] Pennsylvania Gazette, July 27, 1758.

[38] Abercromby to Pitt, July 12, 1758, Pitt Correspondence, I, 297.

[39] James Robertson to the Earl of Morton, December 19, 1758, Military Affairs in North America, 1748–1765 (ed. Pargellis), pp. 429–32.

various types built either on the Hudson or, in the case of whale-boats, at New England wharves could have been completed and portaged with more dispatch and much less difficulty than the vastly greater number now actually needed. Had it been possible for Abercromby to appear at Ticonderoga a month earlier, what would have confronted him? Certainly no force that would have made any effective resistance.

French soldiers had been scattered for the long winter of 1757–8 among the farmhouses lying about Montreal and Quebec.[40] Commissaire of Supplies Doreil, writing to Belle-Isle on April 30, emphasized that the winter had been especially severe,[41] and reference has been made in the preceding chapter to dire scarcity of food in Canada. The Sieur Daine, in charge of the King's domain, in a letter also addressed to the Maréchal under date of May 19, declared: "I am at a loss for terms to describe our misfortunes." [42] Four days earlier Montcalm noted in his *Journal* that "the colony is almost (à deux doigts) lost." [43] In vain all in New France in the spring had waited anxiously for news of the coming from France of supplies — of food above everything else. There could be no concentration of troops without this relief. Not until May 22 did a messenger reach the general with information that the ministry was sending in three convoys from Bordeaux everything necessary to maintain the colony.[44] Then on the 25th two vessels laden with provisions — flour, pork, maize, and codfish — from Cape Breton Island finally moored at Quebec, and the day following two more ships appeared, these from France — one out of twelve of the "first convoy" and another from the "second convoy." [45] Other ships gradually made their appearance. By the middle of June a total of some thirteen merchantmen had at length arrived, bringing in all twelve thousand barrels of flour and some other provisions. This supply, it is true, was, in the words of Doreil, "very trifling in comparison with the vastness of our wants," yet it was enough to enable Vaudreuil to open the year's campaign.[46] In fact, on the last day of May,

---

[40] Montcalm to de Paulmy, April 18, 1758, *Documents Relating to the Colonial History of the State of New York*, X, 699.

[41] *Ibid.*, X, 701.

[42] *Ibid.*, X, 704.

[43] *Journal du Marquis de Montcalm, 1756–1769* (ed. Abbé Casgrain), p. 351.

[44] *Ibid.*, p. 353.

[45] *Ibid.*, pp. 355–6.

[46] Doreil to Belle-Isle, June 16, 1758, *N. Y. Col. Doc.*, X, 717.

Montcalm, with the arrival of the first four provision ships, issued his orders for the departure of the French battalions early in June for the Lake Champlain area.[47]

But the inexpressible relief of the French leaders in Canada in receiving this limited aid — out of so much that the ministry had attempted to forward[48] — with the possibility now of moving the troops, was tempered with news that produced dismay: the *Foudroyant*, bringing not only provisions but all the Indian presents for the year, had sunk off the coast of Newfoundland.[49] However, on June 8 Vaudreuil came to the determination to assemble five thousand soldiers at Ticonderoga.[50] By the middle of June the Chevalier de Bourlamaque arrived there at the head of the Languedoc battalion for the strengthening of the little garrison.[51] But it was not until the 24th that Montcalm was able to leave Montreal for Lake Champlain to begin his campaign. Thus the British, as previously indicated, lost a golden opportunity to strike long before the French could possibly move.

In departing for Lake Champlain Montcalm was far from being a happy man. The Governor General, in fact, had sent instructions to him, for his guidance, that he regarded as "ridiculous, obscure, and insidious";[52] he was especially furious over the preamble of the document, which stated that these instructions had been formed only after deliberating with the general on all matters relating to the colony — something that the latter, in returning them to Vaudreuil, declared was simply not true.[53] Not until the afternoon of

[47] *Journal*, p. 358.

[48] Of thirty-six ships that sailed for the St. Lawrence from Bordeaux in three divisions with provisions and other supplies, only twelve arrived by June 16; of the convoy awaited from La Rochelle and those from Bayonne and Marseille, not one had come (*N. Y. Col. Doc.*, X, 718).

[49] *Ibid.*, p. 362; also excerpts of a letter from Quebec, dated May 30, 1758, Chatham Mss., Bundle 96, P.R.O. (Canadian Archives Transcripts). The *Foudroyant* here mentioned is not to be confused with the great French battleship captured in the Mediterranean that carried the same name.

[50] Montcalm's *Journal*, p. 364.

[51] *Ibid.*, p. 372.

[52] "*Mémoire pour Servir d'instruction à M. de Montcalm*," June 23, 1758, Waddington, *op. cit.*, II, 374. Waddington calls them "as obscure as they were stringy" (*ibid.*, II, 375).

[53] Montcalm records in his *Journal* for June 23 (*ibid.*, pp. 376–7), that Vaudreuil "has never consulted with me on anything; that he never shared with me either the news that he had received or his projects, or his proceedings; and I declared to him positively that I would never suffer this fraudulent preamble to remain at the head of his instructions as a monument reflecting on my reputation."

the 30th was he, accompanied by the Béarn battalion, able to reach Ticonderoga. There he found himself at the head of eight very weak battalions, by reason of the poor quality of the recruits recently sent from France and by the fact that strong detachments from each had been withdrawn by Vaudreuil for de Lévis's projected enterprise to the country of the Six Nations and then against the settlements on the Mohawk. He also found himself with but nine days' provisions and, what was perhaps even more serious, with but a handful of Indians, and these full of insolence and discontent at not receiving their customary presents. In their disappointment, the latter carried away by force barrels of wine from the commissariat and killed cattle. Unable to prevent these outrages for fear of turning his fierce allies into enemies, he could, in fact, only inscribe in his *Journal:* "What a country! What a war!" [54]

Before the arrival of Montcalm at the fort, parties had been sent out to discover the activities of the British at the head of Lake Saint-Sacrement, or Lake George as the English had named it. They returned with prisoners who indicated that a thousand horses and an equal number of oxen were employed to bring to the lake front supplies for besieging Fort Ticonderoga and that an expedition numbering between twenty and twenty-five thousand would take to the water early in July. Bourlamaque had already sent messengers to Vaudreuil with this ominous news, and Montcalm, the evening of his arrival, sent off another courier asking for more provisions, more Indians, and more help in general from the colony. The next morning he set seven of his battalions in motion — some of them to go with Bourlamaque over to the right bank of the river to the end of the portage and some, under his personal command, to occupy both banks at the great falls at the near end of the same. This was done with the idea of ridding the minds of the enemy of the idea that the French were weak and of preventing, if possible, their sudden seizure of the portage road. He then, in company with the military engineers Pontleroy and Desandrouins, made a careful survey of the fort.

Fort Carillon, or Ticonderoga as it was called by the English, stood on a rocky ledge that projected out into the river that drains Lake George just at the point where it flows into Lake Champlain. In the form of a polygon, the fort measured some three hundred and twenty-four feet at its greatest length by some one hundred

---

[54] *Ibid.,* p. 385.

and seventy-four at its narrowest point. Its wall, provided with bastions, was built of squared pieces of oak laid one on top of another and bound together; this was pierced with embrasures designed to permit the cannon to command various points of the approach. The irregular form of the wall, however, did not permit any concentrated fire upon a particular battery that an enemy might direct against it; further, since the ramparts were not more than fourteen feet wide the platforms upon which the cannon were placed were so narrow that upon discharge they were liable in their recoil to run off them. The bastions, having been casemated, served to house the regular garrison, the powder magazine, and other utilities. There were also within the enclosure several stone buildings, two stories high, rising above the ramparts and thus hindering the use of the latter should shot and shell be fired against them. Outside the wall were located various storehouses and sheds, two hospitals, and other conveniences, which were protected simply by a palisade. Half a league to the west of the fort and up the river were the principal falls, and then came the detour by land of half a league along the river to the second falls, called the "portage," to which reference has been made. Finally, about a thousand yards from the fort was a dominating hill bordering the right bank of the river and commanding Ticonderoga and the approaches to it.[55] After Pontleroy had surveyed the fort he wrote pessimistically in a *mémoire:*

> "From this description 'twill be seen how little susceptible of defence is this fort; yet, 'tis the only work that covers Lake Champlain and, consequently, this Colony. Were I entrusted with the siege of it, I should require only six mortars and two cannon." [56]

Clearly, the only means of protecting Ticonderoga was to keep the enemy at a distance from it and therefore Montcalm was correct in concentrating all but one of the battalions about the only feasible approach to it by an enemy moving down Lake George. He also

[55] "Remarks on the situation of Fort Carillon and its approaches" by d'Hughes, enclosed in a letter to Belle-Isle, June 1, 1758, N. Y. *Col. Doc.*, X, 707–10; "Memoir on Fort Carillon by M. de Pont le Roy, Engineer in Chief, *ibid.*, X, 720.

[56] *Ibid.* D'Hughes has the following to say of Fort St. Frédéric at Crown Point: "Fort Carillon once taken, Fort Frédéric would not stand an instant. The latter is built of stone so as to be incapable of resisting four cannon shot, which would be sufficient to tumble it utterly into ruins. All the country in its vicinity is flat and affords, at every step, an easy landing for the largest guns; even firing a few shot at it from pontoons would be enough to render it incapable of answering, it being all shook" (*ibid.*, X, 709).

sent out each day up to July 6 detachments to cruise the lake or scour the woods for sign of the advancing British. On July 4, for example, the Sieur de Langy went out on the lake with one hundred and seventy-eight volunteers to reconnoitre; on the 5th Captain de Trépezec of the Béarn battalion left with some three hundred for the top of Bare or Bald Mountain (Mountagne-Pelée), now known as Rogers' Slide, to observe the movements of the enemy and also to oppose their landing. Langy returned the same day with the news that they were approaching; finally, at four o'clock the morning of the 6th a scouting barge reported that fifteen hundred craft were in sight and were searching for a fit landing.

Thus warned of the immense strength of the enemy, Montcalm the evening of the 5th had sent orders to Bourlamaque to be prepared to retire the next morning with his battalions in the direction of the fort. The latter therefore began his retreat, only waiting with a small detachment to get some report of Trépezec and his men, sent, as indicated, to Bare Mountain; when no news of them arrived, he departed and joined Montcalm at the falls and destroyed the bridge. In the afternoon — after hearing firing in the distance and after the arrival of the remnants of Trépezec's force, which had been decimated by the English now on land — the march back to Carillon began, and early in the evening the troops arrived at a clearing in the neighbourhood of the fort. They thereupon arranged themselves in order of battle and bivouacked for the night.[57]

When Abercromby's army made for a landing on the morning of the 6th at what the French called Contrecœur's Camp, on the west bank of Lake George, there were some three or four hundred of Bourlamaque's rear guard stationed there; but they now retreated, as has been related, and the British, as a result, swarmed ashore without opposition. Still from three to six miles distant from the fort — depending upon the route chosen to approach it — they were able after a brief delay to begin their march in four columns by the more circuitous path to it, veering off to the left and moving through the dense woods, which brought inevitable confusion in their ranks. The columns of rangers, grenadiers, light infantry, and provincials headed by Howe[58] proceeded more rapidly than the others and

---

[57] Montcalm's *Journal*, pp. 385–92; Malartic's "Journal of the Military Operations before Ticonderoga," *N. Y. Col. Doc.*, X, 721–3.

[58] Howe, it may be pointed out, permitted his zeal for the service to do something that caution forbids a commanding officer with great responsibility for the welfare of

consequently, in pushing ahead, unexpectedly fell in with the French detachment under Langy and Trépezec that had gone to Bare Mountain, some miles south of the landing, and was returning to the fort as best it could through the forest — in default of the Indian guides, who had left it to wander about.[59] In the firing that took place the surprised enemy was routed, with a hundred killed and about a hundred and fifty taken prisoner — many of these by the Connecticut troops under General Lyman [60] — but, to the inexpressible grief of the British army, Lord Howe fell mortally wounded at the first exchange of fire.[61] In the words of Abercromby, ". . . he was very deservedly, universally beloved and respected throughout the whole Army, and it is easy to conceive the Grief and Consternation his untimely fall occasioned. . . ." [62] To the provincials also the death of Howe was "an unspeakable Loss." [63] That he had won the hearts of the soldiers of Massachusetts Bay is indicated by the fact that early the following year the Assembly of that colony, as a "Testimony to the . . . Services and Military Virtues of the late Lord Viscount Howe, who fell in the last Campaign fighting in the Cause of the Colonies and also to express the Affection which

an army to do; for he needlessly exposed his life in leading a column of troops liable to be attacked. This he insisted on doing, it appears, "notwithstanding all the remonstrances made him" ("Detailed Statement of Operations at Ticonderoga," *Pennsylvania Archives*, first series, III, 473; the account was apparently written by a Swiss officer attached to the 47th Regiment; it is in French and bears the date July 14, 1758).

[59] *Montcalm's Journal*, pp. 393–4.

[60] Captain Loring to ——, August 13, 1758, Chatham Mss., Bundle 96 (Canadian Archives Transcripts).

[61] According to an account of the skirmish brought to New York by express, but not confirmed in any other account, Howe "was shot dead by a French Officer, after he had entreated him to surrender to good Quarters; and that the French Officer was directly shot dead in his Turn, by the Brigadier's Aide-de-Camp" (*Pennsylvania Gazette*, July 20, 1758). Trépezec, we know, was mortally wounded and was carried by his men to the falls, where he died. Did Howe beg him to surrender on good terms?

[62] Abercromby to Pitt, July 12, 1758, *Pitt Correspondence*. A portion of a letter written on May 31 from New York to a person in Portsmouth, New Hampshire, indicates the basis for his popularity among all troops, both regulars and provincials: "I need not inform you, I suppose, how justly Lord Howe is celebrated here for his robust Soldier-like Constitution, his bold, enterprising Spirit, and every other Military Accomplishment; with how much Care he has been forming his regular Troops to the Method of Bush-fighting all this Season. . . . The Strength of his Constitution enables him to undergo all Hardships. . . . His Soldiers love and fear him, and are willing to comply with his Commands, because he sets them an Example. — What great things might not a few Officers like Lord Howe effect, with an Army of such Men!" (*Pennsylvania Gazette*, July 6, 1758).

[63] Colonel Israel Williams of Massachusetts Bay to his uncle, July 11, 1758, Williams Mss., Mass. Hist. Soc.

their Officers and Soldiers bore to his Command," voted the sum of two hundred and fifty pounds sterling to erect a monument to his memory.[64] As a result, a tablet was placed in Westminister Abbey as a memorial to the young Viscount that embodied these sentiments of devotion to his memory on the part of the people of a colony who, before two decades had passed, were to appear in arms against his brother and the cause he represented.

Had Abercromby been able to call upon either Brigadier General John Stanwix or Brigadier General John Forbes, the loss of Howe might not have been so grievous for the army; but neither was available: the former was up the Mohawk to secure that approach, and the latter was busy with his preparations for the expedition against Fort Duquesne. Colonels Montrésor and Eyre, military engineers, were present, but the former was ill and the latter, after a disagreement with Abercromby over the command of his regiment, was not called upon to act in his most important and specialized capacity.[65] Bradstreet was a great raider and highly serviceable in his sphere, but his influence with Abercromby was limited at this juncture. As for Colonel Gage of the light infantry, he had been with Braddock, had abundantly shown his ineptness in wilderness fighting, and could therefore not be depended upon to supply much military talent of the sort that was so sorely needed. In the words of Captain Loring, whom Pitt had sent over to restore British naval supremacy on Lake George: ". . . so far things had been properly Conducted and with Spirit, But no sooner was his Lordship [General Howe] Dead, then everything took a different turn and finally ended in Confusion and disgrace. . . ."[66]

With the soldiers both bewildered and alarmed, according to Colonel Eyre, at their position in the dense woods after this preliminary engagement, it was decided to return to the landing-place to reorganize and reroute the force. A part of the troops, as a result, spent the night there and in the morning were joined by the rest under Abercromby, who were caught in the darkness and obliged to camp in the midst of the forest.[67] Thereupon it was decided to cross

[64] Records of the General Court of Massachusetts Bay, 1757–59, 22:543, Massachusetts Archives.

[65] Eyre to Robert Napier, July 10, 1758, Military Affairs in North America, 1758–1765, p. 420.

[66] Captain Loring to ——, August 13, 1758, Chatham Mss., Bundle 96 (Canadian Archives Transcripts).

[67] Eyre to Napier, July 10, 1758, op. cit., p. 419.

over to the east bank of the river and to take the direct portage road to the sawmill and falls. This was done without opposition with Bradstreet leading the advance with a mixed body of regulars, bateau-men, rangers, and provincials. Upon arriving he threw a bridge across the stream at that point to take the place of the one that the French had destroyed and, as a result, the entire army found itself late in the afternoon of the 7th again on the left bank of the river but a mile and a half from the fort.

Once more it seemed best to camp for the night, and on the morning of the 8th — after the engineer Lieutenant Matthew Clark had reconnoitred the enemy's breastworks and pronounced them weak — the general summoned to a council of war the commanding officers of the regiments to determine the method of attack against the enemy now concentrated behind its forward defences, well in advance of the fort itself. However, it appears that the only question submitted for their decision had to do with the method of a frontal attack and not the larger and more fundamental one relating to the best means of securing the fort and routing the enemy with the least cost of life.[68] Here was Abercromby's fatal mistake. In defence of him, it may be pointed out that he was labouring under a profound misconception of the strength of the enemy and of its ability to secure, in addition, powerful reinforcements. All this was the result of reports secured from the French prisoners captured on the 6th. They were unanimous in declaring that Montcalm had six thousand troops with him about the fort and that three thousand more were coming to assist him under command of the Chevalier de Lévis.[69] It therefore seemed imperative to attack without delay, and to the general this meant nothing less than a frontal attack on the entrenchments, and, what is important to bear in mind, an attack without support of the artillery, which still rested on the rafts.

How precarious and untenable was the position of the French on that memorable day when they inflicted a decisive defeat upon the British, who outnumbered them almost five to one, can be understood by referring again to the terrain lying adjacent to Fort Ticonderoga. Across the stream that empties into Lake Champlain from Lake George and that dominates the fort is a high elevation, to

---

[68] Ibid., p. 420.

[69] Abercromby to de Lancey, July 18, 1758, Abercromby Papers, No. 445. At the time these men were captured, there were less than three thousand effectives among the French forces (Montcalm to Belle-Isle, July 12, 1758, N. Y. Col. Doc., X, 732).

which reference has already been made, later known as Mount Defiance. Captain Charles Lee of the 44th regiment and later to become a major general in the Continental army, writing with deep feeling of the events of that fatal day, declared:

> "these proceedings must undoubtedly appear most astonishingly absurd to people who were at a distance, but they are still more glaringly so to us who were upon the spot & saw the disposition of the ground. There was one hill in particular which seem'd to offer itself as an ally to us, it immediately Commanded the lines from hence two small pieces of cannon well planted must have drove the French in a very short time from their breast work, the consequence of which wou'd have been that the greatest part of 'em must either have surrendered or drown'd themselves in the Lake . . . but notwithstanding some of our Cannon was brought up & in readiness, this never was thought of, which (one wou'd imagine) must have occur'd to any blockhead who was not absolutely so far sunk in Idiotism as to be oblig'd to wear a bib and bells." [70]

The French military engineer d'Hugues, who was at Ticonderoga before the attack, saw the strategic importance of the hill and the vital necessity of fortifying it.[71] Pontleroy, military engineer in chief, affirmed, as has already been stated, that all that he would desire to reduce the fort would be six mortars and two cannon.[72] While he did not mention this elevation, he must have had it in mind. It was certainly clear in 1777 to General Arthur St. Clair, the American general, that with it in the hands of the enemy the works of Ticonderoga were absolutely worthless as a defence of the place.[73] When Brigadier General Simon Fraser, leading Burgoyne's advance in that year, approached the fort, he immediately realized the importance of Mount Defiance and seized it. "I found this mountain," he reported, "Commanded everything at Ticonderoga . . . any kind of work on the hill took the [American] works . . . *en Revers*, at the medium distance of about 12 or 1300 Yards & it was very practicable to make roads for transporting . . . ordnance to the top of it." [74] St. Clair was therefore fully justified, when Fraser

---

[70] Charles Lee's "Narrative," enclosed in a letter of September 16, 1758, *The Lee Papers*, New York Historical Society, *Collections*, 1871, I, 13.

[71] "Remarks on the situation of Fort Carillon and its Approaches," N. Y. Col. Doc., X, 708.

[72] Ibid., X, 720.

[73] *The St. Clair Papers: Life and Public Services of Arthur St. Clair*, I, 75.

[74] Fraser to [John Robinson], July 13, 1777, Stevens Facsimilies, No. 1561, New York Public Library.

placed a force on the elevation, in deserting the fort with his troops, and a court martial subsequently vindicated his judgment, in spite of uninformed criticism of his conduct.

But Abercromby, instead of detailing a sufficiently large detachment of his troops to proceed to convey some of the artillery — still resting on the rafts — over the portage road and to the mountain top to be used in case he found the enemy too strongly entrenched to dislodge by direct assault, satisfied himself by sending Johnson and his Indians to occupy this vital elevation. After some desultory and ineffective firing with their small arms, the latter thereupon simply settled down to watch the spectacle that unfolded beneath them on the plain.[75]

Montcalm, after returning to the vicinity of the fort on the evening of the 6th, made camp and then early the next morning sent three brigades to the entrance of the woods to begin his abatis or tree barrier in front of the entrenchments located at the top of a slope beyond cannon-shot of the fort. Such a barrier, it will be appreciated, cannot safely be prepared much in advance of a contemplated attack by an enemy, since masses of leaves, twigs, and branches are easily set afire. For the trunks of trees are so laid that the tops project outward and, even with much of the foliage removed and many of the branches sharpened, present an entanglement that is still highly combustible if permitted to dry, and yet which constitutes a temporary formidable barrier to an approaching force. At the end of the day's labour such an abatis was laid down — some seven or eight feet high and a hundred yards in depth — extending from the river to a ravine that bordered Lake Champlain.[76] Behind it the French could now fire in almost perfect security by means of loopholes furnished by capping the tall entrenchments with bags of sand.

That evening some of the French troops — set aside for the expedition against the upper Mohawk Valley but now diverted by Vaudreuil as the result of the alarms sent out from Ticonderoga — put in their appearance, and early on the morning of the 8th de Lévis himself arrived with the rest of the soldiers who would take

---

[75] Montcalm's *Journal*, p. 398.

[76] Malartic's "Journal of Military Operations before Ticonderoga," *N. Y. Col. Doc.*, X, 723; "Detailed Statement of Operations at Ticonderoga, July 14, 1758," *Pennsylvania Archives* (first series), III, 472; Captain Loring to ——, August 13, 1758, Chatham Mss., Bundle 96 (Canadian Archives Transcripts); Colonel Eyre to Napier, July 10, 1758, *Military Affairs in North America, 1748–1765*, p. 420.

LAKE GEORGE

Jnᵒ Lodge Sculp

Sketch of Cheonderoga or Ticonderoga by an English officer, showing Abercromby's advance, 1758.

(From John Almon's *Remembrancer*.)

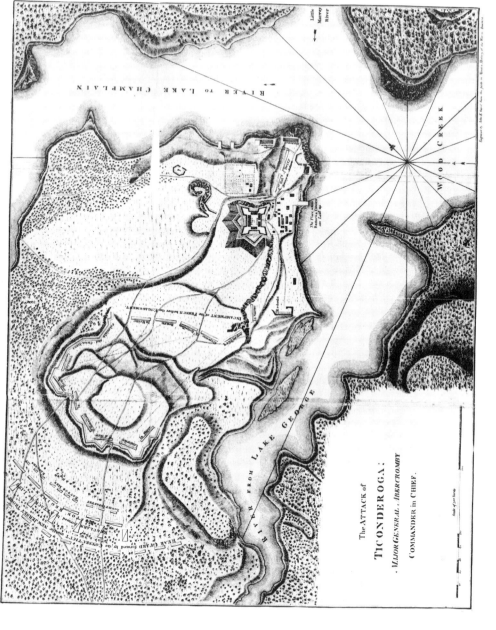

Abercromby's attack on the French entrenchments erected near Fort Ticonderoga 1758

part in the battle. He was immediately placed in charge of the right wing of the defence, with Bourlamaque commanding the left wing and Montcalm himself directing the center. There were now opposing Abercromby the three best field officers that the French had in North America.

The British general, overwhelmed with the necessity for haste, in ordering the grand assault did not feel that he could take the time even to bring up his artillery to support it.[77] Yet Captain Loring, who helped to load it on the rafts, declared that it "lay very Contiguous at the landing place, and could very easily have been Brought up Long before the Atack, had they been Order'd." He also added: "I think we had the finest Train for atacking of Lines that ever was in America," with two hundred rounds of ammunition for each piece.[78] Indeed, by concentrating a heavy artillery fire at particular points and by the use of red-hot cannon balls such as Wolfe made use of at Louisbourg, the abatis, which actually caught fire several times during the engagement,[79] might have gone up in smoke and flames. Further, with the lobbing of shells over the entrenchments upon the heads of the defenders sheltered behind them, their position — without any artillery support except at the fort, the guns of which were out of range — might have become quite untenable. Once they had retreated, it is clear that they would not have attempted to defend the fort, but would have taken to their boats on Lake Champlain, all prepared for such a contingency.

In forming his line of battle for the attack, Abercromby made, it is clear, a suitable disposition of the troops. In the front line were the light infantry, the bateau-men, and the rangers, to be used for sharpshooting work; behind them were the Massachusetts Bay regiments; then came the regulars, who were to carry the burden of the assault; and, finally, there was the rear guard, made up of Connecticut and New Jersey provincials. It was decided in the council

[77] Writing to James Abercromby, Esq., on August 19, 1758, General Abercromby sought to excuse himself for not utilizing his artillery, declaring: "On this Side, the Attack has been censured, in not waiting till our Artillery could be brought up. . . . To accomplish it, must have been the Work of several Days . . ." (Chatham Mss., Bundle 98, Canadian Archives Transcripts).

[78] Abercromby had available, according to Loring, four eighteen-pounders, six twelve-pounders, six six-pounders, a thirteen-inch mortar, and two of ten-inch and eight brass royals, nine eight-inch howitzers, and four of the five-and-two-fifths-inch calibre (Loring to ——, August 13, 1758, Chatham Mss., Bundle 96, Canadian Archives Transcripts).

[79] Montcalm's Journal, p. 401.

of war, however, that the grenadiers and the pickets, the latter made
up also of regulars, should begin the attack, to be followed by the
rest of the regulars in battalion front three men deep,[80] rather than
in column — a decision that Colonel Eyre considered to be a
blunder.[81] All the attacking troops were under strict orders "to
march up briskly, rush upon the Enemy's fire, and not to give theirs
untill they were within the Enemie's Breast-work"[82] — an order
utterly impossible to execute under existing conditions and consequently disregarded.

The battle began at about half past twelve o'clock with troops on
the British right moving to assault the French battalions entrenched
near the river; then the French center was submitted to attack,
and soon the right of center. In the intervals between the attacking
battalions, light-armed troops sheltered by the trees also poured
in upon the enemy "a murderous fire."[83] On the extreme French
right were posted at right angles to the main line, and also behind
entrenchments, the French colonials as well as the Canadian militia. Not being under attack, these troops took advantage of their
position to direct their fire upon the flank of the battalions moving
against the French right-center entrenchments. These British battalions, made up of Thomas Murray's grenadier regiment, the 46th,
and Lord John Murray's Highlanders, the 42nd, continued to return to the assault without either faltering or breaking, according
to Montcalm, and many of these brave men, he also indicated, were
killed within fifteen paces of the abatis — caught by the fire of the
enemy not only in front but on their flank.[84] At about five o'clock,
after bitter fighting, the points of attack were changed: a furious,
concentrated charge of the British battalions was launched against
the entrenchments of the French center, where the regiments of
Guyenne and the left wing of that of Béarn were posted; this
seemed to present such a threat that both Montcalm and de Lévis
were impelled to rush reinforcements to that point to support the
defenders.[85] Then at six o'clock the attack shifted to the French
left of this approach against the Royal Roussillon and Berry bat-

<hr>

[80] Abercromby to Pitt, July 12, 1758, Pitt Correspondence, I, 300; Eyre to Napier,
July 10, 1758, op. cit., p. 420.
[81] Ibid.
[82] Abercromby to Pitt, July 12, 1758, op. cit., I, 300.
[83] Montcalm's Journal, p. 399.
[84] Ibid., p. 400.
[85] Ibid.

talions. But everywhere the French held and everywhere the fires starting in the abatis were quenched by bucket brigades.

Early in the struggle, it should be pointed out, an effort was made to approach the fort by some boats and artillery rafts for the purpose of bombardment; but, coming within range of the guns of the fort, two of the British craft were sunk and the others then retired from the action and no further attempt was made from the water to turn the French left flank. At seven o'clock the assaults ceased and Abercromby's army — deprived now of many of its best regimental and company leaders — began a retreat covered by the fire of the light-armed troops. The heavy losses on that memorable day were almost entirely from the ranks of the regulars, with 464 killed, 29 missing, and 1,117 wounded, according to Abercromby's report, sent in duplicate.[86] The Highlanders suffered especially, with many of their officers either killed or wounded.[87] They lost, in fact, a total of 203 men killed and 296 wounded in their desperate attempts to storm the French breastworks. The retreat, begun in an orderly fashion, soon assumed the proportions of a panic flight. In the words of the general:

> "But tho' the Provincials could scarcely be said to be engaged that Day, the losses which they take credit for, having happened chiefly on the 6th, yet upwards of two thirds of them retired upon the 8th, with great Precipitation to our Landing-Place, and after the Attack was over, I returned to the [ruins of the] Sawmill, so as to post a Guard at the Bridge, to stop the Remainder of them. . . ."[88]

Indeed, it appears that no one was more surprised with the retreat than were the defenders of the fort. According to the reports brought to the English camp at Lake George later by French deserters, it had been fully anticipated that the attack would be re-

---

86 Abercromby to Pitt, July 12, 1758, N. Y. Col. Doc., X, 727–32; and idem to idem, of the same date, Pitt Correspondence, I, 300, for the total casualty figures. Each letter supplies certain details not to be found in the other. The provincial casualty list gives a total of 87 killed, 8 missing, and 239 wounded on the expedition. These latter losses, according to the general, did not occur in the course of the major engagement on the 8th but in fighting on the 6th, the day of the landing (letter to James Abercromby, Esq., August 19, 1758, Chatham Mss., Bundle 98, Canadian Archives Transcripts).

87 Abercromby Papers, No. 425; Pennsylvania Gazette, July 27 and August 3, 1758.

88 Abercromby to James Abercromby, Esq., August 19, 1758, op. cit.; see also Thomas Mante: History of the Late War in America, p. 148. Mante points out that the panic might have resulted in dire disaster had not Colonel Bradstreet prevented the fleeing soldiers from entering the boats, in which case "the greatest part must have perished."

newed the next day with the support then of the artillery. In anticipation that the defence of the entrenchments, under this circumstance, could not be maintained — which, in the words of Captain Loring, "must have Soon been the Case with the Train of Artillery we had with us" — plans were fully made for the main body of the French forces to retreat as far to the north as Fort St. Jean at the lower end of Lake Champlain, leaving as a rear guard at Ticonderoga only enough troops to secure the withdrawal.[89] But Abercromby had had his fill of fighting; the regiments that he most depended upon were now shorn of many of their best officers; nor did he have faith in the fighting ability of provincials, even those who did not flee from the battlefield, but wanted to stand their ground and entrench, as General Lyman's Connecticut line desired to do after the battle.[90] And so with an army that, in spite of its losses, still "had Strength enough Left to have Marcht Through any part of Canada," according to an officer who was to campaign with Amherst,[91] the general proceeded to withdraw to the site of Fort William Henry, where Fort George was soon to be erected.

It may be said that probably no military campaign was ever launched on American soil that involved a greater number of errors in judgment on the part of those in positions of responsibility. Pitt undoubtedly erred, as has been stressed, not only in removing Loudoun from command but also in insisting that a very large body of provincials should be gathered to participate in the expedition and also in setting aside the plan of his late commander-in-chief in North America for a very early drive against Ticonderoga — with his regulars already under arms — before the French could move in the spring. In the words of Abercromby:

"And it is with Concern that I tell you, that, from every Circumstance I have seen, & which has happened, no real Dependence is to be had upon the Bulk of the Provincials — And how can it be other-

---

[89] Captain Loring to ——, August 13, 1758, op. cit. According to the testimony of some who deserted the French army after the battle, "Montcalm was so certain of being defeated . . . that he ordered a Number of Battoes to be kept in Readiness to take in the Garrison of Ticonderoga, as they intended to abandon the Fort and Entrenchments, as soon as our People had brought up their battering Cannon" (Albany advices, Pennsylvania Gazette, July 27, 1758).

[90] Ibid.

[91] Captain Loring to ——, August 13, 1758, op. cit.

wise? the Provinces scarcely began to raise a Man, 'till the Middle of April — Many of those that joined us were hired, in room of others who should have gone — and others draughted or forced, out of the Militia. Their Officers, with a very few Exceptions are worse than their Men. Nay, some of them have actually deserted & shamm'd sick, and we are always much longer in geting them out to their Duty than their Men." [92]

Pitt also erred in his choice of a commanding officer in this most difficult of operations. Either Forbes or Bradstreet joined with Howe would undoubtedly have done much better and probably would have succeeded in carrying the French fort — even with the great delay involved in bringing together the provincials. As for Abercromby, he erred in not taking the necessary steps to secure accurate information respecting the situation of the French at Ticonderoga and elsewhere — in the same way that the enemy kept closely in touch with the movements and strength of British troops. He erred fundamentally in failing to utilize Mount Defiance and also in his unwillingness, after he had committed himself to a frontal attack, to take the time to make use of the artillery that he had brought with him; he thus permitted the useless sacrifice of many of his best soldiers after he was made to realize the extraordinary difficulties of a direct assualt on the enemy; he erred, likewise, in his failure to exert his authority at the end of the battle with the resulting breakdown of the morale of his troops. Finally, Howe, theoretically his subordinate, as has already been pointed out, made his contribution in the ruin of the campaign by permitting himself to commit the glaring error of exposing himself at the head of a column moving in the woods in the direction of the enemy well in advance of all support.

In justice to the provincials — many of whom undeniably acted badly — it may be pointed out that some of the regiments carried on with great credit. Reference has already been made to the firmness of Lyman's Connecticut troops, and particular recognition should be given to the meritorious conduct of Major Putnam's contingent that was with Howe's detachment at the time of the skirmish on the 6th. Indeed, Abercromby had such confidence in Lyman and the men under him that, after the return to Fort George, he was sent out to scout with a thousand troops, including two hundred regulars and light infantry, two hundred rangers, and six hundred

---

[92] Abercromby to James Abercromby, Esq., August 19, 1758, op. cit.

provincials.[93] Some of the Massachusetts Bay troops, too, behaved very well indeed; especially those under command of Colonel Wooster, who after the battle remained steadfast at their posts and did not appear at the place of embarkation until all the other troops had gone aboard the boats on the 9th. Colonel Israel Williams of the same colony also was a man of high spirt and great bravery, who declared in writing to Governor Pownall: "To give up all for lost and quietly to submit our necks to yᵉ Enemy can not be our Duty." [94] In this letter he begged Pownall to come "to set all things to rights, & revive the spirits of yᵉ Army" and was very eager to make another attempt, in which the provincials would alone be employed, would be allowed the artillery train, and would serve under commanding officers to be designated by the governors of the colonies concerned in the late campaign. With respect to the flight of provincials from the battlefield before they had even been engaged and the subsequent scandalous desertion of many of them,[95] it is well to point out that those who took the lead in these disgraceful proceedings were doubtless men without military training or experience, many of them lacking any patriotic desire to play the part of soldiers. Unhappily, after they reached the point of concentration time did not permit the molding of them into disciplined troops before embarking on the boats for Ticonderoga.

Reference was previously made to Colonel Williams's stalwart

---

[93] Abercromby to de Lancey, August 14, 1758, Abercromby Papers, No. 536.

[94] Williams to Pownall, —— 1758, Williams Mss., 2: No. 80 (Mass. Hist. Soc.).

[95] In the October 6 return of men fit for duty at Lake George or to the southward, including Fort Edward and the other posts on the upper Hudson, but four thousand and twenty-nine provincials are listed out of some ten thousand that made the passage to the neighbourhood of Ticonderoga (Abercromby Papers, No. 724). The New Hampshire regiment that arrived at Lake George after the return of the expedition is added to this total. Abercromby writing to Stanwix on July 23 (ibid., No. 468) declared: "I find the Provincial Troops are turning back [home] fast; I will do all in my Power to make them return and shall write to their Respective Governors, if any of them reach home, to return them immediately & make some examples of them." On August 2 he also wrote to Forbes (ibid., No. 500) that the spirit of desertion has now also affected the provincials on the Mohawk and that those stationed at the Oneida Carrying Place from Massachusetts Bay and Rhode Island were going off in bodies. As for the New Hampshire troops, who failed to arrive in time for the expedition, but who at the time of his letter were stationed above Albany, he affirmed that those at Fort Edward would have gone off "night before last" had not Montrésor doubled the pickets and guards. In spite of this bad conduct, he confessed: "I dare not be rigid for Fear of a Total Desertion [of the provincials], in which case it would be impossible to make a Stand here." Desertion from the regular forces, of course, meant death or very severe bodily punishment.

demand for a second attempt that year on Ticonderoga. Abercromby seemed to have dismissed the thought of such a possibility after getting his army back to the head of Lake George.[96] The latter part of August, however, the Swiss Colonel James Prevost and Colonel Thomas Gage submitted a proposal for a new attempt. This involved sending Rogers with a force in boats to the upper part of Lake George; the bateaux would then be carried from Sabbath Day Point over to Wood Creek; thereupon, by moving down this stream, the detachment would be able to get in the rear of Fort Ticonderoga while Abercromby with the main force approached it much after the fashion of the late attempt against it.[97] The general was apparently favourably impressed with the plan and took preliminary steps in harmony with it.[98] He felt impelled, however, to delay putting it into execution until he learned whether or not Amherst — now that official news had arrived that Louisbourg had fallen — was going to move up the St. Lawrence with his army and the fleet.[99] Then early in September came an announcement from Amherst that, while the attempt against Quebec could not be made this year, he was sending six battalions to join the army at Lake George. With this reinforcement Abercromby determined without further delay to execute the project of a second trial.[100]

In calling upon Johnson again to bring up his Indians, he figured that Amherst's battalions would arrive so that he could move against the French fort before the middle of October.[101] But he was not to leave. Amherst, who arrived in Boston with his troops and who was proceeding overland with them to join the forces at Lake George, was called upon by his superior to join him as soon as possible for a conference without waiting for the troops to move up.[102] As a result, upon his arrival a council of war was held, at which Gage, now with rank of brigadier general in America, was also present. It was

---

[96] Abercromby to Amherst, July 18, 1758 (*ibid.*, No. 450).

[97] Prevost to Abercromby, August 20, 1758, *ibid.*, No. 548; *Military Affairs in North America, 1748–1765*, pp. 425–8.

[98] Abercromby to de Lancey, August 28, 1758, Abercromby Papers, No. 574.

[99] Abercromby to Pownall, September 4, 1758, *ibid.*, No. 611.

[100] Abercromby to Forbes, September 6, 1758, *ibid.*, 618. The general's new reliance on Bradstreet, who had gone to Lake Ontario with part of the army against Fort Frontenac, is indicated in a letter addressed to him on September 7 asking him to come to Abercromby without delay as soon as he had returned to the Mohawk (*ibid.*, No. 619).

[101] Abercromby to Johnson, September 26, 1758, *ibid.*, No. 699.

[102] Abercromby to Amherst, September 30, 1758, *ibid.*, No. 704.

agreed that the problem of capturing the fort would now be even more formidable than that presented in July, on account of the strengthening of its outer works.[103] Instead, the troops were sent into winter quarters. Soon after this was done, Abercromby received Pitt's letter of recall, written on September 18, and proceeded to turn his papers over to Amherst, his successor — doubtless with a very genuine sense of relief.[104]

Of all the men who survived the Ticonderoga campaign none appeared to better advantage than did Lieutenant Colonel John Bradstreet. Reared in the colony of Nova Scotia, an ensign there in Philipp's regiment, later a promoter of the expedition against Louisbourg in 1746, in which he played a role of distinction, when the Great War for the Empire broke out he was holding a captain's commission on the regular establishment. Appointed by General Shirley in 1755 to take charge of the bateau service on the Mohawk River, he displayed in that year and in 1756 much talent and activity in organizing companies of bateau-men, in building boats, and in forwarding supplies to Oswego. In 1757 he was given a company in the Royal American regiment and so enjoyed the confidence of Loudoun that the latter made him an aide-de-camp and agreed to permit him to lead an expedition against Fort Frontenac.[105] But Pitt did not include this as an objective and therefore the plan was set aside and Bradstreet, as has been noted, participated under Abercromby in the northern campaign. A man of great energy, bravery, and, it may be added, personal ambition, he left a somewhat spotty record here in America before his death in 1774. But this fact must not obscure his very real qualities of leadership during the years of the war. To Wolfe, he was "for the battoes and for expeditions . . . an extraordinary man." [106]

From the fall of 1756 it would appear that Bradstreet had had his eye on Cadaraqui, where Fort Frontenac stood on the shore of Lake Ontario near the entrance to the St. Lawrence. His intimate relations with General Shirley, indeed, suggests that when the latter proposed the reduction of that place as a primary objective for the campaign in North America in 1757, to be followed by others

---

[103] Abercromby to Pitt, November 25, 1758, *Pitt Correspondence*, I, 299.

[104] *Ibid.*, I, 298.

[105] His instructions, dated January 25, 1758, are among the Loudoun Papers, No. 5460.

[106] Wolfe to Sackville, May 24, 1758, *Hist. Mss. Com. Report* (1910), II, 261.

in the Great Lakes region, it came as the result of his advice.[107] It is clear that he felt strongly that its destruction would be a great step in securing control not only of Lake Ontario but of Montreal as well. After the fall of Fort William Henry in that year he addressed Sir Richard Lyttelton, in England, offering to lead an expedition by way of Oswego:

> "I know and am sensible of the distance, difficulties, & dangers which would attend it and believe few there are who think it practicable, but be assur'd it proceeds from their want of experience of that kind of Service, for so far am I convinced of my being able to go through with it that I will risk my reputation upon the success of it as far as the taking Montreal and all the Forts upon the Lakes and joine the Fleet should they reach Quebec — unavoidable accidents excepted. . . ."[108]

One serious obstacle alone he saw as a barrier to the command of such an expedition — his rank. To overcome this he suggested that he might well be appointed Governor of New Jersey, "with the Rank the King has been pleas'd to give Governors when acting with the Army."[109] In December of that year he placed before Loudoun, as indicated, his plan for an expedition of a more modest character directed only against Frontenac and agreed to carry it out at his own expense, with reimbursement of the costs of it only in case he should capture the fort. With eight hundred bateau-men, he proposed, as soon as the ice broke up on the lake in the spring, to proceed against it while it was still weak and before it was reinforced from Montreal.

Loudoun not only gave his approval of the plan, as has been stated, but agreed to provide Bradstreet with the necessary boats and provisions.[110] With this settled, the latter set to work to build bateaux on the lower Mohawk and was deeply involved in this activity when early in the spring he received His Majesty's com-

---

[107] Correspondence of Shirley, (ed. C. H. Lincoln), II, 292–6.

[108] Bradstreet was, as were Pitt and Wolfe, a man who had great confidence in his own abilities. He began his letter as follows: "Were it not owned by all degrees of People that no person in America is more capable of conducting an Inland Expedition in these parts than I am I would by no means be so presumptuous as to offer My self as a Candidate for the Command of that part of the Forces which should go by way of Oswego as I now do to You should the Scheme be Approved of ("Bradstreet to Lyttelton, September 5, 1757, Chatham Mss., Bundle 95, Canadian Archives Transcripts).

[109] Ibid.

[110] Loudoun to Pitt, February 14, 1758, Pitt Correspondence, I, 194.

mission as deputy quartermaster general to serve with Brigadier General Forbes.[111] To have assumed the duties of this new office would have meant that he must give up the task that he had immediately at hand and so much at heart, in favour of operating in western Pennsylvania, a region to which he was a stranger. As a result, he was permitted by Abercromby, now commander-in-chief of His Majesty's forces in North America, to continue his boatbuilding, and Sir John St. Clair was appointed to fulfil the same duties under Forbes that he had fulfilled under Braddock in 1755.[112] By the latter part of May, Bradstreet had succeeded in constructing fifteen hundred boats; but his plan for diverting a large part of these for the Lake Ontario expedition could not be countenanced by Abercromby, especially in view of Pitt's very definite and binding instructions, which failed to mention Frontenac as an objective.[113] But with the humiliating failure of the army at Ticonderoga, the general was looking desperately for something that might soften the bitterness of his defeat and now lent a sympathetic ear to the renewed proposals of the energetic lieutenant colonel.

On July 13, shortly after the army had returned to the upper end of Lake George and had built stockades for its temporary protection, a council of war was held,[114] out of which came two decisions: first, that a fort should be constructed at the Oneida Carrying Place; second, "that it was proper and advisable to appear in Lake Ontario to distress the enemy" and that in this latter service the provincials of New York, New Jersey, Rhode Island, and one of the regiments from Massachusetts Bay acting with bateau-men and a body of regulars, amounting to some thirty-six hundred men, should be employed.[115] In addition, it was agreed that Stanwix should be strongly reinforced so that two thousand men could be assured him for the building of the fort in question. These operations had in view the staving off of a French attack on the Mohawk settlements, which it was well known from prisoners and deserters had already been projected, but which had been temporarily set aside for the purpose of strengthening Montcalm at Ticonderoga; they were also

---

[111] Pitt to Abercromby, December 30, 1757, ibid., I, 146.
[112] Abercromby to Pitt, May 21, 1758, ibid., I, 252–3.
[113] Pitt to Abercromby, December 30, 1757, ibid., I, 143–51.
[114] At this were not only Abercromby, Haviland, Haldimand, Gage, Grant, Eyre, and Massy, but also Bradstreet and Sir William Johnson.
[115] "Minutes of a Council of War, at Lake George," July 13, 1758, Abercromby Papers, No. 438.

designed to "favour operations to the southward" on the part of Forbes in his drive against Fort Duquesne.[116] In fact, these two objectives were especially stressed in the instructions given to Bradstreet, who was, if he found it advisable, to give battle to the enemy and only, "if found practicable," to attempt, in addition, the reduction of Fort Frontenac.[117]

Bradstreet — with his eyes set on Cadaraqui rather than on giving battle to the enemy on the lake — had asked for a small artillery train, and Abercromby agreed to furnish him with four twelve-pounders and four eight-inch howitzers that he desired, which he would use for the battering and destruction of the enemy fortifications. He was also promised an adequate number of whaleboats and bateaux, out of the number that he himself had built, and other necessaries for his enterprise, as well as the support of some of Johnson's Indians for the purpose of securing intelligence.[118]

As might have been anticipated, the lieutenant colonel, with a display of his unusual vigor, was not long in reaching the lower Mohawk to set his enterprise in motion. But here he was beset with difficulties. He could not lay his hands on a sufficient number of wagons to transport the supplies from Albany to Schenectady for shipment by bateau; nor were the troops ready to leave; it was not until the end of July that the last of his detachments and the matériel left the place of concentration to ascend the Mohawk.[119] Moreover, he had to encounter, it appears, the opposition to the expedition of Lieutenant Governor de Lancey, always a very cautious man.[120] By August 6 he and General Stanwix had reached Herkimer's Fort, and from there he wrote to Abercromby of the great desertions and also sickness among the soldiers assigned to duty up the river and to the Lake Ontario campaign, and added: "never have people gon [sic] on Service with more reluctance than they in general have." He was determined to proceed on his mission, however, and declared that if he could take with him no more than a thousand men, he would embark on Lake Ontario and do

---

116 Abercromby to Bradstreet, July 13, 1758, ibid., No. 439.

117 Ibid.

118 Ibid.

119 Bradstreet to Abercromby, July 24, 1758, ibid., No. 472.

120 "I shall say nothing further on the intended enterprise," wrote de Lancey to Abercromby, on August 20, "it being to little purpose to make objections after a measure is undertaken and carrying into execution: and since Lt. Col. Bradstreet is on his way, I wish he may meet with Success" (ibid., No. 550).

his best to gain his objective.[121] At the Oneida Carrying Place he received his assignment of the troops. These consisted of some twenty-five hundred provincials, not including officers, as well as a company of rangers and a hundred and fifty-seven regulars; these with three hundred bateau-men and seventy Indians gave him a total of somewhat over three thousand men.[122] With this force, after some additional delay at the portage, he was able to move down to Oneida Lake and the Oswego River soon after the middle of August.[123]

One thing that retarded his movement while still on the upper Mohawk was a dispute that arose between him and the five colonels of the provincials. The latter outranked him — as the result of the orders sent out by Pitt the latter end of 1757 respecting the standing of provincial officers in relation to those in the regular service — and therefore refused to serve under him since he was only a lieutenant colonel.[124] Technically, the provincial colonels were on firm ground, but in comparison with Bradstreet's qualifications for the task in hand, including his long years of military training, his experience at Louisbourg in 1746 and elsewhere, his intimate knowledge of the approaches to Lake Ontario and of its navigation, and his leadership of bateau-men, they were all but mere novices. Indeed, to make it possible for the expedition to proceed, Stanwix was finally obliged to send the provincial detachments without their colonels.[125]

---

[121] He indicates that on the night of August 5 one hundred and nineteen of the New Jersey troops deserted, which he thought would be brought back; as to the New York soldiers, he states "hitherto [they] have behav'd well" (ibid., No. 511).

[122] "Stanwix's Return of Troops Detached for Bradstreet," August 20, 1758, ibid., No. 541. According to de Lancey, Bradstreet had 1,112 New Yorkers, 675 Massachusetts Bay men, 412 from New Jersey, and 318 from Rhode Island, together with 155 regulars and 60 rangers (de Lancey to Pitt, September 11, 1758, Chatham Mss., Bundle 96, Canadian Archives Transcripts).

[123] Stanwix to Abercromby, August 20, 1758, Abercromby Papers, No. 547.

[124] They were de Lancey of New York, Williams and Doty of Massachusetts Bay, Babcock of Rhode Island, and Johnson of New Jersey.

[125] Wrote Stanwix to Abercromby (ibid.): "Colonel Bradstreet seemed not a little offend'd that the provincial Colonels would not go upon his Enterprise under his Command, the King having given all these Rank of Colonels wᶜʰ no provincial Colonels ever had before. As you did not settle this at the Lake I could settle it no otherwise than to send these [provincial troops] by detachments without their Colonels, mentioning it in publick Orders that such a number as would compose the Troops agreeable to the inclosed Return, to be detach'd from Every Corps with a proportionable number of Field Officers, Capts. & Subalterns. Wᵗ I most apprehended was that the men would object to going at all without their Colonels. This arose from declarations I

Once the expedition had left the waters of Oneida Lake and had started down the Oswego, it did not take long to reach Lake Ontario, with but one short portage to make, which Bradstreet knew well. It appears that when this was accomplished and the real objective at last became clear, most of the Indians who came with the troops turned back, which undoubtedly had the effect of making Bradstreet very suspicious afterward of the loyalty of the Six Confederate Nations.[126]

To account for this action on the part of the Indians it is necessary to point out that the Indian Superintendent, in addressing the representatives of the Six Nations at Fort Johnson on July 22, had been careful, in calling for the support of their young men, only to mention that a considerable number of troops were assembling to take post at the Oneida Carrying Place for the purpose of building a fort for the security of the Mohawk Valley and for establishing a beneficial trade with the Indians. In other words, what was stressed was that a purely defensive program was on foot in the upper country, of a nature that would appeal to most, if not all, Indians, especially with respect to providing a place of refuge for their women and children in time of danger as well as a trading post most conveniently located. It is true that Johnson called upon his charges to send out scouting parties to watch the movements of the French and asked as many of them as possible to go to the Carrying Place, "where your Brother Col. Bradstreet will acquaint you with the Service you are wanted upon"; but not a word was mentioned respecting the proposed attack on Fort Frontenac.[127] Nor is it probable that Bradstreet even hinted at this to the Indians. Indeed, the success of the campaign depended largely upon secrecy in the matter.

The Confederation policy with respect to the Anglo-French conflict was that it should be kept away from their castles; many of its members were pro-English and many more probably at this moment were pro-French, but all, while willing to fight, wanted quiet to reign about their homes. In fact, an Oneida warrior informed Johnson on August 2 that some of the sachems and warriors of his

had heard of this sort. However, the provincial Colonels settled that affair so amongst their men that I had no trouble about it."

126 De Lancey, writing to Pitt on September 11, 1758, declared that with Bradstreet there were "some Indians, most of whom turned back upon frivolous pretences" (Chatham Mss., Bundle 96).

127 Johnson Papers (ed. E. C. Flick), IX, 952–3.

nation had gone to Cadaraqui to find out if the French were planning to make another descent on the Mohawk and that, should they meet a French army on their way there, they were to acquaint the leaders of it

> "that the 6 Nations desired they would not disturb this part of the Country wch was a road of Peace . . . & therefore to insist with the French that they should not make War in this Quarter but go toward Lake George & fight there. . . ." [128]

It is therefore clear that in refusing to accompany Bradstreet to Cadaraqui those Indians who withdrew were acting in harmony with the views of the Confederation. All did not turn back, however. In fact, some of them even attacked on the lake three French canoes loaded with peltries headed for Montreal and destroyed the occupants — the news of which brought dismay in Canada.[129]

Just as the French, after leaving Fort Frontenac in 1756, concentrated at Niaouré Bay (Sackett's Harbor) preliminary to their assault upon Oswego, so did the British after leaving Oswego on the 22nd before proceeding on to Cadaraqui.[130]

Cadaraqui was the entrepôt not only for all the posts and forts in the Great Lakes region but for those of the upper valley of the Ohio. As such it received from Montreal vast quanities of supplies, which were thereupon sent by lake vessels to the Niagara portage or to Toronto for distribution at the outlying posts; many of the peltries of the upper country were also received preparatory to sending them down the river. While it was no longer important in direct Indian trade, its strategic importance as a factor in maintaining French economic, political, and military control over the vast northern interior cannot be easily overestimated. Less able to make a defence than Forts Niagara or Duquesne or even the fort at Detroit, its integrity was essential if these more powerful posts were not to shrivel and die. Constructed of stone in the form of a square, with bastions located at the corners, Fort Frontenac had on each side an exterior length of about a hundred yards, was provided with permanent barracks, officers' quarters, a chapel, a powder magazine, and other conveniences, and also with some thirty cannon

[128] *Ibid.*, IX, 964–5.
[129] Doreil to Belle-Isle, September 3, 1758, *N. Y. Col. Doc.*, X, 821–2.
[130] *Ibid.* See also "Journal of Occurrences in Canada, 1757, 1758," *ibid.*, X, 852.

in place, with an equal number held in reserve.[131] Beyond its walls were other structures, with the Cadaraqui storehouses located conveniently at the waterside. The garrison at this critical juncture consisted of but a hundred and ten soldiers; there were also present a number of women and children, a handful of Indians, and doubtless a few voyageurs, as well as the sailors who manned the lake vessels. This weak contingent, nevertheless, was responsible for the safety of one of the most important places in New France, with its warehouses at the moment literally bulging with military and other supplies intended for Niagara and Duquesne, as well as with peltries.

When Bradstreet and his men appeared in the neighbourhood of Cadaraqui, the French, usually so alert and well informed of the movements of the enemy, were caught quite off their guard. It is true that prisoners captured by the French operating in the area to the south of Lake George told of the departure of Bradstreet and the purpose of his expedition.[132] But Vaudreuil had sent de Longueuil [133] with two hundred Canadians and Indians into the country of the Six Nations to make sure that their attitude was still as favourable as it had been the preceding year and that they were planning to come again to Canada to talk with him. In a report sent from there, Longueuil indicated to him that the Indians were planning to leave for Montreal in twenty days and also that he was assured by them that the English assembling on the Mohawk were intent only on re-establishing the fort (Fort Bull) destroyed at Oneida Lake. The French Governor General therefore felt assured regarding Fort Frontenac and directed his attention to other pressing matters.[134]

Only when the elderly Chevalier de Noyan, commandant at Cadaraqui, had sent out a small scouting party of Missisauga, who first of all discovered a well-armed barge on the lake, then killed two Englishmen and appropriated their papers,[135] and, finally, detected

[131] Ibid., IX, 875; X, 340.

[132] Journal de Lévis (ed. Abbè Casgrain), pp. 142, 146.

[133] This was the Chevalier Paul Joseph le Moyne de Longueuil, Governor of Trois Rivières, not Joseph Dominique Emanuel le Moyne de Longueuil.

[134] Lotbinière to Belle-Isle, October 9, 1758, N. Y. Col. Doc., X, 893; Vaudreuil to Massiac, September 2, 1758, ibid., X, 822–3.

[135] These papers apparently contained not only Bradstreet's instructions given on August 13 to Captain Wells, who was to leave the Oneida Carrying Place and to scout with a party in the region of Oswego, but also the general orders of Stanwix issued to Bradstreet's force on August 11, which contained a general list of the detachments that

the presence of a large number of craft in and about Niaouré Bay, was the near presence to Fort Frontenac of a large body of the enemy made known to him with the return of the Indians.[136] As a result, he immediately ordered a courier to leave for Montreal, some two hundred miles to the east, with the alarming intelligence. The news reached Vaudreuil the morning of the 26th,[137] thus too late to save the post. In fact, a reinforcement made up of some fifteen hundred soldiers, Indians, and *habitants* — the last brought in from their fields, where they were busy harvesting — was not able to leave the town until the 27th. On that day Fort Frontenac passed into the hands of the British.

Landing on an island in open sight of the French fort and the shipping in the harbour, Bradstreet immediately sent a whaleboat to reconnoitre the shore for a proper landing-place. As the surf was still running high, it seemed best to delay operations until the evening. Then about seven o'clock the entire force landed about a mile from Cadaraqui without opposition. Immediately a body of rangers and those Indians who remained with the little army scouted the woods while the main body of troops remained under arms guarding the bateaux throughout the night.[138] Then early the next morning the artillery was disembarked, placed on gun carriages, and drawn to a point some four hundred yards distant from the French fort. Under cover of a hill Bradstreet now began to bombard it and the guns of the fort replied smartly, although apparently no great injury was done on either side. As soon as it was again dusk, the besieging force moved up to build a new breastwork and to occupy an entrenchment that the French had erected in 1756 some two hundred paces in front of the fort to guard against an attack by Shirley while he was at Oswego with his army.[139] Embrasures in this were cut for the artillery, and at daybreak on the 27th the bombardment began again, this time with real effect. Up to about seven o'clock the garrison replied in a spirited fashion with both their

---

were to go with him with six days' provisions. For these papers, translated into French and signed by Vaudreuil and then translated back into English, see *ibid.*, X, 826–7.

[136] Vaudreuil to Massiac, September 2, 1758, *ibid.*, X, 822–3; "Journal of Occurrences in Canada, 1757, 1758," *ibid.*, X, 852.

[137] Vaudreuil to Massiac, September 2, 1758, *ibid.*, X, 823.

[138] Major Daniel Wall to Governor Hopkins, September 17, 1758, *Rhode Island Colonial Records*, VI, 166.

[139] *Ibid.* See also MacAulay to Gates, August 30, 1758, *Abercromby Papers*, No. 589.

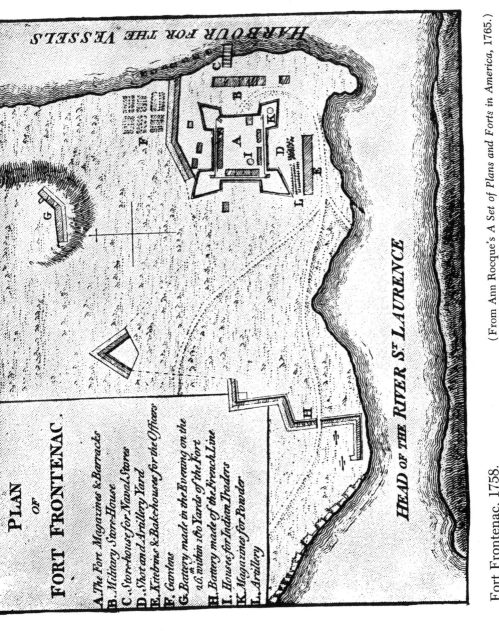

PLAN
of
FORT FRONTENAC.

A. The Fort Magazines & Barracks
B. Military Store-House
C. Store-house for Naval Stores
D. Short and Artillery Yard
E. Kitchens & Bake-houses for the Officers
F. Gardens
G. Battery made in the Evening on the
　26 within 160 Yards of the Fort
H. Battery made of the French Line
I. Houses for Indian Traders
K. Magazines for Powder
L. Artillery

HARBOUR FOR THE VESSELS

HEAD OF THE RIVER St. LAURENCE

Fort Frontenac, 1758.

(From Ann Rocque's A Set of Plans and Forts in America, 1765.)

cannon and their small arms; then it was noticed that the crews of the vessels, moored close under the guns of the fort, were making preparations to sail away. Bradstreet therefore brought two of his twelve-pounders to bear upon the ships, with the result that those on board took to boats and rowed off and the vessels were suffered to drift on shore.

The end had now come for de Noyan and his defenders, for the exploding shells were making havoc within the fort, while the invading force had not suffered the death of a single man in the course of the siege. The French colours were soon lowered and terms of surrender were formulated and signed. The commandant, on one hand, agreed to surrender the fort and its dependencies and all munitions and other supplies accumulated at Cadaraqui; he also agreed that the soldiers at the post should become prisoners of war. Bradstreet, on the other hand, agreed to permit all at the fort to become prisoners on parole and to protect them from insults from the British soldiers and the Indians, and also to care for the sick and wounded; he, moreover, agreed not only to permit them to take as much of their personal effects as could be carried away in the bateaux in which they were to go down the St. Lawrence, and to retain the chapel ornaments and sacred vessels, but also to allow de Noyan, in view of his infirmities, to go without parole to Montreal, under condition that he engage himself to procure as a personal exchange Colonel Schuyler, captured with the New Jersey troops at Oswego in 1756 and still held prisoner in Canada, and likewise the exchange of other British prisoners equal in number to those of the garrison, free under the terms to leave on their parole.[140]

Thus, suddenly, there disappeared not only this great French defence of the upper St. Lawrence, but also French undisputed supremacy on Lake Ontario. Just as suddenly there was snatched from the grasp of the French the supplies destined to support the defence of Fort Duquesne and so sorely needed, in view of the preparations being made by General Forbes to reduce it. As Waddington makes clear, the effect of the fall of Fort Frontenac was nothing less than disastrous to the French interests in North America.[141]

After the surrender on the morning of the 27th the victors were

---

[140] For the terms in French see "Noyan-Bradstreet Surrender Conditions," Abercromby Papers, No. 566; these in English are in the *N. Y. Col. Doc.*, X, 825–6.

[141] *Guerre de sept ans*, II, 389.

busily occupied in collecting the valuable things to be carried away. The evening of that day was a scene of destruction as the fort and other structures were demolished, and most of the French fleet — two snows, two schooners, and three sloops — went up in smoke; only a brigantine and a schooner were spared from the conflagration to carry away the precious booty. The next day, with the place still burning, the ships, loaded largely with furs, departed and were followed by the flotilla of whaleboats and bateaux. With the removal of the more valuable articles from the French vessels at Oswego, these two were consigned to destruction, and thereupon Bradstreet and his force slowly proceeded with their loaded bateaux and whaleboats up the river and on September 13 joined Stanwix and the remainder of the army at Oneida Carrying Place. Could he but have known that Fort Niagara at the time of the completion of his conquest at Cadaraqui had only a garrison of forty men commanded by de Vassan,[142] he would doubtless have moved upon it and thereby added immeasurably to the laurels he and his troops had already won. But this fact was unknown and the specific objective that he had had in mind had been attained without the loss of a single man.

Thus, by the fall of 1758, and in spite of the shocking defeat of the British at Ticonderoga, the French Empire in the New World had been shaken to its very foundations; first through the capture of Louisbourg, the key to the lower St. Lawrence, and later by the destruction of Cadaraqui, the key to the entrance of that river as well as to the Great Lakes region.

---

[142] N. Y. Col. Doc., X, 855.

CHAPTER IX

Forbes Builds
a Road to Victory

JUST AS THE Braddock expedition to the Ohio in 1755 represents, up to its final catastrophic climax, a great military achievement, so does the Forbes expedition of 1758. While having certain things in common, the two movements offer striking contrasts. The one represents the swift movement of a task force supported by an artillery train in order to arrive at Fort Duquesne before the French reinforcements could appear on the scene; the other, the slow, methodical advance, the consolidation of each strategic move, with the idea of holding firmly whatever land was traversed by means of a long line of fortified posts and of finally assaulting the French fort only at a time when the enemy could least depend upon maintaining Indian support. The one illustrates the technique of a powerful raid; the other, that of permanent conquest. Had Braddock's strategy succeeded, his men might have been faced by dire want if not starvation; with the successful outcome of Forbes's strategy, the means were at hand, although difficult enough, indeed, as events proved, to guard against this contingency.

John Forbes, a native of Scotland, was born in Fifeshire in 1707. Although trained in medicine, he came to realize that his real interest lay in a military career. He therefore enrolled in the Scots Greys in 1735, securing a cornet's commission. With his regiment he saw service in the War of the Austrian Succession both in Flanders and in his native land, where he participated in the Battle of Culloden. By the year 1750 he had attained the rank of lieutenant colonel and had won the respect and friendship of many men of influence. Like Amherst, he became identified with the work of military supply and in it attained the rank of deputy quartermaster general in the army. In 1757 he became colonel of the 17th regiment,[1] and late in the spring of that year he came to America and was attached to Lord Loudoun's staff, attaining the rank of adjutant general. Possessing the traditional Scottish sense of loyalty to his leader, he enjoyed the latter's confidence and richly deserved it. When Loudoun's recall was determined upon by Pitt, Forbes, perhaps as the result of the recommendation of Ligonier, who knew him personally, was advanced to the rank of brigadier general and was selected to take command of the expedition against Fort Duquesne. He had never enjoyed, as was true of Amherst, an independent command up to the time of this appointment; he was, moreover, at the time he was notified of his new responsibility, practically an invalid;[2] nevertheless, a man of sound ideas, resourceful, broadly trained in military affairs, with an iron will, he was, in spite of physical handicaps, well fitted for the task that lay before him.

According to Pitt's plan, Forbes was to have as second in command the Swiss Lieutenant Colonel Bouquet of the Royal Americans, with three hundred and fifty troops from this regiment; he was also to have Montgomery's Highland Regiment, numbering over a thousand, the Independent Companies of South Carolina, with a total of somewhat less than three hundred and fifty men, some forty artillerymen from the Royal Regiment of Artillery, with a proper train, and, finally, five thousand provincials.[3] His army, including all regulars as well as all provincials, was, upon the basis of the Minister's distribution of military strength to the three theatres of war in North America, to number somewhat under seven thousand troops. The Independents, however, were obliged to remain in South Carolina along the frontier as the result of the failure of that

---

[1] That there was jealousy of him in the army is evident from the unsupported charge made by Captain Charles Lee that he had received his colonelcy by drinking the health of the Pretender with the Duke of Bedford (Stanley Pargellis: *Lord Loudoun in North America*, p. 349).

[2] "My Infirmitys are really no joke, nor are they to be played the fool with, Both legs and thighs being one absolute sight, and the soals of my feet Blistered, so that it was impossible for me to gett abroad" (Forbes to Loudoun, February 3, 1758, Loudoun Papers, No. 5534).

[3] "Disposition of the Forces in North America," December 30, 1758, Abercromby Papers, No. 851.

province to recruit its regiment to take over that task. North Carolina, it is true, provided for three hundred men, who had to be
equipped; but Maryland remained intransigent with respect to the
support of the war except for purely defensive purposes. The only
men from that province to participate, therefore, were paid and
supported out of Forbes's contingent fund.

It is clear that at the time he received his command of the southern army that was to proceed against Fort Duquesne, Forbes assumed that it would be desirable to bring about the concentration
of its contingents at Fort Cumberland in Maryland and from there
proceed along the Braddock road.[4] In his first instructions to Governor Denny, under date of March 20, he made clear that he proposed to assemble the regular troops and the Pennsylvania provincials on the Conococheague (Conococheaque), which flows into the
Potomac near the old Williams ferry.[5] The next day he wrote to
Governor Sharpe of Maryland about the necessity of having the
road between the ferry and Fort Cumberland to the south of the
river, and especially that portion from Colonel Cresap's home on to
the fort, placed in good condition.[6]

At this juncture Abercromby made one important modification in
Pitt's distribution of assignments of officers that was destined to have
an influence on the southern campaign. Colonel John Bradstreet had
been attached by the Minister to Forbes's command as deputy
quartermaster general in charge of supplies. As has been emphasized
in the preceding chapter, Bradstreet was reluctant to give up his
work of boat-building in upper New York and he also indicated to

---

[4] Under date of February 1, 1758 Forbes drew up a broad plan of military operations in North America which he submitted to Loudoun. Under the heading "Operations on the Ohio" he states: "And for that purpose could assemble early at Fort Cumberland — the 2nd Battn of the R[oyal] A[mericans] & the 1st Highland Battn — which
make 2000 men who joined with the Virginia, Maryland and Pensilvania provinell will
make a body Stronger than any thing that the Enemy can collect . . ." (*Writings of
General John Forbes*, ed. A. P. James, p. 35). In a letter to Loudoun written February
14 regarding this plan, he says: "But send me up my loose thoughts, upon the Generall
plan of operations, as I have neither Scketch nor remembrance of my Ideas at that time
now" (*ibid.*, p. 42).

[5] Forbes to Denny, March 20, 1758, *ibid.*, p. 58. The present town of Williams-
port is located at the old Williams Bac (meaning ferry).

[6] Forbes to Sharpe, March 21, 1758, *ibid.*, pp. 61–2. Forbes also called upon Governor Dobbs to have the North Carolina troops assemble at Wills Creek by May 1
(*ibid.*, p. 60). William Scull's Map of Pennsylvania, made in 1770, shows Williams's
Bac and also Cresap's plantation.

Abercromby that he was an "utter stranger" to the country where he would be obliged to operate with Forbes, and persuaded the general to relieve him of this responsibility. As a result the important office was given to Sir John St. Clair who had been in charge of this work under Braddock.[7] Forbes must have received the announcement with mixed feelings.[8]

On April 2 St. Clair left New York in order to make initial preparations for the campaign.[9] Later in this month Forbes, now also in Pennsylvania, indicated to Abercromby that he was sending St. Clair to Winchester, where a large body of Cherokee warriors had assembled, in order to put the Indians to work.[10] The deputy quartermaster general, significantly, was at the time out at Lancaster in Pennsylvania arranging for supplies for the expedition and for the improvement of roads leading southward; it would appear he was also discussing with frontiersmen the question of the best approach to Fort Duquesne. Nevertheless, the first intimation that the central Pennsylvania approach was being considered, rather than that by way of Fort Cumberland, came in a letter addressed to Washington by an old acquaintance, Forbes's aide-de-camp, Francis Halkett, son of Colonel Halkett, who lost his life in the Battle of the Monongahela. In this letter Washington was called upon to send his Indians to scout by way of Raystown and Franks Town on the south and north branches respectively of the Juniata "to cover our Posts, and Magazines, & keep the Frontiers of the Country quite [quiet], & as the most effectual Route for that purpose. . . ."[11] It is certain that by May 7 Forbes had reached a decision, which was in favour of making Raystown, on the southern branch of the Juniata, the principal base for the expedition against the French fort. On that day he wrote to Abercromby that he was planning on clearing the roads leading westward for the convoy of provisions and would thereupon build a palisaded deposit for his supplies at Raystown.[12] In referring later to this decision, he made clear to Colonel Bouquet

[7] Abercromby to Pitt, May 22, 1758, *Pitt Correspondence*, I, 252.

[8] In 1754 Forbes was hoping to receive the appointment of quartermaster general in America; when he heard of St. Clair's appointment, in a letter to his brother Hugh he referred to St. Clair in not very complimentary terms as "a Mad Sort of Fool" (*Writings of Forbes*, p. 1).

[9] Forbes to Sharpe, April 4, 1758, *ibid.*, p. 64

[10] Forbes to Abercromby, April 20, 1758, *ibid.*, p. 65.

[11] Halkett to Washington, May 4, 1758, *ibid.*, p. 83.

[12] *Ibid.*, p. 87.

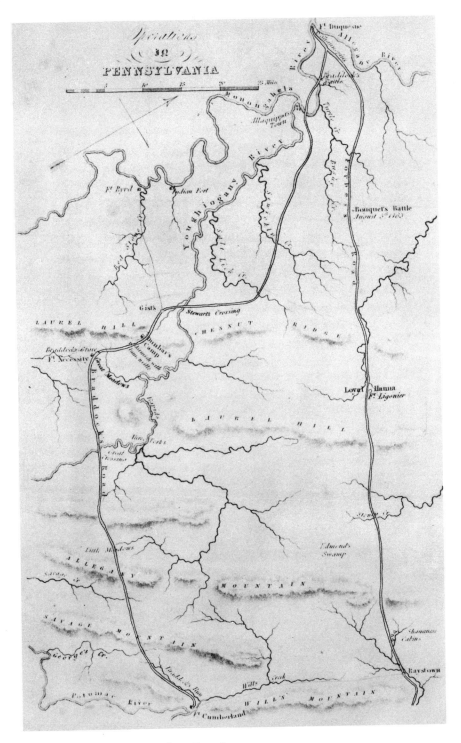

The Braddock and Forbes Roads.
(From Jared Sparks's *Writings of George Washington*.)

that "Sir John St. Clair was the person who first advised me to go by Rays Town. . . ."[13]

Was the decision to go through the heart of Pennsylvania a wise one, especially in view of the fact that Braddock's road was still available? The answer is not a simple one.[14] Involved in it was a great problem in military logistics — a problem of transport and supply. There was also a purely strategic problem. Clearly, by this advance, rather than by way of the Braddock road, there was greater possibility of securing easily, as a means of transport, good horses and wagons from the farmers of Pennsylvania than from those of Maryland and Virginia; there was also the possibility of tapping with much greater ease the most important provision center in North America — Pennsylvania east of the Susquehanna. Again, the road system of Pennsylvania from Philadelphia to Carlisle, located to the west of the Susquehanna, was far superior to that either from the ports of Maryland or from the Virginia tidewater into the back country; further, the distance to the French fort was much less; and, finally, it was possible to avoid the difficult and dangerous crossing of such streams as the Youghiogheny and the Monongahela.

With respect to strategic considerations, it is obvious that the French at the forks of the Ohio anticipated a British advance upon them by way of Fort Cumberland rather than through the center of Pennsylvania; that they therefore took such steps as were within their means to prepare for and frustrate this approach; and that when they were at last made aware of the presence of enemy forces in the area to the west of Raystown, they were still not certain that an attack from that quarter was to be expected, especially in view of the fact that Forbes took the precaution to see that a road from Raystown to Cumberland was constructed that could be used if it was not found to be feasible to cross the difficult barrier of the precipitous Laurel Hill range to the west of his main base of supply.

In favour of the Braddock road, it may, nevertheless, be said that time, always an important factor in military operations, could be saved and also much effort. While it is undoubtedly true that the road during the period intervening since its construction had been overgrown with brush, which would have to be removed, this

---

[13] Forbes to Bouquet, July 6, 1758, *ibid.*, p. 129; see also his letter of July 23, *ibid.*, p. 156.
[14] For an extended discussion of this point see the late Professor Hulbert's *Forbes's Road*.

task was quite different from that involved in making a path through a primeval forest and intervening swamps and over precipitous mountains. Here there was a clear gain in using the Braddock road; for the late general had methodically blasted, filled, and levelled the way. Again, it may be pointed out that provisions and wagons could still be secured in Pennsylvania and sent on to Fort Cumberland by one or more routes — either by way of Conococheague Creek or to the westward of this crossing of the Potomac. Finally, greater speed of movement would have perhaps made it possible to retain the services of a larger number of the southern Indians who came into Virginia by the hundreds in the early spring to participate in the expedition, but who became weary with what they thought was inaction on the part of the English and returned home.

However, in evaluating the evidence for or against the Forbes plan of advance, it should be emphasized that one must not accept uncritically such statements as those made by Washington about the difficulty, even impossibility, of the projected road. The portions of it that aroused the most serious objections are now for the most part identified with one of the busiest arteries of communication until recently within the Commonwealth of Pennsylvania — Route No. 30. Neither to the north nor to the south of this road does the terrain offer so favourable an opportunity to gain direct access to the forks of the Ohio from Carlisle as by way of Shippensburg, Chambersburg, Fort Loudoun, Bedford, and Ligonier. Indeed, once the road was established, this was early recognized. Further, from the strategic point of view, the fact that the final operations against Fort Duquesne were necessarily delayed until very late in the fall proved to be most fortunate even in the face of the desertion of the Indians. All of which tends to support the view that General Forbes, as the commanding officer, did not fail to exercise sound judgment in the course of his campaign, in spite both of frequent embarrassment, as the result of contradictory advice from his subordinates, and of physical incapacity.

No important military movement in North America during the course of the Great War for the Empire, outside of the Braddock march and Wolfe's siege of Quebec, involved such sustained effort, and no other so much real hardship on the part of the participants, as did Forbes's expedition. In launching it he was obliged to rely on colonial support and co-operation. He found Governor Denny of Pennsylvania, Governor Sharpe of Maryland, and President Blair

of the Virginia Provincial Council, as well as the more southern
governors, anxious to give him every assistance within their power.
He also found the general assemblies of both Pennsylvania and Virginia amenable to reason and, all in all, disposed to contribute to
the success of the campaign. As for the lower house of the Maryland
Assembly, consistent with its earlier attitude, it took a strong position against any participation in the war unless the province was
actually invaded, and on May 8 even resolved

> "that No Person [except in case of a foreign invasion] is punishable
> for obstinately refusing to appear & serve in Arms for the necessary
> Defence of this Province by Virtue of . . . the Act . . . which
> vests a power in the Justices of the Provincial Court to fine & im-
> prison [anyone] after . . . Conviction of such obstinate Refusal &
> Disobedience. . . ." [15]

The Pennsylvania Assembly, it is true, took advantage of the
exigency in the affairs of the province to insist on including in its bill
appropriating one hundred thousand pounds to the King's use [16]
certain clauses that caused the Governor to write to it in protest:

> "From your Obstinacy, and the hard Necessity of the Time, I am
> reduced to this Dilemma; I must subscribe My Name to a False-
> hood, Shelter these Men [the commissioners who had disbursed the
> previous appropriation] under an Act of Assembly, and preclude
> myself and the Public from calling them to a future Account, or Suf-
> fer all the Measures concerted for your Safety to stand still, the
> numerous Body of Indians come to our Assistance to return Home,
> and the present Campaign to be as inactive as the former." [17]

---

[15] *Proceedings of the Lower House, Archives of Maryland,* LV, 671. It may be
pointed out that the preceding December and in March of the year 1758 Governor
Sharpe, on the basis of reports that the enemy was operating in western Maryland, had
called out the militia of certain counties to defend the outlying settlements. A good
many people liable to serve refused to answer the call, with the result that Sharpe ordered the justices to proceed against them (*Proceedings of the Council, ibid.,* XXXI, 6).
This action was based upon "An Act for Ordering & Regulating the Militia of this Province for the better Defence & Security thereof," passed in 1715 and made perpetual, according to the Governor and the Council, by the supplementary act of 1752. The lower
house thereupon interfered with the passing of the resolution noted above, which also
stated that Sharpe had exceeded his powers.

[16] *Pennsylvania Statutes at Large,* V, 337–52; *Pennsylvania Colonial Records,* VIII,
80–3.

[17] Denny to the Assembly, April 22, 1758, *Pennsylvania Archives* (fourth series),
II, 928. Denny went on to say in agreeing to sign the bill: "But, I must do it with a
solemn Protestation to all the World, that it is Contrary to my Conscience, and in Violation of Truth, That I am obliged to say that the former Hundred Thousand Pounds is

Denny, however, signed the bill, which made it possible for Pennsylvania to make an important contribution to the success of the campaign by raising two thousand seven hundred men.[18] In Virginia, the frontiers of which were still being ravished by parties of French and Indians, as were those of Pennsylvania, the government under the guidance of President Blair was not long in coming to a decision to support the Forbes campaign. After Blair had laid before the House of Burgesses Pitt's letter of December 30 and Abercromby's of March 15, this body on April 3 readily resolved to bring into the field two regiments rather than one, each of a thousand men, and not only to levy, pay, and clothe the new regiment but to help defray the cost of supporting the Indians who had come to Winchester from South Carolina to engage in the war. Two days later it agreed that as the regiments would be actively engaged in the campaign, the forts on the frontiers, which would otherwise be deserted, should be garrisoned by the militia.[19]

Forbes ultimately had at his disposal therefore thirteen companies of Montgomery's Highlanders and four companies of the first battalion of the Royal Americans, very substantial forces raised by Pennsylvania and Virginia, some three companies sent by North Carolina, who came "in . . . absolute want of everything," [20] and, finally, these Maryland troops, which, under the command of Lieutenant Colonel Dagworthy, had been guarding Fort Cumberland

---

Expended with my Consent. . . ." Forbes in writing to Abercromby the same day observed: "The Money Bill is crammed down the Governor's Throat by the Assembly, and rather than lose any more time he is to pass it this day, although in doing so he is obliged to sign and avow two Notorious falsehoods. In short I never saw such a sett of people, obstinate, & perverse to the last degree" (Writings of Forbes, p. 68).

[18] Pennsylvania Archives (eighth series), VI, 4755–6.
[19] Journal of the House of Burgesses, 1756–1758, pp. 499, 501.
[20] Forbes to Abercromby, September 4, 1758, Writings of Forbes, p. 201. On May 1 the Committee of the Whole of the North Carolina Assembly resolved to bring the total of troops in the pay of the province up to three hundred, which should thereupon march to join the forces under command of Forbes (North Carolina Colonial Records, V, 1003); two days later a bill to this effect was passed. Two hundred of the troops were sent by sea to Alexandria and one hundred more were ordered to march by land to Winchester and arrived there early in July (Forbes to Bouquet, June 16, 1758, Writings of Forbes, pp. 115–39; see also St. Clair's orders of June 24 to the officer commanding the North Carolina detachment, Writings of Washington, II, 224–5). The third company had not been able to join the army under Forbes by September (Forbes to Pitt, September 6, 1758, Writings of Forbes, p. 205); nevertheless, his contingent account for October shows the expense for clothing and supporting three North Carolina companies (ibid., p. 298), although many of them had by the middle of July deserted (ibid., p. 148).

and were supported in the service out of the general's contingent fund. He also had high anticipations of powerful support from the Cherokee and Catawba Indians, which seemed so vital to the success of a movement through mountainous, wilderness country and against an enemy that had at its disposal numerous warlike savage allies.

As has already been made clear in considering military operations in Virginia during the campaign of 1757, fairly large contingents of Cherokee and Catawba had come to Fort Loudoun at Winchester to engage in scouting and in making forays in the direction of Fort Duquesne. Colonel Washington regarded their services highly, but the government of Virginia had not been prepared to reward them suitably for their exertions, and when they returned home at the end of the season there was dissatisfaction in their ranks. Nevertheless, early in April of the new year the Colonel reported that some four hundred had already arrived at Winchester and had gone out to war and that one hundred and forty more were expected at any moment.[21] Moreover, James Byrd III of Westover, who was in New York early in 1758, had assured Forbes that he could bring up five hundred Cherokee[22] and secured Loudoun's authorization to go among the southern Indians for this purpose.[23] By the latter part of March he was in Charleston and while the Superintendent to these Indians, Edmund Atkin, was unable, as the result of illness and the pressure of business, to accompany him into the Cherokee country, he was furnished with credentials and also with a speech to be given to the warriors in the Superintendent's name.[24] Atkin, moreover, was

---

21 Washington to President Blair, April 9, 1758, Writings of Washington, II, 171–2. A Daniel Bush who arrived at Lancaster on April 3 from Winchester brought reports to Colonel Burd that already three hundred Cherokee and Catawba had arrived at that place, that two hundred more Cherokee were daily expected, that by the middle of the month six hundred more of that nation would arrive together with four hundred Creeks; that six hundred more Creeks would leave for the north about May 1, when their corn was hilled. The distance of eleven hundred miles from the Creek country to Winchester, it was estimated, would require forty days of travel and that from the Cherokee country some thirty days (James Burd to Governor Denny, April 3, 1758, Abercromby Papers, No. 104). Had these Indians all arrived, there would have been over two thousand southern Indians engaged in the campaign. But the Creeks did not leave and the number of Cherokee fell far short of the total of eleven hundred.

22 Forbes to Loudoun, February 4, 1758, Writings of Forbes, p. 38.

23 Ibid., p. 43; Atkin to Loudoun, March 25, 1758, Abercromby Papers, No. 73.

24 Atkin to Byrd, March 24, 1758, ibid., No. 70; Byrd to Loudoun, April 30, 1758, ibid., No. 217.

able to inform him that already great numbers of Catawba and Cherokee were moving northward "with English Colours" that had previously been distributed to them and that, in fact, "all the Indians of the Lower Cherokee Towns were gone to Virginia to War." [25] As a result, Byrd had little to do but gather together some sixty Indians who had not as yet started, and with them he arrived at Winchester the latter part of May, also bringing the information that the famous Little Carpenter of the Overhills was on the way with two hundred more warriors.[26]

By April 10 five hundred southern Indians had gathered at Winchester and most of them had left for war, but Washington was greatly disturbed, as they demanded with great insistence suitable clothes and arms and he had no means of supplying them. In his own words: "The Indians are mercenary; every service of theirs must be purchased; and they are easily offended, being thoroughly sensible of their own importance." [27] These needs were at least partially met by Forbes, who sent for their use some light guns, deerskins, and strouds as well as other articles.[28] By May 1 six hundred and fifty had put in their appearance and the general was expecting the total to reach a thousand.[29] But now a problem arose. These southern Indians made war not only upon the French but upon their Indian allies, the western Delawares and the Shawnee. The government of Pennsylvania had been making strenuous efforts during the past two years to detach these two Indian tribes from the enemy and had already held two Indian conferences at Easton with Teedyuscung and his more friendly Delawares living in northern Pennsylvania. These efforts, it seemed, would now come to naught, especially if the southern Indians operated to the east of the Susquehanna. By May 3 a party of Cherokee had arrived at Carlisle. As a result, an express was sent by Forbes from Philadelphia to Colonel Washington calling upon him to prevent the Indians "coming this way." [30] Washington, in reply, made clear that Christopher Gist, Atkin's deputy in Virginia, had used his greatest endeavours to keep them from wandering into the settled part of Pennsylvania, but

[25] Atkin to Loudoun, March 25, 1758, op. cit.

[26] Forbes to Bouquet, May 29, Writings of Forbes, p. 102.

[27] Washington to Stanwix, April 10, 1758, Writings of Washington, II, 173.

[28] Writings of Forbes, p. 70.

[29] Forbes to Pitt, May 1, 1758, ibid., p. 77; Forbes to Abercromby, April 22, 1758, ibid., p. 69.

[30] Halkett to Washington, May 4, 1758, ibid., p. 83.

unsuccessfully, especially since they had been invited into both Maryland and that province the preceding year to receive presents and had expectations of them again.[31] Yet, this difficulty at last surmounted by rearming the Indians,[32] another arose. While the Indians were going out in parties, the English seemed to be holding back, and they demanded action and became increasingly restless. The presents that they had expected in coming northward were also apparently either not forthcoming upon their arrival or too few in quantity, and this embittered them.[33]

Had Forbes had in mind the type of campaign such as Braddock made in 1755, all might have been well. But his plan called for the methodical building of supply depots and fortified posts, with a necessarily slow advance into the area where the enemy was concentrated at Fort Duquesne. As May passed into June and June into July, the Cherokee and the Catawba, no longer to be held, gradually drifted away back home. By July 8 most of them, in fact, had disappeared, with but fifty at Raystown with Colonel Bouquet and but sixty — those brought by Colonel Byrd — at Fort Cumberland. Although Little Carpenter was expected soon to arrive with a hundred more, Forbes now became persuaded that by the time his army was ready to push over the Alleghenies he would be quite lacking in Indian support.[34] It was not until the middle of October that the general was able to send word to Bouquet that Little Carpenter, who had left Winchester to join the army at Raystown, had at length arrived with about thirty of his followers.[35] But the few Indians still with him, he reported, were so spoiled with the presents already given them and so insolent in their behaviour that unless their "sordid and avaricious demands" were met they could not be held. Nor did Little Carpenter's presence relieve the situation; for he surpassed all the others in his unreasonable attitude. Yet Forbes, after putting out so many thousands of pounds for Indian support

---

31 Washington to Halkett, May 11, 1758, Writings of Washington, II, 198–9.

32 Forbes to Abercromby, July 9, 1758, Writings of Forbes, p. 138.

33 When Byrd appealed to the Cherokee in their own towns to come to the assistance of the Virginians, he was impelled to promise each Indian "a Reward in Goods to be deliver'd them at Winchester to the Value of forty weight of Leather . . . to make them amends for the Loss of the Summer hunt" (Byrd to Loudoun, April 30, 1758, Abercromby Papers, No. 217). But both Forbes and Bouquet felt that the only way to hold them was to reserve the presents until the end of the campaign.

34 Writings of Forbes, pp. 139–40.

35 Forbes to Bouquet, October 10, 1758, ibid., p. 228; the same to the same, October 15, 1758, ibid., p. 230.

that at one time promised so much, was not disposed to forfeit what was left of it for the sake of a few more hundred pounds. He therefore met the Indians' virtual ultimatum.[36] Although Little Carpenter, with about a hundred Indians, agreed to accompany the general from Raystown to Loyalhanna, by the middle of November he and his immediate followers from the Overhills had deserted, suddenly departing with the horses, arms, and other equipment liberally bestowed upon them by the general.[37] What was more ominous, other Cherokee, who had deserted earlier, were already making war on the Virginia frontiersmen.[38] Although Forbes sought to waylay the revolted Indians and deprive them of the horses and arms, this effort was not entirely successful.[39] He therefore was forced, as he came into the neighbourhood of the French fort, to rely upon a small band of Catawba, a few Cherokee from the Lower Towns, and a handful of northern Indians that Croghan, the Indian trader and deputy to Sir William Johnson, had brought up. Fortunately, when this desertion occurred, the French at the forks of the Ohio were faced by a similar situation regarding their own Indians, and the tide had about run out for them.

If little dependence could be placed in the Indians by the commander of the expedition, he did have at his disposal provincial troops now experienced in the methods of frontier fighting and also a Highland regiment and a battalion of Royal Americans upon which he could rely. He also had as second in command a talented and experienced officer. Indeed, of all the soldiers that came from the Old to the New World in the service of the British during the Great War for the Empire and who acted in a subordinate position, none left a finer record of achievement than did Henry Bouquet. Descended from a noble family of French Huguenots that had fled from France and had settled in Switzerland, he was born in the canton of Vaud in 1717 and at an early age, as was true of so many Swiss, became a soldier of fortune. After having seen service in

[36] Forbes to Richard Peters, October 16, 1758, ibid., pp. 235-6.
[37] Forbes to Colonel Burd, Loyalhanna, November 19, 1758, ibid., pp. 256-7.
[38] Forbes to Bouquet, October 25, 1758, ibid., p. 248.
[39] Washington to Fauquier, November 28, 1758, Writings of Washington, II, 309-10. However, Little Carpenter did appear in Williamsburg early in the year, "conscious and cast down on Acc[t] of his bad Behaviour," according to Governor Fauquier, who went on to say: "I believe all Differences are accomodated between us, and he seems glad to get off so" (Fauquier to Colonel Byrd, January 23, 1759, Journals of the House of Burgesses, 1758-1761, Appendix, p. 267).

Sardinia and in Holland in the course of the War of the Austrian Succession, in connection with which he attained the rank of lieutenant colonel in the Prince of Orange's regiment of Swiss Guards, he travelled through southern Europe with a member of the English nobility and in 1755 was singled out by James Prevost, a fellow Swiss, as one who would make a desirable officer in the Royal American Regiment that he himself had agreed to recruit among the German-speaking people in America. Bouquet accepted this service with the rank that he had attained in Holland and came to Pennsylvania in 1756, threw himself into the work of recruiting, and then, in 1757, at the head of the first battalion of the newly raised regiment, was sent to North Carolina, as has already been noted, to take command of all the troops designated for its defence. At the close of the year Pitt determined to transfer him and his battalion back to Pennsylvania to assist in the Forbes campaign. Arriving in New York with most of his battalion on April 19, he was occupied for the next three weeks with various matters pertaining to his command and the approaching expedition and on May 5 left for Philadelphia to join Forbes, who had already arrived there.

The two men made a remarkable combination. Each was every inch the soldier; each respected the other; on most military matters they saw eye to eye. One planned and the other executed. And, it may be added, the general received from the Swiss at all times steady, loyal, and highly competent support and in turn gave to the latter his confidence. If one, in his position of extreme physical debility and pain, was at times irascible, the other, in the flood tide of physical vigor, was even-tempered and conciliatory; but both were men of iron and could be firm, even inflexible, when the occasion demanded, and were therefore not easily baffled by obstacles.

By May 20 Bouquet was at Lancaster to put the campaign into motion; [40] two days later he was able to inform Forbes that he had contracted for one hundred and eighty wagons for the establishment of magazines at Raystown. These were to be at Carlisle by June 1 and after being loaded were to begin the journey to that point in stages by way of Shippensburg, Fort Loudoun on the upper Conococheague, and Fort Littleton, with a stage placed midway between Littleton and Raystown, lying some thirty-five miles apart over

---

[40] Bouquet to Forbes, May 20, 1758, Bouquet Papers (Pennsylvania Historical Commission, 1940), Series 21652, p. 7. See Chapter II, footnote 7, for a statement about the Bouquet Papers.

mountainous country. He also assured the general that no time would be lost in erecting the fort at this place of concentration for the protection of the magazines.[41] With some of his Royal Americans and a detachment of Highlanders he reached Carlisle on the 24th. To this place had been ordered the two best Pennsylvania battalions, those commanded by Colonels John Armstrong and James Burd; but he was dismayed at the condition of the provincial troops. He found them in "frightful disorder," their firearms quite unfit for use, the stocks in pieces, and the screw-plates attached to the guns with string; nor did they have tents, kettles, axes, ammunition, or provisions. A thousand muskets, however, were held in reserve in the armory of Philadelphia and he thereupon wrote pressingly to Forbes to get these released to equip the Pennsylvania provincials.[42] For he had decided that these troops, with their long experience on the Pennsylvania frontier, must begin the advance along the road towards Raystown without delay, since the wagon trains would begin moving forward early in June and needed protection, and the roads also would require much improvement.

But there were delays. The Cherokee gathered at Shippensburg had begun seizing the presents intended for them; they had therefore to be quieted. Moreover, the wagons that were to come from Lancaster, York, and Reading had not appeared. The farmers, although guaranteed good payment of fifteen shillings a day, had ignored the orders of the sheriffs. Bouquet thereupon appealed to the local magistrates for press warrants and was prepared, if necessary, to back each constable carrying a warrant with twenty provincial soldiers.[43] His appeals, firm yet tactful, seem to have been effective, for on June 3 he was able to report that there would be enough wagons for his immediate need, with sixty now on hand from Lancaster County, thirty from Berks, and even more expected from York, as well as others engaged apparently about Carlisle in Cumberland.[44] He therefore indicated to Forbes that he planned to leave Carlisle on the 5th with Burd's regiment and enclosed his timetable of operations, which would bring him, he anticipated, to Raystown on the 12th — after having cleared the road of brush, bridged the Juniata, and constructed a stockade enclosure to hold

41 Bouquet Papers, Series 21652, pp. 8, 10.
42 Bouquet to Forbes, May 25, 1758, ibid., pp. 17–18.
43 Bouquet to Forbes, May 27, 1758, ibid., pp. 28–9.
44 Ibid., p. 50.

the crossing of this river.[45] He also requested that two of his Royal American companies still in Philadelphia be sent forward so that with three companies of the Highlanders and four of his own battalion he might be in a position at Raystown to protect the vanguard of the supply train. Having been given permission, moreover, to make what use he saw fit of Washington's Virginia regiment, he had already sent orders for it to concentrate at Fort Cumberland, where a sufficient garrison was to be left and from which point it was to begin cutting a road northward to Raystown.

Colonel Washington in the spring of 1758 was again suffering from such ill health — doubtless as the result of the harassments of his command and overexertion under all sorts of unfavourable conditions — that he was reduced, he confessed, to "great extremity" and even apprehended "an approaching decay." Therefore, since he no longer had hope of military preferment, he was impelled in March to write from Mount Vernon to Colonel Stanwix, before the latter went north, that he was thinking of quitting his command and retiring from all public business.[46] Happily, in the course of the spring his health was restored and in April we find him writing again to Stanwix, now from Winchester, to congratulate him on his promotion to the rank of brigadier general; he also took occasion to express his keen regret that he was not again to have the opportunity to serve under his immediate command; and at the same time asked Stanwix to mention him in favourable terms to Forbes — not as one who sought advancement, but rather as one who would gladly be distinguished in some measure "from the *common run* of provincial officers." [47]

By this time Sir John St. Clair had arrived in Pennsylvania to lay the foundations of the campaign. In accordance with Forbes's first decision, there was to be, as already has been made clear, a concentration of troops on Conococheague Creek before they moved on to Fort Cumberland to take the Braddock road. The news of this concentration in Pennsylvania deeply disturbed Washington, who thereupon wrote to Sir John that he feared that the Indians would take serious exception to that place as they had long been accustomed to resort to Winchester in order to go out to war from, and return to, Fort Loudoun there. This, in fact, was the beginning of

---

[45] Ibid., p. 48.
[46] Washington to Stanwix, March 4, 1758, Writings of Washington, II, 166–7.
[47] Letter of April 10, 1758, ibid., II, 172–3.

Washington's opposition to the plans of his commanding officer,[48] which was to cast its shadow throughout the campaign almost to its final termination. When in May he received orders to concentrate his regiment and thereupon to march to Fort Cumberland, his men were scattered in detachments on garrison duty, some of them two hundred miles distant from Winchester;[49] nor did they have proper arms or tents or other campaign equipment; further, their places in the scattered posts still had to be filled by the Virginia militia. The Virginia colonel therefore hurried down to Williamsburg and laid before President Blair the essentials to be met before his regiment could possibly march.[50] In fact, it was not until the latter part of June, as the result of unavoidable delay, that he could at last begin his advance toward Fort Cumberland, which he reached on July 3 with five companies of his own regiment. Byrd, in command of the new Virginia regiment, arrived on the 7th with eight of his companies and the Indians he had brought up from Carolina. This brings us now to the period of the second and more serious effort on the part of Washington to influence the course of the campaign from the lines laid down by Forbes, so that it might conform to the general pattern of the Braddock advance.

Bouquet had reached Raystown on June 24 with one of the Pennsylvania regiments and a detachment of Virginia troops. With the aid of the engineer Captain Gordon he thereupon laid out the site for a fort to be known as Fort Bedford and started the work of construction. He found, however, that the Virginians would not work unless they received extra pay and was therefore obliged to rely upon the Pennsylvania line, to whom he gave as an inducement to exert themselves a gill of rum each day. But there was an injustice involved in this arrangement and also serious financial considerations should he submit to the demands of the Virginians. Writing to the general on the 28th, he declared:

> "If one wished to put it on the basis of paying the troops in America when they must work, the army would cost nearly four times as much, because no step can be taken without axe or spade in hand. If I had enough troops, I should send them [the Virginians] to Fort

---

[48] Letter of April 18, 1758, ibid., II, 179.

[49] Washington to Forbes, April 23 and to Colonel Adam Stephen, May 24, 1758, ibid., II, 183, 203.

[50] Washington to Blair, May 28, 1758, ibid., II, 205–9.

Cumberland to remove the bad example they give. . . . I am writing to Sir John [St. Clair] to have them relieved as soon as he can, by the [Royal] Americans, the Highlanders, or the companies from North Carolina, in order to enable me to push the construction of this post with necessary diligence." [51]

Two days later Bouquet wrote to St. Clair that he was sending orders to Colonel Washington not only to detach three hundred men to open a communication between Fort Frederick in Maryland and Fort Cumberland, but also, after leaving a sufficient guard at the latter post, to move forward from it with the rest of his troops to make a road to Raystown for the purpose of joining those already there.[52] On July 3, the day after his arrival at Cumberland, Washington — evidently not any too happy over his instructions and almost verging on an attitude of insubordination — wrote to Bouquet: "As I can't suppose you intended to order any part of my Men upon the Roads till join'd in this place by Colo. Byrd, I shall decline sending any upon this Service till his arrival. . . ." [53] Then, after the Byrd regiment appeared, he wrote again to Bouquet, objecting to sending more than three hundred of his men to open communications with Raystown. He declared, among other things, that if his whole force — outside of the detachments ordered to work on the Fort Frederick connection and to guard Fort Cumberland — moved in the direction of the new post, it would be too much encumbered with wagons, which, he felt, must all eventually return; further, that those with whom he had talked were of the opinion that the army would be obliged to proceed to the Ohio by way of Fort Cumberland, where, he was convinced, it would be necessary to establish the principal base for provisions and stores; finally, that Colonel Byrd had assured him that the Indians with him "absolutely refused to march by any other Road than this they are acquainted with." [54] Byrd himself also wrote to Forbes regarding the demand of the Cherokee that the Braddock road be used. This led the general to write to Bouquet:

---

[51] Bouquet Papers, Series 21652, p. 100.

[52] Ibid., p. 105.

[53] Writings of Washington, II, 227.

[54] Washington, however, modified his position when he went on to say: "I was advis'd to hint these things to you, and wait the result of your answer before I put the whole in Motion. Whatever you direct under the Circumstances I shall execute with the greatest punctuality, and Expedition in my power (ibid., II, 231).

> "This is a new System of military Discipline truly; and shows that
> my Good Friend Byrd is either made the Cats Foot off himself, or
> he little knows me, if he imagines that Sixty Scoundrels are to direct
> me in my Measures." [55]

Forbes came to feel, and doubtless correctly, that Washington was
the chief influence at the bottom of this opposition to a new road.
The latter, later in July, went to confer with Bouquet at Raystown
and seems to have exerted himself to the utmost to win him over
to his own point of view, but without success. Upon returning to
Fort Cumberland he wrote despairingly to his old friend Major
Halkett, Forbes's aide-de-camp:

> "I have just return'd from a conference held with Colo. Bouquet. I
> find him fix'd . . . upon leading you a New Way to the Ohio; thro
> a Road, every Inch of it to cut, at this advanced Season, when we
> have scarce time left to tread the beaten Tract; universally confess'd
> to be the best Passage through the Mountains.
> "If Colo. Bouquet succeeds in this point with the General, all is
> lost! All is lost by Heavens! Our Enterprise Ruin'd; and we stopped
> at the Laurel Hill this Winter. . . . The Southern Indians turn'd
> against Us, and these Colonies become desolated by such an Acqui-
> sition to the Enemy's Strength" [56]

When this letter, written in confidence, inadvertently came into the
possession of the General, he saw in this opposition a narrow jealousy
on the part of the Virginians that he was to direct his march through
Pennsylvania [57] — thus providing a new, competing, and perhaps
more favourable route to the Ohio, with all the economic and even
political advantages accruing to the people of the more northern
province. These views of Forbes were supported, it goes without
saying, by the Pennsylvanians.[58] In contrast, Washington was equally
convinced that Forbes and Bouquet, acting under "an evil Geni,"
had been made the dupes, or something worse, of the "Artifice" of

---

[55] Forbes to Bouquet, July 23, 1758, *Writings of Forbes*, p. 157.
[56] Letter of August 2, 1758, *Writings of Washington*, II, 260.
[57] Forbes to Abercromby, August 11, 1758, *Writings of Forbes*, p. 173.
[58] James Young, paymaster for the Pennsylvania provincial forces, declared on July
23 in a letter to Secretary Richard Peters of the province: "The Virginians are making
great interest that our Rout may be by Fort Cumberland, but I hope they will not succeed"; in the same view Colonel John Armstrong of the Pennsylvania line also wrote to
Peters: "The Virginians are much chagrined at the opening of the road through this
government, and Colonel Washington has been a good deal sanguine, and obstinate
upon the occasion" (*Writings of Washington*, II, 264).

the Pennsylvanians, "to whose selfish views," he declared, "I attribute the miscarriage of this expedition. . . ." [59] But, in justice to
the general, it is quite evident that he was quite above local politics
and local considerations.[60]

There were good reasons why Washington honestly despaired of
the success of the expedition. The year was a very rainy one, which
made it especially difficult to move heavily loaded wagons over the
clay roads. Even Forbes at times was very uncertain of his ability to
reach the Ohio during the period available for campaigning. To
the west of Raystown stretched Edmond's Swamp and two mountain ranges and then beyond these towered the Laurel Hill Ridge,
the most formidable barrier of all; still beyond that was the Chestnut Ridge. He himself described the region to be penetrated as

> "an immense Forest of 240 miles of Extent, intersected by several
> ranges of Mountains, impenetrable almost to any thing human save
> the Indians . . . who have paths, or tracts through these desarts, by
> the help of which, we make our roads." [61]

As to surmounting the Laurel Range, by July 14 he began to feel
that it was going to be very difficult upon the basis of reports; but
he called upon Bouquet to "continue to make further tryalls." [62]
Even the man who persuaded him to take the more direct route —
St. Clair — had by that time become convinced "that wee shall not
find a road from Raes Town across the Allegany . . . particularly
the Laurell Ridge." The quartermaster general was indeed now
persuaded that the forks of the Ohio could not be reached without
"going into Braddock's old road." [63]

But Forbes persisted and by August 11 Bouquet had great detachments out carving an opening between the Alleghenies and the

[59] In this letter Washington outlined the steps he had taken in opposing without
avail the construction of a new road and strongly recommended that a full representation of the matter be made to His Majesty. "Let him know," he wrote, "how grossly his
Hon[ou]r and the Publick money have been prostituted." He even expressed the hope
that he might be sent to England in this errand and added: "I think without vanity I
cou'd set the Conduct of this Expedition in its true colours" (ibid., II, 277–8; see also
his letter to Governor Fauquier, dated September 2, which is equally forceful and bitter
(ibid., II, 278–83).
[60] Writing to Bouquet on July 14, Forbes declared: "I am sensible that some foolish people have made partys to drive us into that road . . . but I utterly detest all
partys and views in military operations" (Writings of Forbes, p. 145).
[61] Forbes to Pitt, July 10, 1758, Correspondence of William Pitt, I, 294–5.
[62] Writings of Forbes, p. 145.
[63] Forbes to Bouquet, July 6, 1758, ibid., p. 129

Laurel Ridge and making the pass of the Alleghenies practicable;
the latter also reconnoitred the ground as far west as Loyalhanna,
nine miles beyond the Laurel Ridge, and was optimistic as to his
ability to surmount the ridge itself in spite of the fact that it had
"many bad steps with very steep Ascents and descents at Times."
In fact, St. Clair had by August come to agree that the approach
was fully as good as the first forty miles of Braddock's route to the
west of Fort Cumberland.[64] Indeed, by the latter part of August not
only had the pass over the Alleghenies been made suitable for
wagons, but even one over the Laurel Ridge. Forbes could therefore
write hopefully that they were ready to seize the first favourable
opportunity to visit the enemy with some "pretty large detachments." [65] Further, on September 3 Colonel James Burd arrived at
Loyalhanna with twenty-five hundred men and thereupon began
the construction of an entrenched camp — later given the name
Fort Ligonier — and also the cutting of a road to a point nine miles
west of it.[66] But now the British forces were faced by a very great
danger that might even compel them to retreat from a position
gained with so much effort. For, with the arrival of five hundred
additional troops, Burd found himself with but one day's provisions.
Nor were there horses or wagons to supply his men from Raystown.[67]

It is true that by the middle of July the fort at Raystown had been
provided with storehouses adequate to contain three months' supply
of provisions for an army of five thousand men. But the wagon
trains did not appear there with a sufficient quantity of the needed
supplies; many of the wagons previously contracted for had broken
down along the way, and the draught horses were a sorry lot, not
only by reason of the fact that too many of them were offscouring of
the Pennsylvania farms — horses that under the best conditions could
not pull a full load — but also as the result of privation, through
the lack of forage along the mountainous path and the failure of the

---

[64] *Writings of Forbes*, p. 173. Bouquet also was sure by August 11 of the wisdom
of the direct route. Writing to Forbes on that day from Raystown, he says: "From all
the disinterested persons who have gone from here to Fort du Quesne, I learn that it is
possible to have a Wagon road across the Laurel Hill, and that on the other side there
is nothing but some small mountains which cannot stop us, with forage and water all
the way" (*Bouquet Papers*, Series 21652, p. 111).

[65] Forbes to Peters, August 28, 1758, *Writings of Forbes*, p. 191.

[66] Lily Lee Nixon: *James Burd*, pp. 52–3.

[67] *Ibid.*

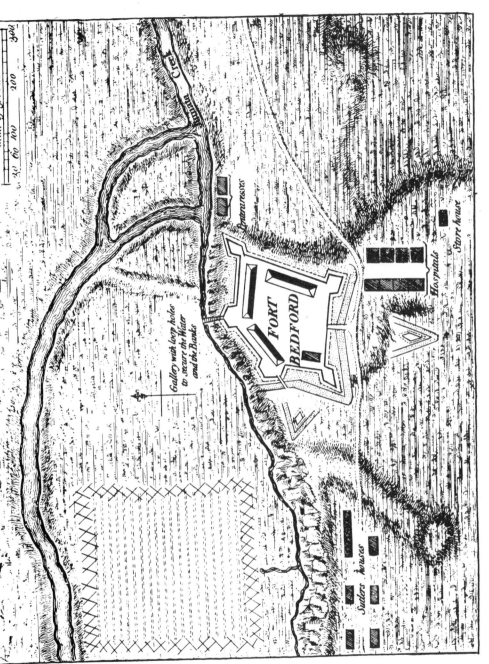

Fort Bedford on Juniata Creek.

(From Ann Rocque's *A Set of Plans and Forts in America,* 1765.)

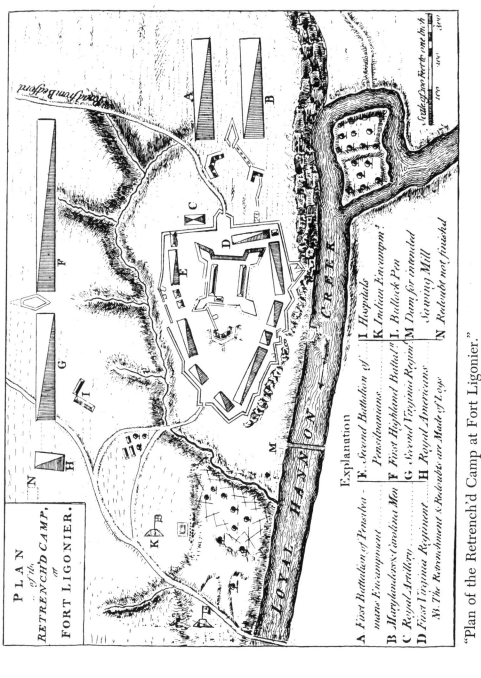

PLAN of the RETRENCH'D CAMP, at FORT LIGONIER.

Road from Bedford

LOYAL HANNON CREEK

Scale 300 Feet to one Inch

Explanation

A First Battalion of Pensilva-
    mans Encampment
B Marylanders & Carolina Men
C Royal Artillery
D First Virginia Regiment
E Second Battallon of
    Pensilvanians
F First Highland Bettal.n
G Second Virginia Regim.t
H Royal Americans
I Hospitals
K Indian Encampm.t
L Bullock Pen
M Dam for intended
    Sawing Mill
N Redoubt not finished

N.B. The Retrenchment & Redoubts are Made of Logs

"Plan of the Retrench'd Camp at Fort Ligonier."

(From Ann Rocque's A Set of Plans and Forts in America, 1765.)

contractors to provide hay and other sustenance for them. By the beginning of September this situation had reached a veritable crisis for the army, now scattered all the way from Fort Loudoun to Loyalhanna.

With some six thousand good wagons and teams available in the settled part of Pennsylvania, according to the best advice, it seemed to Bouquet and Forbes an intolerable thing that a portion of them could not be made available for this enterprise at last reaching a culmination. The latter therefore — in view of the failure of other means employed by Quartermaster General St. Clair to solve the problem, short of an impressment of wagons — appealed directly to Governor Denny in a public letter that a sufficient number of these be supplied without putting the army under necessity of employing "Violent Measures"; in this connection he promised that, should a proper number move forward to Raystown with the desperately needed supplies, their owners would be paid for this service and their wagons thereupon discharged.[68] As a result, the Assembly was led to pass on September 20 an act that provided additional inducements to those who would furnish four good horses and a wagon and would agree to carry from Lancaster to Raystown a load of at least fourteen hundred pounds, in addition to subsistence for the horses.[69]

But things did not mend immediately, although Burd's men were provisioned by depleting the Raystown reserves. At the end of the first week in October, Forbes, now established at Raystown,[70] was quite overwhelmed with the "villiany and Rascality of the Inhabitants," with the wagoners deserting by the dozens and the "Magazines daily Consuming."[71] By the middle of the month, nevertheless, St. Clair was able to give a good report of the great trains of wagons and provisions in motion between Lancaster and Raystown, and the general himself could announce the arrival by that date of two hundred vehicles loaded in Philadelphia.[72] In fact, by the 21st, as the result of the excellent response to his entreaties, he had plenty of provisions to subsist his army for forty days. The grave problem in logistics that had threatened, unless solved, to bring the campaign

[68] Forbes to Denny, September 9, 1758, Writings of Forbes, pp. 207–8.
[69] Statutes at Large, V, 372–4.
[70] Forbes arrived at Raystown on September 15, in a litter carried by two horses.
[71] Forbes to Abercromby, October 8, 1758, Writings of Forbes, p. 225.
[72] Ibid., pp. 227, 233.

to an inglorious end had thus been met and, happily, without the use of force.

With the troops now entrenching themselves at Loyalhanna, where they built Fort Ligonier, it seemed that the time at last had come to feel out the strength of the enemy at Fort Duquesne, hardly more than forty miles to the west. Forbes had had this in mind,[73] and Bouquet, who arrived at the advanced post on September 7, proceeded that very day to give permission to Major Grant of the Highlanders, who enjoyed the fullest confidence of the general, to move forward with a strong detachment of over eight hundred troops made up of his Scots and Royal Americans for the regulars, and contingents from the Virginia, Pennsylvania, Maryland, Delaware, and North Carolina provincials.[74] Bouquet's oral orders to Grant — according to Colonel Burd, who was present — were to march secretly toward the French fort, with scouting parties ahead. When he had reached the high hill in the neighbourhood of the fort, should he see no Indians lying about their fires, he must retreat, since it meant that his movement had been discovered; but should he find them lying before their fires, he was to wait until midnight and then the troops, in white shirts to distinguish one another from the enemy, were to creep up to each fire to take prisoners and destroy as many others as possible and thereupon to retreat.[75]

Grant left September 11 and moved through the wilderness. Early the morning of the 14th, he sent Major Andrew Lewis of the Virginia regiment with three hundred regulars — Highlanders and Royal Americans — and a hundred of his Virginians to make the attack; according to his orders, they were, on getting close, to fire, then, without loading a second time, to use their bayonets; after which they were to retire. To Grant's amazement, Lewis soon returned with his force to report that the night was so dark and there were so many logs to cross that the men had fallen into confusion and he could not proceed.[76] As time was passing and it would soon

---

[73] Forbes to Peters, August 28, 1758, *ibid.*, p. 191.

[74] Abercromby Papers, No. 658; Nixon: *James Burd*, p. 54.

[75] *Ibid.*, p. 56.

[76] Grant to Forbes, September 14, 1758, *Bouquet Papers*, Series 21652, pp. 131–2. Lewis was opposed to the whole project and unhappy about it. Washington on September 25 wrote to Governor Fauquier: "Major Lewis, who chearfully went on this Enterprise (when he found there was no dissuading Colonel Bouquet from the attempt), frequently there and afterwards on the march desired his friends to remember that he had opposed the undertaking to the utmost" (*Writings of Washington*, II, 290–1).

be light, Grant now turned to two of his trusted lieutenants, Robinson and McDonald, who were ordered to take fifty men and attack a place where two or three fires had been seen and, if possible, dispose of a dozen Indians before retreating. They moved forward, but finding no Indians, in retiring they set fire to the large storehouse near the deserted campfires. By this time it was break of day and, after Lewis with two hundred men had been ordered back a mile and a half in the direction of the baggage in order to lie in ambush, Grant directed Mr. Rhor, the engineer, to move forward with Captain McDonald and a company in order to get a sketch of the fort, which Bouquet had requested. This was to be done without exposing themselves too much. At the same time, to put the troops in spirit, the drummers were called upon to beat the reveille.

Now, at last the French and Indians issued from the fort like a nest of angry hornets, and in superior numbers to the British.[77] Separating into three parties, they gradually enveloped Grant's troops. In the course of the engagement the brunt of their attack fell upon the Highlanders, who in an exposed position were shot down in great numbers and at length retreated after their officers had fallen. Grant tried desperately to rally his little army. The Pennsylvanians, a hundred strong and posted farthest away from the enemy, "went off without Orders & without firing a Shott." The other provincials, however, held their ground for a time and "concealing themselves behind Trees and Brush made a good defence." One thing that proved fatal to an effective stand was that Major Lewis, who had put his men in ambush to the rear, on hearing the firing toward the front, moved forward through the trees to support Grant, but in taking a new route missed him. Grant at the same time decided to retire to the baggage to make a stand there where, he supposed, he would find Lewis, but found only Captain Bullett with some forty Virginians, who were holding firm. But without Lewis's detachment no effective resistance was possible. In an attempt to rally more men he therefore moved off to the left, while Bullett, when the enemy appeared, bravely attacked them and held his ground until most of his men were put out of action.

As for Grant, he saw his small detachment diminish each moment, "every Souldier taking the Road he liked best." Surrounded at length by the French, who repeatedly called upon him to surrender,

---

[77] Most of the Indians, deserting their camp close to the fort, spent the night across the Allegheny, but at break of day returned to it.

the major was obliged to accept quarters.[78] Lewis, who, as was stated, had gone forward, was also made prisoner, together with some other officers.[79] The chief losses, as in the attack on Ticonderoga, fell upon the Highlanders.[80] Of over eight hundred who left Loyalhanna, five hundred and twenty-five made their way back.[81] The attack proved one thing: that the French at the fort were still strong and still had at hand a considerable body of faithful Indians. With losses amounting to but eight men killed and eight wounded in the course of the engagement, they were still confident of their ability to deal with the enemy gradually converging upon them.[82]

Fort Duquesne, in fact, did not seem to the French until late in the fall to be in any great danger. The military engineer Captain Pouchot, who reconstructed Fort Niagara and had commanded there, in writing his "General Military Observations on the Frontiers of Canada" in the spring of 1758, stressed the fact that while the English, if given an opportunity, would make profitable settlements about the Ohio, they could depend upon fewer Indians to support them than the French, and their road to that region was so long and difficult that they could only throw out posts, which could be eliminated "either from Canada or from Louisiana."[83] In April

---

[78] For the battle, see the *Bouquet Papers*, Series 21652, pp. 130–4; the *Pennsylvania Gazette*, October 12, 1758; Bouquet to Forbes, September 17, 1758, B.M., Bouquet Papers, Add. Mss., Series 21640, folio 167 (Library of Congress, Transcripts); du Vernys's letter from Fort Duquesne, September 16, 1758, *Journal du Marquis de Montcalm* (ed. Abbé Casgrain), pp. 473–5.

[79] For a list of the officers made prisoner, see Abercromby Papers, No. 655.

[80] According to Bouquet's report (*ibid.*, No. 658), 199 Highlanders, including officers, were killed, wounded, missing, or captured out of a total of some 296 men; as for the Virginians, his figures are lacking except those of six officers killed; a list given in the *Pennsylvania Archives* (fifth series, I, 253–4), however, gives 67 casualties from the Virginia regiment out of a total of 172 engaged; other contingents suffered much less severely.

[81] Abercromby Papers, No. 658. Forbes blamed Bouquet for the defeat, and Bouquet blamed Grant, while the latter affirmed that he had executed his orders faithfully in so far as was possible (Forbes to Abercromby, September 21, 1758, and Forbes to Bouquet, September 23, *Writings of Forbes*, pp. 215–16, 218; Bouquet Papers, Series 21652, p. 134).

[82] The reason for the small French losses may be accounted for by the fact that their Indian allies apparently bore the brunt of the fighting. At least William Peters, writing to Richard Peters on September 29, declared, in referring to the engagement, that the Indians assembling at Easton, Pennsylvania, for a conference should be told that the "French placed their Indians in ye front of the Battle, and ye slaughter on yt side fell chiefly on them, whilst ye French themselves kept for ye most part behind, out of danger" (*Pennsylvania Archives*, first series, III, 547).

[83] *N. Y. Col. Doc.*, X, 695.

the Canadian authorities were able to indicate that everything was well on the Belle Rivière: an abundance of provisions was secured from the Illinois country, and the Canadians and Indians were doing "wonders" there in harassing the English.[84] Reports, it is true, had come in of the efforts on the part of the Governor of Pennsylvania to detach the Indians from the French by showering the Delawares and the Shawnee, as well as the Five Nations, with "carresses, presents, belts, and medals." [85] Yet in July Vaudreuil wrote to the Minister that some Loups (Delawares) of the Mountains [86] had brought belts from the English to their people on the Belle Rivière to invite them to return, but that these had been turned over to the commandant of the fort, M. de Lignery (Lironeris); and that later these same Indians who had come from the English had sent another belt to their fellow Delawares among the French to continue war on the English without giving them rest.[87] However, in view of later reports that preparations were being made to attack Fort Duquesne by way of Fort Cumberland — where a vast number of savages, according to reports, were being collected — the Governor General sent some three hundred and fifty Canadians to reinforce the troops there, which to him seemed to be sufficient to provide for the security of that area.[88] It is true that Doreil, in charge of the King's commissary at Quebec, was, unlike Vaudreuil, deeply apprehensive of the situation at the forks of the Ohio. He declared in a letter written the latter part of May that Dumas, who had in 1755 inflicted the crushing defeat on Braddock's army and had commanded there, had avowed that the fort could not provide security and that it was "fit only to dishonour the officer who was intrusted with its defence." [89] The latter part of August Doreil was still more apprehensive over exaggerated reports that had arrived in Quebec:

> "The English are perhaps at this very moment masters of Fort Duquesne. . . . At least they will be so in a short time, as a force of twelve thousand men with two pieces of cannon and two mortars

[84] *Ibid.*, X, 710.

[85] Montcalm to Belle-Isle, April 18, 1758, "Papers Relating to the French Occupation," *Pennsylvania Archives* (second series), VI, 411.

[86] That is, Delawares who had not gone west to settle on the Ohio among the French.

[87] Vaudreuil to the Minister, July 28, 1758, Archives Nationales, C¹¹A, 103:114.

[88] *Ibid.*

[89] Doreil to M. de Cremille, July 28, 1758, *Pennsylvania Archives* (second series), VI, 418.

must have arrived there. Six thousand have marched by General Bradok's road, and six thousand by another shorter and easier communication. . . ." [90]

De Ligney, nevertheless, was confident in September of being able to resist the enemy's efforts should he be attacked. His only concern seemed to be the want of provisions.[91] In fact, on August 29 he had written from Fort Duquesne that after the British army had advanced six leagues beyond Fort Cumberland, it had retired.[92] He apparently felt that there was little to be feared from the enemy in that quarter during the remainder of the campaigning season. Montcalm, however, when he received this same news of the withdrawal, recorded his conviction that the English were now taking a different route from that of Braddock, as a bearer of a flag of truce from Fort Edward had indicated to him would be the case.[93] He thereupon recorded in his *Journal* that the abandonment of Fort Duquesne, under the circumstances, would be more advantageous than harmful to the colony: "It is a branch that exhausts the trunk. How, with such scarcity of men, food and means, sustain a post so distant, the occasion and instrument of immense expence, a pillage, so to speak, of our resources and without limits?" He also revealed that in a council of war held the preceding year he had favoured blowing up the fort and thereupon making Niagara the barrier of defence of the colony from that quarter.[94]

As to the strength of the forces at Fort Duquesne, according to the Moravian missionary Christian Frederick Post, who went into the Ohio country to confer with the Delawares, there was, at the time of his arrival in the neighbourhood of this fort about the middle of August, some fourteen hundred soldiers there, most of them Canadians.[95] He also noted in his "Journal," on August 25, the arrival of three hundred more troops and reported that six hundred more were expected.[96] At the time of the engagement with Grant's task force in September, however, there were, according to du Vernys, an officer stationed at the forks, but a thousand Frenchmen,

[90] Doreil to Belle-Isle, August 31, 1758, *ibid.*, VI, 420.
[91] Daine to Belle-Isle, October 17, 1758, N. Y. *Col. Doc.*, X, 834.
[92] Montcalm's Journal, p. 462.
[93] *Ibid.*, pp. 462–3.
[94] *Ibid.*
[95] "Post's Journals," *Early Western Travels* (ed. R. G. Thwaites), I, 231.
[96] *Ibid.*, I, 231.

including Canadians, at hand.[97] Post, on the other hand, on September 20 indicated that, according to the best information available, the number in that area amounted to some three thousand — doubtless including those at Fort Machault and beyond who were engaged in forwarding supplies as well as in the work of defence.[98] Even were Post's figures correct — which is not clear — in view of the fact that the prisoners taken in the fight near the fort indicated that seven or eight thousand British troops had gathered in order to visit them with eighteen cannon and mortars, the sudden departure now of many of the French Indians with their booty for their homes brought deep concern to the defenders.[99] For by this time it was clear to them that there was a large concentration of the enemy, not on the Braddock road, but on Loyalhanna Creek, only some forty miles away. It was, in fact, reported that this large force would march forward against Fort Duquesne the latter part of October.[100] Therefore, some action to defeat this plan was demanded, especially since the Louisiana-Illinois militia at the fort must soon return down the river for lack of provisions.

Setting apart as many troops as could safely be spared and collecting from their towns as many Ohio Valley Indians as would go, de Lignery now placed this force under the command of Captain Aubry of the Louisiana troops.[101] The purpose of the expedition, according to the statement of a wounded French prisoner, was to make a surprise night attack on the Loyalhanna encampment. On the morning of October 12, while moving in the direction of the fort in order to deliver the assault that night, the French and Indians unexpectedly stumbled upon an advanced British post. When the firing began, a body of Marylanders rushed to the support of their comrades. Colonel Burd — now in charge of the encampment in the absence of Bouquet — hearing the discharge of arms at a dis-

---

97 Du Vernys to Montcalm, September 16, 1758, Montcalm's Journal, p. 475.

98 "Post's Journals," op. cit., I, 231. The number of French troops at the fort varied greatly, sometimes from week to week, as has already been indicated in Volume VI of this series.

99 Montcalm's Journal, p. 475.

100 Bougainville to de Cremille, November 8, 1758, Pennsylvania Archives (second series), VI, 425.

101 A wounded French prisoner after the engagement at Loyalhanna stated that the entire party numbered over a thousand, including Indians, and that there were between eight and nine hundred Frenchmen (Forbes to Abercromby, October 16, 1758, Writings of Forbes, pp. 232–3). Montcalm gives the figures in his Journal (p. 842) as four hundred and fifty French and a hundred Indians.

tance, sent forward a part of his Pennsylvania battalion to support the troops already engaged, who were being surrounded by the enemy. The latter, however, were too numerous and the provincials were therefore obliged to retreat to the breastworks, although supported now by a third detachment. Once the British troops were collected behind the prepared defences, they showed great steadiness and with the support of cannon and cohorns kept the French and their allies at such a distance that the latter could make little impression. Therefore, after continuing to harass the Loyalhanna defenders throughout the next night, they at length withdrew, gathering up meanwhile a number of horses as their principal booty.[102] Psychologically the French effort was not only a failure but a costly one: it was one factor that led to the desertion of what was left of their Indian support living in the area of the upper Ohio — the Delawares, the Shawnee, and the Mingos. For it appears that the Indians bore the chief losses in this struggle — as well as that of the preceding month near Fort Duquesne — and, after their inflamed minds had cooled, lost their ardor to fight any longer in the French cause.[103]

This is but a part of the explanation for the defection of the Ohio Valley Indians, whose support meant so much to the defenders of the fort at this juncture. Forbes, after becoming acquainted with the local situation, had early determined to win them over, if possible. In view of his increasing disillusionment over effective Cherokee support, he fell in line with the policy previously inaugurated by the Pennsylvania authorities and therefore warmly supported the idea of another and more important Indian conference.[104] As a pre-

[102] *Writings of Forbes*, p. 232; see also Burd to Bouquet, October 12 and 13, 1758, *Bouquet Papers*, Series 21643, pp. 189–90; Montcalm to Cremille, November 21, 1758, *N. Y. Col. Doc.*, X, 901.

[103] Montcalm thought the French had gained a considerable advantage at Loyalhanna, which would have the effect of saving the Ohio, at least, for the year (*Journal*, pp. 482–3).

[104] On April 24, in writing to Abercromby, Forbes showed little sympathy for the idea of appeasing the Delawares and felt that chief reliance for Indian support should be placed on the Cherokee warriors; in his letter of May 4 to the commander-in-chief he indicated that he had sent a message to prevent the southern Indians falling on the Delawares and Shawnee, who were now soliciting a peace with the English; on June 7 he wrote: "I have just now fixed with the Governour to send a solemn message among the Delawares and Shawanese to beg a meeting with them where they choose to appoint, when I hope to persuade many of them at least to remain neutralls for their Campaign"; by the 15th of this month he had given up hope of getting the Cherokee to remain for the campaign; on the 27th he wrote: "I have laboured much to bring those Delawares

liminary to this, a message was sent by a faithful Delaware to the Ohio Valley Indians, and another was carried by the Indian missionary Post and Charles Thomson to the Delawares living in northern Pennsylvania in the Wyoming Valley area.[105] As a result, on July 6, under the leadership of the Delaware Teedyuscung, some fifty Indians, including two from the Allegheny river towns, put in an appearance at the State House in Philadelphia, where they were greeted by Governor Denny. The talks, which lasted until the 12th, centred on the idea of reopening the road of friendship between the English and the western Indians. The latter had appeared to be receptive to the idea. At the same time their deputies who were at the conference were warned that a large British force was about to proceed against the French fort at the forks and that it would therefore be well for them all to move far from it, that their "legs may not be stained with Blood."[106]

As the western Indians through these same deputies had indicated that they saw the English only "at a distance" and would like to have a better view of them, it seemed to be a matter of the first importance that some trusted person should now go directly to them in order to report reliably the work of the conference and to further their inclinations for peace. Post was called upon by the Governor's Council to perform this hazardous task and readily consented to make the trip in company with the Ohio Valley Indians now returning home and also with a small number of Delawares from the Wyoming Valley.[107] This remarkable man had been engaged for the past fifteen years in work among the natives in Connecticut and among the Delawares on the upper Lehigh in connection with the Moravian Church program of Indian conversion. In the course of his devoted labours among them he twice married an Indian convert and lost each of his wives by death; his last wife was, significantly, a Delaware woman baptized as Agnes. Post, who spoke the language of his late wife fluently, therefore went as a tried and true friend of her tribe. This was a means of protection to him, since many of the Ohio Indians had known her as well as him before migrating; he was protected likewise by the fact that he went, as it were, in the capacity of a messenger, who among the Indians

---

now upon the Ohio back to their own Country, at least to come to a Conference" (Writings of Forbes, pp. 72, 85, 109, 113, 127).

[105] Pennsylvania Archives (first series), III, 412–22, 459.

[106] Ibid., III, 454–70.

[107] Pennsylvania Colonial Records, VIII, 147.

was granted a special status. Even so, the hazards that he was obliged to face were very great indeed, moving as he did right into the very heart of the French influence on the upper Ohio.

Leaving Philadelphia on July 15, on August 7 Post came in sight of Fort Machault at Venango and on the 12th arrived at the Indian town of Kuskuskas (Kushkushkee) on the Big Beaver,[108] where King Beaver, a Delaware chief, had his home. There he was received by the Delawares and the Shawnee in a friendly fashion and addressed them, asking them to bring together the chiefs and captains from the other towns that he might announce to all of them "joyful news." On the 17th, accompanied by a French officer and fifteen soldiers, delegates from those Indian groups at Fort Duquesne appeared in a surly mood at the Indian town. An attempt was thereupon made to lure the missionary to the French fort; he insisted, however, that the English were at war with the French, but not with the Indians, and that his mission was to the latter. That he enjoyed the support of King Beaver and most of his Delawares is indicated by the fact that the Frenchmen who sought to take him back to the fort prisoner were kept from doing so.

On the 20th the party appeared at the Indian town of Sankouk, where for a time Post's life was in very real danger, with hatred blazing from the eyes of the Indians. Again, in the presence of a French officer, he read his message to the Indians and again he protested against going to Fort Duquesne — but now in vain. Yet his position as a peaceful messenger saved him. On the way to the fort the party stopped at Logstown, where he met old friends among the Shawnee who had lived in the Wyoming Valley. Arriving across the river from the fort on the 24th, King Beaver called another large conference, where much hostility toward the missionary was manifested and an insistent demand was made by the French that he should be sent over the river and into the fort itself, but again the friendly Delawares and Shawnee refused to deliver him. His life was still in grave danger, however, since a large reward, it was reported, had been offered for his scalp. Upon the advice of his Indian friends, he slept as close to the fire as if he had been "chained there"; and then on the 26th, in the presence of three hundred French and Indians, including a large number of French officers and many of the Fort Duquesne Indians, he made his principal address to "my

---

[108] The location of Kuskuskas on the upper Great Beaver is given in Evans's Map of the Ohio (1755), in my Lewis Evans.

brethren at Allegheny," calling upon the Delawares and Shawnee to return to their homes on the upper Susquehanna, where they would be received with "brotherly love and friendship." The next day, before dawn, he silently left this perilous place by "another road" with six trusted Indian friends.

Returning to Kuskuskas on September 1, there in the presence of a number of Indian chiefs and captains, almost all of whom were inclined to make peace, he had to meet the smouldering suspicion that eventually — in the words of the Indians — "You intend to drive us away, and settle the country, or else, why do you come to fight in the land that God has given us?" This charge the missionary vigorously denied saying: "I am your own flesh and blood, and sooner than I would tell you any story that would be of hurt to you, or your children, I would suffer death. . . . I do assure you of mine and the people's honesty." Still the Indians seemed dissatisfied, fearing a trap, and it was not until the afternoon of the 9th that the missionary, having quieted their minds, was able to secure permission to depart, and then, going by way of little-frequented paths, he and his party finally reached Fort Augusta, at the forks of the Susquehanna, on the 22nd.[109]

To the student concerned with the discussions that took place between the Moravian and the Indians respecting the desire of the English for the lands of the upper Ohio — discussions that are embodied in Post's "Journal" — one fact is evident: the Indians had a much clearer view of the ultimate purposes of the British colonials than did the missionary, whose sincerity cannot be questioned. In the light of the great interest in the Ohio Valley shown by the Virginians as early as 1748, with the formation of numerous land companies such as the Ohio Company; in the light of the elaborate plans drawn up by Thomas Pownall in 1755 to appropriate for settlement every inch of the land bounded by the Allegheny River on the east, Lake Erie on the north, beyond the Ohio on the south, and as far west as the 82nd degree of western longitude; [110] in the light also of Connecticut sea-to-sea claims now being pressed; finally, in the light of the widely advertised project of Samuel Hazard, merchant of Philadelphia, to secure in 1755 from this New England colony

---

109 Post's "Journal," Early Western Travels, I, 185–233.

110 A map and detailed plan by Pownall is to be found among the Loudoun Papers, No. 740, in the Huntington Library. Franklin, Pownall's close friend of the time, also in 1756 laid down his plan for western colonies (Works, ed. J. Bigelow, II, 474–83).

or directly from the King a grant of all the lands lying north of Virginia and Carolina between a line drawn one hundred miles west of the western bounds of Pennsylvania and thence one hundred miles to the westward of the Mississippi [111] for the purpose of erecting a new colony, one must affirm that the Ohio Valley Indians were right in their apprehensions that the coming of the English boded them no good.

The mission, while it did not prevent the western Indians from engaging in hostilities, nevertheless was of great importance with respect to the war, in that it helped to undermine the French influence among them, stirring within them a desire to open up again friendly trade relations with the English. It also was a prelude to the important Indian treaty conference at Easton that opened on October 7 and continued until the 26th. At this notable gathering there assembled over five hundred Indians, including numerous representatives of all the Six Nations and those of nine other Indian tribes. Governor Denny and members of his Council were present at its opening, as was also a committee from the provincial House of Representatives; they also were joined there on the 9th by Governor Bernard of New Jersey. The causes that led the western Indians to go to war with the English were especially stressed and in particular the grievance of these tribes over the sale, by members of the Six Nations at Albany in 1754 to the Pennsylvania Proprietors, of the lands beyond the Appalachian Mountains up to the western extremity of the province. As a concession to Indian goodwill these lands were now released back to the Indians in the name of the Proprietors with the clear understanding that settlement by the English up to the mountain barrier would alone be lawful. Before closing the conference, with its endless talk of digging up the buried chain of friendship and making smooth the road of peace, a message was agreed upon, with the Indians present participating in its formulation, to be carried to the Ohio Indians by two whites, two members of the Six Nations, and one or two Delawares. [112]

---

[111] For the resolutions favouring the Hazard project by the Connecticut Assembly at its May 1755 session, see *Connecticut Colonial Records*, X, 382–3. A broadside "For the settlement of a New Colony to the Westward of Pennsylvania" and another in the form of a petition to His Majesty, dated July 24, 1755, to that same end are to be found among the papers of the New York Historical Society.

[112] For the Easton Indian Treaty of 1758 see the *Pennsylvania Colonial Records*, VIII, 174–223; the formal release of the trans-Appalachian lands came on October 24, 1758 (*ibid.*, VIII, 219).

The Easton Indian Treaty, according to Colonel Bouquet, bringing with it a release by the Pennsylvania authorities of the trans-Appalachian lands within the bounds of the province, was a blow "which knocked the French in the head."[113] For it seemed to confirm fully Post's sincere protestations made to the Indians of the Ohio Valley and therefore took from the French the chief argument for supporting them rather than the English. The treaty, solemnly ratified by His Majesty in Council, became, in fact, with the end of the hostilities in this area, the basis for trans-Appalachian British policy; the whites, moreover, were solemnly warned by a proclamation issued by Bouquet, two years before the famous Proclamation of 1763 was received in America, not to attempt to hunt or to settle west of the mountains without special authorization.[114] That the policy finally broke down was due not so much to lack of sincere desire on the part of the authorities to implement it in order to ensure peace on the frontiers by protecting the interests of the red man, but rather, as will be stressed in a later volume, to the constant pressure of the English settlers against the western barrier and the plans of American expansionists, who were determined to undo this great restriction on the whites embodied in the treaty.

It was of the highest importance that the results of the conference should be brought to the trans-Appalachian Delawares, Shawnee, and Mingos at the earliest possible moment. Even before the final ceremonies at Easton, Post was asked to return again to the Ohio, now in company with Captain John Bull and Lieutenant William Hayes of the Pennsylvania line, who had volunteered to go.[115] For the Indians had indicated that they desired some people to come to them more closely identified with the government of the province than was the Moravian missionary, who was too much one of their own. Leaving Easton on October 25, Post reached Reading two days later, where he was joined by the two Pennsylvania officers and the Indians who had agreed to accompany him. At first it had seemed best to go to the Ohio by the route pursued by Post on his first journey, and Bull and Hayes had been so instructed; but the missionary now brought fresh orders from Denny to go first of all directly to Forbes's headquarters and to receive from him such ad-

---

[113] A. T. Volwiler: *George Croghan*, p. 139.

[114] See Bouquet's proclamation issued at Fort Pitt on October 30, 1761, *Bouquet Papers* (Pa. Hist. Com., 1943), Series 21655, pp. 178–9.

[115] Their instructions, dated October 21, 1758, are in the *Pennsylvania Archives* (first series), III, 556–7.

ditional instructions and messages as he might see fit to give. This the Indians did most reluctantly, fearing greatly that their lives might be in danger from the soldiers stationed along the Forbes road. At Fort Chambers (later Chambersburg) on the 31st the settlers, in fact, threatened them; at Fort Loudoun they picked up a small party of Cherokee going forward; at Fort Littleton the Cherokee who were with them, having received news that the Virginians had killed thirty of their people, called upon the other Indians to turn back, but Post by exerting his influence overcame their fears and on November 7 the party arrived at Loyalhanna, where they were cordially received by the general. After proper ceremonies and after Forbes had penned a special message for the Ohio Indians, the party left on the 9th, escorted by a guard of one hundred men for a distance of ten miles. Then Post, Bull, and Hayes — the last accompanied by fourteen of his own soldiers — and the Indians moved up the Loyalhanna Creek in order to cross the Allegheny River above the forks and reach Kuskuskas on the Big Beaver. As the party was running short of provisions, it was agreed before crossing the Allegheny that Hayes and his detachment had best turn back, which they did, with the unfortunate result that five of his party were killed by the Indians and he and four of the rest were taken prisoner.[116]

Arriving at Kuskuskas on the 16th, Post found that almost all the men, some one hundred and sixty, had again gone out to war against the English. But now the news reached the party that one of Hayes's soldiers held prisoner was about to be burnt at Saweung. To add to the seriousness of the situation, many Indians who had been led by the French to attack Loyalhanna on October 11 were now returning home and were deeply exercised over their losses. Further, the French in their midst attempted to persuade their dusky allies to knock Post and the other messengers on the head and, to further this idea, reported having a letter taken from Hayes that disclosed an English plot to destroy all the Indians. For days the lives of the party hung in the balance. Post, however, gradually won powerful support among the elder men.

On the 20th a most dramatic scene took place when a French officer appeared from Fort Duquesne with a message and a string of wampum. When the string was offered to one of the Indian councillors he refused it. Whereupon in a mood of petulance the French-

---

[116] It was reported that Hayes had been killed.

man threw it to another fireplace, where other Indian leaders were seated, "but they kicked it from one to another, as if it was a snake. Captain Peter [a Delaware] took a stick, and with it flung the string from one end of the room to the other," and taunted the Frenchman to go out with his own young men and fight and no longer depend on the Indians. At which the officer "looked as pale as death." [117]

On the 22nd a warrior arrived with the news that the English general was but fifteen miles from Fort Duquesne, where the French had already uncovered their houses and had laid the roofs around the fort to set it on fire; and on the 24th the Indians actually raised the English flag in their town "in spite of the French." The next day Post delivered the messages from Governor Denny and General Forbes in the presence of a French officer, King Beaver, Chief Shingas, and their followers — their bodies still, in a rhetorical sense, "stained with blood" from the Loyalhanna engagement. There also the letter that had been taken from Lieutenant Hayes was secured by one of the Indians and was found to be one that Post himself had written, the contents of which were most inoffensive in nature, in contrast to the assertion by the French officer that it disclosed a diabolical plot by the English to exterminate the Indians. As one of the Delawares, named Isaac Still, could read, the Indians reacted so sharply against the deception practised upon them that the Frenchman, after being mocked by the Indians, hurriedly left the gathering. But the natives were still troubled about what might still be the secret purposes of the English with respect especially to the settlement of the Ohio Valley lands, and it was not until the beginning of December that Post was able to bring to bear sufficient reassurances on that point to feel free to leave them.[118]

The French accounts of the transactions in the Ohio Valley during this critical period stress the point that the Indians, after participating in the expedition against Loyalhanna, deserted the defenders of Fort Duquesne in order to hunt.[119] This is but half the story. The other half is to be found in the undermining of the French influence among the nations by the conferences in Philadelphia and Easton and by the redoubtable labours of Christian Frederick Post in their midst, overcoming as he did their hatreds as well as their fears and putting their minds temporarily at rest as to what the appearance

[117] "Post's Journal," Early Western Travels, I, 256.
[118] For Post's second trip and his transactions with the Indians see ibid., I, 234–81.
[119] Montcalm's Journal, p. 483.

of an English army moving toward the forks of the Ohio portended to them and to their children.

In turning again to Loyalhanna, it may be noted that when General Forbes finally arrived there on November 2, some five thousand troops had been assembled, and among them were Colonel Washington and his Virginia regiment. The colonel was still deeply pessimistic of success; he described the Forbes road as "indescribably bad," and thought that the campaign must end at the new post.[120] In fact, his views were generally shared by his fellow officers, and at a council of war called by Forbes the general sentiment seemed to be opposed to proceeding farther this season in the direction of the French fort.[121] Then, on November 12, following the council of war, came a French raid under de Corbière on British horses grazing some three miles distant from the Loyalhanna. Forbes sent Colonel Washington with five hundred men to give chase to the enemy and soon afterward sent Colonel Mercer, also of Virginia, with an equal number of men to surround them. Washington and his men succeeded in capturing three prisoners, an Indian man and woman and an Englishman, one Johnson, who claimed that he had lived in Lancaster County but had been carried off by the Indians. When the enemy had fled, the detachment with the prisoners gathered in the dusk of the approaching night about a fire that had been built and soon afterward Washington was in the greatest danger of losing his life. For when Mercer with his detachment suddenly came in sight of the party about the fire and in the gloom saw the Indians, he supposed that he had fallen upon a party of the enemy and immediately opened fire on his fellow Virginians. This fire was returned, resulting in the loss of two officers and thirty-five privates before the tragic mistake was discovered.[122] However, out of this effort to surround the enemy came the information that was so much desired; for Johnson, promptly conveyed to Forbes's headquarters, was told that he had forfeited his life in being found in arms against his King and country and that the only way to save it and make atonement was to give an accurate account of the conditions of Fort Duquesne. With this went a promise of a reward should his statements prove correct and also a warning that if false he would suffer

[120] Washington to Fauquier, October 30, 1758, *Writings of Washington*, II, 300.
[121] The same to the same, November 28, 1758, *ibid.*, II, 308–9.
[122] Forbes to Abercromby, November 17, 1758, *Writings of Forbes*, p. 253; *Pennsylvania Gazette*, November 30, 1758.

death in an "extraordinary manner." According to his circumspect testimony, not only had the Canadians, who had assisted in the earlier attack on Loyalhanna, gone home, but the Ohio Indians had also departed for their towns, and as a consequence the fort was very weak, with few defenders. The Indian male prisoner, later examined, also gave a report that corresponded with that of the white man.

Forbes no longer hesitated. Washington with his Virginians and Armstrong with his Pennsylvanians were ordered out to blaze the way for the advance of the army, and they set to work with great vigour and zeal. From Chestnut Ridge they pushed on to Bushy Run; on the 20th they reached upper Turtle Creek, crossed it on the 22nd, and were now but a few miles distant from the fort. The following day they established a temporary post at a place that they called Bouquet's Camp and apparently acted on Forbes's orders to put it on a state of defence. There they waited for the arrival of the general, borne on his horse litter and accompanied by the main body of troops.[123] Then on the night of the 24th, with the army at last assembled in the hills about Turkey Creek,[124] close to the scene of the defeat of Braddock's army, the sound of a great explosion was heard off in the direction of the forks of the Ohio. The real cause of it was hardly suspected by Forbes and his staff. In fact, it was not until the following evening that the general at last moved forward prepared to brush aside all opposition. When at length his troops, without the slightest interference, came in view of the fort, they beheld a scene of total desolation and wreckage, with the chimneys of the houses alone standing in their stark outlines. As they advanced closer, there appeared another scene that chilled their blood. For on a long row of stakes that the Indians had erected along their well-beaten path to the fort were fastened the heads of Grant's Highlanders, killed or captured, and underneath these were hung their Scottish kilts.[125] As their fellow Scots passed by these gastly

123 For the progress of Washington and Armstrong see *Writings of Washington*, II, 299; *Writings of Forbes*, p. 261. Bouquet's Camp was estimated to be about twelve miles from Fort Duquesne; Forbes, however, thought it more nearly sixteen miles by the path between the two places (*Writings of Forbes*, p. 270).

124 A. B. Hulbert: *The Old Glade (Forbes's) Road*, pp. 157–8.

125 According to a letter written from the fort on November 26, an English boy, who for two years had been held prisoner but who escaped on November 2 and made his way to the army, stated that five of Grant's men who were captured were burnt by the Indians on the parade grounds of the fort, and others delivered to the Indians were tomahawked on the spot (*Pennsylvania Gazette*, December 14, 1756). The torture of

mementoes of Indian victory, from a subdued threatening murmur finally burst into a shriek of rage and grief over this insult to their fallen brothers. Casting their muskets to the ground and raising their deadly claymores, they broke ranks and rushed forward, beside themselves with fury, with but one impulse: that of exacting retribution.[126] But the enemy had fled and was therefore beyond their grasp.

The destruction of Fort Duquesne at the hands of the French themselves came as the sequence of events that have already been considered. The capture in the spring of most of the supply ships, one of them loaded with the Indian presents for the year, and then in the fall the capture of Fort Frontenac by Bradstreet, with the destruction of the great store of provisions and other military matériel stored in the magazines at Cadaraqui and destined for the support of the French forces at the forks of the Ohio and elsewhere, had the most serious consequences with respect to the ability of the French to maintain themselves on the Ohio. De Lignery, faced with a desperate shortage of provisions and with the winter coming on, felt compelled to permit the return down the river of the Louisiana and Illinois militia who had been assisting in the defence of Fort Duquesne. He thus reduced the garrison to not more than three hundred men — placing it therefore on a characteristic winter basis, doubtless with the hope that the reports were true that the English were planning to winter at Loyalhanna.[127]

Governor General Vaudreuil, on receiving news of this forced reduction in the garrison at the forks of the Ohio, took vain comfort in assurances that the commandant at Fort Duquesne would still enjoy the support of the Delawares and Shawnee of the upper Ohio.[128] These warriors, however, were, at the very time of the appearance of the English, attending the peace councils being held in their midst by Post and would no longer raise a hand for the French, whom they had come to realize were weak and in want. When a report arrived at Fort Duquesne of the near approach of

the British soldiers taken to the fort after Grant's engagement is further elaborated in another letter of December 6 (ibid., December 21, 1758).

[126] Winthrop Sargent: History of an Expedition against Fort Duquesne, p. 273.

[127] According to Vaudreuil, de Lignery, who wrote to him on October 30, indicated "that he has been absolutely obliged, by the scarcity of provisions, to reduce his garrison to 200 men" (N. Y. Col. Doc., X, 924–5). Later it is indicated that he had some three hundred.

[128] Ibid.

Forbes's army, de Lignery, now hopelessly weak, anxiously awaited information as to the exact movements of the enemy. On the 19th de Linctot, whom he had sent out to scout, returned to report the presence of a large number of men at the foot of the mountain not many miles distant — apparently the forces under Washington and Armstrong who appeared that day on North Turtle Creek. The commandant, it may be pointed out, was under positive orders "to burn and to remove the artillery, warlike stores and provisions" whenever the enemy should actually come in force in the vicinity of Fort Duquesne.[129] He was, in other words, not to wait to stand a siege. A council of war having been called, it was thereupon agreed that preparations must be made to evacuate the fort, and these were begun with the tearing down of the palisade about the fort and the deroofing of the houses. When Linctot returned on the 23rd from a second reconnoitre and reported that the English army was now but five or six leagues away, de Lignery acted with decision. Placing most of the cannon and the munitions in bateaux, he ordered them down the Ohio to the Illinois country; he also distributed eight days' provisions to those who were to accompany him up the Allegheny; then, for the destruction of the fort, he reserved some fifty barrels of powder in the magazine. Moving with his force a league above the fort, he waited until the roar of the explosion was heard and, having ascertained that the stronghold was now reduced to ashes and rubble, he proceeded up the river to Fort Machault, arriving there on the 28th.[130] With his withdrawal from this strategic centre of trans-Appalachian French power and with the coming of the slowly-dying British general, who raised the British colours where the French fleur-de-lis had so proudly and defiantly flown since 1754 and who named the place Pittsburgh, we pass from one epoch to another in the history of the valley of the Ohio.

There is irony in this event, however, in the fact that it came about as the result of Forbes's close study of French military science and his faithful application of its principles in the building of his chain of protective posts as he gradually moved forward for the purpose of coming to grips with the enemy.[131] He, in truth, mastered the

---

129 *Ibid.*, X, 922.

130 Vaudreuil to the Minister, January 20, 1759, *Wilderness Chronicles of Northwestern Pennsylvania*, pp. 126-9.

131 Forbes to Pitt, October 20, 1758, *Writings of Forbes*, p. 240. In 1754 Lancelot, Comte Turpin de Crissé, published his important *Essai sur l'art de la guerre* in two volumes. The last chapter of Book IV, entitled "*Principe sur lequel on peut établir un*

French by the aid of the French. There is also irony in the event in its portent of a vast future westward expansion of the English-speaking people. Hardly had the echoes died away of Post's protestations to the Indians that the British people were not desirous of taking their lands, hardly had the solemn asseverations of the Treaty of Easton been published to the world, hardly had the occupation of the forks of the Ohio been accomplished for the purpose of driving away the French, when the *New-York Gazette* set forth in the following prophetic statement the true significance of Forbes's great conquest — a statement, incidentally, immediately reprinted in Franklin's *Pennsylvania Gazette* in its issue of December 28:

> "It is not as two Nations at War, contending the one for the other's Habitations . . . but for a vast Country, exceeding in Extent and good Land, all the European Dominions of Great-Britain, France, and Spain, almost destitute of Inhabitants; and will, as fast as the Europeans settle, become more so of its former Inhabitants."

---

projet de campagne," embodied the important conceptions of the building of posts in the progress of a campaign. This work was so highly regarded that it was translated into English by Captain Joseph Otway and published in London in 1761. In his letter Forbes states respecting this work: ". . . you will see the Generall principles upon which I have proceeded."

CHAPTER X

The Continental Colonies and the War, 1759

A S THE YEAR 1758 came to its close, the British at home and overseas could look at the balance sheet of successes and reverses with a good deal of satisfaction. The war in Germany saw the enemies of the Anglo-Prussian alliance retire into winter quarters without being able to claim much advantage, even after the defeat of King Frederick by the Austrian Daun in October at Hochkirch and of Ferdinand's forces near Minden by the French in the same month. For the Prussian King still maintained himself in Saxony and Silesia; while Ferdinand, in spite of the fact that the enemy was once again in control of both banks of the Rhine and again threatening the gates of Hanover from Westphalia, was able by a wise disposition of his troops, including the British forces, to hold his own in the Electorate and in Hesse. Further, upon the coasts of France, to balance the defeat suffered by General Bligh at Saint-Cas in connection with his raid on Saint-Malo, there was the earlier destruction of Cherbourg. Again, on the sea during the year the French had lost, according to Entick, 16 ships of war, either taken or destroyed, as against the loss of but 3 by the British;[1] they had lost 49 privateers as against but 8 on the part of their opponents, and 104 trading vessels as against 313.[2] But the rather favourable

---

[1] John Entick: General History of the Late War, III, 422–3.
[2] Ibid., III, 399–401. J. S. Corbett (England in the Seven Years' War, II, 375), while agreeing that in the course of the war France captured more merchant ships than the British, observed: "The truth seems to be that the bulk of our commerce was so

showing of the French with respect to merchant ships is offset by the fact that much of their overseas trade was carried in neutral ships, particularly those of Dutch registry, and of the neutrals 176 were captured that year, most of them "richly laden with the produce of the French colonies, or with stores of all sorts to enable the French to continue the war" in various parts of the world.[3] The balance was therefore decidedly weighted, in terms of sea power, in favour of the British.[4] On the coast of Africa, in India, and in the West Indies the British not only were holding their own, as will subsequently be emphasized in the next volume of this series, but had scored some striking successes, as, for example, about the river Senegal in Africa, and in Bengal in India. Finally, in America, although on the one hand the year had witnessed the defeat of Abercromby at Ticonderoga, yet on the other it had witnessed not only the fall of Louisbourg, guarding the Gulf of St. Lawrence, but that of Fort Frontenac, supporting French supremacy on Lake Ontario and protecting the upper St. Lawrence region, and that of Fort Duquesne at the forks of the Ohio, the key to the control of the fertile valley of that river.

This is not all. British sea supremacy, joined with the war in Europe, was slowly strangling the economic life of France and of her empire. As has been already noted, Canada was actually living from hand to mouth; Louisiana was greatly distressed and the inhabitants felt that they had been virtually abandoned; and the French West India islands, in order to be succoured, were thrown open to neutral trade as early as 1756. With respect to the French at home, a contemporary historian in summarizing the activities of 1758 is probably not far from wrong, in spite of his patriotic fervour, when he writes:

great that the mere pelagic operations of our enemy, though they absorbed in the end almost the whole of her vitality at sea, could not make a sufficient percentage impression to produce any real warlike advantage."

[3] Entick, *op. cit.*, III, 401.

[4] The dread with which the French looked upon British sea supremacy at this period is indicated by advices from St. Petersburg under date of October 9 in which an excerpt from a paper published by the French Ambassador at that court is given. It reads as follows: "To muster all the Powers of Europe against France, the Word has for a century past been, the Balance of Power on the Continent: But while the English held forth this Phantom to impose upon the Credulity of the Publick, they were incessantly labouring (and have unhappily too well succeeded) to destroy the Balance of Power by Sea, without which, however, that upon Land cannot subsist: This is a Thing to which other nations ought to give the most serious Attention, as it threatens no less than the entire Destruction of their Navigation, and the Usurpation of all Commerce by the English" (London advice, *Pennsylvania Gazette*, February 15, 1759).

"Nothing prospered in their cabinet, nothing succeeded in their operations . . . during the whole year. Their merchants were no longer able to support their credit, their manufactures were at a Stand, and their whole land mourned over the ravages made by the distresses of a bloody, expensive, inglorious, and ruinous War." [5]

In contrast, the same writer pictures the condition of Great Britain and the Empire at this juncture:

"The flourishing state of our colonies, of our islands, of all our settlements and Kingdoms, both for their imports and exports in the course of the year past, exceed all that ever was before. Our merchants and manufacturers, our planters and navigators, were never in so fair a way to serve themselves and their country. Both riches and seamen increased under the protection of a well-regulated and appointed navy. The nation that can best protect their trade, will be always most capable of finding the sinews of war. . . ." [6]

As for William Pitt, "the Darling of the Public," his popularity never reached a higher point; his plans for the next year's campaign were supported by the Cabinet Council, and his demand for funds — eventually amounting to over twelve and three quarters million pounds sterling — to carry these out in the course of the year [7] was readily approved by Parliament. Not only did the Minister see that the great fleet was maintained at the strength it had reached in the fall of 1758, but both public and private shipyards were busily engaged in adding to its offensive power — with ten ships of the line in course of construction in the latter, without taking into account the activities going on at Chatham and at other royal shipyards. [8] At the same time he saw that provision was made for em-

---

[5] Entick, op. cit., III, 427. Pitt on December 9 declared "that all the mighty Efforts of France & her Confederates in Germany, have by the Blessing of God, been totally baffled & render'd abortive, & that the Campaign seems drawing to a Conclusion, so fruitless & humiliating to the Enemy, and so glorious for the Arms of His Majesty and those of the King of Prussia" (Correspondence of William Pitt, ed. G. S. Kimball, I, 424).

[6] Entick, op. cit., III, 427–8. The King's speech from the throne on November 23 also affirmed the flourishing condition of commerce, "not to be paralleled during such troubles" (Parliamentary History, ed. T. C. Hansard, XV, 930).

[7] Entick (op. cit., III, 438–41) itemizes these general grants which took place in December 1758, January, April, and May 1759. See also Journal of the House of Commons, XXVIII, 352, 505–9, 526, 573, 580, 595.

[8] London advices, November 30, 1758, Pennsylvania Gazette, February 22, 1759. By the spring of 1759 thirty new ships of the line were on the stocks in both public and private docks (ibid., May 31, 1759).

ploying sixty thousand seamen in the public service during the following year. As for his next military objectives, while continuing to provide subsidies for Britain's allies in Germany [9] and for a small British army serving there under Prince Ferdinand, in order to keep the enemy fully occupied on the Continent, he determined to proceed not only with the task already begun of conquering Canada but also with the reduction of both of the rich French West India islands of Martinique and Guadeloupe.

With respect to Pitt's American objective, on December 9 he addressed a circular letter to the governors of the continental colonies calling upon them to give their utmost support to the next year's campaign, and particularly those administering the colonies lying north and east of Pennsylvania; they were asked to see that at least twenty thousand men were provided "to join . . . the King's Forces, for invading Canada by the way of Crown Point." Once again he agreed to furnish the provincial contingents with arms, ammunition, tents, and provisions and further indicated, as he had done in his letter of the preceding year, that the King was prepared to make strong recommendations to Parliament that the cost to the respective colonies of levying, paying, and clothing these troops should be likewise reimbursed out of the royal treasury.[10] How did the colonies respond?

Again, as in the earlier years of war, the more northern colonies — not only because of a very direct interest in protecting their borders and in the successful outcome of the war but also on account of the fact that in them there was available a considerable number of people whose ordinary occupational activities made them mobile — gave the best response to the appeal of the Minister. In fact, it may be said that of the southern colonies Virginia alone was disposed to make an effort to contribute to the general cause — and not a great effort at that. Georgia, for example, remained pathetically weak. In 1756, as previously noted, the first of three troops of forty rangers each was raised with the expectation that these contingents would be supported by the royal exchequer. But the matter was passed over by both Loudoun and Abercromby in favour of weightier issues, and in the spring of 1759 the colony was still awaiting authori-

[9] For a brief but excellent account of negotiations between Great Britain and her allies in Germany respecting continued financial support, see C. W. Eldon's *England's Subsidy Policy toward the Continent during the Seven Years' War*, pp. 115–21.
[10] *Pitt Correspondence*, I, 414–20.

zation to bring the plan to realization. Meanwhile, Governor Ellis —
with the colony impotent to assume any financial responsibilities
even of this modest nature — had been subsisting at his own expense
the small body of rangers that had been enlisted.[11] In fact, when
danger seemed to threaten the province, detachments of the South
Carolina Independents were provided, or, as in the situation that
existed in 1757, a company of Virginians was posted on its southern
border.

As for South Carolina, its Governor, who was now William Henry
Lyttelton, had addressed Pitt in November of the preceding year
regarding the plan that he had cherished, ever since taking up his
office in the province, of an attack on the French settlements on
Mobile Bay and the Mississippi River.[12] This, he pointed out, would
be a popular enterprise within the colony and for it the provincial
regiment of but some four hundred men might be recruited up to
seven hundred in strength; out of the militia, numbering between
six and seven thousand, another regiment of a thousand might be
formed; in addition, some two hundred more horsemen might be
embodied in the militia regiment of horse, now with but one hundred; and, finally, these provincial troops might be strengthened
by one of the companies of the Independents. With this combined
force he himself was prepared, he indicated, if authorized to do so,
to march into the Creek country for the purpose of gaining their
support or, if this was not possible, of overawing them and keeping
them neutral while proceeding to move against Fort Toulouse on
the Alabama River and the other French posts and settlements,
with the support at least, he felt sure, of the Chickasaw nation.[13]
The Minister, however, was not disposed to turn aside from his chief
objectives: the reduction of Canada. Only after this had been accomplished was he, in fact, prepared to authorize his commander-
in-chief in North America to proceed, if it seemed possible, with
the more southern enterprise.[14] As a result, the province fell back

---

11 Pitt to Amherst, March 15, 1759, *ibid.*, II, 67.

12 J. R. Alden: *John Stuart and the Southern Colonial Frontier*, p. 65.

13 Lyttelton to Pitt, November 4, 1758, *Pitt Correspondence*, I, 387–9.

14 *Ibid.*, I, 170–1; II, 37–8; Chatham Mss., Bundle 96 (Canadian Archives Transcripts). Amherst, however, had contemplated late in 1758 sending troops to join
the provincials that could be collected for a winter expedition against Mobile and the
Mississippi, feeling that this season of the year would be better for such a campaign than
the summer. He gave up the idea, however, for fear that before it would be terminated
the regulars would be needed for other services. Writing to Viscount Ligonier about the

into its previous attitude of indifference to the support of the war in North America. Therefore, when requested by Pitt to maintain at least seven hundred men under arms during the year, the Assembly, in spite of the Governor's efforts to stir up some spirit for the general cause, in its session in July was willing to go no further than make provision for three companies of foot and two of horse, and these were to be used for local garrison duty only.[15]

Nor was North Carolina disposed to duplicate the exertions it had made the preceding year, when three companies were sent to aid Forbes in the reduction of Fort Duquesne. In fact, it was not until April 9 that Pitt's circular letter of December 9, calling upon the southern governors to induce the assemblies to support the year's campaign, reached Governor Dobbs.[16] He thereupon sent out expresses calling for an extraordinary meeting of the Assembly in May. When it met, there occurred a deadlock between the upper and lower chambers over the supply bill that was offered, with the result that the Assembly was prorogued and therefore no provision was made for the raising of troops.[17] Indeed, as the Governor observed in writing to the Board of Trade, even had the bill been passed, it was already so late in the season that by the time the proposed three hundred troops had been recruited and were prepared to march, the campaign would have been over.[18]

---

matter on January 18, he declared: "I should be lopping off a branch, when it would be time that I should try at the Stem & the Root" (Amherst Papers, Packet 11, Canadian Archives Transcripts).

[15] Alden, op. cit., pp. 66–7.

[16] Dobbs to Pitt, April 11, 1754, Pitt Correspondence, II, 81–2.

[17] The issue between the two houses had to do with the control of the bills of credit to be issued for the raising of troops. The lower house sought to control these funds by inserting special clauses in the bill. The bounty to be paid to those who volunteered for the three companies proposed to be raised by it was reduced from ten to five pounds, a fatal provision in the eyes of Dobbs in view of the fact that even by offering ten pounds enlistment money in 1758, only two hundred men could be recruited rather than three hundred (ibid.). For the bill as rejected, see The Colonial Records of North Carolina, VI, 34–40. One provision of the bill that would have been particularly objectionable not only to the people of Great Britain but to the neighbours of North Carolina was that the bills of credit that were to be issued were to be "a lawful Tender in all Payments whatsoever at Par with Proclamation Money" — in spite of the fact that the North Carolina bills of credit had an exchange value far less than Proclamation money, which was related to sterling at six shillings for the Spanish milled dollar as against four shillings sixpence for the dollar, the sterling rate of exchange. In fact, North Carolina currency by 1759 was so depreciated that it required £133.6.8 of those bills of credit to secure £70 in sterling (see Volume II of this series, pages 151–2, for an analysis of this matter).

[18] Dobbs to the Board of Trade, May 18, 1759, N. C. Col. Rec., VI, 32–3.

Virginia, likewise, while doing much better than its southern neighbours, fell far short of its efforts of the preceding year. When the Assembly met on February 23, Lieutenant Governor Fauquier had not yet received Pitt's letter of December 9 or that of January 23, but he laid before them the Minister's letter of September 18 and one from Amherst of December 13 calling upon the colony to dupli- cate its exertions of the year 1758, and at the same time tactfully recommended that this be done. In his address he congratulated the Assembly on the reduction of Fort Duquesne, which thereby put His Majesty "in Possession of a very extensive, fine and fertile tract of Country," and pointed out the advantages that would accrue to Virginia in making one more great exertion to help bring the war to a conclusion.[19] Then on March 5 he laid before that body Pitt's more recent circular letter, as well as another from Amherst, and again most tactfully urged a hearty response and in this connection stressed the point that the strongest recommendations would be made to Parliament that the province might receive a proper com- pensation for the expenses in which it had already been involved.[20] However, on March 6 an address to the Governor prepared by a committee of the House of Burgesses was read and approved which made clear that "the Incapacity of the Country obliges us to inform your Honor, that we cannot support a greater Number of Forces than one complete Regiment for the ensuing campaign."[21] To this purpose the sum of twenty-six thousand pounds was appropriated for recruiting, clothing, and subsisting the troops.[22] This meant, in reality, that the 1st Virginia regiment was to be retained in service and that the regiment that Byrd had commanded on the expedition against Fort Duquesne was to be disbanded.

But Washington — on whom since the year 1754 had centred the military activities of the province — was no longer to be at the head of this body of men who, in the face of great hardships and also neglect on the part of the provincial government, had, as a group, acquitted themselves so well in the defence of the Virginia frontier and who had played a not unimportant role in the successful though arduous campaign of the preceding year that had terminated at the forks of the Ohio. Soon after his return in December from the site of

---

[19] *Journal of the House of Burgesses, 1758–1761*, pp. 55–6.
[20] *Ibid.*, p. 78.
[21] *Ibid.*, p. 79.
[22] *Ibid.*, p. 112.

the French fort, he had resigned his colonelcy, to the profound regret of his officers. Upon his withdrawal from military life they presented to him an address couched in such sentiments of affection and profound respect as to indicate that the character of the aristocratic Virginian, who was to receive in time the veneration of the American nation, was already moulded to a pattern of high excellence:

> "Your steady adherence to impartial Justice, your quick Discernment and invariable Regard to Merit, wisely intended to inculcate those genuine Sentiments of true Honor and Passion for Glory, from which the great military Achievements have been deriv'd, first heighten'd our natural Emulation, and our Desire to excel. . . . Adieu to that Superiority, which the Enemy have granted us over other Troops, and which even the Regulars and Provincials have done us the Honor to publicly acknowledge. Adieu to that strict Discipline and order, which you have always maintained. Adieu to that happy Union and Harmony, which has been our principle [sic] Cement!" [23]

It is clear that many motives prompted this step. The disappearance of the French from the forks of the Ohio represented in Washington's mind the fulfilment of an objective that he had had at heart for years; it therefore must have seemed to him that the ravaged Virginia frontier would now be quiet once again and that his presence would no longer be needed there. He also must have realized that he could no longer aspire to an appointment on the regular establishment, such as he once had sought, in view of his determined opposition to the policies of his superiors, Forbes and Bouquet — policies that had been vindicated as sound. Further, he was engaged to be married to Mrs. Martha Custis; and, finally, his personal affairs, neglected during the past five years, demanded his attention. So when the year 1759 is ushered in, we find him in a new role as a member of the House of Burgesses from the County of Frederick and with his main attention, as it would be for many years to come, concentrated on plantation management, the marketing of crops, and land speculation, typical activities of the eighteenth-century planter.[24] His colonelcy, which he had carried with so

---

[23] *Letters to Washington* (ed. S. M. Hamilton), III, 143.

[24] *Journal of the House of Burgesses, 1758–1761*, p. 57. See *Writings of Washington* (ed. J. C. Fitzpatrick), II, 318–532.

much honour, was now tendered by Fauquier to Byrd, who accepted it.[25]

Regarding the 1st Virginia regiment, which was retained in service, this body of men, with inadequate clothing, little food, and no shelter, was obliged to return to Virginia from the forks of the Ohio in such bitter winter cold that some of them froze to death. According to Captain Stewart, "the miserable and shameful appearance they made was really moving." [26] Many who survived were ill upon their return and had to receive hospitalization.[27] Indeed, it had been more than two years since their government had provided them with a complete change of clothing, which was now in tatters.[28] As a result the Governor took it upon himself to have each soldier furnished a coat made of a blanket, to offer some protection from the severe winter.[29] And this was in the Virginia that the Reverend Mr. Burnaby visited in 1759 and that impressed him, in spite of the talk of poverty, as a centre of general luxury, viewing as he did the extravagant way of living that was prevalent among the planters! [30] It appears also that many of the men who had served as privates with Washington felt as he did — that they had done their duty — and with the expiration of the period of their service did not re-enlist. As late as the month of May it was officially reported that only four hundred men had been recruited.[31] Nevertheless, the troops that had been embodied in the regiment were already in active service, stationed either at Pittsburgh or at Fort Ligonier.[32] It should also be pointed out with relation to Virginia's war record for the year 1759 that, in addition to providing a regiment of a thousand men to serve outside the colony, which was eventually recruited to its full strength, the House of Burgesses

---

[25] Fauquier to Byrd, January 23, 1759, *Journal of the House of Burgesses 1758–1761,* Appendix, pp. 266–7.

[26] Hamilton, op. cit., III, 133–8.

[27] *Ibid.*

[28] *Ibid.,* I, 286.

[29] *Journal of the House of Burgesses, 1758–1761,* p. 56. The soldiers, according to Captain Hogg, had become riotous, feeling that they had been imposed upon by their government. The only articles of clothing that during the past eighteen months had been given to them, they insisted, was a shirt, a pair of stockings, and a pair of shoes (Hamilton, op. cit., I, 286).

[30] Andrew Burnaby: *Travels through the Middle Settlements of North America,* 1759–1760, pp. 11–14.

[31] "State of the Southern Department," May 11, 1759, *Bouquet Papers* (Pa. Hist. Com. 1940), Series 21652, p. 163.

[32] *Ibid.*

voted to raise five hundred men out of the militia to man the frontier forts and then in April agreed that of this number two hundred should serve as artificers and as such be available for service with the regiment outside of the colony and for aiding in the building of a fort at Pittsburgh.[33] The province is therefore to be credited with raising some twelve hundred men for the general service that year and was so credited by the authorities at home.[34]

As for Maryland, little need be said at this point regarding the discreditable conduct of its Assembly in continuing to insist that local issues involving such matters as the incidence of taxation and the control of the militia, important as they were, were more so than the winning of the war. The differences that developed between the lower house on the one hand, and the Governor and the Council on the other have already been discussed. But it is not without significance that those who have felt impelled to defend the attitude of the popular Maryland chamber have been compelled to seek refuge in a fiction, embodied, it is true, in American national tradition: that the war then raging in North America had little to do with the colonies and their vital interests, but was essentially the renewal of the old European rivalry of England and France in a new setting.[35] It is true that this body, in the general rejoicing over the destruction of Fort Duquesne, was led to reverse its position somewhat respecting the services of Captain Dagworthy and his company of Marylanders. For, against the solemn warning of the lower house, they had loyally continued to guard Fort Cumberland and then had later campaigned under Forbes, all at the charge of the Crown, and, what is more, had played a very creditable part in the movement against the French fort, few as they were. At the conclusion of the campaign the house now voted by a close margin of nineteen to eighteen to make them a present of fifteen hundred pounds,

"for their Alacrity in his Majesty's Service, and their personal Courage and Bravery in repelling his Majesty's Enemies, particularly

[33] *Journal*, pp. 123, 129.

[34] "Provincials raised in 1758, 1759, & 1760," Chatham Mss., Bundle 96 (Canadian Archives Transcripts).

[35] J. T. Scharf gives expression to this traditional point of view in his *History of Maryland* (p. 512): "Maryland from the first saw that this was merely the old standing quarrel of four hundred years, transferred to a new arena; that it was the ancient struggle for supremacy between England and France renewed on this side the Atlantic; and she was not deceived by the pretence that it was a matter in which the colonies were chiefly concerned, and the brunt of which they should bear."

destined to distress the Inhabitants on the Western Frontier of this Province [and for] their Zeal for the Service in General, and their Province in particular." [36]

But with this burst of liberality the representatives of the people settled down again to their obstructionist tactics.

After letters from Pitt, Amherst, and Stanwix had been received calling upon the province to do its part in conjunction with the neighbouring colonies to help make secure the Ohio Valley now that Fort Duquesne had fallen, Governor Sharpe on April 9 sent copies of these communications to the Assembly with an address in which he stated:

> ". . . I cannot think you would wish to lose the Fruits of the late successful Expedition to the Westward, to see the French again in Possession of the Ohio Country, and our Frontier Inhabitants exposed to the dreadful Incursions of their Indian Allies. If you have any Regard for your own Safety, or the Safety and Welfare of Your Posterity; if you have any Regard for the Reputation of the Province, or can be animated by the laudable Example of all your Fellow Subjects in the neighbouring Colonies; or if you have the least Sense of Gratitude to the best of Kings, and your Mother Country, for the powerful Succours which have been sent hither, and supported at a vast Expence, for our Protection; you will, I hope, at this Time, give a convincing Proof thereof by your Actions, by pursuing different Measures from those which you have for a long Time adhered to. . . ." [37]

But nothing could move the majority of the members of the lower house. In fact, the victories that British and colonial arms were winning in the west, instead of animating the body to give a helping hand, had the opposite effect. In the words of the editors of the *Maryland Archives*, "relief from the threat to its frontiers by the French and Indians was to make the Lower House even more Truculent and less willing to contribute to the support of the war." [38] Once again, therefore, its favoured bill — for shouldering upon the Proprietor and the wealthy the financial burdens of supporting an armed force to be raised by the province — made its appearance; once again the lower house denied that the upper house was competent to interfere in financial legislation, insisting that it alone

[36] *Maryland Archives*, LVI, 124, 136–7.
[37] *Ibid.*, LVI, 172–3.
[38] *Ibid.*, LVI, "Letters of Transmittal," ix.

enjoyed such powers as were vested not only in the House of Commons [39] but in Parliament, and that the upper house was not a real legislative body; and once again it presented an appearance of having greatly at heart Maryland's proper contribution to the winning of the war.[40] With his patience exhausted and with no hope of securing a bill of supply along equitable lines, such as, for example, Virginia had repeatedly adopted in connection with the war effort, the Governor on April 17 prorogued the Assembly to July 16.

One reflection may be made at this point. There were many issues of importance facing American colonials, as a free, vigorous, and prosperous people, in the latter half of the eighteenth century, and these will be dealt with fully in the course of the present series. It may be affirmed, however, that had the inhabitants of every part of the old British Empire been afflicted with the myopia that so blinded the members of the popular chamber of the Maryland Assembly in the midst of this greatest of all crises in the life of the American people, it is certain that the power of France in North America would never have been shattered. Had this been the case, had France been permitted to remain entrenched in the heart of the continent, it is indeed highly problematical whether the British colonies on the Atlantic seaboard would have long survived as such. Even were one to assume this survival as the result of some good fortune, had they all followed the reprehensible example of Maryland, is it easily conceivable that there would ever have been held out in animating prospect the grandeur of an American nation that some day would face not only the Atlantic but the Pacific with its teeming millions securely anchored in the vast basin of the Mississippi watershed? Yet by the beginning of the year 1759 a vision of future greatness had dawned in the consciousness of colonials who were willing to aid in the war effort and did so, letting other issues wait. This vision of the significance of recent events as these related to future American trans-Appalachian development made itself felt, it may be noted, in spite of the fact that with the coming of the new year less than four hundred determined men under arms were standing guard over the great gateway to the west at the forks of the Ohio, reclaimed at last from the French after four years of fighting.

---

[39] For Attorney General Charles Pratt's opinion, which was adverse to the pretensions of the lower house, see *ibid.*, LVI, 202–4. This opinion will be given careful consideration in a later volume of this series.

[40] *Ibid.*, LVI, 176–81.

In turning to the province of Pennsylvania, the situation relative to the support of the war was complex and, for an understanding, requires elaboration.

While the Society of Friends was no longer able, in the face of an aroused public opinion, to come out openly in obstructing the war effort, there were many in their ranks or among their supporters who apparently felt that the fight against the Penn family was much more important than bringing the war in America to a satisfactory conclusion and were even prepared, if need be, to sacrifice the fruits of the great victory at the forks of the Ohio rather than abate for one moment their struggle against the Proprietors. The persons of Thomas and Richard Penn were, it is true, inoffensive enough; they neither desired to oppress the people nor sought to do it; they managed their propriety in a businesslike manner without much sentiment, however, and they enjoyed real power, which was resented when they used it. Nevertheless, all elements of the population were thrilled at the good news from the west with the fall of Fort Duquesne and the prospects that this held out in the way of expansion of trade and relief from the savage raiding by the enemy. Therefore, when Lieutenant Governor Denny sent a message to the Assembly on December 21, 1758 enclosing a letter from General Amherst, the new commander-in-chief, in which the latter called upon the province to retain in service, if possible, for the next year's campaign the troops that had participated in the one now completed and also urging strongly the necessity of continued military exertion on the part of Pennsylvania,[41] that body readily agreed to maintain in the pay of the colony fourteen hundred of the provincials until its session early in the new year. Then, it was anticipated, information from England would be available respecting the military plans for 1759.[42]

On February 26 Pitt's letter to Denny of December 9 was placed before the Assembly, together with a second letter from Amherst, and again the Lieutenant Governor urged that the British Minister's request for troops be supported, especially in view of the great burden that the mother country was prepared again to assume for their support.[43] By this time, however, the legislative "Committee on Aggrievances" had reported that the claims of inhabitants for large

---

[41] Pennsylvania Colonial Records, VIII, 236–9.
[42] Ibid., VIII, 241.
[43] Ibid., VIII, 271–6.

numbers of horses and wagons destroyed in the course of Forbes's campaign had not as yet been settled; that many of these were procured from the inhabitants by the soldiers through violent means; and, finally, that in seeking winter quarters for the troops at Lancaster, Chester, and Reading the officers of troops had in some cases extorted billets and in others had been accommodated without making payment.[44] These grievances were now brought to the attention of the Lieutenant Governor, who forwarded them to Amherst. The latter made clear that, on account of the illness of General Forbes, debts owed by the army had not been discharged that should have been and that he would come to Philadelphia shortly to help clear all accounts against it. As to the question of quartering soldiers in time of war, he emphasized the fact that in England itself, during hostilities, soldiers who were obliged to remain in any locality in line of service could, in case of a deficiency of public houses, be legally billeted in private homes, and therefore when the local magistrates refused to provide quarters, the officers could do nothing less than demand accommodations rather than let their soldiers "perish in the Streets." He nevertheless promised that if the troops had been guilty of any irregularities they would be brought to justice.[45] This letter, when brought to the attention of the Assembly, quieted the members.

Meanwhile, work had been progressing on the supply bill for the next year's services and on March 15 a committee of the whole house resolved that immediate provision be made for the support of two thousand seven hundred provincials to act in conjunction with the British forces and those of the neighbouring colonies in such offensive operations as the commander-in-chief should see fit to engage in in these parts, and that to support this service the sum of one hundred thousand pounds be voted to His Majesty in bills of credit, which should be sunk by "a Tax . . . laid on all Estates real and personal, and Taxables within this Province."[46] But now came a hitch to all proceedings of this nature. For a report was spread that Colonel Byrd of Virginia was to command the army on the western frontiers, with the result that the Assembly took alarm and on March 22 sent a committee of two from the house, which waited upon Denny to make clear that should the report prove to be true, "it

---

[44] Votes of Assembly, Pennsylvania Archives (eighth series), VI, 4932–7.
[45] Amherst to Denny, March 7, 1759, ibid., VI, 4942–3.
[46] Ibid., VI, 4947–8.

would be of no service to grant Supplies, as no one [in Pennsylvania] would enlist, and the Indians would take Umbrage at seeing a Virginia Colonel in the Command at Pittsburg." [47] The house, in great apprehension, was even prepared to protest to General Amherst such an appointment from among their southern rivals in the upper Ohio valley and sought the Lieutenant Governor's support in this issue. Their minds were soon put to rest, however, by the arrival of a letter from Amherst announcing that Brigadier General Stanwix, a very real friend of the province and one who had previously commanded the forces to the west of the Susquehanna, was to take over the post that Forbes had held. [48] With this matter settled, the assemblymen again proceeded with the work of supply and sent to Denny soon after this flurry of excitement their proposed act for the raising of a hundred thousand pounds.

It should at this point be made clear that as a result of the protracted dispute between the Lieutenant Governor and the Assembly over the nature of a tax bill to be passed in 1757 for the support of the King's service in the war, the Assembly on February 22 of that year drew up a report on "aggrievances." [49] At the same time it decided to send over to England either Isaac Norris or Benjamin Franklin for the purpose of appealing to the Crown to limit the power of the Pennsylvania Proprietors to bind by instructions their deputy here in the New World. Norris was unwilling to leave, and Franklin was thereupon commissioned and, after a protracted delay in securing transportation because of the war activities, arrived in England on July 26 with the aggrievances. It apparently became clear to him that as these were passed by the Assembly they were too violent in language and too defective in substance to make any appeal to a judicial mind. [50] He therefore redrafted them and under

---

[47] Pa. Col. Rec., VIII, 297.

[48] Amherst to Denny, March 18, 1759, ibid., VIII, 298–9.

[49] For this report see Writings of Benjamin Franklin (ed. A. H. Smyth), III, 370–7.

[50] The report, in insisting that the Pennsylvania Assembly had "all the powers and privileges" of a lawmaking body, referred as a precedent to the House of Commons with its unlimited authority with respect to financial legislation. The Proprietors were, moreover, charged in it with a design "to subvert the fundamentals of this constitution [the Royal Charter] . . . and to assume an arbitrary and tyrannical power over the liberties and properties of his Majesty's liege subjects . . . by their despotic instructions. . . ." It even ventured to present as proof of the liberality of the representatives of the people in supporting the war that five thousand pounds had been appropriated in 1755 to purchase provisions for General Braddock's army and almost three thousand pounds for clearing a road for him, and that in 1756 over ten thousand pounds had been granted to

title of "Heads of Complaints" presented them to the Proprietors in August of that year.[51] The document was short and the complaints, now very general in nature, were reduced to three. The first insisted that the Lieutenant Governor had been restrained by Proprietarial instructions in the exercise of his constitutional functions and of his discretion, as granted by the royal charter, by reason of which sums of money granted to His Majesty for the defence of the province had been rejected; the second laid down the premise that the rights of the Assembly to determine the mode, measure, and time of granting supplies had been infringed by these instructions so that that body must either lose the country to the enemy or give up "the Liberties of the People," and, should they choose the latter course, would still be unable, as the result of the restrictions embodied in the instructions, to provide sufficient funds; the third asserted that the Proprietors had enjoined their deputy to refuse his assent to any act for raising money unless the greatest part of their estate was exempt from such tax — something that appeared to the Assembly and the people both "unjust and Cruel." [52]

As it was quite evident that the complaints were based largely upon the views that the Assembly had of the specific powers of government that had been invested in the original Proprietor and his heirs by the Crown, it seemed important to the Penns to clarify this matter by referring the entire matter to the Attorney and Solicitor General for their opinion. This led to delays, and it was well over a year before the Proprietors were able, with this clarification of their powers, to answer the "Heads of Complaints," which was done by their agent, Ferdinand John Paris, on November 28, 1758.

In the reply it was regretted that the grievances complained of by the Assembly were not made more specific and that this body had not given full powers to its agent to enter into a discussion of these several matters, which, in so far as they related to the Penns personally, might have been speedily adjusted, to the mutual satisfaction of all. However, with reference to "the Rights and Prerogatives of the Crown intrusted to the Proprietaries," the reply stated, "it is hoped the House would not for their own Sakes, desire the Proprietaries to attempt to give up any of them." In this connection,

---

General Shirley for provisions for his campaign and almost three thousand pounds for the support of the Acadians sent to the province (ibid.).

[51] Pa. Col. Rec., VIII, 276.

[52] For this see ibid., VIII, 278–9.

it also declared: "Persons not well inclined to Governors or Government, may, indeed, desire that all Matters whatsoever, should be left to the Discretion of the Lieutenant on the Spot, whom the House might supply [that is, make personal grants to] or not, just as he should yield up that Discretion of his, more or less, to them." But the Proprietors, it was emphasized, had been repeatedly commanded by the Crown to give each successive Lieutenant Governor his instructions and so long as the latter might through "Misbehaviour (if left entirely to his Discretion) bring the Proprietaries' Estate and Franchise into Danger, so long the Proprietaries must . . . give Instructions to, and take Bonds from their Lieutenant Governor." This limitation on their deputy, however, by no means had made it impossible for the Assembly, as alleged, to raise the necessary funds, and the charge in the "Head of Complaints" that the Proprietors had been unwilling to contribute their just proportion to the defence of the colony was "very injust." It was quite true, it was then made clear, that they had instructed their deputy not to assent to any law taxing their quit-rents since they did not think it proper as "Lords of the Fee" to have these taxed "by Representatives of their Tenants"; they nevertheless not only had ordered that five thousand pounds out of the arrears of these taxes be paid to the public service but were prepared to have the annual income of their estate inquired into and thereupon to contribute whatever sum was required in addition, in the same proportion as the inhabitants, should it be found that the above amount was not in that proportion. The report ended with the plea that to avoid all differences in the future the Assembly fully authorize "Persons of Candour" to enter into free conferences with them — something, it was insisted, that Franklin was not prepared to do — so that all measures for the good of the province might be arrived at "in the most agreeable manner." [53]

This formal reply was forwarded to Pennsylvania with a letter from the Proprietors to the Assembly framed in a conciliatory spirit and was presented to the Assembly by Denny on February 27.[54] On March 16, without taking any move to make an answer to it, the House of Representatives voted that one hundred thousand pounds be struck in bills of credit for His Majesty's service and that provision for the sinking of these bills be made by a tax laid on *all* estates

[53] "Answer to the Heads of Complaints," ibid., VIII, 279–81.
[54] Pennsylvania Archives (eighth series), VI, 4918.

real and personal and all taxables within the province.[55] In vain the Governor sought to persuade this body to exempt the Proprietary estate from the bill, in view of the fact that the Proprietors stood ready to make a gift of their proper proportion and, if this gift fell short, to submit to the taxation of their quit-rents and appropriated estates; in vain he offered to approve a bill similar in terms to the one agreed upon the preceding years; in vain he made clear that he was restrained by his instructions to approve any bill for the taxation of the Proprietors' real estate unless commissioners were appointed representing their interest as well as that of the public, by reason of their peculiar position with respect to the province — the Assembly remained firm in rejecting all suggested amendments.[56] Even the presence of General Amherst in Philadelphia and his warning to the house that, should it fail to provide the same number of provincials as last year for the western campaign, he would withdraw the King's forces from the province did not deflect it in its designs to bring under its control the Proprietarial estate.[57]

On April 10 Denny sought the individual opinion of each member of the Governor's Council respecting a new bill drafted by the Assembly on the 4th, which, while modifying certain clauses in the old bill, still embodied the principle that the Proprietarial estate should be taxed in the same manner as all other estates in the province.[58] He found the Council unanimously opposed to sacrificing the interests of the Proprietors by giving in to what seemed to be the unjust demands of the Assembly, and the consensus of opinion within it was that the appearance of obstinacy on the part of the house was mere "Artifice." For should any ill consequence attend the failure of the province to raise supplies and troops, it was felt that the world would blame the Assembly rather than the Lieutenant Governor, especially in view of the fact that the latter had offered to pass a bill such as he had approved the preceding year.[59] The following day, however, Amherst wrote to Denny urging him,

---

[55] Ibid., VI, 4948.

[56] Denny to the Assembly, April 12, 1759, Pa. Col. Rec., VIII, 327-9.

[57] Ibid., VIII, 324.

[58] Pennsylvania Archives (eighth series), VI, 4071-3.

[59] The Governor's Council saw the inevitable destruction of the Proprietary should the Assembly acquire the power it was demanding; since, under the bill, assessors might rate the taxable lands of the Proprietors exorbitantly, with no protection, as afforded in England, against this injustice, and also since the money that the Penn family received on the sale of Pennsylvania lands would be taxable as well as the land itself, in violation of a maxim of English law (Pa. Col. Rec., VIII, 325-7).

as had Loudoun, "for the good of the Common Cause," to waive the instructions that bound him and give his assent to the bill, promising at the same time that he himself would make clear to the ministers the necessity of this unjust demand on the part of the Assembly so that the Governor would face no inconveniences.[60] As a result of this pressure and other reasons that one may only surmise, the Lieutenant Governor gave his assent to the bill in the presence of the Council.[61] By this act, according to estimates that were presented to Governor Sharpe of Maryland, the Penn family was loaded with a tax of some forty thousand pounds sterling toward sinking the bills of credit already issued as well as those soon to be [62] — and at a time when their income was still modest.[63]

Nor did the Assembly stop with this triumph. It attempted through a bill for recording land warrants and surveys to get control of the Proprietarial land office,[64] in spite of the fact that this was generally regarded as most correctly and efficiently managed by the agents of the family,[65] and then, in face of the heated protest of the Governor's Council, brought pressure to bear upon Denny to accept a bill having to do with two distinct objects but joined together by the Assembly to serve its ends: the re-emission of its bills of credit and the granting of a temporary loan of fifty thousand pounds to General Stanwix in order to permit him to start military operations.[66] But under the guise of this laudable purpose the bill

---

[60] Amherst to Denny, April 11, 1759, ibid., VIII, 331–2.

[61] For the act in question see Pennsylvania Statutes at Large, V, 379–96. It will be noted, as has already been emphasized in this series, that the Governor's Council in Pennsylvania had only the power to advise the Governor and therefore not the power to refuse to concur in legislation, as in most of the other British colonies.

[62] Sharpe to William Sharpe, July 13, 1759, Maryland Archives, IX, 351.

[63] About the year 1750 Thomas Penn wrote "that for fifteen years from 1732 to 1747, I laid by but about one hundred pounds a year"; and in 1755, in the midst of the war, he complained that "not one-fifth of our quit-rents are paid" (quoted from an unpublished study of the life of Thomas Penn by Muriel Wilson of Bethlehem). It is true that by the time of the outbreak of the American Revolution, by careful management, the annual amount of remittances from Pennsylvania had reached the sum of twelve thousand seven hundred pounds (Beverley W. Bond: Quit-rent System in the American Colonies, p. 134).

[64] Pa. Col. Rec., VIII, 337–9, 354–5, 362–72, 374–6; Pennsylvania Statutes at Large, V, Appendix, p. 655.

[65] For Lewis Evans's views of the Pennsylvania Land Office, see my Lewis Evans, pp. 136–7.

[66] In view of the fact that funds had not arrived from home in order to liquidate many obligations incurred by Forbes and to pay for present services, Stanwix had asked for a loan of one hundred thousand pounds. But the Assembly cut the amount to one

made it possible for those who had received land grants from the Proprietors to pay their quit-rents on these, not in terms of sterling money as provided for in the instrument of sale, but in paper currency fixed at an artificial rate that would deprive the Proprietors of a good deal of their revenues from these rents when paid.[67]

It is not without significance that in the case of both the supply bill and the re-emission bill the Assembly promptly made Denny a gift of a thousand pounds after he had placed his signature to it.[68] But behind the compliant Lieutenant Governor — fortunately for the Proprietors — there stood the Privy Council and the Board of Trade. When these two acts, together with other provincial legislation, such as the act to provide for the recording of land warrants and surveys, came before the Lords Commissioners by reference the following year, His Majesty's Attorney General, as well as his Solicitor General, appeared before it to support the Proprietors. The Attorney General, in taking up the supply bill, insisted that the Assembly of Pennsylvania had shown a disposition to encroach upon "the rights of the Proprietors, the prerogative of the Crown, and the sovereign government of the mother country," not only by refusing to recognize that the Lieutenant Governor was the representative of the Crown, but by their "almost rebellious declarations" respecting the instruction relating to paper currency, by their denial of the right of the Proprietors to issue instructions to their deputy, and by "other acts of avowed democracy." [69] The Solicitor General also insisted that the Assembly was seeking "to arrogate rights inconsistent with the Constitution." Both the supply bill and that relating to re-emission of paper currency came under their heavy attack, and nothing that the legal counsel of the Assembly could say in defence of its actions could alter the impression that the two laws in

---

half that needed. In contrast the New York Assembly in the spring of 1759, at the request of Amherst, appropriated one hundred and fifty thousand pounds as a loan to permit the campaign in that area to go forward (*Documents Relating to the Colonial History of the State of New York*, VII, 399).

[67] For this act see *Pennsylvania Statutes at Large*, V, 427–43. Richard Peters, secretary for the province, pointed out that this bill was so framed, in contrast to earlier bills, to make it obligatory for the Proprietors to accept payment at the rate of not more than "Sixteen pence Currency for a shilling Sterling, when every other person in the Province for Bills of Exchange would get from Sixty to Seventy-five per C^t, according to the Current Exchange" — which he and the other members of the Council called "a most flagrant Act of Injustice" (*Pa. Col. Rec.*, VIII, 342–50, 353–60).

[68] *Ibid.*, VIII, 333, 362.

[69] *Journal of the Commissioners for Trade and Plantations, 1759–1765*, pp. 109–13.

particular were offensive legislation aimed at the destruction of the Proprietarial rights.

Later, in 1760, the representations of the Board of Trade respecting these acts and others came before the Lords of the Committee of the Privy Council for consideration, and it was thereupon recommended that the re-emission act and that for recording land warrants and surveys should be declared void. With respect to the supply bill, the Lords gave as their opinion that it was "fundamentally wrong and unjust and ought to be repealed," unless amended so as to protect the Proprietors from arbitrary and unfair levies on their property. In the face of this opinion, Franklin and Robert Charles, acting as the London agents for the Assembly, now pledged not only to have the act so amended, but also to see that the Proprietors should be indemnified for any damage they might have suffered through the temporary operation of the act. It was thereupon permitted to stand.[70] So ended the efforts of the Assembly to seek to increase its already great powers by using the war crisis as a club over the heads of the Proprietors.[71]

With Denny's signature of the two acts, however, and before their fate in England — as well as the fate of the Lieutenant Governor himself at the hands of the Proprietors — could be known, the province set to work to aid in the western campaign and, in fact, in the course of the year provided even a slightly larger number of troops than the preceding year to serve under General Stanwix in the valley of the Ohio and the approaches to it.[72] But when it came

[70] *Acts of the Privy Council, Colonial Series, 1745–1766,* pp. 439–42; *Pennsylvania Statutes at Large,* V, Appendix, pp. 655–7. The Proprietors did not object to a fair taxation of their Pennsylvania property by the Assembly and, in fact, urged, in order to re-establish harmony within the government of the province, that the act with the proposed amendments be permitted to stand. The amendments prevented not only the taxation of the unsurveyed lands of the Proprietors, but also the taxation of their uncultivated lands at a rate higher than the lowest rate at which other uncultivated lands were assessed and provided that the rating of their lands located in boroughs should be treated as uncultivated land. These amendments also required not only the Lieutenant Governor's approbation of every issue and application of the money raised by the act, but that provincial commissioners should be named to determine appeals respecting the taxation of lands, and, finally, that payment of quit-rents to the Proprietors should be according to the terms of the respective grants, just as if the legislation in question had never been passed.

[71] The efforts of the Assembly to recall the charter in order to make Pennsylvania a royal colony will be given full treatment later in this series.

[72] In 1758 Pennsylvania is credited with 3,000 troops and in 1759 with 3,060 ("Provincials raised in 1758, 1759, and 1760," Chatham Mss., Bundle 96, Canadian Archives Transcripts).

to the matter of furnishing horses and wagons for the movement of supplies, in order to provide the troops at Pittsburgh and at other western posts the means for campaigning, there was, as will be emphasized in the chapter to follow, a lack of response that made it impossible for the general to carry out any effective operations — outside of maintaining his grasp upon the site of Fort Duquesne and building Fort Pitt to take its place.

In turning from Pennsylvania to its neighbour the royal colony of New Jersey, we move from an area of bitter disputes within the governments of the two proprietary colonies to one where harmony prevailed. By March 20 Governor Francis Bernard was able to write to Pitt that, immediately upon receiving the latter's circular letter of December 9, he had called the Assembly into session and had laid the request for aid before it. This body, he declared, proceeded "with uncommon unanimity & dispatch" to vote to raise the same number of men, one thousand, as had been furnished by the province for general military operations the preceding year, and for that purpose appropriated fifty thousand pounds to the service.[73] To make sure that volunteers living outside as well as inside the province would be attracted to it, a bounty of twelve pounds was given to each man enlisting.[74] In justice to New Jersey in failing to go beyond this grant of men, it may be well to point out that the colony had had the misfortune to lose while in active service in both 1756 and 1757 — in the operations at Oswego and then at Fort William Henry — most of the personnel of its regiment, involving in each case some five hundred soldiers "carried prisoners to Canada & to France."[75] The services of these men were therefore unavailable; in addition, many men were drained off as bateau-men for duty on the Mohawk and the Hudson, and others volunteered as privateersmen. Further, to the credit of the province was the fact that its troops were not only mustered to a man but well, even handsomely, clothed and provided with all the necessaries, and therefore did not suffer from a state of nakedness and want as did the men furnished by Virginia and North Carolina.[76] Thus it is clear that in proportion to its population, estimated to be between seventy and eighty thousand souls,[77] both in the prompt appropriation of money

[73] *Pitt Correspondence,* II, 74–5.
[74] *Pennsylvania Gazette,* March 15, 1759.
[75] Bernard to Pitt, March 20, 1759, *Pitt Correspondence,* II, 75.
[76] *Archives of New Jersey* (first series), IX, 166–7.
[77] *Ibid.*

and in the equally prompt raising of troops for the general service, the record of the colony was praiseworthy and in many respects contrasts with that of Pennsylvania and the provinces to the south of the latter.[78]

What has been said of New Jersey may also be said of New York, another royal province, with respect to the promptness that the Assembly showed in agreeing to raise the same number of men for the approaching campaign as had been provided the preceding year. On February 9 de Lancey sent a message to the Assembly with Pitt's request that had just been received, and by the 21st of that month this body had agreed on a resolution to raise, pay, and clothe two thousand six hundred and eighty men.[79] Then, as it seemed as though there might be some difficulty in securing this number by voluntary enlistment because of the hardships endured by the troops in 1758 and in spite of the extraordinary bounty of fifteen pounds, the Lieutenant Governor sent a message to the house asking that he might be empowered to complete the number by making drafts out of the militia. By a very close margin the Assembly also agreed to this.[80] As a result, it appears that most of the troops, outside of one hundred credited to Albany County, which had furnished many bateaumen and wagoners, were drafted, although it would also appear that a considerable number of New England men, especially those from Connecticut, were attracted to enlist, many of them doubtless to take the place of those whose names were drawn but who preferred to hire a substitute.[81] Further, the members of the Assembly in

---

[78] By the spring of 1759 the debt of the colony, as the result of its war effort, stood at some two hundred thousand pounds (ibid.).

[79] Journal of the Legislative Council of New York, under dates of February 20 and March 6, 1759.

[80] Ibid., under date of March 3, 1759; de Lancey to Pitt, February 28, 1759, Pitt Correspondence, II, 41.

[81] De Lancey to Pitt, March 25, 1759, ibid., II, 76; "Provincials raised in 1758, 1759, & 1760," Chatham Mss., Bundle 96 (Canadian Archives Transcripts). The muster rolls of these troops would perhaps leave the impression that they all enlisted voluntarily. These rolls, it may be mentioned, include the names of a large number of New England men (New York Historical Society, Collections, 1891, pp. 135–212). Governor Fitch of Connecticut, writing to Amherst on April 16, referred to the fact that the inhabitants attracted "by large Bounties were Drawing off into the Pay of the Neighbouring Governments" (Fitch Papers, II, Conn. Hist. Soc., Collections, XVIII, 14). The Connecticut Assembly, at its May 1759 session, also declared that "very many have been induced by large sums offered and given them by persons from other governments to take the places of such of them who ought to have gone to the service" (Connecticut Colonial Records, XI, 251). Most of the Connecticut men entering the service outside the colony were undoubtedly attracted either to the New York or to the Massachusetts Bay service.

hearty accord with the Lieutenant Governor, being now permitted to return home, carried with them into the various counties warrants issued by de Lancey for the purpose of speeding up the draft in order to complete it by April 1, so that the men thus chosen might be ready to serve as soon as the season would permit the campaign to begin. As a final proof of hearty support of the war, the Assembly, upon the request of General Amherst, agreed in June to make him a loan of one hundred and fifty thousand pounds, which was made in July.[82] This action led the general to pay a high compliment to the Council and the Assembly of the province for "their loyalty to the king and their Zeal for his service." [83]

Connecticut, as might have been anticipated — in view of the hearty support given in earlier years and the expressed conviction of the government of the colony at the initial stages of the war that the struggle in North America was primarily for the preservation of the rights and interests of the colonials themselves — could be counted upon to make another great effort in support of the campaign of 1759. Early in the year Governor Thomas Fitch wrote to Amherst acknowledging the receipt of the latter's letter of December 29 and also made clear his satisfaction that the general had in mind both offensive and defensive plans against the enemy in the prosecution of "the important Service the King and these Colonies have so much at heart.[84] To help honour the request of the commander-in-chief for new levies from Connecticut for the campaign, he called the Assembly into special session on February 7. This body he found well disposed to forward the war exertions, but it sought more specific information regarding the extent of the effort that would be expected of the colony as well as the nature of the aid that the troops thus raised might receive this year from the Crown. That this might be available, Fitch wrote to Amherst, after it was agreed that the Assembly should adjourn until March 15 unless called into session earlier by the Governor. With the receipt of Pitt's letter of December 9, however, a call was sent out for the Assembly to meet on March 8. Upon gathering, the Minister's request for the raising of the same number of troops as the colony had furnished the previous year and his assurances regarding the charac-

---

[82] *Journal of the Legislative Council of New York*, under date of July 3, 1759; Amherst to de Lancey, July 8, 1759, *N. Y. Col. Doc.*, VII, 399.

[83] *Ibid.*, VII, 399–400.

[84] *Fitch Papers*, II, 1.

ter of the assistance for their maintenance were presented to them. It was thereupon resolved that three thousand six hundred "good and effective men" should be provided for the general service "to co-operate with and second the extraordinary succours supply'd by his Majesty for the preservation and defence of his subjects in North America."[85] To ensure that this number, at least, should be available, it was further agreed, when Pitt's letter of December 29 arrived, that they should be drafted out of the militia of the colony if sufficient voluntary enlistments could not be secured, and that four hundred men in addition should be sought by purely voluntary enlistment to bring the total number to four thousand.[86] That the men who had previously served with so much credit to the colony might be encouraged to join the forces again, it was provided that the pay of those re-enlisting before April 16 should be continued from December, at the time that they were discharged.[87]

Highly creditable as was this measure for supporting the war — especially in view of the efforts of colonies to the southward — it fell short of the provision made the previous year, when five thousand men were pledged and raised. Amherst, informed of the action of the Assembly, therefore expressed his disappointment in it, especially in view of "this Urgent, Important and decisive Crisis." Further, with a significant emphasis that could not be missed, in writing to Fitch he stated:

> "I trust, therefore, if they [the Assembly] are willing to be Entitled to the Compensation the Secretary of State had the King's permission to make them hope for, in Case of a strong Exertion of their Abilities, that they will . . . proceed to Vote an Augmentation, and fully and in every Respect Answer his Majesty's Expectations."[88]

Fitch, in reply, could only point out that the disappointment that the men had met with in the campaign under Abercromby the preceding year had in some measure "abated the vigor and Spirit of the People." He also added that a considerable number of the inhabitants had already enlisted in the regular forces, others had engaged as bateau-men and drivers of teams, while still others, because of the large bounties paid, had entered the service in other col-

---

85 *Conn. Col. Rec.*, XI, 222–3.
86 *Ibid.*, XI, 251; Fitch to Pitt, April 16, 1759, *Pitt Correspondence*, II, 86.
87 *Conn. Col. Rec.*, XI, 223.
88 Amherst to Fitch, April 6, 1759, *Fitch Papers*, II, 12–13.

onies.[89] In concluding, he urged that, taking all these facts into consideration, the little colony was actually providing "more than its full Proportion of twenty thousand men proposed to be furnished by the Six Northern Governments."[90] Amherst was nevertheless unconvinced that the colony could not equal its record of the preceding year, and his scarcely veiled warning respecting reimbursement of expenses was not without its effect. Already, in fact, the operation of the slow parliamentary and crown machinery for making good the solemn pledges that Newcastle and Pitt had given to the colonies with the permission of the King was in evidence. For in January seven chests of gold and silver Spanish and Portuguese coins had arrived in Boston, consigned to the colony by its London agent, Richard Partridge, as reimbursement for its expenses in the campaign of 1756.[91] Would Connecticut, in the face of this, sacrifice its chance of receiving further liberal aid from the mother country and lose its reputation of being perhaps the most co-operative of all the the continental colonies in the great common task of bringing the war in North America to a successful conclusion?

This issue came before the Assembly at its regular May session when Fitch in his opening address strongly urged this body to preserve the fine record of the colony. It was therefore resolved — in view of

> "the very great importance of exerting ourselves in the present critical and decisive moment for the security of our country, and from a deep sense of our duty to the King and of gratitude we owe to the Kingdom of Great Britain for the very great expence and succours supplied for the immediate defence and for the future safety of our rights and Possessions in America and humbly relying on the gracious assurances which the King was pleased to allow his Secretary of State to give" —

to raise one thousand men in addition to the four thousand previously agreed upon.[92] This was done by providing unusual inducements in increased bounty money, additional equipment, and other

---

[89] For example, the New York Assembly provided that "a bounty Fifteen Pounds, as a Gratuity for his voluntary Enlistment," be given to each man (Pennsylvania Gazette, March 15, 1759); whereas the Connecticut Assembly offered but four pounds lawful money for enlistment (Conn. Col. Rec., XI, 223).

[90] Fitch to Amherst, April 16, 1759, Fitch Papers, II, 14–15.

[91] Ibid., II, 2–5.

[92] Conn. Col. Rec., XI, 251–3.

ways.[93] Fitch was therefore able to assure Amherst by May 21 that the people of Connecticut were again prepared to support the war on the continent for another year "with their Utmost Strength." [94]

In contrast to Connecticut, Rhode Island, saddled as it was with a highly inflated currency, with legitimate trade stagnant,[95] and with an estimated one fifth of its adult male population attracted to privateering by its chance for great profits [96] — and, it also appears, to trading with the enemy in the West Indies [97] — was fired by no great vision of the expansion of the English-speaking people in North America nor by any deep sentiments of attachment to the King or the mother country. The attempt to conjure with paper money had largely cut the merchants of the colony off from profitable commercial relations with those among their neighbours who had preserved the integrity of their own currency; the extreme religious heterodoxy of the colony did not endear it to the people of Massachusetts Bay to the north and to those of Connecticut to the west even in the middle of a century conspicuous for its heterodoxy; nor had the contempt of imperial regulations shown by its Newport shipmasters, especially with respect to the trade and navigation system, won them friends either in Great Britain or in the British West Indies. Its government, as a result, was inclined to act with a certain secretiveness and sought to avoid, as it were, public notice, preferring to be left to go its own way without scrutiny from outside. Governor Stephen Hopkins, was undoubtedly "a firm friend (contrary to . . . private interest in the colony . . .) to His Majesty's interest in America." [98] But he had to move with great caution in view of rebukes that he had received at the hands of the public in 1754 and in 1756 for his disposition to bring the colony into measures of

---

[93] Ibid. See also Fitch to Pitt, July 14, 1759, Pitt Correspondence, II, 140–1.

[94] Fitch Papers, II, 21.

[95] J. Honeyman of Newport, in protesting a tax placed upon that town, stated: "That from sad experience, it is obvious that the merchants of Newport, have lost, in the course of their trade, upwards of two millions of money since the commencement of the present war" (Rhode Island Colonial Records, VI, 212).

[96] S. G. Arnold: History of the State of Rhode Island, II, 217; G. S. Kimball: Providence in Colonial Times, p. 269.

[97] In the petition of Silas Cooke of Newport in behalf of the Spanish owners of a vessel that was seized by the sloop Roby of Rhode Island in the harbour of Monti Cristi on the island of Santo Domingo, it was urged that the ship be released, as there were many vessels with cargos owned by the inhabitants of Rhode Island in the same harbour (R. I. Col. Doc., VI, 184).

[98] Colonel Henry Babcock to the Governor of Rhode Island, July 12, 1759, ibid., VI, 216.

co-operation with the other northern governments that went beyond the mood of the majority of the electorate of the towns. One looks in vain, therefore, for any letters from Hopkins to Pitt and others in authority in response to their own during the year under consideration.[99]

The colony did recognize, however, that it was part of the Empire and that to preserve the ancient and prized charter, so often under attack, it simply would not do for the inhabitants to hold back while the people of Massachusetts Bay and Connecticut were exerting themselves in the war. Further, the possibility of propping up the rickety financial structure of the colony by securing sound money from England in the form of reimbursement of military expenditures as promised by Newcastle and Pitt was a great spur. Rhode Island, in fact, had received about seven thousand pounds sterling — out of a grant to New England, New York, and New Jersey of one hundred and fifteen thousand pounds by Parliament — as a reward for exertions in the campaign of 1755.[100] But when it came to the following year, the colony, since it had by no means distinguished itself for its activity, did not share in the grant made to cover that year, nor did New York or New Hampshire — and this fact was not forgotten.[101]

While Parliament, it is true, took no action to reimburse specifically the expenditures of the colonies for the year 1757, Pitt, as has been previously emphasized, was strongly committed not only to this policy of reimbursement but equally so to the idea that whatever was granted should come as a free gift for peculiar and praiseworthy effort. There was undoubtedly dissatisfaction within the government of the colony [102] — in spite of ugly rumours that had reached England about trading activities of Rhode Island shipmasters — that its claims for 1756 had been ignored while those of its neighbours had been recognized; but there was still hope that recognition would be forthcoming and that the services for the years 1757 and 1758 would also be suitably rewarded. Therefore, after Hopkins had received General Amherst's letter of December 13

---

[99] The only letter written by Hopkins that Dr. Kimball could find for the year 1759 is the very brief and businesslike communication to the House of Deputies in May suggesting that measures be taken for the defence of the colonies (G. S. Kimball: *Correspondence of the Colonial Governors of Rhode Island, 1723–1775*, II, 288).

[100] *Ibid.*, II, 186, 200.

[101] *Ibid.*, II, 297, 304.

[102] *Ibid.*, II, 304–6, *passim*.

and Pitt's letters of the 9th and the 29th of the same month, he called a meeting of the Assembly on February 26. The nature of his recommendations to it, if any, as well as the nature of the discussions within that body, is hidden behind the abrupt and bald statement that begins the record of its proceedings:

> "It is voted and resolved, that the colony furnish one thousand able bodied, effective men, for His Majesty's service, in the ensuing campaign; and that . . . a committee . . . prepare a bill for that purpose, and present the same unto this Assembly, as soon as conveniently may be." [103]

This was done.[104]

It may here be pointed out that in anticipation of a request for men for the campaign of 1759 and in response to the Amherst letter referred to above, the Assembly, to its great credit, did something that none of the neighbouring colonies had the foresight to do. It voted on December 18 to retain in the government service during the winter all soldiers, outside of field and commissioned officers, who had enlisted the preceding year in the Rhode Island regiment.[105] It thereupon agreed to augment these up to one thousand and to provide suitable inducements to those who would enlist. It also, in view of the fact that tavern-keepers and others had been guilty of helping to spirit "out of the government's service many of the soldiers enlisted into the colony's pay," passed suitable legislation to put a stop to this practice.[106] There was reluctance among the inhabitants to enlist, however, and yet the northern provincial troops were expected to be assembled at Albany by the middle of April. As a result, in the May session of the Assembly another act

---

[103] R. I. Col. Rec., VI, 181.

[104] For the act see ibid., VI, 190–4.

[105] Ibid., VI, 172. "The Legislature has certainly given a Proof of its Wisdom and Penetration, in retaining these Troops in Pay during the Winter . . . for by Calculation, it will appear, that the Bounty for Inlistment, with other recruiting Charges, will amount to as much as the Wages and Billeting during the Winter; and it is equally obvious, the Men from their Experience and Duty last summer, will be more capable for action this. If it be further considered, that we have, by these prudent measures of the Government, been released from the Terrors of Draughts and Impresses this Spring, we cannot but think ourselves extremely happy . . . when we reflect on the vast Difficulties our neighbouring Colonies have experienced, by not adopting the same Form of Proceeding with us: Besides, their Levies must in a great Measure be undisciplined and immature in Military Exercises and Fatigue" (Newport advices, April 24, Pennsylvania Gazette, May 3, 1759).

[106] R. I. Col. Rec., VI, 186–7.

was passed "for completing the regiment" by holding out still further inducements to possible enlistees.[107] Likewise, as Admiral Durell had written to Hopkins in February from Nova Scotia about the necessity of securing seamen to man His Majesty's ships stationed at Halifax, an act was passed giving really generous encouragement to those who would join the royal navy for the year's campaign, carrying with it the admiral's assurance that at its close they would be promptly discharged.[108] It was also voted in this connection that those who enlisted in the navy should be accounted a part of the one thousand men that the colony had agreed to provide for the general service. But with all the mechanism devised and the inducements held forth to get the minimum number of troops pledged, even in July Colonel Babcock, stationed with his Rhode Island regiment at Lake George, indicated that he still required two hundred and eighty men to complete it.[109] Whether or not the men were ultimately secured is not clear.[110]

Massachusetts Bay, the pivotal province among the northern continental colonies, had put forth in 1758 such exertion in raising men that it surpassed the previous recruiting record and would not equal the present one during the remaining years of the war. Nevertheless, it was possible in 1759 to raise sixty-five hundred men, only five hundred short of the number secured the preceding year, and, taking all things into consideration, the provincial government must be given great credit for the zeal manifested by the General Court for the continued support of the war in North America. This was largely due, as will be noted, to the influence of Governor Pownall with the legislators and to the indefatigable but unrewarded labours of Lieutenant Governor Hutchinson, not only in connection with the preparation of the complicated military accounts, for submission to Goveral Amherst for repayment of expenses but in other ways.[111]

---

[107] Ibid., VI, 207–8.

[108] Ibid., VI, 198, 208. In addition to the forty shillings sterling offered by Durell it was voted to give each effective seaman six pounds sterling.

[109] Babcock to the Governor of Rhode Island, July 12, 1759, ibid., VI, 216. A part of the troops, those held over from the preceding campaign, left Newport for Albany on April 24 (Pennsylvania Gazette, May 3, 1759).

[110] Rhode Island is credited with one thousand provincials for 1759, ("Provincials raised in 1758, 1759, & 1760," Chatham Mss., Bundle 96), but the question arises, did this figure include those enlisted by Durell in the navy for the year?

[111] See, for example, the letter written by Hutchinson to General Abercromby on January 3, 1759 (Abercromby Papers, No. 866, Huntington Library), indicating the

At the beginning of the year when the Governor met the Assembly, he found that rumors of an approaching peace had so influenced the minds of those deputies who came from the smaller towns that they were not prepared to make any great effort to raise men for the year's campaigns.[112] At the session in question, however, the Assembly settled one problem that had earlier clouded the relations of Lord Loudoun, as commander-in-chief of British forces in North America, with the province and had almost led to a crisis. For an act was now passed that not only facilitated the recruiting of soldiers into the regular regiments but settled for a period the vexed question of quartering the King's troops in Boston itself, rather than at Castle William, across the bay. Under the terms of this measure certain houses in the town were converted into barracks, and the Assembly agreed that while their owners would be permitted to charge the soldiers no more than the customary fourpence a day for quarters as in England, the province itself would assume the burden of an equal amount to cover the actual cost of the quartering.[113] Nor did a fray between soldiers and the inhabitants that took place there later in the spring, in the course of the military concentration of troops designated to go with Wolfe up the St. Lawrence, greatly ruffle the relations between the civil administration and the military authorities.[114] Doubtless one explanation of this spirit of compliance on the part of the authorities of Massachusetts Bay was the fact that the province and Connecticut had been singled out for the receipt of "a free Gift" of money voted by Parliament in general to New England, New York, and New Jersey, amounting to £115,000, as a reward for their outstanding services in the year 1756.[115] Moreover,

extraordinary pains taken by the Lieutenant Governor to protect the interests of the province in its difficult financial transactions with the Crown. "Colonel Burton & Major Barré who were employed by the General [Amherst] at Boston have spoke of Mr. Hutchinson's zeal for the publick Service, and very great Knowledge of the Affairs of his Province in a manner much to his advantage" (Wolfe to Pitt, June 6, 1759, *Pitt Correspondence*, II, 120).

112 Pownall to Pitt, January 19, 1759, *ibid.*, II, 9.

113 In Amherst's letter to Pownall of February 2, 1759 the terms of this measure are discussed (P.R.O., War Office, 34. 27:243–5, Canadian Archives Transcripts).

114 In referring to this fray, Amherst's letter to Pownall of April 19 was a masterpiece of tactful writing. He states that if the people will keep rum away from the soldiers, "the Cause of most Evils Committed by the Troops," he is sure the province will "Covet their Neighbourhood and will be so Sensible of the advantages of having them among them, that they will be the first of asking for a few Battalions" (War Office, 34. 27:289–90. Canadian Archives Transcripts).

115 29 Geo. II, c. 29; Joseph Sherwood, the London agent for Rhode Island, to Gov-

Parliament in 1757 appropriated an additional sum of £27,380 to the colony as reimbursement for the expense of furnishing provisions and stores to its troops during that year.[116] There was, indeed, every reason to feel that this largess on the part of the mother country would continue so long as the people gave their hearty support to the war.

This may also help to explain the willingness of the Assembly — taken together with the idleness of much of the seafaring population during this phase of the war, and also with the probability of impressment at the ports should not sufficient seamen enlist to get the British squadron out of the port at Halifax — to assist in recruiting for the royal navy. This was agreed to when Admiral Durell offered terms similar to those submitted to the government of Rhode Island, to the effect that the men were to be enlisted as sailors for the year's campaign only and were to be counted as part of the colony's contingent of soldiers.[117] As a consequence, it was possible to secure between two and three hundred men for this important service.[118]

It may be mentioned at this point that at the January session Pownall was also able without difficulty to persuade the General Court to agree to build a fort on the Penobscot River, "the only one [river] on the Atlantic now left unoccupied by His Majesty's Arms." This was under an arrangement with Amherst whereby the colony would receive reimbursement out of his military chest for the expenditures involved in its construction.[119] In fact, under these conditions there was no hesitation in taking possession of this fine country, which, incidentally, was claimed by the province and where many families were anxious to settle as soon as it was freed of the menace

---

ernor Hopkins, December 3, 1759, *Correspondence of the Colonial Governors of Rhode Island*, p. 297.

[116] 31 Geo. II, c. 33.

[117] Amherst heartily supported Durell's requisition on the colony. He even indicated that impressment — under the circumstance, with the Quebec expedition taking shape — "must be a natural Consequence of a non compliance" with the admiral's request (Amherst to Pownall, February 12, 1759, W.O., 34. 27:247–8).

[118] Pownall to Pitt, April 19, 1759, *Pitt Correspondence*, II, 923; Boston advices, April 23, *Pennsylvania Gazette*, May 3, 1759.

[119] Pownall to Pitt, January 19, 1759, *Pitt Correspondence*, II, 10. The only expense, according to Amherst, that the colony would be expected to bear would be for raising, paying, and transporting a sufficient force to take possession of the country and leaving an adequate garrison for its defence (Amherst to Pownall, March 2, 1759, W.O., 34. 27:249–54).

of the French and their Indian allies; they, in fact, proceeded with the construction of the fort to apply for lands.[120]

Upon the receipt late in February of Pitt's letter of December 9, Pownall again called the General Court into session and urged the members to give immediate compliance to the request for men contained in it.[121] But it would appear that the disillusionment that spread throughout the ranks of Abercromby's provincials with the defeat before Ticonderoga made itself felt among the members of the Assembly. Even Pownall, who prided himself on his ability to manage that body, had to admit that an "Ill humor . . . reigns throughout the Votes."[122] In writing to Pitt, however, he tactfully indicated that the General Court was only deeply concerned with serious financial problems the province was facing.[123] It seems that the reimbursement funds for 1756, referred to above, had not reached the province and it was felt that the Treasury could not well again support the drain put upon it the preceding year for the payment of bounties, billeting, and wages of soldiers. As a result, only five thousand men were voted for the year's campaign — two thousand less than were furnished in 1758. When the news of this action reached Amherst, who was in New York laying plans for his advance by way of Lake Champlain, he was deeply disturbed. Writing to the Governor, he affirmed:

> "I must Own I cannot but think it [the vote] must be productive of the worst of Consequences, and perhaps subvert the Wise Measures planned at home for the entire Reduction of Canada and the giving a lasting peace to this Country, which . . . could not fail of Success, if the Colonies were to exert themselves . . . both for the honor of their Country, and the quiet and peaceable possession of their Liberties and properties."[124]

He then called upon Pownall to secure an augmentation of the number of soldiers and made clear in detail how he himself was making preparations, by the establishment of royal magazines within the

---

[120] Pownall to Pitt, November 20, 1759, *Pitt Correspondence*, II, 213.

[121] *Acts and Resolves . . . of the Province of Massachusetts Bay*, IV, 232.

[122] General Amherst, after quoting the above from Pownall's letter of March 16, in his reply in a "private" letter to the Governor on March 23 expressed the feeling that he himself should take some public notice of this unfortunate attitude, but refrained from doing so at Pownall's urgent request (W.O. 34. 27:273–6).

[123] Pownall to Pitt, March 16, 1759, *Pitt Correspondence*, II, 70–1.

[124] Amherst to Pownall, March 23, 1759, W.O., 34. 27:267–71.

colony, to relieve the provincial government of much immediate expense. But he was not prepared to meet the desires of the Assembly that he, rather than the colony, should furnish the provincials with fifty per cent more in money, in lieu of provisions, than was allowed to other provincials or to the regulars.[125]

Nevertheless, as the result of the assurances that he was able to give, combined with those of Pitt respecting the continuance of the reimbursement of the expenses of those colonies which made an especial exertion, a report of a committee of the General Court presented late in March recommended that the province duplicate its efforts of the preceding year by increasing the number of soldiers for the general service by two thousand. The house, however, adjourned before coming to a vote on this issue, with the result that the general, informed of the recommendation and hoping to see it carried through the house when it again met, wrote an open letter to Pownall in which he expressed the hope that this body would not "frustrate themselves of the Compensation which the Secretary of State had his Majesty's permission to make them hope for, in Case they did their Utmost upon this Occasion." [126]

This warning — used so effectively at this time to rouse Connecticut to equal its record of the preceding year — was not without its effect upon the more reluctant members of the Massachusetts Bay Assembly and finally led to a vote to supply fifteen hundred men over and beyond the five thousand already pledged and raised.[127] It was agreed that to secure the enlistment of this new increment the very high bounty of ten pounds six shillings and eightpence sterling should be granted to each volunteer.[128] It is clear that this was done

---

[125] *Ibid.*

[126] Amherst to Pownall, April 5, 1759, W.O., 34. 27:283–4. See also the general's "private" letter to the Governor under the same date, in which he expressed regret at the adjournment of the house before the vote was taken and the hope that "neither you nor I shall have the disagreeable Task of Imparting to the King's Ministers the innatention [sic] paid by the Province . . . to His Majesty's Recommendations upon this Urgent, Important and Decisive Crisis" (ibid., 34. 27:279–81).

[127] A correspondent writing from Boston on May 14 stated that Massachusetts Bay "exclusive of upwards of 500 for the Protection of our own Frontiers . . . have now furnished 6500 Men for the general Service of the Year. — Add to this number, all that have engaged as Rangers, Battoe-men, Artificers, etc. etc. and it makes not less than 10,000 of our useful Inhabitants. — Such Exertions from Year to Year, by a Province which did not contain before the War, but about 40,000 Males, from 16 to 70 Years of Age, seems almost incredible" (*Pennsylvania Gazette*, May 24, 1759).

[128] *Acts and Resolves*, IV, 239–41. Hutchinson, who was a member of the joint committee to consider the raising of additional men, wrote on April 24 to his friend

in view of the expectation that this great expense, as well as other charges falling on the government, would ultimately be reimbursed by the mother country.[129]

Upon the shoulders of Hutchinson, it may be pointed out, fell the chief immediate responsibilitiy, as in the past, of guaranteeing that the complicated papers relating to all financial disbursements of the provincial troops in connection with the campaign of the preceding year, as well as the present one, should be in such condition that they would meet the approval of Amherst for reimbursement. This work was done with so much thoroughness — with the elimination of suspected items from the claims, such as, for example, aroused the general in the submission of those of Rhode Island [130] — that the accounts were readily approved.[131] These financial records for securing immediate payment to the province of certain items of expense from Amherst's military chest were, moreover, used as the basis of awarding to the province the generous division in its favour of the sums granted by Parliament as "free gifts." But Hutchinson did not limit himself to the burdensome work of gathering, checking, and approving military accounts. For later in the year Amherst, in thanking him for the zeal he had shown in the public service, expressed his particular appreciation of the fact that the Lieutenant Governor had disbursed his own money in paying the bills arising from the billeting of provincials destined to go to Louisbourg on garrison duty as well as those ordered up the St. Lawrence with Wolfe to serve as pioneers.[132]

Stress has been placed upon the rather angry mood displayed by the General Court at the January session. But this mood changed some-

---

Colonel Israel Williams: "I hope we shall not have occasion hereafter to go into the disagreeable measure of impressing men [as was the case in Connecticut, New Hampshire, and New York]. The Bounty is extravagant & more than I would vote for on the Committee & will be a bad precedent, at least it appears to me who, I assure you, often think of the deplorable State we must be in if we have no reimbursement" (Williams Mss., Vol. II, Mass. Hist. Soc.). But this high bounty money paid was reimbursed by Parliament.

[129] *Acts and Resolves*, IV, 239–41.

[130] Amherst to the Governor of Rhode Island, February 20, 1759, *R. I. Col. Rec.*, VI, 199.

[131] For the approval of the claims of 1758 see Amherst to Hutchinson, March 8, 1759, W.O., 34. 27:261–3. Among the Gunther collection in the Chicago Historical Society is to be found Hutchinson's detailed financial account under title of "Sums due from the General of His Majesty's forces to the Province of Massachusetts Bay." This is under date of February 24, 1759.

[132] Amherst to Hutchinson, June 9, 1759, W.O., 34. 27:313.

what for the better in the course of the early spring. For not only did the Penobscot project of a fort built at the expense of the Crown and garrisoned by Massachusetts Bay troops arouse enthusiasm, but likewise Amherst's proposal, made the middle of March, that the province send twenty-five hundred of its quota of volunteers to engage in garrison duty on Cape Breton Island and in Nova Scotia — thereby taking the places of the regulars stationed there who were ordered to serve under Wolfe on the St. Lawrence River expedition. In writing to Pownall, the general declared:

> "Although His Majesty has not particularly designated the troops of Massachusetts Bay for this employment, yet from their proximity to Nova Scotia, the shortness of the passage from Boston to it; the saving to the public of transporting them by sea rather than by land from different parts of your Province to Albany, and the great inclination the people of your government have to be employed up the St. Lawrence have determined me to give them the preference." [133]

It should be borne in mind that for literally thousands of men living about the ports of Massachusetts Bay the eastern shore of Nova Scotia had before the war been a summer home while engaged in the Canso cod fishery. Others knew well the area about the Bay of Fundy and Minas Basin, where in time of peace they had traded and where, serving under Colonel Winslow, they had assisted in the dispersion of the Acadians in 1755 and had later done garrison duty. What is more, on October 12, 1758 Governor Lawrence of Nova Scotia had issued a proclamation in glowing terms to be distributed in the colonies to the southward in which he declared that he was prepared to make an allotment to new settlers of one hundred thousand acres of the ploughlands and an equal amount of land in pasture, orchards, and gardens that had once been the prized property of the exiles but was now lying waste.[134] The effect of this upon land-hungry New Englanders seems to have been electric. For a few weeks after he had issued it, he was able to inform the Lords Commissioners for Trade and Plantations that "hundreds of families, in the Colonies of Connecticut, Rhode Island and the Massachusett's growing too numerous for their present possessions at home, are

---

[133] Amherst to Pownall, March 15, 1759, *ibid.*, 34. 27:264–5.

[134] This proclamation, among the Nova Scotia papers in the Public Record Office, is in Series A. 62:193–6. For a careful analysis of this proclamation see J. B. Brebner: *The Neutral Yankees of Nova Scotia*, pp. 6–8.

associating and preparing, to take the benefitt of the Proclamation." [135]

It is therefore little wonder that Amherst was able to write to Pownall in April expressing his satisfaction to find "how ready the Massachusetts people are for the Eastern Service." [136] Early in May detachments left Boston to settle down in the heart of old Acadia: at Fort Cumberland, earlier the French Fort Beauséjour on the isthmus of Chignecto; at Fort Edward and elsewhere on the Piziquid, which flows into Minas Basin; and at Annapolis Royal; other detachments soon afterward sailed for Louisbourg and for eastern Nova Scotia, to garrison Halifax and Lunenburg,[137] and also for the St. John, flowing into the Bay of Fundy. It appears that one embarrassment faced those in charge of the movement of these troops. Whole families expected to be transported and carried to these places in company with those who had entered the service. But military regulations forbade this, with the result that they were left behind at the time of embarkation.[138]

The popularity of the move in assigning to the Massachusetts Bay troops the pleasant duty of standing guard over the Acadian country is also attested by the fact that — when it appeared that the regulars who had previously performed this service would not be able to return from Quebec as winter set in — the General Court, without any solicitation from Amherst, "acquiesced cheerfully"

---

[135] Lawrence to the Board of Trade, December 26, 1758, P.R.O., Nova Scotia, A. 62:208.

[136] Amherst to Pownall, April 18, 1759, W.O., 34. 27:289–90. There is reason to believe that a good many Connecticut men, attracted not only by the large bounty offered by Massachusetts Bay, but by the prospect of going into the Acadian country to look for suitable home-sites, were led into this service. Fitch in his letter to Pitt of April 16 refers to the difficulty of raising troops and assigns as one reason that the men of his colony as the result of the large bounties offered "were drawing off into the Pay of the neighbouring Governments" (Pitt Correspondence, II, 85). It is clear that many of the inhabitants of Connecticut had become deeply interested in the prospect of taking up Acadian lands, as indicated by the extract of the letter given above that Lawrence wrote to the Board of Trade.

[137] W.O., 34. 27:297–9; 301–2.

[138] Amherst, in dealing with the above situation, wrote to Hutchinson, left in charge of the government while Pownall was supervising the building of the fort on the Penobscot, that as to the women and children left behind, "if any of them make part of the number allowed to each Corps, Provision ought to be made for them by the Regiment . . . but as it is most probable that those with you are supernumeraries, for which there is no Allowances whatsoever, they must work for their livlihood, which they may easily gain in Boston, if they are not Abandoned and Lazy" (Amherst to Hutchinson, May 19, 1759, ibid., 34. 27:302).

when this proposal was brought to its attention by Pownall to provide for keeping the provincials there.[139] It is also not without significance that the only troops of the colony stationed in Nova Scotia
who expressed deep dissatisfaction with the prospect of wintering
there were those stationed at Halifax, far removed from the Acadian
country.[140]

Yet in other ways the attitude of the province with respect to the
war effort during this year was not so commendable. Colonel Barré,
famed in history as a great friend of the American colonials, was
deeply incensed while in Boston in the spring of the year by the
"spiritless" attitude of even Pownall himself toward forwarding the
preparations for the major aspects of the year's campaign. The Governor, indeed, admitted in conversation with him that the proceedings of the "hardy Provincials" had been "scandalous and infamous."
The colonel, in this connection, in writing to Colonel William Amherst, brother of the general, called into question the nature of the
actual contribution of the province to the general effort and then
declared: "Happy! if I could suggest any expedient to model their
force, & not suffer his Majesty's Ministers & Generals to be imposed
upon by their paper parade of strength!"[141] Of thirty-six hundred
troops of the colony destined to serve in the Lake Champlain region,
only slightly over a thousand had reached Albany by June 9, although the date of concentration of all provincials there was set
for the early part of April, and less than five hundred more were
expected to arrive in the near future.[142] This was not the only evidence of an apparent lack of spirit in favour of bringing the war
to an early termination. Later in the year the general was obliged
to inform the Governor of the "shameful Desertion" in Captain
Smith's company that had been stationed at No. 4 on the Connecticut;[143] and still later, with the campaign in the Lake Cham-

[139] Amherst on November 18 wrote to Pownall asking him to express his deep satisfaction to the Assembly that before his request came it had taken this step to make arrangements to continue to hold the posts (ibid., 34. 27:355–6).

[140] This dissatisfaction, it appears from Governor Lawrence's letter to Pownall dated
December 7, 1759, was because of the lack of provision made for the families that were
left behind and for the sustenance of which the Massachusetts Bay Assembly now made
itself responsible (ibid., 34. 26:3). See also Amherst to Pownall, December 2, 1759,
ibid., 34. 27:361.

[141] Isaac Barré to William Amherst, April 18, 1759, Amherst Papers, Packet 33
(Canadian Archives Transcripts).

[142] Amherst to Pownall, June 9, 1759, W.O., 34. 27:307–9.

[143] Amherst to Pownall, September 9, 1759, ibid., 34. 27:338.

plain region brought to a close, he wrote, again more in sorrow than in anger, that most of the troops in Willard's regiment, who were well, "have taken themselves away." In commenting on this episode, he declared:

> "Such home sick Madness, as will cost too many of them, I fear, their lives, as Some will certainly lose themselves in the Woods and perish. . . . Brig^r. Ruggles [in command of the Massachusetts Bay troops] did on this Occasion, as he has done on every other during the Campaign, everything he could do for the good of the service. . . ." [144]

Nevertheless, the colony, it would appear, in spite of the painfully slow movement of the provincial troops and the mutinous behaviour of some of them, finally furnished the number of men that it had pledged to supply, and most of them, particularly their officers, showed a good deal of steadiness in the course of their service during the year. It also contributed generously to other branches of the service, such as rangers, bateau-men, and artificers.

In turning, finally, to New Hampshire, little need be said regarding its war activities. The government of the province had been as reluctant at the beginning of the year 1758 as it had been the previous year to protect the settlers within the colony living at No. 4 on the upper Connecticut. At the Earl of Loudoun's insistence, however, some fifty men had been drafted to be sent there. [145] Nevertheless, as was true earlier, so it was at the close of that year — the exposed area was chiefly, if not entirely, guarded by Connecticut troops. When Governor Fitch at this juncture ordered back to the colony Captain Ward's company of soldiers, the deeply apprehensive inhabitants sent to Amherst a memorial setting forth their "naked and distressed condition." As a result, the general ordered Captain Cruickshank's New York Independent company to march without delay from Half Moon on the Hudson to the exposed place and also ordered a detail of rangers from Fort Edward to report there as soon as it could be spared. [146] So, for the first few months of the new year, No. 4 was given the protection of the New York Independents in place of the Connecticut provincials. Then in the spring Governor Pownall of Massachusetts Bay proposed that the New

---

144 Amherst to Pownall, November 19, 1759, *ibid.*, 34. 27:358.
145 *New Hampshire Provincial Papers*, VI, 646–7.
146 Amherst to Pownall, January 8, 1759, W.O., 34. 27.

Yorkers be relieved by one of his Hampshire County companies to be raised under the new levy, and Amherst gratefully accepted this offer in view of his need of the Independents in his campaign.[147] This seems to have acted as a challenge to New Hampshire. For the colony, with the final settling of the boundary line between the two colonies, as has been pointed out in an earlier chapter, had acquired No. 4 as well as other townships from Massachusetts Bay against wishes of the settlers. So the province — doubtless to avoid compromising it own position in the eyes of the King with respect to the boundary award — sent one hundred of its new levies also to this place.[148] As a result, we find the old rivals for this area joining together in its protection. Early in September, however, some sixty-four dissatisfied soldiers from Captain Smith's Massachusetts Bay company suddenly deserted the fort.[149] And shortly after that he and the men remaining with him were ordered by Amherst to Lake Champlain.[150] But by this time No. 4 had ceased to be an isolated region and its defence a perplexing problem. Amherst, in fact, for military purposes, had opened up a road to it from Lake Champlain. Lands to the west of it were also now attracting the attention of provincial military leaders. As the year came to a close, it was no longer guarded by either New Hampshire or Massachusetts Bay troops, but once again by Connecticut forces under Colonel Nathan Whiting.[151]

If the province of New Hampshire showed weakness and ineffectiveness in the protection of its own frontier inhabitants, this was at least consistent with the economic and manpower weakness that the government set forth at the beginning of the year in a petition to the King framed by the Governor's Council. In this it was declared not only that as a result of the increase in the taxes in support of the war "the burden on the Inhabitants is Insupportable," but that the colony in its contribution of men for the last campaign — at least if the bateau-men and rangers were included — had given one third of its military effectives to the service; nevertheless, it was affirmed that General Amherst's late request for the same number

[147] Amherst to Pownall, April 5, 1759, W.O., 34. 27:279–81.
[148] Provincial Papers, VI, 621.
[149] Amherst to Pownall, September 9, 1759, W.O., 34. 27:338. Upon Pownall's promise to get the men to return to their duty, Amherst agreed to extend his clemency to them (Amherst to Pownall, September 11, 1759, ibid., p. 338).
[150] Amherst to Pownall, September 21, 1759, W.O., 34. 27:342.
[151] Fitch Papers, II, 33–42.

of troops for the campaign of the new year as had been contributed the preceding year would be cheerfully honoured "that no prejudice may arise to your Majesty's service, through our neglect of duty & obedience, humbly relying that your Majesty will be graciously pleased to relieve us under our present distressed situation. . . ."[152]

The financial plight of the colony, referred to above, was in reality not nearly so serious as presented. For it is abundantly clear from the official records that the province had already received a grant of money out of funds appropriated by Parliament and that this had been thriftily invested in stocks in England by the London agent of the province, John Thomlinson, Esq.[153] In fact, the investment of provincial funds was so profitable that it was felt that the interest drawn on this would be sufficient to liquidate the bills of exchange that the colony was preparing to draw on the agent to pay off the remaining expenses of the last year's campaign.[154] However, no steps were taken respecting commitments for the year 1759 until after the arrival of Pitt's circular letter of December 9 in which he not only requested that the colony again raise a force equal to that of the year then closing but repeated the King's promises of the reimbursement of expenses according to the zeal displayed by the colony. This was sufficient to galvanize the provincial government into action. On March 2 a committee of the two houses reported in favour of complying immediately with the royal requisition and of offering sufficiently high bounties — to be paid later out of the royal exchequer — to secure one thousand men for the general service; the report, however, went on to recommend that should this number not be secured by voluntary enlistments — by reason of the number of men engaged in bateau, ranger, and carpenter service — there should be drafted out of the provincial militia regiments a sufficient number, taken together with those who had freely enlisted, to make a total of eight hundred men.[155] This was done.[156] As has already been indicated, however, one hundred of the latter number was sent to No. 4 to help garrison the fort, so that less than seven

---

[152] Provincial Papers, VI, 700–1. It is by no means clear what disposition was made of this petition passed by the upper house and then sent to the lower house for concurrence. There is no record that the lower branch approved it or that it was ever sent to England.

[153] Ibid., VI, 708.

[154] Ibid.

[155] Ibid., VI, 706–7.

[156] Ibid., VI, 708.

hundred men were available to serve under Amherst.[157] Further, to have at hand the financial resources to meet this expense, taxes in kind, with a fixed valuation in terms of specie, were imposed on the chief products of the colony, as was done in the previous years of the war.[158]

In this survey of the war efforts of the continental colonies for the year in question, one fact among others emerges, as was suggested earlier in this chapter: in passing from the most southern to the most northern of them one moves gradually from an area of relatively slight support of the war into one of really intensive participation. It is clear that three factors account for this. One is that the northern colonies, because of the danger of the near presence of the enemy, felt the necessity of supporting the war effort more immediately than did the more southern colonies not so menaced, especially after the fall of Fort Duquesne. Again, those colonies relying heavily on the plantation slave economy were not so free to contribute men to the general service as were those that were not really dependent upon it. Finally, the granting of reimbursement on the part of Parliament to those colonies which actually exerted themselves in the war was a great stimulus, especially to the northern colonies, to continue their efforts. Among all the continental colonies the record of Connecticut is perhaps the most highly creditable, while that of Maryland is without question the least so. Yet one and all were to benefit immeasurably as the result of the final outcome of the war.

But we must now turn to a consideration of the military activities of Major General Amherst in the Lake Champlain region, of Brigadier General Prideaux in the campaign against Fort Niagara, and of Brigadier General Stanwix in his efforts to consolidate the British position at the forks of the Ohio. It was under the direct command of these three men and in these areas that most of the provincials in arms were destined to see service.

---

[157] "Records of the Provincial Council," ibid., VI, 721.

[158] Ibid., VI, 712. The statement "May be paid in Species" seemed only to provide that those liable to such taxes could, if they did not possess the necessary commodities but did have ready money, so discharge their obligation to the province. These taxes made their appearance in 1756 (see ibid., VI, 516–17, 591, 669–70). In November 1755 an attempt had been made by the lower house to lay a tax of a penny an acre on all lands granted and laid out in townships, whether improved or unimproved, but this was defeated by unanimous vote of the upper house (ibid., VI, 448, 454), with the result that in April of the following year the tax in kind was instituted and thereafter continued for the remainder of the period of the war.

CHAPTER XI

Ohio Valley, Lake Ontario, and Lake Champlain Military Operations, 1759

WITH THE REDUCTION of Fort Duquesne, General Forbes proceeded to make such a disposition of his troops that a small garrison would be maintained for the winter at the forks of the Ohio, with other detachments stationed at the forts leading to it from Carlisle west of the Susquehanna.[1] These were made up of detachments from the Pennsylvania battalions and the Virginia regiment and later also from the regulars.[2] Units from the

---

[1] On December 4, when Forbes left the Ohio, there were two hundred men garrisoned at the forks (*Pennsylvania Archives*, first series, III, 272); early in January 1759 there were three hundred and fifty, with fifty more with orders to march to Pittsburgh when the supply of provisions was adequate; at this latter date there were also four hundred soldiers at Fort Ligonier, thirty at Stony Creek, three hundred at Fort Bedford, and fifty each at Forts Juniata, Littleton, and Loudoun, with a hundred about to be sent to Carlisle (Forbes to Amherst, January 18, 1759, *Writings of Forbes*, ed. A. P. James, p. 282).

[2] *Pennsylvania Archives* (fifth series), I, 274; *ibid.* (first series), III, 580. Forbes had desired to leave at Pittsburgh some two hundred Pennsylvanians and a proportionate number of Virginians and Marylanders, but it was not possible to provision that number of soldiers. Lieutenant Adam Stephen of the Virginia regiment had expected to get the command at Pittsburgh (Stephen to Henry Bouquet, December 2, 1758, *Papers of Henry Bouquet*, Pennsylvania Historical Commission, 1941, Series 21643, p. 199), but this went to Mercer, a Pennsylvanian. As for the Maryland troops, these were all sent to Fort Cumberland, it appears, for the winter. Without pay from their own government and in spite of the efforts of Colonel Bouquet to hold the men there, most of them by spring had deserted (Bouquet to Amherst, March 1, 1759, *ibid.*, Series 21634, p. 1).

latter, after preparations had been completed to place them in cantonments for the winter in the settled part of Pennsylvania and after they had actually proceeded eastward some distance, were ordered to march back so as to support the provincials at Pittsburgh and at Fort Ligonier.[3] These garrisons also had to be constantly provisioned. Therefore during the season of deep snow and ice there took place the steady movement, by pack-horses, of supplies for these isolated groups who were holding this vital line.[4] For Forbes was determined, in spite of his illness, soon to prove fatal, to leave no stone unturned to give them every support within his power — and this he did. At Pittsburgh he left Lieutenant Colonel Hugh Mercer of Armstrong's Pennsylvania battalion in command.[5] The men under Mercer were housed in the temporary barracks that had been constructed before the general left the forks of the Ohio on December 4 and were protected by palisades with log bastions, also temporary in nature.[6] During the long winter Mercer's chief responsibility, outside of seeking information as to the intentions and specific plans of the enemy at Fort Machault on the upper Allegheny, lay in endeavouring to meet the insatiable demands for food on the part of the Indians living about the forks while at the same time attempting to subsist his troops.[7]

The Indians had been brought early in December to the British camp near the site of the French fort by Frederick Post, whose activities preceding the destruction of Fort Duquesne have already been considered in an earlier chapter. It may be noted that when the missionary left Pittsburgh on November 27 for the purpose of inviting the natives to meet with General Forbes, he found, in going down the Ohio to a point beyond Logstown, that the Shawnee had fled from the towns they had occupied, to their chief settlement on

---

[3] Halkett to Bouquet, December 1, 1758, Writings of Forbes, p. 273. On April 4 there were at Pittsburgh over two hundred Pennsylvanians, ninety-eight Virginians, and a hundred and eight regulars, mostly Highlanders (Pennsylvania Archives, first series, III, 580).

[4] Forbes to Bouquet, January 8 and 14, 1759, Writings of Forbes, pp. 276–7, 279. It took about a month and a half for a pack train leaving Carlisle for Pittsburgh to return to the same place.

[5] Parkman was in error in indicating (Montcalm and Wolfe, II, 160) that Lieutenant Colonel Mercer of the Virginia regiment was designated to command at Pittsburgh. George Mercer, who served under Washington, did not remain at the forks of the Ohio.

[6] Mercer to Bouquet, December 19, 1758, Bouquet Papers, Series 21643, p. 206.

[7] Ibid.

the Scioto. As a consequence, most of the Indians whom he succeeded in collecting were Delawares.[8] Since Forbes, by the time the talks with them could be arranged, had left for Fort Ligonier, Bouquet took over this responsibility.

Already George Croghan, acting as Sir William Johnson's agent, had spoken with them respecting the release of the English people held as prisoners among them — in harmony with the agreement arrived at in the Treaty of Easton — and had secured a promise, also made by them to the deputies of the Six Nations, that, during the winter, steps would be taken to gather for release these unfortunate people, many of them held in distant villages not only by the Delawares but by other Indians in alliance with them.[9] Bouquet reminded them of this pledge. He also confirmed the statement — repeatedly made earlier by Post — when he declared: "We have not come here to take possession of your hunting Country in a hostile manner . . . but to open a large and extensive Trade with you, and all other Nations of Indians to the Westward, who choose to live in friendship with us." Further, he made clear that as soon as goods had arrived, this trade, protected from the enemy by a small body of soldiers, would be opened up, and especially stressed the point that the general expected that the Delawares, in view of their declarations of friendship and of his withdrawal of most of his army from their hunting grounds, not only would support the garrison should the enemy come down the river and seek to drive it away, but would compel the French to leave their country. In their reply, delivered the following day, the Indians expressed their satisfaction that General Forbes, after expelling the French from the forks, had, as had been promised to them by Post, departed with his army, leaving only two hundred soldiers "to support and defend the Traders." Again they reiterated their promise to deliver their English prisoners; they further affirmed that they would send a message to the French demanding that they leave these parts; and, finally, they promised, as soon as they had held a council with the more western Indians, to send deputies to meet the general in Philadelphia.[10]

Bouquet, after his departure from Pittsburgh later in the month, realized that Mercer's position might at any time become so pre-

---

[8] For Post's "Journal" of his trip covering the period of November 27 to December 2, 1758, see *Pennsylvania Archives* (first series), III, 560-3.

[9] Ibid.

[10] For Bouquet's address to the Indians and their reply see *ibid.*, III, 571-4.

carious that he would be obliged, in order to save his men from capture, to desert the forks. With the consent of Forbes he therefore drew up rather full instructions to guide the commander. These called upon him to engage the neighbouring Indians to agree to join him in case of an attack by the French — something that they had not as yet agreed to do. He was also to keep spies out all the while at Venango and at Presqu'Isle to the north and also down the Ohio and was to find a suitable place on the other side of the Monongahela where the cohorns, arms, and stores could be secreted in case Pittsburgh had to be evacuated; and should this be necessary in the face of superior forces, he was to burn the new fort, pass over the Monongahela in bateaux constructed for such a contingency, and thereupon retreat to Fort Ligonier.[11]

Happily, the winter came to an end at the forks of the Ohio without incident. But the man responsible for the fact that the region was once again in possession of the British passed away in Philadelphia early in the spring. Fittingly, in the words of the obituary notice that appeared in the *Pennsylvania Gazette*, it was stated of Forbes:

> "By a steady Pursuit of well concerted Measures, in Defiance of Disease and numberless Obstructions, he brought to a happy Issue a Most extraordinary Campaign, and made a willing Sacrifice of his own Life to what he valued more, the Interest of his KING and COUNTRY"[12]

As a recognition of his great services to Pennsylvania, there appeared in the funeral procession the Governor and his Council, the members of the Assembly, the judges of the provincial courts, as well as others holding places of distinction in public and private life, as the body was carried to Christ Church to be placed to rest in the chancel.

On January 23 Pitt, after hearing the news of the destruction of Fort Duquesne and the retreat of the French, had written to Forbes that he had instructed General Amherst to lose no time in coming to agreement with him upon measures either for the rebuilding of the ruined fort or for erecting another at the forks of the Ohio of

---

[11] These instructions prepared at Fort Ligonier are dated December 26, 1758 (*Bouquet Papers*, Series 21652, pp. 145–8). In them Bouquet mentioned the fact that supplies to subsist eight hundred men at Ligonier and Pittsburgh would be sent up and that one hundred regulars and later the same number of provincials would also be ordered to these two posts.

[12] Issue of March 15, 1759.

sufficient strength and in every way adequate "to maintain His Majesty's Subjects in the undisputed Possession of the Ohio."[13] Nor was the importance of providing a strong defence for this region ignored by the commander-in-chief of His Majesty's forces in North America. The latter, in view of Forbes's dangerous state of health, had come to the decision that in case of his death he would send Brigadier General Robert Monckton to take his place.[14] But Pitt had other plans for the brigadier, who, after the capture of Louisbourg, had been sent to the Bay of Fundy to round up the revolted Acadians and operate against Boishébert, the French commandant of a fort on the St. John: in projecting the campaign in North America for the new year, he had resolved to send Monckton up the St. Lawrence as a member of Wolfe's staff.[15] Therefore, as soon as this decision had been made known to Amherst, the general turned, as has been noted in the preceding chapter, to Brigadier General John Stanwix.[16]

Stanwix, upon receiving the appointment, immediately consulted with his superior as to the number of troops he would need to perform the service on the Ohio that Pitt had in mind. The two came to the conclusion that this would require some seventy-two hundred men. Of this number the 1st battalion of the Royal Americans, of less than nine hundred, was the only unit of regulars included; the remainder was to be composed of the two Virginia regiments, of a thousand each, three companies of North Carolinians, each of a hundred men, a Maryland regiment of eleven hundred, and, finally, three thousand men of the Pennsylvania regiments.[17] However, of the sixty-five hundred men that the four colonies named above were called upon to furnish, only twenty-seven hundred were provided by the middle of June, and of this total Pennsylvania furnished two thousand men and Virginia seven hundred. In fact, the battalion of regulars of which Stanwix himself was lieutenant colonel alone met the specifications as to numbers, with North Carolina and Maryland withholding from him all support.[18] Writing to Pitt at this time,

---

[13] *Correspondence of William Pitt* (ed. G. S. Kimball), II, 17.
[14] Amherst to Pitt, February 4, 1759, *ibid.*, II, 33.
[15] Pitt to Amherst, March 15, 1757, *ibid.*, II, 69.
[16] Amherst to Pitt, March 29, 1759, *ibid.*, II, 79. This information was received on March 14 and was contained in Pitt's letter of January 13 in which was given a list of officers who were to go with Wolfe up the St. Lawrence.
[17] Stanwix to Pitt, *ibid.*, II, 13–14.
[18] *Ibid.*

he declared, with some despondency, that the thirty-five hundred men then available were "the utmost of my Expectations." [19]

Nor was the failure of the four provinces to meet their requisitions in soldiers the brigadier general's only trouble. He had inherited a debt from Forbes of one hundred and eighty thousand pounds sterling owing to those who had furnished wagons and horses that had been lost in the campaign and other services as well. His military chest, moreover, was empty. Only Pennsylvania was at all disposed to make him a temporary loan of money to get his campaign in motion and, as we have already observed, the Assembly of that province would advance him no more than fifty thousand pounds and even attached clauses to the bill providing for the loan that were utterly foreign to it and related only to the struggle then taking place between the Assembly and the Proprietors of the province. [20] With all these handicaps, it was well into July before he was able to gather a sufficient number of wagons, horses, and supplies to concentrate his army at Fort Bedford — outside of those troops holding the posts farther to the westward of it, including the post at Pittsburgh. [21] But it was impossible to enter into contracts for carrying provisions and other matériel beyond Bedford. Therefore, it was decided that a thousand pack-horses prepared for the purpose should be employed to traverse the wild, mountainous country over the Forbes road between that place and Fort Ligonier; and then from this fort to Pittsburgh, with the land once again fairly level, a hundred wagons should be used to shuttle forth and back again. [22] By this means, as well as by making use of the Braddock road for provisions coming from Virginia, the storehouses constructed at the forks were filled, although with painful slowness, especially in view of the fact that the forces under Mercer there were gradually increased and the Indians, who flocked to the place in great numbers and expected subsistence, drew heavily on the accumulated stocks. Indeed, the problem of logistics was so difficult to master that Stanwix did

---

[19] Ibid.

[20] Ibid.

[21] In order to get these wagons it was necessary for Stanwix to allocate to each county the number to be furnished, which was done in order to avoid orders on his part for impressing them. See his advertisement of May 4, 1759 (Pennsylvania Archives, first series, III, 628–9).

[22] Bouquet to Mercer, May 26, 1759, Bouquet Papers, Series 21652, p. 170. Wagons were used, however, between Fort Bedford and Fort Ligonier (ibid., Series 21644, p. 153).

not feel free until the latter part of August to move on to Pittsburgh in order to take up his command there,[23] and it was not until September 10 that he felt that he was in a position to begin the building of Fort Pitt, to take the place of the temporary defences that had been erected at the forks.[24]

While there were constant attempts by small parties of French and Indians to break the long line of defence and to destroy the supply trains during the spring and summer, the troops suffered only one serious defeat, when Captain Bullitt with a hundred Virginians, escorting a large number of wagons loaded with provisions going from Bedford to Ligonier, was attacked late in May by St. Blin with a force of French and Indians but three miles from the latter place and was obliged, after the loss of forty of his men, to flee to it with the survivors.[25] It is true that on July 6 an attempt was made to capture Fort Ligonier at a time when the garrison was depleted as the result of convoy duty between Loyalhanna and Fort Bedford. Colonel Adam Stephen in command there employed his artillery to such good effect, however, that the enemy after an effort to storm the fort from all quarters retired.[26]

During this period and until the month of October Colonel Bouquet remained along the line of posts, principally at Bedford, employing every faculty to hurry the movement of supplies and troops. Then he joined Stanwix at Pittsburgh.[27] The garrison there, still under the command of Lieutenant Colonel Mercer, had, before the arrival of General Stanwix in August, been occupied almost exclusively with defensive preparations,[28] including the work of providing guards for the convoys that came from Fort Ligonier and making gardens so as to have a stock of fresh vegetables. The Indians who came and went, while by no means openly hostile, were at the same time not prepared to commit themselves to an open alli-

---

[23] Bouquet to Fauquier, August 25, 1759, ibid., Series 21652, p. 226.

[24] Stanwix to Pitt, November 20, 1759, Pitt Correspondence, II, 211–12.

[25] Adam Stephen to Stanwix, and Stephen to Bouquet, May 25 and 27, 1759, Bouquet Papers, Series 21644, pp. 153, 157. According to the Chevalier Pouchot, who was commanding at Fort Niagara, the party that attacked the convoy was made up largely of Indians of the Six Nations (Memoir upon the Late War in North America between the French and English, 1755–1760, trans. F. B. Hough, I, 156).

[26] Stephen to Stanwix, July 7, 1759, Pennsylvania Archives (first series), III, 669.

[27] Bouquet to Colonel James Burd, October 24, 1759, Bouquet Papers, Series 21652, pp. 270–1.

[28] Bouquet, writing to Mercer on April 13, ordered the commander of the post "to remain on the defensive" (ibid., p. 153).

ance, and they had surrendered few of the whites taken prisoner.[29] Writing to Bouquet from Pittsburgh on May 12, Mercer declared:

> "I can promise you little from the Indians this way. They speak fair to us, and at home are full of Caballs, and propagate a thousand lies, to sharpen each others resentment against us. The French Emissaries have done a world of Mischief, and our best friends among the Delawares begin to think their endeavours to Establish Peace, will be ineffectual for some time." [30]

Nevertheless, sheds were constructed for their entertainment, and in June George Croghan, representing, as was previously indicated, the Superintendent of the Northern Indian District, Sir William Johnson, met there representatives of a number of tribes, among them deputies of his old friends the Wyandots from Sandusky, and, after addressing them, proceeded to provide clothes for some two hundred and fifty of them.[31] The magnet that drew them to the post was not only food, liquor, and presents, but particularly the arrival of trading goods. These were sent up by the Pennsylvania Indian commissioners and by such private traders as the Quaker James Pemberton. This meant that an English market for Indian furs was again available. Thus the expectation that the Ohio Company of Virginia had in 1749 that the forks of the Ohio would become a great Indian trading centre was in the process of realization, although the trade at this period involved, not the company, but Pennsylvania interests.[32]

While the British were thus occupied in their efforts to consolidate their position at Pittsburgh, the French were laying their plans to eject them. In February de Lignery at Venango was able to assure the authorities at Quebec that while the Indian tribes living about the Ohio had retired into the interior of their hunting lands, they appeared to be still strongly attached to the French. Their leaders had assured him that they awaited with impatience his return to the forks in the spring with new forces with which to drive out the English and that they themselves would then be the first to strike the enemy.[33] In March Vaudreuil received equally encourag-

[29] Bouquet to Mercer, April 13, 1759, *ibid.*, p. 154.

[30] *Ibid.*, Series 21644, p. 127.

[31] *Pennsylvania Gazette*, July 19, 1759.

[32] For a return of furs in store at Pittsburgh on May 23, 1759, see the Bouquet Papers, Series 21644, p. 143.

[33] *Journal des Campagnes de Chevalier de Lévis, 1756–1760* (ed. Abbé Casgrain), pp. 166–7.

ing news from the Great Lakes area and from the Illinois country. Not only were the natives well disposed, he was informed, but preparations were being made to forward from the upper Mississippi to the posts about Lake Erie the same quantity of food as the preceding year, which would be convoyed by M. Aubry and his troops by way of the Wabash-Maumee portage.[34]

The Governor General in sending the Chevalier Pouchot to the Niagara to take charge of that most important fort, authorized him to send reinforcements and supplies to de Lignery for both defensive and offensive purposes, especially if there were no threats to the safety of Niagara by way of Oswego.[35] Pouchot, arriving toward the end of April at the post where he had previously commanded, obtained news from English prisoners regarding the weakness of Fort Ligonier and the recall from the forks of the Ohio of the regulars.[36] With everything apparently quiet in the region of the Oswego River, he decided to give to de Lignery at Venango a sufficiently large force to make possible the destruction of both Pittsburgh and Ligonier.[37] It was June, however, before the Chevalier was in a position to send these reinforcements to the Allegheny, together with supplies for the intended expedition against the English posts. Then, in doing so, he informed de Lignery in his final instructions that Aubry and the Chevalier Villiers had reached Lake Erie with between two and three thousand pounds of flour, which would be available for his troops. In these instructions he also recommended that, before embarking on the proposed campaign, it would be well to send out a trusty French officer and some active Frenchmen to examine the country with care, particularly defiles suitable for ambuscades as well as the mountains and rivers that would have to be crossed. In approving Fort Ligonier as de Lignery's chief objective, he then declared:

"If you should be as fortunate as to take Loyal-Anon.[38] you ought to expect all the posts from Raiston [39] to the Ohio would fall of themselves, as they would find themselves abandoned by their own forces, and with no hope of receiving any supplies." [40]

---

34 *Ibid.*, p. 171.
35 *Ibid.*, pp. 172 and 174.
36 Pouchot's *Memoir*, I, 142.
37 *Ibid.*, I, 146–7; *Journal de Lévis*, p. 174.
38 Loyalhanna, where Fort Ligonier was built.
39 Raystown, where Fort Bedford was built.
40 The instructions are given in Pouchot's *Memoir*, I, 152–5.

Thus began the concentration of French forces at Fort Machault at Venango with the purpose of undoing the work of Forbes during the preceding year, which the sporadic raiding by French and Indians had not accomplished. The latter part of June, news reached Pouchot at Niagara that one hundred French and one hundred and fifty Indians from Detroit were about to arrive at Presqu'Isle, preparatory to moving down to Venango by way of Fort au Bœuf and the Rivière aux Bœufs; likewise, that Lintot was bringing six or seven hundred Indians and Rayeul a hundred more; that Aubry from the Illinois country had with him a party of six or seven hundred troops; and, finally, that La Veranderie and Langlade from the upper Great Lakes region were coming down with twelve hundred Indians: Cristinaux, Sioux, Sakis, Folles-Avoines, Saulteur, and Reynards.[41] When, early in July, Croghan sent from Pittsburgh to Venango as spies two Six Nations warriors, who arrived there on the 8th, the latter found already assembled at Fort Machault seven hundred Frenchmen and four hundred Indians. They later reported that both on the 9th and on the 10th two hundred additional Indians arrived there and on the 11th about one hundred and fifty more. Immediately upon the appearance of the natives, representing twelve different tribes, officers set to work, they declared, fitting them out for the expedition, and on the 12th, at a great council, de Lignery, throwing down the war belts, called upon them to be ready to leave the next day.

But this was not to be.

An Iroquois who had arrived at Venango on the 11th boldly rose, after the commandant of the fort had spoken, and warned the Indians that "their Father was rather in too great a hurry and desired them to consider some time on what they were going to do," and he countered de Lignery's war belts with "a large Bunch of strung Wampum." This threw the Indians into confusion. At this critical juncture, moreover, two Indians unexpectedly arrived from Niagara with letters from Pouchot to de Lignery. The latter, after reading these, declared to the astonished assembled savages, according to the spies:

"Children, I have bad news to tell you; there is a great Army of English coming against Niagara with Sir William Johnson who has with him all the Six Nations, with a great Number of other Indians who

[41] Ibid., p. 159.

live that way. I have received Orders to go directly to Niagara and take you with me; we must give over the thoughts of going down this River till we have drove the English away from Niagara. . . . Children, be strong and support your father at this time." [42]

Yet even had no ominous news come from Niagara, there is reason to believe that the expedition for the purpose of capturing Fort Ligonier would not have departed on the 13th. For on that day some of those engaged in the unsuccessful attack against it on the 6th returned to Fort Machault without prisoners and scalps and only to tell of losses; soon afterward on the same day four Indians returned from watching the Forbes road and reported to de Lignery that at Stony Creek they had seen an army of over a thousand men, who, having passed over the Allegheny Mountains with great numbers of cattle and loaded horses, were moving toward Fort Ligonier.[43] The time to strike it had passed.

With the disappearance, as has just been noted, of most of the French and their Indian allies from the region of the upper Allegheny, it was possible to concentrate without interference on the task that had been specially assigned by Pitt to the general commanding in this region: the building of a strong and permanent fort in the neighbourhood of the forks of the Ohio. In the spring of the year Colonel Bouquet had written to Mercer recommending that he should seek to find a better site than the one the French had selected. Indeed, there were certain manifest disadvantages in the position of Fort Duquesne. It could be commanded by elevations in its neighbourhood.[44] Further, it was exposed to the danger of floods; in fact, during the spring freshets of that year the water poured over the entire plain where the French barracks had stood and, it would appear, also covered the floor of the ruined fort.[45] Mercer, therefore, in company with Captain James Robertson, in whose capabilities as an engineer he had great confidence, and one John Wright, set out to discover a better location for the new stronghold and was led to recommend the site first selected by the Ohio Company of Virginia for their fort — a high hill overlooking the Ohio at the point where Chartiers (Shurtees) Creek flows into the Ohio from the south, some few miles below the forks. With respect

---

[42] Croghan to Stanwix, July 15, 1759, *Bouquet Papers*, Series 21644, pp. 191–3.
[43] *Ibid.*
[44] Bouquet to Mercer, April 13, 1759, *ibid.*, Series 21652, p. 155.
[45] Mercer to Bouquet, April 24, 1759, *ibid.*, Series 21644, p. 110.

to the advantages of "Chartrees Hill," Mercer declared in reporting to Bouquet on April 24: "We agree that scarcely a finer Spot for the Purpose could be wishd, every Circumstance conspiring to render the Place, Strong, convenient, healthfull and pleasant." He nevertheless warned that should the fort be erected there, "a quantity of Iron Chain will be requisite, for drawing up water, wood, etc." [46]

It is of interest that Washington, while on his historic journey to the Ohio in 1753, after viewing Chartiers hill, was led to contrast this very unfavourably with the forks of the Ohio as a site for the proposed company post with respect to defence and other obvious advantages.[47] To Stanwix the fact that the proposed location lay beyond the Monongahela, with all that was implied in this — especially the difficulty of preserving intact a line of communication between the new fort and the chain of posts to the eastward — counted heavily against it. Mercer was therefore advised by Bouquet that until the general himself was able to arrive at Pittsburgh, no further steps should be taken regarding a location.[48]

Although Stanwix was not able, as already indicated, to reach the forks until the latter part of August, by the latter part of July he had at least determined to establish permanent entrenchments at Pittsburgh and sent his chief engineer, Captain Harry Gordon, forward to engage in this task;[49] then, early in August, he authorized Bouquet to inform Gordon that if the latter found no objections to the building of the fort "at or near Pittsburgh" — according to the plan of a "Pentagone," which the engineer had drawn up — he should embody in it the works that he had already been ordered to construct.[50] Later in the month Mercer was ordered to employ all of his troops on this activity under the direction of Gordon.[51] The gathering of materials, however, was not to be hurried; sawmills had to be erected, trees felled, and logs shaped; stone was needed for the bomb-proof magazine, and brick for the revetments that faced the two land sides of the pentagon structure. It was therefore not until September 10 that the construction of Fort Pitt itself — in distinction to the outer works, such as the wide ditch that surrounded it and the

---

[46] Ibid.
[47] The Diaries of George Washington (ed. J. C. Fitzpatrick), I, 45.
[48] Bouquet to Mercer, May 8, 1759, Bouquet Papers, Series 21652, p. 160.
[49] Bouquet to Gordon, July 23, 1759, ibid., p. 194.
[50] Bouquet to Gordon, August 2, 1759, ibid., p. 196.
[51] Bouquet to Mercer, August 16, 1759, ibid., p. 217.

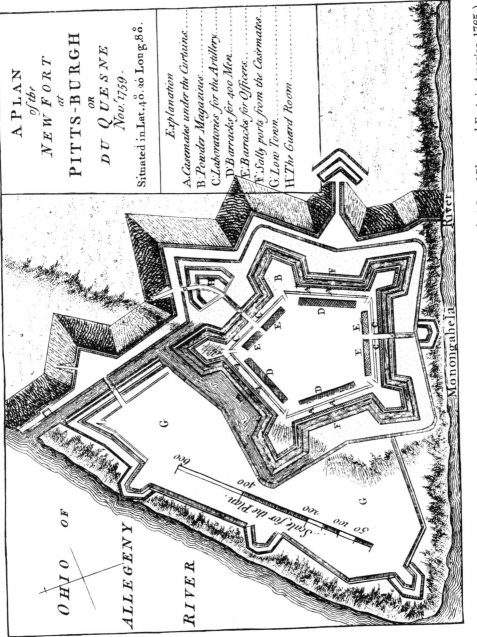

A PLAN
of the
NEW FORT
at
PITTS-BURGH
OR
DU QUESNE
Nov. 1759.

Situated in Lat. 40.°20' Long. 80.°

Explanation

A. Casemates under the Curtains.........
B. Powder Magazines.........
C. Laboratories for the Artillery.........
D. Barracks for 400 Men.........
E. Barracks for Officers.........
F. Sally ports from the Casemates.........
G. Low Town.........
H. The Guard Room.........

OHIO   OF
ALLEGENY
RIVER

Scale for the Plan.
50 100 200 300 400 500 600

Monongahela   River

"Fort Pitts-Burgh," 1759.

(From Ann Rocque's A Set of Plans and Forts in America, 1765.)

pickets on the earthen ramparts — could be begun;[52] and it was not until the summer of 1761 that the main fortifications were completed under Bouquet's supervision.[53]

In taking the place of Fort Duquesne at the forks, Fort Pitt was not a mere trading post, such as the Indians of the Ohio had desired, but a place of real strength. It was indeed built as a token of British possession of the upper Ohio Valley and was therefore designed to be in "every way adequate to the great importance of the sever¹ objects" that Pitt had had in view in sending out his orders for its construction.[54] That it would receive its test in 1763, not from the French, but from the Indians of that area who felt that their hunting grounds were threatened by its presence in their midst, could not be clearly foreseen in 1759, and yet the possibility of it could not have been ignored by those in positions of authority at the forks who were made to realize how strongly opposed were the natives to the permanent military occupation of any part of their lands by the whites.

Just as Fort Duquesne before its destruction in 1758 had been a symbol of the French control of the upper Ohio Valley, so was Fort Niagara with respect to the Great Lakes region and the approaches to the province of Louisiana. In giving to Major General Amherst detailed instructions regarding the operations to be undertaken for the year 1759, Pitt, in his letter of December 29 of the preceding year, had written:

> "It were much to be wished any Operations on the side of Lake Ontario could be pushed on as far as Niagara, and that you will find it practicable to set on foot some Enterprise against the Fort there, the Success of which would so greatly contribute to establish the uninterrupted Dominion of that Lake, and, at the same time, effectually cut off the Communication between Canada, and the French Settlements to the South; and the Utility and Importance of such an Enterprise . . . is, of itself, so apparent, that . . . it is unnecessary to add anything to enforce your giving all proper Attention to the same, so far as the great and main Objects of the Campaign shall permit." [55]

---

[52] Stanwix to Pitt, November 20, 1759, *Pitt Correspondence*, II, 211.

[53] George Dallas Albert: *The Frontier Forts of Western Pennsylvania* (Vol. II of *Report of the Commission to Locate the Site of the Frontier Forts of Pennsylvania*), p. 106.

[54] Stanwix to Pitt, November 20, 1759, *op. cit.*, II, 211.

[55] *Ibid.*, II, 399–400.

Thus it is clear that the Minister was deeply interested in seeing Amherst lay plans for a drive against this fort, provided that this could be done without affecting adversely either the movement against the French in the Lake Champlain area to be undertaken by the commander-in-chief in person, or that up the St. Lawrence, by Wolfe, both of which he had even more at heart. It is equally clear that, before his letter reached Amherst, the latter was weighing the possibilities of such an expedition as the result of the urging of Sir William Johnson, the Indian Commissioner for the Northern District.

On December 13 Amherst had written from the city of New York to Johnson to announce the fact that he had been honoured with the command of the King's forces in North America and to call upon him to enlist the services of as many Indians as he could for the next season's campaign.[56] Although it was not practicable to call a meeting of the Six Nations until early in the spring, Johnson began sounding out the natives and, as a result of informal talks with individual Indian leaders, was able by the middle of February to inform the general that he was optimistic about the outcome of his projected conference with the Confederation and in this connection declared:

> ". . . I flatter myself, and have some Reason to expect that (as Affairs are now Circumstanced) if an Expedition was designed against Niagara, or elsewhere, thro' the Country of the Six Nations, I shou'd be able to prevail upon the greater Part if not the whole of them, to join His Majesty's Arms; This Circumstance I thought it my Duty to acquaint Your Excellency with, in Case such an Expedition was in Agitation."[57]

The profound significance of the above statement cannot escape the student of the history of this people. No longer were the Six Nations bitterly opposed, as they had been the preceding year, to any expedition, whether British or French, that would traverse their lands, and no longer were they prepared to use their influence to preserve Niagara from attack, as they so long had done. On the contrary, they welcomed a campaign through their own villages and were particularly enthusiastic over the idea of participating in it

---

[56] Amherst to Johnson, December 13, 1758, *Sir William Johnson Papers* (ed. James Sullivan), III, 12.

[57] Johnson to Amherst, February 16, 1759, *ibid.*, III, 19–20.

should its objective be Niagara. The explanation for this change is not far to seek. The news of the fall of Louisbourg in July of the preceding year, with the subsequent surrender and destruction of Fort Frontenac near the entrance of the St. Lawrence and the desertion still later of Fort Duquesne at the forks of the Ohio, shook to its very foundation their previous belief in the invincibility of French arms; for not even the defeat of Abercromby by Montcalm before Fort Ticonderoga could offset the loss of these vitally strategic places. Again, there was the psychological influence of the fact that the victor over the enemy at Louisbourg had been appointed to the supreme command of the British troops in North America and had come to New York — and the Six Nations, very humanly, wanted to be on the side of a winner. Further, the loss of the ship bringing Indian goods from France meant that the French could do little to supply their peculiar needs, whereas British trading goods were in abundance at Albany as well as farther to the southward at Philadelphia. Finally, their knowledge that Fort Niagara — now that Frontenac had fallen — was the western depot of furs secured by French traders in the upper Great Lakes region did not fail to arouse their avarice.

One can sense the deep satisfaction with which Amherst learned of the change of heart of the Indians and, in replying to Johnson's letter, assured him that he would furnish suitable light arms for those Indians prepared to fight with the British. Before closing he also declared: ". . . I shall not lose Sight of the Expedition you Mention, and the reasons that induce you to desire it, Shall have the greatest weight with me at it's proper Season." [58] When therefore Johnson held his conference in April with the Six Nations at the Mohawk town of Canajoharie, close to Johnson Hall, rather than at Onondaga, traditional council centre of the Iroquoian Confederation, where French influence had previously been so powerful — another evidence of the revolution in Indian affairs since the spring of the preceding year, when the Indian Superintendent was not even permitted to appear at the Onondaga conference — he found, as anticipated, all the Indians "Urgent that an Enterprise should be taken against Niagara," and was given assurance that if this were to be the objective of a campaign, at least eight hundred of them would participate in it. Indeed, so much did they have this at heart that their chiefs requested him to agree to transmit a special re-

[58] Amherst to Johnson, February 24, 1759, ibid., III, 21.

quest to Amherst that this be undertaken. In doing so he wrote to the commander-in-chief:

> "I am of Opinion the Reduction of Niagara will Overset the whole French Indian Interest, and Trade, and throw it into Our hands . . . and that if You put this Plan in Execution, no Time should be lost, as the Transportation to Lake Ontario grows more & more difficult as the Summer Advances." [59]

Amherst, at the time he received this request from the Indians, was fully occupied in the work of embarking at New York the regiments that would serve under Wolfe up the St. Lawrence. He was able to reach Albany, however, early in May in the process of organizing his own campaign by way of Lake Champlain and thereupon called Johnson into conference. Again the latter reiterated his promise of powerful Indian support, provided that a campaign were directed against Niagara. But the general did not openly commit himself at this time on this important matter. [60] That he was favourably inclined to the idea of an expedition is, nevertheless, evident when on May 5, the day after his interview with Sir William, he ordered three months' provisions for five thousand men to be sent up to Schenectady, on the lower Mohawk. Then on the 8th, without taking anyone into his confidence at the time, he fully committed himself to the idea of an expedition against Niagara and determined to give the immediate command of the forces intended for that purpose to a veteran soldier, John Prideaux, who had become the colonel of the 55th regiment after the death of Lord Howe and who, upon receiving this new command, was now elevated to the rank of brigadier general in America. [61] To support him, the 44th and 46th regiments and the 4th battalion of the Royal Americans, as well as a body from the Royal Artillery, were detached from Amherst's immediate command, as were the Indians. The success of the movement against Fort Niagara depended upon the element of surprise. Therefore, when Johnson appeared for a conference with Amherst

[59] Johnson to Amherst, April 22, 1759, *ibid.*, III, 31. The conference, a long one, lasted from April 4 to the 22nd. For the minutes of this see "Report of Proceedings with the Confederate Nations of Indians, at a Conference held at Canajoharry," *Documents Relating to the Colonial History of the State of New York*, VII, 378–95.

[60] Amherst to Pitt, June 19, 1759, *Pitt Correspondence*, II, 121.

[61] *Ibid.*, II, 122. Prideaux had recently arrived from England, where he called upon General Ligonier while in London. The latter, writing to Amherst on January 23, declared, in referring to Prideaux: "You will find him a very active, diligent officer" (Amherst Papers, Packet 11, Canadian Archives Transcripts).

on the 16th, no hint of this was given to him. In the words of the
general, as recorded in his *Journal:* "I kept my intended operations
secret. If the Indians know them the French will have it. . . ." [62]
By the 19th, however, preparations for the operations were sufficiently advanced so that Amherst felt that he could no longer fail
to confide in Sir William and wrote to him in strict confidence calling upon him to assemble his Indians at Oswego without delay so
as to be ready to join the troops under Prideaux when they arrived
at this rendezvous.[63]

The forces, once assembled in the region of Schenectady, soon
afterward began their movement up the Mohawk in a hundred
whaleboats and a vast number of bateaux. By June 21 they had
reached Oneida Lake; by the 24th they were at the Great Falls of
the Oswego and by the 27th at Oswego itself, on Lake Ontario,
where they were joined by Johnson with his warriors from the Six
Nations. It may be noted that Pitt had ordered the re-establishment
of a fort at Oswego. Amherst, in his arrangements for the expedition, therefore kept this fact in mind and also the vital importance,
in the meantime, of holding effectively this strategic place, especially
while the drive on Niagara was proceeding. This duty was assigned
to Colonel Frederick Haldimand, who, like Bouquet, was a native
of Switzerland and an officer in the Royal Americans, and was
destined to leave, as did his fellow countryman, an impressive record
of military service in the New World. Somewhat over a thousand
troops — one half of the 4th battalion of Royal Americans and
over five hundred of the New York provincials — were therefore
ordered to remain at Oswego.[64] Then, on the 30th, the remainder of
the forces, some two thousand in number, and about a thousand
Indians took to the lake, reaching Ossenodus (modern Sodus Bay)
on July 1, Nidenindequeat (Irondequoist Bay) the following day,
and on the 4th made their landing at the mouth of the Little Swamp
River about three miles to the east of the Niagara River and the
French fort.[65]

This appearance of the British forces came as a complete surprise to the Chevalier Pouchot, commanding at Fort Niagara, and
indicates not only how secretly the movement was planned and

[62] *The Journal of Jeffery Amherst* (ed. J. C. Webster), p. 109.

[63] *Johnson Papers*, III, 42–3.

[64] De Lancey to the Board of Trade, July 24, 1759, *N. Y. Col. Doc.*, VII, 395.

[65] "Orderly Book" of the expedition from June 21 to August 19, 1759, *Johnson Papers*, III, 49–105; *N. Y. Col. Doc.*, X, 977.

how rapidly and efficiently it was executed, taking all things into consideration, but also the extent of the alienation of members of the Six Nations from French interest. Had this not been the case, it is very likely that when the British troops had arrived at Oswego, speedy Indians would have gone overland by well-known trails to Niagara to warn the garrison there. This failure of a warning of impending danger came in the face of solemn promises that this would not be wanting, made by a group of Tonniac and Cayuga warriors to Pouchot on May 28.[66] It is true that he was notified in June by some Cayuga chiefs that Johnson by large belts had won over their nation and that the members of it had a design to pillage the French trading post at the portage on the Niagara river.[67] This he therefore sought to guard against, especially as the Indian trade of Niagara during the months of May and June was unusually brisk. Although in previous years hardly more than one hundred and fifty packs of furs had been taken in there in the course of the whole season, in contrast, during these two months, between seven and eight hundred, brought by the western Indians, passed into possession of the French.[68]

While many rumors of hostile designs on the part of the Six Nations against the French at Niagara were discounted, nevertheless evidence accumulated during the weeks preceding the attack that the fort might be in danger — especially in view of the fact that most of the effective troops stationed there had been sent on June 1 to Venango, as has been noted, for an expedition against Fort Ligonier. Information was now received that some French traders, living hitherto in perfect security and friendship with the natives in a Seneca town not far from the fort, had been taken prisoner; what was even more ominous was the fact that even Joncaire, who had been reared from early childhood within this same nation, was forced to save himself at this juncture by fleeing to the security of Niagara.[69] In an effort to gather reliable information about possible movements of the British, the French commandant sent Sieur de Blainville with a group of loyal Missisauga Indians to Oswego.

---

[66] "If we learn that the English are planning any thing against you, we notify you at once, so that you may not be surprised," declared the Indians (Pouchot, op. cit., I, 150).

[67] Ibid., I, 156.

[68] Ibid., I, 157.

[69] Ibid., I, 156.

Landing there from one of the lake vessels and noting no evidence of the enemy, the party went three or four leagues up the Oswego River and, returning to Niagara on the 27th, reported that it had found no sign of the presence of the English in that area — although at the very time of the visit up the river Prideaux had arrived at the portage about the Great Falls, just two leagues beyond the farthest point that the Frenchman and his Indians had reached.[70] Later, on July 6, the French corvette *Iroquoise* entered the mouth of the river and even then, strangely enough, did not detect the presence of the enemy now established there under Haldimand; nor, in returning, did the French cruise close enough to the south shore of Lake Ontario to get a view of the great British flotilla of whaleboats and bateaux, which, had they been perceived, might have been destroyed by playing upon them the ship's ten or twelve cannon. Indeed, not until late in the afternoon of the 6th, with Prideaux's forces now within operating range of Fort Niagara, was their presence detected. This came after two Frenchmen who had left the fort to hunt had been seized by hostile Indians. A relief of fifty men was thereupon sent out to scatter what was supposed to be a small party of hostile natives; they were received by volley fire, however, which indicated the presence of enemy regular troops.[71] Thus Pouchot and his garrison suddenly found that they were actually besieged.

Fort Niagara, first built in 1725 and later falling into decay, had been in the course of the war to a great extent reconstructed and even replaced by better fortifications. This latter task was begun during the period when Pouchot first commanded there, for he possessed real talent as a military engineer.[72] When he returned late in the spring of 1759 to take over the post again, he immediately proceeded to continue the work of rebuilding the defences and completed, among other things, the raising of the earthen ramparts and the making of casements for the protection of the powder magazine. This construction gave him "a vast storehouse" for the arms of the garrison. Niagara, in fact, was, all in all, at the time of attack, an impressive fort. It comprehended a number of substantial buildings, such as barracks, mostly built of timber, although the com-

---

70 *Ibid.*, I, 158.
71 *Ibid.*, I, 160.
72 *N. Y. Col. Doc.*, X, 466, 694.

mandant's headquarters was a large stone structure some three stories in height.[73] The hornwork connecting the bastions was about seven hundred and thirty feet in length and extended from the Niagara River to Lake Ontario, where a perpendicular cliff formed a natural barrier. Finally, outside of this hornwork was a ditch nine feet in depth and some twenty-three yards in breadth.[74] Thus nature and military science had combined to make it a place of very considerable strength, and so it impressed Prideaux and his men.[75] For its protection Pouchot had about 150 soldiers from four of the battalions of French regulars, some 180 colonial marines, and 133 Canadian militia, together with a small body of artillerymen — numbering in all 486 Frenchmen, who were supported by a body of faithful Indians. Realizing his weakness, when at last on the 7th the presence of large numbers of enemy soldiers was observed by his scouts, he sent off a courier to warn Chabert, commandant of the post at the Carrying Place around the Falls of Niagara, of the danger that threatened and to summon all possible aid from de Lignery at Fort Machault.[76]

Prideaux, meanwhile, was busy consolidating his position upon an eminence on the west bank of the Little Swamp River near its entrance into the lake. By this means he could afford protection to his boats; he also was occupied with the disposition to the best advantage of those of his forces not needed in the work of digging trenches and making an abatis, fascines, and gabions, so as to enclose the enemy. On the 8th, having completed a cordon to the bank of the Niagara at a point somewhat less than half a mile from the fort, he sent Captain Blane (Blaine) of the Royal Americans with a white flag to summon Pouchot to surrender the stronghold to him, since, as he stated, the King of England had invested him with the government of it.[77] To this the French commandant made no reply.

By the 10th it could be observed from the French defences that a zigzag parallel was being dug by the enemy from a dry swamp, some six hundred yards distant, in the direction of the so-called Lake Ontario Bastion of Niagara. In spite of the efforts of the French guns, each day it came ever nearer to the fort. By the 14th it was within some two hundred and fifty yards of the covered way of the

[73] Pennsylvania Gazette, August 2, 1759.
[74] N. Y. Col. Doc., X, 977. Pouchot said the ditch was eleven toises wide.
[75] Pennsylvania Gazette, August 2, 1759.
[76] N. Y. Col. Doc., X, 978.
[77] Pouchot, op. cit., I, 166; N. Y. Col., X, 979.

outer defences; by the 20th it was within eighty yards, and by the
23rd it extended well along the face of the fort, offering protection
to British sharpshooters firing now at close range upon the defenders.
Leading off from the deadly zigzag three boyaux had also been constructed for batteries. The first of these was wrongly located and at
too great a distance to be effective, but the two others, where were
stationed some eighteen-pounders, as well as cannon of lesser calibre
and howitzers for throwing shells, were well within battering
range.[78] By use of shells and red-hot cannon balls these batteries
now began the systematic destruction of the French fortifications.
On the 17th they were aided in this task by a battery of the heavy
guns and two howitzers that opened up on the fort from Montreal
Point across the Niagara River.[79] In the midst of this forward movement of the British came, unhappily, the death of Brigadier Prideaux, who while walking in the trenches was instantly killed by a
gunner who carelessly fired a cohorn.[80] As a result the command was
assumed by Sir William Johnson.

In relating the history of the siege of Fort Niagara nothing as yet
has been said about the activities of Johnson's Indians, who were
at hand to the number of a thousand. It would appear that, after
going into the camp established for them, for several days they
remained all in all rather quiet spectators of the activities taking
place, outside of guarding at night the workers in the trenches. Then,
on the 11th, a Seneca chief, Kaendaé, devoted to the French cause
and encamped with other Indians inside the fortifications, requested
permission of Pouchot to go and speak with those of his nation who
were with the British, in the hope that he could prevail upon them
to leave the besieging army. The Six Nations agreed to a parley to
be held "on the edge of the clearance." As a result of this, they further agreed to send two of their deputies to the commandant of the
fort "to learn his views concerning themselves," provided that a safe
conduct was granted upon the word of Jonaire, who was also in
the fort and who had long been regarded as one of their own chiefs.
This was granted. The deputies, brought blindfolded to Pouchot's
headquarters and questioned, declared that "they did not know how
they had got involved in this war, and that they were ashamed

---

[78] F. H. Severance: *An Old Frontier of France*, II, 289–90.
[79] N. Y. Col. Doc., X, 980–6.
[80] Captain John Knox: *An Historical Journal of the Campaigns in North America for the Years 1757, 1758, 1759, & 1760*, I, 403; *Journal of Jeffery Amherst*, p. 147.

of it." This gave the commandant the opportunity to express his surprise to find in arms against him many who had previously shown him great affection and to indicate to them that all the upper nations were coming to his aid and he hoped that the latter might not have to be called upon to shed the blood of the Six Nations. Members of both the Missisauga and Potawatomi tribes, who were present at the conference, added their voices to those of Pouchot in calling upon the Iroquois to return to the French friendship. The deputies at length left the fort carrying a great belt to reinforce the words that had been spoken to them.[81]

The following day Kaendaé again issued from the fort to counsel again with his fellow Senecas and in the course of the talks, which were held in the presence of Johnson, reproached the latter fiercely for having embarked this nation "in a bad cause." Then in the afternoon he returned to the fort with one Onondaga and two Cayugas. These Indians brought to Pouchot a large white belt of peace and declared that the Six Nations had taken to heart his words and would now quit the English army and go to encamp at La Belle-Famille — some distance to the south of the fort and near the bank of the Niagara. By another belt they requested the commandant to permit Kaendaé and also Joncaire and the Iroquois women and children still in the fort to leave it so that the "kettles" (bombs) might not fall on their heads. Finally, they presented strings of wampum from the Delawares and the Mohegans to the Ottawa and other Indian groups in the fort to engage them to retire to the head of the lake while the white people should fight out the issue, with all the Indians standing aloof. But Pouchot cut this dangerous sort of talk short, and when the deputies proposed to return that same evening, he told them that at night his men fired on everyone who appeared and he would be content if they simply remained quiet as they had agreed to do.[82]

It was clear that whatever were the motives of the Six Nations in engaging in these parleys, they did not want to carry on their shoulders the responsibility of the consequences for the destruction of their fellow Indians in the fort. It is clear also that that very evening they appeared near the fort with a white flag and when Kaendaé went out to speak to them, informed him that in fulfilment of their promise "they had all retired to La Belle-Famille, and that

[81] Pouchot's Memoir, I, 171–3.
[82] Ibid., I, 173–6.

they would remain neutral." On the 14th Kaendaé made his last visit to the Iroquois camp and on returning reported that the Indians there had decided to retire but had subsequently been persuaded to remain when Johnson had promised that, should they do so, they would have the pillage of the fort after the assault, which was to take place within two or three days.[83] Yet, the French noted that no Indians from that time on appeared about the British trenches. They were manifestly holding back, at least until the outcome of the siege was settled.

At this juncture, in line with the desires of Johnson's Indians and also now of those within the French fort, the latter were permitted to leave the place and cross the river with their women to escape the effect of the bombs, and most of them did so. Thereupon, it is of interest to note, these French Indians proceeded to the camp of Chabert, who had had charge of the Niagara Falls portage, deprived him of the oxen and cows that he had attempted to place in security, and, after killing them, actually carried the meat to the English camp. The Six Nations, on their part, gave evidence that they, in turn, remained friendly toward the French. On the 23rd they admitted into their camp four Indians sent by Aubry and de Lignery to carry dispatches to Pouchot and, in the presence of Johnson, held a council with them, at which they accepted five belts and a message, sent by all Indians accompanying the French expeditionary force, calling upon the Iroquois to retire from the British army; in return, they assured these messengers by a belt that they would not mingle in the quarrel; further, to show their good faith, they permitted them to deliver their letters to the French commandant. Moreover, when the latter returned his answer in triplicate, one given to an Onondaga, another to a Delaware from the Ohio, and a third to a Shawnee, the three Indians, upon returning through the British lines with a white flag, were well protected by the Six Nations.[84] All this was highly confusing and seemed to indicate that the Confederation was still committed to its old policy of "balance" in Anglo-French relations.

By the time of the arrival of the dispatches on the 23rd, Pouchot was being desperately hard pressed. His battery at the so-called Flag Bastion had been dismounted and ruined by the heavy British battery facing it; a long breach had also been made in the parapet

[83] Ibid., I, 178.
[84] Ibid., I, 186–9.

at this point; materials for new embrasures were so wanting that furs had to be used for that purpose; blankets and shirts likewise were now torn up for cannon wads; moreover, the fire from the enemy guns and muskets was so steady, heavy, and destructive that the Canadians could no longer be induced to man the parapets, the defence of which now fell solely to the regulars; and as for these, since the 6th no one of them had gone to bed and everyone was overcome with weariness. Then came word from Aubry and de Lignery, in the letters delivered by the Indians, that relief was at hand, with confidence expressed in their ability to engage the enemy successfully and to raise the siege. Indeed, had the hard-pressed Frenchmen at Fort Niagara been able to view the scene as the expeditionary force of six hundred Frenchmen and a thousand Indians entered the upper Niagara River from Lake Erie, their hopes would have been raised to the highest point; for before their eyes would have spread a veritable "floating island, so black was the river with bateaux and canoes." [85]

Aubry and de Lignery had two choices, which Pouchot outlined to them in his reply. If they felt unable to attack the British, they could proceed by way of Chippewa Creek (the Chenondae), on the other side of the river, and thus gain the fort; or they could fall upon one of the three main groups of the besiegers, one of which was now stationed in the neighbourhood of La Belle-Famille; if the latter movement was successful, the siege manifestly would be raised. [86] They made a decision in favour of the approach that involved taking the road leading from Niagara Falls to the fort that passed by La Belle-Famille. Unfortunately for them, before the march began their Indian allies deserted them, with the exception of some thirty warriors led by Marin. This occurred after the natives had shown their willingness to fight and had already overwhelmed and destroyed a party of a dozen British light infantry that was seeking to cross the Niagara River; and also after, as a note of defiance and to terrify others, they had mutilated the bodies of their victims and had stuck the heads on poles. [87] But they did not want to engage in war with the Six Nations, and when, soon after this episode — which occurred early on the morning of the 24th — they had requested Aubry and de Lignery for permission to speak to John-

[85] N. Y. Col. Doc., X, 986.
[86] Ibid., X, 986-7.
[87] N. Y. Col. Doc., VII, 402; Pouchot, op. cit., I, 191.

(From Sir William Johnson Papers.)

Military operations against Fort Niagara, 1759.

PLAN
of Niagara
with the Adjacent Country
SURRENDERED
to the English Army
under the Command
of Sᴿ Wᴵᴸᴸ™ Johnson Barᵀ
on the 25ᵗ of July 1759

A. the Fort
B. Dock and Harbour
C. Burying place
DDDD Approaches
E. 1ˢᵗ Battery
F. 2ᵈ Dᵒ
G. 3ᵈ Dᵒ
H. Head Quarters
I. Bank of Artillery
K. 44ᵗʰ Regᵗ
L. Two Corpˢ of the 4ᵗʰ Battᵗ Royᴸ Americans
M. Part of the New-York Regᵗ
N. 46ᵗʰ Regᵗ
OO Indian Camps
PP. where the Armeʸ and Stores Landed
Q. Garden over the River

THIS RIVER PROCEEDS from LAKE ERIE over OXNIAGARA FALLS

TO THE
Honᵇˡᵉ Sir Willᵐ Johnson Barᵗ
ENGRAVED and PUBLISHED BY
Thomas Jefferys

son's Indians in order to persuade them to try to bring about peace and had been refused, they decided not to act further with the French.[88]

While the impression has been left by some writers that the French, led by Aubry and de Lignery, ultimately fell into an ambuscade,[89] this does not seem to have been the case. Warned fully by Pouchot that they would be obliged to meet a force stationed so as to command the road they had to traverse, they moved forward, in spite of the desertion of their Indians, until about eight o'clock they came in contact with the British, posted, as anticipated, in the Belle-Famille area. To dispute their further progress, they were now faced by Lieutenant Colonel Massy commanding not only a body of over four hundred and fifty regulars drawn from the 46th and 44th regiments and a picket of some fifty Royal Americans, but one hundred New York provincials and some six hundred of Johnson's Iroquois.[90]

The engagement that ensued took place but a mile from the trenches of the besiegers and within view of Pouchot standing on the Bastion of the Five Nations. The British, with bayonets fixed and protected behind a barrier of fallen trees, awaited the onslaught of the French.[91] The attackers "with much confidence" moved forward along the road, some seven or eight feet wide, "with a very great noise and shouting" and soon began discharging their muskets. But there was no response from their opponents until they had approached within some thirty yards of the abatis that flanked them on either side, and then Massy gave the order to fire. Seven rounds were now poured into the ranks of the French before they finally wavered in their attempt to outflank him and his men. Thereupon he commanded the soldiers to leap over their breastworks, which they did

[88] *Ibid.* On the morning of the 24th a group of the Six Nations, according to Captain de Lancey, left him and his New York provincials and went to the French camp to persuade the Indians there not to fight; while they apparently were not permitted to speak to them they were told by the white leaders there that they themselves did not want to fight against the Indians with the British. With that assurance the group returned to La Belle-Famille (*N. Y. Col. Doc.*, VII, 402).

[89] Pouchot, *op. cit.*, I, 194; H. L. Osgood: *The American Colonies in the Eighteenth Century*, IV, 444.

[90] Niagara advices, July 25, 1759, *Pennsylvania Gazette*, August 9, 1759; Colonel Massy to Pitt, July 30, 1759, Chatham Mss., Bundle 49 (Canadian Archives Transcripts); Charles Lee to Sir William Bunbury, August 9, 1759, New York Historical Society, *Collections* (1871), p. 21; Captain de Lancey to ——, July 25, 1759, *N. Y. Col. Doc.*, VII, 402-3.

[91] Pouchot, *op. cit.*, I, 191; *N. Y. Col. Doc.*, VII, 402.

without hesitation, still continuing to fire upon the enemy, who had begun to give way. The retreat soon turned into a wild flight. Only then, it would seem, did Johnson's Indians enter the fray [92] to engage in the pursuit, which continued for some five miles, in the course of which there was a "vast Slaughter" of Frenchmen at the hands of the savages, whose bloodthirst had been aroused and who fell upon them "like so many Butchers, with their Tomahawks and long Knives." In fact, the Indians in their madness could hardly be restrained from destroying the French officers, who had surrendered and who were among the hundred prisoners that fell into Massy's hands. [93] Among the seventeen officers captured were Aubry, de Lignery, Marin, and Repentigny (Repentini), all veterans in wilderness fighting.

While the fate of Fort Niagara was being decided at La Belle-Famille, the French batteries still in condition fired smartly on the British trenches, which in turn replied with equal vigor. Also, to ascertain the truth as to what was actually happening, Pouchot sent a faithful Onondaga through the British lines and received from him on his return early in the afternoon a report on the outcome of the battle. The defenders simply would not believe his story to the effect that the powerful relief had been destroyed or scattered and its officers made prisoner. [94] But at four o'clock they heard the drums

[92] Ibid., VII, 403; Massy to Pitt, July 11, 1760, Chatham Mss., Bundle 49 (Canadian Archives Transcripts). As to the conduct of those on the British side, Massy declared that during the engagement "the Indians all the time [were] running off toward our camp. . . . As I hear the Indians have got great Credit by that day, in Europe, I think I would not do justice to the Regiment [the 46th], I had the Honour to Command, if I wou'd allow Savages, who behav'd most dastardly, to take that Honour, which is deservedly due, to such of His Majesty's Troops, as were in that Action" (ibid.). On the other hand, Johnson, who was not present when the action took place, says that the French "were so well received by the troops in front, and the Indians on their flank, that, in an hour's time, the whole was completely ruined" (Johnson to Amherst, July 25, 1759, Johnson Papers, III, 108–9). But a letter written from Albany on August 6 with reference to the battle states: "It is said all the Indians, except the brave Mohawks, stood Neuter the first Onslot the Enemy made, to see, it is thought, which way the Scale would turn" (Pennsylvania Gazette, August 23, 1759).

[93] Pennsylvania Gazette, August 23, 1759; N. Y. Hist. Soc., Coll. (1871), p. 21; N. Y. Col. Doc., VII, 403. Winsor's statement (Narrative and Critical History of America, V, 535) that Johnson "now went with a part of his force to meet the new-comers . . . beat them, and captured some of their principal officers" is pure fiction, as is the statement by W. L. Stone (Life and Times of Sir William Johnson, II, 97). Sir William remained at his headquarters until the victors returned from the engagement, whereupon in his orders of the day he expressed his thanks to them (Johnson Papers, III, 81).

[94] Pouchot, op. cit., I, 194.

beat the recall from the enemy trenches. The guns in the boyaux now became silent; soon a British officer with a white flag appeared and was admitted to the fort. He was Major Hervey, bringing a letter from Johnson that reaffirmed the testimony of the Indians. Still incredulous, Pouchot and his officers demanded to see the prisoners. Thereupon a captain of the Royal Roussillon battalion was sent to the British camp and was brought into the presence of the wounded de Lignery and his fellow officers. Then at last the measure of the disaster that had befallen the French cause was fully realized.[95] A council of war was hurriedly called. A rapid survey of the situation was taken with respect to the possibility of further resistance, and, face to face with the fact that the hope of reinforcement had disappeared, that the garrison was overcome with exhaustion, and the Canadians no longer willing to fight, and that the defences were crumbling, it was determined to capitulate on honourable terms.

Pouchot demanded the right to march from the fort with the honours of war and to carry his men to Montreal with their effects and those of the French King. But Johnson sent word that he himself was not master of the conditions — otherwise he would accede to the demands.[96] After a period of hesitation therefore the British counter-terms were accepted and signed by all the French officers.[97] These terms provided as follows: for the surrender of the place the following day; for the garrison to march out with arms and baggage and drums beating to the place of embarkation and thereupon to be conducted to New York as prisoners of war; for the deposit of arms at the time of embarkation; for the full protection of the sick and wounded; for the protection of the soldiers from pillage and insult from the Indians; and, finally, for freedom of those Indians who served at the fort to leave without harm. To the great honour of Sir William Johnson and the officers who served under him, the Six Nations were held fairly firmly in check and the garrison was permitted to embark in safety on the 26th in the British bateaux for the journey to Oswego and then down the Mohawk. Fears on the part of the French that the surrender would lead to such a scene of terror and bloodshed as occurred after the British had laid down their arms at Fort William Henry in 1756 were, happily, un-

---

[95] Ibid., I, 195-6.
[96] Ibid., I, 198.
[97] N. Y. Col. Doc., X, 990-2.

founded.[98] Nevertheless, the massacre that took place on the 24th to the south of La Belle-Famille, reminiscent of the still greater massacre that occurred after Braddock's defeat in 1755, must have impressed the French with the fact that the use of savages in warfare between whites was a sword that could cut both ways. Moreover, it could have been said in 1759 as it was in 1777 in the words of Thomes Pownall: "There is not so hellish, so unfair an engine of war as the service of the Indian savage." [99]

It may here be pointed out that when the death of Brigadier Prideaux took place and Johnson assumed command,[100] he immediately requested Lieutenant Colonel Haldimand to come to Niagara from Oswego without delay,[101] but the following day, "on Severall Acc[tts]," countermanded this order.[102] Doubtless one important reason for this was that Haldimand was not disposed to accept orders from a mere colonel of Indians and even insisted on assuming command of the army, but finally agreed to refer the matter to the commander-in-chief.[103] Amherst, aware of this embarrassment with respect to the command of the western forces, immediately on receiving word

---

[98] Pouchot, op. cit., I, 202. The number that became prisoner at Fort Niagara and were carried off to New York was six hundred and seven privates and ten officers (Johnson to Haldimand, July 26, 1759, Johnson Papers, III, 114).

[99] W. Corbett: Parliamentary History of England, XIX, 702.

[100] Johnson's rank was that of colonel, but not on the royal establishment as a regular. Among the regular officers at Niagara Lieutenant Colonel Massy was the senior. He thought that he was entitled to the command of the army, but did not choose to make an issue of this at the time. In writing to Pitt the following year, however, he showed the attitude of the professional soldiers toward Johnson's colonelcy of the Indians: "On the 20th July Brigadier Prideaux and Colonel Johnstone of the Provincials were kill'd. When this happened, I commanded in the Trenches, and was wish'd Joy of the Command of that army, by some of my friends. I thought I had a right to it, as Brigadier General Gage told me the spring before, when . . . I ask'd him shou'd S[r] William Johnson send me any orders, on my march or after . . . how I shou'd Act, his Answer was, not to mind any, as he had no right, to give them" (Massy to Pitt, July 11, 1760, Chatham Mss., Bundle 49, Canadian Archives Transcripts). Captain Charles Lee of the 44th regiment doubtless expressed the view of regular officers toward Johnson when he referred to him as "a very good and valuable man, but utterly a stranger to military affairs" (N. Y. Hist. Soc., Coll., 1871, p. 21).

[101] Johnson to Haldimand, July 20, 1759, Johnson Papers, III, 106.

[102] Ibid., III, 107.

[103] In fact, as soon as Haldimand, at Oswego, heard of the death of Prideaux, he hastened to Niagara in order to take over the command. Johnson in writing to Amherst declared that "as I have His Majesty's Commission as a Colonel since 1756, I did not choose to give it up to him; however, We have Settled it in such a manner, that no dispute may Arise until Your Excellency's Opinion is known" (ibid., III, 116); Amherst's Journal, p. 147.

of the death of Prideaux ordered Brigadier Gage to set out for Oswego to take charge of all operations in the area of Lake Ontario.[104]

With respect to Oswego during the period of operations about Niagara, little need be said. Its position was one of great importance, and could the French have overwhelmed the British force posted there under Haldimand and entrenched themselves, the siege of Fort Niagara would doubtless have come to a sudden halt, and disaster would also have threatened the besiegers. In fact, four days after the departure of Prideaux and his army, scouts returned to Oswego with a report that they had seen one hundred bateaux on the lake. Soon afterward the enemy appeared in force under command of the Chevalier de la Corne, who was aided by the Indians led by the redoubtable Abbé Piquet of La Présentation mission.[105] It had been hoped to carry the British camp by surprise, but the alertness of the British scouts made this impossible. Now the only alternative to retreat was to attempt to overwhelm the garrison. Upon encircling the redoubts that Haldimand had erected out of barrels of provisions, however, de la Corne was received with so brisk a musketry fire that he and his men were obliged to retire to the woods; there they remained for the night. In the morning they again moved upon the encampment, but were again received not only with musketry but also with grapeshot from Haldimand's cannon, and once again retired. At length, after making a series of futile attempts to burn the British bateaux, the attackers, discouraged in their efforts, disappeared down the lake in the direction of the St. Lawrence.[106] This incident represents the last attempt of the French to assume the offensive on Lake Ontario in the course of the war. From now on, their energies were concentrated on the defence of the St. Lawrence — even their post at Toronto was burned and abandoned.[107]

When Brigadier Gage arrived at Oswego on August 16 to assume command of the Lake Ontario operations, he found Sir William Johnson there with most of the little army that had campaigned at Niagara.[108] The great French fort there was now garrisoned with

---

[104] *Ibid.*, p. 147; Amherst to Johnson, August 6, 1759, *Johnson Papers*, III, 119.

[105] According to a French deserter, this force consisted of between two and three hundred of the marines, thirteen hundred Canadians, and one hundred and fifty Indians (*Amherst's Journal*, p. 139).

[106] *Ibid.*, pp. 139–40.

[107] *Johnson Papers*, III, 115.

[108] Johnson's "Diary," W. L. Stone, *op. cit.*, II, 401.

seven hundred British troops under Lieutenant Colonel Farquhar; as for Little Niagara, just below the falls, and the French trading house above it, these had been plundered and then destroyed by the Indians.[109] All that Gage therefore had now to do was to carry out the remaining orders of Amherst, which in turn were based upon Pitt's specific instructions: [110] first, to build a fort at Oswego to take the place of Fort Ontario, destroyed in 1756; and, second, to attempt to occupy fortified La Galette on the upper St. Lawrence.[111] The vital importance of constructing a stronghold at Oswego without delay to take the place of the encampment was clear to all.[112] For should the expeditions against Canada that both Wolfe and Amherst had in hand terminate without success, the French would hardly fail to take advantage of the situation to send a powerful expedition into Lake Ontario to retrieve the capture of Fort Niagara. The loss of Oswego in 1756, moreover, pointed to the necessity of making at that place a really strong fort, especially now that Niagara depended upon it. Accordingly, the day following the brigadier's arrival a site having been agreed upon as well as a plan, work was begun on a new pentagon fort [113] and was continued to its completion.

But the expedition against La Galette and the establishment of a British post there, in terms of Amherst's orders,[114] represented a formidable undertaking. Indeed, in view of all the circumstances, and especially the small number of troops that could be spared for it, a much more energetic leader than Gage might have hesitated.[115]

---

[109] *Johnson Papers*, III, 115–16.

[110] Pitt to Amherst, December 29, 1758, *Pitt Correspondence*, II, 438–9.

[111] There is some confusion regarding La Galette. The name was attached to an island in the upper St. Lawrence now known as Chimney Island, somewhat below the mouth of the Oswegatchi. A French post had been erected there and the island is noted on French maps of the period under consideration. However, the name became transferred to the French fort on the Oswegatchi built to support Abbé Piquet's La Présentation Indian mission. It is described in 1759 as a stockaded fort with five good blockhouses but with no artillery (*Johnson Papers*, III, 133; F. B. Hough: *A History of St. Lawrence and Franklin Counties*, p. 41).

[112] *Johnson Papers*, III, 121.

[113] Johnson's "Diary," Stone, *op. cit.*, II, 401.

[114] *Ibid.* J. R. Alden, *General Gage in America*, pp. 49–52.

[115] Colonel James Robertson of the 60th regiment, who was with Amherst, expressed his doubts whether Gage would be able to carry out his orders to move against Galette. Writing to Loudoun on August 4, he stated that in view of the fact that Sir William Johnson had been obliged not only to leave a considerable force at Niagara but also to detach another large body of troops to convey the French garrison there down the Mohawk, as well as to provide a sufficient number to make Oswego secure for the

The place was but sixty miles distant from Montreal. What is more, the Chevalier de Lévis with eight hundred French troops had reinforced de la Corne's force of over a thousand at Galops Island, just below La Galette,[116] and could also draw reinforcements and supplies easily from Montreal. Again, it was calculated that but one thousand soldiers could be spared from the work at Oswego for this undertaking.[117] These must of necessity proceed out on Lake Ontario in bateaux without artillery protection and face two heavily armed French vessels and then move down the St. Lawrence, the waters of which, as one nears Oswegatchi and the rapids lying below, begin moving with acceleration — so favourable for descending the river, but a serious impediment should a sudden retirement up the stream be required as the result of a military reverse.[118] Should such a reverse entail the loss or dispersion of the expeditionary force in that wild country infested with Abbé Piquet's Indians, the continued control of both Oswego and Niagara would be imperilled. It must thus be clear, in the light of all information now available, that the proposed expedition presented so many grave hazards that Gage, in spite of Johnson's strong urging in favour of it,[119] was fully justified in notifying Amherst on September 11 that it must be postponed and that the few men at his disposal should rather be used to make Oswego a tenable place before winter set in.[120] Amherst, therefore, in rebuking Gage for failure to carry out

---

coming winter, "Gage would now decline taking post where he is ordered" (Loudoun Papers, No. 6133, Huntington Library). Pitt, however, far removed from the local scene, was critical of Gage and wrote to Amherst on December 11: ". . . I will only observe, that the Brigadier's resolution to give over the thoughts of that attempt, was taken on the 11th of Sept^r, a full month before you yourself judged it not too late to attempt, with your whole army, a more difficult and dangerous navigation on the Lake Champlain" (Pitt Correspondence, II, 217).

116 Journal des campagnes du Chevalier de Lévis (ed. Abbé Casgrain), p. 196; Lévis to Bourlamaque, August 30, 1759, Bourlamaque Collection, 3:117–20 (Canadian Archives Transcripts); "Journal de Foligné," A. Doughty: The Siege of Quebec and the Battle of the Plains of Abraham, IV, 194.

117 Johnson's "Diary," Stone, op. cit., II, 418.

118 Henry Young's report of August 31, 1759, Johnson Papers, III, 134; see also Malartic to Count d'Argenson, September 6, 1775, N. Y. Col. Doc., X, 349.

119 "Diary," Stone, op. cit., II, 418.

120 Gage declared that "erecting any other post at La Gallet or elsewhere . . . would require three times my number of men & artificers of all kinds to effect it & after all I could neither furnish it with provisions or artillery without leaving this post or Niagara destitute" (Letter Books, 1759–60, Clements Library). Amherst in his Journal (p. 171), under date of September 21, makes the following notation: "I answered Br Gages Letter I received the 18th, with great concern that he

his positive orders, in his reply to the brigadier's letter was really not in a position, viewing the situation from his headquarters on Lake Champlain, to judge fairly the nature of the task he had set for his subordinate.

Indeed, the commander-in-chief, in spite of his once high hopes of being able to brush aside all resistance and move his army across Lake Champlain and down the Richelieu to the St. Lawrence, was, by the time he had received Gage's letter, pretty well bogged down at the southern end of the lake. He had been called upon by Pitt to invade Canada by way of Crown Point or La Galette and to attack either Montreal or Quebec.[121] For this purpose he was allocated not only most of the contingents raised by the northern continental colonies, as has been indicated in the preceding chapter, but some seven regiments of regulars [122] — giving him a total of about eight thousand men for the invasion when his force reached its maximum strength.[123] According to the Pitt plan, the concentration of these troops was to have taken place by May 1, but it was after the middle of June when Amherst had at hand some seven thousand troops and at last felt in a position to move forward from Fort Edward to Lake George.[124]

had given up la Gallette which the Enemy could not have hindered him from taking and which he had my positive orders for doing; he may not have such an opportunity as long as he lives. I ordered it because I know the situation of the Enemy was such that it could not fail. They found out difficulties where there are none, and must have given them more difficulty than the taking of la Gallette would have done; it is now too late to remedy this." Gage replied to this very effectively on October 2 (Letter Books, 1759–60).

[121] Pitt to Amherst, December 29, 1758, *Pitt Correspondence*, I, 438.

[122] Amherst to Ligonier, April 16, 1759, Amherst Papers, Packet 11 (Canadian Archives Transcripts); Amherst's *Journal*, p. 111; Huck-Saunders to Loudoun, June 19, 1759, Loudoun Papers, No. 6113, Huntington Library. Garrisons had to be left at various points, which cut down the number of troops Amherst could take with him. When he finally embarked he had the following regiments of regulars: the Royals, Prideaux's, Blackneys's, the Royal Highlanders, Montgomery's and Forbes's, as well as Gage's light-armed troops; further, he had three Massachusetts Bay regiments, three of Connecticut, one of New Jersey, one of Rhode Island, and one of New Hampshire (Colonel Robertson to Loudoun, July 20, 1759, Loudoun Papers, No. 6126; Robertson does not mention Gage's troops, which were present).

[123] J. C. Long: *Lord Jeffery Amherst*, p. 94.

[124] *Pennsylvania Gazette*, July 5, 1759; Amherst's *Journal*, pp. 123–4. It is of interest to note that Bradstreet, doubtless in view of his success against Fort Frontenac, proposed to Amherst to lead an expedition early in the spring against Fort St. Jean, located well down the Richelieu midway between the Isle-aux-Noix and Chambly. According to his plan, he would have moved down Wood Creek into South Bay and, leaving a sufficient number of men to keep the garrisons of Ticonderoga and Crown Point

Upon arriving in the vicinity of the lake and near the site of Fort William Henry, he proceeded to lay out the plan for a new fort, which he called Fort George. With other delays it was not until July 21 that he was able to push out into the blue waters of the lake and move toward Fort Ticonderoga. Passing through the Narrows before nightfall, he landed most of the troops the following day without opposition at a place where earlier a French advanced guard had been posted, while the rest of his troops went four miles farther up the river before landing and then proceeded to march by the portage road leading to the sawmill, clearing it of timber that had been laid across it by the French. Then, after the bridge across the river had been repaired so as to stand the weight of artillery, they moved some of their guns over it with very little resistance from the enemy. By the evening of the 22nd Amherst therefore not only was in firm control of the landing-place, the sawmill, and the bridge, but had taken post on rising ground in the vicinity of the French fort.[125] Moreover, the following day he was informed by his advance post that the enemy had struck its tents and gone off in sloops and bateaux.[126] It now appeared that what Abercromby had sought and had failed to gain, in spite of the sacrifice of so many brave soldiers, he was now to realize with little effort or loss of life.

While the broad lines of French strategy involving military movements in 1759 in the defence of Canada will be analysed in the chapter to follow, it should here be made clear that out of sharp divergences in point of view held by Vaudreuil and Montcalm, there evolved a plan for the protection of the province from attack by way of Lake Champlain and the Richelieu River. According to it Brigadier Bourlamaque, a very dependable soldier and military engineer, was placed in immediate command of this area,[127] and was ordered about the middle of April to move the battalion of La Reine and the two battalions of Berry from their winter quarters to

---

"in awe," would have sought to burn the vessels and boats concentrated at St. Jean and then, returning, would have invested Ticonderoga while awaiting the arrival there of the main British army. Amherst, however, failed to approve the plan (Huck-Saunders to Loudoun, June 19, 1759, Loudoun Papers, No. 6113).

[125] Amherst's *Journal*, pp. 141–3; Colonel Robertson to Loudoun, July 20, 1759, Loudoun Papers, No. 6126.

[126] Amherst's *Journal*, p. 143.

[127] Vaudreuil to Bourlamaque, April 16, 1759, Bourlamaque Mss., 5:55–8 (Canadian Archives Transcripts).

Lake Champlain as early as possible in order to strengthen the weak garrisons that had been retained at Crown Point and Ticonderoga.[128] Later he was also given small detachments from battalions of La Sarre, Royal Roussillon, Languedoc, Guyenne, and Béarn.[129] Early in May, with three thousand regulars and a thousand colonial troops, he proceeded up the Richelieu under orders to establish his camp at Fort Ticonderoga.[130] Under instructions received from Vaudreuil on May 5, he had been commanded to complete the entrenchments there and to make the strongest possible resistance should the enemy appear, with the assurance that he would be strongly reinforced should it seem necessary.[131] This was quite consistent with the Governor General's views of an expanded defence of Canada. On May 20, however, after news had reached Quebec respecting the designs of the enemy to attack the colony in force from all quarters, these instructions were superseded by others that, consistent with Montcalm's views, provided for the contraction of the defences of New France so that mutual aid could more easily be extended by those in charge of military operations on the various frontiers. The brigadier was therefore ordered to be prepared to abandon Fort Ticonderoga whenever the enemy appeared in strength on Lake Sacrament (George); in doing so he was to take steps to make the place as useless as possible to the British and was then to fall back behind Riviére La Barbue and remain there until Fort St. Frédéric had likewise fallen; thereupon he was to retire to the Isle-aux-Noix.[132]

By the latter part of May, Bourlamaque was established at Fort Ticonderoga and proceeded to send scouting parties in the direction of Fort Edward to secure information about the movements of the enemy. He was thereby informed of Amherst's march from that place to Lake George, and by deserters from the British army was also made aware of its immediate objective. On July 20 with the news of the approach of the enemy, and in order to delay their operations, he determined to receive them and to make at least a token

[128] Montcalm to Bourlamaque, April 16, 1759, Lettres de M. de Bourlamaque au Chevalier de Lévis (ed. Abbé Casgrain), pp. 308–9.
[129] Montcalm to Bourlamaque, May 20, 1759, ibid., p. 318.
[130] Montcalm to Belle-Isle, May 8, 1759, N. Y. Col. Doc., X, 970. However, Bourlamaque had at Ticonderoga only a force of two thousand three hundred men. The rest of his troops were posted along the way (Bourlamaque to Belle-Isle, November 1, 1759, ibid., X, 1054).
[131] Bourlamaque Mss., 5:199–206 (Canadian Archives Transcripts).
[132] Ibid., 5:215–26.

stand behind the entrenchments that had served so well when Abercromby attacked the French the preceding year. The force of some three hundred Indians that had been sent to him by Rigaud refused to move forward, however, and without their support an advance beyond the fort could not be risked. Then, when it was clear that the enemy had actually landed and were marching along the portage road, and after a report had been received that three thousand men were moving on Fort St. Frédéric, which would place them in his rear, he decided to retreat.[133] But before doing so the following night, he mined the place and left behind as a rear guard a force of four hundred men under Captain d'Hébercourt, a resourceful and energetic soldier who had commanded there during the two preceding winters. D'Hébercourt had orders to delay the enemy as much as possible before blowing up the fort and retiring from it with his rear guard. [134]

It is remarkable that for four days the weak French force held Amherst's large army at bay, vigorously cannonading his advancing lines both by day and by night.[135] It may be noted with respect to this advance that whereas Abercromby had insisted in 1758 that his heavy artillery could not be brought up to support his line without great delay, Amherst by the 24th was bringing up his twenty-four-pounders as well as other guns and by the following day had them in place to support the forward movement of his men against the fort; and, not aware of the actual situation there, by the 26th he was actually in position to pulverize the French bastion.[136] The night of the 26th, however, he and his men saw the glare of fire at Ticonderoga and soon afterward heard the report of an explosion. The French rear guard had finally left, after spiking the guns and setting a match to the fuse of the mine planted underneath the magazine of the fort. D'Hébercourt thereupon rejoined Bourlamaque,

---

[133] For an account of the movements of Bourlamaque at Carillon and his retreat from that place and Fort St. Frédéric, see Bourlamaque Mss., 5:313-24 (Canadian Archives Transcripts).

[134] Bourlamaque to Belle-Isle, November 1, 1759, N. Y. Col. Doc., X, 1055.

[135] Ibid. See also Amherst's Journal, pp. 143-6. When Vaudreuil heard the news of the evacuation and destruction of Ticonderoga by d'Hébercourt, he wrote to Bourlamaque expressing deep regret that the captain did not hold out for fifteen days longer. Bourlamaque replied that, according to a letter addressed to him on June 1 by the Governor General, the latter informed him that he was to conform strictly to his earlier instruction to the effect that "it was better to save the garrison than to gain some days" (Lévis to Vaudreuil, August 10, 1759, Lettres de Bourlamaque, p. 24).

[136] Amherst's Journal, pp. 143-6.

who was encamped two and a half leagues from Carillon, and then the reunited French force retreated to Crown Point. In view of the fact that Fort St. Frédéric there could not be defended against artillery, it in turn was blown up on the 31st. The little army now retired down the Richelieu to Isle-aux-Noix, where the building of defences had been going on since the spring of the year as the result of the directions given by the Chevalier de Lévis.[137]

Bourlamaque with his little army — now increased to some 2,900 men, of which about 1,200 were Canadian militia [138] — was at last prepared to make a determined stand in accordance with his orders. But to protect his flanks he decided that it was necessary to attempt to dam the waters of the Richelieu on either side of Isle-aux-Noix so as to inundate the adjacent woods, which were now dry and passable, whereas earlier in the year they had been swampy. He therefore set about this labour; he also lengthened the entrenchments already constructed on the island and provided embrasures in them for the artillery — all the while anxiously awaiting the appearance of Amherst.[139] As it was by no means clear to him that he could prevent the enemy from reaching Fort St. Jean, the Chambly, and then the St. Lawrence in his rear, he also took steps to concentrate on the island sufficient food supplies so that should he thus be cut off from his main base, he could hold out at least for some weeks.[140]

The movements of the British commander-in-chief were marked with great caution, however. In fact, it was not until the second week in October that he was prepared to move against Bourlamaque's

---

[137] At first it had seemed to de Lévis, and Bourlamaque had agreed with him, that the Isle-aux-Noix was too large in extent and also too far separated by the waters of the Richelieu from the mainland to serve the purpose of defending the approaches to the St. Lawrence by way of Lake Champlain. Bourlamaque, in fact, had strongly preferred to see the real defences established at La Point à Margot, half a league to the south of Isle-aux-Noix, where the river becomes very narrow. One of his chief objections to the island was that he was fearful that the enemy might outflank him by using the Rivière du Sud to get to the Rivière St. Jean below it and thus cut him off (Bourlamaque to Lévis, May 28, 1759, Lettres de Bourlamaque, p. 10). It was found on investigation, however, that the Rivière du Sud was not navigable, and his mind was put to rest as to the defensibility of the Isle-aux-Noix when the Chevalier, after inspecting the place with care late in the month of May, outlined his plan of throwing jetties across the divisions of the river, building redoubts over the water, and massing artillery on the island itself (Lévis to Bourlamaque, May 23 and June 2, 1759, Bourlamaque Mss., 3:83–6, 91–4, Canadian Archives Transcripts; Bourlamaque to Lévis, June 10, 1759, Lettres de Bourlamaque, p. 11).

[138] Ibid., p. 16.

[139] Bourlamaque to Lévis, August 8, 1759, ibid., pp. 13–14.

[140] Bourlamaque to Montcalm, August 7, 1759, ibid., pp. 19–21.

defences. He felt not only that it was necessary to restore Ticonderoga to its former strength, in so far as was possible, and to build a really substantial fort at Crown Point to take the place of Fort St. Frédéric, in harmony with Pitt's orders, but that it was equally necessary, before making an advance, to deprive the French of the control they enjoyed over Lake Champlain because of the presence on its waters of a schooner and three xebecs, all heavily armed with cannon that could easily sink his whaleboats and bateaux.[141] Therefore his troops were immediately employed in fortification construction [142] and in the building of a brigantine and a great radeau or raft, eighty-four feet in length and provided with sails, capable of carrying six twenty-four-pounders. He also, while thus engaged, laid out a road to No. 4 on the Connecticut, sent out parties to scout about Isle-aux-Noix and Fort St. Jean and to explore the source of the Hudson River and the course of Otter Creek, which flows into Lake Champlain from the southeast, and even sought to find an approach, by way of Rivière aux Sables, flowing into Lake Champlain from the west, to Oswegatchi (La Galette) on the upper St. Lawrence.[143] Then, on September 13, he sent out the redoubtable Major Robert Rogers with some two hundred and twenty of his rangers to destroy the settlement of Christian Indians living on the St. Francis River, which flows into the St. Lawrence from the south midway between Montreal and Quebec.

The general had been exasperated with the conduct of the St. Francis Indians in violating a flag of truce sent to them by Captain Kennedy and a party without arms who were trying to make their way to Wolfe's headquarters, as well as by the long history of their bloody forays, especially against the British New England settlements.[144] It may also be added that he could not have assigned a duty more agreeable to the rangers. After going as far north as possible in their bateaux, they moved by stealth through the woods and then on October 5, upon arriving in the vicinity of the Indian village,

---

[141] Bourlamaque to Belle-Isle, November 1, 1759, *N. Y. Col. Doc.*, X, 1055; Amherst to Pitt, October 29, 1759, *Pitt Correspondence*, II, 189.

[142] Three forts at Crown Point were now erected: the Grenadier Fort, the Light Infantry Fort, and Gage's Fort, ibid., II, 191.

[143] *Amherst's Journal*, pp. 148–64.

[144] Rogers declared in his "Journal" that to his knowledge the St. Francis Indians during the six years past had killed or carried off six hundred people; in fact, there was that number of scalps hanging on poles over the doors of their huts when he entered their village (*Reminiscences of the French War Containing Rogers' Expeditions*, p. 91).

divided into three parties. Just before dawn of the 6th they closed in on it and without compunction put the torch to it and proceeded to shoot from the banks those few Indians who, to escape the flames, managed to take refuge in the water.[145] After this retribution had been meted out, the party, separating into small detachments and under the most painful conditions, finally returned to Crown Point in November by way of the upper Connecticut, not daring to retrace the path to their boats.[146]

It may here be pointed out that early in September Amherst received information that Bourlamaque at Isle-aux-Noix was building another vessel pierced for sixteen guns for the purpose of retaining supremacy on Lake Champlain by means of it and the four other vessels already in service. He was therefore led to give orders to Captain Loring to set about the building of a sloop of equal firepower and to send a party of sailors and good swimmers down to Isle-aux-Noix with fire-darts to seek by night to burn the French vessel still on the stocks; but the attempt met with failure.[147] From this time until well into October preparations for the expedition down the lake were continued, and then on the 11th, with the new sloop at last completed and armed and the brigantine and radeau in readiness, the general was at last able to give orders for the advance of his whaleboats and flat-bottomed bateaux. The armada thereupon moved slowly northward in four long columns flanking the radeau and preceded by the brigantine and the sloop, which sailed well ahead in order to engage the enemy fleet and were soon out of sight.[148]

---

[145] For Amherst's orders to Rogers to spare the women and children — orders that were ignored — see ibid., pp. 86–7.

[146] Bourlamaque received information that seventeen British boats capable of carrying two hundred and fifty men had been discovered in the Bay of Missicoui. Suspecting a design against some French settlement or the St. Francis village, on September 29 he sent word to the Chevalier de Lévis and a warning to de Longueil and the missionary to the St. Francis Indians. This warning, however, did not reach the Indian village in time to save it (Bourlamaque to Lévis, September 29 and October 7, 1759, Lettres de Bourlamaque, pp. 49, 55).

[147] Amherst's Journal, p. 168; Bourlamaque to Vaudreuil, September 12, 1759, Lettres de Bourlamaque, p. 44.

[148] According to Bourlamaque, the British who left Crown Point on the 11th numbered between ten and twelve thousand men — a figure greatly exaggerated. He declared that their advance guard consisted of one hundred and sixty bateaux, a brigantine armed with twenty eighteen-pounders, a senau as strong as the French schooner, many bateaux armed with large cannon, and a craft carrying six twenty-four-pounders (Bourlamaque to Lévis, October 17, 1759, Lettres de Bourlamaque, p. 61; Bourlamaque to Belle-Isle, November 1, 1759, N. Y. Col. Doc., X, 1056). With respect to the troops involved

By the 12th the French vessels were sighted by Amherst, who was stationed on the radeau, and he then realized that his own two warships were well in advance of them and could offer no assistance. To guard against disaster he immediately ordered the bateaux to move into one column along the western shore, and the artillery boats to advance abreast. Then as night fell, with the weather unfavourable and the men, who had been rowing, nearing exhaustion, he sought cover in the bay formed by the Rivière aux Sables and ordered his men ashore. During the following week it was very stormy, with a steady, hard wind from the north that held him fast, and, further, the temperature dropped to freezing.[149] On the 14th, while still in the bay, he received a letter from Captain Loring, in command of the two vessels, giving an account of his proceedings.

Loring reported that on the 12th his ships had run aground in chasing the French schooner, but that he luckily had got them afloat without suffering damage; soon after this incident and on the same day he fortunately discovered the three French xebecs and in giving chase ran them into a bay and then stood guard over the entrance during the night to prevent their escape. As a result the enemy, he indicated, sank two of them and ran the third ashore.[150]

Thus culminated Amherst's drive against the Isle-aux-Noix and the upper St. Lawrence. For on the 19th the general, still compelled to keep to the shelter of the protecting bay, but now informed of the capture of Quebec by letters from Gage at Oswego and de Lancey in New York,[151] came to the resolution that since he could hardly reach the French advanced defences within another ten days, it would be impossible to carry out his design to attack Bourlamaque and to send a strong detachment of his regulars to destroy the set-

---

in the expedition, it should be pointed out that Amherst left the provincials at Crown Point to continue the work on the three forts or bastions there and took with him only some forty-three hundred regulars (Amherst to Ligonier, October 22, 1759, Amherst Papers, 11:26–8, Canadian Archives Transcripts; Huck-Saunders to Loudoun, October 13, 1759, Loudoun Papers, No. 6145).

149 Amherst's Journal, pp. 179–82.

150 Ibid., p. 181. The French schooner that, with the xebecs, had given the French control of Lake Champlain succeeded in escaping Captain Loring by slipping into the Bay of Missicoui (Bourlamaque to Lévis, October 17, 1759, Lettres de Bourlamaque, p. 62). The three xebecs, two of which had been sunk in fairly shallow water, and the third beached, as indicated in the text, were soon afterward put afloat and were thus important acquisitions for the British in connection with the advance made the following year.

151 Amherst's Journal, p. 182; J. Appy to Pownall, October 18, 1759, War Office, 34:347–8.

tlements on the south shore of the St. Lawrence and surprise Montreal. He therefore determined to retire with his army.[152] This he proceeded to do without interference and on the 21st reached Crown Point. During the following month he gave his chief efforts to getting the defences there and at Ticonderoga in proper condition for garrisoning part of his regulars and some of the rangers during the winter season and also to getting the provincials, now terribly homesick and in so mutinous a frame of mind that they would no longer work on the fort, back to their respective colonies.[153] Then, in freezing weather, he departed on November 25 with the remainder of his troops for Albany and New York.

In considering the results of Amherst's campaign, it may be said that the driving of the French from their positions at Ticonderoga and Crown Point was highly important from the standpoint of the protection of the Hudson Valley area and the restoration of the British settlements made earlier to the north of Albany in the area of Fort Edward and Lake George.[154] Of equal importance was the forced desertion by the French of three of their vessels, giving to the British, when they were floated, an undisputed command for the first time of Lake Champlain. Whether the general can justly be accused of inaction and timidity in not accomplishing more than he did is by no means clear. It is certain that Bourlamaque was convinced in August that it was feasible for the British during the season of settled dry weather in that month and September to move through the woods around his position and to fall upon weak Fort St. Jean and La Prairie, the latter lying on the south shore of the St. Lawrence; [155] but it is equally certain that the French leader, who had been heavily reinforced early in October, had laid his plans to bring a check, if not disaster, to the British by means of an ambuscade with most of his forces if such an attempt was made.[156] Moreover, it is now evident that Vaudreuil was concentrating at

---

[152] Amherst's *Journal*, pp. 182–3. Amherst to Ligonier, October 22, 1759, Amherst Papers, 11:26–8 (Canadian Archives Transcripts).

[153] Amherst's *Journal*, pp. 183–95. At Crown Point Amherst left the Inniskilling Highlanders and two hundred rangers and at Ticonderoga the late General Forbes's regiment (Amherst to Pitt, December 16, 1759, *Pitt Correspondence*, II, 224).

[154] On September 21, 1759 a proclamation was issued calling upon the people to return to their settlements formed in this region (*New York Documentary History*, III, 556).

[155] Bourlamaque to Vaudreuil, August 7, 1759, *Lettres de Bourlamaque*, pp. 20–2.

[156] Bourlamaque to Montcalm, August 7, 1759, *ibid.*, p. 14; John Knox: *Historical Journal*, II, 180.

Montreal — at the very time when the British general moved down the lake with hope of surprising that place — large numbers of troops,[157] which would have given the British detachment, had it ever arrived there, a very warm reception indeed. Finally, it may be pointed out that Bourlamaque, in indicating that Amherst during the summer season might have been able to outflank him, did not take into account the factor of logistics that confronted the British army — especially with the French still in control of the lake with their heavily armed vessels. That this naval predominance could have been eliminated earlier than it was is hard to believe under actual conditions then facing Captain Loring and his shipbuilders.[158] That Amherst should have attempted to move his forces from Crown Point so great a distance through the woods and swamps on either side of Lake Champlain would hardly have been in harmony with sound military procedure. This is so in view of the fact not only that he had little Indian support, and that quite worthless, but that every mile that carried him in advance through the wilderness would take him farther away from his base of supplies and would bring him closer to Bourlamaque at Isle-aux-Noix and to the very mobile force of French and Indians commanded by the Chevalier de Lévis in the Montreal area which could be counted on to support those stationed at Isle-aux-Noix.

In bringing to conclusion this account of military operations in the regions of the Ohio Valley, Lake Ontario, and Lake Champlain for the year in question, it may be said that all of these were of the utmost significance in relation to the destruction of the French empire in North America. In the valley of the Ohio there had taken place a consolidation of British power with the construction of Fort Pitt; on Lake Ontario, Fort Niagara, the French bastion for the protection of the weak posts in the Great Lakes region, had fallen; and on Lake Champlain, with the loss of Ticonderoga and Crown Point and control of the lake itself, the French had been impelled to en-

---

[157] See the letter written by the Chevalier de Lévis to Vaudreuil on October 15, 1759, *Lettres du Chevalier de Lévis concernant la guerre du Canada, 1756–1760*, p. 238.

[158] Amherst to Pitt, October 22, 1759, *Pitt Correspondence*, II, 190–8. Richard Huck-Saunders writing to Lord Loudoun on October 25, in reply to the "Fault Finders," declared, in defence of Amherst's slowness of movement after the capture of Crown Point: ". . . I say we wanted Vessels of Force on Lake Champlain to face the Enemy, that our Batteaux, which were of themselves bad, suffered much in the Carriage over the Portage at Ticonderoga and wanted repairs, and that it was proper to build a Fort at Crown Point to secure our new Acquisitions and a safe retreat in Case of a Disaster" (Loudoun Papers, No. 6147).

trench themselves to the north of it, no longer able to menace the English to the south of Lake George, but simply to seek to protect from capture Montreal, Trois Rivières, and other settlements on the St. Lawrence still in their possession. Simultaneously with these developments, operations were taking place on that river that were destined to have an importance in world affairs difficult to overestimate. It is to a consideration of this phase of the Great War for the Empire that it is now necessary to turn our attention.

CHAPTER XII

Wolfe Ascends the St. Lawrence

W HEN PITT in the fall of 1758 set to work to evolve his plans for the next year's campaign in North America, it was clear to him that Amherst, as the commander-in-chief of the British forces in North America, should — because of the necessity of carrying on a constant correspondence with the governors and other British officials, both military and civil — remain constantly on the continent; [1] it was equally clear to him that the command of the proposed expedition up the St. Lawrence against Quebec that he expected to launch in the spring should be commanded by Brigadier General James Wolfe.

Wolfe, it may be borne in mind, had been ordered by Amherst after the fall of Louisbourg to proceed to the mouth of the St. Lawrence in a squadron commanded by Admiral Hardy, for the purpose of destroying the French settlements on the lower course of that river and on the gulf, with the hope of alarming the Canadian authorities and thus relieving the pressure they were applying to Abercromby about Lake George. With three battalions on board the fleet, the brigadier left Cape Breton Island on August 28; early in September he appeared in the Bay of Gaspé, where he landed his troops and destroyed the scattered settlement. Detachments were thereupon sent on similar missions to Miramechi Bay and to Pas-Beau, La Grand Rivière au Renard, and Mal-Baye; then, after conferring with Hardy as to the possibility of moving up the river as far as the island of Bic, to which the rear admiral was opposed, Wolfe

---

[1] *Correspondence of William Pitt* (ed. G. S. Kimball), I, 414–20.

determined at least to send a third detachment by land against the
fishing village of Les Monts Louis, located on the St. Lawrence some
thirty-two leagues to the west of Gaspé. With these things accomplished and with a number of the inhabitants taken prisoner, although most of them fled to the woods, the troops were placed on
board the ships and sailed for Louisbourg at the end of the month.[2]
While this feat added no glory to British arms and brought no relief
to Abercromby, it at least, with the disappearance of these fisheries,
served to deprive the people of Canada of some of their remaining
sources of sustenance and to that extent served a military purpose.
Soon after his return to Cape Breton Island the brigadier, having
obtained permission from Amherst to go home in order to regain
his health, set sail in Boscawen's flagship, the *Namur*, on October 1
and reached the Isle of Wight at the beginning of November.

When the report of Wolfe's arrival in England reached Pitt, the
latter was disconcerted. For, with the news of the fall of Louisbourg,
he had sent orders to him to remain in America for the next year's
campaign up the St. Lawrence — and now he suddenly had appeared in England. The brigadier, however, when he had heard of
the Minister's displeasure, was able to clear things up, especially
in view of the fact that the orders had not arrived when he left with
Boscawen and that he now signified to Pitt his readiness to go on the
projected service.[3] Nevertheless, had he been given his choice, he
confessed to a friend that he would have preferred to serve under
Prince Ferdinand on the Continent and in the cavalry, "because
Nature has given me good eyes, and a warmth of temper to follow
the first impressions."[4] In fact, he grumbled to a second friend that
it was his "fortune to be cursed with American service."[5] Yet there
he was, against his own desires, destined as the result of this service
to win immortal fame and the undying plaudits of the English-speaking peoples!

Wolfe was born of Yorkshire parents in southeastern England
in the year 1727. Of Welsh-Irish ancestry, he came of a family with
strong military inclinations. His father, Colonel Edward Wolfe of
the marines, had served with Marlborough in Flanders; after the

---

[2] Wolfe to Pitt, November 1, 1758, *ibid.*, I, 379–82.
[3] Wolfe to Pitt, November 22, 1758, *Correspondence of Chatham* (ed. Taylor and
Pringle), I, 371.
[4] Wolfe to Colonel Rickson, December 1, 1758, Beckles Willson: *Life and Letters
of James Wolfe*, p. 403.
[5] Wolfe to Captain Parr, December 6, 1758, *ibid.*, p. 404.

War of Jenkins's Ear broke out, he received the staff rank of adjutant general of the troops destined for the siege of Cartagena in the New World, and in 1740 young James, although but thirteen years of age, already committed to the idea of becoming a soldier, persuaded the colonel to agree to take him with him. But there were delays on board the fleet before it finally sailed in November, and the boy's weak constitution asserted itself over his desires, with the result that he had to be left behind. His determination to follow a military career, however, was unshaken, and shortly before the beginning of his fifteenth year he received a commission as second lieutenant in his father's regiment, which was at the moment in the area of the Spanish Main. Always a poor sailor and anxious for immediate action, he had an opportunity soon after this appointment to exchange it for an ensignship in the 12th regiment of foot, and with it he saw service on the Continent in connection with the first phase of the War of the Austrian Succession. There he so distinguished himself as acting adjutant in the Battle of Dettingen that he was promoted to the rank of lieutenant. His rise in rank, in spite of his youth, was now fairly rapid, serving as he did in Scotland and then again on the Continent and later in the Highlands on police duty. By the end of the war he had become a major and then in 1750 a lieutenant colonel in the 20th regiment, Lord George Sackville's. It was this unit that he brought to an unusually high level of discipline and morale.

While no student who has read his intimate correspondence is likely to disagree with Beckles Willson, a sympathetic biographer, that Wolfe was "intensely human, subject to error, not without vainglory, quick of temper, sanguine, emotional, vehement to a fault," [6] he was — perhaps because of some of these very qualities, combined with others — an officer of extraordinary ability. His success found its basis in his unceasing solicitude for the welfare of his men, his attention to every detail of his craft, his rigid standard of excellence, his quickness of perception, his ability to reach quick decisions, and his fire and spirit as a leader. While he remained physically weak, as a soldier he was a stranger to fear and he had the rare ability to impress upon those he commanded confidence in his leadership. In fact, among the officers that served with him on Cape Breton Island, there were those who were so impressed with his unusual combination of qualities that three of the most capable colonels (Monckton,

6 Willson, op. cit., p. 415.

Murray, and Burton) urged Amherst to consider him for the command of the St. Lawrence expedition.[7] Pitt therefore, in summoning Wolfe to Hayes, his county seat, and giving him this command, had laid his hand on a man who even with his infirmities was hailed by his associates in arms as a model of a soldier's soldier.[8]

With so heavy a responsibility resting upon the shoulders of this young Englishman, still in his early thirties, to bring the projected expedition, so full of hazards, to a successful termination, Pitt wisely saw that he was given in January the temporary rank of major general and that he should be offered the opportunity to recommend those who would form his staff. His choice fell upon two excellent men as brigade commanders already with American experience: Colonel Robert Monckton, whose activities in connection with the capture of Fort Beauséjour on the Acadian peninsula have been considered in the preceding volume of this series, and an old personal antagonist of the days of the Scottish campaign, Colonel James Murray, who also participated with him in the Louisbourg campaign and in it acquitted himself with high distinction. The third brigade commander was, it appears, recommended by Pitt, in the person of Colonel George Townshend — the brother of the more famous Charles Townshend — and was accepted.[9] Only when the request was made that Colonel Guy Carleton be permitted to act as quartermaster general on the expedition did Wolfe encounter difficulty. The King, who had taken exception to some slighting reference to the Hanoverians that Carleton had made, would only agree to his appointment after Pitt himself had represented to His Majesty the importance of permitting the new commander to have as aids men of his own selection so that, should he fail, he could not justly charge any lack of success to subordinates in whom he did not have confidence.

---

[7] Julian S. Corbett: *England and the Seven Years' War*, I, 398.

[8] There comes to the mind of the student the account left by Lord Temple of the remarkable dinner at Pitt's home at which Temple and Wolfe were the only guests. At this the latter — whether or not he had imbibed too freely before appearing is not known, but at least under the influence of deep emotion over the excesses of the French and Indians in waging war — "broke forth into a strain of gasconade and bravado. He drew his sword . . . he flourished it round the room," boasting of the mighty things it would achieve. All the while the ministers simply sat aghast. After he had left, Pitt, indeed, overwhelmed by the exhibition, lifted his eyes and arms and cried out: "Good God! that I should have entrusted the fate of the country and of the administration to such hands!" (Lord Mahon: *History of England*, IV, 153).

[9] Willson, *op. cit.*, p. 413–14. Townshend had expressed the desire to serve under Wolfe.

He also selected as adjutant general his old friend the energetic Major Isaac Barré, and finally, as chief engineer, Major Patrick Mackellar, already experienced in America. As Corbett points out, it was a "boys' campaign," with only Wolfe and Townshend among the general officers who were not under thirty years of age.[10]

As the enterprise was to be an amphibious operation, Anson had in the fall of 1758 strongly recommended that Rear Admiral Sir Charles Saunders, who had conducted himself well in the Mediterranean in the summer of 1758 and who had subsequently taken over from Hawke the patrol off Brest and the northwest coast of France, should be in charge of the fleet, and he was made a vice admiral for this service alone, as was true of Wolfe's promotion. Wolfe was pleased with this appointment, but not with that of Rear Admiral Philip Durell as second in command of the fleet. Durell, who had served with Boscawen in the Louisbourg campaign,[11] was at the time in American waters, left there by Boscawen with a part of the fleet.

On February 5 the secret instructions for the new commander were signed and sealed.[12] By these instructions he was called upon to embark at Portsmouth on a ship of war and proceed to Louisbourg, where the troops destined for the expedition would be concentrated. After taking over command of them, he was to proceed from Cape Breton Island on or about May 7 to the St. Lawrence to attack and reduce Quebec, if possible; should he be successful, he was to provide a sufficient garrison to retain possession of it and to make such repairs of its fortifications as were needed for this purpose. As to other operations that might to advantage be undertaken afterward that same year, any decision was to rest with him and with the commander of the fleet. After these services of whatever nature had been fulfilled, the troops that were no longer needed should be placed at the disposal of Amherst, as the commander-in-chief, to whom he himself should then report and whose orders he should thereupon follow. Finally, he was enjoined, as was Saunders

10 Corbett, op. cit., I, 409.

11 Writing to Pitt on December 24, 1758, Wolfe, after referring to certain other appointments, stated: "I will add, from my own knowledge, that the second naval officer in command there [in North American waters] is vastly unequal to the weight of business; and it is of first importance to the country that it [that is, the chief command of the navy] doth not fall into such hands" (Willson, op. cit., p. 407).

12 A copy of these is among the Earl of Amherst Papers, Packet 23 (Canadian Archives Transcripts).

in his instructions, to see that a good understanding was maintained between the land and sea forces.[13]

With the above instructions, very general in nature as was proper under the circumstances, Wolfe left Spithead on February 14 in the *Neptune*, Saunders's flagship, on his momentous undertaking. As has already been noted, Rear Admiral Durell had been retained in American waters when Boscawen returned home late in the fall of 1758. The former, who had with him a squadron of some fourteen vessels made up of ships of the line and frigates,[14] was ordered to be ready to begin to cruise in northern waters as early as possible the following spring, just as Hardy had done the spring of 1758.[15] Late in December Pitt wrote to Durell informing him of the proposed campaign up the St. Lawrence and called upon him to prevent by every means any aid arriving at Quebec with the opening up again of navigation, and, for this purpose, to be prepared to sail, as soon as it was safe to do so, up the river as far as the island of Bic, where he was to remain until further orders should come from Admiral Saunders.[16] This strategic move, it may be noted, had five days earlier been urged upon the Minister by Wolfe, who saw the importance of Bic and who had, in fact, sought, as has been made clear, to persuade Hardy, while the two were at the mouth of the river in the fall, to be willing to risk his ships by proceeding two hundred miles up the river as far as this island for the purpose of intercepting the fleet of the enemy preparing to return home from Quebec.[17] But Durell was still at Halifax when Wolfe and Saunders arrived on April 30, held there by ice floes that had up to that time impeded navigation in northern waters, as the result of the very severe and prolonged winter, and also by adverse winds.[18] Indeed, Saunders himself found that it was still impossible to approach Louisbourg on account of the ice packs when he attempted to do so on April 21.[19] Durell, however, ready to sail, was soon able to move

---

[13] The instructions to Saunders are to be found in Admiralty Papers, Secretary's Department, Out-letters, 2:1331.

[14] Boscawen to Pitt, September 13, 1758, *Pitt Correspondence*, I, 351.

[15] On July 28, 1758 Pitt had written to Boscawen ordering him to leave at Halifax for the winter ten ships of the line "with a proportionable number of Frigates" under an officer that the admiral might appoint (*ibid.*, I, 309).

[16] Pitt to Durell, December 28, 1758, *ibid.*, I, 445; Pitt to Saunders, January 9, 1759, A. Doughty: *The Siege of Quebec*, VI, 94.

[17] Wolfe to Pitt, December 24, 1758, Willson, *op. cit.*, p. 408.

[18] Saunders to Pitt, May 1, 1758, *Pitt Correspondence*, II, 92–3.

[19] *Ibid.* Captain John Knox under date of May 24 writes in his *Historical Journal of*

out upon his mission as a result of a change in the wind and the strengthening of his personnel by a detachment of troops, under command of Colonel Carleton, that Wolfe had furnished.[20] But before he could get into the river, two or three French frigates, convoying a number of provision and store ships, had preceded him and were able to reach Quebec.[21]

But while Durell was criticized by his superiors for not getting away earlier, Wolfe and Saunders were not able to keep to Pitt's timetable. April 20 was the date fixed for the concentration of the troops and the fleet at Louisbourg, preparatory to sailing for the St. Lawrence. It was May 13 before they could leave Halifax, and two days later before they were able to enter Louisbourg harbour; not until June 4, moreover, did they finally enter the gulf, with what contemporaries called "the finest squadron of His Majesty's Ships that had ever yet appeared in North-America." [22] Even then Wolfe could only count on a force of somewhat less than nine thousand men, rather than the twelve thousand that had been promised.[23] Many of the ten battalions, however, had already seen service in America, and the rest were eager to win laurels; [24] in fact, the only troops that troubled the general were the four companies of newly raised American rangers, whom he characterized in his customary overtones — doubtless thinking in terms of the superb appearance, discipline, and morale of his old regiment, the 20th — as "the worst soldiers in the Universe." [25] He was pleased, nevertheless, with his

the Campaigns in North America for the Years 1757, 1758, 1759, and 1760 (I, 254) of the presence about Cape Breton of "islands and floats of ice."

[20] Wolfe to Pitt, May 1, 1759, Willson, op. cit., p. 423; Saunders to Pitt, June 6, 1758, Pitt Correspondence, II, 115.

[21] Saunders mentioned seventeen merchant ships in his letter of September 5 to Pitt (ibid., II, 162); but the officers sent by Durell to the admiral when the latter reached Bic declared that "three frigates and ten transports had escaped them" (Captain Knox, op. cit., I, 281); still another officer, who was present, wrote: "At Isle Dubik [Bic] we had intelligence that two Frigates & 14 Transports, with Provisions stores & troops, had got up to Quebeck" (Military Affairs in North America, 1748–1765, ed. S. Pargellis, p. 433). This last total of sixteen ships agrees with the report made to the Minister of the Marine Berryer (the Minister to M. Desclaux, July 22, 1759, Canadian Archives Report, 1905, I, Part VI, 299).

[22] Pennsylvania Gazette, May 10, 1759.

[23] Wolfe to Major Walter Wolfe, May 18, 1759, Willson, op. cit., 427.

[24] The prevailing toast among the officers at Louisbourg was: "British colours on every French fort, post, and garrison in America" (Captain Knox, op. cit., I, 279).

[25] Willson, op. cit., p. 427. To Pitt the general wrote on June 6: "The four new Companies of Rangers are so very bad, that I expect no Service from them unless mixed with the Light Infantry" (Pitt Correspondence, II, 119).

three brigadiers, "all men of great spirit," he called them, and with the great train of artillery that Pitt had provided, and in writing to his uncle while still at Louisbourg, he expressed confidence that if both his army and that of Amherst displayed proper spirit, the war in North America should be brought to a conclusion during the year's operations. Indeed, he thought that with the least enterprise it could have been finished the preceding campaign.[26]

When the fleet raised anchor and headed for its destination, there were under Saunders's immediate command nine ships of the line,[27] thirteen frigates, sloops, and other ships of war, and one hundred and nineteen troop transports and supply and ordnance vessels, with others that were to follow from Boston having aboard pioneers for the work of making entrenchments, whaleboats, and necessary stores.[28] The first days out, the weather was clear but with occasional hard winds; on June 11 the headlands of Gaspé loomed up on the port side; on the 13th to the starboard appeared the deeply wooded and elevated outlines of Anticosti; and on the 15th, in approaching the entrance of the St. Lawrence, it was noted that even so late in the season the highlands on both north and south shores were covered with snow; only on the 16th was there fog, but it soon disappeared.[29] As the fleet moved slowly up the St. Lawrence, retarded by tides and the necessity of sounding, the men on board had full opportunity to observe the scene, so strange to most of them. One of them, Ensign James Miller, of Amherst's old regiment, the 15th, recorded his impressions:

"As you advance higher up, every object appears grand and sublime, nature here displays such luxury and majesty as commands veneration! Rivers like seas! Mountains reaching the clouds, covered with lofty trees; such variety of fish sporting around: sea-cows, seals, and porpuses." [30]

On the 18th the great fleet came to anchor in the neighbourhood of Bic and St. Barnabé.

Durell, who had reached Bic on May 22, where he had been or-

---

[26] Willson, op. cit., p. 429.
[27] Thirteen ships of the line under Durell had gone ahead.
[28] Saunders to Pitt, June 6, 1759, Pitt Correspondence, II, 116; Captain Knox, op. cit., I, 278.
[29] Ibid., I, 279–81.
[30] Ensign Miller's "Memoir of an Invalid," Earl of Amherst Papers, Packet 54, p. 25 (Canadian Archives Transcripts).

dered by Pitt to remain until receiving further instructions from
Saunders, had, however, interpreted these orders broadly and had
already left with most of his squadron so as to move up to the strategic Ile-aux-Coudres, near the rapids and close to Quebec — a wise
and enterprising step — and upon reaching it proceeded on the 28th
to land a detachment of Carleton's troops. There was now a pause
lasting for over two weeks. Then on June 14, mounting the famous
Traverse, some of his ships came to anchor off the Ile d'Orléans that
same day. While too late in arriving in the river, as already noted,
to intercept a convoy coming from France, he did take, as he proceeded up the stream, three other detached provision ships; he also
not only succeeded in laying his hands upon a number of experienced river pilots, who were decoyed to his squadron by the device
of raising French colours on those vessels that formed the van, but
what was perhaps of greater importance, in clearing the rapids successfully he was able to demonstrate that the "French Account of
the Navigation of the . . . St. Lawrence We found to be a Mere
Bugbear." [31] The student must therefore be careful, in seeking to
evaluate the services of those who participated in this great undertaking, not to permit the criticisms levelled by Wolfe and other contemporaries against the admiral to becloud his very genuine contribution to the ultimate success of the expedition.

Meanwhile the main fleet proceeded from Bic slowly up the river,
sounding at frequent intervals, the admiral in his flagship, the *Neptune*, and Wolfe in a thirty-two gun frigate, the *Richmond*. On the
20th the flotilla doubled the entrance of Tadousac Bay; then on the
23rd it came into the area of settlements and those on board beheld
everywhere at night signal fires lighted to warn of their approach.
When they neared Ile-aux-Coudres the necessity for especially careful sounding led to delays. While this was proceeding, the inhabitants along the shore directed a heavy but ineffective fire at the
sounding-boats and other craft, with the result, as Captain Knox
points out, that "these unhappy natives paid dear for this behaviour" [32] — in the subsequent burning of their habitations. On the 25th,
with a French pilot serving against his will on board each transport,
the ships passed the Traverse, called "a place of the greatest difficulty and danger between the entrance of the St. Lawrence and

---

[31] *Military Affairs in North America, 1748–1765*, p. 433; Captain Knox, *op. cit.*,
I, 282.
[32] *Ibid.*, I, 288-9.

Quebec," [33] and thereupon joined Durell's detachment upon the south side of Ile d'Orléans. In this undertaking so favourable was the weather and so skilful were the British navigators that of some two hundred ships not a single one was wrecked or suffered serious damage.[34] There was now presented to those on board the most delightful prospect: an ordered, well-cultivated countryside, undisturbed as yet by war; with its windmills, water-mills, churches, chapels, compact stone farmhouses (some thatched with straw and others with roofs of wood), and, finally, enclosed fields of flax, wheat, barley, and peas.[35] With the landing of the forces on the island the following day, Wolfe was now not more than five miles from his great objective. So near to him and yet, as he would discover soon enough, so difficult to grasp!

In turning now to a consideration of developments in New France, it is clear that the events of the year 1758 had left in the minds of the French in Canada a sense of satisfaction mixed with deep apprehension. There was the great victory of July 8 before Ticonderoga; but there was also the conquest of Louisbourg, bringing with it that of Cape Breton Island and Isle St. Jean; there was likewise the destruction of Fort Frontenac at the hands of the enemy; and, finally, that of Fort Duquesne by its own defenders. Both Vaudreuil and Montcalm felt keenly the desperate need of presenting clearly to the authorities at home the true situation of the colony, each from his own particular point of view. In August of that year Hugues Péan, town major of Quebec and one of a little circle that enjoyed the largest that Bigot dispensed, was sent to France by the Governor General.[36] Then, in November, with the reluctant consent of the latter, Montcalm's close friend and aide-de-camp, the youthful Bougainville, left on the *Victoire* — almost the last boat able to descend the river before it was closed by ice.[37] Also another friend and admirer went in the person of Doreil, commissary at war.[38]

---

[33] *Ibid.*, I, 290. The master of the transport *Goodwill*, according to Knox, who was on board this vessel, refused the services of the French pilot, being an experienced river navigator in European waters (*ibid.*, I, 290–1).

[34] Major Montcrief's "Journal," Doughty, *op. cit.*, V, 36.

[35] Knox, *op. cit.*, I, 292.

[36] *Documents Relating to the Colonial History of the State of New York* (ed. E. P. O'Callaghan), X, 879.

[37] *Ibid.*, X, 856; *Journal du Marquis de Montcalm* (ed. Abbé Casgrain), p. 482.

[38] While the Governor General wrote flattering letters of introduction to the Minister of the Marine and the Minister of War respecting both Bougainville and Doreil, in

Péan, on arriving, drew up a *mémoire* for the consideration of the ministry that emphasized the bad prospects for food the following year and the present near famine in view of the fact that the *habitants* by reason of their war activities had not been able to cultivate the land. As a result, he declared: "Many persons have died of hunger, and the number would have been greater had the King not subsisted a greater part of the people." He affirmed in this connection that the daily bread allotment in the colony had now been reduced from four ounces, a very low ration, to two ounces, and that farmers, who had given their wheat to subsist the army during its operations throughout the summer months, were able to rely only on "some vegetables and wild herbs." He, finally, stressed the point that, for its preservation, Canada must have provisions, ammunition, goods, and more soldiers by the following April, when the ice breaks up on the river.[39]

Bougainville, arriving at Versailles on December 20,[40] had a mission of great delicacy. He was responsible not only for emphasizing in person what Montcalm and Vaudreuil had pointed out in their letters — the great dangers that confronted Canada because of the powerful forces that the enemy was prepared to use in closing in on the colony during the next campaign and the dire need of military supplies and additional soldiers — but also for making clear the discouragements and embarrassments that Montcalm was labouring under, in view of the fact that he did not as field general enjoy the confidence of the Governor General. The differences in point of view between the two must now be considered.

Even after the resounding victory over Abercromby there had developed sharp divergencies between Montcalm and Vaudreuil over the failure of the former to carry out the instructions of his superior to pursue the retreating enemy with his entire army for the purpose of destroying the demoralized British troops — something that he felt was quite impossible under the circumstances. Then, after the surrender of Fort Frontenac, the two did not see eye

---

another letter to Berryer, the first-named Minister, he stated, respecting the two men: ". . . I have the honor to inform you, Monseigneur, that they do not understand the colony, and to warn you they are the creatures of M. de Montcalm" (Vaudreuil to the Minister of the Marine, November 3, 1758, quoted by Parkman: *Montcalm and Wolfe*, II, 172).

[39] N. Y. Col. Doc., X, 897–900.

[40] Bougainville to the Marquise de St. Véray, December 22, 1758, *Canadian Archives Report* (1929), p. 85.

to eye regarding the problem of the defence of Lake Ontario and also of Lake Champlain. Montcalm thought in terms of the concentration of the very limited forces of New France for the most effective defence of Quebec and Montreal; to him the preservation of these two places and the closely settled region between them was really the key to the salvation of the colony when peace should finally be declared. With this paramount objective in mind, he was strongly opposed to the distribution of any large number of his troops at such places as Niagara and Ticonderoga, with the possibility that they might be cut off and sacrificed; instead, he favoured preparing a strong defensive position on the upper St. Lawrence in the neighbourhood of Abbé Piquet's La Présentation Indian mission and another at the lower end of Lake Champlain, where preparations should be made to station powerful contingents. In harmony with this conception he would leave no more than five hundred soldiers at Niagara, which would not be so serious a loss should the place be invested and captured by the enemy with great numerical superiority; nor would he attempt to rebuild Fort Frontenac; further, he would mine both Fort Ticonderoga and Fort St. Frédéric at Crown Point on Lake Champlain so that they might be destroyed, as was Fort Duquesne, should the enemy approach them, also in great force; whereupon the defenders would retreat northward to a position prepared for them in the neighbourhood of Fort St. Jean, from which point the southern approach to the St. Lawrence could be more effectively defended.

In contrast, the Governor General was prepared to concentrate an army of over five thousand men in the area of Fort Niagara and Lake Ontario for the purpose of preserving the fort and re-establishing naval and military domination upon Lake Ontario with the rebuilding of Fort Frontenac. In this connection he was disposed to use these troops against Oswego if the enemy even in great force sought to reoccupy it; nor was he prepared to think of relinquishing the two forts on Lake Champlain without a real battle and, in contrast to Montcalm's views on military concentration, was therefore disposed to station at the two places on this lake during the next campaign between six and seven thousand men. He thus favoured the wide distribution of the colony's limited military power.[41]

As to the respective merits of the two contrasting strategic con-

---

[41] For the *mémoires* embodying Montcalm's and Vaudreuil's strategic conceptions see *N. Y. Col. Doc.*, X, 868–77.

ceptions, the student of military science today cannot easily come to a decision; for each has its undoubted merits. Had the French government been in a position to push up the St. Lawrence a sufficiently large number of transports and supply ships so as to double the actual military strength of Canada and to provision it at the same time, even Montcalm would undoubtedly have hesitated to give up without a hard struggle such places of military importance as Niagara, Ticonderoga, and Crown Point. Yet even with the hope of any such reinforcement dissipated, could a Governor General be expected easily to reconcile himself to the voluntary severance of the vast upper Great Lakes region from the colony and to the withdrawal from those places on Lake Champlain that hitherto had provided attributes of strength to New France? Would he likewise readily call in his forces from the lower St. Lawrence? Near miracles had already saved the colony during the earlier years of the war. Might not these still be expected to continue, so as to preserve it to the end? [42] Would mere numbers of troops, mere material resources, on either side necessarily determine the outcome? It is true that British military preponderance had been decisive in the case of Cape Breton Island and Cadaraqui and might be so in the case of the forks of the Ohio were the British army to advance from Loyalhanna. [43] But there were the brilliant victories at Oswego in 1756, at Fort William Henry in 1757, and at Ticonderoga just this year that seemed to prove that as against not only potential but actual superior numbers of troops and abundant supplies enjoyed by the enemy, leadership of high quality, troops of high spirit, and powerful Indian support more than overbalanced these advantages. Then why weakly surrender any part of His Most Christian Majesty's North American dominions without first defending it to the extreme? Might not such surrender mean permanent restriction of boundaries? What would be the value of New France were it limited at the peace to its three principal towns and the surrounding territory? Should not all be hazarded to preserve at least Canada intact, assuming that the Ohio Valley might be lost?

As against this line of reasoning could be advanced certain logical strategic concepts that coldly brushed aside all sentimental fac-

---

[42] Even Montcalm himself attributed his victory of July 8 to divine intervention (Montcalm to his mother, July 21, 1758, *Canadian Archives Report*, 1929, p. 73).

[43] These views were developed in September before the destruction of Fort Duquesne.

tors — powerful as these are in motivating the actions of men and frequently determining the outcome of such actions — in favour of grim military necessity. Montcalm felt that there were reasonable grounds for confidence in the survival of New France only were he free to limit the range of his military activities to a very restricted area and within it be able to utilize to the maximum his armed strength — and it is of interest that his views were later fully supported by France's greatest living soldier, the venerable Maréchal de Belle-Isle, Minister of War.[44]

When these clashing points of view came before the Council of State in December in the form of letters and *mémoires* received from Vaudreuil, Montcalm, and Bigot, the ministers came to the conclusion that this divergence in military policy between the two leaders was so serious a matter that it must be placed before His Most Christian Majesty in person with the recommendation that

> "it appears necessary that he should be pleased to grant the Marquis de Montcalm his recall, which he has demanded in the letter also annexed hereto, as his health and the debts that he has contracted do not permit him to continue his service." [45]

It seemed, in fact, best to replace him by the Chevalier de Lévis with the rank of Maréchal de Camp. The latter had come over to Canada with the Marquis, was already in line to succeed him in case of accident, could work much more easily with the Governor General, and was generally "beloved and esteemed by all the Troops and Militia of the Colony." [46]

Then it appeared that de Bougainville, armed with additional *mémoires* and able in person to present the views of Montcalm and

---

[44] Writing to Montcalm on February 19, 1759, Belle-Isle declared: "As it is expected that the entire efforts of the English will be directed against Canada, and that they will attack you at different points at once, it will be necessary that you confine your plan of defence to those that are most essential and most connected, in order that being concentrated on a smaller extent of country, you may be always enabled mutually to help one another to communicate with and to support each other" (*N. Y. Col. Doc.*, X, 944).

[45] On July 12, after the victory at Ticonderoga, Montcalm had written to Belle-Isle asking the Maréchal to procure his recall: "My health suffers, my purse is exhausted. At the end of the year I shall owe the Treasurer of the Colony ten thousand ecus. And more than all . . . the impossibility in which I am placed of doing good and preventing evil" (*ibid.*, X, 733). But after the fall of Frontenac he changed his view, feeling that "since the affairs of the Colony are getting bad, it is my duty to endeavor to repair them or to retard their ruin to the greatest extent of my power" (*ibid.*, X, 832).

[46] *Ibid.*, X, 907.

his staff, threw himself into the breach and brought to bear sufficient support for his leader [47] so that on December 28 the ministers reversed themselves, as recorded in one of their minutes which shows that they had come to place a new valuation on the man they had previously determined to recall. It is succinct and reads as follows: "On mature reflection, this arrangement [the plan to recall] cannot take place, as M. de Montcalm is necessary in the present conjuncture." [48]

This was not all. De Bougainville, soon after his arrival, indicated to de Crémille, associated with Belle-Isle at the War Office, that Montcalm would appreciate nothing so much as the rank of lieutenant general. His reply was: "Your general will be satisfied." Not only was this honour accorded to him, so that he now outranked Vaudreuil, but provision was made that he might meet his financial obligations; then, as a final testimony of faith in him, it was agreed by the court to provide that in case of the death of the present Governor General, his rival should take over the administration of New France.[49] To put the new lieutenant general on a surer footing and his mind at rest respecting his military functions and responsibilities, he was also assured, in a letter addressed to him in February of the new year by the Minister of the Marine, that Vaudreuil had been advised to consult him on all operations in the course of the coming campaign.[50] At the same time the Governor General and the Intendant were informed that they should not only do this but seek the field commander's advice on *all* matters of administration that related to the defence and preservation of the colony.[51] Even more pointedly, Vaudreuil was directed that he should not appear in person in the campaign "except it becomes a question of a decisive operation and of the marching of all the militia for the general defence of the colony," but, instead, should remain at the center of the colony and "show himself in the country, to encourage the old

---

[47] See his letter to Madame la Marquise de Montcalm of December 22, 1758 and that to Montcalm's mother of January 16, 1759 (*Canadian Archives Report, 1929,* pp. 85–7). Montcalm refers to Bougainville as "my ambassador" (Montcalm to Bourlamaque, May 15, 1759, *Lettres de M. de Bourlamaque au Chevalier de Lévis,* ed. Abbé Casgrain, p. 313).

[48] *N. Y. Col. Doc.,* X, 907.

[49] *Ibid.,* 939–40; de Bougainville to the Marquis de Montcalm, December 22, 1758, op. cit.

[50] The Minister to Montcalm, February 3, 1759, *Canadian Archives Report* (1905), I, part VI, 291.

[51] The Minister to Vaudreuil and Bigot, February 3, 1759, *ibid.,* VI, 292.

men and women to work the land." [52] In all this can be seen not only the presence of Bougainville but the hand of the powerful Belle-Isle, who now became Montcalm's avowed protector and who pledged the King that he himself would become responsible for his actions.[53]

If the ministry was anxious to place military matters in Canada upon the most effective basis, it was not less so regarding the whole question of the supply of the colony. Reports of notorious abuses had been coming in, particularly with respect to the sale of the King's provisions and goods to private speculators who in turn re-sold them back to the King at an enormous profit. Bigot's office was under suspicion, and yet the full truth of the peculations and frauds committed by the favoured few who surrounded the Intendant, headed by the knave Joseph Cadet, was not to come to light until later. Some facts were already evident, however, particularly the sale of a ship's cargo for eight hundred thousand livres that brought a profit of more than two millions to those engaged in the deal in reselling it to the government. "Can anything be imagined, more opposed to the welfare of the colony and more injurious to the King's interests, than this transaction," wrote the Minister coldly to Bigot. He also asked him as coldly regarding the extravagant sums involved in Indian relations — how it happened, for example, that, according to his accounts, the smallpox among the natives led to a million livres of extraordinary expenditures. As for the flood of card money that the Intendant was spreading about Canada to satisfy the claimants against the government who had furnished provisions and other supplies or labour on the fortifications and who could not be granted true bills of exchange or certificates against the royal treasury to be honoured on sight as payment thereof, he was warned that the colony was fast becoming an insupportable burden and he was forbidden to issue any further notes unless these were counter-signed by Vaudreuil.[54] Yet this device brought little relief.

France — overwhelmed with tremendous financial demands to maintain the armies in Germany, to subsidize other members of the alliance, and to support the war going on in various other parts of the world, and faced with a growing economic paralysis as the result of the destruction of so much sea-borne commerce — could

[52] The Minister to Vaudreuil, February 3, 1759, ibid.
[53] Belle-Isle to Montcalm, February 19, 1759, N. Y. Col. Doc., X, 944.
[54] Letters of January 19, 1757, Canadian Archives Report (1905), I, Part VI, 281; N. Y. Col. Doc., X, 936-9.

only give to Canada limited financial relief at this period, just as she could give but limited relief in the way of supplies and almost nothing in the way of military reinforcements. In fact, were goods and soldiers ever so abundant at home, yet, lacking the ability to send any large convoy across the Atlantic with safety, in the face of the British naval predominance, it would have been necessary for the government, in spite of the most urgent pleas for aid, to reconcile itself to sending but little outside of a new supply of ammunition and provisions for the army. Indeed, Montcalm was warned by Belle-Isle that the King was compelled to depend for the safety of Canada largely upon his "wisdom and courage, and the bravery of the Troops [already there]." [55]

Nevertheless, a fleet of merchant ships was loaded at Bordeaux with provisions that had been ordered by Bigot through his contractor, the Sieur Cadet,[56] and under escort of Captain Kanon left for Canada early in the spring. Only a few other vessels could be promised, however — two converted frigates and four privately owned ships — to be freighted at Brest and at Rochefort with munitions, artillery, clothing, and trading goods, as well as with about five hundred recruits.[57] Not all of this slender supply got through, it is clear.[58] Had it all succeeded in eluding the British ships, it would still have been small in comparison with the vast flotilla of British transports ultimately brought up the river by Saunders and sent from the British Isles and the North American colonies, loaded not only with troops but with an abundance of everything needful to sustain them in the campaign.

---

[55] *Ibid.*, X, 944.

[56] As early as the latter part of 1755 Intendant Bigot instituted the system of contracting with Cadet, who was in Canada, for all supplies to be brought to Canada for the use of the King. This the Minister of the Marine agreed to permit, as it seemed to offer certain advantages (the Minister to Bigot, March 31, 1756, *Canadian Archives Report*, 1905, I, Part VI, 223). This method of provisioning the King's troops in the colony was continued in spite of the appearance of abuses, especially with respect to the high prices agreed to by the Intendant with the contractor (the Minister to Bigot, May 1757, *ibid.*, VI, 238).

[57] The Minister to Vaudreuil and Bigot, February 3, 1759, *ibid.*, VI, 292. In this letter Berryer mentioned not only that supply ships would sail for Quebec from foreign countries under a neutral flag, but that "advantage should be taken of the offers of several English vessels for the same work." I have found no evidence that in the year 1759 any vessels other than French actually reached Quebec, outside of those that came under command of the British admirals. The question of trade with the enemy in the course of the war will be dealt with in a subsequent volume of this series.

[58] Montcalm to Belle-Isle, May 24, 1759, *N. Y. Col. Doc.*, X, 972.

As under the terms of his commission the Governor General was vested with the chief responsibility for caring for the defence of New France, Vaudreuil, after the departure of Bougainville for France, proceeded to develop his strategy along the lines that he had previously laid down, with the idea of preserving intact as much as possible of the King's possessions in North America by spreading out his forces. According to his matured plan of April of the new year for the defence of the outlying posts, de Lignery was to hold himself at Fort Machault on the upper Allegheny with his force to cover the approach to Lake Erie and to support the Indian tribes who were to continue to harass the English at the forks of the Ohio. If obliged by pressure of the enemy, he was to fall back to Presqu'Isle; at this place would be concentrated all the men available from the Illinois region and from Detroit, with the idea that should Niagara be threatened, these, united to de Lignery's force, would be prepared to come to its relief. At Niagara the energetic Captain Pouchot was to be placed in command, and subject to his orders would be between sixteen and seventeen hundred men, as well as the Indians living in the area of Toronto — the Missisauga and other tribes — who were to be assembled in the vicinity of the Niagara River. At Cadaraqui, about the ruins of Frontenac, the Sieur de Corbière was to scout with a detachment of French and Indians; on the upper St. Lawrence in the vicinity of La Présentation and at Pointe-au-Baril somewhat above it, another force of some four hundred was to be held under command of Benoist, and three corvettes were to be launched from Pointe-au-Baril and, when heavily armed with cannon, were to be in a position to re-establish naval supremacy on Lake Ontario.[59] At Fort Ticonderoga the two battalions of La Reine and Berry under Bourlamaque were to be stationed as soon as the season would permit, and these were to be supported by a thousand or twelve hundred Canadian regulars and also by three or four thousand militia, with the understanding that only under great pressure would they retreat north to the upper end of the lake. Finally, on the St. John, flowing into the Bay of Fundy, and at Miramichi Bay, on the Gulf of St. Lawrence, Captain de Boishébert was to encourage the refugee Acadians and the Indians in their activities against the English.

The above plan, involving the dispersion of the defensive power

[59] Before this report was made, two of the corvettes were well along toward completion.

of New France, was based upon Vaudreuil's conviction that the enemy would not undertake to ascend the St. Lawrence to Quebec. Yet even if this presumption proved to be incorrect, he indicated that he was not prepared to alter his primary arrangements. Should information arrive of the approach of the British up the river his supplemental secondary plan called for the evacuation of the farms on its lower banks, the concentration of the families of these farmers about Trois Rivières, the removal of their cattle and crops to Point Levy, on the south shore, and, with the arrival of the enemy fleet at the Isle-aux-Coudres, the attempt to burn it by means of fireships and rafts loaded with fireworks. Should this effort be unsuccessful, then and only then would every man available be utilized by Montcalm and de Lévis to defend the city and render the conquest "of this Colony a work of very great difficulty, not to say of impossibility." [60]

Here we have set forth the strategic conceptions for the defence of New France that Vaudreuil proceeded to implement. They undoubtedly have great merit, in spite of the mockery and scorn heaped upon them by Montcalm.[61] The latter in the spring of 1759, as during the preceding fall and winter, held firmly to his idea of military concentration and remained persuaded that the Governor General was influenced by "prejudices" and that "the Councils of Quacks are followed." [62] He was, very naturally, bitter that he was not consulted in the formulation of the defensive measures and doubtless he should have been.[63] Nevertheless, it is not clear how useful an attempt at collaboration on the part of these two high-spirited men would have been in light of the fact that their views were so far apart and also that the final responsibility for the safety of the colony rested squarely on the shoulders of Vaudreuil rather than Montcalm.

With the arrival of Bougainville at Quebec from France on May 9 bearing letters to Vaudreuil and Montcalm from the ministers, the tension between the two eased somewhat. Neither had gained a complete victory at home and each had been admonished to seek

---

[60] "Summary of the Plan of General Operations for the campaign of 1759," N. Y. Col. Doc., X, 952–6.

[61] See his letters addressed to Bourlamaque of March 8 and 31, 1759, "Lettres du Marquis de Montcalm à M. de Bourlamaque" in Lettres du M. de Bourlamaque au Chevalier de Lévis (ed. Abbé Casgrain), pp. 287–9, 305–8.

[62] Montcalm to de Cremille, April 12, 1759, N. Y. Col. Doc., X, 959.

[63] Montcalm to Belle-Isle, April 12, 1759, ibid., X, 960–2.

concord with the other. While no very fundamental alterations were made in the plan of campaign, a much larger force than the Governor General had previously intended was concentrated in the area of La Présentation when the Chevalier de la Corne, a colonial captain, was now ordered there with fifteen hundred men to guard the upper end of the rapids in the river near that strategic post, in harmony with the views of Montcalm. Also the colonials previously intended to support Bourlamaque's battalions at Ticonderoga were now directed to be stationed at the bottom of Lake Champlain at the Ile-aux-Noix under Rigaud de Vaudreuil, Governor of Montreal, for the purpose of preparing strong defences at that point, to be carried out under the supreme direction of the Chevalier de Lévis, now placed in charge of the defence of Montreal and its environs. These were designed to receive Bourlamaque's forces in case of retreat and constituted another modification of the Vaudreuil plans to conform to the views of his rival.[64]

As Bougainville brought information respecting the plans of the British to send a large army up the river, Montcalm, with other arrangements completed, was permitted to leave Montreal for Quebec on the 21st and, upon arriving there, threw himself vigorously into the work of preparing for the defence of the capital of New France. The day following his coming, five ships, in addition to those that had already appeared under convoy of Captain Kanon, reached the city with the news that a part of the English fleet was now at St. Barnabé, about seventy-eight leagues from Quebec.[65] There was no time to lose. The captains of the ships that had arrived were called into conference and exhorted to co-operate in every way in the use of their vessels and the employment of their crews on land to aid in the construction of entrenchments along the river St. Charles. Montcalm proposed to them that, in order to block the Traverse, ten of the largest ships be sunk at that point, and Captain Duclos agreed to construct a floating battery. That night the signal fires down the river blazed their warning of the approach of the enemy fleet, and with this confirmation of the report brought that very day (the 23rd), the Marquis hurried dispatches off to the Governor General, still in Montreal, and others to the commanders of such troops as had wintered at Trois Rivières and at Montreal and were still available for the protection of Quebec, to hurry down with

---

[64] Op. cit., X, 993.
[65] Montcalm's Journal, p. 523.

them.[66] The night of the 24th Vaudreuil himself arrived and confirmed all of the orders that Montcalm had given in the emergency.[67]
The next day the owners of sheds along the quay of the lower town
were ordered to téar them down, that batteries might be constructed
there — as for the last two years had been contemplated but had not
been carried out.

While they were in the midst of carrying out these defensive
measures, a courier arrived on the 26th from the lower river to report that from fifty to sixty sail were off the island of Bic and ten
at Ile Verte. The effect of this ominous news was to spread fright
among the Quebec people, "who roundly cursed their governor and
his manner of governing." [68] What was equally ominous was that
that very day a northeasterly gale set in — as favourable to speeding
the ships of the enemy up the St. Lawrence to Quebec as it was to
retarding the movement of their own down the river with troops
for its defence from Montreal and Trois Rivières — and it continued
blowing for days, in spite of the prayers to heaven on the part of the
defenders of the city.[69] Nevertheless, the relief troops began to arrive on the 27th and continued to appear during the days that
followed, in face of the adverse wind. On June 8 Montcalm was
therefore able to include among his man-power resources the following units: five French battalions; the marine troops and the militia
of Montreal and Trois Rivières, totalling some five thousand; some
two hundred Indians; and, finally, three thousand men living within
the jurisdiction of the government of Quebec who had not as yet
been mobilized because they were apparently engaged in other
necessary activities. These, with twelve hundred more militia requested from Montreal and Trois Rivières, would make a total of
about twelve thousand men capable of defending the city and its
immediate environs on the north shore. It was found, unhappily, that
neither the Ile-aux-Coudres nor Ile d'Orléans could be secured, and
steps were immediately taken to bring their inhabitants over the
river to the city, so that when Durell finally appeared off these islands he found the homes on them deserted.

While the entrenchments along the St. Charles and those at Beauport were being pushed toward completion as well as the battery in

---

[66] Ibid., pp. 523-4.
[67] Ibid., p. 525.
[68] Ibid.
[69] Ibid., p. 526.

the lower town of Quebec, the preparation for sending the fire-ships against the enemy was rushed. On the 11th these vessels began slowly moving down the river, but still above Quebec, awaiting the critical moment when they should be ignited. By that date thirty-two British ships were counted by the engineer de Léry between Cap Tourmente, in the environs of Quebec, and Bic. If most of these ships could be disposed of, by means of fire and floating batteries placed on rafts, it was felt that it might well be the beginning of a great British disaster. But nature had become an ally of the invaders, and on the 13th another powerful wind from the northeast set in, which not only held back the fire-ships but the following day helped to carry eight of Durell's vessels up the Traverse and to the southeast shore of Ile d'Orléans.[70] An attempt was thereupon made to burn them with red-hot shot when Vaudreuil permitted Mercier of the artillery to cross over to the island with four twelve-pounders and a supporting force. But the British ships moved out of range. Nor was the plan to send rafts prepared with fireworks realized when the Canadians called upon to accompany these in their canoes refused point-blank to go on this perilous mission.[71]

On the 22nd eighty-four of Saunders's vessels were reported to have reached the Islets aux Pelerins, about halfway between Bic and Quebec, and, continuously favoured by the wind, moved forward unimpeded. As a result, on the 27th Montcalm grimly recorded in his *Journal* the presence of an immense line of enemy ships between Point Levy on the south shore of the river and Ile d'Orléans.[72] Nor in doing so was he sparing in his praise of the English navigators who, in making the ascent of the river, had profited by every wind and every tide to move forward even by tacking and who had been able when the ships were in the midst of the narrow Traverse to steer them to safety even when so violent a storm took place that he was persuaded that under similar conditions a French fleet would have perished.[73] And now, at last, the English fleet was massed in the vicinity of Quebec!

---

[70] *Ibid.*, pp. 543–4.

[71] *Ibid.*, pp. 547–8.

[72] *Ibid.*, p. 538.

[73] *Ibid.*, pp. 559–60. It should be pointed out, to clarify Montcalm's reference to the storm, that hardly had Saunders come to anchor off the southeast shore of Ile d'Orléans when a most violent storm of hurricane proportions struck the ships. While the sailors handled the vessels superbly and succeeded in saving every one of them, many of the ships' boats, launches, and even whaleboats were lost (Saunders to Pitt, September 5, 1759, *Pitt Correspondence*, II, 159).

The moment had arrived, it was felt, when, if ever, an attempt must be made to ruin Wolfe's enterprise. The evening of the 28th the French fire-ships and rafts therefore left their moorings and began the descent of the river so as to run into the midst of the English vessels. These, however, were set afire three leagues away from their objectives. One of them exploded prematurely, destroying the captain and the crew, others became stranded and burned even in sight of Quebec, and still others that approached the fleet with grenades bursting were beached by British sailors, who jumped into their boats, grappled these burning infernos, and then rowed for the shore.[74] Although this enterprise failed, the French by this time were thoroughly entrenched below the city along the northern shore with bristling batteries erected at strategic points on the elevation above the beach as far down as the falls of the Montmorency, eight miles below the city.[75] Likewise, in the lower town Montcalm had massed his batteries so that any attempt upon it seemed suicidal; in the upper town the great guns also frowned menacingly upon the enemy; and above the city stretched the lofty rimrock of the cliff with scarcely a break. What would or could Wolfe do against these formidable defences both natural and prepared?

It is clear that the British general had underestimated the military acumen of the French command. For he had laid his plans to throw his army upon the north shore to the west of the St. Charles and to establish strong posts between that river and Beauport so as to cut the city off from any communication with the lower river; he also expected to establish secondary posts on the south shore of the St. Lawrence from the Point Levy west to the Chaudière.[76] But having landed his army on Ile d'Orléans on the 27th, preparatory to taking these steps, and after reconnoitring the enemy's position from the western part of the island, he was made to realize that the northern shore was closed to him and only the south shore was open. As a

---

[74] Ensign James Miller's "Memoir," op. cit. In this connection Miller writes: "Consider what our feelings must have been, when we saw the fire-ships driving down on our fleet; had they [our vessels] been destroyed, we must have surrendered to the enemy for want of provisions." Captain Knox (op. cit., I, 298) also declared: "Nothing could be more formidable than those infernal engines were on their first appearance, with the discharge of their guns, which was followed by the bursting of grenado's, also placed on board in order to convey terror into our army."

[75] See Montcalm's Journal for June 27, 1759, p. 559.

[76] Wolfe to Major Walter Wolfe, May 19, 1759, Willson, op. cit., p. 428.

result he was obliged to limit his immediate action to sending
Monckton with four battalions to occupy unfortified Point Levy,
which was especially necessary in order to provide Saunders with
a more advantageous anchorage for his vessels than they enjoyed in
the narrow passage off the southeast shore of Ile d'Orléans. This
was done on the 30th after some sharp skirmishing with the French,
numbering about a thousand, and thereupon entrenchments were
thrown up at this place and also farther to the west directly opposite the city at Point de Pères, where batteries of heavy guns were
installed for the purpose of bombarding the city.[77]

The movement of Monckton's brigade to the south shore also gave
Wolfe the opportunity of issuing a manifesto to the people of Canada, which was posted on the door of the church at Beaumont, a
village to the south of the point. In this he declared that the King
of Great Britain was not making war on "the industrious peasant,
the sacred orders of religion, or the defenceless women and children" and that the inhabitants were therefore free to remain in
their homes and work their farms without molestation and to enjoy
their religion in security. They were at the same time warned, however, that should they appear in arms, they might expect as a consequence the destruction of their habitations and harvests and the
exposure of their sacred temples to an exasperated soldiery, and all
the distress that would follow in light of the fact that their only
avenue of relief was now cut off.[78]

While studying the problem of a proper approach to the city,
Wolfe sent Brigadier Townshend to establish entrenchments at the
western end of d'Orléans, and by the time these were completed and

---

[77] After the capture of Quebec, Captain Knox was informed by the fort major of
the city and by other officers (*Journal*, I, 307) that Montcalm, fearing the possible
consequences that might result should the British ascend the river and seize Point
Levy, had earlier proposed to Vaudreuil that strong works be erected there and supported by a garrison of some four thousand troops, but was overruled by the Governor
General, who insisted that Quebec could not be effectively bombarded from that point.
As a consequence, it was never fortified. When Montcalm on the 30th saw the beginning of the British movement against it, he hurried into the city from the lines to request
Vaudreuil to send a large detachment there to defend it, but while in conference a body
of Indians appeared with an English prisoner, who, on being questioned, deposed that
a general attack on those French lines extending from the St. Charles to Beauport was
to be made that very evening between ten and eleven o'clock (Montcalm's *Journal*,
pp. 562-3). In light of this report, all thought of detaching any large body of troops
from the main body was given up; instead, those to the east of Beauport were concentrated closer to that place, and the soldiers slept on their arms. But no attack came.
[78] For Wolfe's proclamation see Knox, *op. cit.*, I, 303-4.

manned and the necessary storehouses and hospitals had been erected on the island, he had reached a decision as to the next major move. This was to place a strong division of his army on the northern shore to the east of the Montmorency River and its falls. On the night of July 9, after a bombardment of the French lines by some frigates and bomb-ketches, Wolfe and Townshend carried the troops assigned to the latter across to the north shore, where the brigadier immediately entrenched himself on the heights, not far from the falls; nor did fierce Indian attacks on his rangers on the 17th seriously threaten his position. Now only the Montmorency stood between the British and the French. But the banks of that river were steep, heavily wooded, and forbidding. It is true that below the falls there was a fordable place, as was also true three miles up the river, but at both of these places it was found that the enemy had prepared defences, and the banks of the upper ford were also very steep. The only possibility of getting at the French on the north shore seemed therefore to be to force the lower ford under conditions that might make for success.

While Townshend was establishing his batteries near the Montmorency, those on the south shore, supported by bomb-ketches, opened up a heavy fire on the city the night of the 12th. At first the shells fell short, which led to derisive shouts from the defenders; then the range was found and the lower town, under impact of intermittent but heavy bombardment, began to disintegrate. On the 16th a large conflagration took place when nine buildings, one of them the Cardenat mansion on the edge of the upper town, were burned; and on the 23rd another occurred when the great cathedral church in the upper town and fifteen homes in the lower were consumed in the fire.[79] But even without these conflagrations the work of destruction continued, as buildings crumbled under the impact of cannon balls and shells. It should be pointed out that the very night of the beginning of the bombardment the French under command of Dumas, the victor over Braddock, crossed the river in force to destroy the works at Point Levy. But when it was found that the British entrenchments were stronger than supposed, the attack was delayed until the following night to permit the securing of reinforcements from the northern shore. Unhappily, the troops divided

---

[79] Montcalm's *Journal*, pp. 375, 381. Knox (*op. cit.*, I, 333) gives the date of the burning of the cathedral as July 16. His notation for the 23rd relates only to the fire that raged in the lower town.

into two bodies and, moving through the woods in the darkness, mistook one another for an enemy detachment, with the result they fired on their own men and in panic soon after recrossed the St. Lawrence.[80]

Just as Wolfe had come to see that he had in Montcalm an opponent of extraordinary capacity, so the latter came to realize that Wolfe, known for his impetuosity, was not likely to waste his men in idle assaults, but was settling down behind entrenchments to exhaust his opponent, now cut off from any further assistance from France.[81] Above all things, the British general, it became clear, was seeking to tempt the enemy to divide its forces and also to leave its entrenchments and come out to fight in the open. But the wily Montcalm, supported by two of his best lieutenants, de Lévis and Bougainville, could not be easily baited. On the night of the 18th, however, under command of Captain Rouse, two of Saunders's men of war, with two heavily armed sloops and two transports with troops and provisions, succeeded in passing the Quebec batteries and gaining the upper river, with the batteries at Point Levy supporting the movement by delivering an incessant fire on the city. This permitted a more effective reconnoitring of this area. But even there, as was true of the region below Quebec, no unguarded places were to be found. At Anse des Mères, later close to the scene of Wolfe's penetration, Dumas was now on hand with six hundred troops and his Indians; at Sillery, higher up, a battery did some damage to Rouse's command ship, the *Sutherland*, which led him to move still higher up the river to the settlement of Pointe aux Trembles, some thirty miles distant from Quebec, where Colonel Carleton landed with his grenadiers and Royal Americans; but outside of securing some prisoners, he accomplished little.[82]

Nevertheless, the movement brought consternation to the people of Quebec.[83] Montcalm saw in it the possibility, in case of a landing in force at some point on the northern shore, that all communication with the sources of the city's food and munitions supply might be

---

[80] *Ibid.*, I, 329; Montcalm's *Journal*, p. 572; Wolfe to Pitt, September 2, 1759, *Pitt Correspondence*, II, 150.

[81] *Journal*, p. 574.

[82] Knox, *op. cit.*, I, 337, 342; Wolfe to Pitt, September 2, 1759, *op. cit.*, II, 151–2; Montcalm's *Journal*, p. 578.

[83] Knox, *op. cit.*, I, 344.

cut off.[84] But this was not attempted. It is true that Wolfe, before Rouse and Carleton left on their mission, was hoping to be able to seize St. Michels, just three miles above the city; the place, however, was found on inspection by the general himself from a boat on the 21st to be too strongly defended with artillery to make the attempt practicable.[85] Keeping his own counsel, the British general was trying desperately to devise some plan that would permit him to get at the enemy with some hope of success. In his uncertainty, orders were given but to be countermanded; artillery was shifted from one place to another, while he looked for an opening against his wary opponent.[86] The moves and counter-moves of British and French taking place at this time, in fact, reminded Montcalm of a game of chess, in which Wolfe had greater facility of moving his pawns in an attempt to produce a checkmate than he himself possessed.[87]

A last serious attempt on the part of the French to destroy the British fleet in the basin between Ile d'Orléans and Point Levy occurred on the night of the 27th. They then set adrift a number of schooners and shallops and seventy-two rafts; these were all chained together, not less than a hundred fathoms in length, with the vessels freighted not only with grenades, swivels, gun and pistol barrels loaded to the muzzle, but with other combustible materials, and were ignited by Sieur Courval within musket range of the first of the British vessels.[88] Again the British sailors in the ships' boats courageously met a menace to their fleet by fire; grappling with the blazing monster before it could carry out its mission of destruction, they towed it safely to shore. Yet the expedition was getting nowhere, in spite of all the high hopes of its leaders. Must it at length fail of its objective, move down the river, and return home?

One thing had not been tried: a frontal assault. Wolfe at length determined on this. Two days after the French had launched their gigantic fire-raft he issued orders for a concentration of troops to the east of the Montmorency and at the west point of Ile d'Orléans.

---

[84] *Journal*, pp. 578, 580.

[85] Wolfe to Pitt, September 2, 1759, *op. cit.*, II, 151–2; Willson, *op. cit.*, p. 451.

[86] Doughty: *Siege of Quebec*, II, 451.

[87] Montcalm to Bourlamaque, July 20, 1759, *Lettres de Bourlamaque au Lévis*, p. 337.

[88] N. Y. *Col. Doc.*, X, 1000; Saunders to Percival, September 5, 1759, Doughty, *op. cit.*, VI, 115.

On the morning of the 31st the ships' boats were filled with grenadiers and a part of Monckton's brigade stationed at Point Levy that
they might be landed on the enemy beach; the brigades under
Townshend and Murray east of the Montmorency were likewise
ordered to be in readiness to pass the ford. With the support not
only of massed artillery of some fifty guns stationed on an eminence
above Wolfe's camp on the northern shore, but of the battery of
the *Centurion* riding in the northern channel and of two armed
transports drawing very little water that were now run aground,
facing the camp of the Chevalier de Lévis, it was hoped that the
troops could carry a redoubt that the enemy had established close
to the ford and be able to hold it and from it storm the entrenchments on the heights above. It was not until five o'clock in the afternoon, however, after many feints and movements to deceive the
enemy, that boats with the grenadiers sought to secure a beachhead.
Then, in attempting to land, some were lost when they struck a
ledge of rocks, and the resulting confusion compelled a general
withdrawal. Wolfe thereupon with some naval officers in a flat-
bottomed boat observed the shore at fairly close range and found
a better landing-place. As a result, at six in the evening the assault
took place, led by the grenadiers and two companies of Royal Americans who landed on the muddy beach, beyond which were gullies
formed by the rains and many deep holes. These troops were under
strict orders, after reaching the shore and after carrying the enemy redoubt close to it, to wait until Townshend's troops had crossed the
ford and could join them before undertaking to force the main entrenchments on the heights. But this was not done. The grenadiers,
"impatient to acquire glory," in the words of Knox, would not be
held back, but ran up the "inconceivably steep" hill and made many
efforts to gain the summit over the glacis of trees in front of the
entrenchments upon it — all in the face of the most devastating fire
from the enemy. When they were compelled to retreat to the shore
in disorder, they found there Monckton's troops from Point Levy,
which had meanwhile disembarked from their boats in good order
and the brigades of Townshend and Murray that had crossed the
ford.[89] Yet night was coming on, and also a violent rainstorm had

---

[89] Knox, op. cit., I, 354–8; Lévis to Belle-Isle, August 2, 1759, *Lettres du Chevalier de Lévis, 1756–1760*, pp. 227–33; "Narrative of the Siege of Quebec, published by
the French," *N. Y. Col. Doc.*, X, 1000–1.

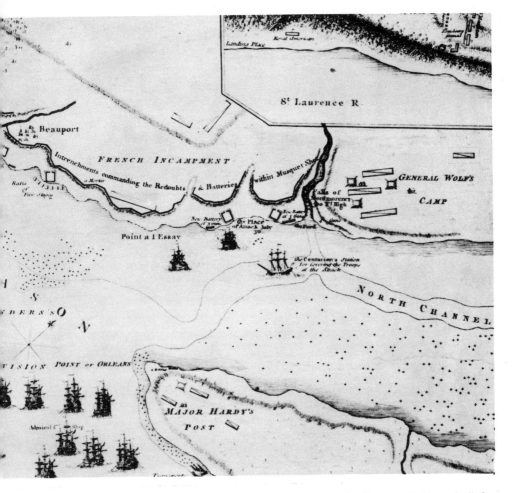

Wolfe's attack near the Montmorency Falls. A Portion of Thomas Jefferys's "Plan of the . . . Siege of Quebec, 1759." (Public Archives of Canada, Division of Maps.)

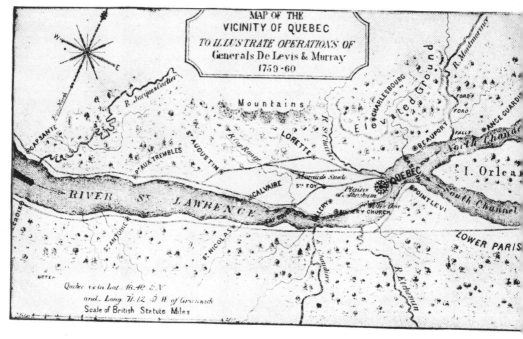

The St. Lawrence above Quebec.

(From Justin Winsor's *Narrative and Critical History of America*

damaged the powder of the assault troops, with the result that
Wolfe now gave the order to retreat while the tide was still favourable. The withdrawal from this dangerous position was carried out
by Monckton without further loss of life. For, outside of a few
French Indians who appeared to secure scalps, there was no movement of the enemy from their secure entrenchments on the heights.[90]

The movement was fairly well planned, but poorly executed, because of the delay of Townshend's contingent in arriving on the
scene across the ford, and on account of the impetuosity of the
grenadiers and the outbreak of the storm as the latter were ascending the precipitous slope.[91] Although the artillery poured some three
thousand shells into the enemy lines in aid of it,[92] this was to no
avail. The British losses in attempting to execute it were about four
hundred and fifty in killed and wounded, mostly grenadiers and
their officers, who suffered severely,[93] as against Montcalm's return
of but seventy French killed and wounded.[94] Yet, even had it succeeded and the French forces been obliged to retreat to the west of
the St. Charles, there would have remained that formidable obstacle
lying between the British and the city, with its precipitous banks,
devoid of bridges, as these would undoubtedly have been destroyed.
With this failure at Montmorency, there undoubtedly weighed on
Wolfe's mind the probability of the collapse of the campaign while
still so near to, and yet so far from, his objective. This sense of frus-
tration is indicated in a letter that he wrote to his mother a month

---

[90] Wolfe to Pitt, September 2, 1759, *Pitt Correspondence*, II, 153–5.

[91] Wolfe, late in the month of August, drew up a detailed report to Pitt on the
operations that had taken place since his letter to the Minister early in June. This was
submitted to Saunders on August 24 for corrections. The admiral felt that the general
had not quite done justice to the important service rendered on July 31 by the navy and
wrote him accordingly (Saunders to Wolfe, August 25, 1759, Chatham Mss., Bundle
55, Canadian Archives Transcripts). On August 30 Wolfe replied with a very circum-
stantial account of the action. In it he freely took the blame for its failure. He declared:
"The great fault of that day consists in putting too many men into boats, who might
have landed the day before [east of the Montmorency] and might have crossed the
ford with certainty, while a small body remained afloat; and the superfluous boats of
the fleet employed in a feint that might divide the enemy's force" (Willson, op. cit.,
p. 462).

[92] Montcalm's *Journal*, p. 385.

[93] Knox, op. cit., I, 358.

[94] *Journal*, p. 385. Knox was later informed that over two hundred of the enemy
were either killed or disabled, largely as the result of the heavy artillery fire from the
heights east of the Montmorency (op. cit., I, 359).

after his defeat, which he must have felt even more keenly on the evening of July 31:

> "The enemy puts nothing to risk, and I can't in conscience, put the whole army to risk. My antagonist has wisely shut himself up in inaccessible entrenchments, so that I can't get at him without spilling a torrent of blood, and that perhaps to little purpose." [95]

---

[95] Wolfe to his mother, August 31, 1759, Willson, *op. cit.*, p. 469.

CHAPTER XIII

The Piercing of the Heart of New France

WOLFE, sick at heart after his repulse near the falls of the Montmorency on July 31, for a time, at least, put aside any thought of attempting to carry the Beauport defences by another assault and turned his attention once again to the upper river. If nothing more could be done, without some unexpected development, than the opening of the way for a possible union of his own forces with those of Amherst, this in itself would hold out possibilities of real military significance. Therefore on August 4 Brigadier General James Murray was ordered to take twelve hundred men up the river above Quebec to co-operate with Admiral Holmes in an effort to destroy the French ships of war stationed at the mouth of the Richelieu, which flows from Lake Champlain. With this done, it was thought that a communication with Amherst, now operating in the Lake Champlain region, might be established. The brigadier also was ordered to seek to engage the French troops posted along the St. Lawrence, if it were possible to do so on anything like equal terms.[1]

Murray, however, in ascending the river in Holmes's ships was not permitted to act without interference. Colonel Bougainville, in view of the British movements, had been ordered by Vaudreuil to follow the enemy squadron with a land force moving along the northern shore and to prevent a landing. Therefore, when the Brit-

[1] Wolfe to Pitt, September 2, 1759, *Correspondence of William Pitt* (ed. G. S. Kimball), II, 156.

ish brigadier sought to disembark his troops on the 8th at Pointe aux Trembles, some twenty miles above Quebec, he was confronted by a force of sufficient strength to frustrate his efforts.[2] In spite of the fact that in this attempt he sustained the loss of well over a hundred men either killed or wounded, he wrote to Wolfe the following day that he was still confident that he would be able within the next few days to "make a stroke." [3] For about a week, after taking post at St. Anthony, a parish on the south shore facing Pointe aux Trembles, he spent the time making incursions into the country round about, laying waste the region.[4] Then for the next two days boats went up and down the river from that point in order to deceive the watchful Bougainville. On the 17th in darkness he proceeded up the river between seven and eight leagues to Deschambault, where the following day he landed and burned a weakly defended magazine filled with military supplies and baggage before the appearance of the French leader with his forces; whereupon he re-embarked his men.[5]

While this operation on the upper river was proceeding, rangers under command of Major Gorham, who for years had campaigned in Nova Scotia, were sent down the river to lay waste the country about St. Paul's Bay on the north side where the people, when the fleet was ascending the river, had fired upon the sounding crews in open boats.[6] Other contingents, supported by some of the smaller vessels, were likewise later sent down the south side — the popula-

---

[2] Vaudreuil to Bougainville, August 9, 1759, Doughty: The Siege of Quebec, IV, 20. One attempt was made at low tide, but ledges of rock prevented the boats from landing; the next was at high tide, when the men on landing were received by such a heavy fire from the partly concealed enemy that it had to be given up; nor could the sailors who sought to destroy the floating batteries stationed there get near enough to them to carry out their work (Major Moncrief's "Journal," ibid., V, 45). Colonel Carleton had early in the course of the campaign about Quebec landed at this point, brushing aside the feeble opposition, and with a number of prisoners had returned to the ships commanded by Captain Rouse.

[3] Chatham Mss., Bundle 50 (Canadian Archives Transcripts). Major Moncrief gives the figure as one hundred and forty (Doughty, op. cit., V, 45).

[4] For a French account of his activities see Doughty, op. cit., II, 219–20.

[5] Major Moncrief's "Journal," ibid., V, 46. When on the afternoon of the 19th the news reached Montcalm of Murray's landing at Deschambault, he was deeply disturbed and immediately left Quebec with his grenadiers to join Bougainville. What he feared was that the British would entrench themselves there. Should they do so, he felt that it would be extremely difficult to dislodge them (Journal, p. 592).

[6] Gorham to Pitt, August 10, 1759, Chatham Mss., Bundle 33 (Canadian Archives Transcripts); Captain John Knox: Historical Journal of the Campaigns in North America for the Years 1757, 1758, 1759, and 1760, II, 9, 17.

tion of which, in spite of Wolfe's proclamation, had repeatedly appeared in arms — to carry out a similar mission of destruction.[7] All the while the bombardment of the lower town was continued, and early the morning of the 9th a shell exploding in a vaulted cellar filled with wines caused a fierce conflagration, which, aided by the wind, gutted most of that quarter of the town, including the Church of la Sainte Victoire.[8]

It was at this juncture that a plan was submitted to the general which had in view the erection of a strong fort capable of containing a winter garrison of fifteen hundred men on the Ile-aux-Coudres in case it was impossible this season to become master of Quebec.[9] It seemed for a time that this project would be executed and it was even expanded so as to provide for a force of three thousand men, but was finally rejected because of the lack of certain building materials and the lateness of the season.[10] It was also proposed, should all other plans fail, as a last desperate measure before the army should be forced to return down the river, to storm the lower city from Ile d'Orléans and Point Levy with the support of part of Saunders's fleet and some thousands of his seamen. But this was also put aside, since, according to Chief Engineer Mackellar, it would expose the ships that attempted to participate to almost certain destruction from the Quebec heights and also since it was by no means clear that, even with the lower town in their grasp, the British could maintain themselves there against the powerful batteries in the upper town, which could deliver point-blank fire at them with impunity.[11] Therefore, Wolfe, while impatiently awaiting Murray's return under orders, was obliged to limit himself to sending out additional parties on both sides of the river to destroy the outlying settlements outside of the places of worship. It is clear that during most of the month of August his mind was filled with deep anxiety. For he seemed no nearer the attainment of his great objective than

7 Saunders to Wolfe, August 18, 1759, Chatham Mss., Bundle 55.

8 Knox, op. cit., II, 13–14.

9 Ibid.

10 Wolfe to Pitt, September 2, 1759, Pitt Correspondence, II, 158; Knox, op. cit., II, 21, 28. The idea had been entertained of sending a ship to Louisbourg to bring up those materials that could not be procured locally. Saunders, in fact, agreed to dispatch such a vessel, but warned that it could not return in less than two months. In the light of this fact, the chief engineer, Mackellar, thought that it would not be possible to find time to construct the buildings that would be required (Mackellar to Barré, August 10, 1759, Chatham Mss., Bundle 49, Canadian Archives Transcripts).

11 Knox, op. cit., II, 24–5, 28.

he had been a month earlier, and time was running short.[12] What is more, the latter part of August it became known that he was laid low at his camp east of the Montmorency with a fever, which filled the soldiers with deep apprehension.

It was on the 25th that Murray and Holmes returned to report the results of their expedition, especially with respect to their success at Deschambault. They also brought some heartening news secured from the prisoners whom Murray was able to capture: that Fort Niagara had fallen to the British and also that the French, in the face of Amherst's advance, had abandoned both Fort Ticonderoga and Crown Point and had retreated to Ile-aux-Noix.[13] As for the French ships that had been stationed at the mouth of the Richelieu, these, by placing their guns and other weighty things on shore, had gone farther up the river over the shallows and beyond the reach of Holmes, who could not strip his ships.[14] He, however, retained most of his weak squadron on the upper river. This fact led to a decision of a French council of war — held in Quebec two days after the brigadier's return to report to Saunders — to rearm five of the French frigates and then seek to destroy these isolated British ships. In accordance with the plan agreed upon, between six and seven hundred sailors, who had been employed in the defence of Quebec, left the city the evening of the 27th in boats and, in spite of heavy fire from the British batteries, reached Pointe aux Trembles; there again they had to submit to another cannonading from Holmes's ships, but in spite of this finally reached Cap Santé, where the frigates were moored. Apparently suspecting some such design on the part of the French who had moved upstream in their bateaux, Saunders the night of the 28th sent up four more ships of war to reinforce Holmes. This led the French to a quick decision to

---

[12] The military engineer Major Moncrief in his "Journal" under date of August 13 records that the batteries at Point aux Pères, just opposite Quebec on the south shore, were now augmented to forty pieces of cannon "either to favour a storm [of the town] by water, or to do the town all possible damage if it could not be taken, which now becomes doubtful" (Doughty, op. cit., V, 44).

[13] This news was confirmed on September 4 when two of Amherst's officers of the rangers and four privates reached the army camped near Quebec with letters dated August 7. They had left Crown Point twenty-seven days earlier; hastening to Boston, they thereupon mounted the Kennebec and descended the Chaudière, which flows into the St. Lawrence five leagues above Quebec; on the last leg of their long journey they met a few straggling French habitants, who, however, did not molest them (Knox, op. cit., II, 51).

[14] Wolfe to Pitt, September 2, 1759, Pitt Correspondence, II, 156; Knox, op. cit., II, 33.

order the frigates not to engage the British after all, but to reoccupy the anchorage at the Richelieu and to return the sailors to Quebec.[15]

Still seriously indisposed, with the month of August soon to end and therefore with but few weeks remaining at his disposal, Wolfe — now that his three brigadiers were again together and in the light of the fact that they would be obliged to assume the responsibility for the termination of the campaign should he become totally incapacitated — felt impelled to submit to them a memorandum in which he asked them to meet together to consider the best method of attacking the enemy. He himself, it is of interest to note, had come back to his original project of an attack against the French army at Beauport. In the memorandum he offered three plans. By the first, a large detachment would move by night up the Montmorency eight or nine miles and, crossing it, press down against the French centre with the support of the rest of the troops, who would cross the ford below the falls. By the second, the troops already encamped to the east of the river would make a night march directly on Beauport with the light infantry detailed to gain the eminence to the east of it, named Woody Hill, and with the grenadiers following them to attack the upper redoubts and hold them while Monckton, with his men in boats lying off the French village, would, with the support of the ships of war, land his men. Finally, by the third, all the strength of the army would be employed directly against the place at the time of low water and apparently in daylight, with a division moving across the ford an hour before the other attack from the boats.[16] The last project was in many respects similar to the one of that fatal day of July 31, although now aimed at the heart of the French lines rather than at the left wing.

The brigadiers in reply drew up on August 29 their report, in which they brushed aside all three of Wolfe's proposals.[17] They questioned the possibility of dislodging the enemy from the Beau-

---

[15] Journal de Foligné, Doughty, op. cit., IV, 199.

[16] Doughty, op. cit., VI, 90–1.

[17] Brigadier George Townshend, as is well known, was at the time very critical of Wolfe's strategy. Writing to Lady Ferrers on September 6, he declared: "Genl Wolf's Health is but very bad. His Generalship in my poor opinion — is not a bit better, this only between us. He never consulted any of us [the brigadiers] till the latter end of August, so that we have nothing to answer for I hope as to the Success of this Campaign" (Doughty, op. cit., V, 195). Murray in later years was also equally critical of Wolfe. Writing to Townshend on November 5, 1774, he referred to the general's "absurd, visionary, attack of the Enemy's Lines at Beauport" (Amherst Papers, Packet 15, Canadian Archives Photostats).

port area between the St. Charles and the Montmorency with the means at their disposal, especially in view of the fact that since the late attack the works had been greatly strengthened. They also questioned the possibility of crossing the St. Charles — should they succeed in gaining Beauport — before the enemy were well supplied with provisions from their ships on the upper river. In fact, they were unanimous in their view that the most practicable way of striking an effective blow would be to leave the camp east of the Montmorency, transferring the troops stationed there to the south shore and thereupon directing all operations toward gaining a foothold above the town on the northern shore. With this accomplished, they declared:

> "The General must fight us on our own terms; We shall be betwixt him and his provisions, and betwixt him and their Army opposing General Amherst.
> "If he gives us battle, and we defeat him, Quebec and probably all of Canada will be ours, which is an advantage far beyond any we can expect by an attack on the Beauport Side. . . ." [18]

In addition to this report, the brigadiers prepared a plan of operations that envisaged the total withdrawal from the Montmorency area in three days, leaving six hundred men for the defence of Ile d'Orléans and the same number for that of Point Levy and one thousand for the batteries, marching the remaining troops to the river Etchemin to the west of the point, where twenty-five hundred of them would be embarked on ships and carried up the river, where they could be landed at some selected point on the north shore and then reinforced by the main body. Their confidence in their ability to get a footing — since Brigadier General Murray had been able to land his troops and had, in fact, passed through several villages unmolested by the people after making an example of those attempting to oppose him [19] — is indicated by the following statement embodied in their plan:

> "There can be no difficulty to effectuate a landing in the night without the least loss, it may be done any where for the extent of a few Leagues, viz., from the heigth of St. John to Cap rouge River. Two attempts may be made, either of which succeeding is sufficient." [20]

---

[18] Monckton, Townshend, and Murray to Wolfe, August 29, 1759, Chatham Mss., Bundle 50 (Canadian Archives Transcripts).

[19] Knox, op. cit., II, 33–4.

[20] "Plan of Opperations" by the brigadiers, Doughty, op. cit., VI, 93–4. They of-

Faced with the united opposition of his brigadiers to his own proposals and apparently uncertain himself as to their soundness, Wolfe admitted to Saunders the day after he had received their reply: "My ill-state of health hinders me from executing my own plan: it is of too desperate a nature to order others to execute." [21] He therefore agreed to carry out that of his subordinates.[22] By the evening of the 29th, the day on which the counter-proposals were made and accepted by the general, preparations were under way to evacuate the troops from the lower northern shores; [23] that same night five more ships loaded with provisions ran past the French batteries at Quebec and gained the upper river to join Holmes.[24] The preparations for meeting the French on more equal terms seems also to have revived Wolfe in both mind and body. For, two days later, he made his first appearance since his recent illness. By the evening of September 3 artillery, supplies, and other matériel, as well as the troops, had been transferred from the Montmorency camp. On the 4th Saunders sent all of his flat-bottomed boats at nightfall above the town, and the same day Wolfe issued orders for the light infantry, the grenadiers, and four regiments to be prepared to march westward of Point Levy the night of the following day so that they could be embarked on the boats awaiting them between the Etchemin and Chaudière rivers.

The movement of the British troops at the point was observed

---

fered an alternative to the plan preferred by them, which would provide that two thousand men should embark in boats at Point Levy at low water at midnight; by daybreak they would be able to disembark at a proper place half a league above the river Cap Rouge; with the ships on the upper river filled with two thousand more troops, there would be four thousand men available to be landed in one tide "without the least jellousy given to the Enemy, and the remainder may be brought over with any number of Artillery, the next [tide] from the Etchmin Camp" (ibid.).

[21] Wolfe to Saunders, August 30, 1759, Willson, op. cit., p. 475. This statement, torn from its context, has been used by writers to prove that Wolfe at the time that he made it had really in mind forcing his way up the Foulon Pass. This must be rejected, not only because of the lack of positive proof, but because he had just pressed upon his brigadiers his proposals to launch a second attack upon the Beauport heights.

[22] Wolfe to Pitt, September 2, 1759, Pitt Correspondence, II, 157. Wolfe's lack of confidence in his own judgment at this critical juncture is also indicated by the following statement in his letter to Pitt: "By the Nature of the River, The most formidable part of this Armament is deprived of the Power of acting; Yet we have almost the whole Force of Canada to oppose. — In this situation, there is such a Choice of Difficulties, that I own Myself at a Loss how to determine."

[23] Knox, op. cit., II, 35.

[24] Saunders to Pitt, September 5, 1759, Pitt Correspondence, II, 161.

by the French generals, and it was judged that some four thousand at least were in the process of moving westward to the river Etchemin and that these would be embarked on the ships that Saunders had waiting for them above the city and would soon attempt to force a landing.[25] The Chevalier de Lévis, who had commanded the right wing of the army between the St. Charles and the Montmorency, had, in order to protect Montreal from an attack on the part of Amherst by way of Oswego and Lake Ontario, been sent with eight hundred troops on August 11 to take post at Galops Island, at the head of the rapids just above that city, where he was ordered to entrench himself.[26] With the troops at his disposal, which included the permanent garrison of Montreal, he was therefore responsible for the general defence of this area from whatever quarter the attack might come, but could not easily bring any support to save Quebec. As to the area on the north shore from Pointe aux Trembles, as already stated about twenty miles above the city, to the Anse [Cove] des Mères, just to the west of it, some of the slender forces available for the protection of this region, to the number of two thousand, were distributed at posts on the heights between Cap Rouge and the environs of Quebec, and the rest, constituting a mobile contingent of cavalry and foot under the command of Bougainville, were free to range along the length of the heights for the purpose of keeping constant watch of the movements of the British.[27] Moreover, the Guyenne battalion was placed for a time in a camp just outside the city near the western gate and remained alert, prepared at any moment to move to support the scattered posts in case of necessity.

Bougainville's responsibility was very great indeed in the eyes of both Vaudreuil and Montcalm. It was by no means clear what strategy the British had adopted. Were they seeking so to weaken the French encampment to the east of the St. Charles that they could attack it again with confidence of success? Or was their real design to force their way, if possible, up one of the passes of the rimrock to the west of the city? Vaudreuil seems to have felt that the latter explained their movement up the stream in force. Addressing Bougainville on September 5, he declared: "I need not say to you, Sir,

[25] Remigny to Bougainville, September 5, 1759 "Correspondance de Bougainville," Doughty, op. cit., IV, 95.

[26] Journal de Foligné, ibid., IV, 194.

[27] Vaudreuil to Bougainville, September 5, 1759, "Correspondance de Bougainville," Doughty, op. cit., IV, 95–7.

that the safety of the colony is in your hands. Certainly the plan of the enemy is to cut our communication by making disembarkations on the northern shore. Only vigilance can prevent it." [28] Montcalm the following day wrote to his friend: "I continue to fear the cutting of the communication. Therefore I am sending 200 more grenadiers to Samos [29] to be placed at your disposal." [30] He, nevertheless, seems to have apprehended, as he expressed himself to Bourlamaque early in September, that Wolfe would "as a gambler playing at *tope et tingue*,[31] having played to the left, and then to the right, would proceed to play to the middle" (that is, directly against Beauport) [32] which, incidentally, Wolfe had determined upon, but had been dissuaded from undertaking by his brigadiers, as has been noted.

Bougainville with his mobile troops had meanwhile taken post at Sillery, midway between Cap Rouge and Foulon, and remained there until the 7th. Then, with the slow movement of the ships of the British squadron under Holmes up the river to a point opposite Cap Rouge on the 7th, 8th, and 9th, he shifted his post to that place. Wolfe on the night of the 6th joined the troops and ships on the upper river, and the following day he issued his orders for his line of battle when a landing should be made.[33] That same day he left with his brigadiers to view the country still higher up the river in the neighbourhood of Pointe aux Trembles and came to a decision to land just a little below that place.[34] That night he ordered the troops to be prepared to move into boats at two o'clock on the morning of the 8th, part of them to proceed up the river under Monckton to make the real attack, and others to make a feint of landing at Cap Rouge in the face of Bougainville's troops awaiting them.[35] But the weather became so stormy, with excessive rain, that no military operations could be undertaken. Therefore, on account of the crowded condition on the transports, over fifteen hundred of the

---

[28] *Ibid.*

[29] Samos is just to the west of the Anse de Foulon.

[30] Montcalm and Montreuil to Bougainville, September 6, 1759, *ibid.*, IV, 99.

[31] A game played with dice.

[32] Montcalm to Bourlamaque, September 2, 1759, *Lettres de M. de Bourlamaque au Chevalier de Lévis* (ed. Abbé Casgrain), p. 348.

[33] For these orders see Knox, *op. cit.*, II, 55–6.

[34] Major Moncrief's "Journal," Doughty, *op. cit.*, V, 48.

[35] Murray to Townshend, November 5, 1774, Amherst Papers, Bundle 15 (Canadian Archives Photostats); Knox, *op. cit.*, II, 58; Admiral Holmes to ——, September 18, 1759, Doughty, *op. cit.*, IV, 295–6.

troops were temporarily landed on the south shore with two days' provisions in order to refresh themselves.[36]

While these troops were ashore, Wolfe reconsidered the whole question of the place for delivering his attack. On the 9th he apparently took a ship's boat and went to the south shore near the Etchemin to view the Anse de Foulon.[37] Then on the 10th, with Holmes, Monckton, Townshend, Carleton, and the engineer Delaune, he again surveyed the Foulon from the same vantage point,[38] and that same day upon returning to the *Sutherland* warned Colonel Burton of the 48th regiment — stationed now with twelve hundred men on the south shore — of his determination to make a landing there rather than higher up the river.[39] On the 11th, according to his own statement, he took with him Brigadier General Monckton, Admiral Holmes, and Captain Shads to Gorham's camp to the east of the Etchemin and to the west of the great battery on the south shore opposite Quebec, in order to study further the situation of the enemy on the heights across the river.[40]

The next day he and Monckton also had some discussion respecting the projected attack. The latter, whose division was to lead it, made clear to Wolfe during this conference that he had perceived a breastwork at the Foulon, as something to take into account, and also stressed the point that he wanted to avoid the disorder connected with a night attack. To this Wolfe agreed and thereupon desired Admiral Holmes to see that the boats arrived on the shore about half an hour before daybreak.[41] While therefore his three brigadiers certainly knew of the change of plan — that the troops would descend from Cap Rouge rather than ascend the river, and that Monckton's troops would lead the attack against the Foulon — it was not clear to them what part each, outside of Monckton, would play and whether the attack would be limited to the one point that had been viewed from near the Etchemin two days before or would include other near-by points. The three therefore wrote to the

---

[36] Townshend to Pitt, September 20, 1759, *Pitt Correspondence*, II, 164; Knox, *op. cit.*, II, 58.

[37] Willson, *op. cit.*, p. 476. Willson does not give his authority for this statement, but it would be in conformity with logical procedure in a matter of such importance as changing the point of attack.

[38] Moncrief's "Journal," Doughty, *op. cit.*, V, 48.

[39] Wolfe to Burton, September 10, 1759, *ibid.*, III, 16–17.

[40] Wolfe to Monckton, September 12, 1759, *ibid.*, VI, 60.

[41] *Ibid.*

general from the *Lowestoft* on the 12th, after Monckton had conferred with him. The following is an excerpt of their letter:

> "As we do not think ourselves sufficiently informed of the several parts which may fall to our Share in the execution of the Descent you intend tomorrow, we must beg leave to request from you, as distinct Orders as the nature of the thing will admit of, particularly to the place or places we are to attack. . . . As we should be sorry . . . to commit any mistakes, we are persuaded you will see the necessity of this application, which can proceed from nothing but a desire to execute your Orders with utmost punctuality." [42]

The letter was a perfectly proper one in view of the fact that up to the time of sending it neither Townshend nor Murray had apparently received any orders and Monckton's orders seem to have been simply by word of mouth. Wolfe in his reply, given the evening of the 12th and directed to Monckton, the senior brigadier, reviewed the incidents of the last two days respecting the maturing of the plan against the Foulon and indicated the nature of the private orders that had been given and the requests made to the navy in line with this. He thereupon stated something that was quite true, but it carried with it an implied rebuke to his brigadiers:

> "It is not a usual thing to point out in the public orders the direct spot of our attack, nor for any inferior officer not charged with a particular duty to ask instructions upon that point. I had the Honor to inform you today that it is my duty to attack the French Army. To the best of my knowledge and abilities I have fixed upon that spot where we can act with the most force and are most likely to succeed." [43]

In reading between the lines of this letter, one cannot fail to detect the fact that Wolfe in his discussion with Monckton that same day had been obliged to invoke his authority as commanding officer

---

[42] *Ibid.*, VI, 59.

[43] *Ibid.*, VI, 60. At the same time that Wolfe sent his letter to Monckton he sent another to Townshend, making clear that Monckton was to lead the first landing and that Townshend, in case of the success of the initial landing, was to see that the troops under his own command were likewise landed (*ibid.*, VI, 60). I have found no similar letter to Murray, setting forth his particular duty, but one must believe that such a letter was written. The general orders issued on the 12th simply state that "the troops will land where the French seem least to expect it," and both officers and men were reminded "what their country expects from them, and what a determined body of soldiers, inured to war, is capable of doing, against five weak French battalions, mingled with a disorderly peasantry" (Knox, *op. cit.*, II. 66–7, in which the italics appear).

of the expedition and to counter strong opposition to his proposal from him as well as from others. In the words of Admiral Holmes:

> "This alteration of the Plan of Operations was not, I believe approved of by many, besides himself [Wolfe]. It had been proposed to him a Month before, when the first Ships passed the Town, and when it was entirely defenceless and unguarded: but Montmorency was then his favourite Scheme, and he rejected it. He now laid hold of it when it was highly improbable he should succeed, from every Circumstance that had happened since [the first proposal in favour of attempting it]." [44]

The decision was, indeed, a critical one. For Holmes had doubts of his ability to bring the troops at night to the right place because of the rapid current.[45] After the event the admiral called the operation "the most hazardous and difficult Task I was ever engaged in — For the distance of the landing place; the impetuosity of the Tide; the darkness of the Night; and the great chance of Exactly hitting the Spot intended, without discovery or alarm; made the whole extremely difficult; And the failing . . . would have brought upon me an imputation of being the cause of the miscarriage of the Attack, and all the misfortune that might happen to the Troops." [46] General Murray, years later, decried Wolfe's

> "desertion of the Sensible, well-concerted, Enterprise to land at the point Au Tramble, where without opposition, with his whole Army, and Artillery, he might have taken Post, and Entrenched himself betwixt the Enemy and their Provinces, [as against] the almost impossible, tho Successful attempt, thanks to Providence, at the Foulon. . . ." [47]

Indeed, had Wolfe's dangerous venture brought disaster to British arms, his brigadiers other than Murray would also doubtless have pointed out the solid advantage that would have come by a determined attack on Pointe aux Trembles with its easy approach. Only a small detachment of one hundred and ninety of the enemy, it is now evident, was stationed there.[48] It could not possibly be

---

[44] Holmes to ——, September 18, 1759, Doughty, op. cit., IV, 296.

[45] Townshend to Murray, October 29, 1774, Amherst Papers, Bundle 15 (Canadian Archives Photostats).

[46] Doughty, op. cit., IV, 296.

[47] Murray to Townshend, November 5, 1774, Amherst Papers, Bundle 15 (Canadian Archives Photostats).

[48] Vaudreuil to Bougainville, September 6, 1759, Doughty, op. cit., IV, 100.

reinforced in time to prevent a landing. For the only troops in reach west of Cap Rouge, where Bougainville had settled down with his mobile force, were two other small detachments: one of one hundred and eighty men at St. Augustine, some distance to the east of Pointe aux Trembles, and the other of two hundred men some distance to the west on the Jacques Cartier, which flows into the St. Lawrence.[49] The traditional assumption therefore that all avenues for landing the British army above the city were firmly closed, outside of the Foulon Pass, is therefore not based upon historical evidence. Nor is it easy to believe that, had Wolfe landed at Pointe aux Trembles and entrenched himself, Montcalm would have ventured to denude the encampment east of the St. Charles as well as the city of most of the defenders in going so far to attack him — especially in light of the fact that the French general apparently remained convinced that Wolfe would still strike against Beauport [50] in a "play to the center." In fact, Saunders did everything on the night of the 12th in the way of lowering his boats, setting up buoys, and engaging in a heavy bombardment to confirm him in this belief.[51] As it was, with the landing at Foulon, just a mile and a half from Quebec, the French general felt free, after leaving a small detachment of but fifteen hundred men at the encampment, to confront Wolfe with almost his entire force stationed east of the St. Charles.

One factor that made for the success of the desperate venture was the fact that for days Holmes, in order to wear out Bougainville's mobile force that followed his squadron, would let his ships ascend fifteen miles and more above Quebec, carried by the high tide, and then with the ebbing permit them to drop down to within a half mile of it. Finally, with his troops "quite overcome with fatigue," the French colonel, no longer willing to play the British game, settled down at Cap Rouge, about eight miles from the city, as has been noted.[52]

At one o'clock the morning of the 12th the division of the army

---

[49] Ibid.

[50] It should be noted that the Guyenne battalion that was to have remained stationed just outside the western wall of the city was brought back to the camp east of the St. Charles and was there on the morning of the 13th (Montcalm's Journal, p. 610). This is clear proof that both Vaudreuil and Montcalm, in spite of their warnings to Bougainville, were deeply apprehensive for the safety of the Beauport camp. Montcalm's Journal at no point indicates there was any difference of opinion on this matter between the general and the Governor General.

[51] Knox, op. cit., II, 63, 67; "Journal de Foligné," Doughty, op. cit., IV, 205.

[52] "Mémoire de Joannès, Major de Quebec," Doughty, op. cit., IV, 225.

encamped on the southern shore opposite Cap Rouge was quietly
brought back to the ships. The light infantry, four of the regular
regiments, a detachment of Highlanders, and the Louisbourg grenadiers — to the number of somewhat less than four thousand in all —
were placed on flatboats at nine o'clock that evening and, with the
onrush of the tide, most of the ships and boats moved up the river in
the darkness following the usual regime as far as Pointe aux Trembles as though to make an attack there; then, aided by a strong
southward wind and the ebbing tide, they moved down rapidly
in the darkness at two o'clock the morning of the 13th, that day so
fatal to New France! [53] At four o'clock, still in the midst of darkness,
the advanced boats, thirty in number and carrying some eighteen
hundred men, with Wolfe, Monckton, and Murray among the number, came to the shore, some just below Sillery and others farther
down just above Cape Diamond, where the city begins. A sentry
detecting one of the boats challenged it with a loud voice and was
told in French not to make a noise as supply boats were stealing
past the enemy to reach Quebec.[54]

The light infantry, commanded by Colonel William Howe —
brother of the late Lord Howe, killed near Ticonderoga, and destined to be commander-in-chief of the British forces in the course
of the American Revolution — had the duty assigned to them of
mounting the Foulon Pass and seizing the post so as to permit the
heavy-armed troops to mount the heights. They found themselves,
however, below the pass and just to the west of the Anse de Mères
on landing. To gain the heights they were therefore obliged to work
their way up a wooded precipice by clinging to trees and bushes.[55]

[53] "Journal de Foligné," ibid., IV, 203; Bigot to Belle-Isle, October 25, 1759, N. Y.
Col. Doc., X, 1052.

[54] Ibid. and Knox, op. cit., II, 67. It so happened that it had been planned to send
a convoy of provisions from the supply ships on the upper St. Lawrence to Quebec that
same night. Information regarding this was circulated through all the posts on the river.
Two French deserters came aboard the sloop Hunter and brought information respecting
this anticipated convoy ("Memoires of Quarter Master John Johnson," Doughty, op.
cit., V, 111–12.). But unforeseen circumstances prevented the bateaux from descending
the river, and the posts were not warned, so "when our sentries saw the enemy's barges
advancing, they took them for ours, and satisfied with the word 'France' which was
returned to the challenge, allowed those barges to pass without giving themselves the
trouble to reconnoitre them" ("Operations of the Army under M. de Montcalm before
Quebec," N. Y. Col. Doc., X, 1038).

[55] Townshend to Pitt, September 20, 1759, Pitt Correspondence, II, 165; Knox,
op. cit., II, 67; "Operations of the Army under M. de Montcalm," N. Y. Col. Doc., X,
1038. Captain de Foligné writes in his "Journal": ". . . Foulon, located along the bank

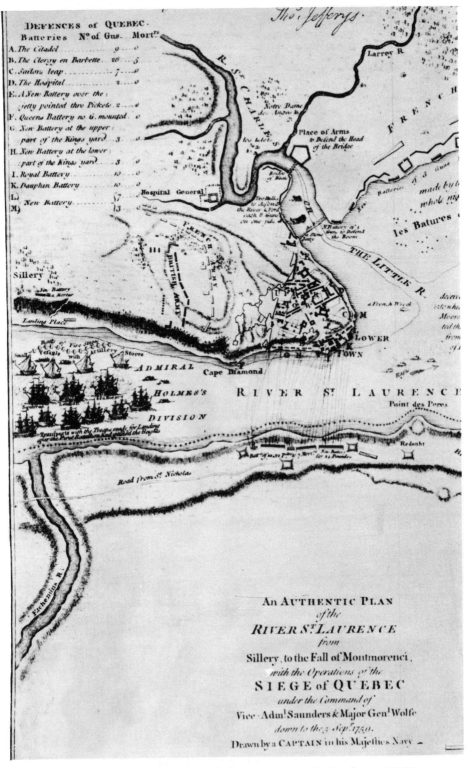

Wolfe's landing and the Battle of the Heights of Abraham, 1759.
(From Thomas Jefferys's "Plan of . . . Operations of the Siege
of Quebec," Public Archives of Canada, Division of Maps.)

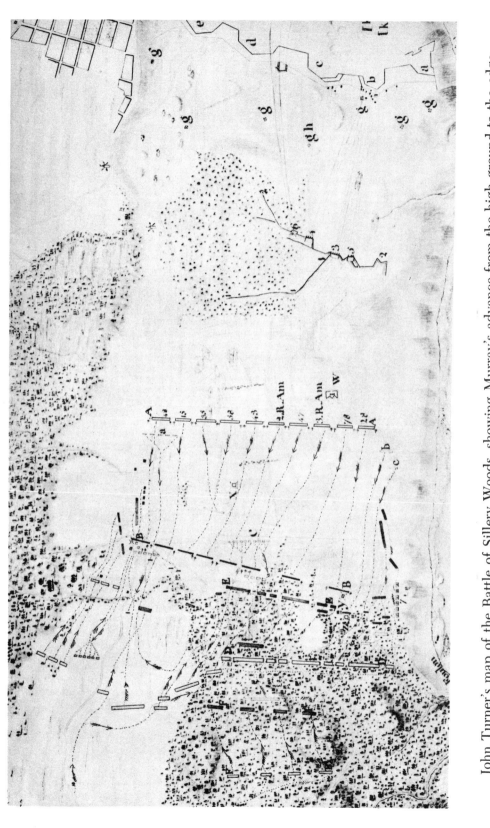

John Turner's map of the Battle of Sillery Woods, showing Murray's advance from the high ground to the edge of Sillery Woods, 1760.

The first detachment to arrive on the plateau in the darkness, when challenged by a sentry, was also able to reply in French through their leader, a Captain McDonald of Fraser's Highlanders and at one time in the French service, that he as its leader had been sent with a large command to take post there and that the sentry should go with all speed to his guard and call off the other men of his party ranged along the cliff.[56] Others followed hard on the heels of this detachment, and with their sudden onrush against the post the little garrison — now reduced to but sixty men — fled after the briefest resistance when their commander, Captain de Vergor, who had likewise been surprised at Beauséjour in 1755, fell wounded and was captured.[57]

Wolfe and Murray had meanwhile gained the heights and the former, it appears, when he heard shots exchanged between the light-armed troops and the enemy, sent orders to his aide-de-camp, Adjutant General Isaac Barré, who was on the beach, not to permit the landing of more troops. In the words of Townshend: "as at the moment he [Wolfe] doubted (and with great reason), of the Success of his Enterprise." But Barré, disregarding these orders, permitted the rest of the troops to land.[58] Thus, not only at the critical

---

at a place most precipitous, was regarded as impossible [of access to the enemy], where a man without impediments could scarcely ascend it" (Doughty, op. cit., IV, 203).

[56] Knox, op. cit., II, 67–8.

[57] "Journal de Foligné," Doughty, op. cit., IV, 204.

[58] Townshend to Murray, October 29, 1774, Amherst Papers, Bundle 15 (Canadian Archives Photostats). Townshend in later years came to admire Wolfe and to revere him in memory as, in contrast, during the operations about Quebec he had distrusted his leadership. So in 1774 we find him defending his one-time leader in a series of letters exchanged between him and General Murray, the latter now showing a very critical attitude toward Wolfe. Copies of these letters are to be found among the Amherst Papers under the above general reference. In the letter just quoted, Townshend went on to say: "The General's view was to support the experiment, if he found it practicable: — that the Colonel [Barré], from the State of things on the Beach, found it more so than the General advanced [to the heights], could determine; and therefore in a state of great responsibility, he seconded the efforts of Mr. Wolfe . . . and decided for his General's wishes, contrary to his orders." Murray, in replying to Townshend on November 5, declared, among other things: "It does not appear to me that it ever was Mr. Wolfe's intention to bring the Enemy to a general action." Barré, however, while later admitting that he did not deliver Wolfe's orders while posted on the beach, "but suffered the troops to land as fast as possible," insisted that Wolfe "was most ardently bent on bringing the Enemy to an Action on any thing like equal terms, & that his ordering him to stop the boats could be only a temporary measure 'till he learnt the Enemy's Forces in the neighbourhood of the landing Place" (Major Caldwell to General Murray, November 1, 1772, ibid., Packet 28).

It is of interest that Intendant Bigot had the same impression as Murray. Writing to

moment of the landing on Cape Breton Island the preceding year, but now at Foulon, Wolfe, it would seem, was permitted to obtain his objective and undying fame as the result of disobedience to his orders on the part of those who were eager to second his efforts.

Warning signals soon appeared at Quebec. But these were disregarded by Montcalm and his staff at the encampment. In fact, the action of Admiral Saunders in placing buoys in the river opposite Beauport on the 11th had been very disturbing. Did it mean the approach of another asault? The battery at that point was thereupon strengthened and the 12th was consumed with this work.[59] The evening of the 12th, with Montcalm's mind still concentrated on this defensive task, other orders for strengthening Beauport were issued and then, before retiring that night, with his aide-de-camp, Marcel, the general visited all the entrenchments. At one o'clock on the morning of the 13th Dumas reported a great noise of moving boats and, as a result, troops were hurried into the entrenchments; at three o'clock it was reported that the enemy boats were opposite the battery of the Canardière. Then shortly afterward appeared the signal from Quebec that something was happening above the city. No notice was taken of it and when, just a little before daylight, firing was heard above the city, it was not doubted that it came from an attempt of the enemy to seize the convoy of provisions that was to come that night to Quebec. At daylight, as all was quiet, the troops left the entrenchments; even the appearance now of a terrified Canadian at the post of the Canardière with a tale that the enemy was in possession of the Foulon and that he alone escaped was not believed, for it was thought that the man was crazy, in view

---

Maréchal Belle-Isle, October 25, 1759, he declared: "I know all the particulars of that landing from English officers of my acquaintance who have communicated them to me; adding, that Mr. Wolf did not expect to succeed; that he had not attempted to land above Quebec [at Cap Rouge], and that he was to sacrifice only his van-guard which consisted of 200 men; that were these fired on, they were all to reëmbark" (*N. Y. Col. Doc.*, X, 1052). The author of a French *Journal*, who, critical of Montcalm, and less so of both de Vaudreuil and Bigot, declared that it had been learned from "divers English officers" that at a council of war Wolfe declared that "as the glory of our arms appear to me to require that we should not retire without making one final attempt . . . I am about to try to get a detachment of only one hundred and fifty men to penetrate through the Sillerie woods, and the entire army will be prepared to follow. Should this first detachment encounter any resistance on the part of the enemy, I pledge you my word of honor that then, regarding our reputation protected against all sorts of reproach, I will no longer hesitate to reëmbark" (*ibid.*, X, 1037).

[59] Montcalm's *Journal*, pp. 609–10. This portion of the *Journal* seems to have been written by Marcel.

of the difficulty of surmounting the heights there.[60] In fact, after talking with the man, Montcalm's aide-de-camp turned in to rest.

But soon the ominous news was verified, and the drums beat the *générale*. The Guyenne battalion that was to have been reposted to the west of the city walls, but was still in the encampment, was now dispatched — Montcalm expressed the conviction that it alone could look after the enemy.[61] He himself, after some delay, left with the Sarre, Languedoc, and Béarn battalions, in order to support the Guyenne, but not before giving orders for other troops to come up. By the time the last-named battalion had been posted on an elevation to the west of the city, some fifteen hundred British troops were drawn up and ready to receive it. The officers therefore decided to await the arrival of the general before bringing on an action.[62] But by the time he had passed over the St. Charles and had appeared on the scene, the boats had brought the second British detachment under Townshend from the ships and other forces from Ile d'Orléans and Point Levy, and he found himself faced by almost four thousand of the enemy,[63] most of them battle-hardened veterans who had shifted from their first position with their backs on the St. Lawrence and were now extended on the Plains of Abraham from the heights of the river on their right to the neighbourhood of the St. Foy road, running through a dense coppice on their left. Reinforced by the arrival of the Royal Roussillon and having at his disposal some fifteen hundred Canadian marksmen and Indians, who under cover of a cornfield on the right and the coppice on the left had been harassing the British line, Montcalm, now with some four thousand five hundred men at hand, decided to deliver his attack at about nine o'clock in the morning without waiting longer for the arrival of Bougainville with his élite corps amounting to some three thousand (by including those detachments in the scattered posts to the east of Cap Rouge).[64]

---

[60] *Ibid.*, pp. 610–11.

[61] *Ibid.*, p. 611.

[62] "Journal de Foligné," Doughty, *op. cit.*, IV, 204.

[63] In all some four thousand, five hundred men were landed but some were needed to guard the shore and the approaches and could not join in the battle. The 48th regiment and second battalion of Royal Americans were ferried across the river and were the last to arrive (Townshend Papers and Major Moncrief's "Journal," Doughty, *op. cit.*, V, 52, 268).

[64] Montcalm, before giving orders to advance on the enemy, declared that as the enemy was entrenching itself and already had two pieces of cannon in place, there was no time for delay; otherwise with the few troops that he had he could never attack

The question immediately arises: Was Montcalm justified in delivering the attack when he did? Should he have waited until Bougainville had arrived and the Montreal battalion had been brought from over the St. Charles? The Chevalier de Montreuil, before Montcalm ordered the advance, told him that he was in no condition to attack the enemy in view of the weakness of his force. Yet in the same breath Montreuil affirms: "Had the Marquis de Montcalm postponed one instance marching against the enemy, they could not have been attacked in consequence of the favourable position they were going to take up, having even begun some entrenchments in their rear." [65] Vaudreuil, on the other hand, insisted that Montcalm acted precipitately, "carried away by his zeal and great vivacity," and attacked prematurely before gathering all the forces that were available. Writing to M. Berryer on September 21 he said that, immediately on hearing that Montcalm had

> "dispatched the pickets of the different regiments, a part of the battalions and Canadians, and advanced himself without communicating his arrangements to me . . . I feared the action would be brought on before the junction of the corps under the command of M. de Bougainville, composed of the élite of our troops; I ordered the advance of the remainder of our forces [about Quebec], with the exception of the posts of the line of Beauport and set out immediately to place myself at the head of the army." [66]

But Vaudreuil brought up his reinforcements too late. Already the day was lost in that vital period of no more than a quarter of an hour from the French attack to their retreat.

While it is clear that before the battle began Wolfe had only two small cannon to support his line and was anxious to secure more artillery before committing himself to a general engagement,[67] it is not clear that he could have strengthened himself greatly had Mont-

---

them. He added to Captain Marcel with chilliness: "Is it possible that Bougainville has not heard of this?" (Montcalm's *Journal*, p. 612. This daily record seems to have been largely if not entirely made by Captain Marcel, the general's aide-de-camp, from July 3 to the end. It ends on September 24). See also Knox, *op. cit.*, II, 68–9; Townshend to Pitt, September 20, 1759, *Pitt Correspondence*, II, 165; and the "Journal de Foligné," Doughty, *op. cit.*, IV, 204–5. For an extended analysis of the battlefield in relation to the present Plains of Abraham, set aside as a national memorial, see Doughty, *op. cit.*, II, 289–309.

[65] Montreuil to Belle-Isle, September 22, 1759, *N. Y. Col. Doc.*, X, 1013–14.

[66] *Ibid.*, X, 1010–11.

[67] "An Account of the Action which happened near Quebec," Cumberland Papers, *Military Affairs in North America, 1748–1765* (ed. Pargellis), p. 438.

calm given him two more hours. At the end of this relatively brief period Bougainville would have been on hand prepared to attack the British in the rear while Montcalm was opening their front. The French general might also have had at his disposal, had he delayed, some two thousand more troops, without leaving Beauport absolutely unguarded, and a train of artillery right at hand at Quebec, instead of being obliged to rely upon but five small field pieces.[68] Had he waited until Bougainville was near at hand and his own line had thus been strengthened and heavily supported with artillery, it is likewise clear that Wolfe would doubtless have felt compelled to attack him on high ground under what well might have been very unfavourable conditions to avoid a death-trap, and history might have therefore recorded a very different story for that memorable day.[69]

The superiority in open-field action on classical lines of an army made up of highly disciplined regulars over one composed to a very great extent of half-trained militia and backwoodsmen was fully demonstrated on September 13, as well as the superiority of the British muskets over the French.[70] The French battalions in Canada had by the fall of 1759 embodied so many Canadians, who excelled only in bush fighting, that they were not adapted to perform the duty that Montcalm now assigned to them.[71] When they were ordered to advance upon the line of the enemy, they dashed forward with loud cries; their first fire, delivered at one hundred and thirty yards, was at such a distance that it made little impres-

---

[68] "Operations of the Army under M. de Montcalm before Quebec" (*N. Y. Col. Doc.*, X, 1040). That Montcalm was refused the use of additional artillery, as was reported, does not seem to rest on very good ground.

[69] A detailed list of "blunders" made by Montcalm on that day is given by an unknown French officer in his "Journal" (*ibid.*, X, 1039–40). Captain de Foligné, writing in his "Journal" regarding the battle, declared that it was the judgment of everyone that had Montcalm awaited the arrival of Bougainville, so that the combined forces could have struck the enemy," not an Englishman would ever have re-embarked" (Doughty, *op. cit.*, IV, 205). Indeed, Bishop de Pontbriand declared that after the battle Montcalm himself, now mortally wounded, admitted that he had resolved to attack too soon ("An Impartial Opinion on Military Operations of the Campaign in Canada, 1759," *N. Y. Col. Doc.*, X, 1061).

[70] Townshend, writing to Amherst on June 26, 1775, declared: "I recollect that in our Service at Quebec the superiority of our Muskets over the French Arms were generally acknowledged both as to the Distance they carried & the Frequency of the Fire, in driving them from their Bushes & holding at a great Distance as Circumstances required" (Amherst Papers, Packet 73, Canadian Archives Transcripts).

[71] *N. Y. Col. Doc.*, X, 1061.

sion;[72] they lay down to reload and then dashed ahead; their second and third fires at closer range were more effective, yet far from devastating. But the silent British lines held firm and reserved their own fire until the enemy had approached within some forty yards, and then their muskets blazed all along the line. The impact on the French columns was instantaneous. They wavered and recoiled. Then it was that Wolfe ordered a bayonet charge. Already the French colonials on Montcalm's right had left the advance to seek the protection of the woods; thus weakened, the right now gave way and in so doing was followed by the centre and the left as the British charged.[73] Soon the entire French army was in wild flight, pursued by Englishmen with their bayonets and Highlanders swinging their heavy claymores in terrifying execution.

What immediate fate might have befallen the French battalions and the city itself is hard to judge had not the Canadians on the British left — concentrated in the woods to the west of St. John's gate of the city and in their native element for fighting — now poured upon the pursuers so steady a fire that it checked their onrush and gave time for the main body of the French army to reach the security of the defences of the city and those along the St. Charles.[74] Swept along in the retreat back to the city gate, Montcalm, who was mounted, received a wound that proved fatal.

Now as to Wolfe, when he ordered the general charge he placed himself on the right wing "at the Head of Bragg & the Louisbourg Grenadiers, advancing with their Bayonets,"[75] and in this exposed position, after having received two lesser wounds, fell likewise fatally stricken and soon expired on the field of battle. Before his death, however, he was assured that the enemy had been routed, and then before passing into unconsciousness he gave an order and uttered his last words: "Now, God be praised, I will die in peace."[76]

---

[72] Speaking of the French advance, Major Moncrief writes in his "Journal" that "their front began to fire before they got within reach, and immediately followed throughout the whole in a wild scattering manner" (Doughty, op. cit., V, 53).

[73] Montcalm's Journal (by Marcel?), p. 613, and "Mémoire de Joannès, Major de Quebec," Doughty, op. cit., IV, 226.

[74] Bigot to Belle-Isle, October 25, 1759, N. Y. Col. Doc., X, 1052; Townshend to Pitt, September 20, 1759, Pitt Correspondence, II, 166.

[75] Ibid.

[76] Knox, op. cit., II, 79. Knox heard many versions of Wolfe's words, but was assured by Lieutenant Brown of the Louisbourg grenadiers, who remained by the general's side to the end, that the above was Wolfe's last utterance (ibid.). Wolfe had a presentiment of death. On the night of the 12th he summoned on board the Sutherland an old

It can be said that he had lived like a soldier and died like one and that the victory he achieved was to have an enormous consequence for the future of the English-speaking world and for North America. This was accomplished with the loss in the battle of but some sixty men killed and about six hundred wounded as against approximately two hundred French killed and twelve hundred wounded.[77]

One may be permitted, before turning from this historic event, to raise the question: Is the commander-in-chief of an expedition of such importance as that sent to the St. Lawrence, and upon whose shoulders rests a vast responsibility not only to the nation that provided the resources to make it possible but for the welfare of so many men immediately under his authority, justified — under the circumstances as presented above — in placing his life in such extreme peril as did Wolfe when he led the grenadiers on their bayonet charge? Did he not violate as clearly as did Lord Howe, near Ticonderoga the preceding year, a time-honoured maxim, not of prudence or caution so much as of common sense, that has been observed by almost all great military commanders? Would Amherst, bearing the King's commission as commander-in-chief of the expedition against Louisbourg, have been warranted in attempting to perform in person the very dangerous service that he assigned to Wolfe of forcing a landing on Cape Breton Island? Were there lacking other officers on September 13 capable of leading the soldiers, only too eager, after submitting to the punishment of the French volleys, to drive their opponents from the field? In other words, did the British general act upon the basis of sound military precepts in his last courageous decision?

Not only was Wolfe killed at the head of the Louisbourg grenadiers, but Monckton, second in command, was shot through the lungs while leading the 47th (Lascelles) regiment in the charge. As a result, the command fell on Townshend, who had been placed in charge of the reserves and was supporting Murray on the left

---

friend, Jervis, and entrusted to him his will and other papers, and also a miniature portrait of the woman he had hoped to marry, Miss Katherine Lowther, which he had up to the present carried with him. In his will and a codicil he made generous provision for his friends, particularly his companions in arms (Willson, op. cit., pp. 482–4).

[77] Major Moncrief's "Journal" (Doughty, op. cit., V, 54; Knox, op. cit., II, 80–1) gives the French losses, according to the enemy's calculations, as "near fifteen hundred, killed, wounded and prisoners" in the course of the engagement. The total British losses during the entire campaign, according to Monckton's return of October 8, 1759, was one thousand and seventy-two, killed, wounded, and missing (Doughty, op. cit., III, opposite page 332).

wing. Hurrying to the centre, the brigadier busied himself in restoring order in the ranks and re-forming the troops after they had returned from the pursuit. Hardly had he done so when Bougainville put in his appearance at the rear with two thousand of his picked troops from Cap Rouge. Immediately two battalions with the two field pieces were ordered to move into position to meet the enemy without leaving the high ground. As Bougainville, now realizing the battle was lost, soon retired into a low region of woods and swamps adjacent to the Plains of Abraham, the British commander cautiously determined not to run the risk of sacrificing the victory by leaving his advantageous position and therefore refused to follow him; instead he set about the entrenchment of his camp.[78]

After eight hundred frightened fugitives had entered the city, the rest of the French soldiers were finally halted without its walls under the defences of its batteries of great guns as well as those posted on the eastern bank of the St. Charles. What could now be done to save the day? The Chevalier de Montreuil thought it best to gather the remnants of the army at the works that protected the bridge over the St. Charles, while Vaudreuil proposed to force the enemy to a new battle by collecting all the Canadians.[79] But the latter, who on occasion had shown so much bravery, were now a frightened, demoralized group that, in the words of aide-de-camp Captain Marcel, "would have had to be driven into battle." [80] So this proposition of the Governor General was dismissed and, with the British no longer pursuing, the battalions and those Canadians who had not deserted once again entered the encampment about Beauport. Thereupon a formal council of war was called by Vaudreuil. It was determined, in view of the lack of provisions, that the battalions should desert the camp and march that same night in three divisions to the Jacques Cartier, each soldier taking with him food for four days and as much ammunition as he could. It was also agreed that the sailors, Canadians, and artillerymen who had served the Beauport batteries should proceed to Trois Rivières. This retreat was carried out silently, but at the same time in the midst of great confusion. On the evening of the 14th the disorganized army had arrived at Pointe aux Trembles, and early the next morning it moved on to the Jacques Cartier, arriving there at noon on the

---

[78] Townshend to Pitt, September 20, 1759, *Pitt Correspondence*, II, 167–8.
[79] *Montcalm's Journal* (by Marcel), p. 614.
[80] *Ibid.*

15th.[81] Thus by the decision of the council of war not only was the Beauport camp virtually abandoned, except for a strong detachment at the St. Charles to keep open the way, but likewise Quebec was left to its fate. Indeed, under the conviction that the city could not long hold out, Vaudreuil, before departing with the army, had drawn up terms for its surrender, which he gave to its commandant, M. de Ramezay.[82]

With a garrison of two thousand two hundred fighting men made up of soldiers, sailors, and militia; with but eight hundred of them to man the extensive batteries of the upper and lower towns; with only from five to six hundred foot soldiers, in addition, for general service, out of which total there were less than two hundred regulars; and, finally, with supplies on hand — according to the report made to the council of war on the evening of the 15th — sufficient to feed the six thousand people gathered within the city (including women, children, sick, and wounded) for but three days, Quebec was doomed, unless extensive relief arrived.[83] Ramezay had been advised by Vaudreuil that should he fail of provisions, he should, without waiting for the British troops to storm the city, hoist the white flag as a sign of capitulation.[84] At the Jacques Cartier, after the arrival there of de Lévis, who, incidentally, strongly censured the army for retreating, the question arose whether supplies could be thrown into Quebec in order to prolong the siege. Bigot agreed to furnish these, and both Vaudreuil and de Lévis to march forward with this relief loaded in eighty carts, with other relief to be sent by boat. For Quebec was still not surrounded and could not be by so small a British force. On the 17th the French army reached St. Augustine, four leagues from the city, when news arrived of the offer of surrender.

After the departure of the army for the Jacques Cartier, a feeling of dread had spread through the city. Montcalm, who had passed away the morning of the 14th, was interred that evening in the chapel of the Ursulines and, with his passing, those remaining in

---

81 *Ibid.*, pp. 615–16.

82 For these see *N. Y. Col. Doc.*, X, 1004–6.

83 "Minute of the Council of War," September 15, 1759; Bernier to Belle-Isle, September 19, 1759; and Daine to Belle-Isle, October 9, 1759, *ibid.*, X, 1007, 1010, 1015. Much of the provisions for the city were in a suburb beyond the walls near the baking ovens west of Quebec and were captured in the advance of the enemy (Bigot to Belle-Isle, October 25, 1759, *ibid.*, X, 1053).

84 *Ibid.*, X, 1004.

Quebec gave up all hope. Women and children refugees who had
been in the woods crowded into the city and demanded food, which
could only be given in small amounts; men of business feared that
their goods would be plundered by the enemy should the garrison
continue to resist and therefore asked for an honourable surrender;
the city itself was largely a ruin, particularly the lower town. On
the evening of the 15th, in the midst of this overshadowing gloom,
de Ramezay called a council of war to determine his course of action
should help not arrive on the 17th. It was decided that he must
then avail himself of the capitulation.[85] The next day, the 16th,
Major de Joannès was sent from the city with an urgent dispatch to
Vaudreuil, but under promise of returning to Quebec that night.
Finding that he could not deliver it in person and honour his pledge
— since the Governor General was some ten leagues away — he sent
it forward and then retraced his steps. On the 17th, as the day wore
on, there was no sign of relief. Although the British land forces
after the battle and up to the 17th limited their activities to the
fortification of their camp, the landing of artillery and stores, the
collecting of fascines, and the beginning of a redoubt to cover a
battery that would be erected to breach the Bastion of St. Ursule,[86]
it was Saunders who forced the issue by sending six of his men of
war opposite the lower town prepared to begin a bombardment.
As a result of this manœuvre in the afternoon, a white flag was flown
from the walls and again Joannès left the city, but this time for
Townshend's camp, bearing Vaudreuil's terms of capitulation.[87]

These terms provided that the troops be permitted to march out
of the city in safety with the honours of war, in order to join the
French army, carrying with them their arms, baggage, and a small
artillery train; that the inhabitants be preserved in their houses,
goods, and privileges and in no way punished for bearing arms;
that the exercise of their religion under the supervision of the Bishop

[85] Of the fifteen officers who made up the council of war, all but one favoured
capitulation should relief not arrive by the 17th, each signing a statement to that effect;
the only one who called for "a defence of the place to the last extremity" was the military engineer, Captain Jacau de Fiedmont (ibid., X, 1008). It was this same Fiedmont
that the French traitor Pichon in 1756 thought could be won over to the British cause
(see Volume VI of this series, page 236).

[86] Major Moncrief's "Journal," Doughty, op. cit., V, 54–5.

[87] Ibid., IV, 228–9. Major de Joannès says that the white flag appeared at four
o'clock but Townshend says that it appeared at noon, "before we had any Battery
erected or could have had for 2 or 3 days" (Townshend to Pitt, September 20, 1759,
Pitt Correspondence, II, 168).

of Quebec be granted to the people of the city; that the wounded be treated in conformity with a cartel signed in February of that year between the two crowns; that before the British troops should enter the city, their guards should be placed before the principal structures; that the King's lieutenant of the city be permitted to inform Vaudreuil of the surrender; and, finally, that the capitulation be executed in its present form without any disavowal of it under pretence of reprisal.[88] At the same time another message was sent to Vaudreuil saying that the defenders would wait for help until evening before giving up. Joannès, on his part, managed to spin out the time in the British camp in a discussion of aspects of the terms with Townshend and Admiral Saunders, who also made his way to headquarters. Then he returned carrying with him an ultimatum that the French would be granted but four more hours in which to surrender upon the British terms; otherwise there would be no further negotiations and the city would be carried by storm,[89] with all that this implied. At the deadline, eleven o'clock in the evening, aid not having arrived,[90] again Joannès appeared at the British camp prepared to agree to the amended capitulation. Thereupon, after considerable discussion, the general and the admiral signed their names to the articles, and at eight o'clock the morning of the 18th the major returned to Ramezay, who placed his own signature to the three copies, two of which were carried back to the British headquarters.[91]

The terms of surrender were much more liberal than were those granted to the French at Louisbourg. The French soldiers were, for example, to be accorded the honours of war and therefore were not to be considered prisoners and as such carried to England, but to be landed under a flag of truce at a port in France; nor were the inhabitants to be uprooted and returned to France, like those of

---

[88] N. Y. Col. Doc., X, 1004–6. Vaudreuil, however, showed his willingness to make the terms more agreeable to the British, if necessary, with respect to the clauses regarding the surrender of the garrison and the treatment of the inhabitants. For he appended to the capitulation certain observations permitting additional concessions (ibid.).

[89] Townshend to Pitt, September 20, 1759, op. cit.

[90] Joannès, it is true, indicates in his mémoire that Ramezay did receive letters from both Bougainville and Vaudreuil. In the first, reference was made to the establishments of individuals where some flour could be found; in the second, aid was promised. He also indicated that the cavalry officer de la Roche-Beaucort, after his own departure for the British camp the second time the night of the 17th, entered the city with sixty horse-loads of bread foods and with a promise of additional aid (Doughty, op. cit., IV, 228–9).

[91] "Journal de Foligné," ibid., IV, 209.

Cape Breton Island, but were to await the final conditions of the peace between the two crowns and meanwhile were to enjoy their property without fear of plundering or any interference; nor were they to be punished for taking arms to defend the city, or to be restrained in the exercise of their religion.[92] In fact, the treatment of the people within the city was, by the terms, so very generous that there were few, if any, of the inhabitants, after these were made known, disposed to make further resistance. Immediately after this formality, in accordance with the desires of Vaudreuil — as expressed in the articles of capitulation that he had given to Ramezay — some companies of British grenadiers entered Quebec and took post at the principal buildings while awaiting the arrival of the garrison that later in the day appeared in the city and took formal possession of it. The next day still more troops were added to the British garrison, bringing with them, not only the train of artillery that was to have been used to batter the walls, but a quantity of ammunition and provisions. Saunders's fleet also on the 19th moored in two lines in front of the city and as far up the river as Sillery and as far down as the falls of the Montmorency. Although the people of Quebec and those living within three leagues of it appeared on the 21st and meekly enough took the oath of fidelity as required by Townshend, in order to enjoy the benefits of the capitulation,[93] a strong French detachment posted on the St. Charles at the Têt de Pont fired sharply on the British troops on the 19th, which led Townshend to send an officer to Ramezay to make it retire. This was done, and thereupon a part of the British army moved into Montcalm's camp at Beauport and took possession of the artillery and other matériel. With respect to the French garrison of about twenty-five hundred that surrendered, some eighteen hundred — regulars, marines, and sailors — were on the 22nd placed on transports to be carried to France and began the next day their voyage down the river. The rest — the Canadians in arms — were released and permitted to remain in the country under the terms of capitulation.[94] But from the battlements of the capital of New

---

[92] The final terms were included in Vaudreuil's letter to M. Berryer written on September 21, 1759 (N. Y. Col. Doc., X, 1011–13). For a collotype of one of the three originals, all in French, which is in the British Colonial Office, see Doughty, op. cit., III, opposite page 280.

[93] "Journal de Foligné," ibid., IV, 213.

[94] Ibid., IV, 214; see also Major Moncrief's "Journal," and "Memoirs" of John Johnson, ibid., V, 56, 110.

France the fleur-de-lis, under which they had served, was never again to float.

The great achievement of piercing the very heart of New France must be attributed to the quality of leadership provided by both Wolfe and Saunders and their lieutenants; further, to the steadiness and splendid morale of British regulars and sailors and to the high quality of the weapons, both heavy artillery and muskets, provided for them; and, finally, to the harmonious co-operation between the two branches of the service throughout the entire operation. The foe that they faced for months and that was only finally vanquished on the heights of Abraham was both superbly commanded and determined. There existed in the French ranks — at least after the appearance of the British fleet before Quebec — much more unity with respect to defensive measures than most historians have recognized in their tendency to overemphasize the effects of the rivalry between Vaudreuil and Montcalm; for there was certainly vastly more unity among all groups who made up the defenders of Quebec than was to have been found among those of Louisbourg.[95] In fact, it was only at the final critical moment when the British appeared on the heights of Abraham that two factors were chiefly responsible for the French defeat: the inferior quality not only of their muskets but of the discipline of the Canadians, who, embodied with the regulars, were called upon to advance in columns upon the weak, extended British line and were unable to bear up under the fire of that line and to break it. Had Montcalm had at his disposal the same number of men, all highly disciplined veterans, of the quality that later under Napoleon swept like a torrent over Europe, who can say with confidence what might have been the outcome of that decisive engagement on September 13?[96]

---

[95] Montcalm, in writing to his friend Bourlamaque on August 19, declared that he and Vaudreuil "were of one mind" and warned the brigadier to pay no attention to the gossip of Montreal. The Marquis also affirmed that should he and the Governor General listen to public clamour, the colony would cease to exist and that the two could be depended upon to do their best to save it (Bourlamaque Mss., 1:575–8, Canadian Archives Transcripts).

[96] Speaking of the French troops who engaged in battle, Marcel, Montcalm's aide-de-camp, writes: "The French soldier no longer knew discipline and in place of becoming a Canadian he acquired all of his defects" (Montcalm's *Journal*, p. 615).

CHAPTER XIV

The Culmination of the War in North America

THE BRITISH OPERATIONS in the Quebec area — preceding the battle of the Plains of Abraham and the capture of the capital of New France — had left, both within the city itself and in the countryside for many miles along the banks of the St. Lawrence, a sad scene of devastation. After describing the widespread destruction that had taken place in the upper and lower towns of Quebec as the result of Wolfe's constant cannonading, Bishop de Pontbriand in a *mémoire,* enclosed in a letter addressed to an unidentified correspondent, indicated the utter misery of the rural population, whose houses, barns, and granaries lying within a radius of thirty-six leagues of the city had been burnt by the British forces and whose subsistence had been carried away.[1] As a result of this unhappy situation there had been a general movement of those dwelling within this region in the direction of Trois Rivières and Montreal in the course of Wolfe's campaign. This movement continued thereafter in spite of the subsequent generous treatment extended by the British not only to the non-combatants but to those who had been in arms and were now disposed to live peacefully.[2]

---

[1] "An Imperfect Description of the Misery of Canada," *Documents Relating to the Colonial History of the State of New York* (ed. E. B. O'Callaghan), X, 1057–9.

[2] Brigadier de Bourlamaque, writing to the Chevalier de Lévis from Isle-aux-Noix on September 29, 1759, declared: "The few Canadians I have here show no bad spirit; but I fear that in learning of the good treatment that the English have given their families they will go off to join them" (*Lettres de Bourlamaque au Chevalier de Lévis,* ed. Abbé Casgrain, p. 48).

While the crowding of these refugees into the Montreal area presented perplexing problems respecting shelter and sustenance, it did have the effect of making available to the Chevalier de Lévis, who was now in immediate command under Governor General de Vaudreuil, the services of many men in his efforts to save the colony. This task he now approached with courage and resourcefulness. To protect those areas which were still under French control, he began the construction of a fort on the Jacques Cartier. At the same time Bougainville, with his mobile force once again taking post at Pointe aux Trembles, from there sent forward not only a detachment to remain at Rivière du Cap Rouge, only three leagues from Quebec, but also from time to time smaller parties that came even within cannon range of the guns of the city in order to harass the victors there.[3] While the Chevalier and Bougainville were thus engaged, Vaudreuil remained at Montreal prepared to send aid in case of need either to Bourlamaque at the Isle-aux-Noix or to de la Corne, stationed at the rapids in the region of Galop's Island near La Présentation and at Fort La Galette on the upper St. Lawrence. But these sectors remained quiet as the winter closed in. Amherst, as has been earlier noted, before leaving Lake Champlain for New York, was chiefly concerned with the comfort and security of his regulars and the rangers left at Crown Point and at Ticonderoga; while Gage, who remained at Oswego with his army until late in the season, gave his major attention to the building of barracks and defences for his men before leaving Lake Ontario under Amherst's orders to assume command at Albany. With everything quiet on the frontier the French regulars, with the exception of those maintained at the advance posts, were therefore widely scattered and settled down as they had done during the preceding winters in the homes of the *habitants*.[4]

Turning now to Quebec, that city of magnificent churches, chantries, and public buildings, which, in the words of Captain John Knox, "would be ornaments in any city in Europe,"[5] when the British came into possession of it there were hardly any among these and other structures large or small that had not suffered serious

[3] Lévis to Belle-Isle, November 1, 1759, *Lettres de Lévis*, p. 244; Captain John Knox: *Historical Journal of the Campaigns in North America for the Years 1757, 1758, 1759, and 1760*, II, 177–8, 203–4, 217.

[4] *Journal des Campaignes du Chevalier de Lévis*, pp. 231–2; M. Pouchot: *Memoir upon the Late War in North America*, I, 222.

[5] Knox, *op. cit.*, II, 146–7.

damage, and many were in utter ruins. Monckton's first task therefore, upon recovering from his wound sufficiently to take command,
was to see that the soldiers destined to engage in garrison duty there
were under proper shelter and provided with other means for facing
the long winter months when they would be quite cut off from the
rest of the world. Deserted houses, stables, and other out buildings
that had been deroofed within the upper and lower towns were now
covered, provisions and military stores were landed from Saunders's
fleet, and detachments to procure fuel were sent out into the country where the *habitants* had been encouraged to gather in their harvests for their own use.[6] By reason of the great extent of Quebec
and the dangers faced should the enemy seek to regain it, it seemed
necessary to leave there a garrison of over seven thousand men.[7] As
the brigadier himself was still too much of an invalid to venture to
remain in Canada for the winter, he determined, before leaving for
New York to recuperate and in view of Townshend's desire to return home, to appoint James Murray Governor of Quebec, and
Colonel Burton Lieutenant Governor;[8] other members of Wolfe's
staff were also ordered to England or to join their regiments posted
elsewhere.[9]

On October 18 Admiral Saunders left Quebec with most of the
ships of the line and a number of transports and on the 26th Monckton embarked and departed. The men of the garrison now realized
that, in this vast, hostile country, their safety lay in their own hands.
With reports constantly received that Vaudreuil and de Lévis were
busy with preparations to retake the city with the aid of the armed
ships still on the upper St. Lawrence, Murray now determined, in
line with Monckton's recommendations,[10] to build twelve floating
batteries, such as the French had constructed and put to good use
in their defence of the city. These, he felt, supported by the two
sloops of war that Saunders had left to winter there, with the still
powerful defences surrounding him and his army, would offer ample protection and would also make it very difficult for the French
to receive any reinforcements that might seek to mount the St. Law-

---

[6] Monckton to Pitt, October 8, 1759, *Correspondence of William Pitt*, II, 177–82.

[7] Murray to Pitt, October 12, 1759, *ibid.*, II, 183; Knox, op. cit., II, 181.

[8] For his general orders dated October 23 see *ibid.*, II, 177.

[9] A. Doughty: *The Siege of Quebec and the Battle of the Plains of Abraham*, VI, 132.

[10] Monckton to Pitt, October 20, 1759, Chatham Mss., Bundle 50 (Canadian Archives Transcripts).

rence in the spring.[11] He was, moreover, very particular with respect to the treatment accorded by the army to the people of the city and to those who had returned to their farms in the country, that their ancient prejudices might be removed and that they would feel reluctant ever again to take up arms against the British.[12] Early in November — in view of the fact that Vaudreuil was seeking to levy contributions from the people of the parishes about the city who had submitted and was also threatening them with destruction by the Indians — he issued a proclamation that was posted on all the church doors. This exhorted the Canadians, since all aid from France was now cut off and a powerful force was in their midst, "to have recourse to a free people, wise, generous, ready to embrace you, to free you from a severe despotism, and to make you partake of the blessings of a moderate and most upright government." [13]

In line with this policy of leniency, the inhabitants of the city, while under regulations such as those which required them not to correspond with their fellow Frenchmen still in arms, to be off the streets by nightfall unless they carried a lantern, and to put out all their lights by ten o'clock at night,[14] were encouraged to carry on their peaceful activities and were treated with respect not only for their persons but for their property as well, including their places of worship. When, for example, objection was raised by them to the soldiers using old fences and ruined houses for fuel, this was forbidden.[15] In fact, it may be said that, as the result of the unusual restraint exercised by the military government in dealing with the people of Quebec, the British soldiers fared far worse during the months of extreme cold than did most of the French within the city. Ensign James Miller of the 15th regiment has left the following vivid picture of the hardships that he and the other men of the ranks had to endure:

> "A severe winter now commenced while we were totally unprepared for such a climate, neither fewel, forage, or indeed anything to make life tolerable. The troops were crowded into vacant houses, as well

---

[11] Murray to Amherst, November 1759, Canadian Archives Report (1912), Appendix I, 94.

[12] Ibid.

[13] For this see Knox, op. cit., II, 185–6.

[14] See Murray's general orders of November 4, 1759, ibid., II, 188–92.

[15] Ibid., II, 187. The robbing or plundering of the inhabitants or any insult offered to their persons was, under orders issued by Murray, to be punished "in an exemplary manner" (ibid., II, 192).

as possible; numbers fell sick, and the scurvy made a dreadful hav-
ock among us. The duty became extremely hard, for after being up
all night on guard, the men were obliged to go near six miles
through the snow to cut wood, and then to drag it home on sledges.
From the severe frost the wood was as hard as marble, and Euro-
peans, who had never been accustomed to cut wood, made but small
progress; a constant and daily supply was however necessary and
required the greatest perseverance. In short, the fatigues of the
winter were so great, that the living almost envied the dead. Liquors
were extremely scarce, and when the men could procure them they
generally drank to excess; it was no uncommon thing in the morning
to find several men frozen to death from that cause." [16]

Yet this honest soldier had words of high praise for the commander-
in-chief, who, he recorded, was "indefatigable, being always present
at guard mountings, visiting the different posts daily, and taking
notice of and rewarding those whom he found attentive and alert." [17]
Murray, while showing great regard for the welfare of his soldiers, was nevertheless a strict disciplinarian. Those who failed in
their duty without proper cause, who incited to mutiny or to desertion, were given the most rigorous punishment, including death.[18]
Further, when proof was forthcoming that the people of the parish
of St. Joseph in the region of Point aux Trembles had revolted from
the oath of fidelity that they had given, he sent a strong detachment
late in November to lay waste the country — and this was done.[19]
Moreover, when he found that it was necessary to do so, he placed
placards about the city threatening severe measures if the inhabitants did not live up to the engagements they had solemnly entered
into.[20] Since the area outside Quebec was subject to constant raiding on the part of the French army, he determined to build a chain
of blockhouses to extend from Cape Diamond, just to the west of the
city, to the suburbs of St. Jean, to the northwest of it, and by the
end of February, in spite of difficulties, they were assuming shape.[21]
Later in the new year traverses were ordered to be built to support

---

[16] "Memoir of an Invalid," Amherst Papers, Packet 54 (Canadian Archives Transcripts).

[17] Ibid.

[18] Knox, op. cit., II, 209.

[19] Ibid.

[20] Ibid., II, 210.

[21] Calendar of events at Quebec from October 27, 1759 to May 8, 1760, Pennsylvania Gazette, June 12, 1760.

them. Most of the efforts of the garrison during the winter, however, were directed toward securing an adequate supply of firewood for use in the iron stoves supplied to the barracks and other places sheltering the men. Each day, when the weather would permit, hundreds of the troops, eight to a sleigh, with others to stand guard with their arms, issued from the city to obtain this essential supply, mostly from the woods of St. Foy, some miles distant, and returned pulling their heavy loads. After this fashion was the season of intense cold endured.

In spite of the embarrassments facing him, the Governor, in writing to Amherst on December 24, was able to express satisfaction with the general situation. He emphasized the fact that the inhabitants of Lower Canada had taken the oath and all in all were behaving well; he also expressed the conviction that, in spite of rumours to the contrary, the French army would make no real attempt to regain Quebec until the spring. In this connection he set forth the view that the city itself would be of little consequence in the next campaign, but that the matter of utmost importance would be the issue of the control of the St. Lawrence.[22]

Not until the end of January was the great river solidly frozen over from the north to the south shore. This fact led Murray to determine to build a blockhouse defended with cannon at Point Levy; especially did this seem to be a matter of urgency in view of reports coming from over the river that French forces were appearing in some strength not far from the point.[23] But before this was undertaken, it seemed necessary to visit punishment on another parish, that of St. Michel on the south shore to the west of the Etchemin, the inhabitants of which, as was true of those of St. Joseph, had repudiated their oath of fidelity and not only had sent their young men to join the French army but had sought to bring other parishes that had submitted to the same resolution. As a result, every house there was reduced to ashes.[24] These stern measures had their effect.

By the beginning of March the garrison of Quebec was combating new enemies that for a time bade fair to destroy it, as fevers, dysentery, and scurvy laid their grip upon it. By that date the army had been reduced from its original strength of seven thousand three

---

[22] *Canadian Archives Report* (1912), Appendix I, 85.
[23] Knox, *op. cit.*, II, 251–3.
[24] *Ibid.*, II, 265.

hundred effective to four thousand eight hundred.[25] The number
of sick and weak men incapable of doing duty was, in fact, so great,
with the hospitals crowded and the duty so severe on those who were
still active, that this became a matter of deep concern to the Governor. What was needed was a supply of fresh provisions; but this
could not be obtained. As a substitute, a plentiful ration of vinegar
was now served to the men, who were also encouraged to drink tar
water to combat these dangerous disorders. Although such measures, taken together with enforced sobriety among the troops and
great care bestowed on those who were being hospitalized, were
somewhat effective — as indicated by a dispatch that Murray sent
to the officer in charge of the British fort on the Bay of Fundy at
the mouth of the St. John [26] — nevertheless, by the end of April
he counted a thousand dead and two thousand "totally unfit for any
Service." [27]

That the French had had in mind a winter attack upon the city
is clear.[28] According to the uniform testimony of deserters and
prisoners, they had planned to surprise and storm the lower town
of Quebec by placing ladders against the walls at various points,
up which the soldiers would swarm. Large numbers of tall ladders,
in fact, were made and the troops, both regulars and Canadians,
were set to work at Montreal to perfect themselves in the art of
moving up them *en masse.* So many serious accidents took place in
the course of these exercises, however, that even the promoters of
the hazardous enterprise, the Canadians, became convinced that it
was impracticable.[29] But the chief obstacle to a winter expedition
was clearly the lack of food such as could be carried by the soldiers, who in the homes of the *habitants* were subsisting largely
on root crops. The mills could not operate to grind the grain because

[25] *Ibid.,* II, 267.
[26] *Canadian Archives Report* (1912), Appendix I, 85.
[27] Murray to Pitt, May 25, 1760, *Pitt Correspondence,* II, 291–2.
[28] *Journal de Lévis,* p. 236.
[29] Knox, *op. cit.,* II, 270–2. The writer of a very interesting *mémoire,* an officer
serving under Bougainville, referred very sarcastically to the many plans suggested by the
Canadians for taking Quebec without artillery: "Amongst the productions of these dis-
tempered brains, that of surprising Quebec by a forced march in winter and . . . by
an escalade was only one of them where there was the least possibility of success. . . .
But . . . the English having seven thousand men in the town . . . it is much to be
believed that we would have lost the half of our army in the attempt and at last, after
a horrible butchery of our men, have been obliged to return shamefully from whence
we came" (*Collection de Manuscrits . . . Relatifs à la Nouvelle-France,* IV, 246–7).

of the ice and, in spite of every effort on the part of de Lévis to secure flour, he was obliged to delay his attempt until the spring thaw
would permit the mills to function.[30] Nevertheless, both he and
Vaudreuil were fully determined to retake the city as soon as the
soldiers were provisioned for a campaign and could move supplies
down the river in their bateaux. They therefore steadily worked toward this end. At the same time they both realized that it was a
matter of supreme importance that effective aid from France should
arrive as early as possible were the colony to be saved.

Vaudreuil, to make sure that the colony would be succoured before it was too late, had determined to send the Chevalier Le Mercier, commandant of the artillery, to France with dispatches before
all navigation must cease.[31] Some eight or ten merchant ships held
in security on the upper river had also been ordered in November
to drop down as far as Sillery to await a favourable opportunity to
run the batteries at Quebec so as to return home for supplies. On
the 21st of the month they had appeared off that point with the
Chevalier aboard one of them; then on the night of the 24th, with
the ebb of the tide and favoured by a fresh wind and extreme darkness, they passed the powerful batteries, in spite of the fact that the
gunners manning these, dimly detecting their presence, fired many
discharges in their direction.[32] Thereupon the ships proceeded on
their mission under command of Captain Kanon, who the preceding
spring had brought the relief convoy to Quebec.

Among the letters sent by the returning ships was one to Maréchal Belle-Isle from the Chevalier de Lévis, under date of November
1, in which he declared:

> "If the King still desires to sustain this colony, he is not without re-
> sources. If he will be pleased to send in the month of May a squad-
> ron in advance of the English with six thousand assault troops
> (*troops de débarquement*) and four thousand recruits for the bat-
> talions and the marine troops here, it will make us masters of the
> river." [33]

Le Mercier, firm in his conviction that, after a French fleet had
ascended the St. Lawrence in May, Quebec would once again be in
the hands of the French, was somewhat more modest in the recom-

---

[30] *Journal de Lévis*, pp. 237–40.
[31] Lévis to Belle-Isle, November 10, 1759, *Lettres de Lévis*, p. 266.
[32] Knox, op. cit., II, 115.
[33] *Lettres de Lévis*, p. 246.

mendations that he made to the ministry in a *mémoire* signed at Versailles on January 7 detailing the needs of the colony. He called for a reinforcement of some four thousand men, which, with the regulars still stationed in Canada, would, he declared, make but eight thousand for the task in hand. The fleet to carry them to their destination, he warned, must be ready to sail by the end of February and must be convoyed by five or six men-of-war. Having arrived before Quebec, these warships would be in position to help the batteries, to be erected on Isle-aux-Coudres, turn back the English fleet when it appeared, and by carrying as ballast some twenty thirty-six-pounders, it would be possible, in addition, to erect batteries on Isle d'Orléans and Point Levy of such a nature as would prevent the enemy ships from anchoring under the protection of the guns of Quebec. In addition to soldiers and artillery, it would be necessary, he further pointed out, to send food supplies and gifts for the Indians. All these, however, must reach the colony before the arrival of the British relief and, to make sure of this, the attempt must be made to ascend the river in the midst of ice floes. Vessels were seldom wrecked by this ice, he affirmed, and then declared that "it would be preferable that such a misfortune should happen to one or two, than to enter the river too late" — otherwise all would be lost.[34]

In the face of these appeals Belle-Isle wrote reassuringly to de Lévis on February 8 that Berryer, Minister of the Marine,

> "orders to be despatched to you, relief of every description in provisions, munitions of war and recruits, by means whereof, despite the advantages the English possess in the occupation of the town of Quebec, which had been too hastily surrendered, you will be able to dispute the ground with them inch by inch, and perhaps to gain some advantage over them, sufficient to arrest their progress." [35]

It is certain that every effort was made to fulfil Belle-Isle's promises. Early in February the Minister of the Marine forwarded instructions to Rostand at Rochefort respecting the freightage for Canada; later in that month signals for each of the French squadrons and for the privately owned vessels destined to carry this aid were also sent to Rochefort in cipher; on the 24th the Comptroller Général and on the

[34] *N. Y. Col. Doc.*, X, 1065–8.
[35] *Ibid.*, X, 1068–9.

25th the Fermier Général were called upon to turn over funds to Rostand without delay so that the expedition might not be retarded; and by the middle of March the ships had fallen down the Charente toward Rochefort. Now there were delays in face of the yearly British blockade, with the result that early in April Berryer wrote to Rostand of his deep distress that the departure of the ships was still held up.[36] On April 14, however, the fleet of some twenty to thirty sail, having assembled at Bordeaux, now finally set out. But the *Machault*, escorting it, was set upon by two English warships and had to retire for repairs; the convoy itself was scattered; and, finally, some of the heavily laden ships were captured. Out of the entire number that sailed, only three by May 17 had arrived at the mouth of the St. Lawrence, and they were too late to render any assistance to de Lévis and his army, with the British fleet by that time in firm control of the river.[37] Thus was the fate of New France sealed by the relentless exertion of superior British sea power.

Buoyed up not only by the hope but by the conviction that ships would be speeded across the Atlantic so as to arrive by way of the Strait of Belle-Isle before the coming of an English fleet, de Lévis pressed ahead with his preparations for a spring assault upon Quebec. In March he distributed elaborate instructions respecting the disposition of the troops to be engaged in it and the order of battle.[38] In an enumeration of the troops, including a battalion of eight hundred to be formed from the inhabitants of Montreal and Trois Rivières, he found that in March he had at his disposal a total of about sixty-seven hundred regulars, some thirty-nine hundred of whom he determined to take with him, together with three thousand militia.[39] To secure the southern approaches to Montreal, Bougainville was now sent to take over the command of Isle-aux-Noix, since Bourlamaque's services were required on the expedition. Pouchot, late commandant of Fort Niagara, who had been taken prisoner but had been exchanged, was also sent in March to the rapids above Montreal to continue the work on Fort Lévis, located on an island some three miles below the mission of La Présentation and Fort

---

[36] *Canadian Archives Report* (1905), I, Part VI, 308–10.

[37] Bigot to the Minister, June 20, 1769, *Collection de Manuscrits . . . Relatifs à la Nouvelle-France*, IV, 271; *Journal de Lévis*, p. 288; advices from Halifax, June 4, *Pennsylvania Gazette*, June 26, 1760. As to the fate of the French relief fleet destroyed in the Ristigouchi by Commodore Byron, see Knox, op. cit., II, 634–5.

[38] For these instructions see *Journal de Lévis*, pp. 243–55.

[39] *Ibid.*, pp. 254–5, 257.

Galette there. It was not until about the middle of April that the ice had broken up on the upper river.

With the preparations at last completed for the enterprise that, it was hoped, would mean so much in deciding the fate of Canada, the army, now provisioned for the campaign, departed from Montreal on the 20th of the month by the north shore, and by the 24th reached Pointe aux Trembles, where the boats and the two frigates carrying the supplies and artillery also arrived that day. The Chevalier had hoped to be able to move down to Sillery, just above the Foulon, made memorable in history, without being detected, and, after surrounding the British troops to the number of some fifteen hundred at the outposts, to attempt to carry the city by surprise, or, if this did not succeed, to besiege it and batter its walls with cannon and mortars collected for that purpose. Murray, however, secured information that the enemy had landed in force at Pointe aux Trembles, and he was able to make his dispositions accordingly, with the result that his outposts, which had extended as far west as Cap Rouge, were drawn in.[40] Therefore there was no surprise when de Lévis's forces moved over the Cap Rouge River and by the evening of the 27th appeared at St. Foy, not far from the city, with the countryside here still wrapped in winter.[41]

Governor Murray now had a choice of measures: either to go out and meet the enemy in the open field with inferior numbers, or to attempt to seal himself firmly within Quebec and stand a siege. He resolved to hazard an action and was persuaded that his fine train of field artillery would help to make up the deficiency in manpower. Therefore early in the morning of the 28th he issued from the fortifications with three thousand men to face a force twice that size. The ensuing battle was fought in the same general area where Wolfe and Montcalm had contested for supremacy in September, but with de Lévis now occupying the Foulon and the ground to the north of it and Murray posted at the beginning of the battle to the

---

[40] Murray to Pitt, May 25, 1759, Pitt Correspondence, II, 292. Murray in this letter does not mention the fact, stressed not only by Captain Knox in his Journal (op. cit., II, 289-90) but by French contemporary writers (see Collection de Manuscrits . . . Relatifs à la Nouvelle-France, IV, 249-50, 267), that when one of the French artillery boats capsized near Cap Rouge, a cannoneer thrown into the water sought to save himself by clambering on a great ice floe, which carried the unhappy man down the river to Quebec, where he was rescued and before expiring gave information of the near presence of de Lévis's army.

[41] Journal de Lévis, p. 258.

west of the line of blockhouses, bastions, and entrenchments that his men had built during the winter and spring from Cape Diamond to St. Jean and even beyond it to the north.

The ensuing action, besides the throwing back of an advancing French column without adequate support at the beginning of the engagement, consisted largely in flank movements, each side making an effort to envelope the wings of the opposing army. So long as the British troops occupied high ground and could be effectively supported by artillery fire, they seemed to have an advantage. When the whole army finally moved forward into low ground where the soldiers had to fight knee-deep in melting snow, this advantage was lost. Further, the light-armed troops on the right wing pushed well ahead of the rest, and although their move forward met with initial success and they started in pursuit of the retreating enemy, they got into such serious difficulty that after great losses they were compelled to retire in so much confusion that they could no longer continue fighting and consequently moved to the rear. To save the situation, Murray sent Otways's grenadiers to strengthen his right wing, and they held firm against two attempts to crush them. At the same time the British left wing advanced and also met with initial success, but could not hold its ground against the pressure of a numerical superiority enjoying the advantages of position, with the result that it in turn was obliged to retire in considerable disorder from its advanced position. This demoralization of both wings of the army now led to a general withdrawal. There was no such panic, however, as had seized Montcalm's troops in September; for in the retreat to Quebec, some three miles distant, the little army was protected by strong rear-guard action on the part of detachments assigned to this duty, which stopped at frequent intervals to fire by volley upon the pursuers. The artillery that had been dragged into the low ground of snow and slush was nevertheless deserted after the guns had been spiked, and the loss in men, including killed, wounded, and prisoners, amounted to some eleven hundred — at least one third of all who took the field that day.[42]

The Battle of Sillery, it may be said, is a testimony to the superiority of de Lévis as a strategist and tactician over his opponent. When Murray placed his army on the Plains of Abraham in battle

---

[42] Murray to Pitt, May 25, 1759, *Pitt Correspondence*, II, 294–5; Knox, *op. cit.*, II, 292–5; *Journal de Lévis*, pp. 263–8; Vaudreuil to Berryer, May 3, 1756, with a "Journal of the Battle of Sillery," *N. Y. Col. Doc.*, X, 1075–86.

formation, his disposition of the troops was sound: he occupied high ground; one of his flanks was covered by the light-armed troops; the other by the mobile rangers and the Quebec volunteers; and his field artillery was well distributed to give proper support to the line. In deserting the elevation, which he never should have done, and in moving toward the enemy, he violated one of the fundamental canons of military science with respect to the surrender of the advantages of terrain and artillery support on the part of a force faced by one of great numerical superiority. In each instance his flanks, which had been permitted to push far in advance of the centre, and beyond the protecting range of the guns, were soon submitted to a devastating fire from an enemy screened by the woods and bushes, which, in the words of Ensign James Miller of the 15th regiment, "gave them an opportunity of cutting us up, they being drawn up under cover and taking aim at leisure, while we could only see them through the intervals of the trees." [43] Consequently, there occurred the retreat of the flanks in the face of sure annihilation or surrender unless a withdrawal took place. Nor could the centre be adequately protected, now posted as it was on the edge of the Sillery woods, where the main body of de Lévis's troops was stationed. To recover the advantages that the British troops had enjoyed at the beginning of the battle was impossible, however, under the circumstances. Murray had no other recourse therefore than to attempt to get his troops back to the outer defences of Quebec. Fortunately for him, de Lévis was not in a position, with his forces overcome with fatigue, to hinder the execution of this movement, which alone saved the British army from disaster and the city probably from recapture.

From April 28 to May 17 Quebec was besieged. With the frost at last leaving the ground, it was possible to dig trenches and parallels where the generally rocky formation of the surface of the ground would permit. This proved to be slow work. Entrenchments appeared, however, and between the 8th and the 13th of May four batteries were finally established, to the west of Murray's chain of blockhouses, and firing began from one of these on the 11th. But even when all four of the batteries were in action — totalling but twenty-one guns and mortars — there was little in the way of results. Only one of the French cannon was in the twenty-four-pounder class; the others were either eighteens or twelves; they were, more-

---

[43] "Memoir of an Invalid," Amherst Papers, Packet 54 (Canadian Archives Transcripts).

over, erected too far distant to batter the walls; and, finally, the supply of powder was so meagre as to compel de Lévis to order that each gun should be fired but twenty times during a period of twenty-four hours.[44] Against these batteries some one hundred and fifty guns, some of large calibre, were shifted from the river defences and most of them ultimately went into action.[45] These by their greater range and fire-power deranged a good deal of de Lévis's offensive arrangements. In fact, the Chevalier, realizing his weakness, was fully counting on receiving from France any day, now that the river was open, aid in the form not only of food supplies and recruits but of a number of real siege guns, such as he had requested, together with an abundant supply of ammunition.[46] With these at his command and with his line enveloping the city from the Foulon to the St. Charles, he felt he would be in a position to finish gloriously the task of reclaiming for his King the capital of New France.

Within the city among the British defenders there were with the beginning of the siege deep apprehensions as to their ability to protect so large a place as Quebec. On the 30th of May, after the returns were in from all the regiments, it was discovered that but two thousand one hundred men were fit for duty.[47] In momentary "panic and fear," according to Captain Knox, the soldiers, many of them intoxicated, committed great irregularities after the battle in order to get at supplies of liquor.[48] Governor Murray was thereupon forced to take stern measures to quell the disorders and to bring about a return of the good discipline that had distinguished the conduct of most of the men up to that time. Yet there was no gainsaying that the situation was most critical. On May 1 the frigate *Racehorse*, which had wintered at Quebec, sailed for Louisbourg and Halifax in order to hasten relief to the army; while on the night of the 4th a French sloop passed the batteries and dropped down the river, also on the same mission. On the 6th there appeared in the countryside on both sides of the river below Quebec signals that seemed to indicate the presence of a fleet.[49] Was it British or French?

---

[44] *Journal de Lévis*, pp. 274–9.
[45] Knox, *op. cit.*, II, 306, 313.
[46] *Journal de Lévis*, p. 279.
[47] Knox, *op. cit.*, II, 298.
[48] *Ibid.*
[49] *Ibid.*, II, 306.

Among the besieged every able-bodied man had meanwhile been set to work in six-hour shifts on the fortifications and new batteries for repelling the enemy. Under this rigid regime, confidence was again restored in the ranks; the men were drawn out of their barracks, and each regiment was encamped as a group at designated points. This confidence was heightened when deserters from the enemy's camp brought reports of the distress of the French army for lack of adequate food.[50] Yet in the background of this restored morale was always the harassing question: what ships are sailing the lower St. Lawrence? The morning of the 9th the defenders of Quebec saw in the far distance a sail moving up the river; for a time all were in suspense, some declaring that it was a French ship, others that it was their own. Then, about eleven o'clock, the speedy frigate *Lowestoft* appeared in the basin and came to anchor.

The excitement and joy of the garrison are not to be described as the men in the very face of the enemy crowded the parapets to shout and wave their hats in the air, beside themselves with excitement, while the artillery thundered with every gun. The commander of the ship, Captain Deane, reported that he was attached to a British squadron that had sailed from England in March under Commodore Swanton. Having become separated from it, he had proceeded up the river alone, but not before he had spoken to Lord Colville's fleet, which had wintered at Halifax but was then cruising off Newfoundland with orders also to ascend the river as far as the island of Bic.[51] Then, on the evening of the 15th, the *Vanguard* with Commodore Swanton on board, the frigate *Diana*, Captain Schomberg, and the armed schooner sent down the river on April 23 put in an appearance. Through the capture on the 16th of a French courier coming from the lower St. Lawrence, it was learned that not only were there scattered ships in the river but that another fleet had entered the gulf.[52] In fact, Colville by the 16th had reached the island of Bic and on the 18th anchored before Quebec.[53] The British were therefore complete masters of the lower St. Lawrence.

---

[50] *Ibid.*, II, 301–7.

[51] *Ibid.*, II, 309–10. By March 20 Colville was ready to take to the sea, but he found that the ice floes in the gulf were so massed that he postponed the date for beginning his cruise to April 14. Then a heavy southerly wind kept him in the Halifax harbour until the 22nd of the month. Sailing even at that late date, he found his passage into the river hindered "by frozen Fogs, compacted Ice and Contrary Winds" (Colville to Pitt, May 24, 1760, *Pitt Correspondence*, II, 290).

[52] Knox, *op. cit.*, II, 317–18.

[53] *Pitt Correspondence*, II, 290.

When de Lévis was informed by an English prisoner captured by the Indians that two large ships seen by his men the evening of the 15th were British — and with his high hopes now blasted — he gave new orders to the two French frigates moored near him on the river. The weather was so unfavourable, however, that the officer who was to deliver the orders could not reach the ships during the night. But at five o'clock in the morning of the 16th the Chevalier could see that the French ships were raising their sails and that three English ships were moving toward them, one in advance of the other, with one of sixty guns bringing up the rear. Cutting their cables, in sight of the now approaching enemy, the French vessels sought safety in flight. The frigate *Pomone*, however, ran ashore and sank in shallow water and was soon afterward burned; the *Atalante*, pursued by the British, moved up the river to Cap Rouge, where it joined the transport ships loaded with provisions and munitions. In view of the fact that the latter would soon be attacked and could not well escape, they were also ordered to be sunk. Thereupon the frigate continued its course up to Pointe aux Trembles and then determined to fight it out with the two enemy vessels. The latter were not long in appearing and for two hours the engagement continued. With his ammunition at length exhausted and after inflicting considerable damage upon his adversaries, the French captain thereupon surrendered his vessel, but without lowering his flag and only after those members of his crew still capable of serving had escaped in the ship's boats.[54]

In view of these losses, the French position in front of Quebec was no longer tenable, especially with the *Vanguard* now directing upon it a heavy enfilading fire. De Lévis therefore proceeded immediately to get his artillery out of the trenches and everything else that could be taken away; the rest, in so far as was possible, he destroyed. The heavier guns brought by the ships were carried to the Anse de Foulon and dumped into the river; the field pieces and those of brass, including the guns lost by Murray in the battle of the Sillery woods were, however, sent off by detachments. Waiting until night had fallen, he thereupon ordered his men out of the defenceless entrenchments and began his retreat.[55] Arriving at Cap Rouge the morning of the 17th, he spent the day there salvaging

---

[54] *Journal de Lévis*, pp. 281–2; Lévis to Vaudreuil, May 18, 1760, *Lettres de Lévis*, pp. 311–12.

[55] *Ibid.*

what he could from the sunken ships and on the following day moved west to the Jacques Cartier. Having passed over it, and at last in a position of some security, he thereupon made a disposition of his troops. Major Dumas, a veteran in wilderness fighting, was given some eighteen hundred men for the purpose of holding Pointe aux Trembles, the fort at the Jacques Cartier, and the church at Dechambeault,[56] where Murray himself had landed with a force the preceding year. The rest of the troops were ordered to their quarters at Trois Rivières and Montreal. As for the militia, by the 21st almost all of the Canadians had deserted and returned home.[57]

De Lévis, upon arriving in Montreal and after conferring with Vaudreuil, was now in a position to estimate the nature of the resources in his possession for continuing the struggle for Canada. Most of the munitions, provisions, and artillery that had been with so much effort gathered together for the campaign just ended had been lost; his battalions were now reduced to an average of two hundred and fifty men; many of the soldiers lacked not only bayonets but even guns; his artillery, at least that which was of any value, had been taken from the enemy, and the supply for each gun did not permit more than a total of forty discharges; further, he no longer had a fleet on the river — only the small *Marie,* which had come from France *en flûte* and had been armed with some old iron cannon, and bateaux still left that could transport scarcely half of his troops. It was true that two semi-galleys were in the course of construction at Montreal, that there were two vessels on Lake Ontario, and a sloop and two small craft on the Richelieu, but they were all poorly manned.[58] It was also true that among the *habitants* were many men capable of rendering effective military service. But the militia had deserted the ranks of his army, and the question therefore arose: could he ever again rally them to join the regulars on the field of battle? The picture was indeed a dark one — with all hope of aid from France at last dissipated and with full knowledge of the vast resources possessed by the British for bringing the war in North America to a victorious end.

In turning to the British plans for the American campaign of 1760, it may be pointed out that on January 7 Pitt had addressed

---

[56] *Journal de Lévis,* pp. 284–5.
[57] *Ibid.;* see also Murray to Pitt, May 25, 1760, *Pitt Correspondence,* II, 296.
[58] *Journal de Lévis,* p. 288.

letters to the governors of the continental colonies, once again, calling upon them to raise at least as many troops as each had furnished in 1759. As in previous years, he had promised that His Majesty would care for the arming and provisioning of these troops and that recommendations to Parliament would also be made that those charges for the levying, clothing, and pay of the men should be reimbursed as the efforts displayed by the respective provinces would seem to merit.[59] At the same time he had called upon Amherst to proceed with the task of reducing Montreal in order "to compleat the glory of His Maj[ty's] arms in North America." This could be done by making such disposition of the forces under his command as seemed best. As to further operations to be undertaken to the south of New York and to the west of Pennsylvania by the regular forces stationed there in conjunction with the provincials, the Minister was not inclined to be definite, only suggesting to the commander-in-chief the possibility of a movement of troops for gaining possession of the Cuyahoga, which flows into Lake Erie from the south, where today the city of Cleveland stands.[60] Again, in February he had written to Amherst revealing his decision to demolish the fortress at Louisbourg and to close the harbour there as effectually as possible and therefore called upon the general to see that these measures were taken.[61] In conformity with this decision, men who had had experience in mining and the use of explosives were formed into companies and sent to Cape Breton Island on the *Vanguard* — destined to ascend the St. Lawrence — and under command of Major Bastide proceeded in the spring and summer with the great task of demolition.

In the mobilization of the forces of the colonies for the approaching campaign, again the northern colonies took the lead. On January 24 Massachusetts agreed to raise five thousand men in addition to twenty-five hundred already in the service who were stationed in Nova Scotia and on Cape Breton Island.[62] However, the number actually raised and credited to the province after the discharge of the troops who had served during the winter was hardly five thousand.[63] Connecticut voted five thousand men and is credited with

59 *Pitt Correspondence*, II, 231–7.

60 *Ibid.*, II, 237–42.

61 *Ibid.*, II, 250–2.

62 Pownall to Amherst, January 22, 1760, War Office 34. 26:9, 13–16.

63 "Provincials Raised in 1758, 1759, and 1760" Chatham Mss., Bundle 86 (Canadian Archives Transcripts); Amherst's *Journal*, Appendix.

this number on the official returns; [64] but great delays were experienced in raising the troops, largely as the result of rumours of approaching peace, and as late as June 12 Colonel Worcester of the Connecticut line expressed the fear upon his arrival in Albany that the colony might fall short by two thousand men of the quota that it had agreed to supply.[65] The New Hampshire assembly in February resolved to put into the field eight hundred men,[66] and Rhode Island, as well, duplicated, it would appear, its effort of the preceding year; [67] both New York and New Jersey indubitably did so. In other words, the colonies to the north and east of Pennsylvania are credited with raising over fifteen thousand men for the general service, whereas all the other colonies, including the populous provinces of Pennsylvania and Virginia, are credited with not even four thousand, Pennsylvania being given credit for twenty-eight hundred, Virginia for seven hundred and sixty-one, and North Carolina for three hundred.[68]

By reason of the "Sloth of the Colonies in raising their Troops and sending them to their Rendez-vous," [69] it was the latter part of May before any of the men from Massachusetts Bay put in an appearance at Albany. From then on, outside of the New York provincials, the contingents from the northern colonies kept straggling in. As late as June 20 Amherst, anxious to begin his operations in earnest, was chafing over their tardy appearance.[70] With the arrival on the 22nd, however, of four New England regiments, he was at last ready to move.[71]

In connection with the plans formulated for the year's campaign, it should be noted that Amherst was obliged to make a diversion of some of the troops as the result of the unexpected outbreak of hostilities on the part of the Cherokee Indians. He was also under the necessity of keeping in mind the importance of strengthening the British position in the valley of the Ohio. To utilize to the best

---

[64] Op. cit.; Conn. Col. Rec., XI, 349–50.
[65] Amherst's Journal, p. 210.
[66] Provincial Papers, VI, 739.
[67] Amherst's Journal, Appendix. For the correspondence between Governor Hopkins and General Amherst covering the support of the campaign of 1760 by the colony, see Rhode Island Colonial Records, VI, 243–5, 254.
[68] "Provincials Raised in 1758, 1759, and 1760," op. cit., see also Amherst's Journal, Appendix.
[69] Amherst to Pitt, June 21, 1760, Pitt Correspondence, II, 305.
[70] Ibid., II, 308.
[71] Amherst's Diary, p. 212.

advantage the forces, both regulars and provincials, to the south-ward of New York and New Jersey, he therefore determined in April to place Brigadier General Monckton in direct charge of south-ern operations, thus relieving General Stanwix of his command.[72] Since the history of the western America frontier from 1760 to the outbreak of the Revolutionary War by reason of its importance re-quires detailed and unified treatment, it seems desirable to reserve consideration of developments there for subsequent volumes of this series and to terminate this volume with an account of the movements made by the British against the last French stronghold in Canada — the final phase of the Great War for the Empire in so far as it involved North America.

Doubtless, in view of the difficulties that he had experienced the preceding year in attempting to invade Canada by way of Lake Champlain, Amherst determined that he would take his main force up the Mohawk to Oswego and from there go by boat across Lake Ontario to the entrance of the St. Lawrence and then down that river.[73] To reach Montreal, however, it would be necessary for him to dispose of the defences that the French had erected between La Galette and the rapids on the upper waters of the stream, and he planned his campaign with this in mind. He also decided that, at the same time he himself was making this move, a smaller force should leave Crown Point for the purpose of attempting to approach the French city by penetrating the Isle-aux-Noix defences on the Richelieu.[74] Further, he expected Murray to move up the St. Law-rence from Quebec and in April had written to him to that effect, and the brigadier had assured him that these orders would be car-ried out.[75]

It seemed to be a matter of first importance for the campaign of 1760 to enlist again the services of the Six Nations. In February Amherst had written to Johnson calling upon him to use his utmost endeavours to that end, and the Indian Superintendent had indicated that this would be done.[76] In this connection it may be pointed out that, at the instigation of Governor General Vaudreuil, representa-tives of twenty-two Indian tribes in alliance with the French had

---

[72] Amherst to Pitt, April 28, 1760, *Pitt Correspondence*, II, 282.

[73] Amherst to Pitt, May 19, 1760, *ibid.*, II, 288–9.

[74] *Ibid.*

[75] Murray to Amherst, May 19, 1760, *Canadian Archives Report* (1912), p. 86.

[76] Amherst to Johnson, February 23, and Johnson to Amherst, March 7, 1760, *Sir William Johnson Papers*, III, 192–3, 197.

journeyed to Onondaga late in 1759 to persuade the Iroquoian Confederation to remain neutral and to send in turn deputies to a council fire at Cagnawaga (Caughnawaga). A report of this conference was given to Johnson by deputies of the Six Nations who gathered at Fort Johnson in February of the new year, and Sir William seized the occasion to emphasize the treachery of the French Indians and also the fact that he had sent repeated messages to them to abandon their white allies and had received assurance from them that they would do so.[77] That the Canadian Indians were now wavering in their loyalty to the French was clear; it was equally clear that the Six Nations had not committed themselves to the proposed neutrality in the war and might be brought into the field once more with proper encouragement, in the way of arms and food supplies. These Amherst agreed to furnish.[78] Before this support could be guaranteed, however, it was necessary to combat a report that the French Indians had circulated among the Confederation which deeply disturbed its members. This was to the effect that after the reduction of Canada by the British the latter planned to turn against all the Indians, friends and foes alike, for the purpose of utterly extirpating them.[79] That Johnson was able to rid the minds of most of them of this apprehension is indicated by the fact that he was successful in rallying six hundred warriors, with whom he proceeded to the rendezvous at Oswego at the appointed time.[80]

In order to speed the preparation for the campaign, Amherst, after ordering two regiments up the St. Lawrence to strengthen Murray, proceeded to Albany early in May and thereupon made a disposition of the forces available for his campaign. He decided that but two regiments of regulars, the Inniskilling Highlanders and Monckton's, supported by the four New York Independent Companies and the Massachusetts Bay, New Hampshire, and Rhode Island provincials, together with a body of rangers and Stockbridge Indians, would move over Lake Champlain and down the Richelieu against Isle-aux-Noix. Colonel William Haviland of the 27th regiment, who had campaigned in America since 1757, had commanded at Fort Edward during the winter of 1757–8, and had exhibited ex-

[77] Op. cit., III, 188–92; N. Y. Col. Doc., X, 1093.
[78] Amherst to Johnson, April 2, 1760, Johnson Papers, III, 206–7.
[79] Johnson to Pitt, October 24, 1760, ibid., III, 272.
[80] Ibid. It may be pointed out that there assembled at Oswego over thirteen hundred Indians, including women and children; before the forces took to Lake Ontario the latter groups were sent back home.

cellent qualities of leadership, was placed in command of this small army, which amounted to some thirty-four hundred men when it sailed northward from Crown Point in August. For the Lake Ontario operations he allotted four regiments, also the 4th battalion of the Royal Americans, the 1st and 2nd of the Royal Highlanders, and six companies of Montgomery's; these were to be supported by the Connecticut, New York, and New Jersey provincials and Sir William Johnson's Indians.[81] Even after the last of the provincial contingents had appeared at Albany late in June, there were unavoidable delays in launching the campaign. Supplies and men moved slowly up the Mohawk by reason of the low water; and two sloops built on Lake Ontario, and alone capable of defending the great flotilla of whaleboats and bateaux that must move the men and matériel over the waters of Lake Ontario in the face of two armed French vessels, had to be provisioned and armed.

Although Amherst left Albany on June 19 for Oswego, it was not until July 9 that he was able to arrive there,[82] and it was as late as August 9 that the last of the colonial contingencies, the New Jersey troops, put in an appearance — the day before he had set for his own departure for the St. Lawrence and that of Haviland for the Isle-aux-Noix, according to orders issued to the latter, so that the movements of the two armies could be synchronized.[83] To clear the way of the hovering French vessels on Lake Ontario and to find the channel of the St. Lawrence, the two sloops, named the *Onondaga* and the *Mohawk* to honour Johnson's Indians — the first manned with a hundred sailors and armed with four nine-pounders, and the second carrying ninety sailors and sixteen six-pounders — had already set sail on the 7th under command of Captain Loring. Therefore, on the appointed morning "at Peep of day" the tents were struck, the soldiers marched to the shore, and soon the expedition had taken to the water and proceeded slowly down the lake in three great columns of row galleys, whaleboats, and bateaux, with an advanced guard made up of Gage's light infantry. On the 14th, before Amherst approached the entrance to the St. Lawrence,

---

[81] Hugh Arnot to Loudoun, October 2, 1760, Loudoun Papers, No. 6256, Huntington Library. According to Richard Huck-Saunders, writing to Loudoun from Oswego on August 6, Amherst's army consisted of fifty-three hundred regulars, forty-three hundred provincials, one hundred and fifty from the royal artillery, and six hundred Indians (*ibid.*, No. 6258).

[82] Amherst's *Diary*, pp. 213-17.

[83] *Ibid.*, p. 222.

he passed Loring's sloops, which had failed to find the channel of the river,[84] and on the following day the invading force moved down the river to Point au Baril — a place where the French had built their two lake vessels the preceding year — which was but three leagues above Fort La Galette.[85]

As has been indicated, the Chevalier Pouchot had been ordered in March to go with a force to take over the direction of the defence of the upper St. Lawrence and had left Montreal on the 17th of that month. Arriving in the neighbourhood of La Présentation mission, where Fort La Galette had been established, he sought no longer to strengthen that place, but to complete the defences on an island a short distance below it, previously known as Isle Orakointon and now named Isle Royale, where Fort Lévis was in the process of construction.[86] With some three hundred men available — regulars, militia, and sailors — he proceeded energetically with the work of completing the barracks, the magazines, and the officers' quarters; he also raised about the whole a rampart some eleven feet in height made of heavy timber and earth, planted batteries on the galleries built along the interior of the ramparts, dug a fosse beyond the latter, and laid down an abatis to the very edge of the river.[87] This little fort, bristling with cannon in the midst of the rapidly moving water, was destined to be the chief, if not sole, defence of the upper St. Lawrence against the army that Amherst was bringing down it. In fact, Fort La Galette on the Oswegatchi had been quite deserted for months because of the fact that it was dominated by elevations and therefore could not be defended against a land force with artillery. Moreover, the numerous Indians of the once flourishing La Présentation mission of Abbé Piquet had for the most part moved from the place to one of greater security, the majority of them settling on a near-by island given the name Isle Piquet.[88] As a result, the buildings of the mission as well as the fort were systematically destroyed in July when it became evident that the British were mak-

---

[84] Loring had been ordered to locate the channel of the river and to proceed down to Isle Royale, where the French had built Fort Lévis. Without a pilot he found the navigation very difficult for his ships moving through the various islands, with the result that he did not succeed in getting down to the French fort until the 19th (Loring to James Rivers, August 29, 1760, Chatham Mss., Bundle 96, Canadian Archives Transcripts).

[85] Amherst's Journal, p. 231.

[86] Pouchot, op. cit., I, 227, 229–30.

[87] Ibid., I, 238–40.

[88] Ibid., II, 8. This island is now known as Galloo Island.

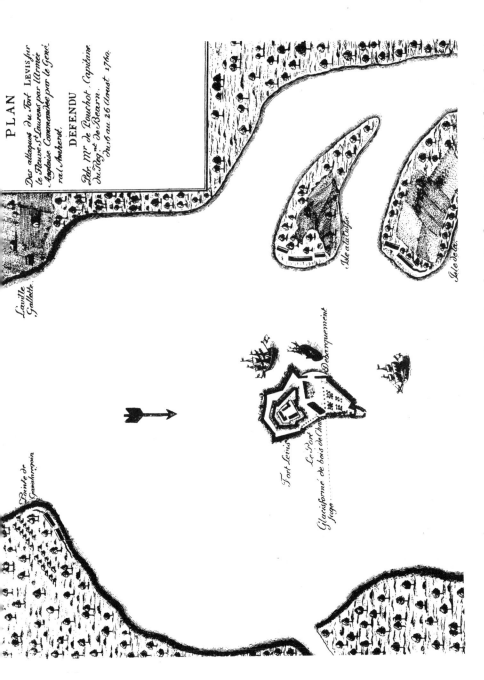

A portion of a map of the Upper St. Lawrence illustrating the attack upon Fort Lévis by Amherst, 1760.

(From Captain Pouchot's *Late War in North America*, 1781.)

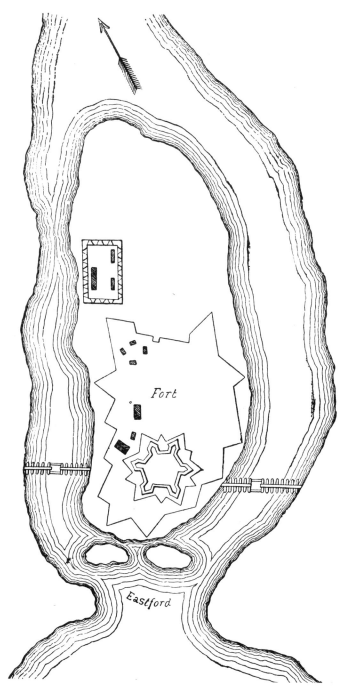

Isle-aux-Noix and its defences, 1760.
(From *Mémoires sur le Canada, 1749–1760.*)

now repaired and stationed above the fort at random-shot distance. It was not until the 23rd, however, that the batteries of twenty-four-pounders were ready to open fire, and Amherst, to bring matters to a head and as a preliminary to storming the island, ordered the three ships to fall down close to the fort and to deliver their broadsides at point-blank range. But the vessels received so much punishment that two of them sheered off and moved down the river out of range, while Loring's own vessel, drifting upon a sandbank close to the French fort, was, after some hours, deserted.[95]

Pouchot, nevertheless, was doomed, with his original four hundred and fifty men on Isle Royale finally reduced to less than three hundred effectives, facing Amherst's ten thousand provided with batteries of heavy guns now playing at will upon the French defences. The four hundred additional troops under de la Corne ordered from Montreal to support him found it impossible even to make contact with him.[96] Therefore, realizing the hopelessness of his situation, surrounded as he was on all sides by the enemy and with Fort Lévis finally reduced to "a litter of carpenter's wood and fascines," with the advice of his officers he determined on the afternoon of the 25th to capitulate — as he had been compelled to surrender to overwhelming force at Niagara the preceding year — and once again he became a British prisoner of war.[97] The fort that he had valiantly defended with his little corps was thereupon given the name of Fort William Augustus. After it had been placed somewhat in a state of repair and garrisoned and after the *Onondaga*, Loring's ship, had also been floated again and repaired, together with the other vessels and the row galleys that had suffered damage in the fighting, the army on the 31st began its movement down the very dangerous rapids and, with the loss of but eighty-four men, forty-six bateaux, seventeen whaleboats, and one row galley, finally moved into the placid waters of Lake St. Francis.[98] To the surprise of the British forces, not a single enemy appeared to oppose their dangerous passage. Yet, it may be pointed out that Johnson and his

---

[95] Amherst's *Journal*, pp. 237–8; Knox, *op. cit.*, II, 411–12; Loring to Captain James Rivers, August 29, 1760, Chatham Mss., Bundle 96 (Canadian Archives Transcripts). These accounts show wide variations respecting the engagement on the 23rd, and especially as these relate to Loring's conduct.

[96] Captain Knox, *op. cit.*, II, 403; *Journal de Lévis*, p. 297.

[97] Pouchot, *op. cit.*, II, 34; Amherst's *Journal*, p. 239.

[98] Knox, *op. cit.*, II, 313–15; Amherst to Pitt, September 8, 1760, *Pitt Correspondence*, II, 329–30.

Indians were present on shore to serve as a cover in case of necessity as the boats moved one by one down the narrow channel of the turbulent, roaring river.

The French forces about Montreal were, in fact, fully occupied with other dangers that faced them, with Governor Murray advancing up the river from Quebec and Brigadier General Haviland moving upon them by way of Lake Champlain and the Richelieu.

With respect to the defences erected at Isle-aux-Noix, these were, as has already been mentioned, entrusted to Bougainville when de Lévis felt the need of the presence of Bourlamaque in the army that proceeded in April against Quebec. To defend the island, he had until the end of June only four hundred and fifty men. But when the English ships began appearing on Lake Champlain and the enemy was otherwise showing signs of activity, he was reinforced by the 2nd battalion of the de Berry regiment, so that he finally had at his disposal some eleven hundred men.[99] Although this sector had remained quiet, as suggested, during the preceding winter and the early spring, when the news reached Amherst at Albany by courier that Quebec was besieged by the French, he ordered Major Robert Rogers of the rangers to create a diversion by taking three hundred men down Lake Champlain from Crown Point; he was instructed, after landing on the west side near the entrance of the Richelieu, to surprise St. Jean, located below Isle-aux-Noix, by moving through the wilderness, and, before retreating, to destroy there all vessels, boats, provisions, and whatever else would aid the enemy.[100]

Early in June Rogers departed on his mission, but, after landing, had the misfortune to be discovered by a French detachment from Isle-aux-Noix on the 6th and, in spite of his success in the engagement, was obliged to return to his boats in the lake. Nevertheless, at midnight of the 9th he landed again and by the evening of the 15th was close to the French fort. St. Jean, however, was much stronger than had been anticipated and was also too well guarded for a successful surprise attack, with the result that he proceeded two leagues farther down the river to Sainte-Thérèse and in open

---

[99] Journal de Lévis, p. 291; Collection de Manuscrits . . . Relatifs à l'Histoire de La Nouvelle-France, IV, 256–7.

[100] For these orders see Reminiscences of the French War containing Rogers's Expeditions, pp. 100–1; Journals of Major Rogers (1769), pp. 178–9.

daylight suddenly rushed through the gate of the stockaded place, burned the houses, the magazines of forage and provisions, and also the wagons for conveying these to Isle-aux-Noix, killed the cattle and horses — and then retired.[101] From this time on until midsummer there was no important move on the part of Brigadier Haviland, busy as he was with preparations for his drive down the Richelieu, which he hoped would carry him successfully to the St. Lawrence after overcoming on the way all resistance at Isle-aux-Noix. Nor did Bougainville for his part do more than send out scouting parties.

Then, on August 11, once more the British army — composed of regulars, provincials, rangers, and a small body of Indians — left Crown Point, with no problem to face such as confronted Amherst the preceding year with respect to the control of Lake Champlain.[102] On the 16th it was landed on the east shore not far south of Isle-aux-Noix and thereupon sought to open a road to communicate with the Rivière du Sud, flowing westward into the Richelieu below the fort, at the mouth of which a small French fleet had been moored.[103] At the same time batteries were erected commanding the island fortifications, and these opened up on the 23rd. Two days later, in the midst of the bombardment, a body of regulars, rangers, and Indians placed under command of Captain Darby moved silently northward through the woods and unexpectedly opened fire on the French river fleet with two light howitzers and a six-pounder. Without giving the enemy time to recover from the surprise, the British rushed on board a large rideau and, by capturing it, were able to train its heavy guns on the other vessels now trying to escape, which grounded and were soon also captured.[104]

This loss — which gave the British command of the Richelieu below Isle-aux-Noix and thus opened an easy way by water to Fort St. Jean and Chambly below it — was a most serious blow to the whole French plan for protecting Montreal. These defences alone stood between a junction of Haviland's army with that of Murray,

---

101 *Ibid.*, pp. 158–70; *Journal de Lévis*, pp. 290–1.

102 Haviland had the 17th and the 18th regiments, four companies of the Royal Highlanders, the Massachusetts Bay, New Hampshire, and Rhode Island provincial regiments, five companies of rangers, and seventy Stockbridge Indians (Knox, *op. cit.*, II, 392).

103 *Journal de Lévis*, p. 297.

104 Rogers's *Journal*, pp. 171–5; Bigot to Belle-Isle, August 29, 1760, *N. Y. Col. Doc.*, X, 1104.

slowly approaching Montreal from the east, and they were now threatened.[105] Moreover, Isle-aux-Noix, as a result of the loss of control of the lower Richelieu, was all but isolated. Could it still hold out?

De Lévis had written to Bougainville from Montreal on the 19th: "I am greatly relying on your post to prolong our defence and to do honour to our arms. It could not be in better hands."[106] This gallant letter, together with one from Vaudreuil, came into the hands of the commandant at this critical moment. Vaudreuil in his message, realizing doubtless the dangers confronting Bougainville and his troops, advised, in contrast to de Lévis, that in case of necessity, if faced by a greatly superior force, he could make his choice: either to capitulate or to retreat.[107] Would he, as de Lévis had requested, make a strong stand and run the risk of capture, or, on the other hand, follow the Governor General's advice and retreat while he still had the opportunity to add his troops to the force that must make a last defence of Montreal? With but two days' supply of provisions at hand he finally decided on the wisdom of the latter course.[108] Yet it was not until the night of the 27th, while the French batteries were still briskly firing, that he carried his men over to the west side of the river, where the flooded lands had offered no opportunity to the enemy to entrench itself, and stole quietly away leaving but forty men to continue the firing of the guns, which they continued to do until noon of the 28th, when a white flag was at last raised.

Although the distance to Montreal was but eight leagues, Bougainville and his little army became confused in moving through the darkness, and after hours of rapid tramping, and almost exhausted, they found themselves to their amazement again close to the Isle-aux-Noix.[109] Nevertheless, starting once more, most of them succeeded, by moving down to St. Jean and Chambly, in reaching Montreal on the 29th. But Isle-aux-Noix had fallen and the protecting fleet on the Richelieu was no more. Was it possible now, even with Bougainville's force, to save Montreal and with it New France? In the words of Bigot, writing on August 29 to Belle-Isle: "Had M. de Bougainville been able to hold out the time that was hoped,

---

[105] Ibid.

[106] Lettres de Lévis, pp. 378–9.

[107] Collection de Manuscrits . . . Relatifs de la Nouvelle-France, IV, 258–9.

[108] Ibid.

[109] Ibid., IV, 260–1.

Canada might have perhaps been saved for this year; such were the appearances, whilst at present it is in great danger." [110]

It was, indeed, in great danger. So overwhelming, in fact, were the other forces, beyond those under the command of Haviland, that were directed against Montreal that it may be questioned whether or not the mere holding of the forts on the Richelieu could possibly have saved New France. Not only was General Amherst approaching Montreal with some ten thousand men from the west, but Governor Murray was moving slowly but relentlessly from the east ever closer to the city.

Although, according to an enumeration of the troops at Quebec on June 15, Murray had at his command some fifty-two hundred men of the rank and file, yet over twenty-three hundred of them were incapacitated, either sick or wounded.[111] He was reinforced, however, before the beginning of July by a number of men who late in the fall had gone southward to New York and other places to recover their health; [112] further, Amherst had ordered two regiments up from Louisbourg to support him.[113] Feeling that, with the British in command of the lower river, Quebec was in no serious danger,[114] the Governor was in a position to carry out Amherst's orders to move against Montreal. He therefore planned to embark most of his troops fit for duty, to the number of somewhat over twenty-two hundred. To these he would also add the Louisbourg reinforcements upon their arrival. To garrison Quebec during his absence, he left under the command of Colonel Fraser seventeen hundred able-bodied men, besides some thirteen hundred still incapacitated.[115] On July 14, the day before his departure, he wrote an interesting letter to Lord Sackville, which indicated that he expected to bring hostilities to a conclusion without any aid from either Amherst's army or that under Haviland:

> ". . . I set out this very day with two thousand two hundred men to do all I can, to facilitate the entire reduction of Canada. Mr. Amherst should be advancing by this time, but I fear he is late; I have no intelligence of his motions; was he near the enemy's frontiers I

[110] N. Y. Col. Doc., X, 1104.

[111] Knox, op. cit., II, 340.

[112] Ibid., II, 346.

[113] Amherst's Journal, p. 198, 201–2.

[114] Murray to Amherst, May 19, 1760, Canadian Archives Report (1912), p. 86.

[115] Murray to Pitt, July 13, 1760, ibid., p. 114.

am positive I should hear of him; he was certainly taking the wrong road; up the St. Lawrence was the sure route, I shall push without hesitation to that Capital; I can do it with safety, because I am master of the river, & if Amherst does not get through, which I much doubt, I shall conquer the country when the reinforcements from Louisbourg join me, & they are hourly expected." [116]

With thirty-two frigates, brigantines, and other sailing vessels, nine floating batteries, and a large number of barges and bateaux, the expeditionary force moved very slowly up the river. Without a strong favouring wind it was found that because of the current no progress could be made unless the tide were coming in. When Point aux Trembles was reached, Murray detached a force to establish a post there; then he passed by the French fortifications at the mouth of the Jacques Cartier and succeeded in surmounting the rapids at Dechambault, three leagues above, at which point the river narrows and then broadens out again. Captain Knox records in his *Journal* the effect of this array of might upon those dwelling along the banks of the St. Lawrence: "The north and south inhabitants are all in arms, terrified, no doubt at their approaching fate; it is not probable they ever saw so numerous a fleet in this part of the country. . . ." [117] But soon the impulse to resist the British gave way to more sober thoughts of the consequences. In fact, on the 19th all the men of the parish of St. Croix surrendered to troops who had landed, and the day following, those of this parish as well as those of the parish of Lobinière took the oath of neutrality; on the 23rd they were followed by the inhabitants of St. Antoine, who, in addition, surrendered their arms. [118] The argument used by the Governor of Quebec, in the presence of deputies of these people of the various parishes, to bring this to pass was potent enough:

> "Who can carry on or support war without ships, artillery, ammunition, or provisions? At whose mercy are your habitations, and that harvest that you expect to reap this summer, together with all you are possessed of in this world? Therefore consider your own interest, and provoke us no more." [119]

---

[116] Germain Papers, Volume II (Clements Library).
[117] Knox, *op. cit.*, II, 348.
[118] *Ibid.*, II, 252–4.
[119] *Ibid.*

News at this time reached Murray that the two Louisbourg regiments had arrived at the Isle-au-Coudre. He therefore sent some of his flat-bottomed bateaux to convey them up the river. This meant delay in the movement of the army. Further, the tide that had aided the ascent of the St. Lawrence quite failed as Trois Rivières was approached, and the men who were rowing the boats found that "without a good breeze of wind the labour of pulling against the stream was excessive." Nevertheless, in the words of Ensign James Millier, as left in his "Memoir":

> ". . . the beauty of the prospect made amends for the fatigue of the body, being beautiful beyond description. Lofty woods, scattered here and there, meadows covered with flocks . . . fields covered with corn, notwithstanding the precarious state of the province; beautiful streams increasing the great river, churches and castles [120] seen at intervals through the trees, all appeared enchanting to men who had passed two such dismal winters." [121]

On August 6 the inhabitants of the parish of Biçancour, just across the river from Trois Rivières, made their submission to "become subjects to his Britannic Majesty," [122] and on the 8th the ascending fleet skirted that town itself, where the Sieur Dumas with his troops behind entrenchments was awaiting to receive the British should they attempt to land. Murray — in conformity with his action in avoiding an engagement at the mouth of the Jacques Cartier — declined, however, to pause and fight, preferring rather to get between the French force and Montreal. This was, to say the least, disconcerting to the French. It led the garrison to file off from Trois Rivières in order to follow the movements of the fleet.[123] De Lévis, writing from Montreal to Belle-Isle on August 7, was obliged to admit: "We possess no means of stopping them; we are making a mere defensive demonstration to retard their march." Those Canadians living in the area that was being penetrated by the invaders, he also confessed, could no longer be relied upon, frightened as they were at the appearance of the fleet and dreading the burning of their homes should they make resistance.[124]

[120] The writer may have had in mind the houses of the seigneurs located on the seigneuries that bordered the banks of the river.

[121] Amherst Papers, Packet 54 (Canadian Archives Transcripts). Captain Knox has likewise left a delightful picture of this region as viewed from his boat (op. cit., II, 361).

[122] Ibid., II, 360.

[123] Ibid., II, 360–2; Journal de Lévis, p. 294.

[124] N. Y. Col. Doc., X, 1102.

While at Berthier, just above Lake St. Pierre, where he had gone to consult with Dumas as to the means of stopping Murray, the Chevalier on the 17th received further ominous news: that two other armies were converging upon Montreal, with that from Crown Point but half a league from the Isle-aux-Noix, and the other moving down the St. Lawrence close to the rapids where the fort that bore his name stood; likewise, the day following he was made aware that Lord Rollo with the Louisbourg regiment — after landing on the north shore and disarming the parishes of Champlain and St. Magdalene [125] — had at last joined Murray, who was now pausing at the island of St. Ignace, located at the upper end of Lake St. Pierre and almost opposite the mouth of the Richelieu or Sorel.[126]

While the British forces were still lingering on the lake, Rollo on the 23rd was detached with a considerable force to raid the southern shore. Falling somewhat down the river by night, the next morning he appeared to the east of the parish of Sorel. He had been ordered, as a warning to other Canadians, to burn the houses of those of the inhabitants there who were still in arms. In this mission he was successful with respect to homes in the lower part of the parish. Yet he did not attempt to force the issue with Bourlamaque, at the head of some seven hundred troops strongly entrenched near the mouth of the Richelieu. Nor did the latter see fit to come out into the open to fight.[127] In fact, the militiamen who made up one half of his force had already shown, he declared, in writing to de Lévis, a very bad spirit and clearly could no longer be easily led into battle. What is more, those from Sorel whose houses were still left standing when Rollo at length returned to the fleet thereupon returned home in a body, and those from St. Ours, situated on the south bank of the river just above Sorel, from now on refused all military service,[128] as did the Canadians who had been with Bougainville at Isle-aux-Noix and had retreated with him. The fear that they spread in returning to such parishes as that of St. Jean had the effect of causing a general desertion from the ranks of the army by the *habitants*.[129] Clearly the situation was getting out of hand even for so experienced a soldier as de Lévis.

[125] Knox, *op. cit.*, II, 364, 371.

[126] *Journal de Lévis*, pp. 296–7.

[127] *Ibid.*, II, 375; Bourlamaque to Lévis, August 12, 1760 *Lettres de M. de Bourlamaque au Chevalier de Lévis* (ed. Abbé Casgrain), pp. 82–4.

[128] Bourlamaque to Lévis, August 22, 1760, *ibid.*, p. 102.

[129] *Journal de Lévis*, p. 300.

By the 28th Haviland, having left Isle-aux-Noix with his flotilla, had appeared on the Richelieu just above St. Jean. To prevent the place from falling into his hands, it was put to the torch, as was Sainte-Thérèse below it on the river, whereupon the French who had garrisoned these places retired to Chambly, still lower down the Richelieu.[130] But even such drastic measures as these could have little effect on the final outcome of the struggle. Murray on the 25th had weighed anchor and started up the river from Lake St. Pierre. Although his fleet could hardly move at times as the result of calms and could at best progress but very slowly, he had three days later moved within four leagues of Montreal — all the while accompanied by a force under Dumas along the north bank, and one under Bourlamaque moving parallel with it along the south bank.[131] On the 31st he landed a body of his grenadiers and light infantry on the latter bank, which proceeded to take possession of the hamlet of Varenne, just below Montreal.[132] This led the following day — after some resistance on the part of the people and the burning of two houses— to the surrender of all living within that rich parish, who came in, delivered their arms, and took the oath; at the same time two other equally flourishing parishes in the neighbourhood sent notice that they would do likewise.[133] Murray's mission was therefore all but complete. Unwilling to move forward without first hearing from Amherst, who, he knew, was moving down the upper St. Lawrence from Isle Royale, he established an encampment at Varenne, while still keeping most of his men in the ships.[134]

Meanwhile Haviland was pushing down from St. Jean, and on September 3 messengers arrived from him at Murray's headquarters bringing word that the brigadier would be at La Prairie — on the south shore above Varenne and just opposite Montreal — in two or three days at most, taking the well-worn road that led from Chambly to that place. For Chambly had surrendered on the 1st, and the people of that parish and of Sorel had taken the oath.[135] Amherst's army — after running on the 4th the treacherous Cedar and Cascade rapids that lie below Lake St. Francis and after spending the night and the next day on Isle Parrot, near the mouth of the Ottawa,

---

130 Ibid.; see also Rogers's Journal, pp. 175–8.
131 Journal de Lévis, p. 300.
132 Knox, op. cit., II, 379.
133 Ibid., II, 381.
134 Ibid.
135 Ibid., II, 382; Rogers's Journal, pp. 177–8.

where the boats that had been damaged were repaired and the oath of allegiance given to the inhabitants who appeared for the purpose of submitting — moved down the river on the 6th and without opposition landed at Lachine, on the island of Montreal.[136]

De Lévis, meanwhile feeling that the menace of the approach of Haviland's army by way of Chambly toward La Prairie was the greatest immediate danger, conferred on September 1 with Bourlamaque, posted on the south shore, and plans were laid for driving it back. These involved the support of the regulars by the domiciled Indians living about Montreal. Having gathered the natives together at La Prairie, de Lévis used all of his powers to rouse them to action. To his dismay, however, a deputy suddenly arrived from one of their villages with the word that peace had been made between them and the British army that was on the upper St. Lawrence. In the words of the Chevalier:

> "In a moment they dispersed leaving M. le Chevalier de Lévis with the officers quite alone. Having been advised at the same time by the Chevalier de la Corne that Fort Lévis had been taken and that Amherst would come down with an army of fifteen thousand men . . . and . . . would be able to reach Montreal the next day, he [de Lévis] thereupon resolved to have all the troops on the south shore fall back to Montreal, a movement that was executed in good order the following morning." [137]

Thus, all the French forces in Canada had concentrated on the island at the time when Amherst arrived at the western end of it; Murray's fleet had by the 6th, moreover, spread along the river to the south of it, ready to disembark the men at any moment; while Haviland, after reducing Fort Chambly, was now moving toward the river, and by that date his rangers under Rogers had actually arrived at Longueuil, on the south bank of the St. Lawrence opposite Montreal and midway between Varenne and La Prairie.[138] It was at this critical juncture, when a ring of steel was being forged about the city, that the last of the Canadians deserted the army and returned home. All that de Lévis therefore had at his command were his regulars, and even among these the married men had joined their wives, leaving him to confront the combined forces of

---

[136] Amherst to Pitt, September 8, 1760, *Pitt Correspondence*, II, 330–1.
[137] *Journal de Lévis*, pp. 301–2.
[138] *Rogers's Journal*, pp. 177–8.

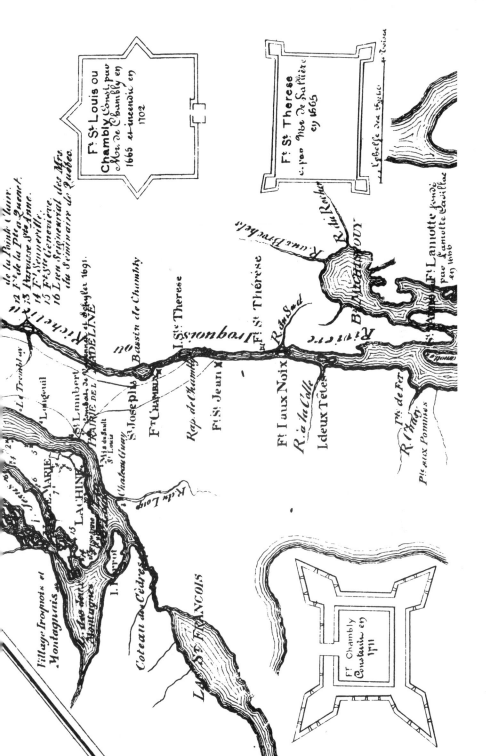

French settlements on the Richelieu River, 1760.

(From P. M. A. Knest's "Carte de la Nouvelle France pour Servir à l'Étude de l'Histoire du Canada. . . ." Clements Library.)

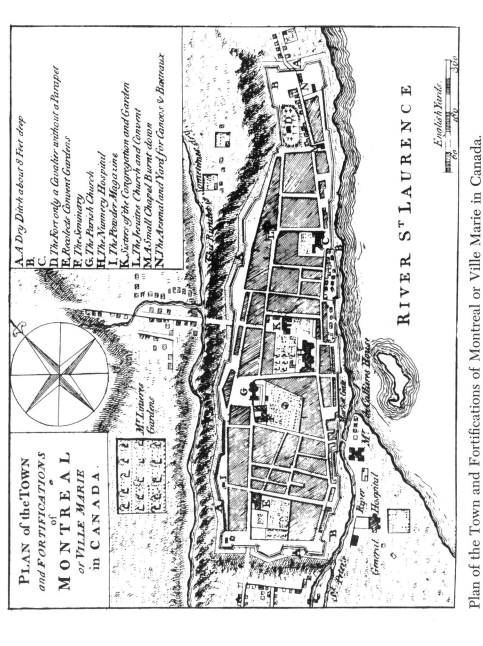

Plan of the Town and Fortifications of Montreal or Ville Marie in Canada.

(From Ann Rocque's A Set of Plans and Forts in America, 1765.)

Amherst and Murray, and also those of Haviland upon the latter's arrival, with scarcely more than two thousand effectives.

During the night of the 6th, with Amherst's army on the island resting on their arms, Vaudreuil conferred at his home with all the principal officers of the land troops and the marines. Intendant Bigot was also present and presented a *mémoire* relative to the capitulation of the colony, setting forth the state of its affairs together with a definite project for surrender. As it was quite hopeless to make any further effective resistance, with the Canadians now out of the war and the domiciled Indians prepared to join Johnson's Indians in arms against their old friends, it was agreed at the meeting that a capitulation honourable to the troops and advantageous to the people of Canada was far preferable to an attempt at defence that could only defer the loss of the city for a matter of a day or two.[139]

Consequently, early the morning of the 7th Lieutenant Colonel Bougainville appeared at Amherst's camp with a letter from Vaudreuil. He made a request for a cessation of arms until a courier had returned, sent down the river by the Governor General to find out whether or not there was peace. Amherst, in reply, told the colonel that he had come to take Canada, would have nothing less, and if Vaudreuil had any proposals to offer, he should make them in writing. Having agreed, however, to a cessation of arms until noon for his own troops — but not those of Murray and Haviland — the general sent Bougainville back to the city. At twelve o'clock came the French proposals, and the negotiations for surrender continued until the morning of the 8th, when Vaudreuil finally agreed to the terms that Amherst had imposed.

The original terms for the capitulation of Canada, consisting of fifty articles, each of which had been framed with great skill, were, it is clear, not drawn up on the spur of the moment. It would appear, in fact, that they had been the subject of the most careful and prolonged consideration on the part of the French at Montreal during the period when the enemy was gradually closing in on all sides and the fate awaiting Canada — without some miracle — could hardly be in doubt. That Bigot himself presented them at Vaudreuil's home for consideration of the council of war in no way militates against the view that he himself was not their chief architect, but only a collaborator in their formulation. Indeed, that he as a civilian should

---

[139] *Journal de Lévis*, pp. 303-4.

have been chosen to perform the formal act of offering them to the council, rather than one holding military rank, was quite in conformity with prevailing conceptions of military honour. In other words, the Intendant, as the leading civilian authority, must be regarded as chiefly the medium, outside his own field, through which the other authorities in Canada, deeply concerned with securing an advantageous capitulation, could find expression at a meeting that they all knew would later become the object of peculiar interest to the French ministry, seeking evidence of any lack of resolution on the part of the leaders of New France in this moment of supreme crisis.

The first twenty-two and the last five articles were exclusively concerned with the military establishment of New France and, among other things, provided that full honours of war should be granted to the troops at Montreal and elsewhere in Canada; that all soldiers, and especially the sick and wounded, should receive full protection and good treatment; and that special regard should be paid to the welfare of the French officers while still in Canada and during their passage to France. Then followed four articles relating to civilian administration involving specifically the protection of the mercantile interests of the contractor Cadet and those of the Compagnie des Indes in connection with its beaver trade. These in turn were succeeded by nine articles having to do with the maintenance of the Catholic religion and the ecclesiastical system in Canada, among which was the stipulation that, even should Canada remain in the possession of Great Britain with the treaty of peace, His Most Christian Majesty would continue to name the bishop of Quebec. Finally, the remaining articles were designed to provide to the inhabitants of Canada the widest measure of choice whether to remain in the New World or return to France, and the fullest protection to their property, including the seigneuries. In this connection it was stipulated that those who chose to abide in Canada, whether Canadians, Acadians, or Frenchmen, should never be forced to take up arms against the King of France, but be regarded as "neutrals" and continue to be governed according to the "custom of Paris, and the laws and usages established for this country; and . . . not be subject to any other imposts than those which were established under the French dominion." [140]

It is remarkable that the British general made few exceptions to

---

[140] N. Y. Col. Doc., X, 1107–19.

this extraordinarly comprehensive document; and even these exceptions were couched in terms of great moderation. In the words of an unknown officer who served under Bougainville at Isle-aux-Noix: "Amherst accorded conditions infinitely more favourable than could have been expected in our circumstances." [141] In returning the proferred terms to Vaudreuil, he indicated that he would insist on the following modifications, among others of less importance: that the French troops must not only lay down their arms but agree not to serve during the remainder of the war; that no protection would be granted to British soldiers who had deserted to the French; that no promise would be made either to permit the bishop of Quebec to be appointed by the French King in case Canada should become a British possession, or to guarantee, until the King's pleasure was known, the privileges of the Jesuits, Recollects, or Sulpicians; and, finally, that all those who decided to remain in Canada must be regarded, not as neutrals, but as subjects of the King of England.[142]

In spite of the liberality of the terms, these were unacceptable to the French military leaders, who felt that they were thereby dishonoured by being required to lay down their arms and to agree not to serve again during the war. De Lévis, in fact, first sent Bougainville to protest this article, but Amherst refused to receive him; then he sent another member of his staff to the British headquarters to request that the article should be modified so that it would apply only to service in Canada and elsewhere in America. In the letter that M. de la Pause carried, the Chevalier denounced "the too rigorous article which you impose on the troops by the capitulation, and to which it would not be possible for us to subscribe.[143] The general, however, had already determined to make an example of the French regular troops and — according to Captain John Knox, whose *Historical Journal* is quite remarkable for its reliability — replied to the French officer that he had

> "fully resolved, for the infamous part the troops of France had acted in exciting the savages to perpetuate the most horrid and unheard of barbarities in the whole progress of the war, and for other open

---

[141] *Collection de Manuscrits . . . Relatifs à l'Histoire de la Nouvelle-France*, IV, 262.

[142] *N. Y. Col. Doc.*, X, 1107–19.

[143] Knox, *op. cit.*, II, 418. It should be noted that the modification requested by de Lévis would, by permitting the troops to serve in Europe, guard against the necessity, under French military practice, of the officers being reduced to half pay which to many would mean financial ruin.

treacheries, as well as flagrant breaches of faith, to manifest to all the world, by this capitulation, his detestation of such ungenerous practices, and disapprobation of their conduct. . . ." [144]

From this position he refused to be moved. De Lévis, after making vocal representations in company with other leading officers to the Governor General against the humiliating terms, then sent to Vaudreuil a letter in which he pleaded with him to break off immediately all negotiations and to make the most determined resistance at Montreal with the resources at their command and, should the Governor General be unwilling thus to sacrifice the city, at least to permit the French troops to go to Ile Sainte-Hélène,[145] where they would willingly expose themselves to every extremity rather than submit to conditions so contrary to the honour of the arms of the King.[146] But Vaudreuil, realizing how very advantageous were the terms by and large that Amherst had agreed to accept, very wisely refused this request and ordered the Chevalier to require the troops to lay down their arms.[147] This was done, but not before de Lévis "desiring to spare the troops some of the humiliation that they were about to endure had ordered their flags to be burnt." [148]

Thus, by this surrender, which included the posts "on the side of Acadia, at Detroit, Michilimakinac, and other posts," as well as the towns of Montreal and Trois Rivières, Anglo-French hostilities on the continent of North America came to a dramatic end.

---

[144] *Ibid.*

[145] A small island lying between that of Montreal and the south shore.

[146] *Journal de Lévis,* pp. 306–7.

[147] *Ibid.,* pp. 307–8.

[148] *Ibid.* Amherst, in explaining to Pitt why it was that no French flags had been surrendered, wrote that only two colours were given up — those taken from the Shirley and Pepperrell regiments at Oswego in 1756. "The Marquis de Vaudreuil, Generals, and the Commanding Officers of the Reg^{ts}, giving their words of honour that the Battalions had not any Colours [declared that] they had brought them six years ago with them, they were torn to Pieces, and finding them Troublesome in this Country, they had destroyed them" (Amherst to Pitt, October 4, 1760, *Pitt Correspondence,* II, 335). That the French officers had previously determined never to let their colours fall into the possession of the enemy, may perhaps be inferred from the fact that in Article 5 of the French terms of capitulation, which refers to the honours of war, while reference is made to their troops marching out of Montreal with drums beating and with their arms, baggage, and artillery, nothing is said, as was customary, about flags flying. The wilful destruction of their flags after the capitulation had been agreed upon was, of course, a serious violation of the rules of war. Vaudreuil therefore was obliged to affirm an untruth in order to save the soldiers from being made undoubtedly prisoners of war without the privilege of parole.

In concluding this volume with the conquest of Canada, it is, however, important to make quite clear that the struggle terminated at the gates of Montreal on September 7, 1760 was but a phase, although an important phase, of a world war. In other words, the permanent acquisition of Canada by Great Britain was still to be determined by the final outcome not only of the Great War for the Empire that continued to be waged elsewhere on land and sea but of the Seven Years' European War with which it was to so large an extent fused while yet remaining distinct — at least in the minds of those who were at the time in authority in Great Britain and also, as will be subsequently noted in this series, of their successors, who in 1763 were responsible for bringing it to an end. It will thus be necessary to give careful consideration to other theatres of this war, the successful conclusion of which was destined to be of such tremendous import to the English-speaking people. To its progress in Europe, in the West Indies, in the Far East, and on the high seas, as well as to its termination in the Peace of Paris, the next volume of this series must therefore be devoted.

Index

Abenaki Indians, support the French, 64; help to destroy an English flotilla on Lake George, 77

Abercromby, Major General James, assigned to go with Loudoun in 1757, 72; at Albany, 153; sends support to New York, 153; warns Robert Rogers, 155; appointed by Pitt commander-in-chief of British forces in North America, 175; limitation of the powers of, by Pitt, 177; early military career of, 211; qualities of, as leader, 211; circular letters of, to all governors, 212; response of colonies to call of, for troops, 212; asks aid from Sir William Johnson, 214; Indian support of, at Ticonderoga, 215; difficulties of, with Massachusetts Assembly, 1758, 216; the expedition of, against Ticonderoga, 218; inability of, to replace Howe, 225; calls council of war, 226; sends Johnson and Indians to occupy Mount Defiance, 228; line of battle and disposition of troops by, 229; retreat by army of, 231; mistakes of, in the attack on Ticonderoga, 233; writes to Forbes of desertions, 234; temporarily dismisses thought of a second attack on Ticonderoga, 235; receives words from Amherst of reinforcement, 235; plans of, for a second attack, 235; calls Amherst to conference, 235; calls a council of war, 235; summons Bradstreet to his aid, 235; the recall of, 236; at a council of war, July, 1758, 238; instructions of, to Bradstreet, 239; modifies Pitt's distribution of officers, 1758, 249

Abraham, Plains of, British appearance at, 417; the battle of the, 419–21; see also battle of Sillery in 1760

Acadia, plan of de Lévis to reconquer, 171; de la Motte censured for failing to reconquer, 186

Acadians, the, efforts to protect the interests of, at the capitulation of Canada, 464

Aetna, the, Captain Balfour, at Louisbourg, 205

Africa, British successes along the coast of, 288

Aiguillon, Duc d', defeats the British at Saint-Cas, 136

Alabama Indians, seek neutrality, 64

Albany, New York, concentration of northern provincial troops at, 315, 329

Aldborough, England, Pitt secures a seat in Parliament from, in 1754, 8

Algonkin Indians, support the French, 64

Allegheny River, military activities along the, see Armstrong, Bouquet, de Lignery, Forbes, Mercer, Hugh

Amherst, Colonel Jeffrey, services of, before 1758, 182; appointed Major General in the American service, 183; to command the forces against Cape Breton Island, 183; arrival of, off Nova Scotia, 186; changes plan of operations against Louisbourg, 192–3; pursues the French troops to Louisbourg, 196; close co-operation between Boscawen and, 202–3; receives the surrender of Louisbourg, 216–7; warns the Pennsylvania House of Representatives regarding the necessity of supplying provincials, 304; pays a high tribute to the Council and Assembly of New York, 310; urges Connecticut to supply its quota of troops, 311; proposal of, that Massachusetts Bay send troops to Cape Breton Island and to Nova Scotia, 322; orders a New York Independent company to New Hampshire, 325; calls Johnson to conference, 344; places Prideaux in charge of the Fort Niagara expedition, 344; instructs Johnson to assemble Indians at Oswego, 345; orders Gage to command operations in the Lake Ontario region, 356; rebukes Gage for disobeying orders, 359; is called upon to invade Canada, 360; number of regiments to support, 360; disapproves of Bradstreet's plans, 361; lays new plans for Fort George, near the site of Fort William Henry, 361; moves upon Fort Ticonderoga, 361; restores Ticonderoga, 365; builds three forts at Crown Point, 365; lays out a road to No. 4, 365; preparations of, for the drive against Isle-aux-Noix, 365; weather

A NOTE ON THE TYPE

This book is set in Linotype Caledonia, belongs to the family of printing types called "modern face" by printers — a term used to mark the change in style of type-letters that occurred about 1800. Caledonia is in the general neighborhood of Scotch Modern in design, but is more freely drawn than that letter.

The book was designed by W. A. Dwiggins and composed, printed, and bound by The Plimpton Press, Norwood, Massachusetts.

A NOTE ON THE TYPE

This book is set in Linotype Caledonia. Caledonia belongs to the family of printing types called " modern face " by printers — a term used to mark the change in style of type-letters that occurred about 1800. Caledonia is in the general neighborhood of Scotch Modern in design, but is more freely drawn than that letter.

The book was designed by W. A. Dwiggins, and composed, printed, and bound by The Plimpton Press, Norwood, Massachusetts.